ORGANIZATIONAL SYSTEMS

Consulting Editor
PHILLIP E. HAMMOND
University of Arizona

ORGANIZATIONAL SYSTEMS

A Text-Reader in the Sociology of Organizations

KOYA AZUMI
Columbia University

JERALD HAGE
University of Wisconsin

D. C. HEATH AND COMPANY
Lexington, Massachusetts   Toronto   London

Published simultaneously in Canada.

Printed in the United States of America.

International Standard Book Number: 0-669-75234-7

Library of Congress Catalog Card Number: 72-1405

CONTENTS

3   THE SOCIAL STRUCTURE OF ORGANIZATIONS

The Problems

The Readings

4 THE INTERNAL CONTROL PROCESSES OF ORGANIZATIONS

The Problems

The Readings

5 THE PERFORMANCES AND GOALS OF THE ORGANIZATION

The Problems

The Readings

6 TOWARD A SYNTHESIS: A SYSTEMS PERSPECTIVE

Introduction
ORGANIZATIONAL PERSPECTIVES AND PROGRAMS

One poignant message of the past decade, and perhaps decades before that, has been the power and pervasiveness of big organizations. To many of us they seem to dominate and control our lives. And this observation is not without much empirical support. Whether the organization is General Motors and its controversial product the Corvair, or the U.S. Army and its involvement in Vietnam, or the C.I.A. and its infiltration in various student movements, or the American Medical Association and its attempts to prevent free medical care, the citizen appears surrounded by large, faceless, bureaucratic machines that make critical decisions and pursue policies that seem contrary to many people's desires. Even the local school or public welfare agency seems beyond citizen control, as frequent demonstrations in front of them have illustrated. In popular parlance, "fighting City Hall" appears fruitless—and there seem to be so many city halls! For this reason many of us feel powerless and can agree with the dire predictions of Weber (1947: 337–40), who felt that the superior efficiency of bureaucracies would mean the probable loss of freedom.

A book such as this one can help people to appreciate how organizations behave. If some control over organizations is to occur, then we first need to understand the hows and whys of organizational behavior. In the course of study one would also realize that if people are to be protected from organizations, then the people must themselves become organized. The best defense is another organization. But beyond the idea of simple protection is another reason why the study of organizations is essential: most of our major objectives are accomplished in the context of one or more organizations. To understand how to make new or existing organizations better; how to structure them—indeed, there is more than one way; how to evaluate a host of other issues; these are the objectives of this text–reader.

1

This does not mean that answers are provided. What is given instead is a description of the present state of the field—its debates and doubts. But also the insights that have been achieved by particular researchers. No one can criticize sociologists for concentrating on trivial issues. The problems discussed in this book are critical ones. But precisely for this reason, the solutions are not easy to come by; they take time. This text–reader tells where we are now.

The term "text–reader" is deliberate. This book is neither a reader nor a text, but a combination of the two. The sociology of organization is in the midst of growing pains. The number of theoretical orientations expressed and problems identified has multiplied in the last few years. Research designs have become more sophisticated, moving from case to comparative studies, employing multiple controls, and becoming increasingly concerned with measurement problems. The rapid proliferation of articles and books about organizations has made it more and more difficult to keep abreast of developments. Although the growth of the discipline is exciting for the researcher, it has nonetheless given him a sense of chaos in the specialty. Some order is called for.

With this much ferment, a textbook would be very difficult to write. The field has too much controversy, too many concepts, and not enough codification to justify the summing up implied in a textbook. Instead the format of a reader seems more appropriate at this stage of development. But at the same time, rapid growth creates problems here as well. There is a limit to the number of articles that can be included, and yet one wishes to have the book reflect the many controversies, both theoretical and empirical, that presently exist. Given the proliferation of material and particularly the general improvement in quality that has occurred, choice becomes difficult and even hazardous. Therefore, it is necessary to have extended introductions describing the development prior to the appearance of the articles, the major problems articulated therein, and the possibilities implied for future research and development. Thus the choice of the name text–reader to describe the program of this book.

The context of the program is dialectical. That is, deliberate attempts are made to specify the debates, the doubts, and the divergent schools—their theses and antitheses—at this moment of development. This does not mean that there are no firm and fixed points of agreement whatsoever. What is relatively agreed upon by sociologists is indicated as well. Nor does it mean that the book is shapeless and spineless, without coherent perspective. Quite the contrary, a definitive perspective, that of a sociological conception of an organization qua system is taken. But what a dialectical program can hopefully accomplish is to let the reader in on the sense of ferment and excitement and perhaps lead to the eventual synthesis of thesis and antithesis and thus contribute to the development of our knowledge about organizations.

The perspective of organizations as sociological systems allows for flexibility in presenting divergent viewpoints and, at the same time, provides coherence, sense of order, and sequence. However, the words *system analysis* have developed a number of different connotations, and the two words *sociological system* must be specified, as they are in the first section of this introduction, so that the hidden assumptions are made clear, if not acceptable. Inherent in perspectives are limits—some would call them blinders—and we would indicate what these are.

Even readers with textual introductions are difficult to organize. There are two reasons for this: any article worth including can be placed in more than one chapter, and there is more than one kind of person. How does one allow for these possibilities and individual preferences? Our solution is to indicate (in the section below) our reasons for selection. The strengths and weaknesses of this reader become apparent as we discuss the criteria both for choosing among available materials and for arranging them. Not all will agree with our decisions, but at least we have tried to do justice to the discipline; perhaps that is all that can be asked. In addition to indicating our criteria of arrangement and choice, we have suggested several other possible sequences, as well as other articles, for those interested in particular problems and issues. In this way the book can be used in a variety of ways. Again, it allows for a fairer presentation of material and perhaps a better realization of our objective of presenting developments in the field as they exist at this moment in time.

Organizational Perspectives

The Sociological Perspective   Just as a painter and a sculptor looking at the same person will see different aspects of the individual, so the psychologist and the sociologist have different perspectives when studying organizations. The psychologist sees an aggregate of individuals and is concerned with their perceptions, cognitions, and thinking processes. Frequently the focus may be on the personality of the leader and how he affected the success of the organization. Since we are all individuals, we have some immediate feeling for personality conflicts and the problem of motivation. These are experiences common to all of us.

In an organization, however, personality conflict may be a consequence of how the organization is structured, i.e., not a matter of personality as such but a problem shared by everyone in exactly the same job position, for example, all students, all workers, or all managers. Some examples of this problem are found in Chapter Four, the selections by Kahn *et al.* and by Corwin. The problem of motivation may not be a consequence of some personality defect but rather a question of company morale or, worse yet, alienation produced by meaningless work in a structure that makes the men at the bottom powerless. Some of these collective counterparts to the problem of motivation—morale and alienation—are discussed in the introduction to Chapter Five.

The sociologist looks at an organization, and very much like the sculptor, sees the pattern and form of human action and interrelationships and not the color and detail of personality and individual differences. The accent is on job titles and what is common to those holding the same position. Thus in looking at a university, the sociologist asks what is common to the job of being a student or a teacher or a dean. Beyond this, and perhaps most important, is the focus on the collective of jobs and how they are integrated; the processes of production and the arrangement of the team into a coherent and effective whole. This is the sociological perspective.

This perspective of organizations is perhaps best grasped by considering two very different objectives. Suppose first that we want to rehabilitate a grandparent after a serious stroke. To do so we will need a vast array of technical experts: physical, speech, and occupational therapists, doctors, some specializing in physical medicine, nurses, perhaps social workers and other ancillary personnel depending on the kinds of psychological and social problems consequent to the physical illness. No single person can master the many different kinds of technical skills needed in this one case alone. More importantly, in *many* instances, when the services of a number of technical experts come into play simultaneously, that is, in a team effort. What we would need in each case is a rehabilitation agency such as a sheltered workshop—in other words, an organization.

Another example is the problem of building an automobile. We could give all the parts, along with several detailed manuals, to each individual worker in the plant. It is unlikely that even after a year we would have many cars built. Organized into an assembly-line process, however, automobile plants are able to produce a large number of cars each year. The principles of organization of an automobile plant are quite different from those appropriate for a sheltered workshop or a rehabilitation agency but, sociologically, they have much in common. There is a pattern and an arrangement, with collective causes and effects.

These examples illustrate the advantage of organizing in a sociological sense, i.e., that we can obtain certain objectives that would be impossible to obtain individually. With a team we achieve these objectives faster, cheaper, and with fewer errors. There are social advantages to organization just as there are mechanical ones to the pulley and the inclined plane and the wheel. A basic problem for organizational analysis is to discover the pulleys, planes, and wheels of organization and determine what advantages they have and for which utilities.

It is also for these reasons of advantages that groups are so different from organizations. Cost or efficiency is of no primary importance in groups. We are not concerned with fast or cheap love or at least we shouldn't be! As soon as this happens friendship becomes a business. Because the objectives of an organization are specific—build a car or rehabilitate a stroke patient—the planning and design can be *relatively* simple. In contrast, the problems of planning an entire institutional process are vastly more complex as the study by Berliner (Chapter One) makes clear. Thus organizations can set their targets and develop some structure and coherence to achieve them.

There is a perspective that combines the psychological and the sociological in the study of organizations. In a social-psychological analysis typically one is concerned with the interrelationships between the characteristics of the job and of the person filling it. What is different about a purely sociological perspective is that it concentrates on how the team operates and does not consider how the individual functions as a member of that team. The latter is the province of the social psychologist. Does this mean that sociologists have lost all sense of people? Not at all. Only note that there is a difference between studying man and mankind.

Thus, the sociological perspective is a very different one. One might ask, if the three viewpoints—psychological, social psychological, and sociological—are all relevant to a complete understanding, why not include all three in a text–reader. The reason why this is not possible is that each has a vast literature in its own right. One could not, at least in our opinion, do justice to all three or even to any two. For this reason most readers on organizations focus on one of the three perspectives. One can then present a coherent viewpoint if not a complete one. This is especially important for the person who is being introduced to a sociological perspective for the first time. Since the sociological perspective is harder to see and less intuitively obvious, it is better to present this single focus so that the person can come to appreciate and even develop a sociological imagination.

To aid the person in this effort and to provide a feeling for organizations qua teams, we have included several case studies about different kinds of organizations and written from different perspectives. In Chapter Two, Blauner writes about the life of the workers in a chemical plant under normal operation. By way of contrast in Chapter Four, McCleery provides us with a view of a prison from the vantage point of the rehabilitators and guards during a period of conflict and upheaval. The Davis and Dolbeare article (Chapter One) lets us see a government voluntary agency, the Selective Service Board in the United States, from the top down, and Crozier (Chapter Three) looks at a government agency in France, where the work is anything but voluntary, from the bottom up. Presthus (Chapter One) shows us that a bureaucratic machine in Turkey can have welfare goals instead of efficiency ones, in sharp contrast to the Crozier selection. In Chapter One, Berliner takes us inside Russian industry, and in Chapter Five, Perrow does the same for American industry. In various ways these studies demonstrate the sociological perspective of organizations.

Kinds of Social Collectives   However much our imagination has been struck by the presence of organizations during the past ten years, these are not the only kinds of social collectives that are of interest to sociologists. Usually we are concerned with at least four basic kinds of collectives: groups, organizations, institutions, and societies (Parsons, 1959). The order of listing is not random and says something about their differences. As we move from groups to societies we are advancing to ever larger collectives that subsume the preceding ones. Thus groups exist in organizations, and both of these kinds of collectives are found in institutions, which in turn are located in societies. Sometimes all four kinds of collectives are lumped together under the generic name of social organization, resulting in some confusion.

The idea of a basic social organization is a simple one. All social collectives exhibit some enduring pattern of social action. The description and analysis of this pattern are what concerns sociology. In a word, how things are *organized* is its basic problem—the causes and consequences of this pattern of social action, the internal sociological quest. Many sociologists believe that eventually one set of variables may be used to describe groups, societies, and organizations, that is, all social collectives, and thus the popularity of the term "social organization." Naturally we hope that this text–reader will contribute to that objective. But social organization to include all kinds of social collectives is not the meaning of organizations that we imply here.

Organizations, as we shall define the term, appear to have some distinguishing properties that make them worth studying in their own right. Some individuals have felt that the most significant property is their size; others have suggested that their complexity is the key; and still others have preferred to emphasize their formality. As a consequence, organizations are frequently called complex organizations, formal organizations, or large-scale organizations. Indeed, these are critical characteristics and, as we shall see in Chapter Three, complexity and formalization go to the heart of describing two basic models of organizational structure, each with its advantages and disadvantages. Likewise Chapter Two explores the impact of size on the social structure of organizations. Therefore, it does not seem that these are the properties that will help us to distinguish between a group and an organization, on the one hand, and an organization and institutions on the other. For now, it seems better to drop the adjectives large-scale, complex, or formal because organizations are not all these things all the time. But, then, what are the defining characteristics of organizations?

The Definition of Organizations as Social Collectives It is easy to point to a large number of examples of organizations: The University of London, the Red Chinese Army, the Vatican, the Kikkoman Soy Sauce Company, Ltd., the Walgreen Drugstore, and the Boston Pops Orchestra are all illustrations. It is somewhat more difficult to determine when a group becomes an organization. We are in the same position as the biologists who can name illustrations of human beings vis-à-vis other mammals but find it somewhat more difficult to decide when ape becomes man.

Our definition of organizations is that they are structured bodies designed to achieve specific objectives that are part of some larger institutional process. Manufacturing plants, wholesalers, retail outlets, banks, etc., are kinds of organizations that produce and distribute the products that are part of our economic institution. Armies, courts, prisons, legislatures, and various government bureaus produce and distribute power, together making up our political institution. Schools, colleges, research institutes are part of the institution of science and education. Hospitals, welfare agencies, rehabilitation agencies form still another institution, what might be called welfare in its broadest sense. This is not an exhaustive list of either institutional realms or organizations but provides some idea of the richness and variety that exist.

Examples of groups that are not organizations are our own families, our peer or friendship groups, certain leisure time clubs and neighborhood associations. What distinguishes these examples from those above is that organizations are designed to achieve specific objectives. Parsons (1956) and others have noted that organizations are literally planned to achieve some specific goals. In contrast, groups, including the family, are formed for the enjoyment of their members. The objectives or goals of groups are diffuse and nonspecific. This is not to say that there are not groups within organizations. They are there precisely because man likes camaraderie. But the purposes of work and play are kept sociologically separate in organizations and groups. Admittedly, in practice it is sometimes hard to demonstrate this. We talk as a professional to another professional about the difficulties with a particular client, and then we shift our conversation to baseball scores because the colleague is also a friend. But a shift does take place and the difference is an important one: What sociologists have labeled as instrumental and expressive communication (Price, 1972).

As in any category, there are borderline cases that are difficult to classify. One example is the family business. Caplow (1954) has noted that some industries depend upon secrecy and therefore need and prefer the bond of blood as well as of money. The Mafia is perhaps the most notorious example, but family businesses have remained in many spheres. Probably most family businesses are more businesslike than familial. The key test is, of course, which is more important, the affectivity of the relationship or the size of the profit. One suspects that the latter probably wins (for a different point of view see Perrow, 1971).

Another borderline case is some voluntary associations. These are collectives where people, at least most of them, work without monetary reward, willingly devoting their time and energy; thus, the name voluntary. Some examples are found in the selections by Davis and Dolbeare (Chapter One) and by Smith and Ari and by Tsouderos (both in Chapter Five). In general, most voluntary associations such as labor unions, professional associations, and lobbying organizations are concerned with specific objectives such as better pay, more work autonomy, or preferential legislative treatment for pet causes, and thus are organizations. However, some associations are concerned with having a good time: garden, golf, and golden age clubs are all examples. These would be considered as groups. Again the test is to ask ourselves how much emphasis is placed on getting a task accomplished and how much on enjoying the relationships among members. There are considerable variations, but somewhere along this specific–diffuse continuum, a group becomes an organization. When it does, there are a number of other changes as well: It is a literal metamorphosis of structure and function. Perhaps the easiest difference to note is the degree of conscious planning that occurs. This is manifested in a variety of ways. Job titles appear, rules develop and are formalized, records are kept, files are maintained, and in Weber's famous words, the social collective becomes rational. Well, perhaps not completely rational, but at least much more so than a group.

One never hears of job titles in a family (unless it is a family business) or in a friendship group. Most families do not do cost-accounting; they keep rather poor files and records, as the Internal Revenue Service people will be the first to testify. The importance of files should not be underestimated, as trivial as they may seem. Perhaps the most dramatic example is the reserve army, an organization that spends most of the year nonoperating. The reserve consists of an army sergeant sitting at a desk with several file cabinets full of personnel folders and a locked warehouse close by full of weapons. Seemingly not much of an organization, and yet, given a crisis, the file cabinets open, telephone calls go out, and a battalion is immediately on the march—as many students have discovered in recent years. Similarly, the record-keeping of organizations has been exploited by researchers such as Chandler (Chapter Five), who has pieced together the histories of the major corporations in the United States, in this instance, DuPont, General Motors, Sinclair Oil of New Jersey, and Sears Roebuck, by nothing more than reading their files.

It is hard to imagine even the most verbose families being studied as effectively.

As we noted above, all social collectives have a basic pattern, but what is distinctive in organizations is that the plan is conscious and well articulated relative to the other three kinds of basic collectives. Presumably this is part and parcel of the need to achieve specific objectives. In addition, organizations and groups can be contrasted on the amount of resources available to them. What makes organizations important is their large size, wealth, and autonomy. In contrast, most groups are puny. There are some wealthy families, but the Du-Pont family qua family does not have the power of DuPont qua corporation. Typically, families and groups seldom acquire more than 20 members, and still fewer more than 100; the average college or high school in the United States, to say nothing of the 200 largest corporations or the various branches of the federal government, is much larger. It is this command over large amounts and varieties of resources that makes the mastery of organization so important. And it is also the reason why the typical response to fighting large-scale organizations is to create other large-scale organizations, such as the labor unions, professional groups, and various consumer groups interested in protections from the prices of self-centered corporations.

How do organizations differ from institutions and societies? Despite Wilson's famous comment that "what is good for General Motors is good for the United States," there are differences, and our definition, to be complete, must take account of them. General Motors is only part of the economy, that institutional realm that produces and distributes goods and services. A moment's reflection leads us to recognize that however big General Motors is, with its sales of $15 billion a year, this is not the whole of the American economy. There are two million businesses, and even the 200 largest do not account for all or even most of the economy. The share of any one given business in the total economy may be too much or too little depending upon one's predilections; the point remains that General Motors' interests and problems are not synonymous with those of the American economy.

Similarly, TVA, as reported in Selznick's study (Chapter Two) is only part of the polity, the institutional realm concerned with the production of power. Again the accent is on specific objectives. For this reason organizations are only part of the institutional processes concerned with the production of basic societal resources such as material goods or power. Finally, society includes all the institutional realms that have the same sovereignty. Thus the United States of America, the Union of Soviet Socialist Republics, Luxembourg, Nicaragua, each is a sovereign nation and each has an economy, a polity, as well as other institutional realms (sociologists are not agreed upon what would be an adequate list of institutional realms and the definitions vary considerably). That General Motors is bigger than the entire economy of Luxembourg does not mean it is an institutional realm. Nor does the fact that United Fruit may own a good chunk of some Central American economies obliterate the distinction between the organization in one economy of one society vis-à-vis an organization in another economy in another society. The point of reference for General Motors remains the U.S.A. Furthermore and most important, the intellectual problems of an institutional realm are different from those of an organization. At the level of the institutional realm one is concerned with how all the organizations articulate together. This is a problem for Luxembourg just as much as it is for the U.S.A. And by keeping these levels of analysis clear we can ask how do the actions of a company such as United Fruit, with its headquarters located in the U.S.A., affect the dislocations of the various economies of other countries where it has plants, warehouses, and other forms of investment?

Again there are several borderline cases that serve to sharpen the difference between organizations and institutional realms. One example is what might be called the multination corporation. The organization with plants in a number of societies—Shell, Unilever, Sony, Fiat, Olivetti—are all examples, none of which is American. Another example is the American university, several of which have built branches overseas. Nor need we point to the ever-present military bases scattered around the world. But although organizations exist across national boundaries as do families, we do not want to lose sight of the fact that they still operate in a societal context. Mr. Ford would be the first to argue that this is the case because British Ford, unlike American Ford, is plagued with a constant series of strikes, as are many British companies. The reasons lie in the differences of the British economy and the British society in comparison with their American counterparts. The problems of multinational organizations, both for themselves and for the societies in which they are located, are only recently receiving attention. As more research is completed, the distinction between where the organization ends and the society begins will become clearer.

Another borderline case, and a more difficult one, is found where the entire economy or polity or other institutional realm seems to be nothing but one big organization. This occurs where there is an attempt to plan an institutional realm as if it were an organization. On the socialist side we have the Gosplan in the USSR, which regulates all major economic organizations, consciously designing quotas, delivery dates, prices, wages, and checking upon internal operations as well (see Berliner in Chapter One). Here it is hard to draw the line between organization and institutional realm. Yet it is clear that there are a variety of different organizations producing different products, even if they are doing so according to a master plan prepared by another organization. One wants to separate the idea of how calculated the overall design of the economy is from the idea of its component parts, namely organizations. We can separate these ideas by noting that different products are being produced and, furthermore, by studying which groups of products have the same leadership in the chain of command stretching from the plant to the Gosplan in the Council of Ministers. An example on the capitalist side is the corporation owned by the Samos family in Nicaragua, a corporation that seems to have the major share of the wealth in that country. The fact that all products are produced by one company makes it difficult to draw any distinctions. Separation by product is at least a first approximation. The way in which the companies are tied together—either by collective control or family enterprise—is essentially an intellectual issue at the level of the institutional realm. How each of these various companies or component parts operates is the level of organizational analysis. For the organizational sociologist the problem of the relationships between companies or organizations is seen as part of the environment and its cause-and-effect relationships with the organization. For the institutional sociologist this same problem becomes one of the operation of the institutional realm. Thus the levels can focus on the same problem but they are phrased differently and as a consequence the perspective is different. This is one of the reasons why the specialized study of different kinds of social collectives is necessary. It helps encourage a dialectic between these perspectives.

Thus we see organizations as consciously articulated to achieve specific objectives. Groups, usually smaller, are not as systematic. Institutions, always larger, may be planned but seldom as effectively because of the magnitude of the task. Groups exist both within and without organizations and a variety of these groups become involved directly or indirectly in the institutional process concerned with the production of some scarce resource.

A Systems Perspective   Since we want to represent the variety of sociological traditions—the technology school, goal analysis, structural-functionalism, as well as the many debates that exist within these various perspectives—we need a framework that is general enough to incorporate these diverse viewpoints and yet at the same time is somewhat systematic and not amorphous. System analysis offers these advantages.

System analysis means more than just the use of the word system, and it is more than just a set of logical categories. It involves several rather critical assumptions that in turn affect how the reader is arranged and what is said in the textual introductions. *The first and most important assumption is that we view an organization as a set of variables that are interrelated in such a way that changes in one variable effect changes in the other variables.* The simplest example is the set of variables in Boyle's Law: a change in temperature affects the volume of pressure and/or the amount of pressure. Our problem in the study of organizations is to identify which variables are the important ones and then discover their interrelationships. The implication is that, when reading, one is searching for important variables and how they are associated. Practically, all the selections in this reader either implicitly or explicitly make this assumption. The two concise and coherent illustrations are the selections by Davis and Dolbeare and by Terreberry, which have been placed in the first chapter. The former gives a flesh-and-blood example in the Selective Service Board, whereas the latter is a more abstract theoretical discussion.

Some of the case studies, particularly those that observe change across time, demonstrate the sense of an organization as a system of variables. In McCleery (Chapter Four), we see the communications system alter and afterwards a large number of other variables as well. In Chandler (Chapter Five), we observe the addition of new technologies and the consequences that it has for the arrangement of management.

Most of the empirical studies present tables on how one or more variables is related to some other variables. And most of the debates and divergent viewpoints in organizational analysis are not over the issue of whether or not an organization is a set of variables but instead over which variables are most important and how they are related, if at all. In reading these various selections, it is important to keep asking in each one, what is the important dimension, what are its causes, and what are its consequences. In this way, one will gradually develop his own sense of the organizational system.

In analyzing the system of organizational variables, one major difficulty is determining which variables are *not* related. In many cases, this is news. Precisely because we keep finding that each organizational variable we study is related to a large number of others, we are particularly interested in the lack of a relationship. Most readers might find this uninteresting, but given the present state of knowledge, it is an important statement. For example, the technology school has argued that this variable affects most others, yet Hickson *et al.* (Chapter Two) suggest that this is not the case, that some variables do not seem strongly related. In contrast (and in the same chapter), Hall *et al.* suggest size is *not* related to two key structural variables. Two other papers (Hickson *et al.* and Blau) present evidence to the contrary.

The second assumption is that the system is part of an environment and in turn the system has particularly key components. If we use the motor of a car as a simple analogy, then we note that there are inputs of gas, oil, water, etc. These come from the environment. There is a throughput (see Katz and Kahn, 1966 for another discussion of this), a process by which power is generated. Finally, the car has various outputs and performances. We can accelerate and drive at a certain maximum speed and, of course, there are pollutants as well.

Organizations in these respects are no different. Like all production processes, they can be conveniently divided into inputs, throughputs, and outputs. The throughput or production process occurs in the context of two major kinds or classes of variables: structuring and process control. These, together with inputs and outputs, begin to provide a more comprehensive conception of a system. (And, not incidentally, a way of titling chapters.)

The chapters are arranged as follows: The first chapter begins with the environment, the origin of the social resources. The second chapter relates the resources to the organization; the third considers the various problems of social structure; the fourth, the issues associated with the various problems of control, and the fifth includes the analysis of goals and performances, including their consequences for the environment. In this way the search for important dimensions, their causes and consequences, becomes more systematic.

The third assumption, and perhaps the most difficult one to accept, is that there are various regulatory processes besides the production process that involve feedback of information. What this means is that an organization, like the motor in our car, has a number of gauges. When something goes wrong there are lights or buzzers. Organizations vary widely in how many gauges they have and how quickly the members may respond at the first sign of trouble, the gauges of an organization are the files and records compiled to keep tabs on certain aspects of the organization's operation, usually an accounting of the fine in the course of the year. These provide some feedback of information and, like the gauges in our car, can warn of mishaps and malfunctions. The Chandler selection on DuPont (Chapter Five) makes this very clear. Likewise, the word feedback is used explicitly in several other selections (Davis and Dolbeare, and Terreberry, both in Chapter One; Blau in Chapter Two; and Hage, Aiken, and Marrett in Chapter Four). We suspect that this aspect of system analysis will be increasingly employed to unravel the complex operations of organizations.

It is in the discussion of feedback that our definition of an organization as being consciously planned becomes important. One aspect of that planning is to establish objectives—gauges—of where the organization is supposed to be at the end of the next year. It may be a sales increase of ten percent or a lowering of a recidivism rate below a certain figure or reducing turnover among the staff. If these changes do not occur, then some response is triggered off by the recognition of the lack of success in meeting these objectives. The information sent from the performance measure to the elites is called feedback. The response or attempt to do better in some way is perhaps the best demonstration that feedback has evoked. The response may be correct or incorrect; successful solutions to lack of meeting objectives is the exception and not the rule.

Sometimes organizational elites have as their goal the elimination or prevention of certain phenomena. Indeed, it is this kind of feedback response that is most familiar. For example, we are all aware of the thermostat in our home, which we set to a desired temperature. As soon as the gauge, the thermometer, indicates that the temperature is falling, then this information signal triggers off the response of more heat, thereby preventing the temperature to drop below a set level. Likewise, prison guards and sometimes university presidents require a sort of thermometer to help in the prevention of riots, a kind of behavior they continuously attempt to keep from occurring. Chapter Four is devoted to the problems associated with this kind of feedback process and some kinds of responses used to prevent internal conflict.

More difficult is the discussion and identification of feedback associated with changes in the environment. Not only must an organization be sensitive to what takes place within it but also it must keep abreast of changes in its environment. For some, certain changes may be a matter of survival. A technological breakthrough, a shift in public tastes, a change in rules or in the number of competitors, are all environmental factors to which organizations must adapt themselves. Chapter Five (especially the selections by Chandler and Tsouderos) at least touches upon how this is done.

Seeing the organization as having various regulatory processes does not mean that it operates like a machine. Indeed, one is impressed at how blind organizational elites remain to various signs of trouble. Both McCleery and Tsouderos document this point nicely. But slow or faulty responses do not mean a lack of information feedback or a lack of control. It only demonstrates that human systems are different from machine systems.

The Choice of Problems   Any text–reader designed to reflect the present development of the field inevitably focuses on the various problems and concerns that sociologists have had. Most of these problems have emerged slowly and in an unsystematic way, as they necessarily must. We have tried to give a fair coverage to most of the problems that have been of concern. For example, in Chapter Three we consider the problem of the internal distribution of power, the problem of rules vs. procedures, the problem of the technical expert and the division of labor. Chapter Four looks at the issues of control and of conflict, while Chapter Five examines the problems of effectiveness and of adaptiveness, plus a number of others.

Yet, despite their seeming ad hoc appearance in each chapter, there are underneath several central themes, one might call them preoccupations. In general, power is a theme that is repeated over and over again. Beyond this is the theme of knowledge. The examination of knowledge and how it affects power is a distinctive sociological concern. Indeed, the interrelations of these two basic dimensions form much of the discussion in Chapters Two, Three, Four, and Five.

Another kind of set or focus is the basic issue of how to construct a viable organization to achieve particular goals. As we noted earlier, this is the essential sociological question, regardless of what the kind of social collective may be.

In Chapter Six, the various problems discussed in the introductions to Chapters One through Five are combined into a general framework. Some readers may prefer to skip ahead and read this chapter, obtaining an overview. Others may find it more helpful to see this framework emerge at the conclusion of reading this text–reader.

Reading Programs

There are as many different ways of reading this text–reader as there are readers. Naturally, we cannot specify all the possible sequences, but perhaps we can propose several general programs that will increase flexibility. But before we do, we might indicate the specific program that we used ourselves, because we felt it would meet the needs of the average reader best.

The Sequence of Selections   Clearly, once one selects a sociological perspective, this excludes a number of articles and books. Perhaps less clear are the various consequences of using a systems perspective. It happens that there are many more articles about the structure of organizations than about most of the other parts and, particularly, about the environment and its impact on the organization and vice versa. If one were to sample all the best articles, one would have different proportions for each part. Instead, we chose to keep the number of articles for each chapter approximately the same. This was necessary for several reasons. We wanted to be sure to cover several critical intellectual problems and debates in each chapter. These require a certain minimum of articles, usually five or six. Equally important, we wanted to present the organization "in the round," so to speak, and this means giving as much attention to the issues of goals and performances as to internal control processes. In the introductory sections we indicate the other articles we would have liked to include and, in addition, the areas we feel are important but relatively undeveloped. We have also included a section on other problems not handled in the reader, with the appropriate references. In this way, the limits of the system perspective as we have employed it are made clear, and the reader can supplement what we have selected according to his tastes and preferences.

Beyond using the basic components of the environment, social resources, social structure, control processes, performances and goals, we employed other criteria in selecting the articles and in editing them. *First,* we tried to represent the major intellectual traditions and debates that are presently important in the study of organizations. For example, the technology school and the size debate are both represented in the chapter on social resources. Similarly, each chapter is organized around three to five major intellectual issues that facilitate reading and provide the theoretical focus needed. In particular, we have tried to do justice to the rapid growth of the field during the past decade. About three-fourths of the selections have been published since 1964, and almost a third in the three years prior to this writing. Furthermore, we have tried to avoid a parochial "buy American" approach to selecting articles and books. About one-fourth of the selections are either by non-Americans or else report on non-American organizations or both. Interestingly enough, some of the best work and most pioneering contributions have been made by three English groups—Burns and Stalker, Woodward, and Pugh *et al.* (the Aston group)—all represented. Besides research on British organizations, Canadian, Turkish, Russian, Japanese, and French organizations are discussed.

Second, we have tried to select articles and parts of books that we feel will still be read some five or ten years from now, even with continued rapid development, because they are seminal and central. Insofar as we have correctly diagnosed the debates and the doubts of the discipline, then the choice of critical works comes relatively easy. Some indication that we may have chosen correctly is afforded by the number of references by the authors themselves to other selections in the text–reader. Certain works are considered critical because they opened a new slant or refuted an old one, and this is what we have tried to include. Although space has prevented us from including all that we would have liked, we have indicated in the introductions other selections worth the effort to get out of the library.

Third, we selected articles that were both theoretical and empirical whenever we could, but we excluded methodological articles and edited from our selections discussions of methodology and of research technique. The latter subject deserves a book in its own right. Perhaps more importantly, Price (1972) has just published an excellent one on measurement of many key organization variables. So there is no need to cover this ground. Even if we wanted to, it would have been difficult, again because of the limitations of size. For the undergraduate reader, the problem of methodology is best left for advanced seminars. In contrast, both theoretical and empirical articles are included because there tends to be a separation between the two, yet they are sides of the same coin. We need to develop hypotheses and we have to have these tested. Theoretical articles tend to concentrate on the former, and, of course, empirical articles on the latter.

Fourth, we have included both case studies and comparative studies. The former provide one with a feeling and data without concepts as well as depth of analysis, whereas comparative studies give one an opportunity for generalization and sophistication of analysis. Both have their advantages and both, therefore, are included.

As we have already noted the articles are arranged in chapters corresponding to the basic parts of an organization. But, again, there is both more and less order than implied in this statement. Since many, indeed almost all of the selections involve more than one variable, it means that frequently there is more than one chapter in which they can be placed. To help the reader follow a particular problem through we have included a large number of cross references, so that these interconnections and the systematic quality are not lost to view. Likewise, we have grouped the articles as much as we possibly can around the basic traditions and the current controversies. Again, cross references allow one to wend his way through these intellectual thickets.

In general, the case studies and the more concrete selections have been placed first in each chapter. This allows the reader to absorb some experiences unencumbered with concepts. Then the more theoretical or sophisticated empirical articles follow. This reflects the development of the field and thus is perhaps a more honest arrangement. But it is also a useful way of studying organizations. By reading case studies first, a fresh mind is maintained. Frequently they can provide the underpinning, the concrete illustrations, needed to make the sophisticated comparative studies and the theoretical discussions more alive. And the juxtaposition of the two kinds of materials creates its own kind of dialectic, much as the telling of the same tale by several witnesses creates a stereoscopic appreciation for what happened.

Different Reading Sequences   For the reader who has never had the opportunity to be an assembly-line worker or a soldier in the army, or a volunteer in some association, our recommendation is that he read all the case studies first regardless of which chapters they are in before beginning Chapter One. In particular, the selections from Blauner, Berliner, Crozier, McCleery, Lawrence and Lorsch, Chandler, Perrow, and Presthus give one the sense of various aspects of an organization. Although most of them, the one exception being McCleery, deal with either business firms or government bureaus, they do so from various viewpoints and even within different countries. These selections can and should be supplemented by reading perhaps more of each of their respective books. In addition, the Blau study of welfare workers (1956), the Caplow and McGee study of university professors (1957), and the Walker study of steelworkers (1957) are helpful and insightful. For those who would like an even more extended list of case studies, they might check Price (1967: 6–7) for a rather complete list of the better ones in the period of 1950–65, which is when most organizational case studies were completed. The importance of this background cannot be underestimated. It is this first-hand experience that makes the abstractions of sociology real. One needs to feel the weight of the hierarchy of authority or to be bounded by a number of rules to really grasp their significance and to appreciate their reality. Being a student in a university is not quite the same experience, unless one is also a teaching assistant or is otherwise employed with a salary and therefore more vulnerable.

Those readers who have been members of organizations, rather than customers or clients, have this background information already stored in their memory. But here, too, experiences may not be broad enough to see general outlines as opposed to idiosyncratic detail. A case study of an organization other than the one with which the reader is most familiar is a useful didactic device. If one has served in the marines, for example, the reading about the problems of the assembly-line worker can make one appreciate both similarities and differences, what is general and what is unique. Again the list in the reference to Price (1967) provides a wide choice range.

Beyond the immediate need for background information are many other possible needs and preferences. To tap these tastes, we have included in our introductions three pieces of information: background work leading up to a particular article (especially when this may not be apparent from reading the selection itself), related work located elsewhere in the text–reader, and additional work that we could not include. This will allow readers interested in particular topics to skip around the book in a systematic way and to supplement what we have done with more depth. Of some twenty major problems discussed, at least some will be of interest to most readers.

Presenting different kinds of problems is not the only way to generate a unique sequence for each reader. We sometimes discover that certain sociologists are on our own wave length, for whatever reasons—and this is more than just a question of their specific focus. We find ourselves attracted by their attack on the issue, their sense of style, and other factors that remain intangible. It is this observation that led us to select several works from each of several authors, in each case the most active ones in the field, rather than to attempt to include as many contributors to the field of organizations as possible. The reader can get a better feeling for the work of Blau, Hall, Pugh, *et al.* (the Aston group), or Aiken and Hage and then can decide whether he wants more. For him who does, we include extended bibliographies to help facilitate these extensions.

Some readers have an interest in only one kind of organization. Business students, educational administrators, welfare workers, etc., have their tastes. We have tried to present a variety of these kinds of organizations. But our objective in doing so is to provide a comparative perspective. It might be a serious error to read only about schools and colleges even if one intends to become a school superintendent someday. The reasons are many. Researchers in particular areas tend to focus on only some things, losing sight of other equally relevant problems. Tradition blinds us as well as provides a pathway for us.

A comparative perspective breaks down at least some of these narrow perspectives. More importantly, certain problems, issues of general scope, are more easily grasped and comprehended in some kinds of organizations than in others. The problem of technology is easier to study in a factory but that does not make it unimportant in a welfare agency. And while Blau (1956) pointed to the problems of clients being maltreated by welfare workers back in the midfifties, Nader and his raiders certainly made this an issue for business organizations in the late sixties. So our recommendation is to read widely about other kinds of organizations even if the major interest lies in a particular kind. Indeed, this is the great strength of a sociological perspective and its accent on patterns common to all kinds of organizations and, beyond that, to social collectives. This does not mean that there is no difference between a school, a factory, and a police station. It does mean that the differences are best comprehended once we understand the similarities.

Finally, as noted in the preceding section, some people prefer to read with a great deal of order and, for this reason, may wish to read the closing chapter before moving into Chapter One. Others prefer, or perhaps one should say understand better, a general framework *only* after having a chance to comprehend the particulars. For these readers, whom we suspect are in the majority, we have placed the set of system coordinates in the last chapter.

The Problem of Reading Numbers It would be pleasant if we could eliminate reporting figures, both arithmetical and schematic. But precisely as the sociology of organizations becomes of more practical value, it becomes more of a science. This means measurement with numbers. It means a steady progression toward mathematics. It means a different kind of reading. We have tried to eliminate as much of the unpleasantness as possible. There are ways of lessening the mystery of statistics, for the principles are relatively simple.

Knowing that many readers might not like to have to wade through a barrage of data, we have considerably reduced the number of tables and have edited them to highlight what we feel is essential. Second, we have arranged the tables as much as possible into several standard formats, namely percentage tables or correlations. Third, we have several guidelines that should aid the reader.

When looking at a percent table or a correlation the major objective is to determine how much two variables are associated. Simply put, on faces with noses do we always find two eyes. This is an important piece of information because if we know that every time we see a nose we see two eyes, we can predict that once we observe the nose coming around the corner, two eyes are not far behind. Indeed, this is exactly what the economists mean by leading indicators.

Both percent tables and correlations are illustrated in Figure 1

FIGURE 1. THREE EXAMPLES OF ASSOCIATION: PLOTS, CORRELATIONS, AND PERCENTAGE TABLES

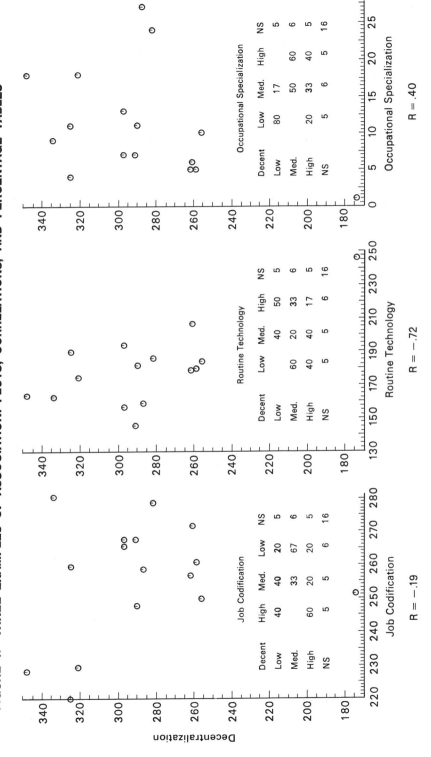

and for the same approximate strength of association between two variables or two categories. We read a percentage table by simply checking which cells have the largest percentages. If we find that 70 percent of one kind of organization has a rules manual but only 34 percent of another kind has one, we can begin to make some predictions about which kinds of organizations have rules manuals, admittedly not with perfect accuracy, because the percentages in the two cells on the diagonal are not 100 percent. Instead of categories, the percentage table can contain variables, and the procedure to read it would be the same. If we find that organizations with a high degree of complexity score low on formalization, then we should look for a cell which tells if those with a low degree of complexity score high on formalization. The key is to observe the cells on the diagonal. And this is true regardless of the number of cells, whether four, nine, or sixteen. (For those who would like to read more about percentages and tables, the best introduction remains, in our opinion, Zeisel's *Say It with Figures.*)

Correlations are much easier to read and require less interpretation, although their computation is more difficult and also perhaps more difficult to understand. In this text–reader, a large variety of measures of association are reported. But simply put and not distorting the theory of statistics too much, like the percentage table, they tell us how much two variables or two categories are associated. For example, the more often we find a rules manual in a large organization and no rules manual in a small organization, the higher the association between the presence of a rules manual and the size of the organization. The degree of association, or the extent to which rules and size go hand in hand in this case, is expressed in the number known as the *correlation coefficient,* which has the maximum score of 1.00. The greater the association, the closer the score gets to 1.00. Sometimes, a negative or positive sign is placed in front of the score but the point remains. Zero means no association and 1.00 means a perfect one. The plus and minus give us direction; if minus, an increase in one variable leads to a decrease in the other. In Figure One, we have diagrammed three common situations and indicated what the percentage table looks like when the measure of association is low, medium, and high.

How much association is enough? There are two ways of answering this question. Statistically, we can and do measure the difference between 0.00 and the correlation we have by determining how many times it could have occurred by chance. The same can be done with the percentage table. Conventions vary, but either one chance in ten or twenty would be considered reasonably low enough to be confident that our association is not just a twist of fate. Indeed, confidence levels are so called for precisely this reason.

But this is not the only standard. Unfortunately, chance and the computation of these confidence levels are largely influenced by the size of the sample. If we have a large enough sample, a correlation of .05 would be statistically significant, and yet common sense tells us that substantively this is pretty uninteresting. We would like an association to be stronger than that. We need to decide whether we find the size of the correlation theoretically interesting, and here conventions are not at all firm. Our own rule is that a correlation above .40 is substantively interesting and one between .30 and .39 is perhaps worth some attention. But in general, those below .30, even with a large sample are not likely, except for special cases, to be of much import. This convention changes rapidly as the field develops. Demographers and economists would find .40 to be too low for their taste, and as the sociology of organizations develops, we can be sure that this substantive level will be increased. But at least it is a rough guideline that the reader can use to work his way through the various selections and debates.

As the measure of association gets higher and higher, substantively it means a stronger association with increasing force. In a sense .40 is twice as good as .30, whereas .60 is eight times as good, and .70 is hard to believe. The reason is simple. Given all the other variables in a complex world and the many problems of obtaining good measures, it is very rare for variables to have associations as high as .70 or more. There are some reported in this text–reader, but they are the exception and not the rule.

To summarize, when reading numbers, we are interested in knowing if two variables or categories are associated. We can determine this by looking at a percentage table or some measure of association. We then ask ourselves if the association is statistically significant, which, if so, is almost always reported, and whether it is also theoretically significant, which is almost never reported. For the latter, we have suggested a rough guideline of about .40.

Conclusions

When we approach a book most of us are interested in knowing how it is integrated and how to maximize its usefulness. This is especially true for a text–reader and readers which tend to be much less structured than textbooks. To help integrate this work, we have chosen what we think is a coherent perspective, what we call a sociological conception of organizations qua systems. Our definition of an organization is that it is a social collective designed to achieve fairly specific objectives, which are only one part of a larger institutional process within a society. Using the system perspective we have selected articles to illustrate the many parts of organizations, namely, their environment, their social resources, their social structure, their control processes, and finally their performances and goals. Also inherent in the system perspective is that the organization can be described as a set of variables, so that a change in one produces a change in one or more others. Some of the variables operate via the mechanism of information feedback. Thus, a critical objective of this text–reader is to identify the important dimensions, indicating where necessary the debates about their utility, and indicating as much as possible how these variables operate together in some system.

The coherence of our system perspective provides one way of integrating the articles. Beyond this, we have included a number of cross references between chapters. Indeed, many of the articles reference other sections themselves. These references are arranged around key problems to provide maximum focus. Additional reading is included so that the reader can supplement according to his desires and in the directions he wants. To further facilitate flexibility, we have suggested various sequences of reading depending upon the kind of reader and his responses to the selections. We have included a short discussion of how to read percentage tables and measures of association, since they afford the simplest way of seeing whether two or more variables operate together as a system. For, while system analysis is our perspective, it still remains a hypothesis about organizations.

Thus, while the field is in ferment, hopefully this text–reader will convey the excitement evident on all sides without inspiring a concurrent feeling of chaos. Indeed, the many debates and divergent viewpoints help in their own way to integrate the work and provide the reader with an abundance of ideas on how to understand and perhaps control the large organizations that are everywhere around us.

1
THE ENVIRONMENT: THE SOCIETAL CONTEXT OF ORGANIZATIONS

Studying the environment in relation to organizations, a relatively unexplored territory, is likely to prove fruitful not only for the sociology of organizations but for sociology in general. In the past, most organizational sociologists have concentrated on the internal arrangements and processes and not on what is external to organizations. Now an increasing amount of curiosity, if not actual research, is being focused on the latter. This concern with the environment has stemmed probably from three sources. One is that as the field moved from case to comparative studies and more systematic data cumulated, we found that relations between variables are inconclusive if not conflicting and, therefore, we are far from discovering universally applicable propositions. Thus, possible and probable variables are sought far and wide, no less in the environment. The second source, though related to the first, is the realization that most organizations deal primarily with other organizations. That is, other organizations constitute a major segment of the organizational environment, and therefore, interorganizational relations are likely to account for at least some of the discrepancies we find in relations among variables about the internal aspects of organizations. The third source is the increased concern over social change. Scholars and concerned citizens want to know what makes for innovation, what environmental forces induce or inhibit change.

In a recent annual meeting of the American Sociological Association, the session on "new directions in research on organizations and professions" amply aired the view that this is the area to which future research ought to be and will be directed. One panelist, Heydebrand, suggested that "we are moving from a psychology of organizations to a sociology of organizations" (1965: 2), in the sense that while psychology claims the person, and sociology, what is external to the person, as their respective units of analysis, the field of organizations is shifting its focus to extraorganizational factors.

Needless to say, no organization stands in a vacuum. No matter how self-contained and autonomous an organization may be, it must still find its own legitimation (Selznick, 1949; Katz and Kahn, 1966; Davis and Dolbeare, 1968, included in this chapter; Perrow, 1970) for existence and survival, and this legitimation must be shared by the outside world at least to the extent of tolerating its being. Though far removed and having little contact with the outside, a Trappist monastery must still be allowed to exist and to recruit new members from the outside. The proliferation of organizations is dependent on certain conditions that prevail in society at large (Eisenstadt, 1959; Stinchcombe, 1965; Azumi, in this chapter), and it is highly probable that the characteristics a given organization can assume are largely determined by its societal context. Its goal-setting, acquisition of resources, the amount of autonomy, wealth, complexity, etc., are limited by the external conditions. The U.S. Army, the General Motors Corporation, the Vatican, the D.A.R., and the Red Cross are all constrained by the world of which they are parts. Legitimation, wealth, knowledge, and labor that they may seek are not necessarily available at the motion of their fingers, and the ways in which they are constrained and their manner of adaptations are surely topics that organizational researchers ought to pursue.

The large number of voluntary organizations, some emerging amorphously as groups with those of like minds and interests, getting together and occasionally growing as social movements that equip themselves with organizational apparatus (Zald and Ash, 1966) is also a function of the environment (Wallace, 1956). There must be, as we suspect, some patterns governing the rise of organizations, the types of organizations fostered, and the course of life that they assume. The sociological task lies in discovering the patterns and basic variables that account for them.

The importance of the environment appears obvious, but there is no consensus on what the environment of an organization consists of or how the relation between the two may be studied.

A reasonable suggestion has been made by James Thompson (1967: Ch. 6) to define the organizational environment as consisting of "exogenous variables" or constraints and contingencies that are beyond the control of the organization. This is in the vein of an earlier statement by Emery and Trist (1965) that organizational environment be defined as components with which the organization actually or potentially transacts and which are comprised of "causal texture." So far this perspective on the environment has been the dominant one. It sees the environment as an independent variable. This perspective is set forth most forcefully in a paper by Terreberry (1968), which is included in this chapter. She sees organizational changes being caused not so much for internal as for external reasons; thus, " 'survival of the fittest is a function of the fitness of the environment" (p. 993).

The direction of influence between the organization and its environment can, of course, be the other way around. Collectively, and sometimes individually, organizations have an impact on the environment. The individual influence of an organization on its environment can be seen in some powerful organizations, and the collective influence of a network of such organizations is obvious. At the very least, they have a powerful hand in setting the conditions and existence for individuals and other organizations in society. The recent outcry from the left against the establishment and the military-industrial complex assumes that some large and powerful organizations and their elites are interlocked and serve to perpetuate and strengthen their position at the neglect of public interest. One recent study, however, reports that while some large organizations in the U.S. are highly dependent upon military expenditures, there is evidence that most corporations would prosper more "if the government shifted to nonmilitary expenditures" (Lieberson, 1971). Further, the propositions by Azumi (in this chapter) suggest that autonomy of a complex of organizations is likely to be reduced in a decentralized environment. At least in the U.S., such a complex is unlikely to develop unhindered by countervailing forces.

For any given organization, the environment consists of environmental agents who are carriers of environmental needs and resources (Azumi, in this chapter). The specific aspects of the environmental agents focused on in the literature vary greatly and defy any attempt at synthesis. Some writers have dealt with culture (Harbison, *et al.,* 1955; Richardson, 1956; Crozier, 1964; Williams, *et al.,* 1966; J. Thompson, 1967; Azumi, 1969), and some with other organizations (Thompson and McEwen, 1958; Evan, 1966; and many others), and with community (Form and Miller, 1960; Schnore and Alford, 1963) or organizational field (Emery and Trist, 1965, Terreberry, 1968; Blau and Schoenherr, 1971).

There is as yet no definitive work that states precisely what it is about the environment that has an impact on the organization and what processes are actually involved in it. In the last selection in this chapter, Azumi makes an attempt in that direction, following the sociological tradition of focusing on structural factors.

In order to discuss the problems of the organizational environment that have been dealt with in the literature, we shall organize the remainder of this introduction in terms of persons, organizations, and, most generally, fields. These are not mutually exclusive categories in reality, but are helpful in presenting what we consider to be the three major problems dealt with so far in the area. They are (1) the problem of societal values (2) the organizational networks or institutional arrangements, and (3) the problem of the organizational fields or markets.

THE PROBLEMS

The Problem of Societal Values

Most fundamentally, no organization can exist without values. It is values that provide legitimation, define needs and goals, and give content to norms that are the means for realizing the goals dictated by values. Culture—the more generic term inclusive of values, ideas, knowledge, and sentiments—serves as a homogenizing influence (Thompson, 1967) for the organization and its environment, and in that sense provides a degree of certainty and predictability in the environment.

Sociologists would like to see that the propositions they make are universally applicable across time and space. Most empirical studies, including comparative ones of the recent past, however, have been conducted in the U.S. and England. As a consequence, we do not know if the findings discussed in Chapters Two through Five have applicability beyond the Western world. In this sense the selection by Presthus in this chapter is highly instructive. Based on a study of a coal-mining firm in Turkey, he suggests that to apply the Weberian conception of bureaucracy to this firm is to see the trees and miss the forest. The overriding societal values make it what he calls a welfare bureaucracy; that is, the importance of hiring the unemployed is above the Western or Weberian preference for efficiency. Once said, this study finds parallels in other societies, especially those with lower standards of living. And yet we lack systematic data to confirm the hypothesis that the welfare bureaucracies decline along with industrialization.

Societal values are called in to explain differences between organizations with the same goals. Richardson (1956), for example, compared two ships, one American and the other British, and argued that the organization must adapt to its particular goals, but at the same time the values and sentiments of its members must also be accommodated. "Variations in organization, then, can be expected to follow from variations of culture from which members of an organization are drawn." What is interesting about this comparison is that the two countries have the same language and even the same naval traditions, but there are still differences.

The Richardson study represents one route to discuss societal values as they influence organizations. That is, persons are defined as carriers of societal values and as such affect some aspects of organization. Institutional as well as organizational arrangements, too, reflect societal values and organizations, too, are carriers of societal values. In this section, however, we shall stress the person as a carrier of societal values.

People have role expectations about employer and employee. Normally mutual role expectations converge and, even if there is a formal contract, there is also what Durkheim called the noncontractual part of the contract, which can be taken for granted. The selection by Presthus may be seen in this manner. Although the organization under study is supposedly a task-oriented one, it is also people oriented, so that its instrumental goal may be sacrificed to some degree. If the management does not accommodate itself to the expectations of its subordinates, the performance of the organization may suffer by way of low morale. A rather dramatic instance of nonconvergence of role expectations occurred in a branch office of an American bank in Japan in the late 1940's (Noda, 1959: 103–105). Employees demanded payment of family and commutation allowances which were commonly paid by other firms in Japan. They asked also that their tardiness due to public transportation failures not be subject to pay cuts. They also reminded the American management that their daily life differed radically from that of the management who had to commute only a short distance in luxury cars and whose breakfast was prepared by servants. The American management indicated a complete disregard for local custom, save the low wages. Their response said that the bank had no responsibility to pay family allowance as it was outside its concern that its employees supported three wives and hatched a dozen children. It did not care where its employees lived. It said that the housekeeping ability of the employees' wives or the reliability of public transportation were outside the bank's concern or responsibility and the life style of the management a private matter, of no concern to the employees.

The subsequent trend among foreign-owned firms to hire local managers is a response to strains arising from nonconvergent mutual role expectations between the management and the workers. If people who come in contact with the organization by becoming either its members or associates can affect it by way of their values and sentiments, then we should find differences between organizations across societies whose values are different. Thus one question that concerns the organizational sociologist is what role, if any, societal values play as a determinant of organizational behavior. In the past, goals, size, and technology have been suggested as the major determinants. While debates over which of these is the primary one continue (see Chapters

Two and Three), we are likely to see societal values added as another variable when cross-societal comparative studies come into being.

There are a number of society-specific case studies (see the rich bibliography in Nath, 1968), but systematic cross-societal comparative studies are almost nonexistent. The reason for this is that, until recently, we lacked a general framework with which to approach a number of different organizations. Now that there are a few general frameworks (Pugh *et al.,* 1963; Hage, 1965; Perrow, 1967; Price, 1967; Thompson, 1967), we should be able to obtain data with which to speak to the issue of values and organizations. If we have standardized ways of seeing and measuring aspects of organizations, the results we get are more comparable and eloquent than those we might get with a number of independent case studies. Some might, however, suggest that these general frameworks themselves are cultural products—social beliefs— that miss the rich and colorful and yet important aspects of organizations in some societies. One must, however, present and interpret the data in such a way that the ideas are readily exportable to other societies and to speak to disciplinary issues rather than to those in a geographical area study. The Presthus selection is much more than a contribution to the study of Turkey, as he places the case in the context of sociological theory by juxtaposing the Weberian conception of bureaucracy against another, which he calls welfare bureaucracy.

The study of values as they affect organizations is a difficult one, especially in empirical research. A part of the difficulty lies in the rising competition of values in a contemporary world, which only adds to the turbulence in the organizational fields that Terreberry speaks of. One mode of analysis is shown by Crozier (1964). We have included in Chapter Three excerpts from the book but not from the section in which he shifts from a structural to a cultural analysis of his data. In the latter part he identifies a set of what he calls permanent French culture traits in an attempt to make sense of French organizations. They are (1) the isolation of the individual, (2) the predominance of formal over informal activities, (3) the isolation of the strata, and (4) [people's] struggles for privileges. These traits indeed appear compatible with earlier observations made in French bureaucracies (some of which are in Chapter Three of this reader). It is important, however, to raise a few questions here. How were these traits identified? By intuition? By systematic observation? Do they constitute the whole of French culture traits, or at least those pertinent to the study of organizations? Are they peculiar to the French? Where, for example, do we find a society in which people do not struggle for privileges? More basically, this manner of explanation tends to be an exercise in tautology as long as culture traits are extracted from structure. Here no analytical distinction is made between culture and society (Kroeber and Parsons, 1958).

What is clearly needed is a general list of values and standardized measures that can be applied to a variety of cultural contexts. Traditionally, those who have studied a single culture have looked at values or some other cultural variable as the major determinant. Those who have taken the comparative perspective have usually, although not always, emphasized structure and other behavioral variables. What is needed is a combination of the two, to assess the relative importance of various variables. And, in particular, cross-societal research in non-Western societies is an important area for future work.

The relation between organization and individual values is, of course, a classic debate that dates back to Weber's additions (1929) to Marx's assumption that individual values are a product of organizational or societal structure. Weber suggested that values could have an independent force or effect. As yet, this debate, which affects all of sociology, is unresolved.

The Problem of Organizational Networks or Institutional Arrangements

While we have considered the societal values primarily through persons, as carriers of those values which influence organizational behavior, we shall here focus on other organizations in the environment. Broadly stated, this is the problem of intra- and interinstitutional arrangements or organizational networks.

While an institutional division of labor is clearly visible in industrial societies, the lines of demarcation between institutions are less clear in underdeveloped societies. That is to say, there is overlapping of functions among institutions, so one finds economic institutions fulfilling some political or welfare functions as well. The selection by Presthus can be interpreted in this way. Although the enterprise he describes is a coal-mining firm, it nevertheless acts as if production of coal as its organizational goal is receded by other goals, including employment of personnel who are not necessarily needed, if one is to consider the production of coal to be the sole and primary aim. The Berliner selection is a case study of factories in the Soviet Union, where the whole economic institution resembles an organization. The Soviet Union is a society in which political values predominate and thus nonpolitical institutions are subjugated to the polity. In the centrally planned economy, each plant is given specific assignments for production, but the shipment of raw materials, etc., does not necessarily proceed according to plan. Managers try, nevertheless, to achieve their goals in reality or on paper by resorting to an extralegal manner of transaction which is called *blatt*. The particular excerpts from Berliner describe the emergence of an informal mechanism to smooth out the rugged path toward meeting production goals.

In sharp contrast to the Berliner selection, the Davis–Dolbeare piece describes an organization that operates in a highly decentralized polity. The local board of the Selective Service System has a great deal of autonomy and thus the subunits of the same organization, supposedly doing the same job, could show much variation in the way they pursue their tasks. We have included this selection for its utilization of a system perspective and for dealing with an organization in the political institution. Decentralization is a major theme in the American polity and it is the local board that decides who is to serve in the nation's armed forces and who is to be deferred. Standardization and control become a problem for the national organization, which in turn is subject to appraisals from a number of governmental offices and agencies. In a way, unlike the Berliner selection, an informal structure is built into the formal system, or the formal system, despite its attempt to standardize practices on the local level, cannot be so rigid as to threaten accommodation to local extralegal mores and sentiments. The Davis–Dolbeare selection is excellent also in that it takes up an issue that Selznick had raised long ago (1949—an excerpt is included in Chapter Two of this book), which is the question of how to have citizen participation in government activities and to democratize government bureaucracies.

There are some other studies on the more specific topic of interorganizational relations. One excellent theoretical exposition is by Evan (1966) who extended Merton's (1957: 368–380) concept of role-set to organizations and coined the term organization-set to suggest a number of promising problems for the field. An organization-set is the complex of organizations that another focal one interacts with, or it may be defined as the complex of organizations that a class of organizations interacts with. Evan identified several dimensions of the concept and suggested also plausible hypotheses linking these dimensions to the autonomy of the focal organization. This is worth reading for inspiration and ideas.

Litwak and Hylton (1962) suggested some features that separate the inter- from intraorganizational studies. The major one is the way conflict is viewed; namely, in intraorganizational studies conflict between organizations is taken for granted. Conflicting values are thought to lead to breakdown in organizational structure. While a fairly well-defined authority structure is assumed to exist in an organization, no such assumption is made for the interorganizational field. So the study focuses on unstructured authority. In the absence of structured authority within the field there is uncertainty and confusion and, thus, a need for coordination. So Litwak and Hylton suggest that coordinating agencies will develop and continue in existence if formal organizations are partly interdependent.

In a study of sixteen social welfare and health organizations, and their interdependence with other organizations, Aiken and Hage (1968) find that those organizations with more complex structures, that is, those with a highly professionalized staff, and a diversified number of occupations, tend to be more interdependent with other organizations, as measured by the number of joint programs. This article implies that as organizations become more complex and decentralized, they will be knit together in coalition with other organizations. The article fails to note that this is probably true only if the environment is decentralized.

The Problem of Organizational Fields or Markets

As we ascend the scale of specificity and concreteness from persons to organizations to institutions, we arrive at the inclusive environment at large which is occasionally referred to as the organizational fields or markets. The Terreberry selection focuses on the fields as the independent variable that causes change in the organization. Her major thrust is that from the viewpoint of a given organization the field varies in its degree of livability or fitness. The organizational field is in a state of flux, to which the organization must adapt in order to survive.

Inquiries into the relation between the environment and the internal structure of organizations have been slow in coming, but there are a few. Burns and Stalker found formalization to be negatively associated with financial success of firms in uncertain environments (1961: 1–10).

Another theoretical exploration in this field was the pioneering paper by Thompson and McEwen (1958). This one links the environment with goal-setting of organization. Their idea was that organizational goals are far from being static and, in effect, are controlled by the environment. Goal-setting, they said, is a recurrent problem for any organization and is essentially a problem of defining desired relationships with the environment (p. 23). Any change in either the organization itself or in the environment demands a modification of goals. The same paper classified the organizational strategies for coping with the environment and its changes into two broad types: competitive and cooperative, the latter of which is further divided into bargaining, cooptation, and coalition. Dill (1958) suggested from a study of two Norwegian firms that managerial autonomy is affected by environmental pressures. Simpson and Gulley (1962) similarly reported that voluntary organizations with diffuse environmental pressures had more decentralized structure and higher internal communication; while those with specific and restricted pressures had the opposite characteristics.

Lawrence and Lorsch (Chapter Four) in a study of six organizations in the chemical processing industry divided their environment into three subenvironments of market, science, and technical–economic, and their organizations into four systems of fundamental research, applied research, sales, and production. The key variable for the subenvironment is certainty. Their study found that the more certain the subenvironment, the greater the formalization of structure in the subsystem. That is to say, an organization operates within a number of subenvironments and, depending on their certainty, the particular parts of the organization associated with the subenvironments change their structure. Schnore and Alford (1963) suggested from their study of 300 suburban communities in the U.S. that the population characteristics of the community are related to the particular form of government that it takes. That is, there are systematic tendencies for the government to assume the more centralized council–manager form if the population of the community is young, mobile, white, and middle class.

Another study which systematically measures the influence of external factors on the internal arrangements of organizations is by Blau and Shoenherr (1971). Employment Security Agencies' state and local offices were the units of analysis in their study, and the environmental factors referred to the respective state in which the offices were located. Aside from some obvious ones, such as the population size of the state and the size of the organization being highly correlated, it appears that the relationships between external factors and organizational structure are weak, and the authors conclude: "The external environment does not exert much influence on the internal differentiation in [State headquarters] or on that in its component branches . . ." (p. 235). We do not yet know, however, how widely applicable this finding may be to other organizations, but it does not refute the importance of considering the environment in studying organizations. As yet, we have explored few environmental variables vis-à-vis organizational resource variables such as size or organizational goals.

Acknowledging that, the Terreberry thesis appears obvious. Once that is pointed out, we need to conceptualize new problems. In the last selection Azumi provides a framework in his discussion of the environmental needs, resources, and agents by looking at two problems within the framework: one is the question of the number and size of organizations and the other is the factors affecting the autonomy of organizations, how some of them become all powerful and, thus, a major influence in the environment.

Additional reading on the problem of the market as one way of conceptualizing the field is Caplow's *The Sociology of Work* (1954: Ch. 7), in which he discusses four models of the labor market. What is important is that these models have very different demand and supply curves, some constant and others liable to quick change. One can extend his thinking to other resources besides the recruitment of staff, such as supply and demand for money, legitimation, and even knowledge.

Still a different line of attack is consideration of the whole problem of research and development in the larger society and how this influences organizations (Hage and Aiken, 1970: Ch. 3). The explosion of research and demonstration development funds has, in turn, triggered off a large number of relevant findings about new products or services. New clients are identified, new problems found, and new solutions proposed. This endless flow of information creates future shock (Toffler, 1970) for organizations. They must constantly change or adapt to a turbulent environment.

THE READINGS

Weberian vs. Welfare Bureaucracy in Traditional Society*

ROBERT V. PRESTHUS

A current focus for organizational theory concerns the utility of the ideal western bureaucratic model for institutional analysis and the guiding of change in underdeveloped societies. How useful are Weber's familiar structural and behavioral components for ordering and understanding organizations in traditional society? There is considerable evidence that the model is indeed useful (Berger, 1958; Heady, 1959: 509–525). Not only does it provide a Platonic ideal against which organizations in underdeveloped countries can be assayed, but its clinical use may help such countries achieve the social and economic goals they have set for themselves.

Despite such advantages, it is very easy to overlook or underestimate the extent to which the Weberian model rests upon certain normative assumptions about time, man, motivation, and society, which are not present in nonwestern societies. While the structural components of bureaucracy are often similar in each milieu, the behavioral manifestations are often quite different. Particularly, one tends to overlook the extent to which the manifest goals of bureaucracies in underdeveloped countries are challenged by their welfare imperatives. Perhaps a useful index for differentiating western and nonwestern bureaucracies is the *relative balance* between Weberian claims for skill, impartiality, predictability, and the achievement of the organization's formal objectives and welfare claims that stress co-operation, full employment, and fringe benefits.

Such a distinction is supported by theoretical considerations and by research. Weber himself noted that bureaucratic structure was not always associated with rationality, and one student of organization recently found in an analysis of 150 organizations in nonindustrial societies that the "bureaucratic" components of Weber's model are

* Reprinted from *Administrative Science Quarterly, 6* (June 1961), pp. 1–24, with minor omissions, by permission of the author and the publisher.

negatively associated with its "rational" elements (Udy, 1959). That is, such "bureaucratic" elements as hierarchical authority structure, administrative staff units, and income gradations according to office were in conflict with such "rational" claims as limited objectives, participation based upon "mutual limited agreement" among members, and "compensatory rewards" whereby those in authority allocate rewards to members in return for participation (Udy, 1959: 793). Such findings suggest a discontinuity between the manifest structure of bureaucracy, as it appears in many underdeveloped societies, and the rational behavioral elements often assumed to be integral parts of Weber's model.

This article attempts to illustrate such disparities by research findings from one traditional society. The study was carried out in 1955 over a six-month period in Zonguldak, a port on the Black Sea where the Turkish coal fields are located, and in Ankara in the public corporation, Etibank, of which Eregli Komurleri Isletmeni (henceforth EKI) is a subsidiary. In addition, officials in other ministries that have some responsibility for EKI were interviewed. Various documents such as personnel records, forms used in the various departments, organization charts, and work-flow diagrams were examined. In the main, the data are qualitative, and the research is best defined as a case study. Most of the one hundred Zonguldak interviews were conducted with high-level staff members in EKI, rather than with line personnel. Since EKI's organization is well structured, and since authority and decision making tend to follow channels rather closely, we were able to secure accurate descriptions of the operation from those in positions of formal authority. Moreover, visits into the coal mines and random observation and conversation with supervisors and miners at the operational level gave corroborative evidence of conditions and attitudes at the working level. We had little chance, however, to attend staff meetings, becoming in effect nonparticipant observers. Also, attempts to build quantitative indexes from questionnaire data on employee opinions, morale, and so on, were not fruitful. Here, the problem of the *social context* of research was engaged: In traditional societies, empirical field research using quantitative methods is outside the experience of even most educated men, since the whole tradition of academic values and educational philosophy is inapposite. Although this problem is steadily being eroded, it provides another example of the cultural diversities with which this articles deals.

Some administrators and students of administration tend to assume that the ethos, behavior, and technology of western bureaucratic organizations can be superimposed upon underdeveloped societies without the necessity of changing to some extent their traditional ideological and structural alignments. While there is some evidence, particularly in Japan, that technological change and economic development can occur without substantial modification of time-honored social patterns, such as the extended family system or the patriarchal authority system (Nimkoff and Middleton, 1960: 109–118) in the Middle East, it seems that extensive modification must occur. In some of these societies, we see "highly bureaucratized" governmental organizations, often the product of French or British rule, but their behavioral consequences and manifest goals are mainly a function of the particular social context in which the bureaucratic apparatus exists. Their underlying social values and class structure bend the organization in ways that document their own major assumptions.

While it is now fashionable to speak of a "cultural revolution" in underdeveloped societies, in the Middle East, one must conclude that social change is painfully slow, despite some isolated evidence of progress toward industrialization, democracy, and so on. The change, for example, from a one-party to a multiparty political system or the drafting of a liberal constitution cannot so easily overcome the authoritarian political and social legacy of the area, as the recent experience of Turkey shows so well. This impasse is surely not because western technology and values have not been brought to bear upon such countries. Rather, traditional ideology and institutions have provided subtle, deep-seated, and pervasive resistance to change. A striking example may be seen in the highly educated elites of underdeveloped society, whose dress, speech, and public style of life often seem typically western, but whose private values about class, mobility, "culture," and political systems remain little changed (Presthus, 1959; Myrdal, 1960: 207–208; Matthews, 1954; Lerner, 1959).

Despite the difficulty of superimposing western values upon underdeveloped countries, it seems that if they choose to follow the West, they must be prepared systematically to redirect traditional values and institutions in rather more pragmatic and rational directions. Above all, the pervasive class stratification of such systems, with attending inequities in educational and economic opportunity, must be eased in order that their latent human resources can be developed. To say this is neither to assume that western values are intrinsically superior nor that nonwestern societies "should" adopt them: it is merely to accept their own choice of economic development as a normative goal, and then to consider the conditions required to achieve it.

Accepting such a goal as a given, let us turn to the problems that confront such societies, as experienced by the so-called technical assistance expert who must go beyond analysis to effect social change. Here, one soon learns that the western bureaucratic model rests upon certain implicit judgments about efficiency, objectivity, motivation, and authority. During the present transitional era, when underdeveloped countries necessarily oscillate between their own norms and those of the West, the introduction of Weberian values is regarded with considerable ambivalence, not only by peasant majorities, but by educated elites, who do not always have a great deal to gain by the social revolution that attends economic development.

These generalizations are sharpened by research in underdeveloped countries, which highlights the normative disparities between western and nonwestern communities and illustrates some of their specific institutional consequences. Such facts of organizational theory can bring us closer to an understanding of how social values and personality press upon administrative behavior. (Presthus, 1961).

Purposes and Organization of EKI

Like basic industry in most underdeveloped countries (those whose annual per capita income is less than $200), the Turkish coal industry is a state-owned enterprise, organized rather like American or British public corporations. The enterprise, charged essentially with coal mining, is completely financed by the state, employs persons with many different kinds of skills, and carries on a broad welfare program, which I shall argue, competes strongly with its manifest function of coal production. Since coal is Turkey's only basic power resource, this is a vital objective.

EKI functions under a director and an administrative committee composed of the director, his assistants, and at least three persons appointed from its remaining officials and employees. The administrative committee formally directs the activities of the enterprise, but the director, who can dictate his views to the committee, is actually responsible for its daily operations and for representing it in its relations with other authorities. He and the other chief officials are appointed by the administrative committee at the recommendation of the national Ministry of Industry, which is charged with planning and co-ordination of all state-owned enterprises. All other employees are appointed by the director, subject only to the right of the Ministry to be informed.

Each year the administrative committee proposes a "work program" or plan of operations for the succeeding year. The director then submits the program with his recommendations to the Ministry's planning group, which discusses it and returns it to him, approved. Modifications of the work program are handled similarly. Copies of the work program are sent to the Minister of Economy, the minister responsible for national economic planning and foreign trade, and to the High Control Board, comprising engineers and economists charged with surveillance of state-operated enterprises and preparation of reports for the prime minister.

Financial statutes limit the responsibility of EKI for debts and prescribe how part of its profits shall be distributed. There is a levy of 10 percent of any profits to cover possible future losses. This levy constitutes a reserve of capital, which continues to be amassed until it reaches a sum equal to one-quarter of the entire capital of the enterprise. The levy is paid into a special account, and may be used at the discretion of the administrative committee, with the approval of the Minister of Industry.

EKI has a special *barem* which governs working conditions, including salary, grades, promotion procedures, and so on. These conditions are generally more favorable than those of the Turkish civil service and presumably better adapted to the needs of commercial-like enterprises. EKI personnel complain, however, because of the restrictions the *barem* imposes on them: they can receive salaries only three to four grades higher than those in the civil service; promotions (with some exceptions) are limited to one every three years; and, the highest basic salary is only about $200 per month. Incentive payments are provided for, however. After a levy of 5 percent of the enterprise's annual profits has been contributed to the reserve fund, up to 57 percent of the remainder may be distributed among EKI personnel, from the director downward. The bonus is proportional to salaries and may not exceed one normal month's salary. There are various other bonuses, most of which tend to be regarded by employees as regular increments to their monthly salaries.

Compared with most industries in Turkey, EKI is a giant enterprise. The number of miners and surface workers involved at EKI during the year is about 30,000, some 13,000 of whom may be called "semipermanent" workers, while the remainder, whose work periods are somewhat less extended and regular, will be called "temporary." Other employees, including both staff (cadre) and "daily-waged," number around three thousand. These include executive and clerical staff who will be called "headquarters" personnel. Alternative designations such as "daily-waged" or "employees" are inaccurate and somewhat misleading, since they could with equal logic refer to the mineworkers who are also on a daily-wage basis. Many departments, all of which are ultimately responsible to the director, have been organized within EKI to employ these people. . . . many departments are staff agencies. Under the director are the secretary-general, private secretary's office, and legal, technical, and financial advisers. There are three assistant directors: one for analysis and development, another for production, and a third for administrative and financial affairs. The personnel, accounting, social welfare, and health departments are under the latter's jurisdiction. Legally, the director is responsible for the entire organization. The administrative committee, composed of assistant directors, chief account, and the director of construction, acts in an advisory capacity directly responsible to him. The director, however, delegates some of his authority. When this study was made, the assistant director for production apparently had considerable influence. Departments which take an active role in production, including several coal-producing districts and the labor department, are under him in the administrative hierarchy. Since periodic labor is supplied by the labor department, its important role in maintaining production is apparent.

The assistant director for production, furthermore, maintains an active interest in other departments not directly under his jurisdiction, e.g., social welfare. This department assists in the preparation of rules and regulations for the training of miners and engineers. The mining school, the state director of education, and the coal-production districts administer such training programs. Furthermore, the department feeds, houses, and clothes the labor force. Consequently, the assistant director for production has been involved in reorganizing the social welfare department and hiring qualified people for it. Since other officials, however, also have authority delegated to them from the same or different sources, such efforts at reorganization may result in internal conflict.

The assistant director for production is assisted by a director of exploitation who is in charge of the districts, the coal washeries, and the archives. Each district is headed by a district director, who is a mining engineer with a Master of Science degree or the equivalent. He is aided by technical and financial assistants, other engineers without Master's degrees, heads of production sections who are engineers, construction engineers, and repair shop supervisors. The production sections are headed by engineers and their assistants, who are responsible to the district director. The district director is the responsible engineer for the entire district and as such carries on coal production in line with policies set by the general management. Although appointed by different departments in EKI, medical doctors, social welfare managers, and labor officers in the district are also directly responsible to the district director. This creates difficulties in standardizing procedures as well as in carrying out departmental policies, since all districts make rules commensurate with their own director's program and interests, and try to carry these out.

The fact that EKI has diverse aims and programs also disturbs its functioning as a commercial-like enterprise. In addition to mining coal, EKI controls the construction of a new harbor, builds state roads, and has important social objectives. Here we see the existence of a welfare bureaucracy, possessing characteristics and objectives quite different from those of the ideal Weberian model. Significantly, the welfare model is increasingly characteristic of western organizations, both public and private, which provide fringe benefits and a co-operative milieu that compete strongly with the rational, task-oriented objectives and ideology of Weber's system. EKI is different from the American or even the nationalized British coal industry, we may say, in that the *balance* between welfare and efficiency objectives leans more heavily in the welfare direction. In sociological terms of goal displacement, we may say that the latent (informal or unintended) functions of EKI compete strongly with its manifest ones.

Thus EKI builds houses, apartments, and barracks for administrators and miners and provides food, training, education, and entertainment for them and their families. In accord with national labor laws, EKI also extends certain other social benefits to its employees, including work clothes, insurance, hospital facilities, grants for children. Then there are other benefits like tennis courts, sports and sea clubs, premiums and bonuses, some of which are peculiar to EKI. Obtaining them depends in part on status, rank, and political factors, as well as on work accomplishment. In this sense, EKI is a social and welfare organization even though its essential function is the production of coal.

EKI is by no means well organized to carry out its major function. There is no plan for job evaluation and analysis. The High Control Board report of 1953 concluded, "EKI does not have a personnel policy." Many departments are spontaneously organized; they change their hierarchical relations periodically. The role of officials in the departments and their duties are not always specified, nor is their scope of authority covered by rules and regulations. There is considerable overlapping of functions, so that the same task or parts of the same task will often be shared by several departments. Obviously, it is impossible to get completely unifunctional departments, but one of the intrinsic objectives of organization is to reduce such diffusion to a minimum. It is clear that EKI has grown haphazardly into its present organizational structure. This happens to every organization, but in some the demands of economy, profit making, or technical change compel periodic modification. At EKI these imperatives seem less demanding. Here, as elsewhere, the very fact of state ownership seems to have affected organization and management, tending to substitute welfare and political goals for economic and technical ones, and resulting in a rather top-heavy administrative structure. This occurred in the British coal industry, where nationalization brought a substantial increase in the number of "headquarters" (i.e., co-ordinating, supervising, and policy-making) personnel, while the number of miners, technicians, and managers directly concerned with coal mining remained virtually unchanged (Presthus, 1949; 1950). EKI's social aims seem partly responsible for the problems it faces in achieving greater operational efficiency. The resulting dilemma is especially vexing because such goals are in themselves necessary and admirable, indicating the government's and the organization's awareness of humanitarian claims.

The Problem of Centralization

A central assumption of western organizational theory is the need for decentralization to meet the demand that authority be delegated to those parts of the organization technically qualified to handle a given problem. Ideally, this prescription not only meets the demands of functional autonomy but insures dispatch as matters are treated at appropriate operational levels, obviating the need for central clearance and the like. In addition, it is often assumed that delegation encourages high morale. Let us set these much-bruited requirements against the situation in EKI.

EKI is characterized by a high degree of centralization. Although the appointment of all higher officials has to be approved by a central ministry, their authorities and responsibilities are to a large extent determined by the director and his immediate staff. Even the administrative committee, the highest decision-making body after the director, actually exists in order to assist him in his decisions. His opinion counts more than any other's in the weekly committee meetings. Although the director's decisions are subject to ministerial approval they are rarely modified, since his decisions are usually in accord with the broad patterns outlined in the approved yearly work programs.

District directors participate to some extent in decision making. They meet weekly with the assistant director for production to discuss problems pertaining to production, miners' wages, and bonus policies. Most of their decisions are subject to formal approval by the administrative committee.

The director infrequently appoints a few assistant directors to study a problem and to return with recommendations. Although they may influence the director in making his decisions, their reports are not decisive. Apart from this, no formal decision-making conferences are held at lower administrative levels. For instance, no conferences are held with the lower-ranking engineers who supervise the miners. Lower-ranking engineers and mine supervisors receive only orders.

The claim is that EKI does not have a sufficient number of qualified engineers to make decision-making conferences productive. According to its cadre, EKI is short about one hundred and fifty engineers. Yet conferences might give all engineers and supervisors a feeling of participation, as well as enlist greater support in carrying out their duties. Knowing clearly what is to be done and sharing responsibility for the decisions might raise the morale of all concerned. They would surely be better informed as to production goals and how to reach them. Furthermore, the higher-ranking engineers who do make the decisions would be better informed about mining conditions and about the capacity of their subordinates to carry on the functions assigned to them. In production planning there is no substitute for the experience and knowledge of the middle-level engineers who are underground daily and thus know best the problems of coal mining.

As it now stands, then, authority is centralized in the director and delegated by him, if he finds a "competent" employee, mainly to his immediate assistants. High-ranking engineers get first priority. We have previously mentioned that the assistant director for production seemingly had more authority than other assistant directors. The power an individual disposes is a function of his personality, political connections, and his area of specialization, as well as his rank. Some employees have less authority than their rank suggests. EKI's personnel director, for example, has little authority over personnel policies and standards (apart from purely legal ones), and thus his influence in determining the qualifications of prospective employees is limited. Consequently, those who are not personally "favored" by their superiors tend to avoid the responsibility commensurate with their rank. Unlike the labor director, who seemed quite secure, the personnel director was reluctant to give us permission to visit his department or to see the personnel files, until we appealed to the assistant director for production, who then informed the personnel director that he should see us. Previously we had had verbal agreements with both officials to that effect.

Centralization, in a word, causes even high-level officials at EKI to seek formal authority from above before acting, causing delay and a general "upward-looking" posture throughout the organization. Furthermore, some departments, like social welfare, mechanization, and labor, do not have rules and regulations covering all their operations. The resulting ambiguity may reinforce the employee's tendency to depend on their superiors for decision making (although in a more positive environment it might have the opposite effect). In all, we were impressed by the lack of delegated authority and fear of initiative evidenced throughout EKI, even by officials whose rank would have seemed to warrant considerable latitude in decision making. Certainly the "commercial-like" atmosphere that the state enterprises seek through the special *barem,* bonus, and similar provisions was conspicuously missing.

The Signature Power   The power of signature is a vital symbol of centralization and of the authority delegated to an individual. This power may be defined as the authority to legitimate a directive, a letter, or any official document on behalf of the organization. In EKI all documents that are sent outside the organization must be signed by two officials. The essential function of the system is to centralize both authority and responsibility. Signature powers have been granted to thirty-four EKI cadre and daily-wage headquarters personnel out of a total of three thousand, about 1 percent. In terms of the total organization, thirty-four people of some 33,000 have this power. Here again, unanticipated consequences and goal displacement follow. Before action can occur, all important documents must be signed by one and often by two of these officials. Unless this power is delegated, and in many cases it cannot be delegated, delay is often inevitable. For example, the head of the labor section in the labor department acts for the director during his absence, mainly when the director goes on recruitment tours for two or three days each month. Yet the head of the labor section cannot sign letters to outside agencies. Similarly, the heads of insurance and compensation of the labor section are the only two officials in the department (besides the director himself) who can sign insurance forms for 30,000 miners. However, these officials have been given the power of signature to a limited degree; they can sign printed forms going to outside agencies. Moreover, subject to the approval of the department's director, all section heads can sign interdepartmental correspondence.

Following the administrative committee's endorsement, the Ministry of Industry must also approve all personnel for power of signature. Theoretically, EKI could dispense with such approvals by not granting this authority to high-ranking employees. But this would only create further difficulties, since the individuals concerned would still have to find someone to sign their official letters and documents. This is often the case with officials who have been newly promoted and are awaiting approval from the Ministry.

In sum, the fetish of signature is another cause and a symbol of centralization at EKI, both reflecting and encouraging the avoidance of action and responsibility by many headquarters' officials. Other results include frequent interruptions of senior officials by subordinates requesting their signature and a resulting reinforcement of the "upward-looking" psychology of the organization.

Deep-seated cultural values underlie such behavior: The patriarchal Turkish family system, which honors age and the authority of the father; the historic idealization of the military, with the attending emphasis upon obedience, rank, and its prerogatives; the educational system which often makes the teacher's authority rather than objective evidence the test of truth; a stratified class structure, reinforced by widespread illiteracy and a consequent monopolization of political skills by a small elite—all provide a social framework for highly structured interpersonal relations in EKI. The delays of the signature system and the general organizational climate must also be seen in terms of prevailing conceptions of *time* in underdeveloped societies. Both the cognition and the valuation of time are sharply different from western assumptions. Far from being viewed as a scarce resource, time is defined as a relatively abundant commodity, to be measured in long-term sequences, e.g., in seasons, which occur relentlessly despite man's wishes. Whereas western man is *personally* concerned with time, by which he measures out his life in hours, days, and years, man in underdeveloped society apparently feels little or no personal affinity with time, over which he seems to have so little influence. This conception of time is bound up with fatalism, with an often well-documented conclusion that man has little control of his personal destiny. Thus the western belief that one can shape his future by the application of logic, rationality, and time is often out of context.

The effects of these social values may be seen in the personnel policies of EKI, particularly in terms of motivation, to which we now turn.

Motivation at EKI

Psychologically speaking, a motive may be defined as a tension which results in behavior leading to need reduction through the attainment of either an original or a substitute goal. In nontechnical language, a motive is a thought or feeling that makes one act. In considering motivation at EKI, we shall be dealing with culturally modified secondary motives. It is possible to think of culturally determined motives as existing in dynamic hierarchical relationship with each other and to regard behavior as a result of such relationships. Several motives are apparent at EKI, including the drive for security and dependence, for status, for self-promotion and income. Some desire on the part of higher executives to maintain status by inculcating subservience is also observable.

In discussing motivation, it is again important to be aware of cultural differences between Turkey and western countries, since these differences bear directly upon the question. Put broadly, western assumptions about incentives and the dynamics of labor must be sharply modified. The aspirations of the Turkish miner and administrator are different from those of, say, their British counterparts, mainly in the sense that western expectations of *participation* in decision making and resulting dividends in higher morale are not shared by Turkish miners. These qualifications must be kept in mind when we examine motivations of EKI personnel. First, however, a comment on leadership is necessary.

As a result in part of the centralization of authority which is characteristic of large-scale bureaucratic organization everywhere and of what may fairly be described as predominantly "dependent" attitudes at EKI, top-level leadership is of primary importance. Such officials have exceptional authority, little of which is delegated, and consequently they must be held partly responsible for EKI's motivational atmosphere. There have been seven directors at EKI during the past fourteen years. One of them, who served between 1943 and 1950, ran the enterprise with an iron hand, and his administration apparently enjoyed a great deal of support among personnel at all levels. Although some younger engineers opposed the centralized system, firm leadership was evidently welcomed by a majority of headquarters staff and workers. In any case, a measure of continuity and control resulted which has not been achieved since.

Here, although the idea is speculative, we suggest that motivation in the Turkish industrial milieu may actually be enhanced by highly structured interpersonal relationships and by centralized authority patterns. There was little expectation of participation in decisions affecting themselves on the part of miners with whom we spoke. This seems to be a cultural phenomenon reflecting such factors as the patriarchal family system and the miners' agrarian background which has not socialized them for an active role in a complex, industrial organization. The absence of a democratic political tradition and limited educational opportunity are also relevant. Thus, paradoxically, motivation may be positively correlated with strong leadership and a minimum of participation, in the western sense of the term. This is a "paradox," however, only from the standpoint of western values.

Motivation of Engineers   We first discuss the leadership potential and motivation of engineers and supervisors. It was mentioned above that the important decisions regarding work and productivity are reached at the top levels in EKI, usually by engineers who have a graduate degree. Engineers who are mining school graduates of Zonguldak technical school do not participate in such decisions because their training is less complete and their technical qualifications are usually not comparable with those of engineers trained in the universities. When subordinates and miners know that this distinction is being made, they tend to feel more obligated to high-ranking engineers than to the low-ranking ones. This tends to fracture lines of command, as well as the execution of orders and work performance, because the miners' most direct contact is with the latter. While all engineers receive on-the-job training in supervision, assigning jobs, and assessing work, this training does not in itself insure effective leadership. Some supervisors, including high-ranking engineers, have a low opinion of the workers which is detrimental to relationships of any kind. Such attitudes again reflect time-honored distinctions between educated elite and the mass in all traditional societies. These engineers are consequently less able to manipulate the miners' needs to meet organizational demands. At the worst, they make the workers hostile to the organization; workers can probably be acculturated to accept authority without accepting a patent lack of respect.

Since regardless of its objectivity, one's definition of a situation often determines his behavior, the following generalizations of an EKI engineer are suggestive as an index of motivation among at least the high-ranking EKI engineers. One such engineer compared the motives of people working for public and private enterprise as follows:

1. *Motive for profit:* This is less in public enterprises.
2. *Chances for promotion:* More chance for promotion exists for superior men in private enterprise, but more exists in public enterprises for those of ordinary competence.
3. *Status quality of the job* (title of the position): Generally, it is more attractive in public enterprise.
4. *Chance for maximum income:* This is greater in private enterprise.

5. *Work conditions:* These are more difficult for top management but easier for lower-level employees in public enterprise.
6. *Work guarantees, retirement pensions, and social assistance:* These are greater in public enterprise.

On four of these variables, the engineer reached a negative conclusion about EKI. Although it is impossible to generalize on this point, it seems that most university-trained engineers felt that private ownership would provide a better work environment for highly trained people. Like most experts, and perhaps because they have often been exposed to western higher education, they resented the political milieu surrounding EKI operations, as evidenced by the rapid turnover of directors mentioned earlier. They honored professional training and certification; they felt that skill rather than political criteria should govern EKI policy. We may say that their values favored ideal, task-oriented bureaucracy over against the welfare objectives that claim much of EKI's resources and energy.

Other factors affect motivation among engineers. It is apparently hard to attract competent engineers to the rather bleak Zonguldak area, some 250 miles north of Ankara on the Black Sea. Regardless of his vocational field, the educated man in Turkey has considerable respect for cultural amenities, such as the theater and music, which are available mainly in Istanbul and Ankara. Thus a feeling of cultural isolation conditions morale and identification among highly trained engineers and geologists at EKI. A similar aversion to living outside the two major cities was noted among professional men in other state enterprises.

Such subjective factors are reinforced by material ones. Given the shortage of trained engineers and the prolific job opportunities brought by U.S. military and technical assistance programs, both the salaries and the self-evaluations of engineers have been inflated during the postwar years. As in most countries, the public service does not and perhaps cannot compete with such increases, even in the state corporations which attempt to operate along the lines of private enterprise. Thus the engineers at EKI complain that their *barem* pay scales are inadequate for their training, *expertise,* and the existing demand.

Nevertheless, production decisions at EKI do not always exhibit a major concern with technical criteria. EKI has increased its labor force repeatedly during the last few years. In order to increase production, a high-ranking engineer once proposed to add a third group of periodic workers to the two groups now in existence. Here again, historical conceptions of investment persist. Underdeveloped society characteristically exhibits a heavy ratio of manpower to machine capital equipment. Since labor has always been abundant and cheap, while capital and machines have been scarce and expensive, even technically oriented men tend to think in this traditional context. Moreover, the expense of importing machinery is aggravated by the absence of technicians who can operate and maintain it. The resulting "multiplier" effect, in which cheap manpower and expensive machinery inhibit technological change, suggests again the multifaceted nature of the economic development problem in traditional societies.

Since there are only about fourteen engineers with graduate degrees in the entire coal field, and they have high administrative posts, technical decisions are not reached at the level where production occurs. There is apparently insufficient co-ordination among these engineers, who remain in headquarters posts, and their subordinates and the miners, who work underground. While the more numerous graduates of the Zonguldak mining school work closely with the miners, operational decisions are ordinarily made by the university-educated engineers, who are intensely status-conscious, though they are only reflecting a general assumption in underdeveloped society that a university degree insures competence and achievement on the job.

Despite such motivational problems, there has been little turnover of engineers (except directors) since 1950, when the political party in power changed. As a matter of fact, on balance, the benefits of EKI's welfare bureaucracy encourage most engineers to remain at EKI. They tend to close ranks when there is an external threat directed toward any of them; they claim generally that the coal field would be unproductive were it not for the engineers. The director (1943–1950), who reported directly to the prime minister and the president, and who is held responsible for originating this attitude, had established a somewhat authoritarian, patriarchal administration. He went so far as to bar all the central government's financial and administrative inspectors from the coal field, apparently believing that EKI should be free from such external controls.

Worker Motivation   We shall now examine the motivations of workers; for convenience we will divide them into two groups, the first of which is comprised of top supervisors and workers' representatives. This group includes workers with training and mechanical specialization, whose daily wages range up to around seventeen liras (about $5.50) a day and who have been working for EKI regularly for at least fifteen years. Their status is nearly the same as that of the young engineers without high qualifications, and both are disadvantaged vis-à-vis the engineers who have a master's degree or its equivalent. Union leaders, labor federation representatives, and labor representatives for the regional labor directorate are also included in this group. At Kandilli, a district far from Zonguldak, there is one individual who does all three jobs. There are not many "qualified" workers at EKI, i.e., those who have been systematically trained and who possess certificates, degrees, or the like. The reliance on periodic labor is in good part responsible for the lack of trained men. Their lack of education is also relevant. At one point, one of the administrative clerks complained that it was hard to make the workers even understand the meaning of bonuses.

For the EKI miner, the economic incentive, so vital in western countries is of much less importance. He is not striving for material things which are not available on a mass basis. Nor is there a liberal credit system which would permit him to buy what is available on a long-term contract and to develop an expanding consumption pattern. He is acculturated to a subsistence level of existence; money income thus has a low point of diminishing returns. While a certain amount of it is desired, the desire for it decreases rather quickly once a subsistence level is achieved.

The labor supply situation at EKI obviously affects motivation and productivity. As noted earlier, EKI depends upon periodic labor, much of which is basically agricultural. The enterprise has a regular, "semipermanent" labor force of approximately 13,000, with a turnover of about fifteen hundred men every six weeks. There is also a huge group of about 17,000 "temporary" miners, half of whom are exchanged every forty-five days. Workers are variously recruited. In the past there have been laws requiring villagers in the Zonguldak area to work in the mines for a certain part of the year; today there is evidence that agents of EKI may combine with the village *muhtar* (mayor) to recruit villagers to come to Zonguldak. During the winter season when there is no work in their villages, workers come to EKI from all parts of Turkey. Others are cared for by self-appointed agents in winter and are sent to Zonguldak in summer when labor is scarce. These agents receive in return a part of the workers' earnings. There are also influxes of permanent workers at times of famine. This fluctuating labor supply and the need to recruit workers on a short-term basis (usually six weeks) to meet EKI's production cycle are among the enterprise's most vexing problems.

EKI favors semipermanent miners and extends social benefits like food, clothing, and low-cost housing to encourage them to come and live in the area with their families. For example, the workers' union in co-operation with EKI and the insurance fund has a 146-unit housing project under way; another company is also building 130 houses for miners in nearby villages. Nevertheless, there is a chronic housing shortage at EKI, which will require several years of such construction to overcome.

The "temporary" miners, on the other hand, are housed in rough barracks, away from their families, under a discipline which some of them resent. For example, welfare officials insist that the miners take daily showers, which the miners resist. The showers are not very clean, and, perhaps more important, there is a cultural aversion to appearing naked, and these are public showers. Although EKI supplies them with horseshoes, nails, and glass and provides them with inexpensive wheat in collaboration with the state Agricultural Bank, the temporary miners and workers do not attract much sympathy from their superiors.

One gets the general impression that both groups of miners at EKI are badly motivated. Much of this undoubtedly stems from the periodic nature of their work. The ordinary miners' role of being ultimately dependent on the land and consequently of becoming more or less an irregular worker must be differentiated from that of becoming permanently identified with the organization. Such workers inevitably look upon mining as an unpleasant, temporary expedient, rather than as a life's work. They are basically agricultural workers, technically unqualified and emotionally unattached to mining. The experience and atmosphere at EKI is essentially foreign to them, and the difficult conditions of work further depress their motivation. Although the welfare program aims at attracting positive support from the miners, even this concession is not decisive, for the quality of benefits is not very high and amenities such as food and housing are regarded as integral parts of their pay, rather than as special dispensations.

It is apparent that most of these workers prefer surface work to work in the mines. This tendency is common in coal mining in every country; work at the coal face is dirty, dangerous, and usually bearable mainly because of higher wage rates and productivity bonuses. Here, in the context of earlier remarks about the difference between "bureaucratic" and "rational" elements in the allocation of rewards, an important point arises: There is no significant pay differential at EKI between surface and underground work. Beginning rates for underground workers are only 25 kurus (about five cents) a day higher. Thus the man who makes yogurt on the surface is paid the same maximum daily wage as the man who works on underground transportation. The *maximum wage* rate (excluding supervisors) is actually higher for surface than for underground workers. Although productivity bonuses and tax exemption provisions for underground workers have an equalizing effect, the wage incentive for those who actually mine coal is not comparatively greater. Thus the "rational" bureaucratic prescription holding that rewards should be allocated for achievement tends to be overcome by the well-known "bureaucratic" propensity to equalize income regardless of function and achievement. In terms of western motivation (which are not always relevant), productivity might be increased by introducing wage differentials more in line with other countries. However, this innovation would require a substantial change in the consumption patterns and material expectations of the Turkish miner.

Other factors affect motivation, including the objective conditions of Turkish mining. Like those in Britain, the Zonguldak mines are not well suited for efficient, highly mechanized production, since geologic conditions are difficult and dangerous. The coal seams are narrow and tilted, and gas is a constant problem. Furthermore, mechanization is at a relatively elementary stage. Men and animal power are still very important sources of production and of transportation in the mines. Safety regulations are not always adhered to. One district director confirmed this by saying that the workers often went ahead in production without taking adequate safety measures: "They were under constant threat of fire." (Late in 1960, 22 miners died in an explosion at the Zonguldak mines.) The present stress on increasing production encourages this tendency to overlook safety regulations.

In sum, motivation among both engineers and miners at EKI is affected by many factors, including not only the conventional difficulties and dangers of mining, but also its dependence upon a large proportion of periodic workers whose experience and identifications are rural and agricultural rather than urban and industrial. For highly trained engineers, the cultural isolation of EKI and its tendency to honor political rather than technical authority also seem relevant. Among the engineers, moreover, status claims compete strongly with economic ones. Finally, the very nature of motivation in Turkish society is different from that in the western world. Economic and material claims, which cannot always be satisfied, do not provide the same degree of incentive as in the West. Thus pay differentials for the vital job of coal mining, as compared with those offered for less important on-the-surface jobs are minimal.

Conclusion

Data from the Turkish coal industry suggest that the western bureaucratic model with its structural and behavioral elements of efficiency, rationality, and control rests upon certain normative assumptions about time, man, and motivation. When such values are absent or when they are sharply challenged by the objectives of "welfare bureaucracy," the mere existence of "highly bureaucratized" organizations, as often seen in traditional society, tells us little about their operational consequences. Where social values do not assign a high priority to objectivity, productivity, and economic gain, the manifest structure of bureaucracy is of little relevance as a guide either to its performance or to its "real" goals.

Factory Management in a Planned Economy: The USSR*

JOSEPH S. BERLINER

. . .

It is in the sphere of industrial procurement that a centrally planned system is supposed to make some of its greatest advances over the decentralized, atomistically competitive market system. Since all plans of all firms are known beforehand, it is theoretically possible to pre-arrange all interfirm shipments of materials, so that no firm will even have to worry about sources of supply after the planning period has begun. But in setting up the formal structure of their industrial procurement system, the Soviet planners have not sought to achieve anything as ideal as this. Their aim was much more realistic and modest. For one thing, not all materials are centrally allocated, but only those which experience has shown to be the most troublesome. In fact, however, these troublesome ones constitute a large proportion of all inter-industrial shipments. The Soviets also recognize that because of the uneven pace of plan fulfillment in different firms, even the most perfectly integrated plan will have to be corrected as the planning period gets under way. Therefore the director is exhorted not to expect his materials to flow into his firm more or less automatically (as the director of a firm in the theoretically ideal system may properly expect), but rather to be ever vigilant over his supply channels, making sure that the flow of materials is never interrupted. In case of an interruption of supply he is charged with making every possible effort to obtain the materials necessary to keep the plant from having to stop work.

Certain formal channels are open to the firm whose inflow of materials is threatened. It may make representations to the ministry, which can then bring the matter to the attention of the supplier's ministry. Or it may try to influence the supplier directly. In a critical case it may call upon the aid of the Party to change or by-pass plans and regulations in order to meet the emergency. Sometimes these formally established channels are used, and with success, but on other occasions they are thought to be unsuitable, either because the particular procurement need of the enterprise would be frowned upon by the higher officials, or because the formal channels would involve an excessively long time. . . .

Rather than face this long drawn-out process whenever a shortage

* Excerpted by permission of the publishers and author from pp. 184–186, 182–183, 186, 205–210, 215–225, 319–320, and 327 of Joseph S. Berliner, *Factory and Manager in the USSR* (Cambridge, Mass.: Harvard University Press). Copyright, 1957, by the President and Fellows of Harvard College.

of some material threatens production, the firm often prefers to turn to the well-established informal procurement system, a major element of which is *blat*. . . .

Blat

The term *blat* (pronounced *blaht*) is one of those many flavored words which are so intimate a part of a particular culture that they can be only awkwardly rendered in the language of another. The word implies the use of personal influence for obtaining certain favors to which a firm or individual is not legally or formally entitled. In the industrial sphere it refers to such actions as obtaining materials contrary to the intent of the plan, or persuading ministry officials to relieve one's own firm of a difficult production task and assign it to another firm with less influence. . . . The particular type of influence needed varies. It may be influence based upon family relationship or close friendship, or it may be merely an entrée into a supplying firm that permits a purchasing agent to propose an unlawful manipulation without fear of being rebuffed or reported to the police. There is an implication of reciprocation of favors, but the reciprocation is usually not a direct *quid pro quo*. A favor done today may not be reciprocated until sometime in the indefinite future. . . . In the industrial sphere the reciprocation is often direct, sometimes involving an exchange of goods or favors. The blat involved in such transactions is the knowledge of which persons are approachable for arranging deals, and the mutual trust which permits the deal to be initiated. . . .

The evasion of economic and bureaucratic regulations involved in blat is looked upon as something perhaps not quite respectable, yet not on the plane of a real moral transgression. In our own society it is similar to black market operations during a period of government controls, or to distilling home brew during the prohibition period. As with the latter analogy, there is a mild tone of naughty humor involved in the use of the term. . . .

Because of the central role of the allocation order in the procurement operations of the enterprise, most of the informal procurement techniques involving the use of blat center around it. Although the evidence leaves little doubt about the importance of blat in circumventing the regulations of the allocation system, the available information on the details of its use is sparse . . . [but] it is possible to document the use of blat at practically every stage of the long process from the securing of the allocation order to the final delivery of the goods to the warehouse of the purchaser.

The most serious problem which an enterprise faces is obtaining a vitally needed material when it has been unable to secure an allocation order for it. It is in such a situation that blat serves its principal function. . . .

The over-all effect of the widespread use of blat is that the advantage of the high-priority enterprise in the formal system is considerably whittled down in the informal shadow world of inter-enterprise relations. The legitimate demands of the important enterprise, on the formal plane of priority awareness, will always take precedence over the legitimate demands of the less important enterprise. But when the less important enterprise turns to the informal channels of blat, it stands a better chance of satisfying its demand for, say, the extra carload of coal.

It should not be thought that the important enterprise is so secure in its priority position that it forswears the use of blat and informal relations entirely. Although it is able to obtain materials more easily through formal channels, and although its plans are reportedly set at a less straining level than the plans of less important enterprises, it is motivated by the same considerations of safety factor and simulation as other enterprises. It is also in competition, on the formal level, with other high-priority enterprises. It therefore also makes use of its blat for obtaining an extra shipment of steel or "work" clothes, or for a somewhat greater appropriation for travel missions. At the least it must make use of its own special purchasing agents to assure that its first-order claim on supplies is not undermined by the well-heeled supply agents of a shoe factory. Blat is therefore of importance to the high-priority enterprise as well.

In general, the effect of blat is to frustrate to a certain extent the purpose of the priority system, and to bring the competitive position of enterprises into somewhat closer conformity with management's effective demand for their products. The penumbral world of informal inter-enterprise relations represents the severely harnessed rudiments of a market economy seeking to break through the hard crust of centralized planning.

.   .   .

Of the various practices of management *blat* depends most of all on the social relationships among persons participating in economic life. One can imagine many types of managerial officials manipulating successfully with a safety factor or simulating plan fulfillment, but the successful practice of blat requires a very special type of person with a very special social character. It is therefore not surprising that a process similar to the division of labor has led to the development of what is in effect, a distinct occupation carried out by those who possess the talent for blat. The literature and the interviews provide a certain amount of information on the nature and effects of the activity of these invaluable persons who contribute so much to the informal operation of the enterprise. . . .

In the pages of the humor magazine *Krokodil* two Soviet humorists have published a poem which tells the story. . . .

The Irreplaceable Anton Fomich

Anton Fomich is irreplaceable,
One feels safe with him, comfortable with him,
However much the official estimates interfere,
He always finds a roundabout way
Of arranging this, or fixing that,
Of working out any business problem
Of getting from the warehouse, without an allocation order,
Everything that is needed and even what is not needed,
And having received a carload of this,
Of exchanging it for that,
Of reducing the plan, of writing something off,
Of concealing resources, and accepting rejects.

He can get for you easily
Anything . . . even pigeon's milk.
For all our shrewd hero has to do
Is pick up the phone, call,
And any supply depot
Without protest
Will rush to help him out.

Iron, nails, lumber, bricks,
Who will get it? Anton Fomich.
How will he get it? Over the "limit."
Where will he get it? From who knows where.
All hush-hush, under-cover,
So that no one can ever trip him up.

Let others pass as shrewd businessmen
He himself is more innocent than a lamb.
When he has made all ends meet,
And concealed all loose ends below the water line
The wisest of the wise
Could never locate the ends.

The bank account has been closed, work has stopped,
There has been a snafu, somewhere, someone, something.
They come running to Anton Fomich:
"Intercede for us!" "I'll intercede."
And he will intercede: slyly, precisely,
He will "formalize," "write-off," "expedite,"
The unimportant order he will ship out as "urgent."
He will cover up any overexpenditure . . .
This is what he is! Everything is child's play
When Anton Fomich is on the job.

One hand, he knows, rubs the other.
And therefore, of all the sciences,
He has mastered one above all,
The interrelations of sordid hands.
This science says that one good turn
Deserves another in return.
If he has done something for you, why not
Do something for him in return?
It is not difficult to do a favor,
A favor is not illegal
For nothing criminal has been done,
No order has been broken:
A favor is not a bribe,
And you can't be put on trial for that!

———————

Anton Fomich is irreplaceable,
And there is no reason to part company with him.
Some say he is an exceptional cheat;
True, he's a cheat, but a valuable one!
A thief? True, he's a thief, but up to now
He has not been caught. So he's not a thief.
A sneak? Probably, but useful.
Impudent? Unquestionably, but pleasant.
A pusher? Yes, but with a head on his shoulders.
A rascal? A rascal, but a business-like one.
Kick him out? No, pity the poor fellow!
Yes, and how about management?
Without him management often
Cannot move a step.
Management is so comfortable with him.
Always, in every kind of weather,
He dives into the deepest water for management,
And always emerges dry.

———————

Involuntarily a question arises,
It is indeed difficult to understand how,
In this day and age, he always manages
To worm his way into an institution,
Such an Anton, such a Fomich!
For the door has long since been closed to him:
Plan, Estimate, Fund, Account, Limit
Have closed the door with a hundred keys
Against all Anton Fomiches.
But, imperceptibly, he gnaws
A little hole here, a little hole there
And finally he crawls through one of them,
Slowly, but wholly . . .

Activity of the "Tolkach"

Anton Fomich is what the Russians call a *tolkach* (pronounced *tull-kahtch*). The word derives from a verb meaning "to push" or "to jostle," and *tolkachi* are people who "push" for the interest of the enterprise in such matters as the procurement of supplies. The *tolkach* is also the name applied to the booster locomotive used to increase the power of a freight train. Various officials of the enterprise may play the part of a tolkach. "Usually these people held some job such as chief of the purchasing department or his deputy," said Informant 26. "Sometimes they are simply called supply agents." If other officials of the enterprise possess the qualities of a good tolkach they may be sent out from time to time on a travel mission (*kommandirovka*) to obtain the needed commodities. . . .

The basis of the success of the tolkach is his blat. He is, first of all, a brazen person who knows how to establish blat with people whom he does not know well. In the stereotype which the informants draw he is depicted as a nervous, energetic man, a master of high-pressure techniques, able to talk his way into enterprises and quickly establish a working friendship with the relevant officials. "They know how to obtain allocation orders and how to get materials on time. They have connections. . . . A good supply agent knows large numbers of people, and where all the warehouses are. . . ." He knows "how to drink with people," and is lavish with gifts and entertainment. (Informant 26.) In this aspect of his activity he must be well supported by his director, who, if he is influential, can do much to smooth the way for the tolkach. First, he must be provided with funds with which to operate, which apparently presents no great obstacle. The enterprise fund, premiums, and various other accounts of the enterprise serve as sources of funds for the tolkachi. How the director feels about the activities of the tolkach is clear: "The director never wants to know how the supply agent operates. All he demands are results," said Informant 384. And in the press we read that there has arisen the opinion that the petroleum industry couldn't survive one day without their services: "For pity's sake, how can I simply throw our funded materials to the mercy of an arbitrary fate.". . .

The attitude of the state toward these activities is somewhat less clear. The more extreme activities such as theft of enterprise materials or money are punishable by imprisonment. From time to time the press carries reports of the discovery and prosecution of guilty parties, but the survival of the "market" as well as the persistence of the reports of prosecutions lends credence to the view that these practices continue to play an important role. But more interesting is the problem of controlling the subtler forms of informal procurement activities associated with blat and the use of tolkachi. For many of these activities are on the borderline of the illegal and quite difficult to pin down.

In the first place, there is a positive exhortation to the manager to show "initiative" and to take vigorous measures to safeguard his flow of materials. The manager who is content to submit his statement of requirements and then sit back and await delivery is considered to be "bureaucratic" and to lack energy. This official approval of initiative and energetic solution of supply problems, rarely accompanied by a specific statement of the lawful limits, provides a cloak of justification for pushing the limits into and beyond the borderline of the lawful. . . .

Recognizing the inevitable imperfection of the information available to bureaucratically organized purchasing organizations about sources of supply, the state is forced to encourage supply agents to manifest their initiative and go looking about for materials. One of the economic functions served by the supply agent is to collect knowledge of sources of supply upon which management can draw for meeting supply problems. The supply agent, by virtue of the experience gathered in the course of his work, thus develops a special competence which is necessary to the system. From this officially encouraged activity it is but a slight step to the tolkach, the person who has not only the knowledge of sources of supply but has also made a wide range of contacts in various organizations. The enterprise can therefore draw not only upon his knowledge, a perfectly legal action, but also upon his informal contacts and blat. . . .

. . . [T]he place occupied in Soviet society by blat and by its master practitioner, the tolkach, will strike many people as strange. More than most modern states, the Soviet state evokes among outsiders an image which stresses the formal, the logical, the homogeneous. Soviet society is often thought of as more "rational" than others, in the technical sense that larger segments of it have been consciously and deliberately legislated into existence. There is a stern neatness in the system of enterprises responsible to chief administrations and chief administrations to ministries; and in plans which flow smoothly from bottom to top and down again from top to bottom. This table-of-organization image is partly the consequence of our enforced reliance upon published sources, which dulls our sensitivity to the role of people in the system. It may seem like a rude intrusion to thrust such activities as blat, and such persons as the tolkach, into a system otherwise so thoroughly automatic and well integrated.

Yet blat and the tolkach are but the most dramatic instances of the important role of personal relations in the operation of the enterprise. One of the strongest impressions that emerge from the examination of the informants' testimony is the all-pervasiveness of the personal factor in the determination of the allocation of resources. While it is impossible to offer a quantitative estimate, it is clear from the interviews that the output plan depends in large measure upon what the enterprise has been able to bargain out of "Moscow," the supply of materials hinges upon how much can be haggled out of the functionary in the State

Economic Committee, the financial plan is based upon currying the favor of some minor official in the Ministry of Finance, and so forth. The cultivation of good relations is a prime principle of plant management. . . .

Point by point these practices conflict with the laws, regulations, and Party pronouncements on how the manager is required to conduct his work. He is expected to propose maximally high production targets, to order supplies and maintain inventories at the minimum levels consistent with his plan. He is supposed to produce his various products in quantities which conform to the plan and to the system of priorities, to maintain high quality and to be thoroughly truthful in his reporting. And all decisions are supposed to be made in accordance with the wishes of the state, rather than with the influence of individuals. The rules which govern actual managerial behavior are clearly not the rules established by the state.

Why then does the manager engage in practices which violate the official rules? Part of the answer is to be found in the circumstances within which he must operate. The manager does not particularly wish to incur the risks involved in applying for a low production target or in reducing quality. The sentiment in the interviews and the published sources is rather that he feels compelled to do so, that the pressures exerted by the economic environment leave him no other way in which to achieve his goals. . . .

With the use of personal influence, as in *blat,* the contribution to the smoother working of the system is more marked. A realistic evaluation of managerial behavior must start not from an assumption of perfect planning but from an awareness that the planning of an entire national economy inevitably involves a great deal of inaccuracy, unpredictability, and plain stupidity. Given a less than perfect system, the function performed by the *tolkach* provides the economy with a useful tool for cutting through the red tape which inevitably ties up the flow of resources into some of the channels in which they are needed. The *tolkach* is an instance of the emergence of an informal system caused by the inability of the larger formal system to take account of the detailed and immediate needs of individual enterprises. *Blat* is the grease in the gears of the economic system which serves to keep the mechanism running more smoothly and quietly.

Disintegrative Forces and Integrative Measures*

JAMES W. DAVIS, JR. and KENNETH M. DOLBEARE

All organizations face problems of cohesion and integration, but Selective Service is peculiarly threatened by centrifugal forces. Structural decentralization and legal autonomy of local units are supported by the dominant grass-roots ethos of the entire organization and the physical isolation of many boards; accordingly, only the most general instructions are given to subordinate elements and this in turn fosters independent and idiosyncratic definitions and applications by state and local units. Also potentially disintegrative are the norms or practices that develop in the many units of the System. If Selective Service is viewed as a system and its state headquarters and local boards as subsystems, the risk is that the subsystem may develop practices that are unrelated or contradictory to the requirements of the system as a whole. Finally, the personal preferences and values of individual organization members are disintegrative forces. No member of any organization is a member *only* of that organization. Local board members particularly belong to a variety of other organizations, are pressured by work situations, experience potential conflicts of interest, etc. In short, they are only marginally subject to the influence of Selective Service in their overall life situations.

With all these disintegrative forces at work, it is clear that national headquarters faces substantial problems. One route toward integration is through formal communication channels. National headquarters issues a variety of publications designed to inform state headquarters and local boards of current regulations, current problems, current practices, and to some extent these may counteract the disintegrative forces in the system. Operations Bulletins, Local Board Memoranda, State Director Advices, Administrative Bulletins, and letters on special problems flow from the national headquarters to the state headquarters and to appeal and local boards. Although there is substantial overlap, these different series have somewhat different purposes. State Director Advices and Administrative Bulletins deal usually with routine organization matters, ranging from savings bond purchases by employees, to warnings about political activity by civil servants, to the care and disposal of records. Operations Bulletins and Local Board Memoranda are more likely to deal with matters relating to classification and induction. Operations Bulletins cover a variety of topics, but most of them detail the procedures to be used or standards to be applied in granting

* Reprinted from *Little Groups of Neighbors: The Selective Service System* (Chicago: Markham Publishing Company, 1968), pp. 39–47, 247–257, with omissions, by permission of the authors and publisher.

**FIGURE 1. OFFICIAL ORGANIZATION CHART OF SELECTIVE
SERVICE SYSTEM**

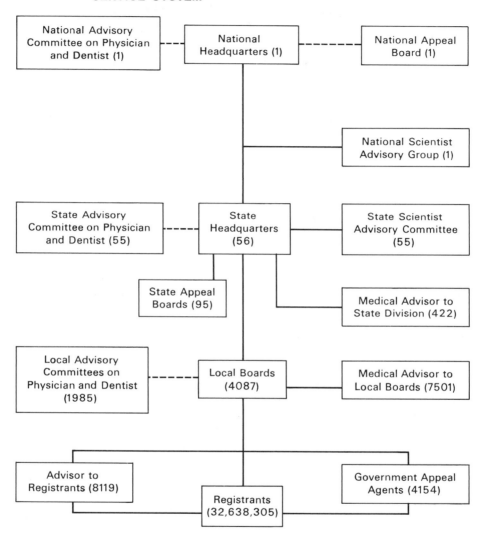

Organization of Selective Service System 30 June 1966. Taken from *1966 Annual Report*, p. 4.
Numbers in parentheses are numbers of personnel or units.

a particular classification. Hardly distinguishable from Operations Bulletins, Local Board Memoranda describe the action that a board (in fact a clerk) should take in particular situations that may arise. Local Board Memorandum 14, for example, describes the steps to be taken when a registrant refuses to submit to physical examination or mental test or fails to report for or submit to induction. Local Board Memorandum 71 describes the public information policies that a local board may follow. This memorandum illustrates national headquarters sensitivity to state headquarters desires and an unwillingness to intrude into a state headquarters bailiwick:

> There are no restrictions imposed by the Director of Selective Service upon the release of publication of lists of names of registrants nor upon the time such lists may be made available for publication. In the absence of any restriction imposed by a State Director of Selective Service upon the local boards under his jurisdiction such local boards may publish such lists of registrants as they in their discretion may deem appropriate.

In other words, national headquarters is telling local boards that they may publish names of men selected for induction, unless they have been told not to by their respective state headquarters.

In spite of all the mailings that the national headquarters sends out, state headquarters and local boards may not receive timely information. Indeed, when national headquarters makes a public announcement of consequence, the press may be informed before either state headquarters or local boards. The result is that some board members complain that, like their neighbors, they must depend on the local newspapers to find out what is happening. The directions of the System are also often quite general and leave much to the interpretation and discretion of state headquarters and local boards. While this can and does lead to substantial variation in performance, it is also true that this may be functional for the organization. When boards can read what they want to into a directive they may be more agreeable and less likely to resist it. An observation recently made by Harold Guetzkow is to the point here: "Because ambiguous messages are open to multiple interpretations, meanings more agreeable to the receiver may be attached. Although at times ambiguity results in slippage between sender and receiver, such slippage also may promote consensus and agreement, which have important value for organizational activity (1965: 557). Of course, what may be functional or advantageous in an organizational context may not appear constructive in a larger context.

The main thrusts of the System's efforts to counteract the centrifugal forces that it faces consist of promotion of a distinctive organizational ideology and a personal loyalty to the Director. Organizational employment of ideology and justification has often been noted by social scientists. Philip Selznick has made this point clearly in his book on the TVA: "Among the many and pressing responsibilities of leadership, there arises the need to develop a *Weltanschauung,* a general view of the organization's position and role among its own contemporaries. For organizations are not unlike personalities: the search for stability and meaning, for security, is unremitting (1949: 47). Daniel Katz and

Robert Kahn make much the same point when they remark that the values of a system, its ideology, may provide a justification for the activities and functions of the system (1966: 51–52). Selective Service, however, has developed its internal ideology well beyond other organizations studied; it, more than many organizations, may be in particular need of justification, both for the benefit of a potentially uneasy membership and for the benefit of a potentially doubting public. The problem may be to convince both members and the public that what is being done is both right and necessary. In contrast a hospital or a school may not need an elaborate justifying ideology since what such organizations do is generally accepted (Downs, 1967: 245).

Beyond justifying the organization, an ideology may also help secure conformity and loyalty. Selective Service in particular may have to rely on ideology to obtain conformity and loyalty since there is so little else it can rely on. Amitai Etzioni has suggested that organizations can be differentiated along the lines of their compliance or authority structure (1961: 1964). Some organizations are coercive, others utilitarian, and still others normative. With regard to its members, as opposed to its registrants, Selective Service is surely a normative organization. It does not pay its board members and certainly cannot coerce them. It must therefore rely on normative appeals and the manipulation of symbols to obtain the behavior it requires. In its ideology it must emphasize personal commitment to the organization if it is to counteract the disintegrative forces in the organization.

In its stress upon ideological justification and promotion of personal loyalty to the director, Selective Service is unrelenting. The chief vehicle is the monthly newsletter entitled *Selective Service,* which is mailed from Washington to every employee, board member, and other participant. In every issue the Director has a personally signed column which by turns justifies, exhorts, and directs. The System is justified in several ways. As the following representative selections show (January 1965–December 1966), it is viewed as necessary to the strength and survival of the nation; military service is a right, an obligation, and beneficial in any event:

> It has been my observation that most of the American people have an image of the Selective Service System as a necessity to insure survival of all.

> Military service is a privilege and an obligation of free men in a democratic form of government. It follows that the induction of a registrant is not, and cannot be, a punishment.

> Armed forces can contribute to the development of youth.

> Any survey of governmental agencies possessing capabilities of training, especially in consciousness of individual responsibility, would place the Armed Forces high on the list.

Nor do board members merely draft men. By deferring others they protect the national interest and encourage enlistments. They act, above all, with fairness, justice, and in the best interests of the nation:

> Education has been considered a process which increases the value of a citizen to this nation.
>
> Deferment is not for the convenience of the individual registrant, although the Nation's interest may at times coincide with the registrant's desires.
>
> The number who have enlisted from the examined and accepted pool illustrate the major dependence of the recruiting service on the Selective Service System.
>
> The Selective Service System earned through a quarter of a century a reputation of fairness, knowledgeability, and effectiveness in operation.
>
> The principles of decentralization of authority, local autonomy, and participation of the Governor in each state have created an image of the Selective Service System that creates confidence in Congress, which has been a large factor in the extension of the Selective Service law, each successive extension being accomplished with less opposition.

Direction and exhortation also appear regularly in the Director's column, occasionally in the form of a eulogy of a deceased member whose performance is set forth as an example for others:

> The personnel of the Selective Service System has adapted well to the everchanging winds of events. Their problem now is to remain alert to the degree of readiness required to be prepared to pursue our present course, to reduce our procurement for the service, or to increase these numbers to some degree or substantially.
>
> There will be a change in the nature of the decisions; more discretion will be required.
>
> Local board members have the knowledge, the experience, and the common sense to make sound judgments. They will make them, remembering that our regulations are adequate.
>
> It must remain clear always that it is the Selective Service System, through its local boards, which determines classifications.

Besides conveying the values of the System to the members of the organization the newsletter is used also to give members of the system factual information and to tell them about each other. Space is taken up with lists of official notices issued during the month, articles on current problems, information about manpower calls, and figures depicting the current classification picture. Special events or activities (for example training meetings being held for Reserve officers) may also be publicized. The newsletter contains much material dealing with the personnel of the System, material best described by the title to a column that began appearing in June 1966: "The Human Interest Stories of People Who Make Up the Heart and Sinew of the Selective Service System." Awards given to members of the System and their visits to national headquarters are duly reported. Particular local boards may rate a story for one reason or another and occasionally an exemplary registrant (one who overcomes obstacles and hardships to register) will gain attention. In general, a homey–folksy air pervades the newsletter and it is easy to conclude that it tries to give the impression that Selective Service is rather a close-knit family.

The newsletter also makes a point of telling members of the System about the Director. In 24 issues of the newsletter, from January 1965 to December 1966, there were 22 articles focused on General Hershey, independent of his signed column. Several of the articles dealt with Hershey giving or approving awards to System personnel and others dealt with Hershey receiving awards. Several articles showed Hershey giving information to various Congressional committees and other articles provided general information about his activities and opinion. Articles were complemented by pictures: General Hershey appeared in almost half of the 26 pictures printed in 16 consecutive issues. In his columns, he expresses convictions which are likely to be shared by board members:

> Patriotism, belief in our country, standards of integrity, and respect for the religion of others, have not been superseded by education. If they have, it is the wrong kind of education.
>
> It is a hope supported [by] some reasonable expectancy that the changing international situation will cause our public to demand more responsible conduct by our registrants and less liberality by our courts toward those failing to perform their obligations.
>
> It weakens the nation when dissent is within legal limits and can be but a termite gnawing at the foundation of government when defying the laws.
>
> Some would turn over to computers the task of fairness and of uniformity, depending more on card punchers than dedicated, unpaid local board members.

The strength of the personal loyalties effectively developed through this and other routes is evident in interviews with board members. There seems little reason to doubt that the Director has made up in personal influence for some of his lack of formal coercive capacity. Amitai Etzioni has phrased the same observation in these terms: "Power used by an organization to control its participants derives either from specific positions or from personal qualities. Personal power is almost always indentitive power; it is based on the manipulation of symbols and it serves to generate commitment to the persons who command it" (1965: 659). Hierarchical power is of little use when it comes to local board members—they are volunteers. State Directors are appointed by the governor and other employees are either appointed by the State Director or are covered by civil service. Since General Hershey's position thus has little coercive power, personal power is required if he is to influence the behavior of other members of the System and counteract the many centrifugal forces.

The foregoing analysis of integrative measures shows that national headquarters has taken at least some steps to counteract the System's disintegrative forces. The grass-roots structure and ethos, for example, may be to some extent counteracted by attempts to portray the organization as a single close-knit body and by attempts to get members to identify with the Director. National headquarters does issue regulations and general guidelines. But perhaps persuaded by its own rhetoric, and in effect a victim of the System's emphasis on decentralization, national headquarters has not done a great deal to counteract disintegration. In this it contrasts starkly with an organization like the Forest Service, of which Kaufman writes: "The Forest Service has made decentralization its cardinal principle of organization structure, the heart and core of its 'administrative philosophy,' " (1960: 83). But Kaufman also describes the number of measures that have been taken to neutralize the risks of decentralization. Detailed rules, preformed decisions, official diaries, reports, inspections, transfers—all these techniques and more are used to keep Forest Rangers acting predictably and according to requirements. Virtually none of these techniques is used by Selective Service national headquarters; it does not in any meaningful sense supervise, control, or review the actions of state headquarters and their local boards. Uniform action is not a goal and national headquarters has not developed performance standards or systematically collected the data required to measure and evaluate either system performance as a whole or the performance of various units. And, of course, there has been no systematic comparison of the performance of different units. Directions are issued and in effect forgotten. What are the criteria that different boards have used in granting deferments? How consistent are the state headquarters in their interpretations and instructions? How much variation is there? These are questions that national headquarters did not find it important to answer, at least until after the National Advisory Commission on Selective Service reported its findings (*President's Commission Report:* Appendix III, IV, VI).

Selective Service and Its Environment: Output and Interaction

"Output" is a generic term which may include several distinct forms of organizational products. Easton uses the term to signify transactions moving from the system to its environment ("authoritative allocations of values or binding decisions and the actions implementing and related to them") (1965a: 126; 1965b: 348). Not all outputs, of course, are functionally task-related. Some are relatively peripheral—mere by-products of basic organizational commitments—and others may even be dysfunctional. The concept of transactions is useful, however, because it suggests continuing exchanges with several publics, and it is inclusive enough to subsume various forms of output.

An analysis of patterns of impact of conscription provides a background of objective reality to the interactions of Selective Service with its environment. In this analysis of the direct output of the organization, we see that impact is segmented according to the registrants' socioeconomic characteristics, so that definable populations bore heavy burdens of military liability and others (at least under conditions of manpower surplus) are relatively lightly encumbered by such obligations (see Davis and Dolbeare, 1968: Chapter 6). These patterns are only the beginning of a characterization of the organization's relationship with its environment, albeit the central reality around which other interaction occurs. A varied set of perceptions and transactions completes the relationship of Selective Service and its immediate environment.

The component units of the Selective Service System operate in environments made up in part of the other elements within the organization and in part from the other actors and institutions of the political system. At each level of the organization, its units are related to a distinct set of external political forces and conditions. The environment of the national headquarters consists of such elements as the Defense Department, the White House, the Armed Services Committees of the two houses of Congress, The National Guard and Reserve Officers' Associations, representatives of the mass media, and ultimately attentive members of the national public. Interaction occurs regularly between the Director and other representatives of national headquarters and the various elements of that environment; when Selective Service rises to national visibility, as it did in the debates of 1966–67, the nature of these interactions may be readily seen from the pages of Congressional hearings, national news media, and popular books. Scholarly inquiries frequently undertake to spell out the character of relationships between agencies and departments of the national government and other elements in the national political scene, permitting comparisons between various agencies, and between times of stress and more normal periods. These are important considerations to have in mind, but they are not our primary focus.

Our data and analyses have been directed at the state and local activities of Selective Service, and it is the interaction between the organization and its publics at this operating level with which we are most concerned. This point of interchange between the agency and the people provides an infrequently used opportunity to assess the character of governmental performance, both in terms of the nature of the job actually done and the satisfactions or antipathies generated in the process.

The environments of the state and local units of the organization are in some respects separable, corresponding to the levels of the System, but we shall treat them jointly. The state headquarters, for example, is almost the only unit to have contact with representatives of the state's press and other media, and it is the primary focus of state interest groups who seek particular policy interpretations or guidance. But the local boards operate in the context of what those media say about Selective Service, and in response to what those interest groups have gained or sought—and our purposes are best served by taking them together. Our identification of the major elements in the organization's state and local environment, therefore, includes media and interest group representatives as well as major employers, veterans' groups, some local politicians, and several distinctive publics: local elites, registrants, attentive citizens, and a broader general public. Most of our attention will be directed at these distinctive publics, but we shall first summarize our findings with respect to the others.

Because it is not economical—or important enough, in most years —for news media to develop expertise among their reporters concerning Selective Service, state headquarters accurately perceives newsmen as ignorant and therefore threatening. The chances are good that an inadvertent phrase or a misplaced emphasis transmitted statewide may seriously embarrass the State Director with the public generally, with registrants or employers, or (more likely, and worse) with his local board members. A report that declares, on the strength of an interview with a state headquarters' spokesman, that the state's Selective Service System *"will do"* certain things is likely to raise tensions among volunteers, who understand no such command relationships to exist; this is particularly likely when, as is often the case, the news item concerns a change in procedure as to which no instructions have yet been received from national headquarters. The state headquarters has many risks and little to gain in its relationships with the press, and it is little wonder that a defensive posture is assumed. The self-fulfilling potential of such action is clear: reporters and public may come to believe that the System is secretive. For the most part, of course, the news media are content with wire service reports of national and state quotas and calls, and it is only in periods of relatively high inductions that problems arise.

In the absence of systematic data on the performance or local impact of the draft—information which the state headquarters does not have—interest groups and employers must base their actions on the sketchy reporting of the news media or on their personal experiences. Their grievances or arguments normally receive a sympathetic hearing from state headquarters officers, whose agreement with them may lead to guidance as to how to enable their members or employees to qualify for deferments, or, in some instances, to general policy statements for the guidance of local boards. There are few ways in which effective pressure can be brought to bear on the state headquarters, and employers' chief reliance must be placed on the officers' acknowledgment of the desirability of minimizing the economic impact of the draft on the state's important industries.

Neither officeholders nor other influential participants in partisan politics play an important part in the System's state and local environment (in Wisconsin, though perhaps they do in some states). This may be due to the tact with which the officers of the state headquarters deflect routine requests for information on behalf of constituents and handle other contacts with such political figures, but it is more likely the product of the peculiar insulation the System enjoys. In this state at least, public disclosure that a politician had obtained special consideration for a registrant would be disastrous to that politician's future and to the image of the System in the eyes of both general public and local board members. While the politician might want to serve an important constituent, he would probably be unwilling to risk public awareness of having done so—an unwillingness that the state headquarters can use to insulate itself against any such attempt. Contacts between the System and the partisan political world are thus frequent and friendly, but do not reach to the point where the actions of the organization are affected.

The several publics with which the System interacts include some intimately engaged and affected by it and some only marginally related to it; the nature of this interaction therefore varies sharply. The most intimately involved public is the semipermanent one made up of local board members. In important ways, of course, board members are members of the organization and communication with them takes place through internal mechanisms and processes; we have conceived of board members as the decision-making appendages of the organization throughout this study. But board members are also a public with which the organization interacts: they are board members in operating capacity only about three to six hours per month, and the rest of the time they are undergoing the experiences and reactions of other similarly situated citizens, albeit from a distinctive perspective. In other words, whatever information is conveyed about the System, whatever events occur and are interpreted, and whatever actions are taken by relevant figures—in the month between meetings—have their impact on board members too. The System must constantly be considering the impact that its actions may have on board members, both as part of the organization *and* as part of the general public. Their limited status as organization operatives, and their plenitude of individual interests and activities, give them this unique dual capacity of member and public.

That the organization does not succeed in converting board members into mere implements of its goals has been demonstrated from the data concerning board members' views on specific Selective Service policies: members, it will be recalled, showed substantial disagreement with organizational policies in the same areas as did the general public. At the same time, they were as a group attitudinally distinct from the other members of the general public in the direction of the organization's goals, so to them the organization's accomplishments were apparent. Considerable effort is expended by the System to maintain the self-image of sacrifice and dedication on the part of these board members, and it may be that much of what appears to be gratuitous or unfounded self-congratulation on the part of the System should be understood as being an effort to maintain good relations with board members. The more board members feel that they are appreciated, the more likely they are to cooperate willingly in carrying out the System's goals.

Overlapping with the local board members, and reached in part through them, is a second critical public: local elites. The recruitment processes employed by the System, as we have seen, draw local board members from the ranks of civically active middle-class entrepreneurs. Board members were shown to be part of a relatively small, circulating body of citizens who fill local public offices and engage in voluntary association activities. If board members are content with the practices of the System and display their satisfactions, these other local leadership elements will probably also consider the System to be working appropriately. In any event, they will have greater confidence in the System if they know those who are serving as board members and interact with them in the course of their daily lives. At stake therefore in the organization's relations with its board members is some portion of the System's acceptance and prospective support from locally significant middle-class elements.

Much more affected by the organization's actions, but much less of concern to it, are the registrants. Those who are even potentially vulnerable to induction have special reasons for attentiveness and concern for the System's actions and statements. The System, however, takes little advantage of this. Very little information of any kind is made available to registrants, and the only direct communication which occurs takes place through the initiative of the registrant. The images of local boards which registrants hold are not favorable; perhaps they could not be under the circumstances, but it seems clear that little is done to moderate the organization's threatening posture.

Those registrants who are "heavy investors" particularly feel threatened by local boards and by the draft; registrants who have experienced some contact with their boards are even more likely to believe them influential in determining applications of conscription policy. Registrants are thus a very special subpublic, and it is not strange that their attitudinal posture should be distinctive. They are more likely to believe that local boards are determinative (make their own policies rather than follow orders) than the general public, and they are slightly more knowledgeable than others about the character and makeup of boards. Much of their information about the System, and hence much of their image of it, comes from nonorganization sources. Registrants reported that their chief source of information about the draft was the news media, and second came their friends and associates; local boards were only the third source of information, closely rivaled by the university itself. The interaction of the System and its primary policy objects is thus an indirect one. Communications are received by registrants from the media, and, perhaps much more important, in the social situation where the effects of friends and other factors may be felt. Board members too, it will be recalled, were found to be close readers of national news media regarding the draft, and probably the availability of this source also serves to detach them somewhat from the direct relationship with the System.

Completing the publics with which the organization maintains some form of contact are two others: that relatively small number of citizens who are attentive to conscription matters (politically conscious persons, parents of registrants, etc.) and the comparatively large number of people who are only marginally aware that there is an organization which carries out the tasks associated with conscription. The latter are probably prepared to accept the organization and its work along with all other governmental activities. Greater effort may be necessary with regard to attentive citizens, many of whom probably perceive the System in terms of a threat. These are the people for whom the symbolic reassurances may be intended, and in many instances at least they are the people whose employees or sons are eventually able to qualify for deferments. As we have seen, they view the draft as unfair somewhat more than persons in less attentive groups, probably due to their peculiar vulnerability, but they switch over to approval of the local board concept in very substantial proportions.

It is apparent that output patterns are indeed complicated: segmented impact on various subpopulations at different socioeconomic class levels is accompanied by varying perceptions and qualitatively different relationships between the organization and its several publics. These findings suggest the probability of several interdependent chains of subsequent response. The greater the manpower surplus, for example, the more the impact of the draft will be concentrated on lower middle-class registrants, and the less the upper- and upper-middle classes will actually be threatened by the draft. Accordingly, both other interactions and subsequently generated demands, organizational characteristics, and public reactions may well follow different channels. In the development of theoretical implications from policy analysis, therefore, considerable attention will have to be paid to the interrelated and varied forms which output may take.

Feedback

Feedback is information concerning the effects of system performance and responses to that performance. It is a vital element in the Eastonian construct because only feedback provides authorities with the information necessary to cope with stress, measure the nearness to attainment of system goals, and modify system behavior and performance to improve achievements and maintain support (1965b: 364–369). Specifically, Easton declares, authorities must know the conditions in the environment and in the system, the supportive state of mind of the members being voiced, and the effects which outputs have produced (1965a: 128–129).

Clearly, feedback is transactional in nature. It implies a state of mind on the part of the authorities within the system, and it imputes to them a certain purposefulness regarding goal attainment and adaptation. In some way, the system must seek to ascertain the nature of its impact and the character of conditions in the system and its environment. And the objects of its actions must develop reactions and be able to communicate them. Both the authorities and the members of the system have parts to play in the mutual accomplishment of the informing function.

As we have noted, the authorities within the conscription-implementing subsystem have made almost no effort to ascertain the effects of their performance. The national headquarters itself has foreclosed some forms of self-assessment by record-keeping omissions and procedures, and compounds this with an unwillingness to ask searching questions concerning performance. Nor have part-time authoritative elements in the subsystem (Congress, Defense Department, President) undertaken examination of effects of performance, with the recent and partial exception of the President's Commission. When the authorities do not seek to learn, can the members bring information to their attention? Let us examine this question in some detail.

Conscription is one of many governmental policies, and Selective Service is one of many agencies of government administering specific functions. Both policy and agency thus compete for public attention (or seek to preserve inattention) in a context of many other governmental activities and world events, most of which have more specific and focused points of contact with the public. For many institutions, public officials, and other political objects, the political parties provide both cues for evaluation and a vehicle for expression of opinion on election day. Others, such as economic policy administration or church–state decisions of the Supreme Court, may be linked to established popular attitudes or values through ideological or religious commitments. No accepted source of similar guidance exists in the case of conscription and Selective Service, however, and perhaps in the case of some other government policies as well. The public thus receives communications from the media concerning Selective Service, and individual members of the public register, are drafted or deferred, or learn of similar events with respect to others, in a field free of basic structuring agents. Reception of such communications and other stimuli is variable and random, and no self-interest investment in the operation or improvement of the policy or its application develops for any sizable group of people.

In this low-saliency, unstructured context, we have found that different factors determine attitudes toward policy and organization, and that separate constituencies exist for each. To the national and state Headquarters of the Selective Service System, the validity of the organization's policy—indeed, the essential nature of the draft—depends on the existence of the local boards. Clearly, for the organization, there is an inherent merger of policy and organizational structure, but by the time these are perceived by the public they have become separated and nearly completely distinguished. Reaction to the draft is marginally favorable while reaction to the local board concept is negative.

Attitudes toward the local board aspect of the System showed sharp cleavages along class lines, with the upper classes strongly favoring and the lower classes as strongly disapproving administration of conscription through local men. Within both categories, those who felt more politically efficacious supported local boards more strongly. Although we cannot demonstrate that the connection is causal, we note that this segmentation of attitudes toward local boards parallels the patterns of impact of the draft that were identified: those who feel the weight of conscription most heavily disapprove of local boards most strongly.

The experience of Selective Service also suggests that the serene administrative consensus (high approval of all forms of government activity) which Janowitz and his associates found to exist at the local level (1958) may have been particular to that place and time, or to specific functions. In our inquiry, the sharp cleavages found regarding local boards were at least as sharp as the cleavages usually associated with elections. Furthermore, the class pattern of approval and disapproval of government was reversed. In the Detroit study, lower classes expected more and sought more from government, and rated it more highly than did the upper classes; here, the lower classes rated local boards much lower than did upper classes.

Perhaps the Selective System is unique in its threatening character, and in this respect should be compared, if at all, only with the (lower-class disapproved) police function in the other studies. More likely, we have another indication of the vital importance of distinguishing between types of policies for the purposes of conceptualizing impact and feedback patterns. Selective Service is an extractive rather than a service-providing agency, at least in the eyes of its potential inductees. Both conscription and law enforcement may be viewed as a service by one class level in the population, and as threatening and exploitative by other class levels. In the Lowi–Salisbury classification schemes, conscription at least is redistributive, and we may hypothesize that redistributive policies will be segmentally received and perceived by the members of the system. The lines of differential reception might not always be class based, of course, but those who benefit from the policy are likely to be more favorable than those who are burdened by the policy under most circumstances.

A further difficulty inheres in the process of feedback from members of the system: There are no available channels through which reactions can be effectively expressed. None of the established instruments of linkage between people and government took up questions concerning conscription implementation. There was no political party or electoral vehicle through which opinion could be felt, nor would it appear that the structure of opinion would make it profitable for a political party or candidate to seek to make conscription an issue—for the subject cuts across party lines and could lose more votes than it would gain.

Diffusion is thus complete. The policy area has very low visibility for most people, with a resulting small and shifting constituency made up for the most part of young men of relatively insignificant political weight. There is further diffusion created by the detachment in public perception between the general policy of conscription and its implementation by local boards, and by differing perceptions and evaluations of the desirability of the present form of local administration on the part of various socioeconomic levels within the population. Additionally, there are no vehicles by which these diffused perceptions and reactions could be communicated to any "authorities." We may add, speculatively, that the whole area is probably overlaid with symbolic attachments to serving one's country in patriotic terms, with fears of communism, and with the general willingness to do what appears necessary to support government commitments.

Under such conditions, there is little likelihood that the effects of system performance or the responses of members of the system will be made known. Given the disinterest of the authorities in ascertaining such matters, the failure of feedback seems complete. With only the occasional and readily dismissible allegations of journalists and popular writers as a source of feedback, it is understandable that both national headquarters and other responsible authorities could cling to rather badly misconstrued images of the efficacy and acceptability of Selective Service (Edelman, 1964). Or, to be somewhat less charitable, it may be that under such conditions the views of those who are the most visible and who carry the most political weight (in this case the middle-class local activists who support local boards and enjoy deferments) are a sufficient source of support and the other factors are dispensable.

The problem of inadequate means of feedback from public to government has consequences which reach well beyond the specifics of Selective Service. The draft is probably only slightly more out of touch with popular views than some other governmental functions, if it is at all. The problem seems particularly well worth raising, however, because of the saliency which the draft appeared to have in 1966 and 1967: it is not often that a government function not in the partisan political arena rises to such visibility, and if a feedback problem exists under these conditions it must be endemic to the subject and perhaps to a broad area of the political system. And where there is a feedback problem, there may also be support problems: if popular preferences cannot effectively be expressed, if there is no way to focus desires on a major governmental function, then surely that function is threatened with a loss of support and, if it is important enough, the system itself may feel the defection.

The Evolution of Organizational Environments*
SHIRLEY TERREBERRY

Darwin published *The Origin of Species by Means of Natural Selection* in 1859. Modern genetics has vastly altered our understanding of the variance upon which natural selection operates. But there has been no conceptual breakthrough in understanding *environmental* evolution which, alone, shapes the direction of change. Even today most theorists of change still focus on *internal* interdependencies of systems—biological, psychological, or social—although the external environments of these systems are changing more rapidly than ever before.

Introduction

Von Bertalanffy was the first to reveal fully the importance of a system being open or closed to the environment in distinguishing living from inanimate systems (1956: 1–10). Although von Bertalanffy's formulation makes it possible to deal with a system's exchange processes in a new perspective, it does not deal at all with those processes in the environment *itself* that are among the determining conditions of exchange.

Emery and Trist have argued the need for one additional concept, "the causal texture of the environment" (1956: 21–31). Writing in the

* Reprinted from *Administrative Science Quarterly, 12* (March 1968), 590–613, by permission of the author and the publisher.

context of formal organizations, they offer the following general proposition:

> That a comprehensive understanding of organizational behaviour requires some knowledge of each member of the following set, where L indicates some potentially lawful connection, and the suffix 1 refers to the organization and the suffix 2 to the environment:
>
> $$L_{11} \ L_{12}$$
> $$L_{21} \ L_{22}$$
>
> L_{11} here refers to processes within the organization—the area of internal interdependencies; L_{12} and L_{21} to exchanges between the organization and its environment—the area of transactional interdependencies, from either direction; and L_{22} to processes through which parts of the environment become related to each other—i.e., its causal texture—the area of interdependencies that belong within the environment itself (1965: 22).

We have reproduced the above paragraph in its entirety because, in the balance of the paper, we will use Emery and Trist's symbols (i.e., L_{11}, L_{21}, L_{12}, and L_{22}) to denote intra-, input, output, and extra-system interdependencies, respectively. Our purpose in doing so is to avoid the misleading connotations of conventional terminology.

Purpose   The theses here are: (1) that contemporary changes in organizational environments are such as to increase the ratio of externally induced change to internally induced change; and (2) that *other* formal organizations are, increasingly, the important components in the environment of any focal organization. Furthermore, the evolution of environments is accompanied—among viable systems—by an increase in the system's ability to learn and to perform according to changing contingencies in its environment. An integrative framework is outlined for the concurrent analysis of an organization, its transactions with environmental units, and interdependencies among those units. Lastly, two hypotheses are presented, one about organizational *change* and the other about organizational *adaptability;* and some problems in any empirical test of these hypotheses are discussed.

Concepts of Organizational Environments   In Emery and Trist's terms, L_{22} relations (i.e., interdependencies within the environment itself) comprise the "causal texture" of the field. This causal texture of the environment is treated as a quasi-independent domain, since the environment cannot be conceptualized except with respect to some focal organization. The components of the environment are identified in terms of that system's actual and *potential* transactional interdependencies, both input (L_{21}) and output (L_{12}).

Emery and Trist postulate four "ideal types" of environment, which can be ordered according to the degree of *system connected-ness* that exists among the components of the environment (L_{22}). The first of these is a "placid, randomized" environment: goods and bads are relatively unchanging in themselves and are randomly distributed (e.g., the environments of an amoeba, a human foetus, a nomadic tribe). The second is a "placid, clustered" environment: goods and bads are relatively unchanging in themselves but clustered (e.g., the environments of plants that are subjected to the cycle of seasons, of human infants, of extractive industries). The third ideal type is "disturbed-reactive" environment and constitutes a significant qualitative change over simpler types of environments: an environment characterized by similar systems in the field. The extinction of dinosaurs can be traced to the emergence of more complex environments on the biological level. Human beings, beyond infancy, live in disturbed-reactive environments in relation to one another. The theory of oligopoly in economics is a theory of this type of environment (1965: 24–26).

These three types of environment have been identified and described in the literature of biology, economics, and mathematics (Emery and Trist, 1965: 24–26; Simon, 1957: 137; Ashby, 1960: Sec. 15/4; Tolman and Brunswick, 1935: 43–72; Ashby, 1960: Sec. 15/8, 7; Chein, 1943: 89–101). "The fourth type, however, is new, at least to us, and is the one that for some time we have been endeavouring to identify" (Emery and Trist, 1965: 24). This fourth ideal type of environment is called a "turbulent field." Dynamic processes "arise from the *field itself*" and not merely from the interactions of components; the actions of component organizations and linked sets of them "are both persistent and strong enough to induce autochthonous processes in the environment" (Emery and Trist, 1965: 26).

An alternate description of a turbulent field is that the accelerating rate and complexity of interactive effects exceed the component systems' capacities for prediction and, hence, control of the compounding consequences of their actions.

Turbulence is characterized by complexity as well as rapidity of change in causal interconnections in the environment. Emery and Trist illustrate the transition from a disturbed-reactive to a turbulent-field environment for a company that had maintained a steady 65 percent of the market for its main product—a canned vegetable—over many years. At the end of World War II, the firm made an enormous investment in a new automated factory that was set up exclusively for the traditional product and technology. At the same time postwar controls on steel strip and tin were removed, so that cheaper cans were available; surplus crops were more cheaply obtained by importers; diversity increased in available products, including substitutes for the staple; the quick-freeze technology was developed; home buyers became more affluent; supermarkets emerged and placed bulk orders with small firms for retail under supermarket names. These changes in technology, international trade, and affluence of buyers gradually interacted (L_{22}) and ultimately had a pronounced effect on the company: its market dwindled rapidly. "The changed texture of the environment was not recognized by an able but traditional management until it was too late" (Emery and Trist, 1965: 24).

Sociological, social psychological, and business management theorists often still treat formal organizations as closed systems. In recent years, however, this perspective seems to be changing. Etzioni asserts that interorganizational relations need intensive empirical study (1960: 223–228). Blau and Scott present a rich but unconceptualized discussion of the "social context of organizational life" (1962: 194–221). Parsons distinguishes three distinct levels of organizational responsibility and control: technical, managerial, and institutional (1960: 63–64). His categories can be construed to parallel the intraorganizational (i.e., technical or L_{11}), the interorganizational (i.e., managerial or L_{21} and L_{12}), and the extraorganizational levels of analysis (i.e., the institutional or L_{22} areas). Perhaps in the normal developmental course of a science, intrasystem analysis necessarily precedes the intersystem focus. On the other hand, increasing attention to interorganizational relations may reflect a real change in the phenomenon being studied. The first question to consider is whether there is evidence that the environments of formal organizations are evolving toward turbulent-field conditions.

Evidence for Turbulence   Ohlin argues that the sheer rapidity of social change today requires greater organizational adaptability (1958: 63). Hood points to the increasing complexity, as well as the accelerating rate of change, in organizational environments (1962: 73). In business circles there is growing conviction that the future is unpredictable. Drucker (1964: 6–8) and Gardner (1963: 107) both assert that the kind and extent of present-day change preclude prediction of the future. Increasingly, the rational strategies of planned-innovation and long-range planning are being undermined by unpredictable changes. McNulty found no association between organization adaptation and the introduction of purposeful change in a study of 30 companies in fast-growing markets (1962: 1–21). He suggests that built-in flexibility may be more efficient than the explicit reorganization implicit in the quasi-rational model. *Dun's Review* questions the effectiveness of long-range planning in the light of frequent failures, and suggests that error may be attributable to forecasting the future by extrapolation of a noncomparable past. The conclusion is that the rapidity and complexity of change may increasingly preclude effective long-range planning (1963: 42). These examples clearly suggest the emergence of a change in the environment that is suggestive of turbulence.

Some writers with this open-system perspective derive implications for interorganizational relations from this changing environment.

Blau and Scott argue that the success of a firm increasingly depends upon its ability to establish symbiotic relations with other organizations, in which extensive advantageous exchange takes place (1962: 194–221). Lee Adler proposes "symbiotic marketing" (1966: 59–71). Dill found that the task environments of two Norwegian firms comprised four major sectors: *customers,* including both distributors and users; *suppliers* of materials, labor, capital, equipment, and work space; *competitors* for both markets and resources; and *regulatory groups,* including governmental agencies, unions, and interfirm associations (1958: 409–443). Not only does Dill's list include many more components than are accommodated by present theories, but all components are themselves evolving into formal organizations. In his recent book, Thompson discusses "task environments," which comprise the units with which an organization has input and output transactions (L_{21} and L_{12}), and postulates two dimensions of such environments: homogeneous–heterogeneous and dynamic (i.e., probably turbulent), he expects an organization's boundary-spanning units to be functionally differentiated to correspond to segments of the task environment and each to operate on a decentralized basis to monitor and plan responses to fluctuations in its sector of the task environment (1967: 27–28). He does not focus on other organizations as components of the environment, but he provides a novel perspective on structural implications (L_{11}) for organizations in turbulent fields.

Selznick's work on TVA appears to be the first organizational case study to emphasize transactional interdependencies (1949). The next study was Ridgway's 1957 study of manufacturer–dealer relationships (1957: 464–483). Within the following few years the study by Dill (1958: 409–443) and others by Levine and White (1961: 583–601), Litwak and Hylton (1962: 395–420), and Elling and Halebsky (1961: 185–209) appeared, and in recent years, the publication of such studies has accelerated.

The following are examples from two volumes of the *Administrative Science Quarterly* alone. Rubington argues that structural changes in organizations that seek to change the behavior of "prisoners, drug addicts, juvenile delinquents, parolees, alcoholics (are) . . . the result of a social movement whose own organizational history has yet to be written" (1965: 350–369). Rosengren reports a similar phenomenon in the mental health field whose origin he finds hard to explain: "In any event, a more symbiotic relationship has come to characterize the relations between the (mental) hospitals and other agencies, professions, and establishments in the community" (1964: 70–90). He ascribes changes in organizational goals and technology to this interorganizational evolution. In the field of education, Clark outlines the increasing influence of private foundations, national associations, and divisions of the federal government. He, too, is not clear as to how these changes have come about, but he traces numerous changes in the behavior of educational organizations to interorganizational influences (1965: 224–237). Maniha and Perrow analyze the origins and development of a city youth commission. The agency had little reason to be formed, no goals to guide it, and was staffed by people who sought a minimal, no-action role in the community. By virtue of its existence and broad province, however, it was seized upon as a valuable weapon by other organizations for the pursuit of their own goals. "But in this very process it became an organization with a mission of its own, in spite of itself" (1965: 238–257).

Since uncertainty is the dominant characteristic of turbulent fields, it is not surprising that emphasis in recent literature is away from algorithmic and toward heuristic problem-solving models (Taylor, 1965: 48–82); that optimizing models are giving way to satisficing models (March and Simon, 1958: 140–141); and that rational decision making is replaced by "disjointed incrementalism" (Braybrooke and Lindblom, 1963: Chs. 3, 5). These trends reflect *not* the ignorance of the authors of earlier models, but a change in the causal texture of organizational environments and, therefore, of appropriate strategies for coping with the environment. Cyert and March state that "so long as the environment of the firm is unstable—and predictably unstable—the heart of the theory (of the firm) must be the process of short-run adaptive reactions" (1963: 100).

In summary, both the theoretical and case study literature on organizations suggests that these systems are increasingly finding themselves in environments where the complexity and rapidity of change in external interconnectedness (L_{22}) gives rise to increasingly unpredictable change in their transactional interdependencies (L_{21} and L_{12}). This seems to be good evidence for the emergence of turbulence in the environments of many formal organizations.

Interorganizational Environment

Evidence for Increasing Dependence on Environment   Elsewhere the author has argued that Emery and Trist's concepts can be extended to *all* living systems; furthermore, that this evolutionary process gives rise to conditions—biological, psychological, and social—in which the rate of evolution of environments exceeds the rate of evolution of component systems (Terreberry, 1967: 1–37).

In the short run, the openness of a living system to its environment enables it to take in ingredients from the environment for conversion into energy or information that allows it to maintain a steady state and, hence, to violate the dismal second law of thermodynamics (i.e., of entropy). In the long run, "the characteristic of living systems which most clearly distinguishes them from the nonliving is their property of progressing by the process which is called evolution from less to more complex states of organization" (Pringle, 1956: 90). It then follows that to the extent that the environment of some living system X is comprised *of other living systems,* the environment of X is *itself* evolving from less to more complex states of organization. A major corollary is that the evolution of environments is characterized by an increase in the ratio of externally induced change over internally induced change in a system's transactional interdependencies (L_{21} and L_{12}).

For illustration, let us assume that at some given time, each system in some set of interdependent systems is equally likely to experience an internal (L_{11}) change that is functional for survival (i.e., improves its L_{21} or L_{12} transactions). The greater the number of other systems in that set, the greater the probability that some system other than X will experience that change. Since we posit interdependence among members of the set, X's viability over time depends upon X's capacity (L_{11}) for adaptation to environmentally induced (L_{22}) changes in its transactive position, or else upon control over these external relations.

In the case of formal organizations, disturbed-reactive or oligopolistic environments require some form of accommodation between like but competitive organizations whose fates are negatively correlated to some degree. A change in the transactional position of one system in an oligopolistic set, whether for better or worse, automatically affects the transactional position of all other members of the set, and in the opposite direction (i.e., for worse or better, as the case may be). On the other hand, turbulent environments require relationships between dissimilar organizations whose fates are independent or, perhaps, positively correlated. A testable hypothesis that derives from the formal argument is that the evolution of environments is accompanied, in viable systems, by an increase in ability to learn and to perform according to changing contingencies in the environment.

The evolution of organizational environments is characterized by a change in the important constituents of the environment. The earliest formal organizations to appear in the United States (e.g., in agriculture, retail trade, construction, mining) (Stinchcombe, 1965: 156) operated largely under placid-clustered conditions. Important inputs, such as natural resources and labor, as well as consumers, comprised an environment in which strategies of optimal location and distinctive competence were critical organizational responses (Emery and Trist, 1965: 29). Two important attributes of placid-clustered environments are: (1) the environment is itself *not* formally organized, and (2) transactions are largely initiated and controlled by the organization (i.e., L_{12}).

Later developments, such as transport technology and derivative overlap in loss of strength gradients, and communication and automation technologies that increased economies of scale, gave rise to disturbed-reactive (oligopolistic) conditions in which similar formal organizations become the important actors in an organization's field. They are responsive to its acts (L_{12}) *and* it must be responsive to theirs (L_{21}). The critical organizational response now involves complex operations, requiring sequential choices based on the calculated actions of others, and counteractions (Emery and Trist, 1965: 25–26).

When the environment becomes turbulent, however, its constituents are a multitude of other formal organizations. Increasingly, an organization's markets consist of other organizations; and regulatory groups are more numerous and powerful. The critical response of organizations under these conditions will be discussed later. It should be noted that *real* environments are often mixtures of these ideal types.

The evolution from placid-clustered environments to turbulent environments can be summarized as a process in which formal organizations evolve: (1) *from* the status of systems within environments not formally organized; (2) *through* intermediate phases (e.g., Weberian bureaucracy); and (3) *to* the status of subsystems of a larger social system.

Clark Kerr traces this evolution for the university in the United States (1963). In modern industrial societies, this evolutionary process has resulted in the replacement of individuals and informal groups by organizations as *actors* in the social system. Functions that were once the sole responsibility of families and communities are increasingly allocated to formal organizations; child-rearing, work, recreation, education, health, and so on. Events which were long a matter of chance are increasingly subject to organizational control, such as population growth, business cycles, and even the weather. One wonders whether Durkheim, if he could observe the current scene, might speculate that the evolution from "mechanical solidarity" to "organic solidarity" is now occurring on the *organizational level,* where the common values of organizations in oligopolies are replaced by functional interdependencies among specialized organizations (1947).

Interorganizational Analysis   It was noted that survival in disturbed-reactive environments depends upon the ability of the organization to anticipate and counteract the behavior of similar systems. The analysis of interorganizational behavior, therefore, becomes meaningful only in these and more complex environments. The interdependence of organizations, or any kind of living systems, at less complex environmental levels is more appropriately studied by means of ecological, competitive market, or other similar models.

The only systematic conceptual approach to interorganizational analysis has been the theory of oligopoly in economics. This theory clearly addresses only disturbed-reactive environments. Many economists admit that the theory, which assumes maximization of profit and perfect knowledge, is increasingly at odds with empirical evidence that organizational behavior is characterized by satisficing and bounded rationality. Boulding comments that "it is surprisingly hard to make a really intelligent conflict move in the economic area simply because of the complexity of the system and the enormous importance of side effects and dynamic effects" (1965: 189). A fairly comprehensive search of the literature has revealed only four conceptual frameworks for the analysis of interorganizational relations outside the field of economics. These are briefly reviewed, particular attention being given to assumptions about organization environments, and to the utility of these assumptions in the analysis of interorganizational relations in turbulent fields.

William Evan has introduced the concept of "organization-set," after Merton's "role-set" (1966: 177–180). Relations between a focal organization and members of its organization-set are mediated by the role-sets of boundary personnel. "Relations" are conceived as the flow of information, products or services, and personnel (1966: 175–176). Presumably, monetary, and legal, and other transactions can be accommodated in the conceptual system. In general, Evan offers a conceptual tool for identifying transactions at a given time. He makes no explicit assumptions about the nature of environmental dynamics, nor does he imply that they are changing. The relative neglect of interorganizational relations, which he finds surprising, is ascribed instead to the traditional intraorganizational focus, which derives from Weber, Taylor, and Barnard (1966: 175–176). His concepts, however, go considerably beyond those of conventional organization and economic theory (e.g., comparative versus reference organizations and overlap in goals and values). If a temporal dimension were added to Evan's conceptual scheme, then, it would be a very useful tool for describing the "structural" aspects of transactional interdependencies (L_{21} and L_{12} relations) in turbulent fields.

Another approach is taken by Levine and White, who focus specifically on relations among community health and welfare agencies. This local set of organizations "may be seen as a system with individual organizations or system parts varying in the kinds and frequencies of their relationships with one another" (1961: 586). The authors admit that interdependence exists among these local parts only to the extent that relevant resources are not available from *outside* the local region, which lies beyond their conceptual domain. Nor do we find here any suggestion of turbulence in these local environments. If such local sets of agencies are increasingly interdependent with other components of the local community and with organizations outside the locality, as the evidence suggests, then the utility of Levine and White's approach is both limited and shrinking.

Litwak and Hylton provide a third perspective. They too are concerned with health and welfare organizations, but their major emphasis is on coordination (1962: 395–420). The degree of interdependence among organizations is a major variable; low interdependence leads to *no* coordination and high interdependence leads to merger; therefore they deal only with conditions of moderate interdependence. The type of coordinating mechanism that emerges under conditions of moderate interdependence is hypothesized to result from the interaction of three trichotomized variables: the *number* of interdependent organizations; the degree of their *awareness* of their interdependence; and the extent of *standardization* in their transactions. The attractive feature of the Litwak and Hylton scheme is the possibility it offers of making different predictions for a great variety of environments. Their model also seems to have predictive power beyond the class of organizations to which they specifically address themselves. If environments are becoming turbulent, however, then increasingly fewer of the model's cells (a 3 $\times$ 3 $\times$ 3 space) are relevant. In the one-cell turbulent corner of their model, where a large number of organizations have low awareness of their complex and unstandardized interdependence, "there is little chance of coordination" (1962: 417) according to Litwak and Hylton. If the level of awareness of interdependence increases, the model predicts that some process of arbitration will emerge. Thus the model anticipates the interorganizational implications of turbulent fields, but tells us little about the emerging processes that will enable organizations to adapt to turbulence.

The fourth conceptual framework available in the literature is by Thompson and McEwen (1958: 23–31). They emphasize the interdependence of organizations with the larger society and discuss the consequences that this has for goal setting. "Because the setting of goals is essentially a problem of defining desired relationships between an organization and its environment, change in either requires review and perhaps alteration of goals" (1958: 23). They do not argue that such changes are more frequent today, but they do assert that reappraisal of goals is "a more constant problem in an unstable environment than in a stable one," and also "more difficult as the 'product' of the enterprise becomes less tangible" (1958: 24).

Thompson and McEwen outline four organizational strategies for dealing with the environment. One is competition; the other three are subtypes of a cooperative strategy: bargaining, co-optation, and coalition. These cooperative strategies all require direct interaction among organizations and this, they argue, increases the environment's potential control over the focal organization (1958: 27). In bargaining, to the extent that the second party's support is necessary, that party is in a position to exercise a veto over the final choice of alternative goals, and thus takes part in the decision. The co-optation strategy makes still further inroads into the goal setting process. From the standpoint of society, however, co-optation, by providing overlapping memberships, is an important social device for increasing the likelihood that organizations related to each other in complicated ways will in fact find compatible goals. Co-optation thus aids in the integration of heterogeneous parts of a complex social system. Coalition refers to a combination of two or more organizations for a common purpose and is viewed by these authors as the ultimate form of environmental conditioning of organization goals (1958: 25–28).

The conceptual approaches of Levine and White and of Litwak and Hylton therefore appear to be designed for nonturbulent conditions. indeed, it may well be that coordination *per se,* in the static sense usually implied by that term is dysfunctional for adaptation to turbulent fields. (This criticism has often been leveled at local "councils of social agencies" [Morris and Randall, 1965: 96–103; Harris, 1964: 34–41; Wilensky and Lebeaux, 1958: 263–265].) On the other hand, Evan's concept of organization-set seems useful for describing static aspects of interorganizational relations in either disturbed-reactive *or* turbulent-field environments. Its application in longitudinal rather than static studies might yield data on the relationship between structural aspects of transactional relations and organizational adaptability. Lastly, Thompson and McEwen make a unique contribution by distinguishing different *kinds* of interorganizational relations.

As an aside, note that Evan's extension of the role-set concept to organizations suggests still further analogies, which may be heuristically useful. A role is a set of acts prescribed for the occupant of some position. The role accrues to the position; its occupants are interchangeable. If formal organizations are treated as social actors, then one can conceive of organizations as occupants of positions in the larger social system. Each organization has one or more roles in its behavioral repertoire (these are more commonly called functions or goals). The organization occupants of these social positions, however, are also interchangeable.

Integrative Framework

Model It is assumed that the foregoing arguments are valid: (1) that organizational environments are increasingly turbulent; (2) that organizations are increasingly less autonomous; and (3) that other formal organizations are increasingly important components of organizational environments. Some conceptual perspective is now needed, which will make it possible to view any formal organization, its transactional interdependencies, and the environment itself within a common conceptual framework. The intent of this section is to outline the beginnings of such a framework.

A formal organization is a system primarily oriented to the attainment of a specific goal, which constitutes an output of the system and which is an input for some other system (Parsons, 1962: 33). Needless to say, the output of any living system is dependent upon input into it. Figure 1 schematically illustrates the skeletal structure of a living system. The input and output regions are partially permeable with respect to the environment, which is the region outside the system boundary. Arrows coming into a system represent input and arrows going out of a system represent output. In Figure 2, rectangles represent formal organizations and circles represent individuals and *non*formal social

FIGURE 1.   STRUCTURE OF LIVING SYSTEMS SUCH AS A FORMAL ORGANIZATION

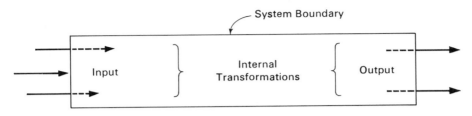

organizations. Figure 2 represents the statics of a system *X* and its turbulent environment. Three-dimensional illustration would be necessary to show the *dynamics* of a turbulent environment schematically. Assume that a third, temporal dimension is imposed on Figure 2 and that this reveals an increasing number of elements and an increasing rate and complexity of change in their interdependencies over time.

FIGURE 2.   ILLUSTRATION OF SYSTEM *X* IN TURBULENT ENVIRONMENT

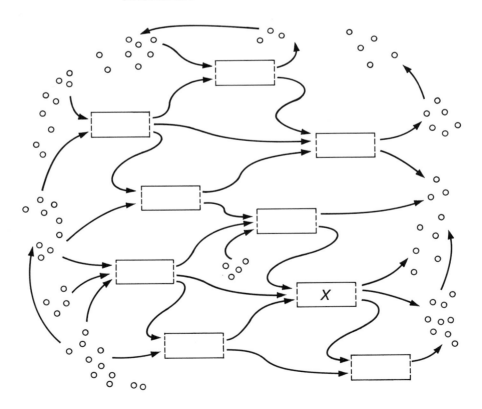

To do full justice to the concept of turbulence we should add other sets of elements even in Figure 2 above, although these are not yet linked to X's set. A notion that is integral to Emery and Trist's conception of turbulence is that changes outside of X's set, and hence difficult for X to predict and impossible for X to control, will have impact on X's transactional interdependencies in the future. The addition of just one link at some future time may not affect the supersystem but may constitute a system break for X.

This schematization shows only one-way directionality and is meant to depict energic inputs (e.g., personnel and material) and output (e.g., product). The organization provides something in exchange for the inputs it receives, of course, and this is usually informational in nature—money, most commonly. Similarly the organization receives money for its product from those systems for whom its product is an input. Nor does our framework distinguish different kinds of inputs, although the analysis of interorganizational exchange requires this kind of taxonomic device. It seems important to distinguish energic inputs and outputs from informational ones. Energic inputs include machinery, personnel, clientele in the case of service organizations, electric power, and so on. Informational inputs are not well conceptualized although there is no doubt of their increasing importance in environments which are more complex and changeable. Special divisions of organizations and whole firms devoted to information collecting, processing, and distributing are also rapidly proliferating (e.g., research organizations, accounting firms, the Central Intelligence Agency).

An input called "legitimacy" is popular in sociological circles but highly resistant to empirical specification. The view taken here is that legitimacy is mediated by the exchange of other resources. Thus the willingness of firm A to contribute capital to X, and of agency B to refer personnel to X and firm C to buy X's product testifies to the legitimacy of X. This "willingness" on the part of organizations A, B, and C, however, can best be understood in terms of informational exchange. For example, A provides X with capital on the basis of A's information about the market for X's product. Or B refuses to refer skilled workmen to X since B has information on X's discriminatory employment practices and also knows of consequences to itself from elsewhere if it is party to X's practice. Technology is also sometimes treated as an input to organizations. We use the term, however, to refer to the complex set of interactions among inputs, which takes place in the internal region shown in Figure 1. It is technology which transforms the inputs of the system into the output of the system. Transportation and communication technologies, however, are of a uniquely different order; the former constitutes an energic and the latter an informational transcendence of space–time that enabled the evolution of the more complex environments (L_{22}) which concern us here. Automation and computer technologies are roughly equivalent (i.e., energic and informational, respectively) but on an intraorganizational (L_{11}) level.

Our attention to "legitimacy" and "technology" was tangential to our main theme, to which we now return. Our simplistic approach to an integrative framework for the study of organizations (L_{11}), their transactional interdependencies (L_{21} and L_{12}), and the connectedness within their environments (L_{22}), give the following conceptual ingredients: (1) units that are mainly formal organizations, and (2) relationships between them that are the directed flow (Cartwright, 1959: 254–271) of (3) energy and information. The enormous and increasing importance of informational transaction has not been matched by conceptual developments in organization theory. The importance of information is frequently cited in a general way, however, especially in the context of organizational change or innovation. Dill has made a cogent argument on the need for more attention to this dimension (1962: 94–109).

The importance of communication for organizational change has been stressed by Ohlin, March and Simon, Benne, Lippitt, and others (Ohlin, 1958: 63; March and Simon, 1958: 173–183; Benne, 1962: 232; Lippitt, 1958: 52). Diversity of informational input has been used to explain the creativity of individuals as well as of social systems (Allport, 1955: 76; Ogburn and Nimkoff, 1964: 662–670). The importance of boundary positions as primary sources of innovative inputs from the environment has been stressed by March and Simon (1958: 165–166, 189) and by Kahn *et al.* (1964: 101–126). James Miller hypothesizes that up to a maximum, which no living system has yet reached, the more energy a system devotes to information processing (as opposed to productive and maintenance activity), the more likely the system is to survive (1955: 530).

Evolution on the biological level is accompanied by improvement in the ability of systems to discover and perform according to contingencies in their environments. The random walk which suffices in a placid-randomized environment must be replaced by stochastic processes under placid-clustered conditions, and by cybernetic processes in disturbed-reactive fields. Among biological/psychological systems, only man appears to have the capacity for the purposeful behavior that may permit adaptation to or control of turbulent environments. There is some question, of course, as to whether man actually *has* the capacity to cope with the turbulence that he has introduced into the environment.

Analogous concepts are equally applicable to the evolution of social systems in general and to formal organizations in particular. The capacity of *any* system for adapting to changing contingencies in its environment is inversely related to its dependence upon instinct, habit, or tradition. Adaptability exists, by definition, to the extent that a system (L_{11}) can survive externally induced (L_{22}) change in its trans-actional interdependencies $(L_{21}$ and $L_{12})$; therefore viability equals adaptability.

Hypotheses

Hypothesis 1.   *Organizational change is largely externally induced.*

Any particular change may be adaptive or maladaptive, and it may be one of these in the short run and the other in the long run. There is *no* systematic empirical evidence on the relative influence of internal versus environmental antecedents to organizational change. The empirical task here is to identify organizational changes, and the internal or external origins of each change.

It is crucial to distinguish change on the organizational level from the multitude of changes that may occur in or among subsystems, only some of which give rise to change on the system level. Many social psychologists, for example, study change in individuals and groups *within* organizations, but with no reference to variables of organizational level. Likert's book is one noteworthy exception (1961). The important point is that change on the organizational level is analytically distinct from change on other levels.

Organizational change means any change in the kind or quantity of output. Ideally, output is treated as a function of inputs and of transfer functions (i.e., intraorganizational change is inferred from change in input–output relations). Haberstroh illustrates the use of these general system concepts in the organization context (1965: 1171–1211). An excellent discussion of the efficiency and effectiveness of organizations, in an open-systems framework, is given in Katz and Kahn (1966: 149–170).

However, the input–output functions in diversified industries and the outputs of many service organizations are resistant to objective specification and measurement. An empirical test of this hypothesis, with presently available tools, may have to settle for some set of input and internal change that seems to be reasonably antecedent to output change.

The identification of the origin of change is also beset by difficulties. An input change may indeed have external antecedents, but external events may also be responses to some prior internal change in the focal organization. And internal change may be internally generated, but it may also be the result of an informational input from external sources. Novel informational inputs, as well as novel communication channels, often derive from change in personnel inputs. Increasingly, organizations seek personnel who bring specialized information rather than "manpower" to the organization. The presence of first, second, and higher order causation poses a problem for any empirical test of this hypothesis.

Hypothesis 2. System adaptability (e.g., organizational) is a function of ability to learn and to perform according to changing environmental contingencies.

Adaptability exists, by definition, to the extent that a system can survive externally induced change in its transactional interdependencies in the long run. Diversity in a system's input (L_{21}) and output (L_{12}) interdependencies will increase adaptability. The recent and rapid diversification in major industries illustrates this strategy. Flexible structure (L_{11}, e.g., decentralized decision making) will facilitate adaptation. Beyond this, however, adaptability would seem to be largely a function of a system's perceptual and information-processing capacities (Ansoff, 1965: 162). The following variables appear crucial: (1) *advance information* of impeding externally induced (L_{22}) change in L_{21} or L_{12} transactions; (2) *active search* for, and activation of, more advantageous input and output transactions; and (3) *available memory store* (L_{11}) of interchangeable input and output components in the environment.

Advance information and active search might be empirically handled with Evan's concept of the role-sets of boundary personnel, along with notions of channel efficiency. For example, overlapping memberships (e.g., on boards) would constitute a particularly efficient channel. Likewise, direct communication between members of separate organizations, while less effective than overlapping memberships, would be a more efficient channel between agencies A and B than instances where their messages must be mediated by a third agency, C. Efficiency of interorganizational communication channels should be positively associated with access to advance information, and be facilitative of search, for example. The members of an organization's informational set may become increasingly differentiated from its energic set. Communication channels to research and marketing firms, universities, governmental agencies, and other important information producing and distributing agencies would be expected to increase long-run viability. The third variable, memory store, is probably a function of the efficiency of past and present informational channels, but it involves internal (L_{11}) information processing as well.

Lastly, *any* internal change that improves an organization's transactional advantage (e.g., improved technology) will also be conducive to adaptability. Since organizational innovation is more often imitation than invention (Levitt, 1966: 63–70), these changes are usually also the product of informational input and can be handled within the same integrative framework.

Summary

The lag between evolution in the real world and evolution in theorists' ability to comprehend it is vast, but hopefully shrinking. It was only a little over one hundred years ago that Darwin identified natural selection as the mechanism of evolutionary process. Despite Darwin's enduring insight, theorists of change, including biologists, have continued to focus largely on internal aspects of systems.

It is our thesis that the selective advantage of one intra- or interorganizational configuration over another cannot be assessed apart from an understanding of the dynamics of the environment itself. It is the environment which exerts selective pressure. "Survival of the fittest" is a function of the fitness of the environment. The dinosaurs *were* impressive creatures, in their day.

Environmental Needs, Resources, and Agents
KOYA AZUMI

The general framework envisaged here conceives of the organization as extracting resources from its environment in order to meet certain articulated environmental needs. Needs as well as resources are represented by environmental agents, the key ones of which are suppliers, consumers, integrators, and competitors. In analyzing the relationships between the environment and the organization, there are at least two major problems. One issue is how characteristics of the environment affect the number and size of organizations. A second problem is how characteristics of the environment affect the relative power or autonomy of an organization. Implicit in much of the discussion is the assumption of Gouldner (1959) that organizations will strive to maximize autonomy. But while this may be a truism it is also clear that some organizations have become much more powerful than others.

Environmental Needs

The existence of organizations presupposes the existence of environmental needs. Organizational goals are *ipso facto* articulated needs that are believed to exist in the environment. Organizations differ in the scope and variety of needs they purport to meet, and a gross generalization that may be made is that the more industrialized a society, the more specific the perceived needs and hence goals of organizations found in it. The environmental needs that we speak of here are not as fundamental and general as the functional prerequisites or imperatives of society that have been a major theoretical concern in sociology (Parsons, 1951; Levy, 1952; and others). These fundamental needs —(there is no agreement among sociologists on exactly what they are)—are those without whose fulfillment a society cannot survive, and they remain a constant for all societies regardless of the degree of differentiation.

The articulated environmental needs whose fulfillment becomes the primary goal of an organization may be considered ultimately related to one or more of the functional imperatives, but they are distinguished from the latter in the degree of specificity and the scope of market. An organization is established to meet relatively specific needs which are carried by a relatively limited segment of the environment. On this level the needs are countless and are highly correlated with the general degree of differentiation of the surrounding environment. To cite some examples, new technologies in weaponry have increased the need to ensure their non-use, thus the Disarmament Agency and numerous organizations to promote peace. The increased use of barbituates has led to the establishment of organizations to deal with drug addiction and related problems. The societal need to maintain a high birth rate in traditional societies is now obsolete for most if not all nations. More pregnancies are now being defined as unwanted and thus a need for sex education, contraceptives, and abortion and vasectomy services. Each of these has resulted in specialized services in existing organizations such as the schools and clinics in the United States or even new organizations. Contraceptives are sold in specialized stores in Great Britain. There is a Ministry of Family Planning in India. The care of small children has been usually entrusted to the family, but we find that some parents through no fault of their own are defined by others as unfit to provide proper socialization even to preschool children. At the same time many parents now having little or no access to those who may have shared in the task under traditional arrangements find child-rearing a stifling chore from which they seek occasional release. In France, the care of the child by organizations with this objective starts almost immediately after birth. A working mother can leave her child all day in a crèche until age three, then the child attends a nursery school until five, when he starts at a regular school. All of these are separate organizations, organizations designed to socialize children to become participants in society, social men and women.

When we speak of needs we must recognize of course that there are hierarchies of needs for different social entities. Beyond the basic ones, individual needs differ between persons and over time. The same can be said for social collectives, and for each the needs are partly dictated by societal values. Environmental needs change over time due to new knowledge, greater differentiation, change in the structure of environmental agents, and change in values and standards. That it is the change, turbulence, and uncertainty in the environment that causes organizational changes has been stressed by some writers (Terreberry, 1968, included in this chapter; Thompson, 1967). More specifically the environment determines by and large the goal-setting of an organization (Thompson and McEwen, 1958). An organization may not be even permitted to withdraw its goals despite its own desires, lest the environmental needs it has met go unattended (Perrow, 1970).

The law of supply and demand of the economist is useful in thinking about the determinants of the hierarchy of needs, and of environmental agents. Many of the propositions suggested later are formulated with this in mind.

Environmental Resources

If there are environmental needs whose fulfillment are the goals of organizations, then resources are the means by which the needs are met. The environmental resources are physical, social, and cultural items that entail at least some utility, and include natural resources, labor, wealth, knowledge, legitimation, coercive power, and any others that could conceivably be used for the attainment of some ends. Each organization extracts or acquires some resources from the environment in order to achieve its goals, and thus resources become inputs of organizations. In the next chapter, the primary focus is on four basic kinds of social resources: knowledge, including the idea of training, skills, ideas, etc.; power or autonomy, to make decisions about policies, allocate resources internally, etc.; funds; and finally staff. All of these resources vary in their availability.

Environmental Agents for Organizations

The environmental needs and resources are carried or represented by environmental agents. Agents vary in terms of the kinds, specificity, and amount of needs and resources carried. An agent may be a person, a group, an organization, or more elusively a community, the public, or society at large. For my purpose, there are four key environmental agents relative to any focal organization: suppliers, consumers, integrators, and competitors. For a university, the key suppliers of resources are the state legislature (if it is a state university), other universities, and foundations. Other universities supply staff and also knowledge including new ideas and techniques. Legislatures set limits on the autonomy of the university. Its main customers are students. Its integrators are accreditation bodies, professional organizations, and some governmental agencies. Its main competitors are other universities. The fact that universities supply each other with staff and knowledge about new technologies and yet at the same time are competitors means that the nature of competition is much less than it would otherwise be.

How Many Organizations?

Evidence is overwhelming that organizations proliferate in environments that are urban and industrial, with populations that are well educated (Lipset, 1960: 45–76). One can safely predict that the more industrialized a society, the greater the proliferation of organizations. On the basis of facts one can also predict just as assuredly that the more industrialized a society, the greater the proportion of its labor force that is salaried rather than self-employed or unpaid family workers. We can perhaps make a few more predictions of similar generality, but beyond that sociology can tell us little. There are no grounded theories for us to make our predictions more precise. We cannot predict, for example, the number, the size, the institutional distribution of organizations in a given society, let alone their relations with each other or their internal structures.

A beginning must be made somewhere, and there are bits of scattered information that tickle our curiosities.

Proposition 1. The greater the articulated environmental needs, the larger the number of organizations.

Proposition 2. The greater the environmental resources, the larger the number of organizations.

As we have stated, the major components of resources are knowledge, power, wealth, and population. And thus:

Proposition 2.1. The greater the knowledge in the environment, the larger the number of organizations found in it.

Proposition 2.2. The greater the power in the environment, the larger the number of organizations found in it.

Proposition 2.3. The greater the wealth in the environment, the larger the number of organizations found in it.

Proposition 2.4. The larger the population in the environment, the larger the number of organizations found in it.

As the size of knowledge, power, wealth, and population increases in society, so does the societal ability to have a larger number of organizations. Increased resources imply larger numbers of new products and services, occupations (or specializations), responsibilities, customers, and further new needs. These propositions are yet to be empirically demonstrated, however. A cursory examination of limited data, however, finds that they are likely to be supported. Confined to economic organizations in one nation (U.S.), we find, for example, the number of corporations increased from about 341,000 in 1916 to 925,000 in 1956 (U.S. Bureau of the Census, 1960: 572) to almost one-and-a-half million in 1966 (U.S. Bureau of the Census, 1969: 479). During the 1930's (the decade of depression) the number declined, supporting proposition 2.3 above. When one examines the particular industries, one finds that even in agriculture the number of corporations increased during the period. In 1916, the U.S. had a population of about 100 million and in 1956, about 168 million, and thus corporations grew in number faster than the population. The institutions of higher learning numbered 563 in 1870, 951 in 1910 and nearly 2,500 in 1968 (U.S. Bureau of the Census, 1960: 211; 1969: 126).

Differentiation of society, which results from growth in environmental resources, atomizes its members. The process frees men from diffuse bonds to establish new affiliations, or it increases the organizational capacity of populations, to use the phrase by Stinchcombe (1965). There is evidence that the higher the educational attainment of a person, the greater the tendency for him to belong to at least one voluntary organization (Gendell and Zetterberg, 1961). Similarly, the higher the income, the more likely that he belongs to at least one voluntary organization. When the general educational attainment (correlated with knowledge) and general wealth of society rise, the more likely it is that a large number of voluntary organizations are to be found in it.

The very rapid growth in knowledge resources, as represented by the amount of money allocated to science and education, has resulted in a proliferation of a large number of new kinds of organizations. Among others are the spread of sheltered workshops, the creation of nursing homes, the very specialized nonprofit think organizations like Systems Development Corporation and Rand, the very new group homes and halfway-houses for patients with mental illness. The discovery of new inventions has led to whole new industries being created: photo-copy, polaroid, laser beams are only a few illustrations.

We would also like to predict the relative distribution of organizations among various sectors of society. By studying how much of the society's total revenue is allocated to various sectors such as science and education, polity, economy, we can make at least some inferences about whether there might be more economic organizations than educational organizations. However, much remains to be done on this problem yet. It is here that values may play a key analytical role. There are also countervailing tendencies, namely for organizations to grow in size.

Obviously, one person cannot constitute an organization and the applicability of proposition 2.4 has its limits. An organization is a team of men who accomplish tasks more efficiently together than these same men would separately and individually. Thus, we need a proposition to consider the size of organizations.

Proposition 3. The greater the resources in the environment, the larger the average size of the organizations found in it.

In the U.S. again, the average size of manufacturing establishments increased from about 8 in midnineteenth century to about 25 around 1900 and to 55 in 1954 (U.S. Bureau of the Census, 1960: 409). The average membership per church for all religious bodies in the U.S. grew from 235 in 1926 to 382 in 1965 (Demerath, 1968: 402). Although the number of separate units of government bureaucracies in the U.S. is not readily available, we can reasonably infer their growth in size from the total number of employees: 4.5 million in 1940, 6.4 million in 1950, 8.4 million in 1960, and 12.8 million in 1969 (U.S. Bureau of the Census, 1960: 709 1969: 215).

This proposition, too, has its limits of applicability. While the maximum size of an organization is the population of its environment, this would be far larger than its optimum size. The sheer number of persons in an organization affects its shape and function (Haire, 1959), its formalization, authority structure, and morale (Tsouderos, 1955, included in Chapter Five). With more complete data one would be able to calculate even the birth and death rates of organizations separated by institutional sectors and correlated by environmental variables.

There are several other variables that affect the size of organizations. One is the current tendency to proliferate new units iike plants or university centers or recreational branches. Thus the parent organization grows larger and larger while its many units actually may decrease in size. How far this trend can go without causing great coordination problems is hard to say. But it has the critical consequence of slowing the speed with which new organizations are created.

Seen in terms of employed labor force in factories, the average Russian worker is working in a much larger factory than his American counterpart (Granick, 1961: 210). How can we account for this difference? Is it a consequence of central planning and its rationality in U.S.S.R. and lack of it in the U.S.? Do Russian people tolerate or prefer working in a large organization more than do Americans? In the Soviet Union in 1954–1955 well over 60 percent of workers in factories (with more than 20 persons) were in plants in which there were more than 1,000 workers, compared with 35 percent for the American and less than 9 percent for the Japanese counterparts. By 1967, the Japanese figure had risen to 23 percent, however. Does this indicate that the economy of scale demands larger factories whereby small and presumably inefficient plants are eliminated?

The average size of organizations in a given environment is a consequence of a number of variables, so we would necessarily have to qualify each proposition with the clause "when other factors are held constant." The bits of data above must of course be strengthened with additional information, but the following tentative propositions are suggested.

Proposition 4.1. The more centralized the environment, the larger the relative size of the organizations found in it.

Proposition 4.2. The more centralized the environment, the fewer the number of organizations found in it.

A good case in support of these propositions is found in the political institution, in which the legitimate use of coercive power is entrusted. By necessity coercive power is centralized. Thus the military is normally under one command and so is the government, though the degree of centralization varies from nation to nation.

We have suggested that enhanced resources result in not only more organizations but also larger ones, but other factors remaining equal, organizations tend to be larger as their environment is more centralized.

How Autonomous Is an Organization?

The inputs of organizations are gained from among environmental resources. The outputs of the organizations are placed back into the environment for consumption, and in the consumption certain needs are met. What is implied is that in the transaction between the environment and the organization there is a reciprocal exchange (Levine and White, 1961). In saying this, a picture may be implied in which organizations are holding hands with their environmental agents in a state of harmonious bliss where everyone's needs are met to his satisfaction. As in relations between persons, however, not all organizational transactions are horizontal.

Equality does not pervade the organizational environment. Some agents are more important than others, and some organizations exert more influence than others. That is, organizations differ in degree of autonomy and the question before us is what is organizational autonomy a function of? In discussing the question a series of propositions are suggested with the autonomy of the organization as the dependent variable. The propositions necessarily require the qualification, "when other factors are held constant."

How many organizations there are in a society affects how many agents, that is suppliers, customers, integrators, and competitors there are. In turn, this has consequences for the autonomy of any particular organization. For how many suppliers and customers there are for any focal organization has considerable impact on its capacity to decide its new goals and policies. This leads to the next few propositions.

The following set of propositions concern the input and output environmental agents of the organization.

Proposition 5.   The larger the number of suppliers and consumers of an organization, the greater the autonomy of the organization.

Proposition 6.   The lower the integration of suppliers and consumers of an organization, the greater the autonomy of the organization.

The more suppliers and consumers there are for an organization, the less the degree of dependency of the organization on any one particular agent. In the extreme opposite case, when the organization has just one supplier of an indispensable resource or just one consumer on the output side, then the organization's dependency on the agent is maximized and its autonomy minimized. However, if the suppliers and consumers become integrated (through communication and coordination of action) as in the case of consumers' boycott of a particular product (e.g., California table grapes) or products of a particular organization, the organizational autonomy is threatened. Thus one obvious pathway for organizations to gain greater power is to seek out multiple customers and suppliers. This holds even for public organizations. Federal funding for state universities has meant less dependence upon state legislatures and wealthy alumni. The same increase has occurred for local welfare agencies who are increasingly receiving funds from other sources than the local dollar.

The focal organization's environment is here thought to extend beyond "an input and an output organization-set" (Evan, 1966: 178). Another kind of environmental agent is the competitor.

Proposition 7.   The fewer the number of competitors of an organization relative to any particular product or service, the more autonomous the organization.

The fewer the competitors for the same inputs and outputs of an organization, the greater its autonomy. We normally consider the competitors of an organization to be those having the same products, but those having different outputs compete for at least some of the same resources (Yuchtman and Seashore, 1967: 899). Competition introduces an added element of uncertainty or turbulence in the environment and an organization attempts to create a more stable and, hence, predictable environment by way of either coalition with competitors or else by their elimination.

Which pathway is to be taken to gain control over the environment —coalitions with or elimination of competitors—depends upon the internal characteristics of the organization: its technology, structure, and product policies. Works of Thompson (esp. 1967) suggest that centralized organizations are likely to eliminate competitors and absorb suppliers, whereas differentiated organizations are likely to form coalitions and proliferate new products. Coalition comes about through each party giving up a part of its autonomy, as if to entrust it to a newly created unit that envelops the parties, but in doing so they increase their collective autonomy.

Another manner in which an organization attempts to create a more stable and predictable environment is to appeal to integrators to control its competitors. Regulatory agencies, courts, trade organizations serve the functions of integrators. A case in point is the American textile industry's continued efforts to have the government erect tariff barriers and other pressures against foreign imports.

While it need be stated that the more decentralized the institutional sector in which an organization is located, the greater the autonomy of the organization, we cannot neglect the increased amount of autonomy that an organization shares as a result of coalition with other organizations.

Evan's concept of organization-set (1966) is very useful in discussing the collective power of organizations. An organization-set here refers to the complex of organizations a focal organization deals with (although it is possible to divide, as Evan did, the set into finer parts). A discussion of alliances of organizations and their growth in power will have to consider the extent to which the various sets of the organizations overlap.

Proposition 8. The more overlap there is among the sets of organizations in a given set, the greater the autonomy of the set.

If a group of environmental agents finds that they can complement each other's needs sufficiently to the extent that no other agents are needed, then that group is self-sufficient. And further,

Proposition 9. The more closed an organization-set, the more autonomous the set is.

The phenomenon of *zaibatsu* in pre-World War II Japan is an illustration of these propositions. The family-based financial magnets of that time had their own banking, mining, manufacturing, sales, and shipping organizations, each of which secured the majority of its suppliers and customers from other organizations within the same *zaibatsu*. This occurred, however, in a context marked by a high degree of centralization, in each institutional sector as well as in society as a whole.

In a centralized economy such as the Soviet Union there is little that any given organization can do on its own, but in a decentralized economy such as the U.S. an organization has much greater freedom to change suppliers and customers and even goals. Thus, the autonomy of any given organization is likely to be greater in a decentralized context, but the autonomy of an organization-set is likely to be greater in a centralized context.

2
THE SOCIAL RESOURCES OF ORGANIZATIONS

Organizations have certain inputs to work with. Traditionally, economists have talked of the four factors of production: land, capital, labor, and entrepreneurial ideas. A sociological conception of resources includes these factors but differs from the economists' view in emphasis. Land is generally not considered important. Capital as a resource has not been studied as such; instead sociologists speak of the size of an organization, usually meaning the scale of its operations, combining capital and labor. Beyond this, sociologists have spoken of the autonomy of an organization, or the amount of power it has, and the technology of an organization, or its pool of machines and skills and techniques. In the preceding chapter, we looked at how the environment affects what resources an organization has to work with. Here we are primarily concerned with their impact on the structure and operation of the organization.

The problem of how the acquisition of resources affects organizational structure has been one of the more exciting and recent developments. Within the past few years, a number of articles and books about the impact of technology have appeared. Indeed, now one begins to talk about the technology school, so distinguished by its central tenet that the major independent variable in the analysis of organizations is technology. More recently, an older tradition has been revived by some very sophisticated analytical techniques—the studies of growth or size and their effects on structure. Along with the increased interest in this variable has come a debate about the importance of size as a determining factor.

These two intellectual traditions, while the most popular and current, are not the only ones that need to be explored. Almost twenty years ago, long before the idea became part of a radical critique, Selznick raised the fundamental issue of organizational autonomy and what this might mean for the survival of democracy. Unfortunately, few other writers have followed his exploration. Only recently has an empirical measure for autonomy been developed. Along with size and technology, autonomy represents another critical resource variable of an organization.

THE PROBLEMS

The Problem of Technology

Although there had been various hints about the importance of technology, especially in the industrial relations literature (Mann and Hoffman, 1960; Walker, 1957; Richardson and Walker, 1948; Whyte, 1948), it did not become a distinctive force within the sociology of organizations until several key studies were published in the midsixties. Blauner's (1964) work of the impact of four kinds of technology on alienation in the United States and Woodward's (1965) of three kinds on various aspects of organizational structure in Great Britain changed considerably everyone's perspective.

Both studies classified industries in a simple but effective way. Here we might use three of Blauner's four categories: craft, mass production, and continuous process industry. Subsumed under these labels were a large number of differences, as can be seen in the selection from Blauner, which discusses continuous process but with an implicit contrast to mass production.

Blauner's exploration of technology grew out of an interest in the question of how it affects a worker's sense of alienation. Raising a basic theoretical issue of Marx and using his perspective, it was perhaps only natural that technology and its possibilities for the meaninglessness of work and the self-estrangement of the worker would become obvious. In our first selection, we have included excerpts from his analysis of the chemical and oil refinery workers, who appear to be relatively less alienated. Other chapters in his book report the high alienation of the automobile workers in the assembly line and the relatively low alienation of the printers (his example of craft industry) and of the textile workers (his example of the fourth category, the machine tenders). Alienation has been a popular research theme during the sixties in sociology but few have linked it with technology. A recent exception is Shepard's (1971) work (which builds directly on Blauner's work) on the consequence of automation.

Woodward came to appreciate the importance of technology by an empirical pathway. After testing and finding wanting a number of management theories about span of control, she discovered that her data fell into place with a simple distinction between three kinds of industries, which she called unit and small batch (Blauner's craft), large batch and mass, and process. It might be noted that her book was written about the same time, so there was little opportunity for mutual influence. In the first few chapters of her book she documents a large number of differences between these three kinds of technologies: the span of control is larger in the mass production and smaller in the other two; the ratio of direct to indirect labor is smallest in the continuous process and largest in the craft industries; the number of levels of management are the greatest in the continuous process and smallest in the craft, etc. What we have selected for inclusion in this chapter is the very intriguing finding of what happens to the success of a company if it uses other than the average span of control for its type of technology. We know of no other example of analysis like this, perhaps because of the difficulties of measuring success, a point to which we shall return in Chapter Five.

Inherent in her table is a way of thinking that may go a long way towards resolving a number of the debates that presently exist in sociology about the effects of various factors. Most important is the implication that we need to look at the association between variables, in this instance, span of control and success, while controlling or including types of variables describing different kinds of organizations. Her findings also suggest, although she does not argue for a kind of determinism, that it is the kind of technology employed that commands a structure most appropriate for success of the organization. Considering the large number of organizations in her study, even though they are from a single city in England, the findings are important ones.

We have included one study in Chapter Four that directly builds upon both Blauner and Woodward, but especially the former. Fullan relates technology to worker integration. This study was selected because it measures a variable that is seldom researched, namely, social integration. Also, it is a study of Canadian industry as opposed to American or English, and this is to be preferred because of our concern about the generality of organizational findings beyond cultural contexts of societies. Essentially, Fullan finds that Blauner's work is supported. But, more importantly, he notes that within each of the three types there is considerable variation, a variation associated with differences in integration. In other words, the type classification of Blauner and Woodward is perhaps too crude. One needs one or more variables for describing the differences between kinds of technology.

Since the publication of Woodward's book, the perspective of technology has been broadened in two directions, one theoretical and the other empirical. The theoretical push has come from Perrow (1967) in a piece that we would like to have included in the reader. He has suggested that a critical and major dimension of technology is what he calls the routine-nonroutine. In addition, he attempts to derive systematically four types of technological bases, largely relying on the knowledge relative to the task, and then relate these four kinds to the kinds of social structures and the kinds of goals the organization has. For the advanced student, this article is well worth extended study, and the bibliography on technology prior to the date of its publication is the best there is. Since then some of Perrow's ideas have been tested by Hage and Aiken (1969) in social welfare agencies and have received empirical support. Perhaps a more accessible exposition of Perrow's theoretical ideas on technology, for the undergraduate, is to be found in his recently published book (1970: Ch. 3). Among the most interesting aspect of his writings is his belief that structure may be largely determined by technology but goals are not, a point discussed in Chapter Five.

Also of theoretical interest, albeit somewhat tangential to the main thrust of this text–reader is the theoretical discussion of technology by Litwak (1968). It indicates some of the major components involved in the meaning of the term technology and illustrates the considerable differences between groups and organizations because of the organizational imperative of technology to achieve specific objectives.

The empirical thrust has come from the various attempts by the Aston group (Pugh, Hickson, et al.), another excellent group of English researchers, to operationalize and measure the various dimensions that were subsumed in Woodward's discussions. In the piece by Hickson et al., we see one of the clearest discussions of the different meanings of technology. The authors distinguish three types: operations technology, materials technology, and knowledge technology. Their effort is primarily concerned with the first of these conceptualizations because it appears to be critical to Woodward's definition, which they carefully review and quantify.

The conclusion of the selection is interesting, for it suggests that size is more important than technology for a number of the variables of structure, at least as these have been measured in the work of the Aston group. (See their selections in this chapter and the next.) Thus the authors question whether technology is the single most important determinant as some have argued. They carefully document the differences between their sample of organizations and that of Woodward. It is always important to read carefully the descriptions of samples because they can materially affect the findings. In the Birmingham sample, all of the organizations are larger than 250 in size. Had we used this limit as a criterion, almost all of the other selections in this text–reader would have had to be eliminated. In other words, there is a considerable variation along this resource variable of size in the various organizations that they researched. In a recent reanalysis of the published data by way of path analysis, Aldrich argues that technology is more important an organizational variable than the Aston group has assumed (1972).

Another interesting point is the adjective *operations.* Would knowledge technology, assuming that one could develop some measures for it, be as limited in impact vis-à-vis the three factors of structure as operations technology? We do not know, but the work of Perrow points more in the direction of concern with knowledge technology.

Lawrence and Lorsch (1967: 234–245), in their book *Organization and Environment* suggest that as knowledge grows in the environment, mechanization does as well but at a slower pace, thus linking the two ideas of operation and knowledge technology together. However, they do not measure technology per se and their idea must remain an intriguing insight. A similar point is made by Hage and Aiken in their book *Social Change in Complex Organizations* (1970), namely, the growth of research, and, thus, knowledge is a powerful environmental force that affects both techniques and skills, the technological resource available to the organization.

And here is perhaps the major problem for many organizations— technology can reside in people's brains and fingers. Call them professionals or experienced managers, but the fact remains that much of the technology is not in a machine or an arrangement of machines such as an assembly line. Level of training is at least one crude measure for knowledge technology. This was one of the findings of Woodward: skill levels were lower in the mass production and higher in the continuous process and the craft industry. Along these lines is the work by Hage and Aiken (Chapter Five) and Hage, Aiken, and Marrett (Chapter Four), both of which show the influence of professionalism, and in particular the importance of professional associations. In a similar vein is an article by Peter Smith (1969) about the extra organizational associations of managers. Are the effects of technology in structure that we see due to the skills of the people or the arrangement of the work flow or both? As yet we don't know.

The Lawrence and Lorsch selection in Chapter Four also raises the needed point that organizations have more than one technology. It is hard to speak of *the* technology of an organization that produces even only one product because there is the technology of marketing, the technology of management, of research, etc., relative to just one product.

One variation on the theme of technology that we have not included in the reader is the problem of automation. This has received some attention in organizational research. So far, however, most of the work is largely descriptive. The case studies of Mann and Hoffman (1960) and of Walker (1957) are of interest. More recently, Meyer (1968) has investigated the impact of automation on the span of control and

Shepard (1971), on alienation. Both of these works note that the problem of automation vis-à-vis organizations as opposed to societies, where it becomes the problem of unemployment, is essentially much like that of the continuous process industries studied by Blauner and included in our selection from his writings.

All in all, technology is an important factor shaping the structure of organizations. It also seems important for various other components of an organization. Technology has been related to the control processes, performances, and goals. In turn, the environment and its impact on technology is part of the way in which environment and structure, and performance can be linked.

The Problem of Size

Almost from the beginning of the study of organizations by sociologists, size—that is the number of people working for the organization—has been seen as one of the critical aspects of organizations. The early work focused on two different problems, one of which was the pattern of growth (Haire, 1960, is probably the most well known), and the other was the impact on various measures of configuration, including the proportion of administrative staff (Anderson and Warkow, 1961, being perhaps the most influential). The best review of this work is to be found in Starbuck (1965) who explores it from almost every conceivable angle. Some are also reviewed succinctly in two of our three selections, the one by Hall *et al.* and the other by Blau. Two important points about this early work might be noted. First, the analysis tended to be much more sophisticated than was true of much of the other kinds of organizational analysis; it marked the appearance of comparative research and also of various mathematical attempts to describe organizations. Second, the results were inconclusive and somehow disappointing.

Recently, interest in the impact of size has been revived, and along with it, the advance of analytical technique. Again, there is a debate about the relative importance of the variable size. Hall *et al.* present the case for the negative and Blau and Pugh *et al.* present the case for the affirmative. Furthermore, while Hall *et al.* talk of complexity and Blau of structural differentiation, a close examination of their indicators makes it apparent that the two variables are essentially the same. Pugh *et al.*'s factor structuring of activities is largely a combination of complexity and formalization, although they have more indicators and not always the same ones.

It will be some time before the debate is concluded, but several points should be kept in mind when reading these three selections. The analysis of the data is quite different and the sample of organizations is also not the same. That Blau has concentrated on a single kind of organization is perhaps an important reason for his findings. Similarly,

Pugh *et al.* appear to have a more restricted sample than Hall *et al.* More importantly, the graph approach of Blau allows for much more understanding than is true in a threefold percentage table. Another reason why the results of the work on size may be somewhat inconclusive is that there are one or more other variables, as in Boyle's Law, which have to be held constant before some pattern emerges.

The Pugh *et al.* selection in this chapter defines size both in terms of personnel and in terms of assets, which in their sample proved to be strongly associated with each other. They find that size is highly associated with what they call structuring of activities. Although they have only organizations with more than 250 members, it is still hard to argue with an association of .69. We have already observed in the Hickson *et al.* selection that size appeared to be more important in the same sample of organizations than their various measures of technology. Here we can assess the relative importance of size vis-à-vis number of other possible determining factors. Indeed, this is the great strength of this paper: its consideration of a number of what they call contextual variables, of which size is only one. They present another piece of evidence that perhaps the debate over size will be resolved as size being another important resource variable that must be considered.

But what is clear from Blau's work is that if there is an impact it is a complicated one, and we have to move away from simple forms of analysis to more mathematical ones. The advanced student who is not bothered by this will find the recent work of Pondy (1969) and Klatzky (1970) on size to be well worth the effort. Both of them consider alternative models for their data. They represent the probable wave of the organizational future, not only for the substantive importance of size but more importantly for analytical rigor. Also, one should see the expanded book by Blau and Schoenherr (1970).

Beyond these two articles size tends to appear as one of the most frequently used controls in multivariate analysis. While we may not be sure of the importance of size, it is generally agreed that if one wants to demonstrate that a relationship does exist, size is the first variable that is considered as a candidate for an alternative explanation of the data. Woodward, in another part of her book (1965), does this for the relative importance of technology and finds that it holds. Another example is found in the selection by Hage and Aiken (Chapter Five), who use in this instance a log scale of size as a control variable. In much of the work of Tannenbaum (1968) and his colleagues, the same approach is used; relationships are explored with size held constant. We might mention here that almost all empirical studies of organizations have been cross-sectional studies, that is, studies at a given time. When organizations are studied over time, that is, longitudinal studies, we can observe if the predictions made from cross-sectional studies in fact hold up. Obviously, this is one fact that future research should take advantage of.

Despite this, size as cause has not enjoyed the popularity of technology. Corwin is the first to relate it to conflict in the selection of Chapter Four, although a prior analysis by Smith (1966) inferred its effect on conflict. Although the measures are different from one kind of organization to another, the secondary analysis by Smith of the various organizations studied by Tannenbaum (1968) and his colleagues is a model of thinking, one of the best illustrations of testing alternative variable chains or paths. In this instance, the dependent variable is conflict, but one of the hypothetical chains of reasoning is the impact of size on complexity and in turn its consequences for conflict. Unfortunately, this kind of thinking is best tested in longitudinal research, which as yet is rare in the sociology of organizations. With measures across time we discover the effects of size from other kinds of effects. What is of special interest about the Smith article is that the size set of consequences is weighed vis-à-vis two other equally plausible chains of variables.

Size has been related to effectiveness by Price (1967: Ch. 7) in a different chapter from the one selected for inclusion in Chapter Five. Likewise, Yuchtman and Seashore (1967) have suggested that size be used as a proxy for a measure of effectiveness. But, in general, size has not been related to many other variables outside of these two, conflict and effectiveness, and in turn these have not been examined with the same detail as the association between size and span of control and other measures of configuration and of complexity. In this respect the Hall *et al.* work, while presenting negative evidence, and the Pugh *et al.* work, while presenting positive evidence, are both important because they are implicitly raising the issue of considering size vis-à-vis other aspects of structure, particularly the development of rules and procedures. Similarly, the relationship between the environment and size has not been well explored.

The Problem of Autonomy

The selection by Selznick probably speaks to many who have witnessed the events of the past decade. Can we make big government responsive to local needs? Selznick's answer is perhaps a disturbing one because it suggests that bringing local participation into decision making may lead to a displacement of goals.

Selznick's selection should also be juxtaposed against the case studies by Presthus and Berliner (Chapter One). Russian industry is charged with the goal of maximum rate of development; the consequence is not much organizational autonomy in a centrally planned economy. The successes of the Soviet economy are well known and need not be repeated here. Likewise, welfare goals in Turkish bureaucracies subvert objectives of efficiency. Here is a basic organizational dilemma and one that is not easily resolved. Which is more important, organizational autonomy or the realization of certain goals?

Until Pugh *et al.* developed scales for autonomy and independence, there seemed to be no way of measuring how much power was given to an organization. It would be helpful to read the Pugh *et al.* selection in Chapter Three in conjunction with this one. Conceptually, they have considered autonomy as a part of the internal distribution of power and thus included it in their concentration of authority factor. We have placed the articles in the reverse order in which they have been written, not only because of their topic relevance but also because they are somewhat easier to read in this order. In the selection of Chapter Three they find that autonomy and centralization form a factor because they are highly interrelated. This finding is summarized in Table 1 of their selection in this chapter. Perhaps we should mention that some recent unpublished works call into question the relationship between autonomy and centralization suggested by the Aston group. Next question is what determines the concentration of authority or more specifically, autonomy.

Pugh and his colleagues explore several contextual variables besides autonomy and those that go to the heart of some of Selznick's analysis: public accountability and dependence. They find that both of these variables are highly associated with concentration of authority. In other words, public accountability tends to lead to centralization, a finding with many implications for those who would like to make organizations more responsive to their clients.

But perhaps the most important point of this selection is their argument for a multivariate approach to the analysis of organizational structure. Here we see an emerging synthesis of the technological, size, and other resource variables, looking at the joint impact on social structure. The great value of the Pugh *et al.* work has been the large number of resource variables with their clear operationalizations. We have edited out their discussions of measurement, which form the major part of their articles and contributions. For those readers who are interested in measurement problems, we highly recommend reading their articles in full (1963, 1968, and 1969a). Also, Price's (1971) discussion of their work is invaluable.

Other Problems

The resources of manpower or size, political power or autonomy, and mechanical power or technology are not the only ones organizations have. Most readers will probably wonder why capital investment or financial power has been left out. The paradox is that while wealthy organizations are indeed powerful ones, little work has been done on the exact nature of how wealth of an organization per se affects its internal operations. Perhaps this has been ignored because it is obvious. We find some hint of it in the Blauner selection, where the capital investment per worker is noted, but here it is really seen as an indicator of technology. Price (1971), in his discussion of the measurement of size, suggests that wealth be included with size under the general rubric of scale of operations. Pugh *et al.,* in their selection in this chapter, report such a high correlation between size and assets that the distinction does not seem worth making. However, high associations can still have different consequences for an organization.

What may be accomplished by considering wealth as an independent variable is exemplified in the recent work of Klatsky (1970) on organizational inequality. She found that public employment offices in more wealthy states were able to hire more professional staff, which in turn were more successful in getting more money from the federal government for their states. Thus the rich get richer and the poor, poorer as someone once said. We need more studies like this to understand the exact impact of wealth or investment. Beyond this is the question, if we want to talk about the power of an organization to affect its environment: is the source of this power in its wealth, its size, or its autonomy from the environment, or maybe even in the level of professionalization and mechanization that has occurred?

Still another problem, which we have not included, but which may be of interest, is the impact of the client on organizational structure and operation as represented in the work of Lefton and Rosengren (1966). They suggest that the greater the client's life space the organization is concerned with, both in terms of the number of areas and the period of time, the more complex the division of labor. It is hard to know, however, if the organization's decision to treat the whole client or simply one of his characteristics, such as mental retardation, represents an organizational input or whether it represents goals. But it does represent still another distinctive approach to the problem of what determines social structure.

The variables operating variability and diversity in the Pugh *et al.* selection may be the manufacturing counterparts to what Lefton and Rosengren have in mind. As can be seen in Table 2 of the former selection, they have some impact, but not as much as some of the other resource variables.

Their selection also points to the twin issues of age and location. Both of these variables are difficult to interpret. They are probably representative of various forces in the environment or of the resource variables to the organization, but it is difficult to single them out. They have not been explored much and they appear to be less important than technology, size, and autonomy, but they might be of interest to some readers. The few other major references are cited in Pugh *et al.*

THE READINGS

Technology, Integration, and Alienation*
ROBERT BLAUNER

Automated production was well developed in oil refining and industrial chemical plants long before the recent concern with this new industrial trend; in fact, these industries were "automated" years before the term "automation" was invented. Oil and chemicals are the two most important examples of continuous-process technology. Extremely advanced technologically, economically, and socially, these industries may portend the conditions of factory work and employment in a future dominated by automated technology. Therein lies the special importance of an intensive analysis of alienation in these industries. At the same time we must guard also against overgeneralizing from this limited case, for even a predominantly automated economy will have considerable diversity, and present knowledge already indicates that automation takes many different forms, depending on the industry's technology and economic situation before automation.

A continuous-process plant is quite different from a typical factory. There are no recognizable machines and very few workers visible. Except for a few maintenance workers in colored helmets welding or painting pipes, you see very few people doing anything and nobody making anything. Instead, one sees a large number of individual buildings with vast areas of open space between them, huge networks of pipes, and large towers and other equipment, which one later learns are various types of distillation units or chemical reactors. The chemicals which are made and the oils which are refined flow through these pipes from one stage of their processing to another, usually without being handled at all by the workers. They are processed in large reactors where raw materials are combined or separated. Generally, oils and chemicals must pass through a number of reaction operations before the product is completed. The flow of materials; the combination of different chemicals; and the temperature, pressure, and speed of the processes are regulated by automatic control devices. The automatic controls make possible a continuous flow in which raw materials are introduced at the beginning of the process and a large volume of the product continually emerges at the end stage. Ultimately, it is the

* Reprinted from Robert Blauner, *Alienation and Freedom: The Factory Worker and His Industry* (Chicago: The University of Chicago Press, 1964), pp. 124–140, 146–153, 157–158, 164–165, with omissions, by permission of the author and the publisher.

liquid or gaseous nature of most products and raw materials that makes possible a continuous-flow technology.

Continuous-process technology is the most highly mechanized of the various forms of manufacturing. Capital investment is enormous. So much of the process is carried out by the machine system that relatively few manual workers are required. Thus in the most highly automated industry, oil refining, the capital investment per production worker is $110,000, compared to the average of only $15,000 in all manufacturing industry. In the chemical industry as a whole, the ratio is $28,000 per production worker; and in the branch of this highly diversified industry which manufactures heavy chemicals, it is considerably greater.

The oil refining industry is a key industry in the economy. The value of its products shipped in 1954 was almost twelve billion dollars, a figure exceeded only by the food industries and perhaps by the steel and automotive industries (National Industrial Conference Board, 1960: 184). And yet it has only two hundred thousand employees, ranking nineteenth in size of employment among the twenty major manufacturing industries (*ibid.,* p. 183). Not surprisingly, the individual worker in a continuous-process industry is more productive than workers in other industries, in terms of the value he adds to the product by his participation in the manufacturing process. Thus, another indicator of the high level of mechanization is the fact that the value added by manufacturing, per production worker, is highest in the chemical and petroleum industries. Each chemical production worker adds $12,772 a year to the total value of the products of the industry, in contrast to the $4,577 which a textile worker adds. The more highly mechanized an industry's technology, the greater is the investment in the physical plant and machinery, and therefore expenditures for maintaining and repairing this equipment increase. In oil refining, 44 percent of the entire payroll is earmarked for maintenance expenses, the highest figure among twenty manufacturing industries. In chemicals, the proportion is 22 percent, the third highest industrial figure, and almost twice the proportion for manufacturing industries as a whole.

The continuous-process industries are both relatively new industries. Industrial chemicals is still at an early stage of its growth cycle. The industry has experienced meteoric expansion in the war and postwar years and is now the fastest growing major manufacturing industry. Whether measured in terms of capital investment, trends in total output, or employment, oil and chemicals are dynamic growth-industries. Important factors sustaining this growth and economic prosperity are the high level of scientific research and the expenditures for new plants and equipment, which far surpass those in other industries.

The dynamic change inherent in the chemical industry is due to its competitive market situation; its youthfulness; and particularly its close relationship with, and dependence on, science. Chemistry, like all sciences, is inherently dynamic; the discovery of new chemicals and processes is sooner or later reflected in new forms of industrial production. Although the chemical industry does not have the kind of price competition we find in the older small-firm industries, there is considerable competition among the major companies in developing new products and processes. It spends more money on basic research than any other manufacturing industry.

The science and research emphasis is naturally reflected in the industry's occupational structure. Twelve percent of its total labor force in 1950 were professionals (including 23,500 chemists and 21,000 engineers), compared to only 4 percent of the labor force in the automobile industry (U.S. Department of Commerce, 1955: 36). The large number of professionals and scientists in the industry is a cause, as well as an effect, of its dynamic character, since the role of an industrial scientist is to stimulate change and experimentation.

Because of the extremely complex technology and the high level of capital investment necessary to produce industrial chemicals and the products of the oil industry, the continuous-process industries are dominated by large companies. Oil refining is one of the most concentrated of all industries; it has a concentration ratio of 99. The chemical industry, with a ratio of 59, is somewhat less concentrated; however, small operators predominate in sectors of the industry other than heavy industrial chemicals. In 1949, the three largest companies—DuPont, Union Carbide, and Allied Chemical and Dye—held 50 to 60 percent of the total assets in the industry (Lambert, 1949: 17–19); the eight largest companies control approximately 80 percent of the total assets (*Hearings, Subcommittee on Economic Stabilization,* 84th Congress, 1st Session).

Despite the size of the major companies, individual plants do not employ as many workers, on the average, as in the automobile industry. Whereas 55 percent of the automobile workers are employed in plants with more than 2,500 men, only 19 percent of the chemical employees and 28 percent of the oil workers are in such large establishments (National Industrial Conference Board, *op. cit.,* p. 183). This is because automation has reduced the size of the work force in the continuous-process industries and also because of a conscious policy of decentralization. The large companies have preferred to operate many middle-sized plants rather than a few big establishments. Large establishments are more characteristic of the oil industry, 53 percent of whose employees work in plants with more than 1,000 people, than the chemical industry, only 40 percent of whose employees work in factories with more than 1,000. The average chemical plant has about 69 employees; the average oil refinery, 142 employees; the average automobile factory, about 334 employees.

Decentralization is a decisive feature of the continuous-process industries, expressed not only by the distribution of the plants of a single company but also by the organization of individual plants. Continuous-process technology results in a layout of work that is very different from textile and automobile production, where the bulk of machine and assembly-line operations and the majority of the workers are concentrated under one roof. Chemical and oil refining operations are divided among many buildings or subplants with large stretches of open space between the buildings. In a sense, a chemical factory or a refinery does not consist of one plant, but of a large number of plants, in each of which a particular product or a particular reaction is processed. The 400 blue-collar employees of the Bay Chemical Company are dispersed throughout the ammonia plant, the caustic plant, the chlorination plant, the latex plant, the methionine plant, the xanthate plant, the mercaptan plant, and the electrolytic-cell plant, in addition to several maintenance buildings. The danger of fire and other hazards, as well as the range of products and processes, makes such decentralization necessary. Even in the largest continuous-process establishments, the "social density" of the work force is very low. The 3,500 workers employed at one of northern California's largest oil refineries are spread out over 3,500 acres of grounds.

In this chapter, I shall examine the ways in which the distinctive technological, economic, and sociological features of the continuous-process industries affect the alienation of the blue-collar workers. In contrast to the numerous studies of the automobile assembly line, there has been little research on work in continuous-process plants, an indication of their newness, but more importantly of the concentration of research on negative work environments. The emphasis will be on the chemical industry, particularly its most automated heavy industrial chemicals branch, rather than oil refining, since the former was the major focus of my field investigations. Before considering the specific dimensions of alienation, let us look at the employment situation, occupational structure, and the new type of blue-collar work brought about by continuous-process technology.

Job Security and Careers: Their
Technological and Economic Bases

Workers in the continuous-process industries are far more secure in their employment than employees in most other industries. In an automated technology, the volume of output is not a function of the number of production workers, as it is in pre-automated systems, but depends largely on the capacity of the technical equipment. Individual plants do not hire and fire as consumer demand rises and dips, as is common in the automotive industry. The number of workers necessary to operate and maintain the equipment has already been reduced by automation to the minimum number required for safety and efficiency. For these reasons, labor tends to be a semifixed or fixed cost in production rather than a variable cost, and the "core labor force" in an automated technology therefore has an unusually high degree of job security, as James Bright has emphasized (1958: 202–203).

Another contributing factor has been a persistently steady demand for oil and chemical products which has made the long-run economic situation in the continuous-process industries extremely favorable. The oil industry's most rapid growth was in the 1920's; however, production levels remained high even during the depression, and oil workers had considerably greater job security during the 1930's than other factory workers. Oil employment stabilized during the 1940's and actually declined for a period in the 1950's as economic recessions and continued automation took their toll. On the other hand, the chemical industry's growth rate has not slowed down. Between 1940 and 1960 the number of its wage and salary employees increased by approximately 100 percent. In the ten years between 1950 and 1960, while the number of production workers in oil refining decreased from 136,000 to 116,000, the blue-collar work force in chemicals expanded from 494,000 to 539,000 (U.S. Department of Commerce, 1961: 208–210).

The chemical industry is also considerably less subject to short-run business fluctuations than the automobile industry, for example. This is partly due to the wide range of its products, which means that a drastic drop in demand for any one product does not depress the entire industry. The industry is also less dependent on the vagaries of consumer spending, since much of its production is sold to other companies (often other chemical firms) for use in production, maintenance, and sanitation.

Of all major manufacturing industries in 1949, the oil refining and chemicals industries had the highest proportions of employees who worked fifty or more weeks. Eighty-eight percent of all oil workers and 79 percent of chemical workers worked virtually the entire year, compared to only 57 percent of the automobile workers and 67 percent of all factory workers. Between 1958 and 1961, when the average monthly layoff rate in the automobile industry was 3.6, it was only 0.8 in the chemical industry and 0.6 in the oil refining industry. In all factory industries, 2.1 workers were laid off per month, on the average, in this period.

The attitudes of continuous-process workers in the Roper survey suggest almost no fear of job loss. Only 2 percent of the oil and chemical employees thought they were likely to be laid off in the next six months. These were the lowest figures for any industry and contrast with 29 percent of the automobile workers and 14 percent of all factory workers. Similarly, 94 percent of the chemical employees and 92 percent of the refinery workers felt that they could have their jobs as long as they wanted, so again oil and chemicals were the two most optimistic industries.

Because of the high degree of responsibility that continuous-process technology demands, management is particularly interested in a permanent, stable work force; and indeed, employment in the oil and chemical industries is often for life. The economist Richard Lester has stated that these industries have moved from a commodity to a welfare concept of employment: "The employer and the prospective employee think of employment in terms of a whole work career—a long-term relationship in which the employer takes on an increasing burden of fringe benefits covering the man and his family, and the employee acquires tenure, job rights, and rights to promotion opportunities" (Lester, 1959: 3.1–3.11).

Job security in the continuous-process industries is enhanced by the proliferation of welfare benefits. The petroleum industry (and, to a lesser extent, the chemical industry) has a "cradle-to-the-grave" series of employees' benefits which includes paid sick leave, company contributory savings plans, pensions, and death benefits. In 1959, a survey of the National Industrial Conference Board found that almost 40 percent of all the company savings plans in the country were in the oil industry (Fox, 1960: 2). In 1957, this industry averaged 78 cents per payroll hour for fringe benefits, compared to only 45 cents for all manufacturing.

The welfare concept of employment in these young industries partially reflects the socially progressive viewpoints of their managerial elites, who are usually college trained. It is a conscious policy, but one which stems naturally from the economic basis of production in continuous-process plants. These policies are made financially possible by the high profits of the industries and the relatively small numbers of blue-collar workers. Because these industries are so highly capital-intensive, labor is a relatively minor aspect of cost; high wages and fringe benefits therefore do not "hurt" as much as they would in such relatively labor-intensive industries as automobiles and textiles.

Workers in the continuous-process industries are therefore able to face the future with fewer economic anxieties than workers in other industries. In the Roper study the highest proportion of employees who said it was likely that they'd be able to retire from work at the age of 65 and live the rest of their lives "in reasonable comfort on . . . savings, pensions, and social security payments" was in the chemical industry, where 63 percent were this optimistic. Fifty-one percent of the oil workers were optimistic, compared to 43 percent of all factory workers and only 33 percent of the automobile workers.

Automated Work: Responsibility and Variety

It is the work of operating the automatic equipment that exemplifies the distinctive technology of continuous-process production, just as the assembly-line operative's job epitomizes the work situation of the automobile industry. Jobs in maintenance and distribution do not differ greatly from similar work in other industries. For this reason, my analysis of the work and the alienation of the chemical worker focuses on the chemical operator.

Very little of the work of chemical operators is physical or manual, despite the blue-collar status of these factory employees. Practically all physical production and materials-handling is done by automatic processes, regulated by automatic controls. The work of the chemical operator is to monitor these automatic processes: his tasks include observing dials and gauges; taking readings of temperatures, pressures, and rates of flow; and writing down these readings in log data sheets. Such work is clearly of a non-manual nature.

Workers characterize their jobs as being more "mental" or "visual" than physical. When asked if they do any manual work, they will often say that they turn valves occasionally, an expenditure of physical energy which is not much greater than the office manager's adjustment of the controls on the office thermostat. On the whole, the operators interviewed like this lack of physical effort, although it was not a major element in their over-all work satisfaction. A few regretted the absence of physical activity. They felt jobs were becoming too easy and that a man could get soft with too much "push-button stuff." Workers with farm backgrounds seemed more likely to express such opinions.

The development of machine and assembly-line technologies greatly reduced the number of traditional craft skills necessary for manufacturing production; with the emergence of automated continuous-process technology, traditional craft skill has been completely eliminated from the productive process. Even the talent for unskilled manual work, or "knack," so important on the assembly line, has been eliminated by the automated processes. In the place of physical effort and skill in the traditional, manual sense, the major job requirement for production workers in continuous-process technology is responsibility. As the French sociologist Alain Touraine phrases it, "Their responsibility defines their professional skill" (Touraine, 1955: 123).

Within each of the buildings that make up a continuous-process plant, a small crew, generally numbering from three to seven workers per shift, is responsible for the particular products or processes of their subplant. Each team is directed by a head shift operator who has considerable training and experience, and each is made up of workers of diverse levels of training and with varying degrees of responsibility.

Chemical operators are responsible for the quality of the product, for the continuing, trouble-free operation of the processes, and for the extremely expensive automatic equipment. Almost all of the Bay Company operators interviewed felt that their jobs involved a high degree of responsibility. Only two out of twelve had worked previously at jobs in other industries which they felt required more responsibility than their work in the chemical plant. However, the extent of an operator's responsibility depends on his position in the hierarchy of his departmental work team. The closer to the bottom his job, the more likely the worker was to minimize his own responsibility and to stress the over-all responsibility of his head shift operator upon whom he could call when something was seriously wrong.

The responsibility of a head shift operator is extremely great; he co-ordinates the work of all the members of his team, arranges for maintenance priorities and for the transport of materials and products to and from his plant, and serves as the link between his work team and management.

As we shall see later, the long-run change in the nature of blue-collar work from manual skill to responsibility provides new avenues for meaning and self-expression in work.

Variety and Diversity   The extreme rationalization and division of labor in the textile mill and on the automobile assembly line result in jobs which are the ultimate in repetition and routine. The variety of the jobs of chemical workers in a continuous-process plant is considerably greater. For maintenance workers, who make up 40 percent of the plant force, the very nature of their work disallows a repetitive cycle of operations, except for those tasks involved in regular preventive checks of equipment. Scheduling of maintenance work is determined by what piece of equipment breaks down, and there is obviously no way to standardize this. There is also an inherent variety, though to a lesser extent, in the jobs of the distribution workers who load and un-load trucks and tank cars or pump the product from one part of the plant to another.

Process operators have a certain amount of standardized work, but the contrast with the repetitive, subdivided operations of the auto-mobile worker is striking. Virtually all jobs require more than the ten operations that only a favored minority of auto workers enjoy. While the typical job cycle of the assembly-line worker is one minute, the chemical operator's most standardized operation is his periodic round of readings, which he takes every two hours. On such a round, an operator may check the readings on more than fifty different instruments located at widely dispersed points in his patrol area. There is a consid-erable variety, then, even in the most routine of the chemical operator's job tasks.

Jobs are not as limited in scope in the continuous-process indus-tries because chemical processes cannot be subdivided to the extent that the mechanical operations in assembly can be. Chemicals are not discrete units upon which a number of operations can be performed very quickly, but liquids and gases that flow continuously through a series of automatic operations, each of which takes a considerable amount of time. Job design must be organized around the entire process the chemical undergoes in its production. Automation also greatly reduces the number of operators necessary for production, so that the work is divided among fewer employees.

The large number of subplants, products, and processes in an industrial chemical factory makes for a highly diversified work environment. This diversity adds greatly to the variety in work, especially when job rotation allows many workers to divide their time between different parts of the plant. At the Bay Company, many craftsmen and distribution employees were on a job-rotation program. The maintenance responsibilities of the instrument repairmen, for example, are divided into five zones, each of which includes one or more buildings of the plant. A man works in one zone one week, another zone the second week, and so on, in a five-week rotation cycle.

Even the work of those operators who do not rotate from one subplant to another gains variety from the large number of chemicals produced in a single process. An automobile worker might produce scrap that can be shoveled into a scrap barrel; there is no equivalent to the waste products, by-products, or co-products made in a chemical process, each of which must be controlled and looked after.

Freedom in the Automated Factory: Free Time and Free Movement

The special technological and economic characteristics of the continuous-process industries give workers a great deal of control over their immediate work processes. Due to the interplay of a large number of factors, the alienating tendencies of modern industrial organization, so pronounced in the case of the automobile assembly line, are reduced to a virtual minimum and the personal on-the-job freedoms of the operatives are enhanced.

A New Work Rhythm in the Factory Unlike textile and automobile workers, chemical workers are free from constant pressure on their jobs and, in fact, have a great deal of free time. The Bay Chemical Company workers interviewed were virtually unanimous on this point. A typical comment of a middle-aged operator was:

> There's no great pressure. They give you a job to do, and you do it. If things are running smooth, there's no problem. Nobody is pushed around here unless you're lax. There's no real incentive to get out two pounds more than yesterday, nothing like that.

The lack of constant job pressure in continuous-process plants is not a product of management's humanitarian concern for the employees but is principally due to the nature of an automated technology. The monitoring of automated processes and equipment need be done only periodically, not constantly. Because it is mental work and requires great care and responsibility, if not necessarily elaborate knowledge, workers cannot be rushed or pressured. The defective work of an automobile assembler is usually easily remedied by the repairmen after the car is off the line. But in continuous-process production mistakes are extremely costly. Turning the wrong valve can ruin thousands of pounds of product. And because of the inevitability of problems and breakdowns which must entail all the energy of the work force, the standardized operations are scheduled to take up only part of a worker's time, leaving large quantities of free time to deal with such emergency situations if they arise.

Therefore, instead of the steady work characteristic of other types of manufacturing, the work of the chemical operator has an irregular, even erratic, rhythm. It is a rhythm which consists of long periods of relative inactivity and occasional, though unpredictable and usually brief, periods of extremely arduous activity. Most of the time, things are going well. The operator has only his regular monitoring to do, which takes up about half his time. When a stranger enters the control room of a chemical plant or an oil refinery, he sees many operators sitting around and talking. He wonders why so many more men are kept on the job than seem to be needed, particularly since unions in the oil and chemical industries generally have not been strong enough to maintain the "featherbedding" that exists elsewhere. The answer is that all these men are needed, and needed badly, in crisis situations. When something goes wrong with the process, it is necessary for everyone to work extremely hard in order to locate the trouble and set things right as quickly as possible, so that the loss of the product is minimized. The extra cost that management incurs by such work-scheduling is much less than the savings it can gain by getting production quickly back to normal, since the huge capital investment makes "down time" exceedingly expensive. An operator's story captures management's attitude:

> I remember once the boss came into the control room and he said, "When I see you guys sitting around I know everything is going all right. When I see everybody up and running around then I know something's wrong."

Although the chemical worker's freedom from pressure is principally caused by technological factors, it is supported by the economic conditions of the industry. High profits and economic prosperity and growth greatly contribute to the relaxed atmosphere. The cost structure of the industry also works to the advantage of the manual workers. In a highly capital-intensive industry, it is more profitable to exploit technology than the work force itself. In the labor-intensive textile industry, as we have seen, the worker rather than the machine system is pushed and pressured.

Chemical workers control the pace of their work; they do not, however, control the pace of production. For operatives in other factory industries, work is production. The conveyer belt which forces the automobile worker to work at a predetermined rate compels him to produce at that rate. But with automated technology, the work of operators, even though they are still called production workers, becomes separated from direct production per se. The chemical operator can determine the pace at which he monitors the automatic equipment, but the automatic processes taking place within the chemical reactors determine the speed of production. The operator can, of course, and sometimes does, control this rate by adjusting the controls; but the approved pace of output is established by engineers in the front office, and not by him.

For this reason the chemical worker is similar to the automobile worker in his inability to control the quantity of his output. But for him it does not appear to be a restriction of freedom but a necessary fact inherent in the nature of automatic technology. The automobile worker's lack of control over output is an integral part of his lack of control over work pace and the pressure of the assembly line and is therefore an additionally distasteful feature of his work environment.

Quality of Product   But unlike automobile workers, chemical workers are able to control the quality of their production. In fact, control of the quality of the product is their major job responsibility. Although the instinct of workmanship has been removed to a different level by the elimination of manual skill, it is still important. Putting out a good quality product is one of the most important sources of satisfaction and accomplishment for the operators interviewed.

Control over the quality of production can be frustrated not only by assembly-line pressure, forcing would-be craftsmen to work sloppily, but also by completely automatic quality control which insures a perfect product. The ability of an operator to feel a sense of accomplishment because "our product is now coming out 100 percent yield . . . I'm tickled to see that," depends on the *problematic* nature of the process. It might be expected that improvements in automatic processes would eventually eliminate these areas of uncertainty and thereby eventually reduce the operator's sense of accomplishment. Industry experts deny this. Each advanced stage of automation, they say, brings its own technical problems and potential for breakdown.

Methods of Work   Chemical-process work is not as standardized as work on the automobile assembly line or in the textile mill. The worker has more freedom to determine techniques of doing his job. This results from the variety inherent in the work; the lack of time pressure, which allows experimentation and change; and the new situations for which new solutions must be found. Even on such a relatively routine job as instrument-reading, much variation in the sequence of work is possible.

The high level of this freedom is suggested by the fact that 50 percent of the respondents in the Davis survey replied that they usually plan how they do their jobs; 34 percent frequently do this; and only 6 percent seldom or never are able to plan out their work. In the same study, 89 percent of the workers reported that they "decide what needs to be done" on their jobs either usually or frequently.

In the Roper survey, 64 percent of the chemical workers and 59 percent of the oil workers said they could try out their own ideas on the job, compared to only 49 percent of the total sample, 47 percent of the automobile workers, and 38 percent of the textile employees. Only in two craft industries, printing and transportation equipment, did higher proportions of workers command this job freedom. The technology and work organization of the continuous-process industries thus give the worker a certain amount of freedom to exercise choices and to make decisions in the course of his job.

However, even this degree of freedom is not as great as many workers desire. When I asked Bay Company workers whether they could try out their own ideas, many expressed a wish for more opportunities to display initiative in their work. The introduction of a suggestion system was frequently proposed to improve this situation.

Social Integration in Chemical Plants

The technology, economic situation, and social structure of the chemical industry also contribute significantly to the integration of the work force in a cohesive industrial community. Of first importance is the small size of the plants in the industry and the decentralized organization within the plant. In small plants and small departments, the anonymity and the impersonality of bureaucratic large-scale organization are found less than in large, centralized factories. Communication between workers and management representatives is more frequent and is especially likely to be two-way communication in which advice is sought, as well as orders given.

A second critical factor, already discussed in the above section, is team production. Auto assembly workers are rarely members of clearly defined and interdependent work teams, and this consequence of assembly-line technology reduces the cohesion in the industry. But chemical-process operators are clearly identified with a particular shift and a particular department; the departmental work teams are not only clearly defined, they also have an explicit hierarchy of authority and status. Maintenance workers, too, are members of specific departments made up of others in the same craft. Work teams in the chemical industry develop identities: teams on different shifts strive to outdo each other in the quality of their product; retired workers often continue to inquire after their old work crews. As a pumper in one of the Bay Company's process plants, who had worked in the steel industry, puts it:

> A chemical plant is more compact. There are less employees, and they are more closely knit. Just more people that you know. In a big plant like the steel mill you're one of many. Here there is closer knit contact. In a big company you are just a number to them. In my plant there's twenty shift men and two men on days. I got a chance to know all these people.

The high degree of cohesion brought about by team production within small, decentralized plants is suggested by a number of research findings. At the Bay chemical plant, Davis found that blue-collar employees ranked "friends at work" as that element of the total job situation which they most liked more consistently than ten other job factors, including interesting work, security, and pay. A number of workers mentioned their surprise at the readiness with which more experienced employees taught them their jobs and helped them with their problems —exclusiveness and withholding of skills and knowledge had been common in other industries. And in the Roper survey, 57 percent of the chemical workers felt most of their fellow workers were doing very good work and 40 percent felt that they were doing pretty well. Fewer workers proportionately than in any other industry said their workmates could do a lot better.

A third element contributing to integration is the quality of supervision in continuous-process plants. The overbearing supervision characteristic of past industrial practices is unlikely in a modern continuous-process plant. Chemical production requires responsible workers who will not need to be watched too closely. Due to the decentralized operations, the large amount of outdoor work, and the considerable physical mobility possible, individuals often work far out of the range of their immediate supervisors. As for operators, three-quarters of the time they are working nights or weekends, when there may be only one supervisor on duty in the entire plant.

The chemical workers interviewed all felt that the load of supervision was light and that they were given considerable scope to do their jobs in their own way. A construction laborer reported that he kept looking around him all the time during his first few months with the company, expecting someone to be breathing down his neck. On his previous job he had had to be in front of his machine eight hours a day. The other workers at the chemical company kidded him, and it took him quite a while to get used to the different atmosphere.

This freedom is possible because the work team which runs an individual plant takes over many of the functions of supervision in other technological contexts. A worker will come to work and do his job well, not out of fear of a particular boss, but because he feels the other operators in his crew are depending on him to do his part of the total work. Many of the co-ordinating and administrative functions of supervision fall to the head shift operator, the leader of each plant's work crew. Since the head operator is an hourly blue-collar employee and the most experienced man in the particular department, his guidance is not felt to be oppressive supervision. The fact that he has previously worked at each of the jobs in his department in the course of working his way to the top is an important basis of his authority and respect.

The chemical operator probably has more personal contact with persons in higher levels of supervision than do workers in mass-production industries. These contacts generally are for consultation on production problems and are therefore more satisfying than administrative or disciplining contacts. In automated production, when the workers' function becomes responsibility rather than skill, consultation with supervisors, engineers, chemists, and other technical specialists becomes a regular, natural part of the job duties. Because the operator is responsible for an important and expensive process, he can initiate interaction with those higher in status. Because he is the person close to the actual operations, he must be listened to. These facts have great implications for the dignity of the chemical worker. Automobile assemblers and textile operatives may call upon a foreman or maintenance machinist when some mechanism is not working perfectly, but their own advice is rarely consulted by their superiors. Technical consultation with superiors does take place in craft industries, but since craftsmen have a more independent domain, it is built into the system less than in continuous-process technology.

The result is that the social atmosphere of the plant becomes an all-important aspect of the work situation in an automated technology, as Alain Touraine has emphasized. A climate of collaboration is necessary for successful operations because of the interdependence of work teams and the importance of individual responsibility (1955: 118–119, 173–183). Because the technology, work organization, and social structure of chemical plants allow the worker to become integrated into the company through his work group and to identify with the enterprise, the quality of supervision is extremely salient. Of course, co-operative relations between workers and supervisors are not automatically determined by a continuous-process technology but depend also on the practices of management and the orientation of the individual foreman. For this reason, the extremely high morale and integrated atmosphere in the Bay plant partly reflect its successful management. We would expect to find some plants in the chemical industry, though not as many as in the automotive industry, with considerably less integration and lower morale.

Status Structure, Advancement, and Loyalty to Company

A fourth factor which influences integration in the chemical industry is its status structure. An elaborate system of superior and inferior ranks supports a normative structure because those in higher positions have presumably internalized the goals of the enterprise and more clearly express its values. The existence of achievable higher positions also serves to motivate those of lower status to accept the goals of the organization and to act in accordance with its norms.

The technological requirements of continuous-process production encourage a finely elaborated status structure, since, as we have seen, a balanced skill distribution emerges, made up of employees at all levels of training and responsibility. This differentiation is further developed within each operating department, where the jobs make up an elaborate hierarchy. A typical operating department consists of seven men in seven different job grades, from a beginning helper to the responsible head shift operator. Each job is a step on a natural ladder of promotion. Workers start in the department at the bottom, and the assumption is that the men will work up, one step at a time, and eventually reach the top position. At each step, there is an increase in training required, job duties (particularly responsibility), pay, and status.

Georg Simmel has written of the "inevitably disproportionate distribution of qualifications and positions," which means that all social organization involves a "contradiction between the just claims to a superordinate position and the technical impossibility of satisfying this claim. . . ." Simmel observes that among the ordinary workers in a factory there are certainly very many who could equally well be foremen or entrepreneurs (1950: 300–303). The highly differentiated stratification in the chemical plant is possibly one of the best solutions to this problem of the inevitable injustice of all social systems. The elaborate hierarchical arrangement probably allows the maximum number of people to be in positions where there are others below them in rank, and this is another force for social integration.

The high level of advancement which a stratified blue-collar world makes possible is a fifth factor which supports normative integration in the continuous-process industries. The situation differs considerably from that of the automobile, textile, and other industries. Many Bay Company workers commented that in other industries a man is hired to do a particular job and it is assumed he will stay on that job. The job histories of these chemical workers show a great deal of upward movement. Of the twenty-one workers interviewed, twenty had some job advancement; only one had experienced no job change.

A representative case is that of a thirty-three-year-old operator who started with the company thirteen years ago as a bus boy in the cafeteria. After three years he moved into the ammonia plant, where he worked in succession as a janitor, a cylinder painter, and a cylinder filler. After three years in the ammonia plant, he moved into the methionine plant and began climbing its job ladder. He started as a helper, moved up to finishing operator, then to ion operator, then to mercaptan operator, and finally to his present job as hydantion operator, fifth highest on a ladder of seven jobs. Above him are the acrolein operator and the head shift operator. After reaching these two steps, the salaried position of process foreman is his goal.

In addition, skilled maintenance craftsmen in the continuous-process industries are recruited from the ranks of the less-skilled employees through formal apprenticeship and training programs. In an auto plant studied by Robert Guest, only 6 percent of the maintenance craftsmen had started their careers on the assembly line (1960: 322): fully skilled craftsmen were hired from the outside. In direct contrast, at one of the largest oil refineries, 90 percent of the 1,000 skilled workers in 1937 had originally started in the plant as unskilled laborers (Larson and Porter, 1959: 382).

A study of a major oil refinery similarly reports that "the method of upgrading, whereby all new hires start out in the labor pool and branch out from there into specialties," contributes to general job satisfaction. "After a short stay in the labor gang it is almost inevitable that a worker progress. . . . Under this scheme the majority of our long term respondents have experienced considerable mobility in the refinery" (Union Research and Education Projects, 1956: 15).

The Roper survey results confirm the superior advancement opportunities in the chemical industry. Seventy-nine percent of the chemical workers, compared to only 47 percent of all workers answered that their jobs led to promotions if they did them well. This was by far the highest proportion among the sixteen industries and was exactly twice as large as the proportion of automobile and textile workers who expected promotion. The second highest figure, 63 percent, was in the petroleum refining industry.

Advancement opportunities for chemical workers exist largely within the blue-collar manual sector; the route into supervision, engineering, and higher management is not as open. However, chemical workers may have slightly better chances of rising out of the blue-collar ranks than workers in other industries because the industry's rapid growth creates more openings.

Jobs in the automobile industry rarely allow a worker to show those qualities of skill and leadership that he may possess. Chemical operating and maintenance jobs not only permit their use; they often develop such potentialities. This fact and the relative lack of a worker–management cleavage in the industry result in greater feelings of equity concerning the distribution of promotion than exist in other industries. The advancement progress of each employee is reviewed periodically in the continuous-process industries, and this means that misunderstandings and resentments about promotions can be "aired out." In addition, such bureaucratic procedures as seniority provisions and the public posting of job openings also diminish the sentiments of injustice and inequity. Although individual workers have their own grievances, there seems to be no general feeling that advancements within departments are awarded unfairly, in contrast to the situation observed by Chinoy at the ABC automobile plant. However, there is considerable dissatisfaction about the age limit which kept middle-aged operators out of craft apprenticeship programs. And resentment against the length of time necessary to transfer from shift work to day jobs appears to be common in many continuous-process plants (Union Research and Education Projects, 1956: 27–28).

The structuring of advancement opportunities in continuous-process technology enhances the integration and cohesion in these industries; conversely, the high level of integration increases an employee's motivation to advance and is therefore an incentive toward superior performance. An insightful operator, who had worked in four other industries and developed a comparative perspective, makes this point:

> There's more place to advance here than in other places. At the can company I was at the top but there's not much difference between the bottom and the top. In the brickyard there's no difference at all—you stay on the same job all your life. Here the difference between my job and the top job is about $1,200 a year. That makes an incentive to do your best and to get promotions. I guess that's the way the company sees it.

However, I must qualify this highly positive picture. The institutionalization of mobility routes through formal job ladders and the company's encouragement of aspiration and training result, naturally enough, in a high level of expectation of upward movement. In addition, the industry's employment security has been so consistent that workers are not as preoccupied with holding on to their jobs as are the automobile workers and textile workers. When the job is secure, advancement becomes even more important psychically. And since promotions are rarely as rapid as workers would like them, considerable dissatisfaction often results.

The economic downturn of the past few years has decreased the rate of advancements in the industry sharply and thus has aggravated this crisis in expectations. Taking advantage of the general postwar prosperity and its own growth position, the chemical industry expanded very rapidly in the late forties and to a lesser extent in the early fifties. Advancements were quite rapid. When other industries were laying off workers during recent recessions, it was able to avoid unemployment because of its superior economic and growth situation: workers who quit or retired were simply not replaced. However, in this period, advancement has slowed down drastically.

We have seen that continuous-process technology results in a distinctive plant social structure, many aspects of which contribute to a high degree of social cohesion and normative integration. It is fortunate that these natural, spontaneous, social processes work in this direction because automated production requires an integrated manual work force for its successful operation. Not only does the responsibility demanded of the operator necessitate more loyalty to the enterprise than when work is standardized, but the constant technological change inherent in continuous-process production also makes an integrated work force essential.

The continuing economic and technical advances in the oil refining and chemical industries would be impossible if workers in these industries were disposed to resist innovation and change, as are many industrial workers. The high degree of integration, the relative lack of conflict, and the high level of job security in the chemical industry provide an atmosphere in which technological change is more accepted by workers and unions than in the automobile industry, where, because of its history of labor-management strife and its irregular employment pattern, workers are naturally suspicious of the motives and effects of technological innovation.

The Chance for Growth and Development   Continuous-process technology is highly dynamic, and one of the consequences of a changing work milieu is that it challenges the self-estrangement inherent in personal stagnation. Chemical workers stress the fact that even though they have become perfectly competent to handle their jobs they are not through learning because something new comes up all the time. An operator who had been on his job two years told me: "You never know everything that's needed to know on it. I know the basic things. But sometimes I doubt if I know anything. You scratch your head and just wonder when something goes wrong."

To carry on experimental work on new processes and products, chemical companies establish pilot plants, often on a short-time basis, to which regular operators are assigned. Work in such plants increases the diversity of a man's job experience and provides an opportunity for growth and development. Even within regular departments, the frequency with which new equipment or new processes are introduced means that learning is more or less constant. A young operator, in comparing the chemical plant with his previous job in the paper industry, emphasizes the heightened interest which change and new experience bring about:

A chemical plant is more technical. There are more interesting jobs. There (at the paper factory) you grab a box, it's all manual labor. Nothing to hold you, you do the same thing every day. Here, the operations are constantly changing. It holds your interest. You get something going; you wonder what's going to happen, how it will come out.

A technical and changing work environment obviously requires a different kind of work force than an environment in which jobs and processes are relatively unchanging. A student of labor conditions in the chemical industry writes: "A continuous result of new development is the regular change in jobs and in methods of work. Modifications of duties on the job and introduction of new types of duties demand workers of fairly high ability" (Lambert, 1949: 15). In recent years, chemical companies and oil refineries have generally limited their hiring to high-school graduates, in an attempt to get workers who are intelligent and adaptable. Although many workers are not able to change fast enough to keep up with changing technology, their environment itself tends to produce workers who are more alert, more technically minded, and more adaptable than the average.

In order to help the work force keep up with technological change, companies in the continuous-process industries have instituted extensive training programs. At a major oil refinery in the Bay area, all of the operators had recently completed one week's schooling on the job. In addition, technical courses at evening schools and junior colleges are actively encouraged by management, which often pays a portion of the worker's tuition.

Social Integration Through Responsible Function: A New Source of Dignity and Non-Alienation in Blue-Collar Work?

For chemical workers, then, work means much more than the pay check, the major factor binding automobile assembly-line workers to their job. Certainly the instrumental purpose of work is important for chemical employees, as it must be for all except perhaps a minority of creative artists and intellectuals; the critical difference is that the job includes many features which are inherently fulfilling. It was for intrinsic, immediate, job-content reasons that most chemical workers interviewed preferred their present work over past jobs in other industries; in contrast, the X plant workers studied by Walker and Guest preferred automobile-industry employment only for such extrinsic considerations as pay and security. Since the intrinsic nature of the work —its challenge, learning opportunities, and social function in production—is meaningful to an employee in a continuous-process chemical plant, the job is therefore not solely the means to an end which it tends to be in other industrial settings. The chemical worker is less likely to be subjectively alienated than the automobile worker.

In stressing the unique combination of technological, economic, and social forces which counteract alienation in the chemical industry, I do not want to unduly exaggerate the well-being and happiness found in these work environments. There are undoubtedly many chemical companies where workers are more dissatisfied than at Bay, a plant with a remarkably high degree of morale and social cohesion. Even in the latter plant, one meets a number of workers who are clearly alienated and express marked negative feelings about the work of an automated operator. It was my impression—unchecked by systematic statistics—that young, highly intelligent, and ambitious workers were the most likely to be dissatisfied. They viewed the work as insufficiently challenging, advancement opportunities as too long range, and probably also resented general working-class status and income. The overall argument is simply that there are proportionately fewer of these alienated workers in continuous-process industries.

The chemical worker's freedom is the result of an automated continuous-process technology and constant technical change, rather than tradition. Based on the responsibility required by the non-manual work of controlling an automatic technology, it reflects new conditions and job requirements which result from the needs of management rather than the consequences of the worker's superior power position. Although in this sense chemical employees are more dependent on their companies than printers, the responsibility for automated production confers a new source of dignity and worth on manual employment—a possibility not foreseen by many students of alienation, who assess manual work by the yardstick of traditional craftsmanship.

Technology, Span of Control, and Success*
JOAN WOODWARD

Technology and Success

One of the objectives of this survey was to find out how far the principles and ideas which formed the basis of the teaching of management subjects were accepted and applied in practice, and whether such acceptance and application ensured business success. In approximately half of the firms studied, these principles and ideas were reflected in the form of organization established—but there seemed to be no direct link between them and business success. As far as organization was concerned, successful firms seemed to have little in common. Indeed, in analysing the research data the only variable found to be demonstrably related to variations in organization was the system of production in operation.

At this point in the analysis, the research workers thought it might

* Reprinted by permission of the Clarendon Press, Oxford, from: Joan Woodward, *Industrial Organization: Theory and Practice* (London: Oxford University Press, 1965). pp. 68–80, with omissions.

be useful to take a second look at the organizational characteristics of firms graded as above and below average in success in each production category.

Of the twenty firms in the above average category, five were unit production firms, a further five were large batch and mass production firms, and six were process production firms. The remainder operated combined systems; in one, the combination was of mass production with unit production, and in three, of process production with mass production. Of the seventeen firms classified as below average, five were unit production firms; six were mass production firms; four were process production firms, and two had combined production systems. In each production category there were both successful and unsuccessful firms; the figures suggesting that chances of success might be slightly higher in process production than in other types of manufacture.

The re-examination of the organizational figures revealed one other interesting fact; the five successful unit production firms had organizational characteristics in common; so had the five large batch and mass production firms, and the six process production firms. It was found that the figures relating to the organizational characteristics of the successful firms in each production category tended to cluster round the medians for that category as a whole, while the figures of the firms classified as "below average" in success, were found at the extremes of the range.

The figures relating to the span of control of the chief executive, the number of levels in the line of command, labour costs, and the various labour ratios showed a similar trend. The fact that organizational characteristics, technology, and success were linked together in this way suggested that not only was the system of production an important variable in the determination of organizational structure, but also that one particular form of organization was most appropriate to each system of production. In unit production, for example, not only did short and relatively broadly based pyramids predominate, but they also appeared to ensure success. Process production, on the other hand, would seem to require the taller and more narrowly based pyramid.

It was also interesting to find that, in terms of Burns's analysis (1960: 23), successful firms inside the large batch production range tended to have mechanistic management systems. On the other hand, successful firms outside this range tended to have organic systems.

There were administrative expedients that were linked with success in one system of production and failure in another. For example, the duties and responsibilities of managerial and supervisory staff were clearly and precisely defined on paper in most of the successful large batch production firms studied and in none of the unsuccessful firms. In process production, however, this kind of definition was more often

FIGURE 1.   AVERAGE SPAN OF CONTROL OF FIRST-LINE
SUPERVISOR ANALYZED BY BUSINESS SUCCESS

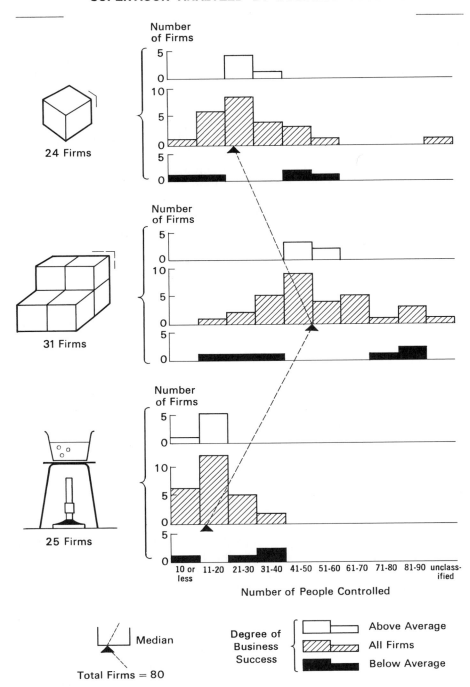

associated with failure. It was found too that as technology became more advanced, the chief executive seemed able to control an increasing number of direct subordinates successfully. All the successful firms in which the span of control of the chief executive was ten or more were process production firms.

In general, the administrative expedients associated with success in large batch production firms were in line with the principles and ideas on which the teaching of management subjects is based. In all the successful large batch production firms there was not only a clear definition of duties and responsibilities of the kind already referred to, but also an adherence to the principles of unity of command; a separation (at least on paper) of advisory from executive responsibilities, and a chief executive who controlled no more than the recommended five or six direct subordinates.

The tendency to regard large batch production as the typical system of modern industry may be the explanation of this link between success and conformity with management theory. The people responsible for developing management theory no doubt had large batch production in mind as they speculated about management. In general, the experience on which their generalizations were based had been obtained in large batch production industry.

In the final analysis the conclusions reached earlier had to be modified. While at first sight there seemed to be no link between organization and success, and no one best way of organizing a factory, it subsequently became apparent that there was a particular form of organization most appropriate to each technical situation. Within a limited range of technology this was also the form of organization most closely in line with the principles and ideas of management theory. Outside the limited range, however, the rules appear to be different; the most suitable form of organization being out of line with these principles and ideas.

Assessing the Effects of Technical Change

The demonstration of a link between technology, organization and success has practical significance for the industrial manager; it can lead not only to the development of techniques helpful in the appraisal of organizational structure but also make it possible to plan organizational change simultaneously with technical change. The industrial manager need not wait to see the effects of technical change before modifying organizational structure. Investigation showed that any technical changes which did not radically affect the nature of the production system only resulted in minor modifications to organization. On the other hand, the kind of technical change involving change in the production system was followed by a fundamental organizational change. This was as true of the change resulting from developments that made possible the more efficient realization of original objectives as it was of the changes resulting from modifications of objectives.

For example, automatic devices for the control of individual machines introduced into unit and small batch production had relatively little effect on anything other than the nature of the work done by the machine operators themselves. The introduction of the transfer-line for the manufacture of cylinder blocks led to modifications in the size and composition of primary working groups and affected supervisor–subordinate relationships on the job, but because so small a percentage of total production operations was affected, the overall organizational picture remained as before. On the other hand, in those firms where technical change had transformed what had been either large-batch production or a combination of process production with large batch production into continuous-flow production, fundamental organizational changes had come about.

The work done by Scott and his colleagues (1956) on technical change and social structure in a large steel works (1956), showed that significant organizational changes resulted from the introduction of the continuous strip-mill. This is in line with the results of this survey, for the introduction of the new strip-mill was a technical change of the kind that involved a fundamental change in the production system of the firm. Traditionally the manufacture of steel was a batch production process, but recent technical developments had turned it into a continuous-flow process.

In South Essex most of the organizational changes that had followed changes in production systems were neither dramatic nor planned for in advance. Organizational problems seemed to have arisen as a result of technical changes, and the finding of solutions to these problems had led to modifications in the organization. For example, in firms where large batch production had been superseded by continuous-flow production, the command hierarchy had lengthened, the span of control of the chief executive had widened, and the ratio of managers and supervisors to total personnel had increased. In the firm which had reverted to unit production (Woodward, 1965: 45), abandoning the standardized production of parts, the reversion had been followed by organizational change of a dramatic kind, the command hierarchy being reduced overnight from eight levels of authority to four.

The fact that organizational change brought about by technical change resulted in modifications to structure in line with the results of the survey, suggests that facts and figures of the kind given in this report could help the industrial manager to foresee the organizational results of any technical change he contemplated. Thus, no problems need arise from technical change to which at least partial solutions cannot be found from the accumulated experience of manufacturing industry. This implies, of course, that such experience must be adequately documented and systematized information made available. There is a pressing need for more factual description of manufacturing situations. Information of this kind would also be helpful if amalgamations or take-overs were contemplated, enabling the parent company to understand the organizational problems of any subsidiaries that were concerned with production processes different from its own.

Technology and Social Structure

There appears to be some conflict here between the findings of this research and those of other researches carried out by social scientists in the industrial field (W. H. Scott, *et al.,* 1956: 73). Generally speaking, social scientists seem to find more conscious planning of formal organization in the firms they study than was found here. A possible explanation of the discrepancy might be found in the way the firms were chosen for this present study. The research covered a geographical area in an intensive way and probably brought in smaller and less well-known firms of the kind that normally escape the social science net. It seems reasonable to suppose that, in general, firms likely to be approached by social scientists and to accept them would be the more progressive, and therefore more organization-conscious firms.

The survey findings did confirm, however, that conscious planning of organization rarely seems to be based on technical considerations. In many firms those responsible for making organizational decisions had only a limited knowledge of the manufacturing processes, the majority of organization specialists being non-technical people.

In the final stages of the survey the research workers tried to find out not only whether organizational changes accompanying technical changes had been planned in advance but also whether the managers of successful firms were conscious of the requirements of their production systems, or had tried to satisfy these requirements in making organizational decisions. This appeared to be the case in only three firms. On the whole managers had a limited awareness of the requirements of their production systems. Many, when discussing particular administrative expedients, made some such comment as "it would not work here"; they all seemed to regard their own situation as unique. People with industrial experience will no doubt be familiar with this kind of comment. Management consultants, for example, would probably regard them as evidence of rationalization or prejudice against new ideas. The research workers recognized that there was an element of prejudice in them; nevertheless, in as much of what was said, there was an implicit recognition of the situational demands of the production system. But this recognition seldom became explicit; it was found, for example, that although all the successful unit production firms had short-command hierarchies, there was little evidence to suggest that the lines had been kept short as a result of deliberate decisions. The managers concerned did not even seem to be aware that the command hierarchies in their firms were short in comparison with those of other firms in the area.

Against the background of facts and figures linking technology, formal organization, and success, it must be remembered that the firms studied fell into two approximately equal groups: those in which formal organization had arisen imperceptibly and gradually from informal organization, and those in which it had been consciously planned. It was interesting to find that among the successful firms in the first group, unit and small batch production and continuous-flow production predominated, while the majority of successful firms in the second group were in the large batch production category. This suggests that conscious planning produces better results in some kinds of industry than in others.

There may be a simple explanation of this. Conscious planning is based on the principles and ideas of classical management theory. These principles and ideas were the result of the speculative thinking of individual managers, the majority of whom obtained their industrial experience in large batch production. Basically, therefore, conscious planning may be no more than the formalization of the informal pattern of relationships found to be most appropriate in the management of large batch production.

This would support the assumption that formal organization depends more on technical considerations than is generally realized, and that any tendency to divorce it further ought to be resisted.

Technology, because it influences the roles defined by formal organization, must therefore influence industrial behaviour, for how a person reacts depends as much on the demands of his role and the circumstances in which he finds himself, as on his personality. There can be occasions when the behaviour forced on him by his role is in conflict with his personality. If so, role considerations may lead him to alter or modify his personality, or to leave his employment and seek a more congenial job elsewhere.

It will be remembered that at one stage in the analysis of the survey data the research workers considered whether the differences between firms both in organization and achievement could be attributed to differences in the ability of their senior managers, and rejected this as a complete explanation. In considering the personality differences between managers, it did appear, however, that senior executives in the firms in each production category had characteristics in common. This might imply that one of the ways in which situational demands impose themselves is by bringing individuals to the top of the management ladder whose personal qualities best fit the technical background in which they have to operate.

In general, the senior executives of firms in the batch production categories where efforts were continuously being made to push back the physical limitations of production, seemed to have more drive and push and to be more ambitious than their counterparts in unit production or process production. Whether this was the result of natural selection or conditioning it is, of course, impossible to find out through studies of this nature.

The research results suggested too that some technical environments impose greater strains than others on individuals at all levels of the hierarchy. Reference has already been made to the differences in communication behaviour. Both inter-managerial relationships and employee-employer relationships seemed to be better at the extremes of the scale than they were in the middle; pressure was greater in the middle and it seemed more important to build mechanisms into the organizational structure which would resolve the conflicts likely to occur.

Thus it seems that an analysis of situational demands could lead not only to the development of better techniques for appraising organizational structure and for conscious planning, but also to an increased understanding of the personal qualities and skills required in different industrial situations, and to improve methods of training directed towards giving those concerned a better understanding of the strains and stresses associated with the roles they are likely to occupy.

Operations Technology and Organization Structure: An Empirical Reappraisal*

DAVID J. HICKSON, D. S. PUGH, and DIANA C. PHEYSEY

Objective of This Study

The objective of the research reported here is to test the proposition of a "technological imperative" at the organizational level of analysis. It tests the broad hypotheses that technology and structure are strongly related, utilizing data from a wider study (Pugh et al., 1969a, 1969b) of the context of organization structure (context including size, ownership, dependence, operations technology, etc.).

This paper describes a classification of concepts of technology, and the operationalization of the concept used in this study. Two measures of technology were used, one suitable for non-manufacturing as well as for manufacturing organizations, and the other designed specifically for manufacturing industry. Only seven variables of structure

* Reprinted from the *Administrative Science Quarterly, 14* (September 1969), pp. 378–397, with omissions, by permission of the authors and the publisher.

were found to be related to technology, but from these and from the reconciliation of the overall negative results with Woodward's (1958, 1965) seemingly contradictory outcome, a revised hypothesis is developed.

Concept of Technology: A Classification

Conceptualization of an organization's technology is still at a stage where the word technology may have varying meanings. The concept has three facets, which taken together encompass the range of meanings that have been developed; *operations technology, materials technology,* and *knowledge technology.*

The concept of *operations technology* is used by Pugh *et al.,* who define an organization's technology as "the techniques that it uses in its workflow activities" (1963: 310). To Thompson and Bates it is "those sets of man–machine activities which together produce a desired good or service" (1957: 325), a view represented later in the "serial interdependence" of acts in Thompson's (1967) "long-linked technology." Udy (1959), Woodward (1958, 1965), and Burack (1966, 1967) all base their operationalizations on this view. The concept may be defined as the *equipping and sequencing of activities in the workflow.* The term workflow is taken from Bakke (1959) to mean producing and distributing the output. In the wide sense it is not only factories that have workflows, but also public utilities and service organizations. A transport undertaking has equipment (buses) and a sequence of operations (bus routes). An insurance office has its pens, paper, and calculating machines, and sequences of operations in the issuing of policies, obtaining of premiums, and meeting of claims.

Materials technology, an element in the construction of Perrow's (1967) theoretical scheme, broadens the notion of technology beyond the bounds so far described. To Perrow, technology is "the actions that an individual performs upon an object . . . in order to make some change in that object" (1967: 195). This includes the characteristics of the object itself or raw material (as Perrow also calls it), which Perrow categorizes by its perceived uniformity and stability and Rushing (1968) by its hardness. Thompson (1967) categorizes as "intensive technology" those situations where what is done is determined by the state of the object or material itself. So this concept of technology concerns characteristics of the *materials used in the workflow.*

Knowledge technology is a concept developed in this field primarily by Perrow (1967). The generalized view of organizations as systems functioning under uncertainty, epitomized by Cyert and March's (1963) approach, is applied by Perrow to the workflow as "the number of exceptional cases encountered in the work" (1967: 195) and the degree of logical analysis achieved. Although he regards ability to "understand" the raw material as a characteristic of the material, this would be more appropriately an aspect of knowledge. Thompson (1967: 86) makes use of the same idea. Knowledge technology is therefore the characteristics of the *knowledge used in the workflow.*

The overlap between concepts of technology and the meanings of such terms as charter, purpose, goal, and function presents a problem. Pugh *et al.* (1963) defined these separately, and operationalized them separately, so that the number of kinds of outputs an organization creates and their variation to customer demand, for example are treated as aspects of charter or purpose (Pugh *et al.,* 1969a); that is, what the outputs are and whether they are changed are seen as elements of charter or goals, not of technology, which has more to do with the means by which outputs are created. Taken in this sense, Harvey's (1968) operationalization of "major product changes" in terms of retooling, materials changes, and design changes is nearer the conceptualization of charter than of technology; as is also Thompson's (1967) categorization of the "primary function" of an organization as "mediating technology."

Subconcepts of Operations Technology

The project described here uses only the *operations technology* concept, as already defined, which itself consists of a number of subconcepts.

First, a salient characteristic of equipment is how automated it is. As Amber and Amber put it, "The more human attributes performed by a machine, the higher is its 'order' of automaticity. Automaticity is here considered to be the self-acting capability of a device" (1962: 2). This gives a constitutive subconcept of the *equipment used* in terms of *automation of equipment.*

The sequence of operations performed can be more or less rigid. This depends, according to Thompson and Bates, on "the extent to which the appropriate mechanics, knowledge, skills, and raw materials can be used for other products" (1957: 329). It also depends on the extent to which operations are linked in series. There is therefore a constitutive subconcept of the *sequence of operations* in terms of *workflow rigidity.*

All work organizations have means of assessing the operations performed, whether against exact standards or merely by personal opinion. This gives a third constitutive definition, in terms of the *specificity of evaluation of operations.*

All three subconcepts of operations technology can apply to all work organizations, whether manufacturing or service. *Workflow integration* is achieved through automation of equipment, a rigid sequence of operations and the precision demanded by specificity of evaluation.

A fourth subconcept is the continuity of the units of throughput (work in process) in the customary engineering terms of single-unit jobbing, batch, mass, or continuous-flow production. This subconcept, *production continuity,* is central to Woodward's (1958) approach on manufacturing technologies.

A similar approach to identifying subconcepts such as these is taken by Burack (1966: 5).

Other possible variables that might be utilized in further work, but were eventually excluded from the project because of difficulties either in conceptualization, operationalization, data collection, or effective discrimination, were: 1. Throughput complexity (for example, number of pieces assembled, technical knowledge required); 2. Throughput cycle (time to produce a unit of output); 3. Throughput rate (outputs per time unit); 4. Operations performed (for example, extracting, assembling, disassembling, processing, fabricating, conveying, etc.); 5. Operating continuity (for example, weekdays only, 24 hours continuous); 6. Variety of sequences ("production lines"); 7. Uniformity of equipment (range of types used).

Sample and Data Collection

The concepts of workflow integration and production continuity were operationalized on data from 52 diverse work organizations with a minimum of 250 employees each, in the Birmingham area in England.

Of these organizations, 46 were a random sample drawn from an official list of registered employers in the area, stratified by product or purpose and by size.

Of these 46 organizations, 31 were manufacturing and 15 were service organizations. Manufacturing is defined as the creation of new physical outputs whether solid, liquid, or gaseous; therefore the manufacturing organizations included food-processing firms and a brewery, as well as engineering factories, etc., but excluded retailing, omnibus services, education, and water supply. Relationships were examined across all 46 organizations, and also among the 31 manufacturing organizations alone.

Test on 31 Manufacturing Organizations

On the 31 manufacturing organizations, there was a striking lack of association between workflow integration and all three *dimensions* of organization structure (Table 1, column 1). As in the full sample, it is size that is overwhelmingly related to structuring of activities (Table 1, column 2). The irrelevance of technology is emphasized when the effects of size are removed. The correlation of (log) size and workflow integration is 0.30 on the manufacturing subset. Then holding size constant, the partial correlation coefficient between workflow integration and structuring of activities is merely 0.10. Conversely, if the effects of workflow integration are held constant, the correlation of size with structuring is almost unchanged at 0.76.

The workflow integration measure of operations technology is not associated with the dimension of concentration of authority or with line control.

Scores on structural dimensions, compounded of scores on several linked scales, might obscure more intricate relationships between technology and these component scales; but the correlations do not show this. Workflow integration is not substantially correlated with any of the main structural variables listed, and where some positive association is indicated, it is again overwhelmed by the correlations with size. Equally, if the scales which are the components of the workflow integration measure are examined, the outcome is very similar. The only relationships that remain are with job-count variables of configuration. Within manufacturing industry, these are the proportions of personnel in the employment side of personnel work, and in buying, stock control, and storekeeping. The more integrated the technology, the fewer these are, implying decreasing problems in the acquisition and retention of both human and material resources.

This result draws attention to the risks of generalizing from single cases. The study by Scott *et al.* (1956) of greater mechanization in a steel plant describes increases in what in Table 1 are called role specialization and overall formalization. Fensham and Hooper (1964) describe increases in vertical span and in workflow superordinates (managers) in textile mills. But the correlations in Table 1 imply that these effects of changing technology may not be true of very many cases. Indeed, they point to a much stronger positive relationship of each of role specialization, overall formalization, and vertical span, with *size*. Thus a multiorganization multivariate approach suggests that in these case studies, the effects which were attributed primarily to technology were as likely to be due to the simultaneous growth in size of the organizations observed. Burack's (1967) analysis distinguishes "scale-of-operation effects" from "technological change," but implies that they are of equal importance. The present data suggest that operations technology has only a limited specific effect compared with size.

Even though the technological concepts embodied in the items of the workflow integration scale apply readily to manufacturing, and a good discrimination is achieved between such organizations, the results obtained with it could be questioned if they were not supported by criteria intended specifically for manufacturing. Woodward's (1958) classification was intended solely for manufacturing production systems. Use of this classification affords a further test of the hypothesized connection between technology and organizational structure, particularly as Woodward's (1958, 1965) own findings on a range of firms in South-East Essex are principal evidence in its favor.

TABLE 1. CORRELATION* BETWEEN SCALES OF OPERATIONS TECHNOLOGY AND OF SIZE AND SELECTED SCALES OF STRUCTURE

	31 Manufacturing Organizations			
	Work-flow inte-gration	Size (log of no. of em-ployees)	Production continuity	Produc-tion con-tinuity (size par-tialled out)
Structural Dimensions	(1)	(2)	(3)	(4)
Structuring of activities	0.17	0.78‡	0.41†	0.07
Concentration of authority	0.00	—0.20	0.11	0.24
Line control of workflow	—0.05	0.13	—0.17	—
Structural Variables				
Overall role specialization	0.25	0.83‡	0.52‡	0.26
Overall standardization of procedures	0.19	0.65‡	0.35	0.07
Overall formalization (documentation)	0.04	0.67‡	0.27	—0.07
Overall centralization of decisions	—0.05	—0.47‡	0.00	0.28
Autonomy of the organization	0.02	0.23	—0.07	—0.19
Configuration of structure variables:				
Chief executive's span of control	—0.09	0.29	0.08	—0.07
Subordinate-supervisor ratio	0.02	0.04	—0.09(0.36)	—
Vertical span	0.15	0.77‡	0.51‡	0.26
Percentages of total number of employees:				
Direct workers	—0.17	—0.46‡	—0.14	0.10
Workflow superordinates	0.02	—0.31	0.13	0.33
Nonworkflow personnel	0.22	0.53‡	0.22	—0.04
Design and development	—0.08	—0.04	—0.18	—
Methods	0.07	0.15	—0.03	—
Inspection	0.07	—0.08	—0.15(0.62)	—
Employment	—0.45†	—0.03	0.04	—
Buying and stocks	—0.42†	—0.12	—0.10	—
Workflow control	—0.17	—0.35	—0.44†	—0.33
Transport and dispatch	0.32	—0.18	0.45†	—
Maintenance	0.05	0.13	0.20(0.46)	—
Size (log of no. of employees)	0.30	—	0.47‡	—

* Product moment coefficients of linear correlation (*r*): with correlation-ratio coefficients of nonlinear correlation (*η*) in parentheses in column 3, production continuity.
† Beyond 95 percent level of confidence.
‡ Beyond 99 percent level of confidence.

Test Based on Woodward's Classification

The 10-category classification in Table 2 is that proposed by Woodward (1958: 11, Figure 1). To Woodward (1958: 12), this was "a scale of technical complexity. This term is used here to mean the extent to which the production process is controllable and its results predictable." There is certainly a conceptual ordering in the arrangement of the categories, which suggests that they might be treated as a scale, potentially usable in correlational analysis. But the category headings are not stated primarily in terms of degrees of control and prediction, but rather in terms of the unit of throughput: unit, batch, and flow process. The conceptual ordering might therefore rather be regarded as denoting the degree of continuity of throughput units present in the production workflow, from the one-by-one of jobbing to the continuous flow of process production. This view is also taken by Starbuck (1965), who says: "It is not really accurate to call the technological variable 'complexity,' since this complexity seems to correspond to *smoothness* of production, but this was Woodward's term."

The further operationalization of these categories shown in Table 2 was therefore conceptualized as representing a production *continuity* variable. Woodward's (1958) original 10 categories were retained, rather than those used in her revised version (Woodward, 1965: 39), where categories not exclusively within one or other of the three broad production groups of unit and small batch, large batch and mass, and process are removed (that is, her "mixed" categories V and VIII). Since this either destroyed the sequence, or shortened the scale, it was less useful for the analysis presented here. The main problem in further defining Woodward's categories was with the idea of "batch," particularly the question, "How small is a small batch?" Woodward's headings were in general terms and their application was not specified. The concept of time was therefore introduced, and batch size was defined by time units selected to discriminate within the particular sample. Time intervals have the advantage of being clearly definable and can be varied to suit different samples. The distinction between small batch and large batch at weekly resetting of equipment was appropriate to the data available here, but in further work can be adjusted as required.

Finally, criteria mentioned in Woodward's categories but extraneous to the continuity concept were excluded, such as, whether production was to customer's orders or consisted of liquids, gases, or solids.

Correlation coefficients between the production continuity scores (on the seven categories in Table 2 for which there were organizations), and the structural dimensions and variables appear in Table 1 (column 3). At first sight there did seem to be a relationship here between technology and structuring of activities, albeit a moderate one. It was repeated in the correlations for the variables of specialization, standard-

TABLE 2. PRODUCTION CONTINUITY: A FURTHER OPERATIONALIZATION OF WOODWARD'S CLASSIFICATION OF PRODUCTION SYSTEMS

Woodward classification Unit and small batch: I through V Large batch and mass: V through VIII Process: VIII through X	Scale of production continuity†	Manufacturing organizations ($N = 31$)
I. Production of simple units to customers' orders	*Simple units:* units basically *single-piece* not assemblies; produced one by one	0
II. Production of technically complex units	*Complex units: assemblies,* produced one by one	0
III. Fabrication of large equipment in stages	*Fabrication:* one by one; workpeople come to the unit of output (which moves about very infrequently) rather than the unit moving to different workpeople	2
IV. Production of small batches	*Small batches:* equipment reset *every week* or more often, for outputs measured in *items*	11
V. Production of components in large batches subsequently assembled diversely	*Large batches:* equipment reset at intervals *longer than a week* for outputs measured in items: *but* items *assembled diversely* (i.e. variety of assembly sequences, including assembly by unit and/or small batch methods)	3
VI. Production of large batches; assembly line type	*Large batches:* as in V, but with *large-batch assembly*	5
VII. Mass production	*Mass: batch size, measured in items, is indefinite* (i.e. change of batch requires decisions on (a) design modification, (b) retooling, which are beyond the normal authority of the line production management and production planning to vary production programs)	4
VIII. Process production combined with the preparation of a product for sale by large-batch or mass-production methods	*Process:* throughputs measured by *weight or volume; but* outputs become *items at finishing stage*	0
IX. Process production of chemicals in batches	*Process:* but *ingredients* (i.e. recipes) of the throughputs *change periodically*	3
X. Continuous-flow production of liquids, gases and solid shapes	*Process:* but *constant ingredients;* (i.e. recipe change beyond the normal authority of the line production management and production planning to vary production programs)	3

† The predominant technology of an organization was assessed giving particular weight to its highest degree of "continuity."

ization, and formalization, from which scores on that structuring dimension were made up; and there was a 0.51 correlation with vertical span (number of levels). But again the size variable had to be reckoned with. On the present manufacturing sample, it correlated 0.47 with the technology measure (production continuity), 0.78 with structuring of activities, and 0.77 with vertical span. Again using the partial correlation technique, when (log) size was held constant, the correlation between structuring of activities and production continuity disappeared to just 0.07, and between vertical span and production continuity dropped to only 0.26. The correlations between production continuity and the structural variables with size partialled out (where the coefficient was greater than $=0.2$) are given in Table 1 (column 4). Again the prima facie relationship with structure does not survive closer examination.

Even so, a few remaining relationships are found once more among the job-count variables of configuration, where the percentages of employees in workflow control (Table 1, column 4) and in transport (column 3) respectively have some negative and some positive link with production continuity over and above their connections with size.

However, in general, even the use of this different scale, approximating a classification devised specifically for manufacturing organizations, fails to show widespread significant relationships with structure. Although the scales of workflow integration and production continuity are not dissimilar, being correlated 0.46, they are far from identical. Can this be reconciled with Woodward's own study where technology was thought to be the only factor that did vary with structural features?

Comparison with Woodward's Study

The two studies are difficult to compare directly. First, the operationalization in the form of the production continuity scale might categorize slightly differently from the way Woodward may have applied her categories, although the effect on the ordering of organizations should be negligible. There are then differences in data analyses. The analysis reported here was mainly by correlation, using categories along the scale; Woodward did not herself use her proposed 9- or 10-point classifications in presenting her results, but charted and compared the distributions of firms in each of three broad production groups only.

Most critical are the differences in sample. The biases in the industrial compositions of the two regions were reflected in the distribution of organizations. In South-East Essex in 1954–55, Woodward found firms in every production category, particularly chemical and similar plants at the process end of the continuum. The Birmingham sample in 1962–1964, however, left three categories vacant and had a high proportion of organizations in the batch production categories in the middle of the continuum due to the prominence of engineering industry in the region. There were also variations in sample sizes: 31 throughout

TABLE 3. COMPARISON WITH WOODWARD'S FINDINGS (1958, 1965)

South-East Essex findings		Equivalent Birmingham results ($N = 31$)	
Structural Variable	Relation-ship*	Structural Variable	Relation-ship†
"Length of line of command" ($N = 80$)	Positive linear	Vertical span	0.26‡§
"Span of control of chief executive" ($N = 80$)	Positive linear	Span of control of chief executive	0.08
"Ratio of direct to indirect labour" ($N = 75$)	Positive linear	Not available (total hourly paid indirect labour not separated from total nonworkflow personnel)	—
"Ratio of managers to total personnel" ($N = 45$)	Positive linear	Percentage of workflow superordinates to total employees	0.13
"Ratio of clerical and administrative staff to manual workers" ($N = 75$)	Positive linear	Percentage of nonworkflow personnel to total employees	0.04‡
"Span of control of first-line supervisors in production departments" ($N = 78$)	∩-shaped curvilinear	Subordinate–supervisor ratio	—0.09(0.36⁼)

* Relationship with "technological complexity" over three production groups; unit, batch-mass, process.
† Product-moment (linear) correlation with production continuity scale.
‡ Correlations with size shown in Table 1.
§ Not significant.
⁼ Correlation-ratio coefficient of nonlinear correlation (η).

in the Birmingham project, and 45, 75, 78, or 80 (from among 80 firms used in comparisons) on the several variables in South-East Essex. Finally, there is an important difference in the size range of the organizations. In Birmingham, this was 284 to 25,052 employees; in South-East Essex, Woodward (1965: 41) reported 35 of the total 92 firms available being between 100 and 250 employees, and only 17 over 1,000.

Table 3 summarizes the comparison on equivalent variables of structural *configuration*. Woodward presents data only on configuration variables, not on the other aspects of structure summarized in this study by the dimensions of structuring of activities and concentration of authority.

Table 3 shows that none of the univariate *linear* relations between configuration and technology suggested in South-East Essex were repeated in the Birmingham organizations. Yet Woodward (1965: 40) found relationships with "technological complexity" alone; for to her "there appeared to be no significant relations" between structure and size. It may be noted that in South-East Essex organizations technology and size appear to be unrelated.

Nor were the several *curvilinear* relationships with technology suggested in the discussion in Woodward's text (and not shown in Table 3) found in the Birmingham organizations. These were with a number of specialists, definition of duties and responsibilities (Woodward, 1965: 64), and amount of paperwork (1965: 67), all of which in the Birmingham sample were strongly and monotonically related to size (Table 1, column 2).

On the other hand, the ∩-shaped (concave curvilinear) relationship expected with first-line supervisor's span of control (i.e. subordinate–supervisor ratio, Table 1) *was* possible in the Birmingham results. This variable was not linearly correlated with production continuity, and reference to Table 1 (column 2) shows that it is among the few not also linked to size. Comparison as close as possible with Woodward's published data, that is, using only the broad unit production, batch–mass, process groupings, gave the confirmatory patterns shown in Table 4. The number of subordinates was greatest in the middle of the technology range, in large batch and mass. This is shown both in terms of median figures, as first published by Woodward (1958), and in the form of means calculated from her 1965 data, based on her revised 9-category classification of production systems.

A more precise indication of this relationship in the Birmingham data is given by the correlation-ratio coefficient of nonlinear correlation when η was found to be 0.36 (Table 1, column 3). This correlation might be greater were it not for the limited range of the Birmingham sample, in which the unit and process technology extremes were less well represented than in South-East Essex.

Relation of Operations Technology to Certain Structural Characteristics Only

This result on subordinate–supervisor ratio agrees with the assumptions in Burack's (1966) models, and with Starbuck's (1965: 509) thorough and sophisticated review, where six other studies, as well as Woodward's, were found to be consistent with the assumption of a ∩-shaped function on the variable of workers per foreman. More than that it suggested that other structural variables not linearly related to technology might show a curvilinear relationship. Such variables are found only in the configuration aspect of structure; once again, they are job-counts. Table 1, column 3, shows in parentheses the nonlinear coefficients with the two further variables where curvilinear relationships with production continuity were established; that is, the percentage employed in inspection and the percentage in maintenance. The proportions engaged in both these functions increase up to the large-batch stage of production and then tend to decline, as does the subordinate–supervisor ratio. Such relationships were not found in any other configuration variables, nor with the workflow integration scale.

Therefore, although a sweeping "technological imperative" hypothesis is not supported, a residual seven variables have been identified in the tests on manufacturing industry that do have associations with technology. These are:

Related to

Structural Variables	Production continuity	Workflow integration
Subordinate–supervisor ratio	∩-shaped curvilinear	—
Proportion in inspection	∩-shaped curvilinear	—
Proportion in maintenance	∩-shaped curvilinear	—
Proportion in workflow (production) control	negative linear	—
Proportion in transport and dispatch	positive linear	positive linear
Proportion in employment (personnel) specialization	—	negative linear
Proportion in buying and stocks specialization	—	negative linear

What is distinctive about these variables, as compared with the large number not related to technology? Subordinate–supervisor ratio is an element of organization at the level of the operative and his immediate superior. Obviously the number of men a supervisor requires to run a row of lathes differs from the number he requires to run the more continuous integrated workflow of an automatic transfer machine. Thus, subordinate–supervisor ratio is a structural variable which reflects activities directly bound up with the operations technology itself. This is true of the next four variables also. The relative numbers engaged in inspection and maintenance are linked to the variety of equipment and operations, which tends to be greatest in batch production. Workflow (production) control tends to decline in proportion after the batch stage, for it shows a negative linear relation, but this is complicated by the intrusion of some size effects. The transport and dispatch specialization largely reflects internal transport activities related to the workflow system. Thus these four specializations are activities visibly linked to production work. By comparison, activities such as accounting or market research are not so linked, and the proportions of employees in these activities do not correlate with technology. In

TABLE 4. SUBORDINATES PER FIRST-LINE SUPERVISOR IN MANUFACTURING ORGANIZATIONS

	Subordinates per first-line supervisor*			
	No. of firms/ organi- zations	Unit and small batch	Large batch and mass	Process
Medians† for each production category:				
South-East Essex	80	between 21 & 30	between 41 & 50	between 11 & 20
Birmingham	28‡	30	40	27
Means§ for each production category:				
South-East Essex	78‖	22	46	14
Birmingham	28‡	35	42	31

* First-line supervisor defined by Woodward (1965: 267), as "the lowest level official who spends more than half his time on the supervision of production operations. Working charge hands are not included. The classification, "production operators," includes the total staff of all production departments including laborers and others not necessarily on direct production work." Defined for the Birmingham study as the mean number of workflow (production) subordinates per first-line supervisor (that is, the lowest job in the hierarchy which does not include *prescribed* direct work on the throughput).

‡ Woodward's omission of firms in the "combined system" categories V and VIII of her 10-category classification and removal of the categories from her revised 9-category classification requires, for comparison, the omission of the three Birmingham organizations in these categories.

‖ Woodward's 1965 data on "averages" are on two firms fewer than her 1958 data on medians.

† Birmingham data calculated as from 10-category classification (Woodward, 1958: Figure 1); South-East Essex data from Woodward (1958: Figure 3).

§ Birmingham data calculated as from revised 9-category classification (Woodward, 1965: Figure 11); South-East Essex data from Woodward (1965: Figures 19, 20).

this light, it may be speculated that the otherwise puzzling relationships between the workflow integration scale and the proportions engaged in employment, and buying and stocks, might be due to the intermediate position of these activities. They are closer to the production work itself than is, say, accounting; but not so close as, say, inspection.

A two-part hypothesis emerges from these results. Associations with operations technology will be found only among variables of structure that are centered on the workflow. Such variables are likely to be job-counts of employees on production-linked activities, and not features of the wider administrative and hierarchical structure.

But the size of the organizations in South-East Essex ranged down to 100 employees, whereas the Birmingham sample had a minimum size of 250; and there were proportionately fewer multithousand units in Essex than in Birmingham.

Hence the two projects may not be irreconcilable if the hypothesis is construed to take account of size: *Structural variables will be associated with operations technology only where they are centered on the workflow. The smaller the organization the more its structure will be pervaded by such technological effects: the larger the organization, the more these effects will be confined to variables such as job-counts of employees on activities linked with the workflow itself, and will not be detectable in variables of the more remote administrative and hierarchical structure.*

This interpretation breaks the stalemate between the classical management theorists and the behavioral scientists. The management theorists may well be right (up to a point): in bigger manufacturing organizations—and it is with such organizations that the better known management writers have been most associated—the basic activities of management and their structural framework are probably not much affected by the particular operations technology employed. The behavioral scientists may well be equally right (up to a point): technology makes all the difference at "shop-floor" level, and throughout smaller organizations, where nothing is far removed from the workflow itself.

Interorganizational Relationships: Autonomy and Displacement of Goals*
PHILIP SELZNICK

In the wake of the general centralization of social (and especially economic) life, has followed inevitably the centralization of public authority. But this, like the centralization in other fields, is not unequivocally bad. Just as centrally managed private enterprises have achieved lowered costs, more efficient and wider distribution, and the advancement of science and invention, so too, centralized government has brought improvements which cannot be denied out of hand. Above all, it is necessary to see that in the ambiguous results of centralization there is a problem, a dilemma, which must be recognized explicitly and boldly faced so that new techniques of organization may be devised which, while preserving the essential good, will eliminate the more critical evils. This problem is pressing, for the disappearance of small units and local controls "lays bare the peculiar hazard of this modern

* Originally published by the University of California Press; reprinted by permission of The Regents of the University of California, from Philip Selznick, *TVA and the Grass Roots* (Berkeley, California: University of California Press, 1949), pp. 22–30, 37–44, 69–74, with omissions.

world: the danger implicit in vast size, the disaster consequent when power is exercised far from those who feel the effect of that power, remote and alien to their lives." (Lilienthal, 1940, mimeo.)

The recent history of American democracy has been in significant part, according to TVA doctrine, a history of the simultaneous broadening of the responsibilities and the field of intervention of national government. Although not without difficulties, and certainly without complete uniformity, the executive, legislative, and judicial departments of the federal government have alike accepted a widened view of the fields of regulation and positive construction in which Washington agencies might operate. These new national responsibilities have been accepted in response to (1) acute needs, such as unemployment, impossible to ignore and yet beyond the power of the states to handle; (2) the demands of large interest groups, including labor and agriculture, organized on a national scale and viewing the power of the federal government as both objective and instrument; (3) the growth of centralized industry requiring the counterbalance of a federal government strong enough to meet it on something like equal terms; and (4) the growth of collectivist ideology, supporting and justifying the trend toward over-all integration. National problems have demanded national recognition, and doubtless will continue to do so. This trend is irreversible; it would be idle to attempt to turn back the clock, to return to methods which offer no answer to the real and urgent problems posed by modern society and its technology.

At the same time, we are told, the question must be raised: is it necessary that the exercise of federal functions be identified with top-heavy organizations centered in and administered from Washington? For the most part this identification has been made. As statutes have been enacted recognizing new obligations of the national government, their administration has been delegated to existing departments and *ad hoc* agencies with headquarters in Washington, thus increasing the staffs, responsibilities, and functions centered at the national capital. If this procedure has sometimes effectively provided the services required, it has done so while retaining and extending the basic conception of a national government centrally administered.

This historic extension of centralized power has, in Lilienthal's view, created a justified feeling of uneasiness and distrust. Ordinary people and, increasingly, men in responsible posts in business and government have been understandably fearful of an unchecked growth of a vast administrative apparatus in Washington. It is in this proliferation of Washington-oriented agencies rather than in the mere grant of power to the federal authority that there is reason for fear. "This country is too big for such a pyramiding of direct responsibilities. For in spite of our triumphs over time and space, Washington is still remote from the average citizen and is sheltered from participation in his daily struggles" (1939: 4).

This fundamental evil of overcentralized government is accompanied by another: the inhibition of action through the proliferation of red tape. A centralized agency, remote from the field of operation, lays a deadening hand upon its officers "on the line" by relieving them of the responsibility for significant decision. In the interests of standardized practice and accountability in detail, the national headquarters is driven to insist that all important problems, and many that are not so important, be referred up the hierarchy, "through channels," for action. The consequences of this procedure are well known: delays when action is contemplated and the stifling of initiative in the face of a justified fear of being pitted against the resistance of the bureaucracy.

From these observations Lilienthal derives a fundamental dilemma. On the one hand, it must be conceded that increasingly large powers ought to be intrusted to the federal government, for there are too many basic problems which cannot be handled through the organs of local control; on the other hand, the centralization of large powers is always a menace to democracy. "It must be recognized that there is genuine peril if the powers of federal government are hopelessly outdistanced by the trend to centralized control in industry and commerce and finance"; still, "the dangers of centralized administration are all too evident. They cannot be ignored" (p. 7).

There is, of course, no single remedy, but it is believed in TVA that the theory of administrative decentralization, properly understood and wisely applied, will serve to check the growing tendency toward excessive centralization of federal administration. This is not a new idea, for there has been for some time an increasing awareness in Washington of the need for a greater measure of decentralization. But for the most part we have seen no fundamentally new departure, for the attempt by federal departments to set up regional offices and otherwise establish important nucleuses of administration in the field has left the old structure of control intact. The reins are held by the central offices and their various control divisions; these in turn are subject to the manifold restrictions (such as laws regulating procurement and accountability) which serve to crystallize and perpetuate the existing system of centralized control.

There has been, however, one federal agency which serves as an example of and an experiment in the decentralization of federal function. This is the Tennessee Valley Authority, "the boldest and perhaps most far-reaching effort of our times to decentralize the administration of federal functions. If it succeeds, if its methods prove to be sound, we shall have added strength to the administrative defenses which protect the future of our beleaguered democracy" (1939: 10). The TVA is invested with the authority of the national government, and derives its power from the exercise by the federal government of its constitutional prerogatives as interpreted in our time. At the same time, administration of these powers is effectively decentralized.

When the TVA was established, the programmatic responsibilities of the federal government for the control of the natural resources of water and land were brought together and treated as a unit in order to deal effectively with the watershed of the Tennessee River as an integrated area, a single problem in resource development. Thus one agency, located in the area of operation, represented the federal government in relation to a complex local problem. The TVA was not appended to any existing department, but was given freedom of action and a substantial measure of autonomy, subject only to the direct control of the President and Congress. The TVA Act, the agency's basic charter, was so framed as to give the Authority the power to make its own decisions, and thereby such flexibility as would make possible a maximum adjustment to local conditions. This delegation of discretion is the heart of the idea of grass-roots administration.

Thus the social problem to which the grass-roots theory is directed is of sweeping proportions. And though the technique of federal decentralization is not presented monolithically, as an only answer or a panacea, still it is clear that, in the mind of its chief proponent, it is more than a modest device linked to special problems within the federal system.

In a decade of existence as a decentralized federal agency, the TVA had the opportunity to formulate the special requirements which differentiate actual decentralization from the kind which represents little more than lip service. The goals have been variously stated, but uniformly include the following elements:

1. *The responsible agency in the area of operation is permitted the freedom to make significant decisions on its own account.* This assumes that the organization is to be independent, that it will not be made a part of some larger administrative agency having the power to write rules and regulations signed by the top administrator in Washington and hence immediately applicable with the force of law to the local operating organization. It further assumes that the field officers will be of a capacity and standing which will permit them to exercise broad discretion in adapting general policies to particular local situations, and to do this in such a way that their authority in local matters will be recognized by the local public. Moreover, this independent agency, if it engages in business functions, is to be permitted wide corporate freedom in the exercise of such managerial responsibilities as the selection of personnel, procurement, and disposition of operating funds.

2. *There must be active participation by the people themselves in the programs of the public enterprise.* The services of state and local agencies are to be utilized, with the federal government providing leadership that will strengthen rather than weaken or eliminate the existing agencies. Management should devise means to enlist the

active and conscious participation of the people through existing private associations as well as through *ad hoc* voluntary associations established in connection with the administration of the agency's program.

3. *The decentralized administrative agency is given a key role in coordinating the work of state, local, and federal programs in its area of operation; and a regional development agency should be given primary responsibility to deal with the resources of the area as a unified whole.* The place for the coordination of programs is in the field, away from the top offices which are preoccupied with jurisdictional disputes and organizational self-preservation. Coordination should be oriented to the job to be done, centering federal authority and its administrative skills and power upon the special needs and problems of the area.

These minimum essentials may be more clearly understood if they are examined as (1) the concept of managerial autonomy, (2) the partnership of TVA and local government, and (3) the ideal of basing unity of administration upon the natural unity of a region as an area of operation in resource development.

Managerial Autonomy

The TVA itself, as an autonomous administrative agency, "a corporation clothed with the power of government but possessed of the flexibility and initiative of a private enterprise" (Message of the President, 1933), embodies the first of the essentials of decentralized administration: the freedom to make significant decisions on its own account. This freedom from centralized control is in turn a condition for the realization of the second essential, for the decentralized agency must be able to make its own choices, on the basis of its experience in the field, in order to maximize the "participation of the people themselves."

To this end, the TVA has demanded managerial autonomy in its relation to the federal government. The Authority has insisted that if effective decentralization is to be achieved the organization must be permitted to retain real administrative powers unhampered by the administrative controls ordinarily exercised over government departments. Considered broadly, this demand has a wider significance than the establishment of the conditions of decentralized administration. It is also intended as revolt against the conception of government as a necessary evil and government officials as inherently tainted. In the eyes of some TVA officials, the stringent controls over personnel and financial policy normally exercised by civil service and budgetary agencies represent a cultural lag, still attuned to a governmental structure limited in scope and essentially parasitic rather than playing a significant positive role in social and economic life. The rationale of strong housekeeping controls seems to be weakened rather than strengthened by the conditions of the new state with its ever broadening functions. A new problem arises: not one of restricting the powers and functions of government, but of developing new techniques which will permit, within the framework of positive government, the exercise of initiative and the kind of independence which can forestall the rise of centralized bureaucracy. Can the benefits of anticorruptionist controls be obtained outside of the old administrative devices? This question, in the opinion of the Authority's leadership, can now be answered positively.

It is doubtful that the experience thus far accumulated is sufficient to permit any exhaustive listing of the administrative freedoms necessary for that degree of managerial autonomy required by administrative decentralization and yet consistent with a reasonable measure of broad control by the President and Congress. But it is possible to state three such conditions of autonomy which are considered fundamental by TVA:

1. Freedom from control by the Civil Service Commission.
2. Freedom from control by the General Accounting Office.
3. Freedom to apply revenues to current operational expenses.

The Partnership of TVA and the People's Institutions

After some difficulties and initial disagreements, but still very early in its history, the Authority defined its approach to cooperation with the agencies and institutions already existing in the Valley. The alternatives seemed to be two: either to take a line which assumed that the TVA itself could and should carry out its programs by direct action; or to accept as legitimate and efficient a method which would seek out and even establish local institutions to mediate between the TVA and the people of the area. It was felt that an imposed federal program would be alien and unwanted, and ultimately accomplish little, unless it brought together at the grass roots all the agencies concerned with and essential to the development of a region's resources: the local communities, voluntary private organizations, state agencies, and co-operating federal agencies. The vision of such a working partnership seemed to define "grass-roots democracy at work."

In the Authority's view, the fundamental rationale of the partnership approach is found in its implications for democracy. If the TVA can be "shaped by intimate association with long-established institutions" (H. A. Morgan, 1941, mimeo.), that will mean that its vitality is drawn from below. By working through state and local agencies, the Authority will provide the people of the Valley with more effective means by which to direct their own destinies. The TVA may then become more integrally a part of the region, committed to its interests and cognizant of its needs, and thus removed in thought and action from the remote impersonal bureaucracy of centralized government.

The moral dimension of the grass-roots approach has been emphasized many times. The methods of TVA are proffered as more than technical means for the achievement of administrative objectives. They include and underline the responsibility of leadership in a democracy to offer the people alternatives for free choice rather than ready-made prescriptions elaborated in the fastnesses of planning agencies. By 1936, Lilienthal had formulated the bases of such a policy.

> This matter of making a choice available, which is the duty of leadership, seems to me critically important. There are two ways of going about many of these matters. There, for example, is a steep slope which has been denuded of trees by the farmer. He has to make a living. He needs this steep slope to grow the things that will keep his family alive, and so he cuts the trees down and plants his corn, and the soil is washed off in a few years, and the nation has been robbed of just that much of its capital assets. . . . Now one way of going about it is to say, "We will pass a law that any farmer who cuts down the trees and cultivates a slope steeper than a certain grade is incapable of farming. He is injuring the community and the nation, and by this law we will take his land away from him and turn it back into forest or meadow." That is one way. . . . Then there is the other method, which the TVA has pursued, of giving the farmer a chance to make a choice; recognizing that the farmer does not cut down those trees because he enjoys cutting down trees or because he likes to see the soil washed off and destroyed but because he has a problem of feeding his family and making a living. Give him a choice—a free choice—by making it possible for him to use his land in such a way that he will not only be enabled to support his family but at the same time protect that soil against depredation. This is only one illustration of many of this conviction I have that a man must be given a free choice, rather than compelling a choice or having super-men make the choice for him. (Lilienthal, 1936, mimeo.)

In this way the Authority has applied a moral sanction to its program of giving the people and the existing institutions in the area a chance and the means to participate in an over-all program.

The orientation toward local agencies is also a product of the conception that the resources of a region include its institutions, in particular, its government agencies. The Authority deems it part of its obligation in connection with resource development that these local governmental institutions be strengthened rather than weakened, that they be supplemented rather than supplanted. In doing so, the Authority directs its effort toward developing a sense of responsibility on the part of the local organs and, what is equally important, toward providing them with a knowledge of the tools available to put that responsibility into action.

The TVA's policy of strengthening local institutions is linked to its broad responsibilities for regional development. Thus Gordon R. Clapp, formerly general manager and now chairman of TVA, has emphasized that maximum regional development is a function not only of the physical resources of a region but of administrative or managerial resources as well (1945). This must be evident to all who understand the difficulty of bridging the gap between a recognition of the needs of a region and the establishment of suitable methods for their fulfillment. Moreover, the plans of engineers and scientists depend for their effectuation upon the decisions and efforts of the people who actually operate upon the soil and other resources of the area. To attain the cooperation of these people is a matter not of simple exhortation, but of persuasion and organization, of practical attempts through the solutions of their individual problems to link them with the public goals of the TVA.

A list of agencies with which the TVA has maintained some form of cooperative relationship includes nearly all of the governmental institutions in the area: municipal power boards, rural electric cooperatives, school and library boards; state departments of health, conservation, and parks; state and local planning commissions, agricultural and engineering experiment stations, state extension services, and others. In developing these relationships TVA has applied the rule that "wherever possible, the Authority shall work toward achieving its objectives by utilizing or stimulating the developing of state and local organizations, agencies and institutions, rather than conducting direct action programs" (April 1943). In addition, a number of federal agencies, notable technical bureaus of the U.S. Departments of Agriculture and the Interior, the Army Engineers, and the Coast Guard, have cooperative arrangements with the TVA. Notable also are the *ad hoc* organizations and conferences which have been established as vehicles for cooperation among the administrative agencies within the Valley. These include, among others, a semiannual conference of directors of extension services and of agricultural experiment stations of the seven Valley states, the U.S. Department of Agriculture, and the TVA; the Tennessee Valley Trades and Labor Council, bringing together fifteen international unions of the American Federation of Labor Building and Metal Trades; an annual conference of contractors and distributors of TVA power; and the Tennessee Valley Library Council. Such gatherings help to lay a sound foundation for regional unity, focusing the efforts of many agencies on the region as a central problem.

The form of cooperation with state and local agencies varies, but the pattern of intergovernmental contract has been most fully developed. Such contracts often include reimbursement by the Authority for personnel and other facilities used by the state in carrying on the cooperative program. In many cases, the ideal outcome is viewed as the tapering off of TVA contributions until, as TVA's responsibilities recede in importance, the local agency carries on by itself. Thus the states have in some cases begun planning work through their own commissions with the material help of TVA; later, state funds have been secured with a view to continuing the work when TVA's responsibilities for the readjustment of reservoir-affected urban communities would terminate. In cooperating with the local governments, TVA attempts to establish a pattern which may be continued after TVA aid has ceased.

The objective of stimulating local responsibility among governments and associations within the area is basic to the grass-roots approach. But there are other reasons which support it as sound administrative policy. The existing facilities of the states, even though they may be inadequate, are used to capacity, thus avoiding the establishment of duplicate services and personnel with parallel functions. The TVA is not anxious to have its own men in the field and is willing to forego the prestige that comes from identification as "TVA men" of agents performing services paid for out of TVA funds. The staff is educated to feel most satisfied when it can show evidence that a local organization has carried on TVA work and been permanently strengthened by the experience and in the eyes of its public. In addition, utilization of existing agencies permits TVA to shape its program in conformity with the intimate knowledge of local conditions which such agencies are likely to have; at the same time it is possible to restrict the size of the Authority's direct working force.

The attempt to create a working partnership between the TVA and the people in carrying out a common program for regional development goes beyond the strengthening of existing governmental agencies, though this objective is vital. The meaning of the partnership is contained as well in the use of the voluntary association as a means of inviting the participation of the people most immediately concerned in the administration of the program. In this way, the farmer or the businessman finds a means of participating in the activities of government supplemental to his role on election day. If there is fertilizer to be distributed, farmers are invited, on a county and community basis, to participate in locally controlled organizations which will make decisions as to the most effective means of using that fertilizer in the local area. If government land is to be rented, a local land-use association is organized so that the conditions of rental can be determined with maximum benefit for the community. If power is to be sold in a rural area, a cooperative provides a consumer ownership which retains profits in the community and makes possible a management guided by community problems and local needs. If the business area of a city must be modified because of newly flooded lands, let a locally organized planning commission work out the best possible adjustment of special interests and long-range planning goals. Thus, at the end-point of operation, the specific consequences of a federal program may be shaped and directed by local citizens so that its impact at the grass roots will be determined in local terms. This procedure is not only democratic and just, but undoubtedly adds measurably to the effectiveness of the programs, which will be conjoined to the special desires of those affected and thus have the benefit of their support and aid.

The policy of consciously working with and through local institutions is, in the Authority's view, integrally related to its relatively autonomous position within the federal system. It is precisely the flexibility accorded to the TVA management which has enabled it to keep in mind its broad concept of regional development and at the same time to seize upon whatever opportunities might arise to implement the concept concretely. Nationally directed restrictions as to employment of personnel, a host of regulations framed in national terms, would doubtless greatly restrict the ability of TVA to establish procedures attuned both to its substantive objectives and to the grass-roots methods by which they are carried out. It would surely inhibit the freedom to search out techniques uniquely adapted to the special situations of some particular state government or community if TVA did not have the power to make its own decisions and to take the initiative in fostering cooperative relationships. Moreover, the absence of discretion might well be psychologically decisive in hobbling the TVA stall by binding it to the customs and traditional modes of action laid down by the broader hierarchy into which it might be absorbed.

Decentralization and Regional Unity

While the problem of method is the nub of the TVA approach, the latter may not be divorced from the program which called it into being. The outlook of the TVA leadership stresses decentralization as vital not only for the future of democratic government but also as an indispensable tool for the effective development of regional resources. The TVA idea is also a regional idea which looks toward the formulation and execution of a unified program for resource development; and it is believed that responsibility and authority for the fulfillment of such a program should be allocated to a single agency. This does not mean that a single agency will actually carry out all the necessary activities, but it does mean that it will provide over-all direction in terms of regional goals. It means that governmental initiative, localized and focused in an agency which has responsibility for unified development, will be available to seize opportunities as they may arise, and to make the most of them.

Any general extension of the TVA idea must plainly be rooted in a recognition of the diversity of needs and potentials which characterizes the various sections of the United States. This diversity demands flexibility on the part of federal authority and the use of a method which can adjust a national program to the special problems of the area of operation. It is difficult and perhaps impossible to specify in any exact way how the lines may be drawn around an area to say this is a Region (Lilienthal, 1945: 167). That will have to be done in terms of the existence of a problem area, or a resource base, or some other criterion or combination of criteria which will serve to reflect the practical unity which ordinary men understand when they associate together for regional objectives. What is important is not precise specification or neat boundaries, but the recognition of focuses of potentiality and need which, treated as wholes, can contribute most effectively to regional development and thereby to national welfare. Diversity in nature and tradition requires diversity in program and policy; for the idea of regional administration is frankly opposed to those forces which strive to introduce uniformity into all aspects of government programs.

The decentralized regional agency offers a means of creating a center of regional responsibility, planning, and coordination within the framework of the existing federal system. Through it, functions too broad to be undertaken by a single state and yet not actually national in scope may be initiated at the proper level and given direction and scope in terms of the special problems of an area, at the same time that national policy may be brought to bear upon regional needs. Such staff agencies as the Bureau of the Budget and a National Resources Planning Board can, as integral parts of the Presidency, direct from the national government matters of broad perspective. The decentralized regional agency is, however, not the same as the regionalization of national agencies through the establishment of field offices. Such federal outposts are not charged with responsibility for integral regional development; and, equally important, regional unity demands the continuous development of a program based on study and decision in the field. A truly regional agency is multifunctional and single purposed. It has the means and the authority to engage in or to initiate several major and many lesser projects in accordance with the developmental needs of the area. At the same time, the outlook of the agency is integral, devoted to the unified and conservative exploitation of the region as a whole.

A regional agency is the reflection of the physical unity of the resource base of the region. In the Tennessee Valley, the control of water in the river channel is bound to the control of water on the land. The river requires a unified system of dams and reservoirs; the land requires the development of sound agricultural practices and the wider use of phosphatic fertilizers. These jobs require different techniques and specialized personnel, but the development of the area demands that they be seen as a whole, as they affect each other. A regional agency can undertake to bring those perspectives together; it can also take into account the social consequences of its programs as the TVA does when it aids communities to intelligently readjust themselves to newly created reservoirs, and flooded-out farmers to relocate. The interrelation of social phenomena makes for a spreading network of consequences following in the wake of action; as a result, a special public emerges. It is this public, plus the national interest ultimately involved, which forms the political basis for the decentralized structure of the regional agency.

So runs the official doctrine.

Inherent Dilemmas

Tension and dilemma are normal and anticipated corollaries of the attempt to control human institutions in the light of an abstract doctrine. Social structures are precipitants of behavior undertaken in many directions and for many purposes. Mutual adaptation establishes only an uneasy equilibrium. This in turn is continuously modified and disturbed as the consequences of action ramify in unanticipated ways. Practical leadership cannot long ignore the resistance of social structure, and is often moved thereby to abandon concern for abstract goals or ideals —for which it is often criticized out of hand by the moralists and idealists who lack experience with the vicissitudes of practical action. (Merton, 1945: 413). But a leadership which, for whatever reason, elects to be identified with a doctrine and professes to use it in action, is continuously faced with tensions between the idea and the act. Ideological symbols may fulfill useful functions of communication and defense and may be long sustained as meaningful even when effective criteria of judgment remain lacking; but an act entails responsibility, establishing alliances and commitments which demand attention and deference.

This is not to suggest that ideals are futile and abstractions useless. Tension does not mean defeat, nor does dilemma enforce paralysis. It is precisely the problem of leadership to find a means, through compromise, restraint, and persuasion, to resolve tensions and escape dilemmas. But in doing so, attention must be directed to the real forces and tendencies which underlie its difficulties. This is the constructive function of analysis which seeks to take account of structural rigidities and the indirect consequences of executive action. Where such analysis is considered destructive, it is usually because doctrine, assuming an ideological role, is not meant to be analyzed. In extreme cases, unanalyzed doctrine ceases to operate in action at all, and the real criteria of decision are hidden is a shadowland of unrecognized discretion determined opportunistically by immediate exigency.

The TVA, in relation to its policy of grass-roots administration, is not immune to such difficulties. Though seldom made explicit, sources of tension are recognized by members of the staff, and have already entered into the process of administrative decision. Among these may be noted:

1. *There is a dilemma of doctrine and commitment, or of the abstract and concrete* (1939: 11). This dilemma is the most general source of the tensions inherent in the grass-roots approach, for it inheres as well in all behavior which involves both the verbalization of ideas and a set of specific activities. Doctrine, being abstract, is judiciously selective, and may be qualified at will in discourse, subject only to the restrictions of sense and logic. But action is concrete, generating consequences which define a sphere of interest and responsibility, together with a corresponding chain of commitments. Fundamentally, the discrepancy between doctrine and commitment arises from the essential distinction between the interrelation of ideas and the interaction of phenomena. The former is involved in doctrine, the latter in action. Of course this is the ground of the normal necessity to revise decisions and even over-all doctrine in the light of events. The tension between the abstract and the concrete is resolved through continuous executive action. However, where doctrine itself creates commitment, as in the institutionalization of policy, executive decision is not readily reversible. Policy which ostensibly should be determined on the basis of a scientific appraisal of practical means for the achievement of formal ends becomes invested with prestige and survival value and may persist as official doctrine despite a weakening of its instrumental power. Whatever instrumental capacity the policy does have is related to informal rather than professed goals.

2. *There is also the dilemma of consent and conformance (1939: 10), or of selective decision and total involvement.* Democracy as method, and the grass-roots policy as method represent processes of decision. Decision, however, demands only the partial consent of the participants, who are involved only obliquely in their capacity as voters or choosers. But the execution of decision is a matter of action, which tends to involve the participants as wholes. Hence cooperative action, as Barnard says, "requires substantially complete conformance."

   In other words, while the choice of a given course of action may be conceived of as involving the individual or group only to a limited degree, in fact there is a tendency for circumstances to demand more extensive involvement. Organizational action, once initiated, tends to push onward, so that the initiator may be enmeshed in new relationships and demands beyond his original intention. Here again the key word is "commitment." Every executive knows that the initiation of a new course of action is a serious matter precisely because of the risk involved that the establishment of precedents, of new machinery and new relationships, the generation of new and complex interests may make greater demands upon his organization than he can presently foresee. The problem is not one of inner impulse, but rather of the structural forces which summon action and constrain decision. This structurally induced tendency is roughly comparable to the notion of adience as applied in the theory of animal drive.

Conformance, indispensable to the completion of the movement begun by decision, has therefore a qualifying effect and creates an inescapable tension. This means, in respect to the TVA, that while its decentralist policy may be instituted for special reasons (referable in part to the ideals of the leadership as well as to other factors), nevertheless there will be a tendency for the organization as a whole to be shaped by the process of conformance. It will have to go farther in carrying out the policy than it may have originally intended; the formal process of consent will have been transformed into concrete institutional relationships, generating new and unlooked-for demands. Generally, the problem of checking conformance is present in all administrative decisions concerning relationships established under the grass-roots formula.

3. *So far as discretion is delegated, bifurcation of policy and administration is reinforced.* It is basic policy inside the Authority that planning and execution should be united in a single administrative organ. But the delegation of functions involved in the grass-roots approach makes insistence upon this principle of unity somewhat anomalous. The channeling of programs through independent agencies necessarily delegates discretion, hence programs may be extensively modified in execution. The dilemma is only made more explicit if controls are instituted which operate objectively to transform the independent local agency into an administrative arm of the Authority: execution may be brought into line with policy, but the grass-roots objective will have been undermined. The dilemma is mitigated to the extent that a denial is made of the possibility of a difference in objective between the initiating and the executing agency. An attempt in this direction made in the TVA's agricultural program will be described in a later chapter.

4. *Theories about government become preempted by social forces.* It is unrealistic to estimate the implications of a theory of government on the basis of its abstract formulation. The propagation of a point of view carries with it an often unwished-for alliance with others who, for their own reasons, are espousing the same or a convergent doctrine. A theory about method may at any given time be linked with a special substantive doctrine; support for the method may imply a position on program, and conversely. Thus TVA finds itself

in the camp of the supporters of "states' rights" both in its criticism of over-centralization in government and in its support of the state governments—as "regional resources"—in its area of operation. But at the same time, in respect to the complex of political issues summed up in the extension of "positive government," the Authority's point of view is very far from that of the general run of supporters of local sovereignty. TVA is therefore in the continuously ambivalent position of choosing between an emphasis on method and an emphasis on substantive program, or more accurately, of assigning a priority to one or the other. To the extent that the movement for planning and a strong federal government oriented along welfare lines is identified with the existing federal structure, the TVA leadership tends to emphasize method as basic and cut itself off from the general welfare movement. But it cannot divorce itself completely from its antecedents, and the ambivalence persists.

5. *Emphasis on existing institutions as democratic instruments may wed the agency to the status quo.* A procedure which channels the administration of a program through established local institutions, governmental or private, tends to reinforce the legitimacy of the existing leadership. This is especially true when a settled pattern claims the exclusive attention of the agency, so that other groups striving for leadership may find their position relatively weakened after the new relationships have been defined. In strengthening the land-grant colleges in its area, the TVA has bolstered the position of the existing farm leadership. There is some evidence that in the process of establishing its pattern of cooperation, TVA refrained from strengthening independent colleges in the area not associated with the land-grant college system. Again, the relatively dominant role of the American Federation of Labor unions in TVA labor relations, especially as constituting the Tennessee Valley Trades and Labor Council, is objectively a hindrance to the development of labor groups having other affiliations. In general, to the extent that the agency selects one set of institutions within a given field as the group through which it will work, the possibility of freezing existing social relationships is enhanced. At least in its agricultural program, TVA has chosen to limit its cooperative relationships to a special group so that the potential or inherent dilemma has been made explicit.

6. *Decision at the grass roots may be inhibited by the system of national pressure groups.* When important issues become crystallized in the program of a group organized on a broad scale with a national leadership, local decisions may be influenced primarily by their effect on the outcome of over-all controversy. The local problem is appraised not for its own sake but for the influence of a local decision on the general bargaining position of the leadership. Thus a

local branch of the American Farm Bureau Federation of a CIO union may have its attitudes framed for it by a long-run national strategy, as by a pending bill in Congress for the transfer of functions from one agency to another, or an impending organizing drive, or a national election. To the extent that a decentralized governmental agency is influenced by decisions made by local groups in national terms, it would appear that the grass-roots approach becomes the victim of the growing centralization of political decision.

7. *Commitment to existing agencies may shape and inhibit policy in unanticipated ways.* When the channels of action are restricted, programs may be elaborated only within the limits established by the nature of the cooperating organizations. The traditions and outlook of an established institution will resist goals which appear to be alien, and the initiating agency will tend to avoid difficulties by restricting its own proposals to those which can be feasibly carried out by the grass-roots organization. Where the grass-roots method is ignored, new institutions may be built, shaped *ab initio* in terms of the desired program. An attempt to carry forward a policy of nondiscrimination (as against Negroes) will not proceed very far when the instrument for carrying out this policy—usually as an adjunct of some broader program—has traditions of its own of a contrary bent. Moreover, the grass-roots policy voluntarily creates nucleuses of power which may be used for the furtherance of interests outside the system of cooperation originally established. Thus the TVA distributes electric power through electric power boards which are creatures of municipalities, with the contractual reservation that surplus income shall be used only for improvements in the system or for the reduction of rates. But the question has been raised: what if pressure arises to use surpluses for general purposes, that is, to finance nonpower functions of the municipal governments? And what if the state governments undertake to tax these surpluses, because of a restricted tax base and unwillingness to institute a state income tax? The logic of the grass-roots policy might force the Authority to agree. However, it is perhaps more likely that the Authority's commitment to function as a successful power project would take precedence over the grass-roots method.

8. *Existing agencies inhibit a direct approach to the local citizenry.* The participation of local people always takes place through some organizational mechanism, notably voluntary associations established to involve a public in some measure of decision at the endpoint of operation. But such associations are commonly adjuncts of an administrative agency which jealously guards all approaches to its clientele. If, therefore, a federal agency establishes cooperative relations with such an agency, it will be committed as well to the system of voluntary associations which has been established.

Hence the channels of participation of local people in the federal program will be shaped by the intermediary agency. In respect to its closeness to the people, the status of the federal government may not, in such circumstances, be materially altered. Viewed from this perspective, the grass-roots method becomes an effective means whereby an intrenched bureaucracy protects its clientele, and also itself, from the encroachments of the federal government.

Organizational Size, Complexity, and Formalization*

RICHARD H. HALL, NORMAN J. JOHNSON, and J. EUGENE HAAS

The relationship between organizational size and organizational structure has been a persistent subject in the literature. However, interest in this area, which has been expressed at both the inferential and empirical levels, has not resulted in a definitive set of propositions or findings. The present study, based on data from 75 organizations, examines the relationships between the size factor and measures of organizational complexity and formalization.

Size

It is commonly noted that the size of an organization somehow "makes a difference" in other structural characteristics. Caplow (1957: 484–505; 1965: 25–28) and Grusky (1961: 269), among others, have assumed that large organizations are, by definition, more complex and formalized than small organizations, while Blau and Scott (1962: 7) and Zelditch and Hopkins (1961: 470) have argued that size may not be such a critical factor. At the same time, these latter authors appear not to question the relationship between size and other structural components. In short, there is agreement that size affects structure, but there is no agreement on the relative importance of size *vis-à-vis* other aspects of organizational structure.

Empirical studies using size as a major variable also have come to rather contradictory conclusions. For example, Chapin (1951: 835–836) and Tsouderos (1955: 206–210) suggest that increased size is related to an increased degree of bureaucratization. Hall (1963: 38–46), on the other hand, found that size was not a major factor in determin-

* Reprinted from the *American Sociological Review, 32* (December 1967), pp. 903–912, with permission of the authors and the publisher.

ing the degree of bureaucratization in organizations. Despite the limited scope of these studies, they do begin to suggest that some assumptions about size must be systematically investigated before the fact that an organization is "large" can be taken as an indicator of other important structural characteristics.

The growing number of investigations of the relative size of the supportive or administrative component of organizations provides additional evidence that the present state of knowledge about size is inconclusive. While the relative size of the administrative component is not central to this study, the nature of the findings in this area is indicative of the problems associated with the utilization of size as a major analytic variable. Terrien and Mills (1955: 11–14) suggest that the administrative component increases disproportionately in size as organizational size increases. Anderson and Warkov (1961: 23–28) and Bendix (1956: Table 7, p. 222), on the other hand, found that larger organizations contained a smaller proportion of personnel engaged in administration. Recent studies by Hawley et al. (1965: 252–255), and Haas et al. (1963: 9–17), suggest that this relationship may be curvilinear, with the administrative component at first increasing disproportionately in size and then decreasing with further organizational growth. It should be noted that the administrative component has been defined somewhat differently in each of these studies.

Regardless of the exact nature of this relationship, the studies noted share a number of characteristics which are part of the problem confronting research on organizations in general. First, many studies include one or only a few organizations as the "sample." This obviously limits the study to inferences in regard to size, since comparisons within the same research context and across organizational types are not available. A second factor is that those studies which have included a larger number of organizations have typically concentrated on only one type of organization, such as mental hospitals, manufacturing firms, or school districts. If the size factor is important in its relationships to other organizational phenomena, this importance should be demonstrable in a large sample of varying types of organizations.

Determination of organizational size for this study was quite simple. The total number of paid employees in an organization was taken as an accurate measure of size. In cases where all or most of the organizations' members were either part-time or voluntary workers, a technique was devised to convert these members to "full-time equivalent" members. This standardized measure was used for all organizations.

Complexity

The importance of complexity as a variable in organizational analyses has been stressed by Zelditch and Hopkins, who note: "Large size, in our view, is not in itself a critical characteristic of organizations.

Rather what appears to be important here is complexity, which is often indicated by size but is quite distinct from it (1961: 470)." Blau and Scott also suggest the centrality of complexity when they comment: "Since formal organizations are often very large and complex, some authors refer to them as 'large-scale' or as 'complex' organizations (1962)." These authors then suggest that usage of "complex" in naming a whole area of analysis (complex organizations) is misleading because of the wide variations in complexity which exist among organizations.

While there appears to be agreement that the degree of complexity of an organization is important in organizational analysis, there is only a limited number of attempts to operationalize the concept. Hage has suggested that, "The complexity, or specialization, in an organization is measured by the number of occupational specialties included and the length of training required by each. The greater the number of occupations and the longer the period of training required, the more complex the organization (1965: 294)." The emphasis on occupational types and the amount of training required of these types suggest that only one aspect of complexity, in this case specialization, is considered in this approach. A broader view of the complexity issue is offered by Pugh, Hickson, *et al.*, in their discussion of the components of organizational structure. While the term they use is "configuration," their meaning appears to be closer to the more general issue of structural complexity. They suggest that, "Every work organization has an authority structure. . . . The shape or configuration of this structure may be compared in different organizations (1963: 305)." Components of this configuration (structural complexity) are vertical and lateral spans of control, the criteria for segmentation and the number of positions in various segments. These authors also suggest that size is apt to be a major determining factor of organizational structure.

In a similar vein, Kahn, Wolfe, *et al.*, suggest that, "With increased size, the structure of the organization becomes much more complex. The division of labor becomes more differentiated and specialized; more levels of supervision are introduced to maintain coordination and control; and more people become involved in organizational planning (1964: 75)."

These approaches to complexity suggest that it is a structural condition which itself contains a number of components. While such discussions imply that structural complexity is related to complexity in interpersonal and intraorganizational relationships, the concern here is simply structural complexity approached through multiple components or indicators. The definition of complexity, which appears to encompass the considerations discussed above, is the degree of internal segmentation—the number of separate "parts" of the organization as reflected by the division of labor, number of hierarchical levels, and the spatial dispersion of the organization. The indicators used are:

A. Division of Labor—General
   1. The number of distinct organization goals—multiple goals indicating a necessary division of labor beyond that required by a single goal.
   2. Presence of more than one major organizational activity.
B. Division of Labor—Specific
   1. The number of major divisions or departments (horizontal differentiation).
   2. The most specialized department (number of distinct subdivisions under major departmental headings).
   3. Mean intradepartmental subdivision (the total number of subdivisions divided by the number of departments).
C. Hierarchical Differentiation
   1. Number of levels in the deepest single division.
   2. The mean number of hierarchical levels for the organization as a whole (the sum of the number of hierarchical levels within every department divided by the number of departments).
D. Spatial Dispersion
   1. The degree to which physical facilities are spatially dispersed.
   2. The location (distance from the organizational headquarters) of spatially dispersed facilities.
   3. The degree to which personnel are spatially dispersed.
   4. The location of spatially dispersed personnel.

No assumption is made about the priority of these indicators. While Hage considers the division of labor or specialization to be the key factor, the other indicators also appear to be central to the complexity concept. The measurement of these indicators will be discussed below.

Formalization

The concept of organizational formalization has been rather explicitly defined and utilized. Hage (1965: 295), and later Aiken and Hage (1966: 499), have suggested that formalization "is measured by the proportion of codified jobs and the range of variation that is tolerated within the rules defining the jobs. The higher the proportion of codified jobs and the less the range of variation allowed, the more formalized the organization." Pugh, Hickson, *et al.* note that "formalization or standardization . . . includes statements of procedures, rules, roles, and operation of procedures which deal with (a) decision seeking (applications for capital, employment, and so on), (b) conveying of decisions and instructions (plans, minutes, requisitions, and so on), and (c) conveying of information, including feedback (1963: 303–304)."
     As in the case of complexity, a series of indicators is used to

measure the degree of formalization in the organizations examined following the broader meaning of the concept used by Pugh, Hickson, *et al.* Here again, no priority among the indicators is assumed. The indicators of formalization used in this study are:

A. Roles
    1. The degree to which the positions in the organization are concretely defined.
    2. The presence or absence of written job descriptions.
B. Authority Relations
    1. The degree to which the authority structure is formalized (clear definition of the hierarchy of authority).
    2. The extent to which the authority structure is formalized in writing.
C. Communications
    1. The degree of emphasis on written communications.
    2. The degree of emphasis on going through established channels in the communications process.
D. Norms and Sanctions
    1. The number of written rules and policies.
    2. The degree to which penalties for rule violation are clearly stipulated.
    3. The extent to which penalties for rule violation are codified in writing.
E. Procedures
    1. The degree of formalization of orientation programs for new members (systematic socialization for all new entrants).
    2. The degree of formalization of inservice training programs for new members (systematic and continuing socialization of new members).

Methodology

The present research includes organizations ranging in size from six members to over 9,000 members. The organizations represent a wide range of types, such as educational, commercial, military, governmental, manufacturing, religious, and penal organizations.

The list in Table 1 represents a selection, rather than a sample, from the organizational universe. Selection was based, to a degree, on the fact that purposeful inclusion of certain types of organizations was desired and that budgetary and time factors were of some consequence. A more central point is that there is no clearly defined organizational universe from which such a sample could have been drawn. Organizational research sampling necessarily has to be purposeful and non-random.

TABLE 1. ORGANIZATIONS INCLUDED IN STUDY

Organizational Type	N	Organizational Type (N of 1)
Manufacturing Plant	8	County Political Party
State Penal Institution	6	City Recreation Department
Delinquent Reformatory	4	Post Office
Retail Store	3	Public Utility
State or Area Church	3	Fund Raising Agency
Trade or Lobbying Assn.	2	Railroad
University	2	Trucking Firm
Bank	2	Law Enforcement Agency
Labor Union	2	Municipal Airport
Govt. Regulative Agency	2	Public Transit Firm
Marketing Organization	2	Insurance Company
Hotel-Motel	2	Private School
Restaurant	2	Church Congregation
Public School System	2	Parochial School System
Private Welfare Agency	2	Medical Association
Farm Cooperative	2	School for Mentally Retarded
State Hospital	2	Private Hospital
Racial-Ethnic-Religious Assn.	2	Quarry
Newspaper	2	Military Command
Television Station	2	Private Country Club
		Religious Order

Data were gathered by tape recorded interviews in the 75 organizations. In addition, supporting materials in the form of all printed matter relevant to each organization were examined, and the process of categorizing each of the organizations on each cf the variables was begun. The majority of the categorizations were accomplished with little difficulty. On variables such as size, number of hierarchical levels, and the number and specificity of written rules and policies, the range and distribution of the data provided "natural" categories.

On variables such as the degree of emphasis on written communications or the degree to which the authority structure is formalized, the task of categorization was more difficult. The research team itself decided upon the final classification. Where the data from the original interviews were insufficient for agreement on proper placement, additional organizational information was obtained. The final categorizations represent the nature of the data and the judgments of the researchers.

The data were such that statistical analysis was limited to the use of Kendall's Tau C as a measure of association (1960: 319–324). While some information appeared to be continuous, such as size and number of departments, there was no assurance that this sample represented the universe. Most of the data were in the form of discrete categories.

Where necessary, categories were combined in order to follow standard statistical procedures.

Findings

In general, the findings of this study in regard to size are similar to those of previous research which utilized size as a major variable; that is, the relationships between size and other structural components are inconsistent. As Tables 2 and 3 indicate, there is a slight tendency for larger organizations to be both more complex and more formalized, but on only a few variables does this relationship prove to be strong. On others, there is little, if any established relationship.

The complexity indicators related to size fall within three major categories. The first of these is spatial dispersion. This conclusion, in which both physical facilities and personnel are considered, is congruent with the suggestion of Anderson and Warkov (1961) that the relative size of the supportive component is also related to spatial dispersion. On a common sense basis, such dispersion is possible only for sufficiently large organizations. A decision to add dispersed facilities may require a secondary decision to add more personnel, rather than the reverse. It also appears that a very large or extensive "market" for the organization's product or service is necessary to support a very large organization. Apparently, such an extensive market is more easily or economically reached through physical dispersion. Thus, it could be argued that both size and complexity are dependent upon available economic "input," and to the extent to which such potential "input" is dispersed, large organizations will also be more complex in regard to physical dispersion.

A second set of significant relationships is found in regard to the hierarchical differentiation. Although Woodward has noted differences in the "width" of the span of control according to the technological stages of industry (1958), the generally accepted principle of limiting the number of subordinates supervised by one person seems to be operative here. More hierarchical levels are found in larger organizations.

The third set of significant relationships is in the area of intradepartmental specialization or the specific division of labor. While the number of divisions is not related to size, this form of internal differentiation is. Performance of the major organizational activities plus such prerequisites as accounting and personnel management apparently are accomplished by departmentalization regardless of organizational size (Haas, et al., 1963: 16). Further specialization may take place within the existing departmental structure as the organization grows in size.

In general, the relationships between size and the complexity indicators appear to be limited to a few factors. Even in those relationships found to be statistically significant, enough deviant cases exist to cast serious doubts on the assumption that large organizations are necessarily more complex than small organizations.

The same general conclusion can be reached in regard to the formalization indicators as demonstrated in Table 3. Relatively strong relationships exist between size and the formalization of the authority structure (B–1), the stipulation of penalties for rule violation in writing (D–3), and orientation and in-service training procedures (E–1 and E–2). A general association does exist to the extent that larger organizations tend to be more formalized on the other indicators, even though the relationship is quite weak.

The most immediate implication of these findings is that neither complexity nor formalization can be implied from knowledge of organizational size. A social scientist conducting research in a large organization would do well to question the frequent assumption that the organization under study is necessarily highly complex and formalized. If these two general factors are relevant to the focus of his research, he will need to examine empirically, for each organization, the level of complexity and formalization extant at the time. The ideal research procedure would be to have standardized measures of these phenomena to allow comparative research. At the minimum, the degrees to which these phenomena are present should be specified, at least nominally.

A second implication of these findings lies in the area of social control. Increased organizational formalization is a means of controlling the behavior of the members of the organization by limiting individual discretion. At least one aspect of complexity, hierarchical differentiation, also is related to social control in that multiple organizational levels serve as a means of maintaining close supervision of subordinates. It seems rather clear, on the basis of this evidence, that a large organization does not necessarily have to rely upon impersonal, formalized control mechanisms. At the same time, the fact that an organization is small cannot be taken as evidence that a *gemeinschafft* sort of social system is operating. An organization need not turn to formalization if other control mechanisms are present. One such control mechanism is the level of professionalization of the work force as Hage (1965: 300) and Blau *et al.* (1966: 184), have suggested. The organizations with more professionalized staffs probably exhibit less formalization.

These findings suggest that size may be rather irrelevant as a factor in determining organizational structure. Blau *et al.,* have indicated that structural differentiation is a *consequence* of expanding size (1962: 185). Our study suggests that it is relatively rare that the two factors are even associated and thus the temporal sequence or causality (expanding size produces greater differentiation) posited by Blau and colleagues is open to question. In those cases where size and

TABLE 2.   COMPLEXITY INDICATORS BY ORGANIZATIONAL SIZE

	Size		
	Less than 100 (N = 20)	100–999 (N = 35)	1,000 or more (N = 20)
A. Division of Labor—General			
1. Number of Goals			
1	30%	29%	20%
2	45%	46%	45%
3 or more	25%	25%	35%
Kendall's Tau C = .08			
2. Presence of Second Major Activity			
No second activity	65%	69%	70%
Second activity present	35%	31%	30%
Kendall's Tau C = .04			
B. Division of Labor—Specific			
1. Number of Major Divisions (Horizontal Differentiation)			
1–4	30%	20%	25%
5–6	20%	37%	25%
7 or more	50%	43%	50%
Kendall's Tau C = .02			
2. Divisions within Most Specialized Single Department			
1–3 subdivisions	55%	23%	5%
4–6 subdivisions	20%	26%	45%
7 or more subdivisions	25%	51%	50%
Kendall's Tau C = .27			
3. Mean Number of Subdivisions per Department			
1 or 2 subdivisions	70%	29%	20%
3 subdivisions	20%	29%	25%
4 or more subdivisions	10%	42%	55%
Kendall's Tau C = .35			
C. Hierarchial Differentiation			
1. Number of Levels in Deepest Single Division			
two or three levels	55%	14%	10%
four levels	35%	43%	40%
five or more levels	10%	43%	50%
Kendall's Tau C = .35			

TABLE 2 (*Continued*)

	Size		
	Less than 100 (*N* = 20)	100–999 (*N* = 35)	1,000 or more (*N* = 20)
2. Mean Number of Levels for Organization as a Whole (Vertical Differentiation)			
two or three	90%	60%	50%
four or more	10%	40%	50%
Kendall's Tau *C* = .31			
D. Spatial Dispersion			
1. Dispersion of Physical Facilities			
All in one location	45%	46%	25%
Mostly in one location, some in field	30%	37%	35%
Mostly in field (dispersed)	25%	17%	40%
Kendall's Tau *C* = .14			
2. Location of Physical Facilities			
1 location	45%	46%	20%
Within city or county	35%	17%	20%
State-national-international	20%	37%	60%
Kendall's Tau *C* = .23			
3. Degree of Dispersion of Personnel			
All in one location	35%	34%	16%
Mostly at one location, some in field	25%	34%	47%
Mostly in field (dispersed)	40%	32%	37%
Kendall's Tau *C* = .06			
4. Location of Personnel			
1 location	35%	34%	15%
Within city or county	40%	20%	15%
State-national-international	25%	46%	70%
Kendall's Tau *C* = .24			

complexity are associated, the sequence may well be the reverse. If a decision is made to enlarge the number of functions or activities carried out in an organization, it then becomes necessary to add more members to staff the new functional areas. Clearly, what are needed

TABLE 3. FORMALIZATION INDICATORS BY ORGANIZATIONAL SIZE

	Size		
	Less than 100 (N = 20)	100–999 (N = 35)	1,000 or more (N = 20)
A. Roles			
1. Concreteness of Positional Descriptions			
Low	45%	17%	20%
Medium	35%	46%	55%
High	20%	37%	25%
Kendall's Tau C = .12			
2. Presence of Written Job Descriptions			
None	35%	26%	20%
Present only at some levels	40%	23%	50%
Present throughout organization	25%	51%	30%
Kendall's Tau C = .01			
B. Authority Relations			
1. Degree of Formalization of Authority Structure			
Low or medium	58%	32%	26%
High	42%	68%	74%
Kendall's Tau C = .25			
2. Codification of Authority Structure in Writing			
Not codified	58%	26%	47%
Codified	42%	74%	53%
Kendall's Tau C = .08			
C. Communications			
1. Degree of Emphasis on Written Communications			
Low	35%	17%	30%
Medium	55%	57%	55%
High	10%	26%	15%
Kendall's Tau C = .05			
2. Emphasis on Using Established Communications Channels			
Low	35%	23%	15%
Medium	25%	37%	30%
High	40%	40%	55%
Kendall's Tau C = .13			

TABLE 3 *(Continued)*

	Size		
	Less than 100 (*N* = 20)	100–999 (*N* = 35)	1,000 or more (*N* = 20)
D. Norms and Sanctions			
1. Number of Written Rules and Policies			
Less than 12	32%	17%	21%
More than 12	68%	83%	79%
Kendall's Tau *C* = .08			
2. Penalties for Rule Violation Clearly Stipulated			
No	65%	44%	47%
Yes (for at least some members)	35%	56%	53%
Kendall's Tau *C* = .14			
3. Stipulation of Penalties for Rule Violation in Writing			
No	70%	50%	42%
Yes (for at least some members)	30%	50%	58%
Kendall's Tau *C* = .22			
E. Procedures			
1. Formalization of Orientation Program for New Members (Only Programs for All New Members Included; *N* = 57)			
No program or low formalization	83%	63%	50%
High formalization	17%	37%	50%
Kendall's Tau *C* = .26			
2. Formalization of In-service Training Program for New Members (Only Programs for All New Members Included; *N* = 36)			
No program or low formalization	77%	47%	50%
High formalization	23%	53%	50%
Kendall's Tau *C* = .26			

are longitudinal studies which examine the preconditions of staff increase as well as the structural consequences of such increases.

While size and organizational structure are not closely related, size is an important variable in other kinds of analyses. The individual in a large organization might feel "lost" in the great numbers of people. Organizational size also is an important variable in interorganizational relations since size and organizational power are probably positively related. Similarly, larger organizations probably have more financial resources. Thus, organizational size should not be dismissed as a variable but should rather be utilized where is is likely to have more predictive significance than it has for complexity and formalization.

A Formal Theory of Differentiation in Organizations*
PETER M. BLAU

The objective of this paper is to develop a deductive theory of the formal structure of work organizations, that is, organizations deliberately established for explicit purposes and composed of employees. The differentiation of a formal organization into components in terms of several dimensions—spatial, occupational, hierarchical, functional—is considered to constitute the core of its structure. The theory is limited to major antecedents and consequences of structural differentiation. It has been derived from the empirical results of a quantitative study of government bureaus. The extensive analysis of these empirical data on the interrelations between organizational characteristics, too lengthy for presentation in an article, is reported elsewhere (Blau and Schoenherr, 1971). . . .

Formal Structure

Formal organizations cope with the difficult problems large-scale operations create by subdividing responsibilities in numerous ways and thereby facilitating the work of any operating employee, manager, and subunit in the organization. The division of labor typifies the improvement in performance attainable through subdivision. The more com-

* Reprinted from the *American Sociological Review, 35* (April 1970), pp. 201–218, with omissions, by permission of the author and the publisher, The American Sociological Association. In reprinting the article, parts of text, Figures 2, 4, and 5, as well as all expository footnotes, are deleted.

pletely simple tasks are separated from various kinds of complex ones, the easier it is for unskilled employees to perform the routine duties and for skilled employees to acquire the specialized training and experience to perform the different complex ones. Further subdivision of responsibilities occurs among functional divisions, enabling each one to concentrate on certain kinds of work. Local branches may be established in different places to facilitate serving clients in various areas, and these branches may become functionally specialized. The management of such a differentiated structure requires that managerial responsibilities too become subdivided among managers and supervisors on different hierarchical levels. . . .

The central concept of differentiation in organizations must be clearly defined in terms that permit translation into operational measures. A dimension of differentiation is any criterion on the basis of which the members of an organization are formally divided into positions, as illustrated by the division of labor; or into ranks, notably managerial levels; or into subunits, such as local branches, headquarters divisions, or sections within branches or divisions. A structural component is either a distinct official status (for example, employment interviewer or first-line supervisor), or a subunit in the organization (for example, one branch or one division). The term differentiation refers specifically to the number of structural components that are formally distinguished in terms of any *one* criterion. The empirical measures used are number of branches, number of occupational positions (division of labor), number of hierarchical levels, number of divisions, and number of sections within branches or divisions.

The research from which the theory of structural differentiation has been derived is a study of the 53 employment security agencies in the United States, which are responsible for administering unemployment insurance and providing public employment services in the 50 states, the District of Columbia, Puerto Rico, and the Virgin Islands. These are autonomous state agencies, although they operate under federal laws and are subject to some federal supervision.

First Generalization

Increasing size generates structural differentiation in organizations along various dimensions at decelerating rates (1). This is the first fundamental generalization inferred from the empirical findings. From it can be deduced several middle-range propositions, which subsume additional empirical findings. One can consider this theoretical generalization about the structure of organizations to comprise three parts, in which case the middle-level and lower-level propositions are derived from the conjunction of the three highest-level ones. In this alternative formulation, the three highest-level propositions composing the first basic generalization about the formal structure of organizations are:

(1A) large size promotes structural differentiation; (1B) large size promotes differentiation along several different lines; and (1C) the rate of differentiation declines with expanding size. The assumption is that these generalizations apply to the subunits within organizations as well as to total organizations, which can be made explicit in a fourth proposition: (1D) the subunits into which an organization is differentiated become internally differentiated in parallel manner.

A considerable number of empirical findings on employment security agencies can be accounted for by the generalization that differentiation in organizations increases at decreasing rates with increasing size, and none of the relevant evidence conflicts with this generalization. The operational definition of size is number of employees. When total state agencies are compared, increases in size are accompanied by initially rapid and subsequently more gradual increases in the number of local branches into which the agency is spatially differentiated; the number of official occupational positions expressing the division of labor; the number of levels in the hierarchy; the number of functional divisions at the headquarters; and the number of sections per division. The profound impact that agency size has upon differentiation is indicated by its correlations of .94 with number of local offices; .78 with occupational positions; .60 with hierarchical levels; and .38 with functional divisions. Logarithmic transformation of size further raises these correlations (except the one with local offices); for example, that with number of divisions becomes .54; and that with sections per division, which was before an insignificant .16, is after transformation .43. The improvements in the correlations logarithmic transformation of size achieves reflect the logarithmic shape of the regression lines of the numbers of structural components on size, and thus the declining rate of differentiation with expanding size. For an illustration of this pattern, the scatter diagram for agency size and number of hierarchical levels is presented in Figure 1.

The internal differentiation within the subunits that have become differentiated in the agencies assumes the same form. The larger a local branch, the greater the differentiation into occupational positions ($r = .51$), hierarchical levels (.68), and functional sections (.61). . . .

The larger a division, the larger is the number of its occupational positions, hierarchical levels, and functional sections; and differences between very small and medium-sized divisions have again more impact on variations in these three aspects of differentiation than differences between medium-sized and very large divisions. Moreover, this tendency for differentiation at decelerating rates to occur with increasing size is observable in six separate types of divisions with basically different function and thus provides some support for the claim that the same tendency will be found in other organizations which have different functions from those of employment security agencies.

**FIGURE 1.   SIZE OF AGENCY AND NUMBER OF HIERARCHICAL
LEVELS AT HEADQUARTERS**

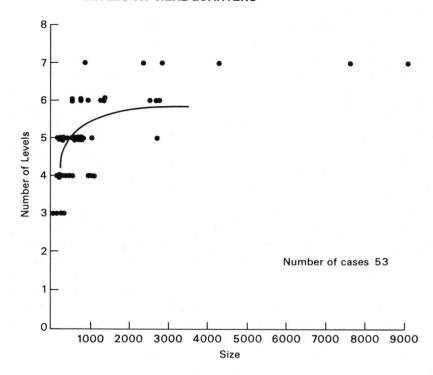

Proposition 1.1   The first proposition that can be derived from the first
fundamental generalization is the following: as the size of organizations
increases, its marginal influence on differentiation decreases (1.1). As
a matter of fact, this is hardly a derived proposition, since it is merely
a restatement of one part of the original proposition (1C). But by
translating the initial proposition into different concepts, the new
proposition directs attention to a distinctive implication and an important parallel with the economic principle of diminishing returns or, in
technical terms, of the eventually diminishing marginal physical productivity. In the words of Boulding: "As we increase the quantity of
any one input which is combined with a fixed quantity of the other
inputs, the marginal physical productivity of the variable input must
eventually decline" (1955: 589).

In a factory, production output can be raised by adding workers,
but the marginal increment in output resulting from adding more and
more workers without changing plant size and equipment eventually
declines. In parallel fashion, a larger complement of employees in an
organization makes its structure more differentiated, but as the number
of employees and the differentiation of the structure increase, the marginal influence of a given increase in personnel on further differentia-

tion declines. It seems that the differentiation produced by the expanding size of organizations stems the power of additional expansions in size to make the structure still more differentiated.

But why does the marginal influence of size on differentiation in organizations decline? If the analogy with the economic principle of diminishing returns is appropriate, it should provide some clues for answering this question. The reason for the eventually declining marginal productivity of increments in only one type of economic input is that such increments create an imbalance of inputs and the growing need for other inputs depresses productivity. For example, additional workers cannot be efficiently utilized in production without parallel increases in equipment and space. We may speculate that the influence of increasing organizational size on differentiation produces a growing need which in turn diminishes the influences of further increases in size.

The existence of differentiation in formal organization implies a need for coordination. There are at least two inputs, using the terminology of economics, on which the development of structural differentiation in organization depends. The first is a sufficient number of employees (the measure of size) to fill the different positions and man the various subunits, and the second is an adequate administrative machinery to meet problems of coordination. The advancing differentiation to which an increasing number of employees gives rise intensifies the need for coordination in the organization, and this need restrains the further development of differentiation, which is reflected in the declining marginal influence of increasing size on differentiation. The implication of these considerations extrapolated from economic theory is that differentiation in organizations creates pressures to find ways to meet the need for coordination. We shall later return to the analysis of this problem, after discussing five other propositions that can be derived from the first basic generalization.

Proposition 1.2 The second derived proposition is that the larger an organization is, the larger the average size of its structural components of all kinds (1.2). This proposition logically follows from the principle of the decelerating rate of differentiation with increasing organizational size (1C). . . . If the structural components increase more slowly than organizational size, the average size of these components necessarily becomes larger. . . . Two examples are the mean size of local branches, which variable has a zero-order correlation with agency size of .65, and the number of incumbents of the average occupational position, which variable is correlated .94 with agency size.

Thus, the large size of an organization raises the average size as well as the number of its structural components. Large agencies have more and larger local offices than small agencies, more and larger headquarters divisions, and the same hold true for every one of their structural components. The large size of the local offices within an agency and of its headquarters divisions, whatever their function, in turn tends to increase both the number and the average size of sections, and both the number of occupational positions and of managerial ranks and the mean number of employees occupying each position and each rank.

This double effect of organizational size has the paradoxical result that large offices and headquarters divisions constitute at the same time a more homogeneous and a more heterogeneous occupational environment for most employees than small ones. For larger offices or divisions contain comparatively many employees in nearly every occupational specialty, providing a congenial in-group of colleagues for most employees—often not available in small organizational units—and they simultaneously contain a relatively great variety of different specialties, enhancing opportunities for stimulating contacts with people whose training and experience are unlike their own. However, the greater opportunity for social interaction with a colleague in-group in larger offices may prove so attractive that social contacts with persons from different specialties are rarer there than in small ones, despite the fact that opportunities for out-group contacts are better in large offices too.

Proposition 1.3   A third derived proposition is that the proportionate size of the average structural component, as distinguished from its absolute size, decreases with increases in organizational size (1.3). This follows directly from (1A): if the number of structural components, the criterion of differentiation, increases as organizational size does, the proportion of all employees who are in the average component must decrease. Hence, most groups or categories of employees in big organizations are larger in absolute numbers but constitute a smaller proportion of the total personnel than in small organizations. A consequence is that the average (*mean*) relative size of employee complements on a given dimension decreases with increasing organizational size, though not necessarily the proportion of any particular complement.

But we may reformulate this proposition (1.3) into a probability statement about groupings of employees: *ceteris paribus,* chance expectations are that the proportionate size of any personnel complement decreases with increasing organizational size. The empirical data show that this proposition applies to various kinds of administrative overhead or supportive services for the majority work force. The size of an agency is inversely related to the proportionate size of its administrative staff ($r = -.60$) and of its complement of managerial personnel ($-.45$). (The terms "manager" and "supervisor," unless qualified, are used interchangeably to refer to all levels.) The proportion of managers is also inversely related to size in local offices (—.64) and in headquarters divisions regardless of function.

When a certain personnel complement is singled out for attention —the staff or the managerial component—and exhibits the expected decrease in proportionate size with increasing organizational size, the remainder of the total personnel—the line or the nonsupervisory employees—must naturally reveal a complementary increase in proportionate size. This is mathematically inevitable, and it indicates that the reformulated proposition (1.3) cannot possibly apply to both parts of a dichotomy. The plausible assumption is that the residual majority actually consists of numerous personnel categories while the specialized personnel complement focused upon can be treated as a single one, which implies that the proportion of the minority complement is the one that should decrease with increasing organizational size. The data support this assumption. If employees in various organizational units are divided into clerical and professional personnel, the proportion of whichever of the two is in the minority tends to decrease as unit size does. The conclusion that may be drawn, which extends beyond what can be derived in strict logic from the premise, is that the proportionate size of any supportive service provided by a distinctive minority to the majority work force is likely to decline with increasing organizational size.

Proposition 1.4 Another proposition can be derived either from the last one (1.3) or from the one preceding (1.2): the larger the organization is, the wider the supervisory span of control (1.4). If chances are that the proportionate size of any organizational component declines with increasing size (1.3), and if this applies to the proportion of managers, it follows that the number of subordinates per manager, or the span of control, must expand with increasing size (1.4). Besides, if chance expectations are that the absolute average size of any structural component or grouping of employees increases with increasing size (1.2), and if this applies to the various work groups assigned to supervisors, it follows that the size of the group under each supervisor, or his span of control, tends to expand with increasing size (1.4). Here again the logical implications specifying the *mean* absolute and proportionate size for *all* components have been translated into *probabilities* or statistical expectations referring to *any* component. Whether these derived propositions apply to a *particular* personnel component, like the managerial staff, must be empirically ascertained. If the evidence is negative, it would not falsify the theory, though it would weaken it. If the evidence is positive, it strengthens the theory, and makes it possible to extend it beyond the limits of its purely logical implications by taking into account the empirical data confirming this particular application of the merely statistical deduction from the theory.

The empirical data on employment security agencies confirm the proposition that the span of control of supervisors expands with increasing organizational size. This is the case for all levels of managers and supervisors examined in these agencies and their subunits. The larger an agency, the wider is the span of control of its director and the average span of control of its division heads. The larger a headquarters division, whatever its function, the wider is the span of control of its division heads, the average span of control of its middle managers, and the average span of control of its first-line supervisors. The larger a local office is, the wider the span of control of the office manager and that of the average first-line supervisor. Moreover, the size of the total organization has an independent effect widening the supervisory span of control when the size of local offices is controlled. Big organizations and their larger headquarters divisions and local branches tend to have more employees in any given position with similar duties than small organizations with their smaller subunits, as we have seen, thus making it possible to use supervisors more efficiently in large units by assigning more subordinates with similar duties to each supervisor.

The additional influence of the size of the total organization, independent of that of the size of the office, on the number of subordinates per supervisor, may reveal a structural effect (see Blau, 1960). The prevalence of a wide span of supervisory control in large organizations, owing to the large size of most of their branch offices, creates a normative standard that exerts an influence in its own right, increasing the number of subordinates assigned to supervisors; and the same is the case, *mutatis mutandis,* for the prevalence of a narrow supervisory span of control in small organizations with their smaller branches. To direct attention to the substantial influence of organizational size on the supervisory span of control is, of course, not to deny that this span is also influenced by other conditions, such as the nature of the duties.

Propositions 1.5 and 1.6 Organizations exhibit an economy of scale in management. This proposition (1.5) is implicit in the two foregoing ones. For if the proportion of managerial personnel declines with size (1.3) and their span of control expands with size (1.4), this means that large-scale operations reduce the proportionate size of the administrative overhead, specifically, of the complement of managers and supervisors. In fact, the relative size of administrative overhead of other kinds, such as staff and supportive personnel, also declines with increasing size, as has been noted. The question arises whether this economy of scale in administrative overhead produces overall personnel economies with an increasing scale of operations. The data on employment security agencies are equivocal on this point. The only index of personnel economy available, the ratio of all employees engaged in unemployment benefit operations to the number of clients served by them, is inversely correlated with size, but with a case base of only 53 agencies the correlation is too small ($-.14$) to place any confidence in it. Logarithmic transformation of size raises the correlation to —.24, which suggests that large size might reduce the man-hour costs of benefit operations slightly.

Whereas this finding is inconclusive, not inconclusive are the numerous findings that indicate that the relative size of administrative overhead declines with increasing organizational size. Large-scale operations make it possible to realize economies in managerial man-power. This can be explained in terms of the generalization that the number of structural components increases at a declining rate with increasing size (1), which implies that the *size* of work groups under a supervisor, just as that of most personnel components, increases with increasing size, and that the *proportion* of supervisors, just as that of most personnel components, decreases with increasing size, and these relationships account for the economy of scale in management.

A final derived proposition in this set is that the economy of scale in administrative overhead itself declines with increasing organizational size (1.6). This proposition follows from two parts of the basic gener-alization (1A and 1C) in conjunction with one derived proposition (1.3). If the number of structural components increases with increasing orga-nizational size (1A), the statistical expectation is that the proportionate size of any particular personnel component decreases with size (1.3). The empirical data showed that the proportion of managerial personnel and that of staff personnel do in fact decrease as size increases, in accordance with these expectations. But since the increase in the number of components with expanding size occurs at a declining rate (1C), the decrease in the proportionate size of the average component, implicit in this increase in number, must also occur at a declining rate with expanding organizational size. Reformulation in terms of statis-tical probability yields the proposition that chance expectations are that the proportionate size of any particular personnel complement decreases at a decelerating rate as organizations become larger.

Whether this statistical proposition about most personnel compo-nents holds true for the managerial and staff component is an empirical question, and the answer is that it does. The proportion of staff person-nel decreases at a declining rate as organizational size increases (see Figure [2]), and so does the proportion of managerial personnel at the agency headquarters as well as in local offices. . . . The marginal power of organizational size to produce economies in administrative overhead diminishes with growing size, just as its marginal power to generate structural differentiation does. Both of these patterns are implied by the generalization that the number of structural components in an organization increases at a declining rate with expanding size.

Second Generalization

Structural differentiation in organizations enlarges the administrative component (2), because the intensified problems of coordination and

**FIGURE 2. SIZE OF AGENCY AND PERCENT STAFF
PERSONNEL**

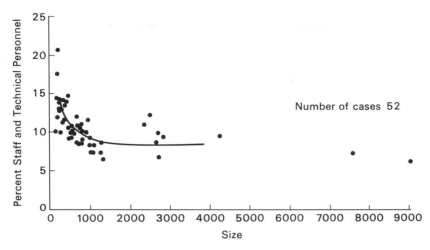

communication in differentiated structures demand administrative attention. In this second fundamental generalization of the deductive theory, the first part subsumes many empirical findings, whereas the second part introduces theoretical terms not independently measured in the research but inferred. The assumptions are that differentiation makes an organization more complex; that a complex structure engenders problems of communication and coordination; and these problems create resistance to further differentiation; that managers, the staff, and even first-line supervisors spend time dealing with these problems; and that consequently more supervisory and administrative manpower is needed in highly differentiated structures than in less differentiated structures. Although these assumptions of the intervening connections are not empirically tested, the implications of the conclusion are. If, in accordance with the inferred assumptions, much of the time of supervisors on all levels in the most differentiated structures is occupied with problems of communication and coordination, it follows that these supervisors have less time left for guiding and reviewing the work of subordinates.

Hence, the more differentiated the formal structure, the more administrative personnel of all kinds should be found in an organization of a given size, and the narrower that span of control of first-line supervisors as well as higher managers. This is precisely the pattern the empirical findings reveal. Vertical differentiation into levels and horizontal differentiation into divisions or sections are both positively related to the proportion of supervisors among the total personnel, controlling size, in the whole organization, in local branches, and in the six functional types of headquarters divisions. They are also positively related to the proportionate size of the staff in agencies of a given size.

Moreover, both vertical and horizontal differentiation, with size held constant, are negatively related to the span of control of managers and supervisors on different levels in local offices and in headquarters divisions, regardless of function. The finding that the second generalization and its derivations discussed below are supported when the span of control of supervisors on a given level is substituted for the ratio of all supervisors is of special importance. The more levels organizations of a given size have, the larger is necessarily the proportion of their supervisors, that is, of their personnel above the lower level. The positive relationship of number of levels with proportion of supervisors does not merely reflect this mathematical nexus, which would make it trivial, as demonstrated by its positive relationship with supervisory span of control, which is not affected by this nexus. Hence, the empirical data support the principle that hierarchical as well as horizontal differentiation, presumably by engendering problems of coordination, enlarges requirements for managerial manpower.

Propositions 2.1 and 2.2   One derived proposition is that the large size of an organization indirectly raises the ratio of administrative personnel through the structural differentiation it generates (2.1). If increasing organizational size generates differentiation (1A), and if differentiation increases the administrative component (2), it follows that the indirect effect of size must be to increase the administrative component. Decomposition of the zero-order correlations of size with various ratios of managerial and staff personnel in multiple regression analysis makes it possible to isolate the indirect effects of size mediated by differentiation from its direct effects. In every problem analyzed, the empirical findings confirm the prediction that the indirect effects of size mediated by both vertical differentiation into levels and horizontal differentiation into divisions or sections raise the ratio of administrative to total personnel. This is the case whether the dependent variable under consideration is the staff ratio or the managerial ratio at the agency headquarters; the ratio of supervisors on all levels; or the span of control of first-line supervisors in any of the six types of functional divisions or in local branches. In all these instances, the indirect effects of size mediated by the differentiation it generates and its direct effects are in opposite directions. The savings in administrative overhead large-scale operations make possible are counteracted by the expansion in administrative overhead the structural complexity of large organizations necessitates.

Another derived proposition is that the direct effects of large organizational size lowering the administrative ratio exceed its indirect effects raising it owing to the structural differentiation it generates (2.2). This is a logical consequence of propositions (1.5) and (2.1). If the overall effect of large size reduces management overhead (1.5), and if large size, by fostering differentiation, indirectly increases management overhead (2.1), it follows that its effect of reducing overhead must outweigh this indirect effect. All the decompositions of the zero-order correlations of size with various measures of management reflect this, as they inevitably must. For example, the direct effect of agency size on the managerial ratio at the agency headquarters, which is represented by the standardized regression coefficient when three measures of differentiation are controlled, is —1.13, whereas its overall effect, indicated by the zero-order correlation, is —.45, the difference being due to the strong counteracting effect mediated by differentiation. For the staff ratio at the agency, with the same conditions controlled, the direct effect of size is —1.04, and its overall effect is —.60, revealing again a substantial indirect counteracting effect due to structural differentiation. The direct and indirect effect of the size of a division on its managerial ratio and of the size of a local office on its managerial ratio reveal parallel differences. *Ceteris paribus,* a large scale of operations would effect tremendous savings in administrative overhead, but these savings are much reduced by the structural differentiation of large organizations. Consistently, however, the economies of scale exceed the costs of differentiation, so that large organizations, despite their greater structural complexity, require proportionately less administrative manpower than small ones.

Proposition 2.3 The last proposition to be derived is that the differentiation of large organizations into subunits stems the decline in the economy of scale in management with increasing size, that is, the decline in the decrease in the proportion of managerial personnel with increasing size (2.3). The derivation of this proposition is rather complicated and must be approached in several steps. The new proposition is not as well knit into the system as the others and should be regarded as a mere conjecture.

The concept of economy of scale in administration refers to the fact that the proportion of various kinds of administrative personnel decreases with the increasing size of the organization or its subunits. The operational indication is a negative correlation between any of these proportions and size, which is represented on a graph by a negative slope of the regression line of the proportion on size. These negative correlations and slopes are evident in all empirical data on employment security agencies: size of local branch and either proportion of all managerial personnel or ratio of first-line supervisors to operating employees (the reverse of span of control); size of functional division and either ratio of all managerial personnel or ratio of supervisors to subordinates on three levels; size of total agency and either proportion of staff personnel, or proportion of managerial personnel at the headquarters, or proportion of managerial personnel in the total organization.

A decline in this economy of scale means that the *rate of decrease* in the ratio of managerial personnel itself *decreases* with increasing size. This is reflected on a graph by a curve in the negative slope of the regression line of the ratio on size that shows that the ratio of overhead personnel drops first sharply and then more gradually with increasing size. The percent of supervisors in local offices illustrates a decrease at such a decreasing rate . . . , and so does the ratio of staff personnel in the agency (Figure [2]) and that of the supervisors at the agency headquarters . . . , and the same pattern is observable in most other relationships mentioned in the above paragraph. The major exception is that the proportion of managerial personnel in the total agency does not reveal such a declining rate of decrease but a fairly linear decrease with increasing agency size. Although this appears to be a deviant case, the principle it expresses can be deduced from the propositions in the theory.

In local offices, the smallest organizational unit examined, the proportion of all supervisory personnel drops rapidly as size increases from ten, or fewer, to about fifty employees, but it drops much more slowly with further increases to one and two hundred employees. . . . From a projection of this trend, one would expect that further increases in size to several thousand employees are hardly accompanied by any decline in the proporiton of supervisory personnel. As the size of the entire organization increases from about one hundred to several thousand employees, however, the total proportion of supervisory personnel decreases on the average at a constant rather than declining rate . . . though there is much scatter. Although this decline is not pronounced, it is by no means inconsequential; the zero-order correlation is —.34, which compares with a correlation of —.46 between size of office and its proportion of supervisors. (However, the latter correlation is raised to —.64 if size is logarithmically transformed. In contrast, the former correlation is reduced to —.23 by such a transformation, which is another indication that the regression line does not exhibit a logarithmic curve.) Why does the decrease in the proportion of managerial personnel with increasing size, which is already very small as office size expands beyond fifty employees, not become virtually zero but is again considerable as agency size expands from several hundred to several thousand? The answer suggested by the theory is that the differentiation of large organizations into many branch offices (and divisions), while raising the proportion of managers needed, simultaneously restores the economy of scale in the managerial component, that is, it recreates the decline in the proportion of managerial personnel with increasing size observed among very small organizational units.

The growing need for managerial manpower resulting from the structural differentiation engendered by expanding size (2.1) increasingly impinges upon the savings in managerial manpower that a large scale of operations realizes (1.5), which helps to explain why the economy of scale in management declines as size and differentiation increase (1.6). In other words, the *rate* of savings in management overhead with increasing size is higher among comparatively small than among comparatively large organizational units, although, or perhaps because, the management overhead is bigger in small than in large organizational units. Differentiation in a large organization (1A) means that it consists of relatively many smaller rather than relatively few larger organizational subunits, such as local offices. Inasmuch as the *rate* of savings in management overhead is higher in smaller than in larger organizational units, the reduction in the size of units created by differentiation raises this rate of savings and stems the decline in the economy of scale with respect to management overhead that would be otherwise expected once organizations have grown beyond a certain size (2.3).

Conclusions

. . . Organizing the work of men means subdividing it into component elements. In a formal organization, explicit procedures exist for systematically subdividing the work necessary to achieve its objectives. Different tasks are assigned to different positions; specialized functions are allocated to various divisions and sections; branches may be created in dispersed locations; administrative responsibilities are subdivided among staff personnel and managers on various hierarchical levels. The larger an organization and the scope of its responsibilities, the more pronounced is its differentiation along these lines (1A, 1B), and the same is the case for its subunits (1D). But large-scale operations, despite the greater subdivision of tasks than in small-scale operations—involve a larger volume of most organizational tasks. Hence, large organizations tend to have larger as well as more structural components of various sorts than small organizations (1.2).

The pronounced differentiation of responsibilities in large organizations enhances simultaneously intra-unit homogeneity and inter-unit heterogeneity. Inasmuch as duties are more differentiated and the amount of work required in most specialties is greater in large organizations than in small ones, there are comparatively many employees performing homogeneous tasks in large organizations. The large homogeneous personnel components in large organizations simplify supervision and administration, which is reflected in a wider span of control of supervisors (1.4) and a lower administrative ratio (1.3) in large than in small organizations. Consequently, organizations exhibit an economy of scale in administrative manpower (1.5). At the same time, however, the heterogeneity among organizational components produced by differentiation creates problems of coordination and pressures to expand the administrative personnel to meet these problems (2). In this formulation, the unmeasured concepts of intra-unit homogeneity and inter-unit heterogeneity have been introduced to explain why large size has two opposite effects on administrative overhead, reducing it owing to the enlarged scale of similar tasks, and raising it owing to the differentiation among parts.

By generating differentiation, then, large size indirectly raises administrative overhead (2.1), and if its influence on differentiation were unrestrained, large organizations might well have disproportionately large administrative machineries, in accordance with the bureaucratic stereotype. However, the administrative ratio decreases with expanding organizational size, notwithstanding the increased administrative ratio resulting from the differentiation in large organizations (2.2). Two feedback effects of the administrative costs of differentiation may be inferred, which counteract the influences of size on administration and differentiation, respectively. The first of these apparently reduces the savings in administrative manpower resulting from a large scale of operations, as implied by the decline in the rate of decrease of administrative overhead with increasing organizational size (1.6). (Although differentiation into local branches may keep the rate of overhead savings with increasing size constant [2.3], it also raises the amount of overhead.) The second feedback process, probably attributable to the administrative problems engendered by differentiation, creates resistance to further differentiation, which is reflected in the diminishing marginal influence of expanding size of differentiation (1.1) and the declining rate at which size promotes differentiation (1C).

In short, feedback processes seem to keep the amount of differentiation produced by increasing organizational size below the level at which the additional administrative costs of coordination would equal the administrative savings realized by the larger scale of operations. Hence, organizations exhibit an economy of scale in administration, despite the extra administrative overhead required by the pronounced differentiation in large organizations, but this economy of scale declines with increasing size, on account of this extra overhead due to differentiation. The feedback effects inferred, though not directly observable, can explain why the influence of size on differentiation, as well as its influence on administrative economy, declines with increasing size. Figure [3] presents these connections graphically.

A final question to be raised is how widely applicable the theory is to organizations of different types. Since the theory was constructed by trying to formulate generalizations from which the empirical findings on employment security agencies can be derived, the fact that these data conform to the propositions advanced does not constitute a test of the theory. But it should be noted that several of the specific propositions included in the theory are supported by findings from previous empirical studies of other kinds of organizations, for example, that administrative overhead in organizations decreases with size and increases with complexity or differentiation (see Anderson and Warkov, 1961; Pondy, 1969 and references therein), and that its decrease with size occurs at a declining rate (Indik, 1964). Moreover, an empirical

FIGURE 3.   CHART OF CONNECTIONS

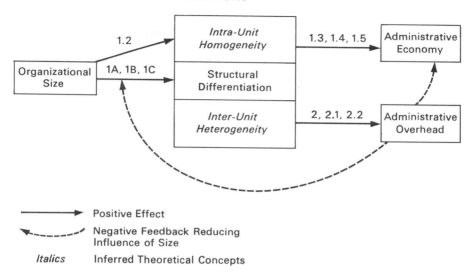

test of the entire body of theory has been conducted in a study of another type of government bureau, the 416 major finance departments
of American states, large cities, and large counties. This independent
test confirms the propositions implied by the theory. Whether the
theoretical generalizations are also valid for private and other public
organizations, and how they must be modified or refined to make them
widely applicable, only further research can tell.

The Context of Organization Structures*

D. S. PUGH, D. J. HICKSON, C. R. HININGS, and C. TURNER

The structure of an organization is closely related to the context within
which it functions, and much of the variation in organization structures
might be explained by contextual factors. Many such factors, including
size, technology, organizational charter or social function, and interdependence with other organizations, have been suggested as being
of primary importance in influencing the structure and functioning of
an organization.

* Reprinted from *Administrative Science Quarterly, 14* (March 1969), pp. 91–114, with
omissions, by permission of the authors and the publisher.

There have been few attempts, however, to relate these factors in a comparative systematic way to the characteristic aspects of structure, for such studies would require a multivariate factorial approach in both context and structure. The limitations of a unitary approach to organizational structure have been elaborated elsewhere (Hinings *et al.,* 1967), but its deficiencies in the study of contextual factors are no less clear. Theorists in this area seem to have proceeded on the assumption that one particular contextual feature is the major determinant of structure, with the implication that they considered the others less important. Many writers from Weber onwards have mentioned size as being one of the most important causes of differences between structures, and large size has even been considered as characteristic of bureaucratic structure (Presthus, 1958). Others argue for the preemptive importance of the technology of production or service in determining structure and functioning (Dubin, 1958; Perrow, 1967; Woodward, 1965; Trist *et al.,* 1963). Parsons (1956) and Selznick (1949) have attempted to show in some detail that the structure and functioning of the organization follow from its social function, goals, or "charter." Eisenstadt (1959) emphasized the importance of the dependence of the organization on its social setting, particularly its dependence on external resources and power, in influencing structural characteristics and activities. Clearly all of these contextual factors, as well as others, are relevant; but without a multivariate approach, it is not possible to assess their relative importance.

A previous paper described the conceptual framework upon which the present multivariate analysis is based (Pugh *et al.,* 1963), and a subsequent paper its empirical development (Pugh *et al.,* 1968). It is not a model of organization in an environment, but a separation of variables of structure and of organizational performance from other variables commonly hypothesized to be related to them, which are called "contextual" in the sense that they can be regarded as a setting within which structure is developed. Table 1 summarizes the framework.

The design of the study reported in the present paper treats the contextual variables as independent and the structural variables as dependent. The structural variables are (i) *structuring of activities;* that is, the degree to which the intended behavior of employees is overtly defined by task specialization, standard routines, and formal paper work; (ii) *concentration of authority;* that is, the degree to which authority for decisions rests in controlling units outside the organization and is centralized at the higher hierarchical levels within it; and (iii) *line control of workflow;* that is, the degree to which control is exercised by line personnel instead of through impersonal procedures. The contextual variables were translated into operational definitions and scales were constructed for each of them. These were then used in a multivariate regression analysis to predict the structural dimensions found.

This factorial study using cross-sectional data does not in itself

TABLE 1. CONCEPTUAL SCHEME FOR EMPIRICAL STUDY OF WORK ORGANIZATIONS*

Contextual variables	Structural variables
Origin	*Structuring of activities*
Ownership and control	Functional specialization
Size	Role specialization
Charter	Standardization (overall)
Technology	Formalization (overall)
Location	
Dependence	*Concentration of authority*
	Centralization of decision making
	Autonomy of the organization
	Standardization of procedures for selection and advancement
	Line control of workflow
	Subordinate ratio
	Formalization of role performance recording
	Percentage of workflow superordinates

* Pugh *et al.* (1968).

test hypotheses about *processes* (e.g., how changes in size interact with variations in structuring of activities), but it affords a basis for generating such hypotheses.

Sample and Methods

Data were collected on fifty-two work organizations, forty-six of which were a random sample stratified by size and product or purpose. The sample and methods have been described in detail in a previous paper (Pugh *et al.*, 1968). For scaling purposes, data on the whole group were used, but for correlational analyses relating scales to each other, and for prediction analyses relating contextual variables to structural ones, only data on the sample of forty-six organizations were used. None of the data was attitudinal.

Contextual Variables

Origin An organization may have grown from a one-man business over a long period of time, or it may have been set up as a branch of an already existing organization and so develop rapidly. During its development it may have undergone many or few radical changes in purpose, ownership, and other contextual aspects. An adequate study of the impact of these factors on organizational structure must be conducted on a comparative longitudinal basis (Chandler, 1962); but even in a cross-sectional study such as this, it is possible to define and make operational aspects of this concept.

Impersonality of origin. This variable distinguishes between entrepreneurial organizations, personally founded, and bureaucratic ones founded by an existing organization. Impersonally founded organizations might be expected to have a higher level of structuring of activities, whereas personally founded organizations would have a higher degree of concentration of authority. The data on the present sample are given in Table 2. They show no relationship between impersonality of origin and structuring of activities ($r = -0.04$), but a strong relationship between impersonality of origin and concentration of authority ($r = 0.64$). (With $N = 46$, all correlations 0.29 and above are at or beyond the 95 percent level of confidence.) To a considerable extent this relationship is due to the fact that government-owned, and therefore impersonally founded, organizations tend to be highly centralized. Such organizations tend to be line controlled in their workflow, thus contributing to the relationship ($r = 0.36$) between impersonality of origin and line control of workflow. The lack of relationship with structuring of activities, which is common to all three scales of this dimension, underlines the need to examine present contextual aspects in relation to this factor rather than historical ones.

Age. The age of the organization was taken from the time at which the field work was carried out. The range in the sample varied from an established metal goods manufacturing organization, founded over 170 years previously, in 1794, to a government inspection department, which began activities in the area as a separate operating unit 29 years previously. No clear relationship was found between age and impersonality of origin ($r = -0.20$). Stinchcombe (1965) has argued that no relationship should be expected between the age of an organization and its structure but rather between the structure of an organization and the date that its industry was founded. The present data support this conclusion in that no relationship is found between age and structuring of activities ($r = 0.09$) or line control of workflow ($r = 0.02$). Age was related to concentration of authority ($r = -0.38$), older organizations having a tendency to be more decentralized and to have more autonomy.

Ownership and Control The differences in structure between a department of the government and a private business will be due to some extent to the different ownership and control patterns. Two aspects of this concept, public accountability and the relationship of the ownership to the management of the organization were investigated. For wholly owned subsidiary companies, branch factories, local government departments, etc., this form of analysis had to be applied to the parent institution exercising owning rights, in some cases through more than one intermediate institution (e.g., committees of the corporation,

TABLE 2. ELEMENTS OF ORGANIZATION CONTEXT

Elements of context	Product-moment correlation with structural factors		
	Structuring of activities	Concentration of authority	Line control of workflow
Origin			
Impersonality of origin	—0.04	0.64	0.36
Age	0.09	—0.38	—0.02
Ownership and control			
Public accountability	—0.10	0.64	0.47
Concentration of ownership with control	—0.15	—0.29	—0.21
Size			
Size of organization*	0.69	—0.10	—0.15
Size of parent organization*	0.39	0.39	—0.07
Charter			
Operating variability	0.15	—0.22	—0.57
Operating diversity	0.26	—0.30	—0.04
Technology			
Workflow integration	0.34	—0.30	—0.46
Labor costs	—0.25	0.43	0.32
Location			
Number of operating sites	—0.26	0.39	0.39
Dependence			
Dependence	—0.05	0.66	0.13
Recognition of trade unions	0.51	0.08	—0.35

* Logarithm of number of employees.

area boards, parent operating companies, which were themselves owned by holding companies, etc.). The ultimate owning unit is referred to as the "parent organization."

Public accountability. This was a three-point category scale concerned with the degree to which the parent organization (which could, of course, be the organizational unit itself, as it was in eight cases) was subject to public scrutiny in the conduct of its affairs. Least publicly accountable would be a company not quoted on the stock exchange; next, organizations that raised money publicly by having equity capital quoted on the stock exchange, also public cooperative societies; and most publicly accountable were the departments of the local and central government. On the basis of the classical literature on bureaucracy as a societal phenomenon, it might be hypothesized that organizations with the greatest exposure to public accountability would have a higher degree of structuring of activities, and a greater concentration of authority. The data on the present sample show relationships more complicated than this, however.

First, it must be emphasized that although this sample included eight government departments, all the organizations had a nonadministrative purpose, which could be identified as a workflow (Pugh, *et al.,* 1968). This is not surprising in this provincial sample, since purely administrative units of the requisite size (i.e., employing more than 250 people) are few outside the capital. The relationships between public accountability and structure must be interpreted in the light of this particular sample.

No relationship was found between public accountability and structuring of activities ($r = -0.10$). This structuring factor applies to the workflow as well as administrative activities of the organization, and it appears that government organizations with a workflow are not differentiated from nongovernment organizations on this basis. On the other hand there was a positive relationship between public accountability and concentration of authority ($r = 0.63$), standardization of procedures for selection and advancement ($r = 0.56$), and line control of workflow ($r = 0.47$). These all point to centralized but line-controlled government workflow organizations (Pugh *et al.,* 1969). The scale of standardization was a bipolar one, and a high score meant that the organization standardized its procedures for personnel selection and advancement, and also that it did *not* standardize its procedures for workflow. The relationship between public accountability and this standardization scale suggests that the government workflow organizations standardize their personnel procedures, but rely on professional line superordinates for workflow control.

Relationship of ownership to management. The concepts of Sargent Florence (1961) were found most fruitful in studying this aspect of ownership and control, but the method used was the selection of variables for a correlational approach, rather than classification on the basis of percentages. Florence studied the relationships of shareholders, directors, and executives. Where these groups were completely separate there was full separation of ownership, control, and management; where they were the same, then ownership, control, and management coalesced. Between these two extremes, the scales were designed in the present study to measure the degree of separation.

As would be expected, there was a negative relationship between public accountability and concentration of ownership with control ($r = -0.51$); the more publicly accountable the ownership, the less concentrated it was, with central and local government ownership epitomizing diffuse ownership by the voting public.

The discussion about the effects of differing patterns of personal ownership on organizations and society originated with Marx, and has since polarized into what Dahrendorf (1958) has called the "radical" and "conservative" positions. It is generally agreed that there has been a progressive dispersion of share ownership following the rise of the corporation, but there is little agreement, or systematic evidence, on the effects of this. The radicals (Burnham, 1962; Berle and Means, 1937) argue that present ownership patterns have produced a shift in control away from the entrepreneur to managers, who become important because of their control over the means of production and the organization of men, materials, and equipment. The result then of dispersion of ownership is likely to be dispersion of authority. However, the conservatives (Mills, 1956; Aaronovitch, 1961) argue that the dispersion of capital ownership makes possible the concentration of economic power in fewer hands, because of the inability of the mass of shareholders to act, resulting in a concentration of authority.

The results obtained with this sample support neither of these positions. The correlation given in Table 2 of concentration of ownership with control with concentration of authority ($r = -0.29$) might suggest that concentration of ownership is associated with dispersion of authority; but it must be remembered that this correlation is obtained for the whole sample, which includes government-owned organizations, whereas the discussion of the effects of ownership patterns has been concerned entirely with private ownership. When the government organizations were extracted from the sample, the correlation disappeared ($r = -0.08$ for $N = 34$). No relationships were found between the structure of an organization and the ownership pattern of its parent organization. This lack of relationship is quite striking, particularly in view of the extent of the correlation found with other contextual variables. Since ownership and control seemed to have its impact through the degree of public accountability, and the other variables did not have an additional effect, there seemed to be grounds for not proceeding with them in a multivariate analysis.

Size   There has been much work relating size to group and individual variables, such as morale and job satisfaction, with not very consistent results (Porter and Lawler, 1965). With few exceptions, empirical studies relating size to variables of organization structure have confined themselves to those broad aspects of the role structure which are here termed "configuration" (Starbuck, 1965). Hall and Tittle (1966), using a Guttman scale of the overall degree of perceived bureaucratization obtained by combining scores on six dimensions of Weberian characteristics of bureaucracy in a study of twenty-five different work organizations, found a small relation between their measurement of perceived bureaucratization and organization size ($\tau = 0.252$ at the 6 percent level of confidence).

In this study the aspects of size studied were number of employees, net assets utilized, and number of employees in the parent organizations.

Number of employees and net assets. It was intended that the sample be taken from the population of work organizations in the region employing more than 250 people, but the sample ranges from an insurance company employing 241 people to a vehicle manufacturing company employing 25,052 (mean 3,370; standard deviation 5,313). In view of this distribution, it was felt that a better estimate of the correlation between size and other variables would be obtained by taking the logarithm of the number of employees (mean 3.12; standard deviation 0.57).

"Net assets employed by the organization" was also used, because financial size might expose some interesting relationships with organization structure that would not appear when only personnel size was considered. The sample ranged from under £100,000—an estimate for the government inspection agency whose equipment was provided by its clients—to a confectionery manufacturing firm with £38 million. The attempt to differentiate between these two aspects of size proved unsuccessful, however, as the high correlation between them ($r = 0.78$) shows. Taking the logarithm of the two variables raised the correlation ($r = 0.81$). For this sample, therefore, a large organization was big both in number of employees and in financial assets. The logarithm of the number of employees was therefore taken to represent both these aspects of size.

The correlation between the logarithm of size and structuring of activities ($r = 0.69$) lends strong support to descriptive studies of the effects of size on bureaucratization. (This correlation may be compared with that between actual size and structuring of activities, $r = 0.56$, to demonstrate the effects of the logarithmic transformation.) Larger organizations tend to have more specialization, more standardization, and more formalization than smaller organizations. The *lack* of relationship between size and the remaining structural dimensions, i.e., concentration of authority ($r = -0.10$) and line control of workflow ($r = -0.15$) was equally striking. This clear differential relationship of organization size to the various structural dimensions underlines the necessity of a multivariate approach to context and structure if oversimplifications are to be avoided.

Indeed, closer examination of the relationship of size to the main structural variables underlying the dimension of concentration of authority (Pugh *et al.,* 1968: Table 4) points up a limitation in the present approach, which seeks to establish basic dimensions by means of factor analysis. As was explained in that paper, the structural factors represent an attempt to summarize a large amount of data on a large number of variables to make possible empirically based comparisons. But the cost is that the factor may obscure particular relationships with the source variables which it summarizes. For some purposes therefore, it may be interesting to examine particular relationships. The lack of relationship between size and concentration of authority, for example, summarizes (and therefore conceals) two small but distinct relationships with two of the component variables. There is no relationship between size and autonomy ($r = 0.09$), but there is a negative relationship between size and centralization ($r = -0.39$), and a positive one between size and standardization of procedures for selection and advancement ($r = 0.31$). The relationship with centralization has clear implications for the concept of bureaucracy. Centralization correlates *negatively* with all scales of structuring of activities except one: the more specialized, standardized, and formalized the organization, the *less* it is centralized. Therefore on the basis of these scales, there can be no unitary bureaucracy, for an organization that develops specialist offices and associated routines is decentralized. Perhaps when the responsibilities of specialized roles are narrowly defined, and activities are regulated by standardized procedures and are formalized in records, then authority can safely be decentralized. Pugh *et al.* (1969) discuss the interrelationship of the structural variables in particular types of organization.

Size of parent organization. This is the number of employees of any larger organization to which the unit belongs. The literature on bureaucracy often implies that it is the size of the larger parent organization that influences the structure of the sub-unit. The important factor about a small government agency may not be its own size, but that of the large ministry of state of which it is a part. Similarly, the structure of a subsidiary company may be more related to the size of its holding company. The number of employees in the parent organizations ranged from 460 to 358,000 employees. The size of the parent organization correlated positively (after logarithmic transformation) with structuring ($r = 0.39$) and concentration of authority ($r = 0.39$) but not with line control of workflow ($r = -0.07$). The classical concept of bureaucracy would lead to the hypothesis that the size of the parent organization would be highly correlated with structuring of activities and concentration of authority; therefore the support from this sample was relatively modest. The correlation with structuring ($r = 0.39$) is much lower than the correlation of *organization* size and structuring ($r = 0.69$). The impact of the size of an organization is thus considerably greater than the size of the parent organization on specialization, standardization, formalization, etc. But a relationship with concentration of authority is not found with organization size ($r = 0.10$). Thus large groups have a small but definite tendency to have moie centralized sub-units with less autonomy. This relationship would be partly due to the government-owned organizations, inevitably part of large groups, which were at the concentrated end of this factor.

Charter

Scales. Institutional analysts have demonstrated the importance of the charter of an organization; that is, its social function, goals, ideology, and value systems, in influencing structure and functioning (Parsons, 1965; Selznick, 1949). To transform concepts which had been treated only descriptively into a quantitative form that would make them comparable to other contextual aspects, seven ordered category scales were devised. Four of them characterized the purpose or goal of the organization in terms of its "output," the term being taken as equally applicable to products or services: (i) multiplicity of outputs—ranging from a single standard output to two or more outputs; (ii) type of output—a manufacturing-service dichotomy; (iii) consumer or producer outputs or a mixture of both; and (iv) customer orientation of outputs—ranging from completely standard outputs to outputs designed entirely to customer or client specification. Three scales were devised for ideological aspects of charter: (v) self-image—whether the ideology of the organization as indicated by slogans used and image sought emphasized the qualities of its outputs; (vi) policy on multiple outputs—whether the policy was to expand, maintain, or contract its range of outputs; and (vii) client selection—whether any, some, or no selectivity was shown in the range of customers or clients served by the organization.

Operating variability. This factor, accounting for 30 percent of the variance was highly loaded on the variables, consumer or producer outputs, customer orientation of outputs, and type of output. It was therefore conceptualized as being concerned with manufacturing non-standard producer goods as against providing standard consumer service. The manufacturing producer end of the scale was linked with an organizational emphasis on self-image, whereas the consumer service end emphasized outputs. The scale was therefore constructed by a weighted summing of the scores on all these variables (the weighting being necessary to equate the standard deviations) and then standardizing the sums to a mean of 50 and a standard deviation of 15. The lower scores distinguished organizations giving only a standard service (e.g., teaching, transport, retailing) from organizations (with high scores) producing non-standard producer outputs to customer specification (metal goods firm, engineering repair unit, packaging manufacturer, etc.), with those organizations having a standard output range in the middle.

Operating diversity. This factor of charter, accounting for 20 percent of the variance, emphasized multiplicity of outputs, policy on whether to expand the range of kinds of outputs, client selection, and self-image. The more diversely operating organizations were a glass manufacturer, a metal manufacturer, and a brewery; the more restricted were a motor component manufacturer, a domestic appliance manufacturer, and a scientific inspection agency.

Eisenstadt (1959), Parsons (1956), Selznick (1949, 1957), Wilson (1962), and Clark (1956) have discussed the effects of the goals of an organization on its structure, but there has been almost no detailed empirical work on the actual relationship between goals and structure. Selznick (1949) showed how the goal of democracy led to decentralization in the TVA, and also suggested that the role structure of an organization is the institutional embodiment of its purpose. Wilson (1962) suggested a relationship between goals and methods of recruitment and means of selection. Clark (1956) as well as Thompson and Bates (1957) emphasized both the marginality and the degree of concreteness of the goal as a determinant of the direction of organization adaptation. Blau and Scott (1962) made one of the few attempts to classify organizations by their goals, suggesting that internal democracy goes with mutual benefit goals, efficiency with business goals, a professional structure with service goals, and bureaucratic structure with commonweal goals.

Scales of organizational charter were related to structure, and operating variability was shown to be strongly associated with line control of workflow ($r = 0.57$). Thus the more an organization is concerned with manufacturing non-standard producer goods, the more it relies upon impersonal control of workflow; the more it is providing a standard consumer service, the more it uses line control of its workflow through the supervisory hierarchy. Organizations showing operating diversity, however, tended to be more structured in activities ($r = 0.26$) and more dispersed in authority ($r = -0.30$).

Technology

Scales. Technology has come to be considered increasingly important as a determinant of organizational structure and functioning, although comparative empirical studies of its effects on structure are few, mainly case studies on the effects on the operator's job and attitudes (Walker, 1962). Thompson and Bates (1957), however, compared a hospital, a university, a manufacturing organization, and a mine for the effects of their technologies on the setting of objectives, the management of resources, and the execution of policy. The main work on the classification of technology in relation to organization structure has been that of Woodward (1965). She related mainly "configuration" aspects of the structure of manufacturing organization (e.g., number of levels of authority, width of spans of control) to a classification of their production systems according to the "controllability and predictability" of the process.

In the present study the need to develop suitable measurements of overall organizational technology made the level of generality achieved by the Woodward classification desirable; but the need to develop concepts of technology that applied to all the organizations in the sample precluded the direct adoption of that scale. A full account of the development of scales of technology and their relationship to organization structure is given in Hickson, *et al.* (1969). Only the scales included in the present analysis are described here.

Technology is here defined as the sequence of physical techniques of the organization, even if the physical techniques involve only pen, ink, and paper. The concept covers both the pattern of operations and the equipment used, and all the scales developed are applicable to service as well as to manufacturing organizations. Five scales of related aspects of technology were developed. These are effectively summarized under the title "Workflow Integration" (p. 270).

There were no clear relationships between workflow integration and the variables of size, origin and history, or concentration of ownership with control and negative relationship with public accountability ($r = -0.35$), largely because the government-owned organizations in the sample were predominantly service and therefore at the diverse end of the workflow integration scale. The correlations between workflow integration and operating variability ($r = 0.57$) and diversity ($r = 0.33$) reflect the close relationship between the ends of the organization and the means it employs to attain them.

Workflow integration showed modest but distinct correlations with all the three structural factors, the only contextual variable to do so apart from labor costs, as can be seen from Table 1. The relationships of technology are therefore much more general than is the case with size, for example, which has a greater but more specific effect. The positive correlation between workflow integration and structuring of activities ($r = 0.34$) would be expected since highly integrated and therefore more rigid technologies would be associated with a greater structuring of activities and procedures. Similarly, the correlation with concentration of authority ($r = -0.30$) suggests that because of the increasing control resulting directly from the workflow itself in an integrated technology, decisions tend to become more routine and can be decentralized. But the fact that the correlations are not higher than this emphasizes that structuring may be related to other contextual factors, such as size. The relationship of technology to line control of workflow, however, was very clear ($r = 0.46$); the more integrated the technology, the more the reliance on impersonal control. It must be emphasized, however, that these relationships were found on the whole sample of manufacturing and service organizations. When manufacturing organizations only were considered, some of the relationships showed considerable change (Hickson *et al.,* 1969).

Labor costs. This is a second related, but conceptually distinct, aspect of the technology of the workflow and is expressed as a percentage of total costs. The range in the sample was from 5 to 70 percent, with engineering organizations scoring low and public services high. The scale correlated with workflow integration ($r = -0.50$), high integration being associated with reduced labor costs. Its correlations with the structural factors are comparable with those for technology (after adjusting the signs).

Location

The geographical, cultural, and community setting can influence the organization markedly (Blau and Scott, 1962). This study controls for some of these effects in a gross way, for all organizations of the sample were located in the same large industrial conurbation, and the community and its influence on the organizations located there were taken as given (Duncan *et al.,* 1963). Compared with the national distribution, the sample was overrepresented in the engineering and metal industries, and unrepresented in mining, shipbuilding, oil refining, and other industries. Because of the location, however, regional cultural differences of the sort found by Thomas (1959) as to role conceptions, were avoided.

One aspect of location which discriminated between organizations in the sample, was *number of operating sites.* The range formed a Poisson distribution, with 47 percent of the sample having one site; but six organizations had over a hundred sites, and two over a thousand. This distribution did not appear to be a function of size ($r =$ 0.14) but of the operating variability aspect of charter ($r = -0.56$). Manufacturing organizations were concentrated in a small number of sites (the largest number being nine), whereas services range across the scale. The number of operating sites was therefore correlated with the workflow integration scale of technology ($r = -0.58$), and with public accountability ($r = 0.34$), this last correlation reflecting the predominantly service function of the group of government-owned organizations.

This pattern of inter-relationships among the contextual variables led to the expectation of relationships between number of operating sites and the structural dimensions which would be congruent with those of operating variability and workflow integration. The correlations of number of operating sites wtih structuring of activities ($r = -0.26$), concentration of authority ($r = 0.39$) and line control of workflow ($r = 0.39$) confirm the relationships with charter and technology, and suggest a *charter-technology-location* nexus of interrelated contextual variables having a combined effect on structure.

Dependence

The dependence of an organization reflects its relationships with other organizations in its social environment, such as suppliers, customers, competitors, labor unions, management organizations, and political and social organizations.

Dependence on parent organization. The most important relationship would be the dependence of the organization on its parent organization. The *relative size* of the organization in relation to the parent organization was calculated as a percentage of the number of employees. This ranged from under one percent in two cases—a branch factory of the central government, and a small subsidiary company of one of the largest British private corporations in the country—to 100 percent in eight independent organizations. The distribution was Poisson in form with a mean and standard deviation of 37 percent. The next scale was a four-point category scale concerned with the *status* of the organization in relation to the parent organization: (i) principal units (8 organizations) where the organization was independent of any larger group although it might itself have had subsidiaries or branches; (ii) subsidiary units (18 organizations) which, although part of a larger group, had their own legal identity with, for example, their own boards of directors; (iii) head branch units (4 organizations) which did not have separate legal identity although they were the major operating components of the parent organization and the head office of the parent organization was on the same site; (iv) branch units (16 organizations) operating parts of a parent organization which did not satisfy the preceding criteria.

The third aspect of the relation between the organization and the parent organization was given by the degree of *organizational representation on policy-making bodies.* This three-point scale ranged from the organization being represented on the policy-making body of the parent organization (e.g., board of directors, city council), through the organization being represented on an intermediate policy-making body (e.g., board of directors of an operating company but not of the ultimate owning holding company, committee of the city council), to the organization having no representative on any policy-making body of the parent organization. As would be expected, these three variables were highly correlated.

A related variable was the number of *specializations contracted out* by the organization. In many cases these would be available as services of the parent organization to the organization, although account was also taken of the various specialist services (e.g., consultants) used outside the parent organization. The specializations were as defined in the structural scale of functional specialization (Pugh *et al.,* 1968: Appendix A), and ranged from one specialization contracted out (two engineering works, a printer, and a builder) to no less than fifteen of the sixteen specializations contracted out (an abrasives manufacturer and a packaging manufacturer) with a mean 7.2 and standard deviation 4.0.

Dependence on other organizations. The suppliers and customers or clients of the organization must also be considered. The operating function of the organization can be regarded as being the processing of inputs and outputs between supplier and client, and the degree to which the organization is integrated into the processual chain by links at either end can be measured. Five category scales were developed to elucidate this concept. They were concerned with the integration with suppliers and clients, and response in the output volume to client influence, etc. To establish a single dimension measuring the degree to which the organization was integrated into this system, the five scales were transformed into biserial form. Item analysis was carried out on the 18-item scale generated and yielded a mean item analysis value of 0.70, which seemed to justify the addition of the items into a total scale, *vertical integration*. At one extreme was a confectionery manufacturer and an engineering components firm supplying goods from stock with a large number of customers after obtaining their supplies from a large variety of sources; at the other extreme were organizations (vehicle components, civil engineering, scientific research) obtaining their resources from a small number of suppliers and supplying their product or service to a small number of clients (often the owning group only) who had a marked effect upon their workflow scheduling.

For *trade unions,* a scale of five ordered categories was developed of the extent to which unions were accepted as relevant to the activities of the organization. The scale was (i) no recognition given; (ii) only partial recognition given (i.e., discussions for certain purposes, but not negotiations); (iii) full recognition given to negotiate on wages and conditions of service on behalf of their members; (iv) full recognition given plus facilities for union meetings to be held regularly on the time and premises of the organizations; (v) as in the preceding plus the recognition of a works convenor to act on behalf of all unions with members in the organization. Organizations in the sample were located in all the categories, with the modal position being full recognition; but five organizations did not recognize unions, and eleven gave the maximum recognition including a works convenor.

Examination of the intercorrelations between these variables of dependence and of their correlations with other important aspects of context shows considerably higher correlations with size of parent organization than with size of organization, and considerably higher correlations with concentration of ownership with control (a variable applied to the parent organization) than with operating variability or workflow integration (variables applied to the operations of the individual organizations themselves). This pattern lends support to the view that these measures are tapping aspects of the dependence of the organization, particularly its dependence of external resources and power as in Eisenstadt's (1959) formulation. The one exception was the variable of recognition of trade unions, which had its largest contextual correlation with organization size, and is therefore concerned with a different aspect of interdependence. Impersonality of origin (from origin and history) and public accountability (from ownership and control) show the same pattern of higher correlation with the parent organization than with the unit, indicating that impersonally founded organizations are likely to be more dependent on their founding organizations; and that more publicly accountable organizations are more likely to be dependent on outside power with government-owned organizations being the extreme case.

These relationships suggested the application of factor analysis to a correlation matrix containing seven variables—relative size of unit, status of unit, representation on policy-making body, specializations contracted out, vertical integration, impersonality of origin, and public accountability. A principal-components analysis applied to the matrix produced a large first factor *dependence* accounting for 55 percent of the variance, which was heavily loaded on all seven scales (on six of the seven, the loadings were above 0.7; the remaining loading on vertical integration was 0.58). The scores for dependence were obtained by an algebraic weighted sum of the scores on the four more highly loaded component scales, the weightings being obtained by a multiple regression analysis of the component scales on the factor. A high score characterized organizations with a high degree of dependence, which tended to be impersonally founded, publicly accountable, vertically integrated, with a large number of specializations contracted out, small in size relative to their parent organization, low in status, and not represented at the policy-making level in the parent organization (e.g., branch units in packaging, civil engineering, and food manufacture, a central government repair department, and a local government baths department). Organizations with low dependence were independent organizations characterized by personal foundation, low public accountability, little vertical integration, few specializations contracted out, and where the parent organization was the organization itself (e.g., a printing firm, the very old metal goods firm, a chain of shoe repair stores, and an engineering component manufacturer).

The correlation of dependence with the structural factors was focused largely on concentration of authority ($r = 0.66$), in every case, for dependence and its component scales the correlation being much greater than with the other factors, as Table 1 shows. Dependent organizations have a more centralized authority structure and less autonomy in decision making; independent organizations have more autonomy and decentralize decisions down the hierarchy.

The relationships between dependence and the component scales of concentration of authority vary. Centralization, as defined and measured in this study, is concerned only with the level in the organization which has the necessary authority to take particular decisions (Pugh *et al.*, 1968: 76); the higher the necessary level, the greater the centralization. No account was taken of the degree of participation or consultation in decision-making as in Hage and Aiken's (1967) formulation of the concept. These were regarded as aspects for study at the group level of analysis. Neither is it possible for such a statement as the following to hold: "The decisions were centralized on the foreman since neither the superintendent nor the departmental manager had the necessary experience." In the present formulation this would be regarded as relative decentralization. Autonomy was measured by the proportion of decisions that could be taken within the organization as distinct from those which had to be taken at the level above it. Thus independent organizations of necessity had more autonomy, since there was no level above the chief executive, and the correlation between dependence and this component of concentration of authority was $r = -0.72$. The relation of centralization (which is concerned with the whole range of levels in the hierarchy) with dependence is less, but still high ($r = 0.57$). Dependent organizations also have a distinct tendency to standardize the procedures for selection and advancement ($r = 0.40$), a major component of concentration of authority. So dependent units have the apparatus of recruitment routines, selection panels, formal establishment figures, etc., of their parent organizations.

The Multivariate Prediction of Structure from Context

The variables in Table 3 are now used as independent variables in a prediction analysis of the structural dimensions. The pattern of these correlations, that is, that where they are high they are specific, and where they are low, they are diffused, indicates that the predictions should be attempted on a multivariate basis. In this case consideration had to be given to choosing not only predictors with high correlations with the criterion, but also having low intercorrelations among themselves. If high intercorrelations among the predictors were allowed, then, since the high correlations with the criterion would be aspects of the same relationship, the multiple correlation would not be increased to any extent. If the intercorrelations between the predictors were low, then each would make its distinct contribution to the multiple correlation.

These problems can be illustrated from the attempt to obtain a multiple prediction of structuring of activities from the three contextual variables correlated with it (Table 3). Size is clearly the first predictor, with a correlation of $r = 0.69$, and the question is whether taking account of size of parent organization and workflow integration will increase predictive accuracy. In spite of its greater correlation with the criterion, the size of the parent organization would be expected to make a smaller contribution to the prediction than workflow integration, since it has a strong correlation with the first predictor ($r = 0.43$); whereas the technology measure is not correlated with organization size ($r = 0.08$).

The existence of the charter-technology-location nexus referred to above is supported by the fact that when any one of these variables is used as a predictor, the remaining two do not add to the multiple correlation. Table 3 shows the multiple correlation of 0.75 obtained by

TABLE 3. MULTIPLE PREDICTION ANALYSIS OF STRUCTURAL FACTORS

Contextual predictors of structural factors	Single correlation	Multiple correlation	F ratio	Degrees of freedom	Level of confidence
Structuring of activities					
Size	0.69	0.69	39.6	1:44	>99%
Workflow integration	0.34	0.75	8.2	1:43	>99%
Size of parent organization	0.39	0.76	1.9	1:42	NS
Concentration of authority					
Dependence	0.66	0.66	34.2	1:44	>99%
Location (number of operating sites)	0.39	0.75	12.5	1:43	>99%
Age of organization	—0.38	0.77	2.5	1:42	NS
Operating diversity	—0.30	0.78	3.0	1:41	NS
Workflow integration	—0.30	0.78	0.0	1:40	NS
Size of parent organization	0.39	0.79	0.4	1:39	NS
Line control of workflow					
Operating variability	—0.57	0.57	20.7	1:44	>99%
Workflow integration	—0.46	0.59	1.7	1:43	NS
Number of sites	0.39	0.59	0.1	1:42	NS

using the location measure together with dependence as predictors. When the technology scale of workflow integration is substituted as the second predictor, the multiple correlation is 0.71; when the operating diversity scale of charter is used, the multiple correlation is 0.70.

The prediction of line control of workflow shows this same phenomenon, where the addition of predictors, because of their interrelationships, does not improve on the original single correlation of operating variability with the criterion.

The size of the multiple correlations obtained with the first two factors, each 0.75 with two predictors, together with the small number of predictors needed, strongly supports the view that in relation to organization structure as defined and measured in this study, salient elements of context have been identified. Thus a knowledge of the score of an organization on a small number of contextual variables makes it possible to predict within relatively close limits, its structural profile. Given information about how many employees an organization has, and an outline of its technology in terms of how integrated and automated the work process is, its structuring of activities can be estimated within fairly close limits. Since in turn the score on the organization on structuring of activities summarizes an extensive description of broad aspects of bureaucratization, the organization is thereby concisely portrayed in terms of this and similar concepts. Likewise, knowing the dependence of an organization on other organizations and its geographical dispersion over sites tells a great deal about the likely concentration of authority in its structure. *Size, technology, dependence, and location* (number of sites) are critical in the prediction of the two major dimensions (structuring of activities, concentration of authority) of the structures of work organizations.

The predictability of the structural dimensions from contextual elements serves as external validating evidence for the structural concepts themselves. It has now been shown that besides being internally consistent and scalable, as previously demonstrated, they can also be related in a meaningful way to external referents. Indeed the size of the correlations inevitably raises the question of causal implications. It is tempting to argue that these clear relationships are causal—in particular, that *size, dependence, and the charter-technology-location nexus largely determine structure.*

3
THE SOCIAL STRUCTURE OF ORGANIZATIONS

The study of social structure, the best developed area in the sociology of organizations, reflects the pervasive influence of Max Weber. Working in a military hospital during the first world war in Vienna, he came away from military service with a conception of what he called bureaucracy. This model of organization is based on a rational–legal system of authority arranged in a hierarchy of offices filled by technical experts. Rules and files provide internal control and ensure impartiality in dealing with the outside world. Weber felt that eventually this model would be the dominant form of organization because of its superior efficiency. Weber's model is significant for its sociological treatment of organization, in that it was a new way of thinking about social structure.

Perhaps we need to define what is meant by the social structure. Although definitions vary, most sociologists agree that the idea of patterned action is an essential ingredient. This is easily seen within organizations, probably more so than in other kinds of collectives. Diverse individuals perform diverse tasks while interacting with diverse individuals. These tasks are called *jobs* in an organization (*offices* to use Weber's term), and *positions* in a collective (to use the more generic label). The crux of social structure is how to arrange these jobs or positions into some coherent whole. The task for the organizational sociologist has been to isolate important patterns of action that are both theoretically relevant and empirically measurable. Most of the following readings speak to this issue.

For a full decade after the English translation of Weber's work, researchers investigating organizations based their work (usually case studies of single random organizations) on the model Weber had constructed (examples are Gouldner, 1954; Blau, 1955; Harrison, 1959; and there is a good review in Pugh *et al.,* 1963). It turned out to be a fruitful point of departure. In the sixties both thought and research began to shift. Newer structural models equally as viable as Weber's, came under consideration. Research was becoming comparative, by exploring more than one organization at a time; as a consequence, a more exacting test of Weber's ideas was possible. Although organization theory has now advanced beyond the Weberian model of bureaucracy, essentially we still remain indebted to Weber for shaping some basic questions sociologists are working to answer.

The fundamental problem has been to identify what kinds of models of social structure exist. The next step was to explore and study at length a number of critical properties common to the model of structure. As expressed in Weber's terms, they are the hierarchy of authority or the distribution of power; the utilization of rules; and the role of the technical expert within the division of labor. Although the bulk of the research on structure has focused on these properties, another one has been equally important: the problem of configuration, the morphology or shape of the organization. Although not strictly a Weberian conceptualization, it articulates in various ways with other properties, because it is frequently seen as a way of inferring these other characteristics. Thus we have the following five most important issues, which become our foci for discussion of the readings: (1) the diverse models of organizational structure, (2) the internal distribution of power, (3) the rules, (4) the technical expert, and (5) the problem of configuration.

THE PROBLEMS

Models of Organizational Structure

Since the first model of organizational structure was Weber's legal–rational authority model, we have selected Crozier's case study of a French bureaucracy as an excellent description of what it is like to work inside one. We see how impersonality pervades all aspects of the organization. In the same regard the case study by Presthus (in Chapter One), is also an excellent introduction to a number of key ideas in Weber's model, if only in the sense of how Weber's principles of bureaucracy can be violated. Yet it is also clear from reading about the chemical workers (Blauner in Chapter Two), and contrasting their experiences with the French clerks, that this model is not the only empirical one that exists. Most of the selections in this chapter focus in one way or another on the problem of how to construct a team that can function effectively to achieve specific goals. Is there only one viable model of organizational structure? Or are several models equally viable?

The Burns and Stalker selection in this chapter provides an excellent review of Weber's model of bureaucracy as well as of the several other approaches that developed as antitheses to Weber's work. Then emerge two models of organizational structure, the *mechanistic,* which is basically Weber's bureaucracy minus the technical experts, and the *organic.* What is indeed helpful in their description of the differences between the mechanistic and the organic models is that they specify the categories that differentiate them. (We would have liked to include some of their case studies of Scottish electrical firms. For those who want some additional empirical examples, their book *The Management of Innovation* [1961] is rich in anecdote.)

Increasingly, the selection by Burns and Stalker included here is becoming one of the most widely referenced works in the literature. Since the formulation of their mechanistic and organic structures, a number of other individuals have found some empirical support for these models. Woodward (1965) found that her craft and continuous process industries were largely organic, whereas the mass production firms were mechanical. Aiken and Hage (1971) explicitly tested a number of propositions implied in Burns and Stalker's description and found them empirically supported. Lawrence and Lorsch (1967a) found the models a helpful way of conceptualizing the impact of the environment on organizations, although they have developed and advanced some of Burns and Stalker's original insights considerably.

One of the reasons for the centrality of the Burns and Stalker work is that not only does it suggest two organizational models, one of the first to do so, but also that these models are dictated by the nature of the organizational environment. We have already seen how important this is in the Terreberry and the Azumi selections (both in Chapter One) which develop this idea considerably. And the Lawrence and Lorsch selection in Chapter Four is a further refinement, observing that different parts of the organization may need different structures because of their different environments.

The McCleery selection in Chapter Four is an interesting case study that indicates how an organization can shift from one structural arrangement to another. The traditional structure of the prison prior to the arrival of the men interested in rehabilitation, while perhaps an extreme example, provides an illustration of Weber's bureaucratic model; whereas the new structure represents the most common alternative model to be considered viable by many but not all organizational sociologists.

As further illustrations, each of the case studies gives us a glimpse of what organizations might be like. The Chandler piece (Chapter Five) also illustrates the process of change from one form to another, in this instance in a chemical company. And while both of these are viewed from the top of the structural pyramid, the bottom is illustrated by contrasting the Blauner selection with Berliner's contribution. Together they give us a sense of the variations in constructions.

In the selection by Hall, we find still another review of Weber's work, this time pointing out which theorists in sociology have emphasized what aspects of bureaucracy as being theoretically relevant. The point of Hall's work is to develop dimensions for describing the model and then to see if these dimensions are associated, which is the implicit hypothesis of Weber. Hall finds that they are not all interrelated and provides empirical evidence for the need for more than one structural arrangement. His article is critical because it is one of the first attempts to test Weber's ideas both empirically and comparatively, in a study examining ten different organizations.

Also, Hall's article calls attention to an interesting problem: which property of the model is most important? Hall concludes that the hierarchy of authority is primary, a finding with which Weber would probably agree, because his three models of organization (the other two, charismatic and traditional, were more of historical interest than importance in understanding present-day organizations) were largely built upon the problem of power and authority and their basis of legitimacy. Hall bases the conclusion about the hierarchy of authority on the pattern of associations between the dimensions.

As interest grew in consolidating what was already known in the field, various attempts were made to create a more systematic theory about social structure. The axiomatic theory by Hage is perhaps the most systematic effort so far. Like the Burns and Stalker piece, it builds upon several traditions but does so in a different way. The reader might compare the terms used by Weber, reported in the Burns and Stalker article, with those in Hage's theory of organizations. The latter attempts to develop a more general formulation, with variables that are easily measured, thus facilitating the testing of hypotheses. Like Burns and Stalker, Hage presents two models, but unlike them, he indicates that there are many more models between the two extremes and that evolution is probably forcing organizations toward what Burns and Stalker would call the organic model.

Here, at best, is an unresolved question: is a particular model of structure likely to be more viable in the future? Weber's (1947) original conception was that bureaucracy would triumph over all. Hage suggests the opposite. Elsewhere Hage and Aiken (1970: Chapters Three and Five) have given a number of reasons as to why changes in the environment are forcing more organizations toward some kind of organic form. Writing independently, Lawrence and Lorsch (1967a), in their book *Organization and Environment,* and others have come to the same conclusion. Not everyone agrees, however; Perrow (1971) takes exception and argues for Weber, claiming that the bureaucratic model, in essentially the form he outlined, will be with us for some time. Here we have a fundamental theoretical issue which requires more research to resolve.

For those who like to read about the theory of organizational structure, several other formulations are well worth studying. One should start by reading the Henderson and Parsons translation (1947) of Weber, especially pp. 330–340. We have not included Weber's original discussion because he is variously reviewed in a number of selections (Burns and Stalker; Hall; Hage; and Blau). The contrast in their interpretations is illuminating and more insightful than just reading Weber's work in isolation. It also tells us something about the various interpreters. Victor Thompson's *Modern Organizations* (1961) is also a good introduction to basic issues. As noted in the selection by Hage, Thompson explicitly argues that conflict exists between specialists and the hierarchy of authority, which is one of the central issues in the argument favoring the necessity for more than one model of organizational structure. For the more advanced, James Thompson's *Organizations in Action* (1967), is worth close scrutiny and much thought. Price's *Organizational Effectiveness* (1967), a chapter of which is reprinted in Chapter Five, also has much to offer.

Perhaps still more interesting is the number of similarities in the formulations of what might be important models of organizations. Although the words, emphases, and conceptions differ, there are still many agreements on a number of points. The essential agreement between Burns and Stalker, and Hage, is noted by the latter. One might also compare their work with that of Price (1967), and although Blau does not refer to any of these works, his article in this chapter is in accord on certain issues. Again, this concurrence on basic issues reflects the intellectual debt the field owes to Weber.

How much evidence is there that a number of the propositions in Hage's theory are correct? Several of the empirical articles, which were written after he developed the theory, give some additional support. In addition to the article by Blau in this chapter, another article he coauthored (Blau, Hydebrand, and Stauffer, 1966) also gives evidence for several of the propositions. The selection in Chapter Five by Hage and Aiken represents one of the series of research studies specifically designed by them to test some of the propositions. Others in the series include Aiken and Hage (1966 and 1971) and Hage and Aiken (1967b). A more detailed exposition of the available empirical evidence is to be found in their book *Social Change in Complex Organizations* (1970). A study reported by Palumbo (1969) largely confirms a number of the propositions. At the same time the evidence is not all positive. Pugh *et al.,* in this chapter, give some positive and some negative evidence, indicating again support for the idea that complexity and centralization are negatively related but raising the question of whether there might not be more procedures in the organic model than in the mechanistic one, in contrast to the description by Burns and Stalker and the hypotheses by Hage.

Naturally, we need still more evidence, especially in rigorous longitudinal research, before we can be sure of the accuracy of the hypothesis. Probably we also need a much more sophisticated formulation than the axiomatic one. The latter does have the advantage of being simple to understand and it can organize one's reading. But our intuitions tell us that just as the studies of the impact of size on structure have been forced to ever more sophisticated mathematics, the description and analysis of organizational structure will have to undergo the same treatment.

When two contrasting models are suggested, one always wonders why only two. Are there three, four, five, or fifty? Some writers have suggested that there are more than two, whether conceived as two types, as in Burns and Stalker, or as a continuance, as hypothesized by Hage. These diverse formulations are well worth exploring. Perrow (1967) in his article on technology, suggests four basic kinds, two essentially similar to the mechanistic and organic forms, and two interesting derivations. His basis of classification, as we noted in the introduction to Chapter Two, is technology. Routine technology leads to the mechanistic form and nonroutine to the organic, but the other two are admixtures. Another earlier example of adherence to four existing models is the classification of Blau–Scott (1962), based on the principle of who benefits from the organizational achievements.

For those who like the number three, there is Etzioni's (1961) typology, based on the kind of sanction used to achieve compliance. This tradition is represented in the article by Julian (Chapter Four). It might also be noted that both the Blau–Scott and Etzioni typologies have been researched by Hall, Haas, and Johnson (1967b) and found wanting.

Another seeming advocate of three models is Litwak (1961), who in an early article suggested the necessity of having more than one. However, his third is really the middle between the two extremes and these bear a close resemblance to Burns and Stalker's description; Litwak, however, arrived at these independently in the same year as Burns and Stalker's contribution, based on experiences with different kinds of organizations in a different culture.

Of some more recent empirical and quasi-empirical approaches to the problem of a typology of organizations, probably the two best are the work of Pugh et al. (1969b) and Samuel and Mannheim (1970). The latter has a good review of the different ones that have been suggested. Both of these examples, along with Perrow's, have the advantage of being much more systematically derived than most of the others. However, what distinguishes all of them is their basis of classification: environment (Burns and Stalker), technology (Perrow), structure (Pugh *et al.*), control (Etzioni), and beneficiaries (Blau–Scott). This is probably a question of taste. And the links between them go to the heart of the issue, the system of variables and how these variables articulate together.

More importantly, the attempt to create typologies always represents an early state in the development of a field. The study of organizations has now advanced to the point where many recognize the greater advantages of concentrating on variables and hypotheses. This is reflected in a number of attempts to build theory, many of which are reprinted in this text–reader (Blau in Chapter Two, Hage in this chapter, and Price in Chapter Five).

A separate issue is the problem of prediction. Can we state the probability for the likelihood of encountering one or the other kinds of structures? As already noted, one school suggests the key factor to be various dimensions of technology. Size is held as another possibility. The importance of the environment has already been noted in a number of places. Hage suggests that the tension is inherent to the structure itself; that is, complexity or division of labor is the major driving variable. Still other answers are to be found in later chapters.

So far the theorist of organizations who has done the best job of attempting to unite some of these perspectives is James Thompson (1967). Noteworthy is his conceptualization of structure as the resultant of a number of forces, the major two being the nature of the environment and the nature of the technology. This is probably the most likely proposition, but the larger task of synthesis, as noted in the Introduction, still remains to be done. It is one thing to say that synthesis is desirable and another to achieve a meaningful merger of thesis and antithesis.

The Problem of the Internal Distribution of Power

This is a subject that seems to fascinate everyone. (For example, see the new reader on the subject edited by Zald, 1970.) It certainly attracted the attention of Weber, who described his three different organizational structures primarily in terms of their authority or power distributions. One of the major problems involved in the question of power is really why anyone should obey orders. Weber's answer was that the legitimacy of orders in a rational–legal hierarchy of authority, the power structure of bureaucracy, rest on the legitimacy of the position. Indeed, this is the reason for his term rational–legal. This theme has since been elaborated upon by various students of organizations in various ways.

The problem of how to define power is raised in the selection by Mechanic, in what we feel is the most simple and straightforward discussion of the problem in the literature on organizations. After duly noting his basic debt to Weber, Mechanic attempts to handle a most un-Weberian kind of question—what gives power to what he calls the "lower participants"? Or, humorously rephrased, why should the boss obey his secretary's orders? His answers provide insights into how organizations work as a give and take between the power bases of the superiors and those of the subordinates.

A straightforward measure of how much influence each level of organization has over the other levels, especially over the higher ones in the hierarchy, is presented in the control graph work of Tannenbaum and his colleagues (1968), an example of which appears in Chapter Five, in the selection by Clagett Smith and Ari. Here we see a measure designed to tap the power of Mechanic's lower participants.

The question "what are the bases of power?" is another way of asking "why do subordinates obey an order?" This problem is discussed in two articles, each representing a different approach. Julian (Chapter Four) builds upon the Etzioni (1961) thesis of three different forms of compliance, examining the theory vis-à-vis patients in a hospital. This thesis sees three kinds of control: coercive, renumerative, and normative. Etzioni rationalizes that physical force, money, and ideas or norms are the reasons why people obey orders. A similar answer is found in the work of Warren (1968).

For those who would like to read more about this issue, perhaps one of the most accessible analyses is by Peabody (1964), a case study of the reasons why teachers, policemen, and welfare workers obey orders. Unfortunately few have followed his empirical approach of simply asking why. His findings are instructive: teachers in an elementary school were most likely to say they obeyed because of the competence of their superior, welfare workers out of deference to position or, in Weber's terms, legitimacy, and policemen, who were more divided, out of respect for position or personal qualities. Again in this work, there is an excellent review of the literature.

Another useful source in the same vein is the second case study of French bureaucracy by Crozier (1964), which we were unable to include here. He asks how anyone can have any power in a highly centralized and programmed organization. His answer is that uncertainty provides a basis of power. This approach to the problem of power is important in that it differs considerably from the power conceptions of Mechanic, Julian, Warren, and Peabody. It has, in turn, inspired a number of interesting research studies on the problem of why some departments have more power than others. Following through on this insight, Lawrence and Lorsch (Chapter Four) note that power is most likely to accrue to departments with uncertain environments.

Before we move on to the problem of centralization (and the various other terms for describing the internal distribution of power across all positions or all departments), we might note that a very important question involved in the issue of power is the appropriate span of control for the superior. Should a boss have four assistants or one? Six subordinates or none? For many years, conventional wisdom suggested that five or six was the maximum one could have. When Sears, Roebuck kept making higher profits (Worthy, 1950), and showed that one could have fifty subordinates, conventional wisdom became less wise. During the past decade, a large amount of work on span of control has been done. Its popularity is reflected in the selections by Woodward; Hall et al.; and Hickson et al. in Chapter Two, and by Blau, and Pugh et al., in this chapter.

In the latter article, on the dimensions of organizational structure, the authors quantify several variations of a theme: the span of the chief executive and the subordinate ratio. The subordinate ratio is an important part of their third factor—line control of work-flow—on organizations, although the chief executive's span is not, suggesting, like Woodward, different spans for different levels, perhaps influenced by different variables. In the Hickson et al. selection (Chapter Two), the supervisory–subordinate ratio is a replication in Birmingham, England, of what Woodward had already done in South Essex. This led them to conclude that operational technology may be critical for this variable because it is the point in the structure where the production process—in the sense of machines—exists.

Among other articles, for those who are interested in this problem, we especially recommend Udell (1967) and Meyer (1968a and c), both of whom give additional bibliography. The upshot of most of the work has been to discover that span of control still varies considerably, and we have no conclusive explanation. Meyer suggests that more qualified people are placed in shorter spans, but this contradicts Udell's findings. Again, there may be a need to make the kinds of distinctions made by Woodward—in terms of technologies and of levels within the organization. Closely akin to the idea of span of control is that of supervisory styles. This is a traditional social-psychological concern and therefore beyond the province of this book. However, sometimes span of control is used to infer the kind of supervisory style that exists. It might be better to measure it directly.

The Mechanic and Julian, selections focus primarily on the power of a particular position and not on the distribution of power among a number of different positions. This latter conception, which Weber termed the authority structure, comes across most clearly in the selection by Blau, who notes the necessity for making a distinction between what he calls the professional and the bureaucratic.

Equally important is the problem of how one measures power across a number of different positions. A variety of methods are represented in the selections given in this text–reader. The oldest tradition, and a very effective one, is represented in the control graph work of Smith and Ari (Chapter Five). For those wanting to read more about this approach, and about the various variables to which this measure has been related, Tannenbaum's *Control in Organizations* (1968) is excellent. In the paper by Pugh *et al.,* we see the variable of centralization, which is determined by noting at what levels decisions of various kinds are made. On research in England, the Aston group (Pugh, Hickson, *et al.*) investigated what factors determine particular power distributions, whereas what determines the consequences, of such aggregates of power is the focus of Tannenbaum and his colleagues. In the Hage and Aiken selection in Chapter Five we find that power is measured in two ways. The first is based on some items reported in this chapter from Hall's study, which measure control over work decisions. The second is a measure of participation in basic decision making. Again, the accent is on consequences of particular power distributions, which they also call centralization, for effecting innovation in the organization. In Chapter Four, the Hage, Aiken, and Marrett selection raises the same question but this time vis-à-vis communication variables. For those who are especially interested in the measurement problems of power distribution, the Price (1972) book on measurement gives the explicit and concrete items that are used in these various studies. And another article by Hage and Aiken (1967b) explores which measure of power is more important, participation in decision making or Hall's hierarchy of authority. Their answer is the former.

Together these various selections indicate that internal power distributions are related to a large number of other kinds of variables, both as causes and as consequences. Those wishing to read more about various hypotheses regarding power should consult the Hage theory. Beyond this, Price (1967) and James Thompson (1968) offer much food for thought. In particular, the latter has raised a number of issues regarding the kinds of coalitions that form in organizations, a relatively novel approach to the problem of organizational power. Traditionally, organizational sociologists have tended to see the power structure as somewhat static. Thompson's work leads to a more dynamic conceptualization.

Another way of reflecting about the internal power distribution is to ask what are the maximums of centralization or decentralization. Here, some of the case studies are insightful, providing some understanding of how power structures are moved or not moved, as the case may be. The McCleery piece in the next chapter is a study designed to see how a power distribution alters across time, in part as a consequence of the addition of technical experts and in part as a consequence of alterations in the communications system. Berliner's case study makes clear that too much centralization is ineffective, forcing the Gosplan to allow more decentralization than it would prefer, in order to make the system work at all. Chandler's case study of

DuPont (Chapter Five) indicates the same to be true for organizations in a capitalist country. Thus another source of change is negative feedback from too much centralization. Still another study—Harrison's, on the American Baptist Church (1959)—provides another part of the puzzle, suggesting that power structures cannot be too decentralized because, if so, they lose in their efficiency and strength—again, presumably an example of negative feedback operating to bring about a change in the internal distribution of power. Together, these three case studies allow us to understand the typical by exploring some of the extremes. However, the problem of a changing power distribution is best handled by comparative, longitudinal research. This we will have to wait for in future research designs.

The Problem of Rules

If the most important component of Weber's bureaucracy is the hierarchy of authority, the second most important is probably rules. Again, there has been much research on this topic, as seen in the large number of studies attempting, in one way or another, to measure rules and procedures. The discussion of measurement is to be found in Price (1972). However, the work of Hall (this chapter), Hall, Johnson, and Haas (Chapter Two), Blau (this chapter), and Hage and Aiken (Chapter Five) are typical of the approaches that have been taken. By far, the most extensive work, however, has been done by Pugh *et al.*, whose many measures of standardization are summarized in their selection in this chapter.

What causes rules and why do people obey them? At first glance, this question might seem the same as that inquiring why people obey orders, but there are some differences. In a famous case study by Gouldner (1954), we read that one reason for the existence of rules is that they are a convenient substitute for supervision. Thus they are seen as mechanisms of control which handle problems in close supervision. Still another answer is given by Haas and Collen (1963) in their case study of an academic department. They observed that the more frequently an event occurred the more likely there was to be a procedure developed to cover it.

One of the problems in discussing rules has been this: just what are the differences between rules and procedures? Interestingly enough, Hall (this chapter) developed a measure indicating that indeed they may be different and may have different causes as well. Which of the two is measured may lie at the source of some of the conflicting findings regarding formalization and size. Size may result in the proliferation of procedures but not necessarily rules. There may be a difference between (1) rules that carefully codify behavior and sanctions for violation, thus becoming substitutes for close supervision, as in the

Gouldner study, and (2) procedures that give guidelines, the standards that are necessary when something occurs frequently, as in the Haas and Collen study.

Certainly rules vary considerably in their obnoxiousness. We might be upset with a no-smoking rule but be quite willing to accept a different safety rule, a point Gouldner observed in his discussion of the different kinds of rules, even down to which are considered acceptable and which not. For those interested in this problem, the pioneering work by Goudner is still the best discussion.

Like centralization, the variable of formalization is an attempt to measure distribution—this time of rules—throughout the whole organization. And in a similar way, formalization has been related to a variety of causes and consequences, albeit with more mixed results than have been obtained in the various studies of power distributions. Again, this diversity probably reflects the basic confusion over kinds of rules.

The Problem of the Technical Expert and the Division of Labor

As in the case of power, this problem has been conceived on two levels and thus in alternative ways. On one level, it has been the problem of the technical expert, to use a Weberian term, or the problem of the professional, to use the most common label in the literature. On another level, it has been conceived as the problem of the division of labor or the degree of complexity in the social structure of the organization. Next to power, this issue has been the most popular topic in the organizational literature, probably because the first two formulations of the problem, one in a famous footnote by Parsons—his discussion of Weber's views on power and authority (1947: 58–60)—and the other in a famous study by Dalton (1950) on the conflict between line and staff, were themselves related to the problem of power. Each suggested that the technical expert on the staff would not accept centralization of power but instead would demand at least to share in the distribution of power.

The problem of the professional, with his demands for power, was noted by Blau and Scott (1962) in their text *Formal Organizations,* as one of the basic dilemmas of organizations. Since then a large amount of work has indeed accumulated on the problems of the professional. One of the better reviews is by Kornhauser and Hagstrom, on the various conflicts between scientists and managers in industry (1962). Hall has written several articles and a monograph on the problems of the professional in a bureaucratic setting (1967, 1968, 1969). Most of these researches indicate that the professional had different values and orientations, and thus different goals or objectives, which in turn can become the basis of conflicts.

Blau, in a selection in this chapter, suggests that different authority structures are necessary as well. A similar argument has been made by Hage and Aiken (1967b), building upon the work of Victor Thompson (1961), who in turn was influenced by Dalton's findings. The professional, in fact, has been the particular focus of Hage and Aiken's work (see Chapter Five), with the finding, in general, that professional activity has a more important impact than professional training, at least as the two variables were measured by them. The findings of Corwin in his study of teachers, reported in the next chapter, in turn appear to suggest that professionalism in organizations is a cause of conflict. All these various works and findings suggest that professionals demand a share of the power structures and are willing to fight for it. Their training and, perhaps even more important, their involvement in professional activities reinforces a different set of goals and commitments that facilitate both their demands for autonomy and their likelihood of conflict with the powers that be.

Traditionally parallel to the problem of the technical expert in a bureaucratic setting has been the issue of the complexity of the social structure, or what Durkheim called the division of labor (1933). Victor Thompson (1961) suggested that the key to structure lies in separating the organization into various parts, usually by occupation, and then reintegrating it into an articulated whole. He made a very careful distinction between *person* specialization in the professions (for example in Blau in this chapter) and *task* specialization on the assembly line (for example in Crozier also in this chapter). It is the former that creates a complex division of labor, which in turn generates consequences for the organization. Most of the articles in the next chapter in one way or another deal with the problem of reintegrating the scattered pieces. Lawrence and Lorsch make this their explicit focus and, in a series of research findings, indicate the many behavioral and attitudinal differences between the departments of an organization. Likewise, Hage, Aiken, and Marrett, in the next chapter, attempt to develop a theory on how structure can be integrated and coordinated.

In this chapter most of the selections suggest that a consequence of the increasing complexity of organizations is the change in power distribution toward decentralization, in one way or another. This idea is found in Burns and Stalker; Hage; Blau; Pugh *et al.,* and to a lesser extent, in Mechanic. Empirically, it is substantiated in Blau, Pugh *et al.* and McCleery (Chapter Four), The other major link again, largely implied in Burns and Stalker, and made explicit in the selections by Hage, Aiken, and Marrett; and Hage and Aiken is the increased communications and innovations that would seem to result from greater complexity in an organization's social structure. What is perhaps surprising about these findings is that most of them were anticipated by Durkheim in his book *The Division of Labor* (1933), which dealt with society. Perhaps this is the reason behind Burns and Stalker's suggestion of the terms *mechanistic* and *organic,* terms used by

Durkheim to describe two ways in which societies could be integrated and coordinated.

The question of what causes increased complexity has already been raised in the previous chapter. In general, the approach has usually been Durkheimian. The answer according to Durkheim, lies in increased size and, more importantly, population density. This is one reason why the Pugh *et al.* selection on the contexts of organization is so critical. It suggests the importance of considering several variables as causes at the same time, moving beyond a single causal model of structural differentiation.

The Problem of Configuration

Running through many of the selections is an attempt to measure organizational structure by counting its most visible aspects, namely, its parts. Thus, departments can be contrasted by the number of levels they exhibit (Hall, Haas, and Johnson; and both Blau selections) and by the span of control at various levels (Blau, in this chapter; Woodward, in the previous one; and Pugh *et al.*). The attractiveness of these measures is that they are easy, or relatively so, to obtain. They have the appearance of being much more objective. One is unlikely to make many mistakes counting the number of departments in an organization or to misperceive what is a department.

Yet, at the same time, these measures have been used indirectly for other variables such as complexity and centralization, thus becoming indirect measures of these variables. What is complicated is that different people have used the same indicator to mean different things. One argument runs that a longer span of control means less supervision, and another that a shorter span of control means less supervision. Some, such as Blau in this chapter, have suggested that many levels in a hierarchy are associated with decentralization, whereas others have argued that this would be a measure or an indicator of centralization (see Udy, 1959b). Perhaps it is for these reasons that the results so far have been inconclusive regarding these various properties. But one reason for this lack of conclusiveness may be the failure to follow up Woodward's lead. Clearly her table on technology, span of control, and success is a pattern that one can easily grasp and that has much significance.

A more direct approach to the problem of configuration is represented in the Pugh *et al.* selections in this and preceding chapters. Here we see numerous and diverse measures one can employ to explore the shape of the structure. In their factor analysis, the authors obtain a major dimension which they call line control of work-flow. Here, configuration is studied in its own right and not as a proxy for some other variable. For those interested in this aspect of structure, the articles by Pondy (1969) and by Kaufman and Seidman (1970) are among the best reading, along with that already referred to in our discussion about span of control. All of them also offer good reviews of the literature.

What are the causes and consequences of configuration? Except for the unequivocal findings of Woodward, which are also suggested by Hickson *et al.,* this remains a bit of a mystery. It is not at all certain that configuration, as visible as it is, is an important aspect of social structure. What is clearly important is the distribution of power across a number of levels. It may not be important how many levels there are. Moreover, if the number of levels is used at once to indicate differentiation and centralization and decentralization, then we cannot hope to find any consistent results. Equally controversial is the relationship between complexity and the number of departments or levels. This configurational aspect may not be as important as the number of specialisms (Pugh *et al.*) or occupations (Hage and Aiken; Hage, Aiken, and Marrett). The great advantage of configuration is its ease of measurement. The great disadvantage is that we are not yet sure of its effects. What is more, considerable differences of opinion obtain about which particular aspects of the configuration matter. Again, we confront an area requiring more research.

Other Problems

We would have liked to include other articles that speak to still more issues in the study of social structure and that appear to be equally important. The distribution of money and prestige, the status pyramid, is one topic deserving some attention. In the selection by Hage, it is made a part of the theory of organizational structure. But there have been relatively few studies focusing on this problem. In part, this may reflect the general assumption that power and status are the same thing and that, of the two, power is the more important. Indeed, the distribution of salaries has been suggested as a measure of centralization, reflecting this viewpoint (Price, 1972). Perhaps the most promising study has been done by Seeman and Evans (1961), who report their work on the relationship between stratification and hospital care. What is of special interest about this study is the careful attention paid to measurement. Few studies have been so rigorous and so provocative. Unfortunately, others have not followed their lead.

Closely akin to the problem of the distribution of money, the question of succession in organizations has been well studied, with interesting results. Here the work of Grusky, who spent much time working on various aspects to this problem stands out (1970). The Gouldner (1954) case study can also be read with profit because it raises a slightly different issue, that is, succession from outside of the organization. Closely analogous to various measures of configuration are what might be called the ratio measures. Interest in these first developed with the original work on size, when researchers were exploring its relationship to the proportion or number of administrative staff, an association that was felt to be the essence of bureaucracy. For example, in the selection by Pugh *et al.* in this chapter, the variable, proportion of clerks, is used to raise the question of whether size increases the proportion of administrative staff.

Again, many of the findings have been either somewhat inconclusive or else point to more complicated relationships than simple one-to-one associations (see Blau and Schoenherr, 1970). The best analysis is the article by Pondy (1969) and the best research the selection by Hickson *et al.* Pondy's "administrative intensity" is perhaps the wisest label but, as the Hickson *et al.* selection makes clear, organizations can be intense in many ways. And each research study tends to represent particular kinds of organizations, although counting clerical staff or "clerks," as the English call them, is perhaps almost universal. Pondy's work argues that besides technology, one needs to consider other variables including that elusive phenomenon, managerial discretion.

Just as we can be concerned with the problem of how best to construct an organization, we can also raise the issue regarding the best way to construct a job or position. Except for a vast literature on personnel selection, which is mainly psychological in nature, surprisingly little has been done of a sociological nature. One study, perhaps one of the most provocative pieces in the entire literature, is never or hardly ever referenced, perhaps because few have raised the issue of how best to construct a social position. Andrews (1964; also see Pelz and Andrews, 1966) found that one could obtain higher levels of productivity and innovativeness by working less than 100 percent of the time on research and by combining research jobs with either teaching or administration. Yet, during the great conflict between students and universities of the sixties over absent professors, this article was, to our knowledge, never cited. Unfortunately, Andrews does not report what happens to teaching under these circumstances. Nevertheless the implications of the findings are staggering because they open a whole new way of thinking about the problem of social structure and the ways in which an organization can be constructed. Two other studies, both from the social-psychological and psychological literature, and each with extended bibliography, are Douglas Hall and Lawler's (1970) work on job characteristics and Cummings and El Salmi's (1970) work on role diversity. Both aim at how to construct a job for maximum contribution to an organization while maintaining the job satisfaction of the workers.

THE READINGS

Bureaucracy, Integration, and Alienation*
MICHEL CROZIER

The Parisian Clerical Agency is the Parisian branch of a large public agency, part of a government department. This branch is quite a large-scale organization by itself. At the time the data we will use were collected, it employed 4,500 people, mostly women, in a single establishment. Its size—in any case huge for an administrative organization —sets it apart from the other establishments of the same public agency, since it employs four or five times more personnel than the biggest provincial establishment. Its purpose is to handle, on a daily basis, simple financial operations requested by a great many customers.

It is a public service run for the public benefit and not for profit. However, since it provides the French nation with huge sums of money on a short-term basis, it has a great importance for the French treasury.

The Clerical Agency's most important present characteristic is its steady growth. This growth is due not only to the general economic growth of the country, but also to the changing habits of the French public. It is not viewed with great favor by the managements of the Agency and of the Parisian branch, since it brings them many difficulties and no rewards. The managements must abide by Civil Service rules, since increase of staff and all other new expenditures are part of the National State Budget. Because of the habitual thrift of the French Ministry of Finance and the usual distrust of parliament for the executive, the necessary authorizations for budgetary expansion always lag behind. The organization must be managed in a parsimonious way incompatible with the requirements of its development.

The main problems are the number of personnel and shortage of office space. New jobs are not created until the need for them is very great; it is thus impossible to build up reserves of personnel and to devote enough time to training. There is a heavy emphasis on productivity, but productivity tends to decrease because of the large percentage of young and ill-trained employees, and because of the poor working climate and the high rate of turnover. The working-space situation is even worse. It had been temporarily solved by introducing shift work, which made it possible for twice as many people to work in the same rooms. But the Agency has now been obliged to utilize rooms

* Reprinted from *The Bureaucratic Phenomenon* (Chicago: The University of Chicago Press, 1964), © 1964 by the University of Chicago, all rights reserved. Chapters 1 and 2, with omissions, by permission of the author and the publisher.

formerly considered unsuitable, and this has started continuous bickering with the unions about the hygiene of working conditions.

Office installations, the internal layout, and general maintenance are equally inadequate. There are insufficient toilets, washing facilities, and locker-rooms for the increased personnel. Workrooms are extremely noisy. Tables and filing equipment are old. The whole building is cold and unattractive. The poor standard of cleaning makes it even sadder.

The technology of the Agency's work is simple and it has remained basically unchanged for thirty-five years. The employees, all female, work in production units on heavy cross-tabulating accounting machines (with six or two tabulators). A pneumatic system facilitates quick communication. Work organization is also simple. It does not involve advance planning, since everything is done on a daily basis, according to the demands of the public. The most important qualities for a successful member of management are experience of possible difficulties and a relentless drive for control. All in all, however, this system is very efficient. The Parisian branch, like all the other branches, provides extremely good service, both quick and trustworthy.

The hierarchical organization is also uncomplicated. It is a pure line organization, with no staff function at all, at least at the branch level. The basic unit is the workroom, with about one hundred employees working in two shifts of fifty each. The workroom is further divided into the regular workroom, and the special section, where half a dozen senior employees and a few members of the supervisory grades handle mistakes, special cases, and requests for information. Two inspectors—one for the special section and one for the regular workroom—and four *surveillantes* form the supervisory staff of each shift. A section chief heads the two shifts and co-ordinates their work. There is one division head over ten such workrooms. He has about a thousand employees to care for and has two senior section chiefs and a secretary as his own personal staff. At the time of our study there were three regular divisions, with a fourth one in charge of all auxiliary work, incoming and outgoing mail, new accounts, the printing shop, maintenance, etc. Over the four divisions there was one senior division head, the formal head of the branch. He also has a very small staff—one personal secretary, a dozen clerks for handling mail, and a special office, likewise very poorly staffed, for all employment records, the delivery of pay-checks, and many odd jobs. As one would expect, this manager does not plan ahead and direct the adjustment of the organization. His function is, rather, to coordinate the action of the four division heads, to arbitrate among them when necessary, and to try to make them work according to the imperative rules of the Central Office.

The Agency is not autonomous, and its national management is part of the Ministry's bureaucratic structure. Executives are promoted from one section of the Ministry to another more frequently than from the field to the Central Office. National management has many echelons but not a very large staff. Its organization also is very rigid. Most of its bureaus theoretically have only advisory functions. In fact, however, they operate as the actual heads of the line organization and issue orders that must be applied in the field. These orders usually are presented not as special decisions but as general rules for all branches throughout France. Only the Parisian branch frequently receives special treatment because of the problems created by its size, but even this is done quite reluctantly.

The Organization of Work and Productivity

The basic units of work organization are the four-girl work teams. These teams, to which more than 60 percent of the employees belong, are in charge of the direct productive function of the Agency—i.e., the carrying out and accounting of the customer's orders. Many employees, of course, do not belong to these teams, but are doing preparatory work or handling special cases and mistakes. Among them are the people working in the special workrooms and all those employed in the fourth division. The Agency as a whole, however, remains a rather rare example of a large modern organization in which everything still revolves around a large set of autonomous and parallel productive units, working independently of one another.

The work-flow in such an organization is extremely simple. Sorting out the incoming mail in the early morning and a second mail in the late morning, processing operations, preparing the outgoing mail, and balancing the accounts of the day—these daily tasks never vary. The main characteristics of this system of work are the daily rhythm, the lack of interdependence between the teams. Every work team has to do the same thing and does not have to cooperate with other work teams to accomplish its tasks. These tasks are daily tasks, and even their quantity cannot be fixed by human decision. One principle is followed, as a sort of golden rule: All the traffic arriving on time must be handled the same day.

Work, therefore, does not depend on supervisory decisions and group relationships, but on the impersonal pressure of the public at large. The only possible scapegoat for one shift is the other shift, whose alleged slowness and neglect may be seen as having made it necessary for the group to stay overtime.

Within the work team, on the other hand, there are division of work and a great deal of interdependence. Two girls work at the tabulating machines and two at checking. The work process begins with a check of the customer's credentials, then the girl at the first (six-tabulator) machine types, at one time, all documents necessary for carrying out the order. The figures are then checked by the third employee; and they are finally tabulated again, for balancing the accounts, by the fourth. The girl who initiates the work process by checking the customer's demands must be the most experienced, since she has the responsibility of deciding whether or not the order can be carried out. More important, in practice she sets the pace of work for her colleagues. She is considered, therefore, the team leader, although her role is not officially acknowledged and she does not receive any recognition for it.

Obviously such a system of organization de-emphasizes the role of supervision. Supervisors need not organize the work-flow; they do not have to decide about the work to be done and the people to do it.

Most of the time of the *inspecteurs* is devoted to small personal tasks, especially to collecting data for statistical purposes. The functions of section chiefs are of a more supervisory nature. They handle all minor problems of discipline, take care of personnel administration, and prepare the individual ratings of their subordinates.

At a higher level, the main problem concerns the distribution of the work load among the different sections. Such a distribution cannot be made daily according to the requirements the organization has to meet and the resources it has at its disposal. It is made indirectly and permanently by making each section and each work team within the section responsible for all the traffic which a certain number of customers they service will eventually bring.

Each team is solely responsible for handling the traffic of its own customers. But when there are traffic peaks the work load becomes too heavy; bigger units, by allowing for reserve and planning ahead, could handle them much better.

To solve this problem, the managers of the Agency put a great deal of pressure on the personnel by imposing very harsh discipline and by relying, in times of crisis, on the direct authority of the supervisors. Employees are not usually subject to arbitrary interventions, but they cannot bargain over the amount of the work load. The discipline to which they must submit is impersonal and its means of action are limited, since firing anyone is practically impossible. But it is sufficient to hold in check a woman employee whose feelings are easily manipulated by threats of public humiliation, such as official reprimands and insertions of criticism in the personal files. No kind of absenteeism is tolerated; mistakes are traced to the girls administratively responsible for them and written excuses are demanded from each of them.

In times of crisis, the supervisor's role of watching and checking, which ordinarily does not seem to have much importance, suddenly takes precedence. The social system of the Agency itself seems to be set up for a regular alternation of long periods of routine with short periods of crisis. During the periods of routine the authoritarian structure of the organization will all but disappear behind its impersonal system of action; subordinates are left alone, and supervisors take care of their own tasks only. But when crises come, a complete transformation into a very painful climate of excitement and nervous stress occurs. A state of emergency reigns. People adjust to it, the superiors by becoming active interventionists and the girls by accepting an obedient role.

Employees' Social Participation and Integration

There is a definite contrast between employees' attitudes toward work and their job and their attitudes and behavior in terms of social participation within the organization. The girls working in the Clerical Agency do not dislike their jobs more than the employees in other large-scale administrative organizations dislike theirs; but a general climate of apathy and social isolation such as prevails in the branch is very uncommon. The girls do not manifest any pride in belonging to the Agency or to their branch. They are not interested in participating or getting involved in any way in the branch life. Furthermore, they do not seem to interact much among themselves when on the job, nor to be able to form stable supportive clique relationships. Finally, the kind of solidarity that does develop is expressed against the higher-ups and the formal structure of the Agency.

Social Isolation and the Lack of Friendship Ties

The poor morale and the disintegration of the old-fashioned *esprit fonctionnaire* can easily be understood. However, the lack of friendship ties among a personnel made up of young and lively girls is curious. Nevertheless, interviews indicate that there is such a lack.

Forty percent of the interviewees say that they have no friends at all in the branch. Another 40 percent say that while they may have friends in the branch, they prefer to have their friends outside. Only 20 percent feel positively about their workmates as potential friends. The flavor of the comments we get are even more striking:

> From a thirty-year-old working-class girl from Brittany:
>
> I have my friends on the outside. Here in the branch one cannot get to be friends as in a small office.
>
> From a thirty-year-old working-class girl from Paris:
>
> I have my friends more outside. I would not like having friends here. . . . I may see some of them (my colleagues) outside work, but they are not actually friends, but acquaintances only.
>
> From a twenty-year-old lower-middle-class girl from Paris:
>
> We are work pals but not friends. We do not say "tu" to each

other. In the work team everything is fine, although there are always jealousies, you know. . . . I have my friends outside. I would not like to have my friends here. I am not so sociable, and then most of the girls come from the country; it is not the same.

From a twenty-eight-year-old middle-class girl from the southwest:

It is only at the work team level that one can get to be friends. Anyway here I have work pals but not really friends. It is difficult to make friends.

The Negative Solidarity of the Personnel and the Extent of Union Activities

Employees, we have seen, do not identify themselves with the Civil Service, they are not interested in the purposes and the functioning of their organization, and they feel completely neglected. This moral isolation is not compensated by a warm atmosphere of friendship ties derived from belonging to a cohesive and diversified group. Thus individuals are left quite on their own, with the only possible support being that of their small work team. This isolation, however, forms only one side of the employees' social relationships. One must recognize the existence, at a deeper level, of a strong group solidarity—albeit a negative one. It is manifested against the branch as an institution, against management, at times even against trade unions—but never positively.

This general feeling of negative solidarity was very well expressed in the strike that took place in 1953, exactly eight months before the interviews. This strike was not the outcome of a dispute restricted to the branch, but a part—and a small part—of a successful general strike of all civil servants in France. But if the girls at the branch did not take the initiative, they certainly seized the opportunity to express with great eagerness their pent-up discontent. In that respect, it is characteristic that the girls who had struck, when interviewed eight months later, talked most of the time about the strikes as if they had forgotten that it was a general strike and remembered it only as their own personal strike. At any rate, it had taken a bitter turn at the branch and had lasted almost one full month, with about half of the girls striking till the very end.

We asked the girls whether they had been strikers and whether they had struck until the end. We also asked them for their comments on the way the strike had been run and about its results.

The Agency officials in the Ministry thought of the strike as a trade-union affair and presented us with the usual stereotypes about strikers as hotheads and poor workers excited by trade-union agitators. Our interviews made it possible to check interpretations of the strike more accurately. To our own surprise, the results were extremely unambiguous. The simplest cross-tabulations showed clearly that the girls who stayed on strike until the last minute were (1) the team leaders (all of them but one), and (2) the people attached to their work who had favorable attitudes toward friendship ties in the branch. All staunch trade unionists, of course, had struck; but otherwise there was no relationship between feelings toward the unions and participation in the strike. Strikers were not hotheads; on the contrary, they were the most responsible and best workers. This was corroborated by a cross-tabulation with the evaluations supervisors had made of them. Seventy-seven percent of the girls considered excellent by their supervisors struck until the end; only 33 percent of those considered merely good workers and 20 percent of those considered mediocre stayed out as long.

Authority Relationships

We had asked several questions: "What do you think of first-line supervisors?" "Will *your* supervisors go to bat for you?" "Are they friendly with you?" "Could you trust them?" The first question is general, the others more specific. They were never directed toward one individual, since the employees interviewed had to deal with two different supervisors. The questions elicited many comments, often rich and well balanced—but surprisingly enough, almost never emotional or even personal. Our respondents remained within the functional frame of reference they were given; they took great pains to express themselves clearly and moderately; they were often sharp, but did not lose their tempers or their tolerance.

For example, one of the sharpest answers by a serious, experienced woman who had a great deal to say:

> Generally, I think they [the supervisors] worry too much about their career and possibilities of promotion. They are jealous and awfully competitive. They are also sectarian. Often there is a lot of hostility between sections, and they are all responsible for it; each one of them wants to have his little kingdom. . . . They are too far above the actual work problems to understand what is actually going on. . . . I do not think they understand clearly how the work is done; they miss most of it—and most of what people feel too.
>
> They should be less numerous. The role of the *inspecteur* is not clear enough. Section chiefs have to take responsibilities, but the *inspecteur* never has to.

And when asked whether the supervisors would go to bat for employees:

> Supervisors defend us inasmuch as they think it will help them. If not, they would eventually trample on the employees. Our own section chief is very self-seeking.
>
> They are moody, very distant and cold with some employees, almost intimate with others. In the last analysis, relationships are not bad; one feels free toward them and I myself do not scruple to tell them what I think.
>
> They never talk with us about work. They say hello once in a while, convinced they will never have to learn anything, although I feel they could benefit most from contact.

It seems clear that this employee is very critical of her section chief. She is, at the same time, perceptive and rather tolerant. She analyzes the situation of a supervisor as if she were able to forget her own stake in the relationship.

Authority relationships at the first level can therefore be considered as tolerant, reasonably cordial, and not at all tense. Against this rather moderate background, the comments made by the employees about their division heads, i.e., the second-line supervisors, appear unexpectedly personal.

We had asked only one question: "What do you think of the big bosses?" Forty-four percent of the interviewees made no comments. They stated that, having had no direct relationships with them, they could not make any fair evaluations. But 28 percent gave sharply hostile comments, such as:

> He is a no-good; he is a real skunk; they are very harsh.

Or showed some highly emotional fear:

> He makes me feel helpless, paralyzed.
>
> I have seen him only once, with a delegation, but I understood right away. He prevents people from saying anything. I could not speak one word. He did not let us explain. . . . I do not want to see him, I feel paralyzed.

Besides this group of violently hostile employees, a smaller group (9 percent) were moderately critical, and a group of 20 percent were favorable.

We have already described the quasi-militaristic chain of command with the division head on top, the section chief and the *inspecteurs* in the middle, and almost no functional staff. The division head has only two senior section chiefs to help him. Yet he has to make all decisions necessary to the functioning of the division—not only the general decisions, such as fixing new goals to co-ordinate the sections' operations, and prescribing new ways of working. He also must make the specific decisions pertaining to the daily life of the em-

ployees that affect problems of work—e.g., the possibility of post-
poning a number of operations when the section is delayed—as well
as discipline and other personnel problems.

Placed in such a situation, division heads have neither the capability nor the desire to delegate their responsibilities. Thus they have
the final word on a multitude of trivial matters—e.g., whether or not
to allow an employee one day off for personal convenience, or whether
to blame an employee who has made errors in posting an operation.
Since they themselves, even with the help of their two assistants, cannot possibly have an adequate knowledge of what is involved, they
must rely heavily on the information they receive from the section
chiefs. The section chiefs, however, are not in a position to provide
reliable information. All ten of them are running parallel identical
units that have to compete for scarce resources. Therefore, they have
no relationships of interdependence and no common positive interests
among themselves, and tend to view each other only as competitors.
Thus they are likely, first, to bias the information they give in order to
get the maximum of material resources and personal favors with which
to run their sections smoothly; and, second, to put pressure on the
division head to prevent him from entering into a close relationship
with another colleague and to favor the latter over them.

As a result, division heads are condemned to get only unreliable
information and to remain isolated from the daily problems of work.
Their decisions tend to be impersonal routine decisions, i.e., decisions
based on the letter of the rules and not on equity. The only possible
exceptions are a few, more personal decisions resulting from chance
encounters from an informal network of information—and these decisions will very likely be the cause of accusations of favoritism.

In view of the pressures arising from this kind of arrangement, one
should not be surprised to discover that the employees blame the division heads, while remaining tolerant of the first-line supervisory staff.
The latter are well situated to placate their subordinates by pretending
to do whatever they can to defend them against the harshness of an
impersonal system manifest in the division head. Indeed, it is interesting that the only really discriminating item in the comments of the employees relating to their first-line supervisors concerns this problem of
defending subordinates. The girls do not trust their supervisors very
much; 44 percent of them say that it is very difficult to know, and only
12 percent seem to trust them completely. A solid discrimination could
be made, finally, on the negative side, where the decisive argument
was, "My supervisor will surely not go to bat for us," and not "He is
harsh."

The Ministry's behavior tends to reinforce this pattern. It resists
vigorously any pretensions of the section chief to a part in managerial
prerogatives. As we have already seen, it does not leave the section
chiefs much initiative on either personnel or on work organization

matters. Materially, it does not want to give them the status of supervisors. At the time they were interviewed, the section chiefs' main demand was to have management give them, when modernizing the workrooms, separate cubby-holes with real supervisors' desks. Management successfully resisted their request by affirming that they did not have to be isolated from their subordinates.

No wonder that the section chiefs tend to side with their employees! They have nothing to gain by assuming a managerial attitude. And defending their employees, or at least putting on a show of defending them, gives them a chance of fostering a better climate and may even please management by keeping them out of trouble. They prefer —and one easily sympathizes with them—to have cordial relationships with their subordinates at the expense of the division head than to assume, in place of their superiors, responsibilities which the latter refuse to relinquish.

It is also not surprising that the Ministry views the supervisors as apathetic and unreliable. They are, as a matter of fact, lackadaisical; they refuse stubbornly to be involved in management's plans. They feel—and it is rational enough—that they have not much to gain and a great deal to lose by giving their support to management. Management is not strong enough to reward them, and they would be vulnerable to criticism by the employees, the unions, and their peers. Section chiefs, as a matter of fact, are as critical of management and as suspicious of its motives as *inspecteurs* and *inspecteurs-adjoints.* Discussing with the researcher the problem of the *controleurs* who do not have a function corresponding to their status, only one of thirty-one section chiefs did not give an explanation devoid of any derogatory connotation.

To summarize the situation, we would like to propose the following hypothesis: Management's complaints come from its inability to have any influence on its supervisory staff. The supervisory staff's behavior is primarily directed by its desire to prevent management from interfering in its affairs.

We have frequently pointed out the fact that responsibilities within the Agency are centralized, with no staff functions to help carry them out. This means that decisions must be made by people who have no direct knowledge of the field and of the relevant variables, and who must rely on the information given them by subordinates who may have a subjective interest in distorting the data. In this sense, one can state that the power of decision in this system tends to be located in a blind spot. Those who have the necessary information do not have the power to decide, and those who have the power to decide cannot get the necessary information.

Now, let us analyze the case of an executive faced with the problem of making a decision which can hurt or further the feelings and interests of some of his subordinate units without being able to ascertain the value of their conflicting arguments. He is most likely to try to find some impersonal rules, or at least some precedent, on which to rely. His decision will probably be inadequate; but given his special predicament, it will be the best solution in the long run.

Our division head might make better decisions if he tried to establish for himself some special channel of information, or if he were ready to trust one or several of his subordinates. But if he did either, he would probably have to combat accusations of favoritism and to face the possibility of a serious deterioration of the climate, whatever the soundness of the end result. If he were to grant all the claims of his subordinates, he would not be able to run an organization where the constraint of scarcity remains. Routine remains the safest way for him, whatever his own feelings. One may wonder more about the (very infrequent) innovating decisions than about the reiteration of routinized behavior.

We have already noticed that there is a parallel impossibility of communication on the same subject between the first-line and the second-line supervisors. The second-line supervisors are frightened at the possibility of discriminating between units in order to help them improve productivity. They refuse to allow any breach in the rules and will alleviate the work load only at the last minute, when there is no alternative. Thus both groups, first-line and second-line supervisors, evade conflict and the use of direct authority. For them, routine is a protection. The same interpretation can apply at the higher level. It also seems clear that management prefers the impersonality of rules and statistics to the risks of a more responsible course of action.

Routinism, of course, is reinforced at all levels by the special training that comes with the established career patterns. And one may even grant that some kind of self-selection may operate, that people come to work or remain at work in such an organization because it fits their personality needs or corresponds to their value system. But sources of routinism should not be sought first in the personality traits of the civil servants, but in the respective situations of the different groups to which they belong in the work organization. Patterns of behavior which have become internalized during long formative years must be considered. They must be taken into account, not as explanations of this situation—people do not refuse to take responsibility because they have been trained not to—but as an added weight to the stability of the system, as a decisive factor in understanding why change is so difficult.

Viewing the situation from another angle, we may argue that communications are biased and behavior routinized because there is too great a gap between the prescribed patterns of action and the requirements of the task. If this is so, the only solution is to add a few other impersonal rules. Since these rules will disturb some already established patterns, they will have to be imposed over the resistance of the intermediary echelons; and they will finally appear as a further step toward greater centralization. Reform will most probably take the aspect of, and appear as, a threat of centralization. It will not benefit from the good will and the experience accumulated below, and will be all the more difficult accordingly. Most people will refuse to become involved. Those who do will be accused of favoritism; the pressure for preserving equality of treatment will become irresistible.

In the present case the basic question seems to be: why did a system develop which blocks executives and supervisors in a situation of routine and produces many frustrations among employees, and how can it resist all kinds of pressure for change?

In other words, why do people build organizations where impersonal rules and routine will bind individual behavior to such an extent? Why do they build bureaucracies? Anticipating our future analysis, we should like to suggest that they are trying to evade face-to-face relationships and situations of personal dependency whose authoritarian tone they cannot bear.

Models of Mechanistic and Organic Structure*
TOM BURNS AND G. M. STALKER

As industrial enterprises grew in size and as the variety of individual tasks increased with the division of labour and the development of technology, the consequential task was created of directing, co-ordinating, and monitoring the activities of large numbers of men, women, and children. The first spontaneous attempts at comparatively large-scale organization used a system of sub-contracting. Bendix, in his study of industrial management in England during the Industrial Revolution, cites evidence that this system prevailed in iron-making and cutlery, in engineering, building, textiles, pin-manufacture, clothing, match-industry, boot- and shoe-making, printing, paper, mining, and railways, and remarks "It was obviously up to these sub-contractors to deal with their 'underhands,' whom they recruited, employed, trained, supervised, disciplined, paid and fired" (1956: 53; Clapham, 1932: 124–33).

The incorporation of the sub-contractor (and his "underhands") into the concern itself, first as agent and then as foreman, gradually pruned away many of these functions from him. For most of the

* Reprinted from Tom Burns and G. M. Stalker, *The Management of Innovation* (London: Tavistock Publications Ltd., 1961), pp. 103–12, 114–16, 118–25, with omissions, by permission of the authors and publisher.

nineteenth century, however, the scale of enterprise was such that what functions were removed from the salaries agent or overseer reverted to the owner–manager himself. It is the last hundred years that have seen the absolute and relative growth of the salaried officials of industry. Bendix (1956: 214) has worked out estimates for the period c. 1900–c. 1950 for Britain, France, Germany, Sweden, and the United States. According to his findings, the proportion of "administrative employees" to "production employees" rose in Britain from 8.6 percent in 1907 to 20 percent in 1948. In Sweden, where this proportion grew most rapidly, it rose from 6.6 percent in 1915 to 21 percent in 1950.

Increase in scale had two aspects: sheer growth in numbers employed, and increase in productivity. Both are equally familiar developments, and both depended largely on the expansion of the consumption of standard products which enabled industrialists to break down manufacturing processes into small individual cycles of activity which could be converted into machine processes or semi-skilled routines. The whole system depended on holding demand for the same product steady enough and on technical development being slow enough for large-lot production. The history of the motor-car industry is characteristic of the general industrial trend.

The standardization (through publicity and through price reductions) of consumer demand enabled the major industries to maintain relatively stable technical and commercial conditions. Under such conditions not only did concerns grow in size, not only could manufacturing processes be routinized, mechanized, and quickened, but the task of ensuring co-operation and of co-ordination, of planning and monitoring, could also be broken down into routines and inculcated as specialized management tasks.

The growth in the numbers of industrial administrative officials, or managers, reflects the growth of organizational structures. Production department managers, sales managers, accountants, inspectors, and the rest, emerged as specialized parts of the general management function as industrial concerns increased in size. Their jobs were created, in fact, out of the general manager's either directly, or at one or two removes. This gives them and the whole social structure which contains their newly created roles its hierarchic character. It is indeed—what one would expect to emerge from the spontaneous sub-contracting phase of management if history followed set patterns —a quasi-feudal structure. All rights and powers at every level derive from the immediate superior; fealty, or "responsibility," is owed to him; all benefits are "as if" dispensed by him. The feudal bond is more easily and more often broken than in feudal polities, but loyalty to the concern, to employers, is regarded not only as proper, but as essential to the preservation of the system. Chester Barnard makes this point with the utmost clarity and emphasis: "The most important single contribution required of the executive, certainly the most universal qualification, is loyalty, domination by the organization personality" (1938: 220). And, as A. W. Gouldner has said, "Much of W. H. Whyte's recent study of 'organization man' is a discussion of the efforts by industry to attach managerial loyalty to the corporation" (1958: 416).

In drawing a contrast between the spontaneity of the first phase of industrial management and the highly structured formalistic nature of the second, we do not imply in either case that their adoption by shrewd and competent and successful business men was anything other than a reasonable solution for their immediate problem. Each was—and is—appropriate to specific sets of circumstances, circumstances which include the knowledge available of the working of administrative systems. At the time of the creation of formalized management systems, this knowledge was limited largely to the experience of large, stable bureaucracies—civil service establishments and ecclesiastical hierarchies—and to military forces and ships' companies. Industry, when the time came, inevitably adopted bureaucracy as its management system because, during this phase, stability was a basic presumption of growth.

The formal organization of industrial management along bureaucratic lines coupled with the concurrent growth of national armies and governmental administration, especially in Western Europe, suggested to sociologists that "bureaucratization" was as intrinsic to the character of modern society as was scientific and technological progress. For Weber, the founder of the study of bureaucracy, it exhibited the same feature of rational thought applied to the social environment as does technology in the case of the physical environment.

Bureaucracy, then, stands as the "formal organization" of industrial concerns. The formulation given by Weber is a generalized description of the "ideal type" of bureaucracy—i.e., a synthetic model composed of what are understood in society at large to be the distinguishing features of actual bureaucratic organizations, military, ecclesiastical, governmental, industrial, etc. These distinctive characteristics are (1947: 329–334):

(i) The organization operates according to a body of laws or rules, which are consistent and have normally been intentionally established.

(ii) Every official is subject to an impersonal order by which he guides his actions. In turn his instructions have authority only insofar as they conform with this generally understood body of rules; obedience is due to his office, not to him as an individual.

(iii) Each incumbent of an office has a specified sphere of competence, with obligations, authority, and powers to compel obedience strictly defined.

(iv) The organization of offices follows the principle of hierarchy; that is, each lower office is under the control and supervision of a higher one.

(v) The supreme head of the organization, and only he, occupies his position by appropriation, by election, or by being designated as successor. Other offices are filled, in principle, by free selection, and candidates are selected on the basis of "technical" qualifications. They are appointed, not elected.

(vi) The system also serves as a career ladder. There is promotion according to seniority or achievement. Promotion is dependent on the judgement of superiors.

(vii) The official who, in principle, is excluded from any ownership rights in the concern, or in his position, is subject to discipline and control in the conduct of his office.

These general principles underlie every subsequent definition given to formal organization in industry; they can even be read, in garbled form, in Henri Fayol's principles of management (1948), although it is extremely unlikely that Weber's work was known to him. Fayol's definitions of management, organization, and so on amount to no more than a thesaurus of synonyms, but the visible symbol of formal organization—the organization chart—originates with him and remains, along with the "organization manual" of job descriptions, the chief instrument of industrial organization (Norman, 1958; Brech, 1953: 25). Industrial consultants, the disciples of Fayol and of F. W. Taylor (whose discrepant views about the necessity of unified command and functional specialization still survive actively in the dilemma of the line and staff organizational structure) have refined and developed the bureaucratic conception of organization in keeping with the growth in technical complexity and scale of twentieth-century industry.

In discussing management systems, social scientists have usually followed one of two paths. They have either accepted the organization chart and manual conception as the "formal organization"—an imposed system of control, information, and authority to which seniors try to get their subordinates to conform—or have harked back to Weber's ideal type of bureaucratic structure and proposed this as a rationalistic interpretation of the working organization of a concern.

The first case seems to entail the notion of a concern as two mutually opposed social systems. The Manichean world of the Hawthorne studies (the chapter of *Management and the Worker* dealing with these matters is headed "Formal *versus* Informal Organization") has been left behind, but it has been succeeded by a crudely Freudian dualism, with formal organization in the role of consciousness, and the concealed or repressed informal organization up to all kinds of mischief.

The *theory* of formal organization is, in itself, quite simple. It holds that throughout the organization there is a strict definition of authority and responsibility. Similarly, there is an equally precise definition of the function of every department. . . . In addition to the described attributes of formal organization, there are several implied assumptions. The first of these is that formal organization is necessary to achieve organizational goals. It is necessary because it is by nature impersonal, logical, and efficient. An organization can function best when individual idiosyncrasies, sentiments, and prejudices do not interfere with official activities. . . .

The second assumption of formal organization is that it is the only organization. . . .

Although formal organization is designed to subject production to logical planning, things never seem to go "according to plan." This is evidenced by the many "problems" managers encounter. They find that no matter how carefully they organize, despite the concern in anticipating problems, unanticipated ones always arise. For these eventualities formal organization offers little guidance because it is created as a guidepost for the routine, the typical, and the foreseeable (Miller and Form, 1951: 159–60).

For an explanation of these unanticipated consequences, the authors prescribe a study of the "informal organization."

The second view construes the bureaucratic structure as one of two possible "models" of the working organization. Gouldner (1958: 405), suggests that the bureaucratic model is a consequence of a rationalistic view, in contrast with the "natural-system" model (such as that presented by Selznick in his *TVA and the Grass Roots*) which arises from the realization that the commercial or administrative "goals of the system as a whole are but one of several important needs to which the organization is oriented. Its component structures are seen as emergent institutions, which can be understood only in relation to the diverse needs of the total system. The organization, according to this model, strives to survive and to maintain its equilibrium, and this striving may persist even after its explicitly held goals have been successfully attained. This strain towards survival may even on occasion lead to the neglect of distortion of the organization's goals. Whatever the plans of their creators, organizations, say the natural system theorists, become ends in themselves and possess their own distinctive needs which have to be satisfied." Waldo (1956) has even identified four different models, each interpreting the working organization from a different point of view: the "machine model" conceived in terms of efficient procedures; the "business model" with activities interpreted in terms of their profitability; the "organic model," which presents the relationships of the concern and its members with the total environment; and the "pure system" model, emphasizing the nature of any organization as a system with special systemic needs. These four models are, however, easily reducible to Gouldner's two when structure and function are considered together; the "machine model" is, after all, a structural representation usually associated with the manipulation of the resources of a concern in the interests of profit (the "business" model); and the "pure system" model, as Gouldner has seen, is merely the "organic model" seen from the point of view of the total needs which the organic system is created and maintained to satisfy.

What all these kinds of views have in common is the assumption that they are concerned with the same thing, that all working organizations are analysable in one or other set of terms, the choice depending not on the difference between working organizations but on the different standpoints of the writers. Variations in working organizations themselves are attributed to departures from normality, or from the overt purpose of the concern, which may be read as inefficiency (Fayol, etc.), irrationality (Weber, etc.), pathology (Mayo, Barnard, etc.), or the superior strength or inflexibility of "informal" institutions (Selznick, etc.).

In the last few years, however, there have emerged some attempts at a synthetic appreciation of the concern which will accept the fact that it is both a bureaucratic institution with a specific social purpose to fulfil *and* a community of people with distinct purposes and institutional forms. One empirical study aimed in this direction is Gouldner's own study of the "succession crisis" in a gypsum mine and factory, when an "outside man" took over the management (1956). The particular form taken by any working organization, he suggested, was the result of the predominance of one or two distinct bureaucratic patterns, either of which took its shape from the intentions and aspirations of chief managers and from the responses and counter systems evolved by subordinates. A "representative bureaucracy" is one in which the organizational rules are initiated and maintained by a majority of all the individuals, managers and workers, on the grounds that the rules are means to ends they all, in some measure, desire. (A "mock bureaucracy" may also exist as a tacit, collusive system in which the formal rules are disobeyed and remain unenforced.) The second pattern is "punishment-centred," a system by which rules are enforced on the grounds on the authority vested in superior office, subordinates are ordered to do things divergent from their own ends, and resistance from subordinates counterbalances the stress on obedience as an end in itself (1958: 403).

The point of the study lies not so much in the formulation of varieties of bureaucracy as in the way in which the actual conduct of a bureaucracy of either kind is displayed as a matter of "informal cooperation and spontaneous reciprocity . . . the latent function of bureaucratic rules (being) to provide a managerial indulgency, in the form of withholding applications of the rules" (1958: 403). In this sense, Gouldner's variable faintly echoes our third independent variable, "direction."

The second attempt at a synthesis is associated, so far as sociology is concerned, with the name of H. A. Simon and with the development of organization theory.

The main preoccupation of organization theory is again with the internal structure of organizations and their efficiency, but students have directed their attention especially to what had previously been accepted as a datum—the rationality of the formal organization. It is, as Eisenstadt says, "concerned with the conditions which make for maximum rational behaviour, calculation, and performance within a given structural organizational setting, or, conversely, the extent to which various structures and organizational factors limit rational calculation and efficiency" (1958: 106).

In itself an eclectic branch of sociology, drawing on classical economic theory, communication theory, the study of small groups, and industrial sociology, organization theory has become associated with a number of other parallel developments which are relevant to the study of working organizations. Further, it is identified with a much wider movement in the social sciences at large.

Organizing for Change

In many of the social sciences, one focal point of interest during the past decade has been the attempt, increasingly determined, to replace or supplement the static theoretical models of their textbooks with dynamic models. The data of economics, of psychology, and of sociology are largely events and transactions, although these happenings may be often, even largely, repetitive, or routine, or customary. These studies are also concerned with the conduct of actual people, although the existence of a large number of abstract terms in common usage and technical language allows us to ignore this for quite long stretches of time. Awareness of this has led to a number of assaults on accepted theories, which presume an order in equilibrium, or of attempts to square the accepted theories with the facts of life.

Both in psychology and sociology, however, there seems to be little more at present than some dissatisfaction with the existing state of affairs. Social psychologists have been less inhibited, at least in America; there is a lively interest in experiments on cooperation and competition (Deutsch, 1949), gambling (Edwards, 1953), and the performance of groups with work to do or problems to solve (Christie *et al.,* 1952; Bales, 1950; Bavelas, 1952). Undoubtedly, however, it is economists who have formulated most explicitly (and modestly) the criticisms of static theories and have produced the most fertile and rapidly exploited ideas on which to construct an "economic dynamics."

In particular, the development of conceptual models which will take account of the empirical situation of people confronted with decisions to make has proved of exceptional interest for sociologists. This is not only because of the intrinsic interest of what G. L. S. Shackle has made of the notions of belief and potential surprise (uncertainty) in developing his model of decision-making, but also because this line of theorizing has concurred, and finally joined up, with the gradual concentration of interest among sociologists on the "decision-making" function as the central element of the role of business manager (Simon, 1957: especially Introduction to 2nd ed.; Barnard, 1938: especially Chs. XII and XIV).

Put simply, the general thesis expounded by Shackle (1949; 1955; 1958) and accepted by those who have since joined forces and issues with him, runs thus: the course actually followed by a firm, or by an isolatable section of a firm, or, in the last resort, by the individual business man, is set by choices between two or more possible courses of action. Business decisions hinge on (a) the relative gain or loss attached to the various outcomes, and (b) the strength or weakness of the belief accorded to each expectation. The attractiveness of courses of action will be a function of the several combinations of profitability (or its reverse) and feasibility (or unlikelihood) which they represent.

The controversial part of this conception, and that which has proved the most fertile ground for later development and speculation, is the reconstruction of "feasibility" of expectations in terms other than those of orthodox notions of probability which is "measured by the relative frequency of favourable cases among all possible cases, provided these are equally possible" (Georgescu-Roegen, 1958: 14), or, in other words supplied by W. B. Gallie, is "the ratio between one particular sort of result to (*sic*) all other allegedly possible results in a theoretically repeatable experiment" (Gallie, 1954). The innovation here lies in deserting the assumption that business (and most other) decisions are based on any frequency-ratio. "Mathematics has shown in probability theory how to derive knowledge concerning aggregates of future events from aggregates of past events, but this technique is irrelevant to personally unique and crucial occasions of decisions by an individual" (Shackle, 1954: 100). We may observe that Toulmin has also argued, more generally, that statistical calculations of probability are in fact no more than refinements of the guarded conclusion or the qualified conclusion of common usage and not statements of a totally different logical status.

As usual with new departures initiated by a sense of the inadequacy of existing theory, great difficulty has been experienced in determining the boundaries of the constellation of meanings to be attached to expectation in this new guise. The focal concept is uncertainty—the ignorance of the person who is confronted with a choice about the future in general and in particular about the outcomes which may follow any of his possible lines of action. Since he must choose, if he is to remain operative (as a business man or any other agent), he acts in accordance with his belief about the future and the specific possibilities. These possibilities will always be differentiated in his mind according to the degrees of belief with which they are credited.

Types of Decision-Making Situations

H. A. Simon approaches the theme of discontinuity from a totally different point of departure—what he calls "the facts of life that we will discover when we make actual empirical studies of the formation and use of expectations in business decision-making" (1958). What transpires is very closely akin to what Shackle has treated in terms of "seriable" and "non-seriable" decision-making. "Seriable" decisions are those which are very frequently repeated, with expectations relating quite specifically to past experience in similar circumstances. Seriable decisions involve virtually no uncertainty and the lowest potential surprise, and are next in order of uncertainty to decisions which are insurable against consequent losses (and are therefore equivalent to "dead certs"). The discussion of decision-making proper, for Shackle, begins with "non-seriable" decisions.

Simon suggests that, by common knowledge, a large number of the decisions we ordinarily make, in business and elsewhere, fall within the limits of a "programme": "Under certain circumstances when an individual or an organization is confronted with a situation requiring decision, the decision process goes off quickly and smoothly—almost as though no decision were being made at all, but the matter had been decided previously." By contrast, "non-programmed" decisions involve "much stirring about, deliberation, discussion, often vacillation." The distinction is said to resemble that drawn by other, psychologist, students of decision-making between "habitual behaviour" and "genuine decisions" or between "routine" and "critical" decisions.

The grading introduced by this kind of division seems at first sight to be different from Carter's discontinuous array of fields of decision. But what Simon is doing amounts to no more than substituting "doubt" for "potential surprise." In programmed decisions the choice made is to some extent a foregone conclusion, although it may be necessary to perform a complicated series of calculations before a single choice is actually made. In fact, it corresponds to our conception of interpreting local and technical information in relation to a specific choice between courses of action. Simon instances driving a car to a destination, which involves almost exclusively programmed decision-making, although a good deal of computation (most of which is done "unthinkingly") takes place based on information obtained through the eyes. Experience in driving counts, but the more experienced the driver, the nearer the approach to a fully programmed series of decisions—i.e., he knows what to do "automatically" on every occasion of choice. There is no substantial dissimilarity, says Simon, between this and what happens in practice when a monthly schedule is planned in a factory.

Programmed decision-making is what it is because of the existence of an institutional framework around the individual. "The pattern of behaviour in a business firm in which this particular decision" (the choice of an aggregate production rate for a factory) "represents one small detail, may be regarded as a mosaic of such decision-making programmes. . . . So far as any of the programmed decision processes is concerned, all the other programmes that surround it are a part of its environment."

This squares with an earlier thesis of the same writer on "composite decision" as the process by which an organization influences the decisions of each of its members—supplying these decisions with their premises. "It should be perfectly apparent that almost no decision made in an organization is the task of a single individual. Even though the final responsibility for taking a particular action rests with some definite person, we shall always find, in studying the manner in which this decision was reached, that its various components can be traced through the formal and informal channels of communication to many individuals who have participated in forming its premises" (1957: 221).

In non-programmed decisions "the alternatives of choice are not given in advance, but must be discovered" by a rational process of searching. Not that in non-programmed decisions the chooser is compelled to calculate in terms of expectations and his degree of belief in them; Simon suggests that such searches for alternatives are conditional upon a higher level of aspiration, when satisfaction will have to be sought outside the routine, habitual, programmed courses of decision-making.

Guides for action, epistemic moduli, or institutions are not wholly private to the individual. They are, as Parsons has pointed out in another connexion, functions of interaction between persons. As such, their existence depends on a pre-existing *"common culture—* that is, a commonly shared system of symbols the meanings of which are understood on both sides with an approximation to agreement" (1952). Non-verbal conduct, as well as objects and language, is involved in such symbol systems.

The sets of patterns of considerations taken into account in decision-making may therefore be regarded as aspects either of the individual person (biographically determined) or of the social context in which a decision is made. Neither will yield, by itself, a comprehensive statement about the framework of belief in which a decision is made. But in working organizations decisions are made either in the presence of others or with the knowledge that they will have to be implemented, or understood, or approved by others. The set of considerations called into relevance on any decision-making occasion has therefore to be one shared with others or acceptable to them.

Our own studies suggest that there are industrial concerns for which non-programmed decision-making is a normal function; indeed, that this kind of activity takes up most management time, and is its most important function. Such firms, in so far as they are successful, have either spontaneously or deliberately worked out a kind of management system which will facilitate non-programmed decision-making. In exploiting human resources in this new direction, such concerns have to rely on the development of a "common culture," of a dependably constant system of shared beliefs about the common interests of the working community and about the standards and criteria used in it to judge achievement, individual contributions, expertise, and other matters by which a person or a combination of people are evaluated. A system of shared beliefs of this kind is expressed and visible in a code of conduct, a way of dealing with other people. This code of conduct is, in fact, the first sign to the outsider of the presence of a management system appropriate to changing conditions.

Mechanistic and Organic Systems

We are now at the point at which we may set down the outline of the two management systems which represent for us the two polar extremities of the forms which such systems can take when they are adapted to a specific rate of technical and commercial change. The case we have tried to establish from the literature, as from our research experience exhibited in the last chapter, is that the different forms assumed by a working organization do exist objectively and are not merely interpretations offered by observers of different schools.

Both types represent a "rational" form of organization, in that they may both, in our experience, be explicitly and deliberately created and maintained to exploit the human resources of a concern in the most efficient manner feasible in the circumstances of the concern. Not surprisingly, however, each exhibits characteristics which have been hitherto associated with different kinds of interpretations. For it is our contention that empirical findings have usually been classified according to sociological ideology rather than according to the functional specificity of the working organization to its task and the conditions confronting it.

We have tried to argue that these are two formally contrasted forms of management system. These we shall call the mechanistic and organic forms.

A *mechanistic* management system is appropriate to stable conditions. It is characterized by:

(a) the specialized differentiation of functional tasks into which the problems and tasks facing the concern as a whole are broken down;

(b) the abstract nature of each individual task, which is pursued with techniques and purposes more or less distinct from those of the concern as a whole; i.e., the functionaries tend to pursue the technical improvement of means, rather than the accomplishment of the ends of the concern;

(c) the reconciliation, for each level in the hierarchy, of these distinct performances by the immediate superiors, who are also, in turn, responsible for seeing that each is relevant in his own special part of the main task;

(d) the precise definition of rights and obligations and technical methods attached to each functional role;

(e) the translation of rights and obligations and methods into the responsibilities of a functional position;

(f) hierarchic structure of control, authority, and communication;

(g) a reinforcement of the hierarchic structure by the location of knowledge of actualities exclusively at the top of the hierarchy, where the final reconciliation of distinct tasks and assessment of relevance is made;

(h) a tendency for interaction between members of the concern to be vertical, i.e., between superior and subordinate;

(i) a tendency for operations and working behaviour to be governed by the instructions and decisions issued by superiors;

(j) insistence on loyalty to the concern and obedience to superiors as a condition of membership;

(k) a greater importance and prestige attaching to internal (local) than to general (cosmopolitan) knowledge, experience, and skill.

The *organic* form is appropriate to changing conditions, which give rise constantly to fresh problems and unforeseen requirements for action which cannot be broken down or distributed automatically arising from the functional roles defined within a hierarchic structure. It is characterized by:

(a) the contributive nature of special knowledge and experience to the common task of the concern;

(b) the "realistic" nature of the individual task, which is seen as set by the total situation of the concern;

(c) the adjustment and continual re-definition of individual tasks through interaction with others;

(d) the shedding of "responsibility" as a limited field of rights, obligations and methods. (Problems may not be posted upwards, downwards or sideways as being someone else's responsibility);

(e) the spread of commitment to the concern beyond any technical definition;

(f) a network structure of control, authority, and communication. The sanctions which apply to the individual's conduct in his working role derive more from presumed community of interest with the rest of the working organization in the survival and growth of the firm, and less from a contractual relationship between himself and a non-personal corporation, represented for him by an immediate superior;

(g) omniscience no longer imputed to the head of the concern; knowledge about the technical or commercial nature of the here and now task may be located anywhere in the network; this location becoming the *ad hoc* centre of control authority and communication (cf. Klein, 1956: Ch. 2);

(h) a lateral rather than a vertical direction of communication through the organization, communication between people of different rank, also, resembling consultation rather than command;

(i) a content of communication which consists of information and advice rather than instructions and decisions (Burns, 1954);

(j) commitment to the concern's tasks and to the "technological ethos" of material progress and expansion is more highly valued than loyalty and obedience;

(k) importance and prestige attach to affiliations and expertise valid in the industrial and technical and commercial milieux external to the firm.

One important corollary to be attached to this account is that while organic systems are not hierarchic in the same sense as are mechanistic, they remain stratified. Positions are differentiated according to seniority—i.e., greater expertise. The lead in joint decisions is frequently taken by seniors, but it is an essential presumption of the organic system that the lead, i.e., "authority," is taken by whoever shows himself most informed and capable, i.e., the "best authority." The location of authority is settled by consensus.

A second observation is that the area of commitment to the concern—the extent to which the individual yields himself as a resource to be used by the working organization—is far more extensive in organic than in mechanistic systems. Commitment, in fact, is expected to approach that of the professional scientist to his work, and frequently does. One further consequence of this is that it becomes far less feasible to distinguish "informal" from "formal" organization.

Thirdly, the emptying out of significance from the hierarchic command system, by which cooperation is ensured and which serves to monitor the working organization under a mechanistic system, is countered by the development of shared beliefs about the values and goals of the concern. The growth and accretion of institutionalized values, beliefs, and conduct, in the form of commitments, ideology, and manners, around an image of the concern in its industrial and commercial setting make good the loss of formal structure.

Finally, the two forms of system represent a polarity, not a dichotomy; there are, as we have tried to show, intermediate stages between the extremities empirically known to us. Also, the relation of one form to the other is elastic, so that a concern oscillating between relative stability and relative change may also oscillate between the two forms. A concern may (and frequently does) operate with a management system which includes both types.

The organic form, by departing from the familiar clarity and fixity of the hierarchic structure, is often experienced by the individual manager as an uneasy, embarrassed, or chronically anxious quest for knowledge about what he should be doing, or what is expected of him, and similar apprehensiveness about what others are doing. Indeed, as we shall see later, this kind of response is necessary if the organic form of organization is to work effectively. Understandably, such anxiety finds expression in resentment when the apparent confusion besetting him is not explained. In these situations, all managers some of the time, and many managers all the time, yearn for more definition and structure.

On the other hand, some managers recognize a rationale of nondefinition, a reasoned basis for the practice of those successful firms in which designation of status, function, and line of responsibility and authority has been vague or even avoided.

The desire for more definition is often in effect a wish to have the limits of one's task more neatly defined—to know what and when one doesn't have to bother about as much as to know what one does have to. It follows that the more definition is given, the more omniscient the management must be, so that no functions are left wholly or partly undischarged, no person is overburdened with undelegated responsibility, or left without the authority to do his job properly. To do this, to have all the separate functions attached to individual roles fitting together and comprehensively, to have communication between persons constantly maintained on a level adequate to the needs of each functional role, requires rules or traditions of behaviour proved over a long time and an equally fixed, stable task. The omniscience which may then be credited to the head of the concern is expressed throughout its body through the lines of command, extending in a clear, explicitly titled hierarchy of officers and subordinates.

The whole mechanistic form is instinct with this twofold principle of definition and dependence which acts as the frame within which action is conceived and carried out. It works, unconsciously, almost in the smallest minutiae of daily activity. "How late is late?" The answer to this question is not to be found in the rule book, but in the superior. Late is when the boss thinks it is late. Is he the kind of man who thinks 8:00 is the time, and 8:01 is late? Does he think that 8:15 is all right occasionally if it is not a regular thing? Does he think that everyone should be allowed a 5-minutes grace after 8:00 but after that they are late?" (Haire, 1956: 54)

Settling questions about how a person's job is to be done in this way is nevertheless simple, direct, and economical of effort. We shall, in a later chapter, examine more fully the nature of the protection and freedom (in other respects than his job) which this affords the individual.

One other feature of mechanistic organization needs emphasis. It is a necessary condition of its operation that the individual "works on his own," functionally isolated; he "knows his job," he is "responsible for seeing it's done." He works at a job which is in a sense artificially abstracted from the realities of the situation the concern is dealing with, the accountant "dealing with the coats side," the works manager "pushing production," and so on. As this works out in practice, the rest of the organization becomes part of the problem situation the individual has to deal with in order to perform successfully; i.e., difficulties and problems arising from work or information which has been handed over the "responsibility barrier" between two jobs or departments are regarded as "really" the responsibility of the person from whom they were received. As a design engineer put in, "When you get designers handing over designs completely to production, it's 'their responsibility' now. And you get tennis games played with the responsibility for anything that goes wrong. What happens is that you're constantly getting unsuspected faults arising from characteristics which you didn't think important in the design. If you get to hear of these through a sales person, or a production person, or somebody to whom the design was handed over to in the dim past, then, instead of being a design problem, it's an annoyance caused by that particular person, who can't do his own job—because you'd thought you were finished with that one, and you're on to something else now."

When the assumptions of the form of organization make for preoccupation with specialized tasks, the chances of career success, or of greater influence, depend rather on the relative importance which may be attached to each special function by the superior whose task it is to reconcile and control a number of them. And, indeed, to press the claims of one's job or department for a bigger share of the firm's resources is in many cases regarded as a mark of initiative, of effectiveness, and even of "loyalty to the firm's interests." The state of affairs thus engendered squares with the role of the superior, the man who can see the wood instead of just the trees, and gives it the reinforcement of the aloof detachment belonging to a court of appeal. The ordinary relationship prevailing between individual managers "in charge of" different functions is one of rivalry, a rivalry which may be rendered innocuous to the persons involved by personal friendship or the norms of sociability, but which turns discussion about the situations which constitute the real problems of the concern—how to make products more cheaply, how to sell more, how to allocate resources, whether to curtail activity in one sector, whether to risk expansion in another, and so on—into an arena of conflicting interests.

The distinctive feature of the second, organic system is the pervasiveness of the working organization as an institution. In concrete terms, this makes itself felt in a preparedness to combine with others in serving the general aims of the concern. Proportionately to the rate and extent of change, the less can the omniscience appropriate to command organizations be ascribed to the head of the organization; for executives, and even operatives, in a changing firm it is always theirs to reason why. Furthermore, the less definition can be given to status, roles, and modes of communication, the more do the activities of each member of the organization become determined by the real tasks of the firm as he sees them than by instruction and routine. The individual's job ceases to be self-contained; the only way in which "his" job can be done is by his participating continually with others in the solution of problems which are real to the firm, and put in a language of requirements and activities meaningful to them all. Such methods of working put much heavier demands on the individual. The ways in which these demands are met, or countered, will be enumerated and discussed in Part Three.

We have endeavoured to stress the appropriateness of each system to its own specific set of conditions. Equally, we desire to avoid the suggestion that either system is superior under all circumstances to the other. In particular, nothing in our experience justifies the assumption that mechanistic systems should be superseded by organic in conditions of stability. The beginning of administrative wisdom is the awareness that there is no one optimum type of management system.

The Concept of Bureaucracy:
An Empirical Assessment*

RICHARD H. HALL

Students of organizations from the time of Weber to the present have used the bureaucratic model as the basis for conceptualizing the system of interrelationships in organizations. This acceptance of the bureaucratic model has served as the point of departure for studies of the development and modification of organizational structure, the place of the individual within such a structure, and various associated problems. This paper examines the bases of the bureaucratic model, the dimensions of organizations that are characteristically cited as bureaucratic attributes by measuring the degree to which these dimensions are present in a variety of organizations.

Bureaucratic Dimensions

Max Weber, in his formulative work on bureaucracy, described bureaucratic organizations from the dimensional perspective (1947). That is, he listed a series of organizational attributes that, when present, constitute the bureaucratic form of organization. These dimensions, including division of labor, hierarchy of authority, extensive rules, separation of administration from ownership, and hiring and promotion based on technical competency, have served as the basis for subsequent delineations of bureaucratic structure (1947: 330–334).

Those students who have used this theoretical model as the basis for empirical research or theoretical development have typically made the assumption that the dimensions are present in the first case or would be present in the latter case in the organizations under study or consideration.

This assumption was the source of Gouldner's concern (1948: 396). In a later publication (1950: 53–54), he more specifically questions much of the current usage of the bureaucratic model:

> It is instead an *ideal type,* in which certain tendencies of concrete structures are highlighted by emphasis. Not every formal association will possess all of the characteristics incorporated into the ideal-type bureaucracy. The ideal type may be used as a yardstick enabling us to determine in which particular respect an organization is bureaucratized. The ideal-type bureaucracy may be used much as a twelve-inch ruler is employed. We would not expect, for example, that all objects measured by the ruler would

* Reprinted from *The American Journal of Sociology*, *69* (July 1963), pp. 32–40, with omissions, by permission of the author and The University of Chicago Press. © 1963 by the University of Chicago.

be exactly twelve inches—some would be more and some would be less.

Stated in other terms, Gouldner, and later Udy (1959), imply that bureaucracy is a condition that exists along a continuum, rather than being a condition that is either present or absent. This point may be expanded to state that bureaucracy is a form of organization which exists along a number of continua or dimensions.

In regard to the dimensionality of bureaucracy, Udy's findings are relevant. In his study of formal organizations in non-industrial societies, Udy utilized seven characteristics of bureaucracy. These characteristics, subdivided into "bureaucratic" and "rational" elements, were also treated as dimensions (1959: 791–95). Using a present versus absent dichotomy for each characteristic, he found a variation among the associations in the pattern of presence versus absence for the seven dimensions. The characteristics were not either all present nor all absent in any one organization. Instead, some had certain configurations of present versus absent characteristics, while other organizations had other configurations. These findings support the contention that the bureaucratic model is best approached from the dimensional perspective.

Six dimensions were chosen for use in this study on the basis of frequency of citation and theoretical importance. (See Table 1.) They are:

1. A division of labor based upon functional specialization.
2. A well-defined hierarchy of authority.
3. A system of rules covering the rights and duties of positional incumbents.
4. A system of procedures for dealing with work situations.
5. Impersonality of interpersonal relations.
6. Promotion and selection for employment based upon technical competence.

In the ideal-type bureaucracy all of these dimensions would be present to a high degree, while non-bureaucratized or simple organizations would ideally have a low degree of all the dimensions present. Stated more directly, a highly bureaucratized organization would be characterized by an intricate division of labor; a multilevel, closely followed hierarchical structure; extensive rules governing on the job behavior; well-developed and systematically followed work procedures; interpersonal behavior, both between organizational members and toward outsiders, governed by norms that stress the importance of the positional rather than the personal basis for interaction; and the importance of successful performance as opposed to senti-

TABLE 1. CHARACTERISTICS OF BUREAUCRACY AS LISTED BY MAJOR AUTHORS

Dimensions of bureaucracy	Weber	Friedrich	Merton	Udy	Heady	Parsons	Berger	Michels	Dimock
Hierarchy of authority	*	*	*	*	*	*	*	*	*
Division of labor	*	*	*	*	*	*		*	*
Technically competent participants	*	*	*	*		*	*		
Procedural devices for work situations	*	*	*		*		*		*
Rules governing behavior of positional incumbents	*	*	*				*	*	
Limited authority of office	*		*		*	*			
Differential rewards by office	*			*					
Impersonality of personal contact			*						
Administration separate from ownership	*								
Emphasis on written communication	*								
Rational discipline	*								

* Cited by author.

ment as a basis for both hiring and promotion practices. The non-bureaucratic organization would be characterized by a relatively flat and often by-passed hierarchy, simpler division of labor, and so on.

In order to delineate more accurately the actual structural characteristics of organizations in relation to the bureaucratic dimensions, and to test the proposition that bureaucracy actually exists in degrees along the six dimensions, the following hypothesis was tested: The bureaucratic characteristics described above are not highly inter-correlated; thus, organizations that are highly bureaucratized on any one dimension are not necessarily so on the other dimensions.

This hypothesis assumes that the bureaucratic dimensions do in fact exist in the form of continua and that these continua are measurable. Both of these assumptions will be demonstrated.

Methodology

Scales were constructed for measurement of each of the six dimensions. The format of the Likert internal-consistency technique was employed together with other methods (Hall, 1961). The scales were then pretested to eliminate irrelevant items and, perhaps even more importantly, to eliminate any interdependency among the scales.

The six scales that were developed on the basis of these considerations were comprised of items to which organizational respondents were to respond. The responses were based on a five-point scale designed to indicate how closely each statement corresponded to an accurate description of the organization. Examples of items from each scale are:

1. Hierarchy of authority scale: "A person can make his own decisions without checking with anyone else."
2. Division of labor scale: "One thing people like around here is the variety of work."
3. System of rules scale: "The time for coffee breaks is strictly regulated."
4. System of procedures scale: "We are to follow strict operating procedures at all times."
5. Impersonality scale: "We. are expected to be courteous, but reserved, at all times."
6. Technical competence scale: "Employees are periodically evaluated to see how well they are doing."

In their final form, the scales were quite brief, five contained ten items each, while the sixth contained twelve items.

The scales were designed to be administered to the personnel of the organizations selected for study. The organization was assigned a score on each dimension based on the mean of all responses from that organization. The mean scores yield an ordinal score for each organization (Whyte, 1949: 308).

Data were collected from the employees of ten organizations. In each organization a systematic random sample of employees was selected that was designed to include members of both "management" and "worker" categories in order to reduce bias from either perspective. Respondents from the various internal segments of the organizations were similarly included to avoid any departmental bias.

The selection of organizations for study was purposive to the extent that organizational variety in terms of type, age, and size was desired in order to demonstrate the relationship between the several dimensions. If there is concomitant variation in the magnitude of the dimensions, it should be present when a series of organizations are compared. On the other hand, if inter-organizational comparisons indicate that the dimensions do not vary concomitantly, then the dimensional nature of bureaucratic structure will be further demonstrated.

The final sample included organizations that performed a number of different functions. The organizations ranged in size from 65 to 3,096 employees and in age from four to sixty-three years (Hall, 1961).

Findings

The major hypothesis was tested by use of the Spearman rank–order correlation method. A rank was assigned to each organization on each dimension. Rank–order co-efficients between each dimension and every other dimension were computed and are shown in Table 2.

None of the coefficients reach the .05 level of significance, upholding the central hypothesis. In the organizations studied, there is not concomitant variation in the presence–absence patterns among the dimensions. The relatively small number of organizations included

TABLE 2. RANK–ORDER INTERCORRELATION COEFFICIENTS BETWEEN DIMENSIONS* (N = ORGANIZATIONS)

	Hierarchy of Authority	Division of Labor	Rules	Procedures	Imper- sonality
Division of labor	.419				
Rules	.594	.134			
Procedures	.660	.678	.167		
Impersonality	.678	.266	.194	.624	
Technical qualifications	.032	.300	.627	—.303	.170

* The ranking of each organization was from most bureaucratic to least bureaucratic on each dimension.

in this study indicates that caution should be exercised in the interpretation of these findings. The results of this analysis are suggestive, however, of the variability with which the degree of bureaucratization can exist.

Analysis of the matrix of rank correlation coefficients in Table 2 suggests that the "hierarchy" dimension may be the central dimension in the determination of the over-all degree of bureaucratization. This can only be looked upon as a tentative proposition, however, because the data from this research do not yield significant conclusions in this direction.

Another possibility that should be considered is that organizations of similar types may be found to have similar configurations of dimensional magnitude, with the corresponding concomitant variation among the dimensions. Two organizations, both marketing divisions of large national firms, which were *not* included in the final organizational sample due to inadequate sample size, were found to have quite similar dimensional configurations. Although the data were insufficient for analysis, they are suggestive of the possibility of such common configurations.

Although there may be similar configurations of bureaucratization among organizations of the same type, evidence obtained during the course of the research indicated that the commonly noted factors of organizational size and age were not related to the degree of bureaucratization on the six dimensions. As Table 3 indicates, none of the rank–order correlation coefficients indicated any significant relationship between age or size and degree of bureaucratization.

The fact that the size and age of the organizations studied were not highly related to the degree of bureaucratization should not be

TABLE 3. SIZE AND AGE OF ORGANIZATIONS CORRELATED WITH MEAN SCORE ON BUREAUCRATIZATION DIMENSIONS* (N = 10 ORGANIZATIONS)

	Rank-order correlation coefficients	
Dimension	Size	Age
Hierarchy of authority	.227	—.409
Division of labor	.362	.423
Rules	.398	.411
Procedures	—.201	—.171
Impersonality	.133	.001
Technical qualifications	.403	.368

* Organizations ranked 1–10 from most bureaucratic to least bureaucratic. Size and age ranked 1–10 from largest and oldest to smallest and youngest.

taken as conclusively ruling out the effects of these factors. If a larger organizational sample were taken, covering a wider range of age and size, the importance of these factors could be more easily determined. It may well be, however, that these factors have been overestimated as the important determinants of bureaucratization. From the evidence here, the type of organizational activity appears to be of greater importance.

It must be stressed, however, that the organizations studied did not yield any significant patterns either in the interrelationships among the dimensions or in over-all organizational configurations.

These findings raise some serious questions about bureaucratic theory as it has been commonly formulated, and about many empirical studies done in "bureaucratic" settings. First, the findings indicate that what is commonly approached as a totality (bureaucracy) is not such an integrated whole in reality. The configurational nature of the degree to which the dimensions are present suggests that organizations are indeed composed of the commonly ascribed dimensions, but these dimensions are not necessarily all present to the same degree in actual organizations. The bureaucratic concept would appear to be more descriptively accurate if it were rephrased in these dimensional terms, with an emphasis on the continual nature of the dimensions. This would allow continuity in the over-all discussions of "highly" bureaucratized organizations, but in a more sophisticated manner. It would also allow other organizations to be studied from the bureaucratic perspective with less conjecture as to their degree and type of bureaucratization.

Second, many of the empirical studies of conditions within the bureaucratic setting and of the setting itself might be re-examined. There is little empirical evidence presented in many studies that yields any reliable estimate of the degree to which the organizations are bureaucratized along the dimensions cited by the authors themselves. Indeed, some research in this area has simply stated that the organizations under investigation are bureaucratic without any attempt to demonstrate their degree of bureaucratization. From the evidence presented in this study, a reassessment of certain assumptions included in past and contemporary research is warranted. A more exacting delineation of the degree to which the organizations being studied are bureaucratized would aid in the over-all systematization of findings from the field.

Third, the direction of the relationship between the "technical qualifications" dimension and three of the other dimensions is negative, as Table 2 indicates. This finding, while not conclusive, does raise the question of the appropriateness and utility of the inclusion of the dimension in the bureaucratic model. If technical competence is taken to encompass a general high level of training and ability, then it may not be an appropriate dimension. In a highly bureaucratized situation (along all dimensions) the highly competent person might not be able to exercise the full range of his competence due to specific procedural specifications, limited sphere of activity, limited authority due to hierarchical demands, etc. The generally competent person in these terms could easily manifest the symptoms suggested by Merton (1957) and others (Brown, 1954: 259–68). If, however, this dimension were rephrased to specify that technical competence is required only to the degree necessary to fulfil each job requirement within the hierarchical structure, the dimension might have more verifiable utility.

These findings are similar to those of Udy in certain regards. In distinguishing between the "bureaucratic" and "rational" elements of organizational structure, he notes that there are high interrelationships among the attributes of each element. There was also, however, a negative association between the attributes of the two elements (Udy, 1959: 794). The dimensions of the present study, while essentially on the "bureaucratic" side of Udy's distinction do include one dimension which could be termed as "rational."

The "technical qualifications" dimension can be viewed as a "rational" aspect of the over-all concept of bureaucracy used here. As noted above, this dimension was generally negatively associated with the other dimensions. The findings of Udy and this study thus concur on this point. As Udy suggests, the distinction made may be operative in contemporary society as well as in the non-industrial societies that he analyzed.

Conclusion

While additional evidence is needed to demonstrate conclusively the validity of the findings reported in this paper, certain conclusions can be drawn. First, the bureaucratic dimensions are meaningful organizational structural attributes. Second, when measured quantitatively, the dimensions exist in the form of continua rather than as dichotomies. Third, the magnirute of the dimensions varied independently in the organizations studied.

Factors related to the degree of bureaucratization along each dimension were examined. From the data available, it appears that the type of organizational activity may be highly related to the degree of bureaucratization. Additional research in this area may indicate that certain organizational activities are related to particular degrees of bureaucratization on one or several dimensions. For example, organizations that regularly deal with a large volume of customers or clients may develop a high degree of impersonality. At the same time, a rather low degree of procedural specificity could be present if there is much variation in the type of interaction involved. While the activity factor appears to be related to the degree of bureaucratization, the factors of age and size did not emerge as important factors in this study.

The use of this dimensional approach could also lead to a more accurate delineation of the organizational form that is most "rational" for the pursuit of particular organizational goals. For instance, an intense emphasis on procedures may be very useful in one type of organization but not in other types. It is within the realm of possibility that there are optimal or most rational forms of organization for particular organizational activities. Bureaucracy, as it has commonly been used, may not be that rational form described by Weber, but particular configurations of the bureaucratic model may be the most rational form for particular activities.

If human life is increasingly becoming organizational life, a better knowledge of the organizational structures in which such lives are led may allow a more realistic confrontation of the problems associated with such a life. The mere fact that the "organization man" is a symbol of modern life for some people is not enough for the understanding of the organizational forces that produce such a man. Inasmuch as all organizations are not equally bureaucratic, there are undoubtedly a variety of organizational factors that contribute to a variety of different types of "organization men." More adequate knowledge of such factors is thus essential to the understanding of the over-all significance of organizations for contemporary life.

An Axiomatic Theory of Organizations*
JERALD HAGE

The major purpose of this paper is to suggest a theory of organizations in an axiomatic format (Zetterberg, 1963). Eight variables are related to each other in seven simple, two-variable propositions. These seven propositions are then used to derive twenty-one corollaries. An eighth proposition, which sets limits on these propositions and corollaries, completes the theory. It defines two ideal types of organizations. The propositions and corollaries provide twenty-nine hypotheses, which are used to codify a number of research studies and to analyze the problems of organizational change.

Although the original variables were selected on an *ad hoc* basis, they have some theoretical justification. The four ends were suggested by the work of Parsons, Bales, and their associates (1958) on the four functional problems of a social system (although they might disagree with the author's interpretation). Production is equivalent to their goal

* Reprinted from *Administrative Science Quarterly*, 10 (December 1965), pp. 289–320, with omissions, by permission of the author and the publisher.

TABLE 1. THE EIGHT VARIABLES

Variable	Indicators*
Organizational means	
Complexity (specialization)	Number of occupational specialties.
	Level of training required.
Centralization (hierarchy of authority)	Proportion of jobs that participate in decision making.
	Number of areas in which decisions are made by decision makers.
Formalization (standardization)	Proportion of jobs that are codified.
	Range of variation allowed within jobs.
Stratification (status system)	Differences in income and prestige among jobs.
	Rate of mobility between low- and high-ranking jobs or status levels.
Organizational ends	
Adaptiveness (flexibility)	Number of new programs in a year.†
	Number of new techniques in a year.
Production (effectiveness)	Number of units produced per year.
	Rate of increase in units produced per year.
Efficiency (cost)	Cost per unit of output per year.
	Amount of idle resources per year.
Job satisfaction (morale)	Satisfaction with working conditions.
	Rate of turnover in job occupants per year.

* Two indicators are used for each variable because of the possibility of errors in measurement. In general, the first indicator should be the stronger one, with the second accounting for exceptions.
† The time unit of a year is used to level out random variation resulting from specific and idiosyncratic organizational events. This time period also has the advantage of corresponding to one which is used by many organizations in the compilation of their records.

achievement; efficiency is equivalent to their integration; job satisfaction is equivalent to their tension management; and adaptiveness is equivalent to their adaptation. The four means are major characteristics of organizations: complexity is a measure of how many specialties are utilized, centralization is a measure of how power is distributed, formalization is a measure of how many rules are used, and stratification is a measure of how rewards are distributed. Table 1 lists these eight variables and the indicators by which they can be measured.

The Axiomatic Theory

Central to the theory are seven propositions, which have been drawn from the writings of Weber, Barnard, and Thompson (Weber, 1947: 324–340; Barnard, 1964: 46–83; and Thompson, 1961: 3–113). The first three propositions summarize much of Weber's model of bureaucracy, while the second three are extracted from Barnard's discussion of the functions of status systems. A seventh proposition is obtained from Thompson's work. Combining the seven propositions makes it possible to derive twenty-one corollaries. In some instances, these corollaries are discussed in one or more of the writings of these three organizational theorists, but many of the corollaries are not mentioned. Some of the derived corollaries appear to represent entirely new hypotheses, indicating areas for future research.

The major theme running through this axiomatic theory is the idea of functional strains, as discussed in the writings of Parsons, Bales, and their associates (1958: 88–90, 180–185), or the concept of organizational dilemma, as it is called by Blau and Scott (1962). This means that an increase in one variable results in a decrease in another variable, or that the maximization of one social means results in the minimization of another. Although this dependence of one variable on another is an old idea, the problem is to specify which variables are in opposition, and perhaps more important, why they are. This is exactly what the theory attempts to do.

The Seven Propositions The essence of Weber's model of bureaucracy is a hierarchy of offices where the duties are clearly codified by rules and regulations (1947: 330–331). Although he was describing the administrative staff, his principles can be applied to other areas of the organization, such as production, as illustrated by the production of the Ford Model T. Weber felt that the bureaucratic arrangement was superior to other forms because it had more precision and speed, and reduced both material and personal costs (Gerth and Mills, 1958: 214). Part of his reasoning for the efficacy of bureaucracy was its superior discipline and control of role performance (Gerth and Mills, 1958: 197; Weber, 1947: 334), for he specifically stated that if officials were elected instead of appointed, discipline and control would be weakened (Weber, 1947: 335). The high formalization of offices or jobs results in the development of expertise in a limited area and therefore greater efficiency in performance with fewer errors being made. The combination of centralization and formalization is nothing more than coordination (Blau and Scott, 1962: 32). There are individuals who supervise and who have rules or standards by which to evaluate the performance of their subordinates, which not only results in more uniformity of behavior but in a higher volume of production as well. Weber's model can be formulated into the following three propositions:

I. *The higher the centralization, the higher the production.*

II. *The higher the formalization, the higher the efficiency.*

III. *The higher the centralization, the higher the formalization.*

Barnard was concerned with the consequences of status systems (Etzioni, 1961: 82–98). He viewed stratification as a method for ensuring the incentive to work hard because it not only provided an objective, promotion, but also specified a clear line of advancement, an idea very similar to Weber's concept of bureaucratic career (1947: 334). While Barnard believed the motivation to work hard resulted in increased production because of greater effort, he saw some dysfunctional consequences as well. Stratification satisfies the man at the top, but not the men at the bottom. It builds in failure because there are a limited number of jobs at the top. Barnard (1964: 71–83) also noted that status systems tended to reduce mobility or circulation of elites, the second indicator used to measure stratification; this in turn lowered job satisfaction, and in fact, resulted in injustices. Blau and Scott (1962: 122) have noted that status differences result in the reduction of informal relationships, and the lessening of emotional support, thereby producing dissatisfaction.

Barnard also noted that stratification reduced adaptiveness. Thompson suggests that status systems encourage the *status quo.* In part, the elites remain unaware of the need for change, and in part, with their right to veto, they discourage suggestions for change. Status systems diminish communications that are critical of the system and that bypass it. Blau and Scott (1962: 100) suggest that stratification reduces adaptiveness because changes are likely to have upsetting consequences for the status system, and therefore, those who have the most to lose are likely to oppose changes. This is, of course, Veblen's concept of vested interests. All of these ideas can be expressed in three propositions:

IV.   The higher the stratification, the lower the job satisfaction.

V.   The higher the stratification, the higher the production.

VI.   The higher the stratification, the lower the adaptiveness.

In sum, Barnard pinpointed a crucial organizational paradox. Stratification makes employees work harder, but they do not like it, and it tends to turn them into organizational men, who will not criticize superiors for fear of loss of advancement.

Thompson noted that a proliferation of occupational specialties, particularly those requiring long periods of training, results in an undermining of hierarchical authority (1961: 83–100). In part, this dilemma stems from the increasing difficulty of a person in an authority position having the requisite knowledge in all areas of specialization found in complex organizations. To make decisions, he must consult the job occupants of the appropriate specialties, thus sharing the decision making with the specialist. The specialist has access to information, and by giving or withholding information, he has a source of power over the decision maker. He has channels of communication, usually informal, that cut across hierarchical lines of authority. Specialists need information from different areas of the organization, and they are consulted by job occupants in different areas. Consequently the elites lose some control. Gouldner (1959: 400–428) has discussed a motivational assumption that tends to encourage these processes, which he calls the functional strain towards autonomy. He assumes that specialties or occupations strive for the right to make their own decisions and this results in decentralization of the organization. Blau and Scott (1962: 247–250) have called this phenomenon the dilemma of managerial coordination and individual initiative. These ideas can be summarized as proposition VII.

VII.   The higher the complexity, the lower the centralization.

The Corollaries   On the assumption that the eight variables form a closed system of interrelated variables, it is possible to derive additional hypotheses by applying the simple rules of the syllogism; for example:

The higher the centralization, the higher the production.   (Prop. I)

The higher the stratification, the higher the production.   (Prop. V)

The higher the centralization, the higher the stratification.   (Corol. 19)

In other words, combining propositions I and V gives a corollary that is essentially Michel's iron law of oligarchy.

In the same way, a total of twenty additional corollaries are derived. Table 2 lists the propositions and corollaries of the theory. The corollaries are numbered in the sequence in which they were derived. Table 3 presents a schemata of the association between each of the eight variables along with the number of the proposition or corollary that describes the relationship. It should be noted that each corollary can be obtained in several different ways depending upon the sequence in which they are derived. Together, the seven major propositions and the twenty-one corollaries represent all the possible two-variable relationships, when order does not make a difference. The resulting twenty-eight hypotheses explicate all the interrelationships of this organizational system of eight variables, making research easier.

Some corollaries merely specify ideas already contained in the writings of the organizational theorists: corollaries 1, 2, and 8 are found

TABLE 2. MAJOR PROPOSITIONS AND COROLLARIES
OF THE THEORY

Major Propositions

    I.   The higher the centralization, the higher the production.

   II.   The higher the formalization, the higher the efficiency.

  III.   The higher the centralization, the higher the formalization.

  IV.   The higher the stratification, the lower the job satisfaction.

   V.   The higher the stratification, the higher the production.

  VI.   The higher the stratification, the lower the adaptiveness.

 VII.   The higher the complexity, the lower the centralization.

Derived Corollaries

  1.   The higher the formalization, the higher the production.

  2.   The higher the centralization, the higher the efficiency.

  3.   The lower the job satisfaction, the higher the production.

  4.   The lower the job satisfaction, the lower the adaptiveness.

  5.   The higher the production, the lower the adaptiveness.

  6.   The higher the complexity, the lower the production.

  7.   The higher the complexity, the lower the formalization.

  8.   The higher the production, the higher the efficiency.

  9.   The higher the stratification, the higher the formalization.

 10.   The higher the efficiency, the lower the complexity.

 11.   The higher the centralization, the lower the job satisfaction.

 12.   The higher the centralization, the lower the adaptiveness.

 13.   The higher the stratification, the lower the complexity.

 14.   The higher the complexity, the higher the job satisfaction.

 15.   The lower the complexity, the lower the adaptiveness.

 16.   The higher the stratification, the higher the efficiency.

 17.   The higher the efficiency, the lower the job satisfaction.

 18.   The higher the efficiency, the lower the adaptiveness.

 19.   The higher the centralization, the higher the stratification.

 20.   The higher the formalization, the lower the job satisfaction.

 21.   The higher the formalization, the lower the adaptiveness.

Limits Proposition

 VIII.   Production imposes limits on complexity, centralization, formalization, stratification, adaptiveness, efficiency, and job satisfaction.

in Weber's discussion of bureaucracy; corollaries 15 and 21 have been suggested by Thompson. Some corollaries are found in different areas. Corollary 4, which relates job satisfaction and adaptiveness, is found in the human relations writings, where the idea that dissatisfied workers will resist change is a principle of research. Corollaries 11, 14, and 20 along with proposition IV represent three of the organizational conditions that produce alienation, as suggested by Seeman (1959: 783–791), a point discussed below. Some corollaries are new hypotheses that deserve study. Corollaries 5, 12, and 18 relate to the problem of organizational adaptiveness, a relatively unexplored area. Thus the axiomatic theory, by making explicit all the implicit hypotheses,

TABLE 3.   THE INTERRELATIONSHIPS BETWEEN ORGANIZATIONAL MEANS AND ORGANIZATIONAL ENDS*

| | Organizational means | | | Organizational ends | | | |
	Complexity	Centralization	Formalization	Stratification	Adaptiveness	Production	Efficiency	Job satisfaction
Organizational means								
		−	−	−	+	−	−	+
Complexity		(VII)	(7)	(13)	(15)	(6)	(10)	(14)
			+	+	−	+	+	−
Centralization			(III)	(19)	(12)	(I)	(2)	(11)
				+	−	+	+	−
Formalization				(9)	(21)	(1)	(II)	(20)
					−	+	+	−
Stratification					(VI)	(V)	(16)	(IV)
Organizational ends								
						−	−	+
Adaptiveness						(5)	(18)	(4)
							+	−
Production							(8)	(3)
								−
Efficiency								(17)
Job satisfaction								

* The Roman numerals refer to the seven basic propositions, and the arabic numerals refer to the corollaries that are derived from these propositions. A plus sign means a positive association between the two variables; a minus sign means a negative association between the two variables.

makes it possible to integrate previously isolated schools of thought as well as suggesting new avenues of thought.

If job satisfaction is taken as an indicator of alienation from the organization and its work activities, the axiomatic theory not only includes many of the ideas suggested in the literature on alienation but provides new hypotheses. The following relationships between job satisfaction and the other seven variables are indicated:

The higher the stratification, the lower the job satisfaction.   (Prop. IV)

The higher the production, the lower the job satisfaction.   (Corol. 3)

The lower the adaptiveness, the lower the job satisfaction.   (Corol. 4)

The higher the centralization, the lower the job satisfaction.   (Corol. 11)

The higher the complexity, the higher the job satisfaction.   (Corol. 14)

The higher the efficiency, the lower the job satisfaction.   (Corol. 17)

The higher the formalization, the lower the job satisfaction. (Corol. 20)

Proposition IV is a restatement of the idea of estrangement, while corollary 11 describes the condition of powerlessness. Corollary 14 is the condition of meaningfulness: when person specialization is practiced, the work is much more meaningful, and job satisfaction is correspondingly higher. The condition of normlessness (which is indicated by no formalization), is not represented in the theory, nor is the condition of social integration. The theory indicates that too many norms or high formalization leads to alienation as represented by lower job satisfaction.

High efficiency, indicated by lower wages and salaries and fewer fringe benefits, lowers job satisfaction. On the other hand, high production is associated with low satisfaction because high volume indicates an emphasis on speed, as indicated by Blauner's study (1964) of the automobile industry.

Similarly, we can examine the hypotheses that relate complexity with the other seven variables. Two of the seven logical possibilities, proposition VII and corollary 14, have already been discussed. The remaining five are:

The higher the complexity, the lower the production.   (Corol. 6)

The higher the complexity, the lower the formalization.   (Corol. 7)

The higher the complexity, the lower the efficiency.   (Corol. 10)

The lower the complexity, the higher the stratification.   (Corol. 13)

The lower the complexity, the lower the adaptiveness.   (Corol. 15)

Corollary 15 is a summary of some of Durkheim's ideas (1947). Although society was Durkheim's unit of analysis, the corollary is equally applicable to organizations. It might be added that specialists have access to channels of information, both internal and external to the organization, which makes them more aware of the need for innovations, whether the innovations represent a response to internal or external strains. From the organizational viewpoint, the more occupational specialties that organizations have, the more closely organizations are linked by communication networks with other organizations. As has already been discussed, specialists establish internal informal channels of communication, which not only tend to undermine the hierarchy of authority but also the status system.

Corollaries 6, 7, and 10 appear to be more provocative and have not received as much discussion in the literature as the other corollaries. In an organization with high complexity, there is apt to be less efficiency or lower productivity because of higher cost for the specialists' salaries and because of lower formalization, which itself decreases efficiency. The strain between complexity and formalization has been called the dilemma of the professional and the bureaucracy by Blau and Scott, and by others (1962: 244–247). These vary inversely with each other, as Thompson has also hypothesized. The lower volume of production is, as a consequence of high complexity, likely to result from an organizational emphasis on the quality of product or service being produced. The differences between craft and mass-production industries are examples of this phenomenon of low-volume, high-quality production versus high-volume, low-quality production.

Two Ideal Types   It is possible to examine each of the eigth variables as job satisfaction and complexity have been examined, but another way of examining the theory is to consider the two extreme types of organizations that it suggests (see Table 4). Some of the same characteristics of the two types are described by Burns and Stalker (1961: 119–125). The mechanistic model is described as "the precise definition of rights and obligations and technical methods attached to each functional role" (high formalization), "hierarchic structure of control, authority and communication" (high centralization). The organic model is characterized by "the adjustment and continual redefinition of individual tasks" (low formalization), "a network structure of control, authority and communication" (low centralization). Burns and Stalker also suggest other differentiating characteristics, which are not among the eight variables given here. The content of communication in the organic model is information and advice; in the mechanical model it

TABLE 4.   TWO IDEAL TYPES OF ORGANIZATIONS PREDICTED BY THE AXIOMATIC THEORY

Organic model (Emphasis on adaptiveness)	Mechanistic model (Emphasis on production)
High complexity	Low complexity
Low centralization	High centralization
Low formalization	High formalization
Low stratification	High stratification
High adaptiveness	Low adaptiveness
Low production	High production
Low efficiency	High efficiency
High job satisfaction	Low job satisfaction

is instruction and orders. The mechanical model requires loyalty to the organization and emphasizes local knowledge; the organic model requires commitment to the tasks of the organization and emphasizes expertise.

Burns and Stalker suggest that the emphasis on adaptiveness, and, correspondingly, on organic or mechanistic structural arrangement, is directly related to the rate of change in technical or market conditions. Several factors other than production can affect the relative emphasis on adaptiveness as the dominant organizational end. The nature of the output of the organization has an effect. When the outputs are services to clients rather than manufacturing products, the organization is apt to show more adaptiveness, because there is less opportunity for standardization of tasks. If the organization is competing with another firm that has a particular social means, for example, high centralization, then it is likely to adopt a similar means. Under conditions of extreme threat, the organization is likely to move toward high centralization. Some organizations, such as military units, are more likely to have this environmental condition than others (Berelson and Steiner, 1964: 370). The dominant value patterns in the society may favor high centralization in government, and this will tend to be reflected in other kinds of organizations. Similarly, the society may consider one social end more important than another, resulting in the adoption of certain means to maximize the desired ends. In fact, most ideological disputes about organizations can be translated into an argument over the relative importance of the volume of production and efficiency *versus* job satisfaction and adaptiveness.

The Limits Proposition   Although each ideal type has advantages and disadvantages, there is a limit to how much the decision makers can emphasize one organizational end over another. If there is no codification of jobs, then a condition of normlessness prevails, and there is likely to be low job satisfaction. If new programs and techniques are not adopted, the organization is apt to fail in the face of an ever-changing environment. On the other hand, too high a rate of change in new programs and techniques is likely to have the same consequence because of spiraling costs. There are limits on each of the eight variables, beyond which an organization dare not move. This idea can be expressed in the following proposition:

VIII.   *Production imposes limits on complexity, centralization, formalization, stratification, adaptiveness, efficiency, and job satisfaction.*

The determination of the actual limits requires a considerable amount of research; yet, this would appear to be a strategic area for study. By examining the consequences of extreme scores, a better understanding of organizational dynamics is achieved. The limits proposition provides the basis for explaining the failure of organizations, because it suggests that extremes in any variable results in the loss of production, even in an organization that has the means that maximize this end.

The logical consequences of the limits proposition are complex. One consequence is that all of the relationships specified in the previous propositions are curvilinear ones. If centralization becomes too high, production will fall; if stratification becomes too low, job satisfaction will drop. Exceeding the limits then results in a reversal of the hypothesized relationships. Another consequence is that the reversal of these relationships would manifest itself first in declining production figures. These represent important qualifications to the axiomatic theory.

Available Evidence

The findings reported here represent a variety of methodologies and even variations in definitions; therefore some interpretation is necessary. The research cited includes voluntary associations, hospitals, colleges, schools, prisons, corporations, and others. Many of the studies involve only a single organization, and a few represent multiple organizations or units within organizations. Although the author attempted to review a large number of studies, the review was hardly exhaustive, if only because there are so many. In general, research reviews have been relied upon, because they usually attempt some exhaustive search in particular areas and because they usually provide bibliographies of pertinent studies.

The findings reported below are organized around three variables, each of which corresponds to an organizational problem: (1) adaptiveness or the problem of organizational change, (2) centralization or the problem of organizational democracy, and (3) job satisfaction or the problem of organizational morale. The last two problems have been frequently discussed, whereas the first problem is seldom mentioned. Since the variables are interrelated, there is some obvious overlap in the discussion of the research findings; for example, adaptiveness, as stipulated by the theory, is associated with low centralization and high job satisfaction. At the same time, this organization of findings around three key organizational problems helps clarify what the theory says about them, thereby making its practical import easier to understand.

Adaptiveness In a series of studies of adaptiveness, Mort and his associates developed a scale of 176 innovations in school techniques and programs (Ross, 1958). In a study of 43 school systems, Buley (1947), using Mort's scale, found that adaptiveness correlated positively with complexity as measured by professional training and experience of the teachers; but correlated negatively with the efficiency of the school system, as measured by expenditures per pupil (corol. 10, 15, 18). Georgopoulos and Tannenbaum used two attitudinal questions to measure adaptiveness in 32 organizational units of a business organization (1957). They found adaptiveness highly correlated with the lack of strain between supervisor and employees, but the correlation with volume of production was much lower. If the lack of strain is considered to be one of the elements of job satisfaction, then the findings support corollaries 3, 4, and 5. The study also lends support for the necessity of proposition VIII; there must be some job satisfaction in order to have production at all.

Several case studies have examined the organizational consequences of increases in adaptiveness, whether the addition of new techniques or the addition of new programs. In a study of the military, Janowitz (1959: 198–212) disclosed that the increasing technology of warfare was leading to increased complexity and resulting in a decentralization of decision making. In a case study of a community hospital, the introduction of a new department of medical education led to decentralization of decision making and increased costs (corol. 10, prop. VII) (Hage, 1963). Introducing the changes was easiest in those departments of the hospital that had the highest degree of specialization and a history of adaptiveness (corol. 15). The department that resisted change the most not only had little history of adaptiveness, but was also low in specialization and higher in stratification (prop. VI, corol. 13).

Blau and Scott (1962) reviewed the literature relating stratification and adaptiveness and concluded that status differences tended to reduce criticism of the ideas of those superior in power and prestige. Ronken and Lawrence (1955) in a case study of change found that status differences severely restricted communications, lowered job satisfaction, and as a result, retarded the addition of an assembly line for the manufacturing of a new electrical tube (prop. IV, VI). The well-known French and Coch study (1948: 512–532) suggested that low job satisfaction, created by piece rates, led to resistance to change, implying low adaptiveness. This was successfully overcome by decreasing centralization and allowing the workers to discuss changes. The workers made suggestions in their group discussions with management that resulted in even more changes being made. This study provides partial support for the hypothesized relationship between high satisfaction, low centralization, and high adaptiveness (corol. 4, 12); it also represents some negative findings about the relationship between adaptiveness and production (corol. 5). As a consequence of the increased worker satisfaction, production was higher than it had ever gone before. The only explanation that can be provided for this negative finding is that job satisfaction was so low that it had exceeded the minimal limit suggested by proposition VIII, having negative consequences for production.

Cillie (1940: 96), using Mort's scale, contrasted the degree of adaptiveness in 16 decentralized and 16 centralized schools in districts which were matched in socio-economic characteristics. (All 16 centralized schools were part of one system.) He found that the decentralized schools had adopted more of the 176 items on the list than the centralized schools; significantly, they were more likely to have adopted techniques and programs that increased their capacity for change. The changes allowed for greater individual attention to the pupil, a greater scope of instructional services, and for the teachers to participate more in decision making. In contrast, the centralized schools were more likely to have adopted practices that increased efficiency (corol. 2, 12).

Centralization   In an experiment conducted by Morse and Reimer (1955: 120–129), centralization was increased in one department and lowered in another. At the end of a year the centralized department had a higher rate of production but a lower rate of job satisfaction (prop. I, corol. 3). A similar finding was obtained in the communication studies of Bavelas and his associates (1960: 669–682). The centralized nets had higher production and fewer errors (an indication of efficiency), but lower job satisfaction among the members in the occupants of peripheral positions. The centralized nets tended very quickly to develop a formalized procedure for passing messages, whereas the decentralized nets did not standardize their work. Although these were experiments conducted in a laboratory, they suggest that centralization increases production, efficiency, and formalization, while lowering job satisfaction among the lower-ranking members (prop. I, III, and corol. 2, 11).

If the number of levels in an organization is accepted as a rough indication of centralization, then Udy's study of organizations in non-industrial societies provides cross-cultural evidence for some of the hypotheses (1959: 36–40). He found that the more centralized organizations, which he called bureaucracies, were more likely to have task specialization, i.e., low complexity, and to distribute rewards on the basis of office, i.e., high stratification (prop. VII, corol. 19). Michel's iron law of oligarchy (corol. 19) has received partial support in the Lipset, Trow, and Coleman study (1956). They suggest that the International Typographical Union had a lower level of centralization because of a number of factors that tended to limit stratification in the union. There were fewer status differences between the leaders and members, more specialization per person and less task specialization on the job, and an occupational community apart from the organizations involved.

Hall developed a series of scales to measure several dimensions of Weber's model, which he called hierarchy of authority, division of labor, system of rules, and system of procedures (1963: 32–30). The hierarchy of authority had high correlation with a system of rules and procedures and lower correlation with division of labor, which in turn had almost no correlation with the use of rules. Centralization and formalization, as defined by Hall, are highly correlated (prop. III). The studies of assembly-line work, as reported by Blau and Scott, showed that the routinization of tasks (high formalization) was associated with high centralization, higher production, higher productivity (efficiency), but lower job satisfaction and higher levels of turnover (1962: 211, 251). These studies support Weber's theory applied to areas other than administration; they also reinforce the Bavelas findings (prop. II, III, corol. 1, 20).

Blau and Scott (1962: 48) also discussed the reverse relation, noting that group decision making (low centralization) is slow and highly inefficient. Harrison's study (1959) of the Baptist Church is a single example of low centralization of decision making being associated with the absence of rules and regulations. An independent management-consulting firm rated the effectiveness of the organization and found it to be low, but there is no report of what criteria were used. The same firm rated the Roman Catholic Church and found its effectiveness to be high. The two religious organizations represent an example of two ideal types, with the Baptist Church approximating the adaptive organization and the Catholic Church approximating the productive organization.

Thompson's basic hypothesis of increasing complexity leading to a decentralization of decision making has support in several different research studies. The studies of staff-line conflict reflect how complexity undermines hierarchical authority (Blau and Scott, 1962: 172). In a study of five correctional institutions, Zald (1962: 335–345) found that the control structure was much more decentralized in treatment organizations, where specialization of persons was much higher and more individual attention was given to the inmates. The more decentralized organizations had a higher inmate-staff ratio as well, suggesting lower efficiency (corol. 10, prop. VII). Becker's case study (1961: 243–251) of teachers in schools suggests some of the mechanisms that they use to decrease supervision and authority over their work, that is, centralization. Another revealing case study made by Lipset (1950) explores how centralized and formalized bureaucracies reduce adaptiveness (corol. 12). Hage, in a study of 142 hospitals, observed that those with more highly specialized staffs of physicians tended to have more decentralized authority structures.

Although the decision-making study of the American Association of University Professors did not relate the increased complexity of universities to its findings of increased decentralization, this seems a highly plausible interpretation, since most of the universities in their sample did add many new occupations in the period covered (1955: 62–81). Lazarsfeld and Thielens (1958) found in a study of 70 colleges that the faculty had more influence in high-quality schools, where quality was measured by an index composed of the proportion of faculty having a Ph.D. (a measure of technical skill), the cost per student (efficiency), and the number (production) of students awarded a Ph.D. degree. Although this measure mixes several variables, it does seem that low centralization is related to high complexity and low efficiency.

Job Satisfaction   March and Simon (1958) reviewed the factors that affect job satisfaction and reported that it was higher when there was a high level of skill, i.e., high complexity; many programs, i.e., low formalization; and autonomy in decision making, i.e., low centralization (corol. 11, 14, 20). Two case studies of changes in the degree of formalization, as measured by the number of rules and their enforcement, suggest that there are very definite limits to the relationships between job satisfaction and formalization. In Gouldner's study of a gypsum plant, increases in formalization led to decreases in satisfaction. But Guest's study of an automobile plant disclosed that relaxing bureaucratic rules and especially their enforcement led to increases in satisfaction and increases in both production and productivity (Blau and Scott, 1962: 239–240). Therefore, increases or decreases in the scores of variables should be viewed in terms of proposition VIII, because a limit, whether maximum or minimum, may have been exceeded. There is some suggestion of this in Guest's work. Tsouderos's study (1955: 206–210) of voluntary associations disclosed that increases in formalization resulted in raising larger amounts of funds (high production) and lower costs, but that memberships dropped. Although voluntary associations are different from businesses, Tsouderos's findings support many of the hypotheses in the theory.

This brings us to what is probably the most controversial hypothesis in the theory: corollary 3. There have been many studies of morale and volume or production, but the results have been conflicting (Berelson and Steiner, 1964: 409–411). About one-half of them report a small positive correlation between high morale and high production, contrary to the hypothesis. Another third of the studies indicate that there is no relationship. The studies use a variety of definitions, of course, and the definition of high morale varies.

There is some support for a number of the hypotheses, and even though the evidence for specific hypotheses is not strong, there is considerable support for the theory. As Zetterberg (1963) has suggested, it is easier to prove a theory than specific hypotheses. Most of the studies involve only two or three of the hypotheses of the theory. Some of them, such as corollaries 6, 7, 9, and 16, do not appear to

have been examined by researchers. Some of them have both supporting and negative evidence. Certainly, the relationships between
job satisfaction and volume of production, and between either complexity or adaptiveness and volume of production are not completely
clear.

Two explanations are possible for the negative evidence. One
explanation is that when the limits of a variable are exceeded, there
is a reversal of the usual hypothesized relationship. Proposition VIII
stipulates both minimum and maximum levels, which must be maintained before the predicted relationships can hold. Another explanation is that the contradictory studies are using different levels of the
same variables or even different definitions. But one must also be
cautious about accepting the positive evidence. Perhaps the major
qualification that must be made is that the scales that have been employed in the various organizations are not the same.

Organizational Change

If the theory is a general one, it should be able to explain, at least
within a narrow scope, the problem of organizational change. There
are two aspects to this problem: the Parsonian distinction between
change within the system and change of the system of variables (1951).
The former aspect is the variable of adaptiveness, defined as the rate
of change in new programs and techniques; the latter aspect is the
consequence of a change in one variable as related to the other seven
variables, which effects a change in the entire system of variables.
Decision making becomes decentralized or status differences decrease.
The axiomatic theory indicates how the scores on the other variables
should change as a consequence.

Several of the studies reported in the previous section, e.g.,
Morse-Reimer, Bavelas, Tsouderos, were longitudinal ones. They indicate how changing one variable affected the scores on other variables. Although the number of longitudinal studies of organizations
is small, they are extremely useful because by examining whether a
change in one variable leads to changes in other variables, a more
exacting test of the hypotheses is possible. Longitudinal experiments
also allow a test of the validity of proposition VIII.

One study that investigated societies over a very long span of
time, 125 years, is Ben-David's study of medical research in France,
Great Britain, Germany, and the U.S. (1962: 305–328). It indicates that
for a period of time, the countries with centralized medical research
had much higher production but also higher stratification, as indicated
by slow rates of mobility among medical researchers. The countries
with decentralized medical research kept adding new specialties and
new techniques and programs, as well as research laboratories. The
lack of adaptiveness by the centralized organizations for a long period

of time gradually resulted in a reduction in production. This study suggests the importance of the limits hypothesis, proposition VIII. Without at least some adaptiveness in the organization, production drops and the advantages of centralization are lost.

The reverse problem is represented in a case study of the General Dynamics Corporation, which kept adding new programs and services in its various divisions at a very rapid rate. This resulted in a high adaptiveness score, but procedures for coordination were not set up and the organization suffered staggering losses until centralization and formalization were increased (Smith, 1962: 64; 1962: 120). The same point is made in Sloan's reminiscences of General Motors during the days of Durant (1963: 135). Durant kept adding new programs and services, but made no attempt to effect some centralization of decision making and formalization of procedures. The consequence was loss of efficiency and the near-bankruptcy of the company. In contrast, Ford used the policy of one product under rigid control with high production and high productivity, but, in the long run, the company's lack of adaptiveness resulted in a loss of sales to General Motors, which was pioneering new techniques, until Ford itself became much more adaptive.

All of these studies indicate that the continued emphasis on one organization end to the neglect of another gradually results in the exceeding of the limits, as suggested by proposition VIII. It should be noted that both maximum limit and minimum limit are exceeded simultaneously. In the Ben-David studies of Great Britain and France, the maximum of centralization and stratification is exceeded while the minimum level of adaptiveness is not reached. The General Motors study suggests that the maximum of adaptiveness was exceeded while the minimum of efficiency was not reached. In contrast, Ford Motor Company illustrates an exceeding of the maximum on centralization and formalization along with a failure to reach the minimum of adaptiveness. Thus, these case studies document not only the interrelationships between the variables, but how they can articulate as a system.

As is well known from a number of studies of changes in organization, the introduction of a new program or a new technique is known to lower satisfaction temporarily during the implementation. Increases in complexity and adaptiveness can produce temporary conflicts between groups, but the theory attempts to predict permanent changes in variables, rather than these temporary consequences. An illustration is the McCleery study of a prison (1957: 376–399). Before the introduction of a rehabilitation program, which resulted in the addition of new occupations and new techniques, the prison was described as having high stratification, high centralization, and high formalization. The rehabilitation program resulted in temporary conflicts and considerable job dissatisfaction among the guards. The permanent consequences were reduced stratification, centralization, and formalization. These findings are supported by another study of a prison, reported by Grusky (1959: 452–472). The adoption of the therapeutic technique in handling prisoners reduced status differences between guards and prisoners, increased interaction between them and the staff, resulted in a decentralization of authority, and a reduction in the use of bureaucratic procedures (lower formalization).

It should be noted that these case studies do not provide measures of the amount of change in adaptiveness or centralization or other variables. Consequently it becomes impossible to state how much of an increase in adaptiveness is necessary for a reduction of a given unit in centralization or how much increased formalization is necessary for an increase of one unit of efficiency. Such statements require the development of metrics such as the coefficients of the variables, the power values of the variables, and the limits suggested by proposition VIII. Metrics are the necessary first step before precise prediction can be made. Once this is done, then a much more exacting test of the hypotheses is possible.

Summary

Although a large number of research studies have been codified by the axiomatic theory, several qualifications must be made. The major qualification is that the definition of the variables used in the wide diversity of organizational types is not the same. The evidence for some of the hypotheses is negative; this may be a definitional problem or a limits problem. Since there are no metrics, a precise test of the hypotheses in the axiomatic theory is not possible; predictions cannot be made and then either verified or denied. At the same time, there is enough supporting evidence to indicate that the development of metrics and the consideration of definitions is a worth-while undertaking. It would appear that this axiomatic theory is pointing in the right direction toward the understanding of organizations.

Sources of Power of Lower Participants in Complex Organizations*

DAVID MECHANIC

This paper explores various factors that account for the power of secretaries, hospital attendants, prison inmates, and other lower participants within organizations. Power is seen as resulting from access to and control over persons, information, and instrumentalities. Among

* Reprinted from *Administrative Science Quarterly*, 7 (December 1962), pp. 349–364, with omissions, by permission of the author and the publisher.

the variables discussed affecting power are normative definitions, perception of legitimacy, exchange, and coalitions. Personal attributes related to power include commitment, effort, interest, willingness to use power, skills, and attractiveness. Finally, various attributes of social structure are discussed which also help to account for the power of lower participants: time spent in the organization, centrality of position, duality of power structures, and replaceability of persons.

It is not unusual for lower participants (Etzioni, 1961) in complex organizations to assume and wield considerable power and influence not associated with their formally defined positions within these organizations. In sociological terms they have considerable personal power but no authority. Such personal power is often attained, for example, by executive secretaries and accountants in business firms, by attendants in mental hospitals, and even by inmates in prisons. The personal power achieved by these lower participants does not necessarily result from unique personal characteristics, although these may be relevant, but results rather from particular aspects of their location within their organizations.

Informal Versus Formal Power

Within organizations the distribution of authority (institutionalized power) is closely if not perfectly correlated with the prestige of positions. Those who have argued for the independence of these variables (Bierstedt, 1950: 730–38) have taken their examples from diverse organizations and do not deal with situations where power is clearly comparable (Dahl, 1957: 201–15). Thus when Bierstedt argues that Einstein had prestige but no power, and the policeman power but no prestige, it is apparent that he is comparing categories that are not comparable. Generally persons occupying high-ranking positions within organizations have more authority than those holding low-ranking positions.

One might ask what characterizes high-ranking positions within organizations. What is most evident, perhaps, is that lower participants recognize the right of high-ranking participants to exercise power, and yield without difficulty to demands they regard as legitimate. Moreover, persons in high-ranking positions tend to have considerable access and control over information and persons both within and outside the organization, and to instrumentalities or resources. Although higher supervisory personnel may be isolated from the task activities of lower participants, they maintain access to them through formally established intermediary positions and exercise control through intermediary participants. There appears, therefore, to be a clear correlation between the prestige of positions within organizations and the extent to which they offer access to information, persons, and instrumentalities.

Since formal organizations tend to structure lines of access and communication, access should be a clue to institutional prestige. Yet access depends on variables other than those controlled by the formal structure of an organization, and this often makes the informal power structure that develops within organizations somewhat incongruent with the formally intended plan. It is these variables that allow work groups to limit production through norms that contravene the goals of the larger organization, that allow hospital attendants to thwart changes in the structure of a hospital, and that allow prison inmates to exercise control over prison guards. Organizations, in a sense, are continuously at the mercy of their lower participants, and it is this fact that makes organizational power structure especially interesting to the sociologist and social psychologist.

Clarification of Definitions The purpose of this paper is to present some hypotheses explaining why lower participants in organizations can often assume and wield considerable power which is not associated with their positions as formally defined within these organizations. For the purposes of this analysis the concepts "influence," "power," and "control" will be used synonymously. Moreover, we shall not be concerned with type of power, that is, whether the power is based on reward, punishment, identification, power to veto, or whatever (French and Raven, 1960: 607–23). Power will be defined as *any force that results in behavior that would not have occurred if the force had not been present.* We have defined power as a force rather than a relationship because it appears that much of what we mean by power is encompassed by the normative framework of an organization, and thus any analysis of power must take into consideration the power of norms as well as persons.

I shall also argue, following Thibaut and Kelley (1959), that power is closely related to dependence. To the extent that a person is dependent on another, he is potentially subject to the other person's power. Within organizations one makes others dependent upon him by controlling access to information, persons, and instrumentalities, which I shall define as follows:

(a) *Information* includes knowledge of the organization, knowledge about persons, knowledge of the norms, procedures, techniques, and so forth.

(b) *Persons* include anyone within the organization or anyone outside the organization upon whom the organization is in some way dependent.

(c) *Instrumentalities* include any aspect of the physical plant of the organization or its resources (equipment, machines, money, and so on).

Power is a function not only of the extent to which a person controls information, persons, and instrumentalities, but also of the importance of the various attributes he controls.

Finally, following Dahl (1957: 201–15), we shall agree that comparisons of power among persons should, as far as possible, utilize comparable units. Thus we shall strive for clarification by attempting to over-simplify organizational processes; the goal is to set up a number of hypothetical statements of the relationship between variables taken two at a time, "all other factors being assumed to remain constant."

A Classic Example Like many other aspects of organizational theory, one can find a classic statement of our problem in Weber's discussion of the political bureaucracy. Weber indicated the extent to which bureaucrats may have considerable power over political incumbents, as a result, in part, of their permanence within the political bureaucracy, as contrasted to public officials, who are replaced rather frequently (1952: 18–27). Weber noted how the low-ranking bureaucrat becomes familiar with the organization—its rules and operations, the work flow, and so on, which gives him considerable power over the new political incumbent, who might have higher rank but is not as familiar with the organization. While Weber does not directly state the point, his analysis suggests that bureaucratic permanence has some relationship to increased access to persons, information, and instrumentalities. To state the hypothesis suggested somewhat more formally:

H1.   Other factors remaining constant, organizational power is related to access to persons, information, and instrumentalities.

H2.   Other factors remaining constant, as a participant's length of time in an organization increases, he has increased access to persons, information, and instrumentalities.

While these hypotheses are obvious, they do suggest that a careful scrutiny of the organizational literature, especially that dealing with the power or counterpower of lower participants, might lead to further formalized statements, some considerably less obvious than the ones stated. This kind of hypothesis formation is treated later in the paper, but at this point I would like to place the discussion of power within a larger theoretical context and discuss the relevance of role theory to the study of power processes.

Implications of Role Theory for the Study of Power

There are many points of departure for the study of power processes within organizations. An investigator might view influence in terms of its sources and strategies; he might undertake a study of the flow of influence; he might concentrate on the structure of organizations, seeing to what extent regularities in behavior might be explained through the study of norms, roles, and traditions; and, finally, more psychologically oriented investigators might concentrate on the recipients of influence and the factors affecting susceptibility to influence attempts. Each of these points of departure leads to different theoretical emphases. For our purposes the most important emphasis is that presented by role theorists.

Role theorists approach the question of influence and power in terms of the behavioral regularities which result from established identities within specific social contexts like families, hospitals, and business firms. The underlying premise of most role theorists is that a large proportion of all behavior is brought about through socialization within specific organizations, and much behavior is routine and established through learning the traditional modes of adaptation in dealing with specific tasks. Thus the positions persons occupy in an organization account for much of their behavior. Norms and roles serve as mediating forces in influence processes.

While role theorists have argued much about vocabulary, the basic premises underlying their thought have been rather consistent. The argument is essentially that knowledge of one's identity or social position is a powerful index of the expectations such a person is likely to face in various social situations. Since behavior tends to be highly correlated with expectations, prediction of behavior is therefore possible. The approach of role theorists to the study of behavior within organizations is of particular merit in that it provides a consistent set of concepts which is useful analytically in describing recruitment, socialization, interaction, and personality, as well as the formal structure of organizations. Thus the concept of role is one of the few concepts clearly linking social structure, social process, and social character.

Many problems pertaining to role theory have been raised. At times it is not clear whether role is regarded as a real entity, a theoretical construct, or both. Moreover, Gross has raised the issue of role consensus, that is, the extent to which the expectations impinging upon a position are held in common by persons occupying reciprocal positions to the one in question (Gross, Mason, and McEachern, 1958). Merton has attempted to deal with inevitable inconsistencies in expectations of role occupants by introducing the concept of role-set which treats differences in expectations as resulting, in part, from the fact that any position is differently related to a number of reciprocal positions (1957b). Furthermore, Goffman has criticized role theory for its failure to deal adequately with commitment to roles (1961: 85–152)—a factor which Etzioni has found to be related intimately to the kind of power exercised in organizations

(1961). Perhaps these various criticisms directed at role theory reflect its importance as well as its deficiencies, and despite the difficulties involved in role analysis, the concept of role may prove useful in various ways.

Role theory is useful in emphasizing the extent to which influence and power can be exercised without conflict. This occurs when power is integrated with a legitimate order, when sentiments are held in common, and when there are adequate mechanisms for introducing persons into the system and training them to recognize, accept, and value the legitimacy of control within the organization. By providing the conditions whereby participants within an organization may internalize the norms, these generalized rules, values, and sentiments serve as substitutes for interpersonal influence and make the workings of the organization more agreeable and pleasant for all.

It should be clear that lower participants will be more likely to circumvent higher authority, other factors remaining constant, when the mandates of those in power, if not the authority itself, are regarded as illegitimate. Thus as Etzioni points out, when lower participants become alienated from the organization, coercive power is likely to be required if its formal mandates are to be fulfilled (1961).

Moreover, all organizations must maintain control over lower participants. To the extent that lower participants fail to recognize the legitimacy of power, or believe that sanctions cannot or will not be exercised when violations occur, the organization loses to some extent, its ability to control their behavior. Moreover, insofar as higher participants can create the impression that they can or will exert sanctions above their actual willingness to use such sanctions, control over lower participants will increase. It is usually to the advantage of an organization to externalize and impersonalize controls, however, and if possible to develop positive sentiments toward its rules.

In other words, an effective organization can control its participants in such a way as to make it hardly perceivable that it exercises the control that it does. It seeks commitment from lower participants, and when commitment is obtained, surveillance can be relaxed. On the other hand, when the power of lower participants in organizations is considered, it often appears to be clearly divorced from the traditions, norms, and goals and sentiments of the organization as a whole. Lower participants do not usually achieve control by using the role structure of the organization, but rather by circumventing, sabotaging, and manipulating it.

Sources of Power of Lower Participants

The most effective way for lower participants to achieve power is to obtain, maintain, and control access to persons, information, and instrumentalities. To the extent that this can be accomplished, lower participants make higher-ranking participants dependent upon them. Thus dependence together with the manipulation of the dependency relationship is the key to the power of lower participants.

A number of examples can be cited which illustrate the preceding point. Scheff, for example, reports on the failure of a state mental hospital to bring about intended reform because of the opposition of hospital attendants (1961: 93–105). He noted that the power of hospital attendants was largely a result of the dependence of ward physicians on attendants. This dependence resulted from the physician's short tenure, his lack of interest in administration, and the large amount of administrative responsibility he had to assume. An implicit trading agreement developed between physicians and attendants, whereby attendants would take on some of the responsibilities and obligations of the ward physician in return for increased power in decision-making processes concerning patients. Failure of the ward physician to honor his part of the agreement resulted in information being withheld, disobedience, lack of co-operation, and unwillingness of the attendants to serve as a barrier between the physician and a ward full of patients demanding attention and recognition. When the attendant withheld co-operation, the physician had difficulty in making a graceful entrance and departure from the ward, in handling necessary paper work (officially his responsibility), and in obtaining information needed to deal adequately with daily treatment and behavior problems. When attendants opposed change, they could wield influence by refusing to assume responsibilities officially assigned to the physician.

Similarly, Sykes describes the dependence of prison guards on inmates and the power obtained by inmates over guards (1961: 191–197). He suggests that although guards could report inmates for disobedience, frequent reports would give prison officials the impression that the guard was unable to command obedience. The guard, therefore, had some stake in ensuring the good behavior of prisoners without use of formal sanctions against them. The result was a trading agreement whereby the guard allowed violations of certain rules in return for cooperative behavior. A similar situation is found in respect to officers in the Armed Services or foremen in industry. To the extent that they require formal sanctions to bring about cooperation, they are usually perceived by the superiors as less valuable to the organization. For a good leader is expected to command obedience, at least, if not commitment.

Factors Affecting Power

Expertise Increasing specialization and organizational growth has made the expert or staff person important. The expert maintains power because high-ranking persons in the organization are dependent upon him for his special skills and access to certain kinds of information. One possible reason for lawyers obtaining many high governmental offices is that they are likely to have access to rather specialized but highly important means to organizational goals (*New Yorker,* April 14, 1962: 62).

We can state these ideas in a hypothesis, as follows:

H3. Other factors remaining constant, to the extent that a low-ranking participant has important expert knowledge not available to high-ranking participants, he is likely to have power over them.

Power stemming from expertise, however, is likely to be limited unless it is difficult to replace the expert. This leads to two further hypotheses:

H4. Other factors remaining constant, a person difficult to replace will have greater power than a person easily replaceable.

H5. Other factors remaining constant, experts will be more difficult to replace than nonexperts.

While persons having expertise are likely to be fairly high-ranking participants in an organization, the same hypotheses that explain the power of lower participants are relevant in explaining the comparative power positions of intermediate- and high-ranking persons.

The application of our hypothesis about expertise is clearly relevant if we look at certain organizational issues. For example, the merits of medical versus lay hospital administrators are often debated. It should be clear, however, that all other factors remaining unchanged, the medical administrator has clear advantage over the lay administrator. Where lay administrators receive preference, there is an implicit assumption that the lay person is better at administrative duties. This may be empirically valid but is not necessarily so. The special expert knowledge of the medical administrator stems from his ability legitimately to oppose a physician who contests an administrative decision on the basis of medical necessity. Usually hospitals are viewed primarily as universalistic in orientation both by the general public and most of their participants. Thus medical necessity usually takes precedence over management policies, a factor contributing to the poor financial position of most hospitals. The lay administrator is not in a position to contest such claims independently, since he usually lacks the basis for evaluation of the medical problems involved and also lacks official recognition of his competence to make such decisions. If the lay administrator is to evaluate these claims adequately on the basis of professional necessity, he must have a group of medical consultants or a committee of medical men to serve as a buffer between medical staff and the lay administration.

As a result of growing specialization, expertise is increasingly important in organizations. As the complexity of organizational tasks increases, and as organizations grow in size, there is a limit to responsibility that can be efficiently exercised by one person. Delegation of responsibility occurs, experts and specialists are brought in to provide information and research, and the higher participants become dependent upon them. Experts have tremendous potentialities for power by withholding information, providing incorrect information, and so on, and to the extent that experts are dissatisfied, the probability of organizational sabotage increases.

Effort and Interest   The extent to which lower participants may exercise power depends in part on their willingness to exert effort in areas where higher-ranking participants are often reluctant to participate. Effort exerted is directly related to the degree of interest one has in an area.

H6.   Other factors remaining constant, there is a direct relationship between the amount of effort a person is willing to exert in an area and the power he can command.

For example, secretarial staffs in universities often have power to make decisions about the purchase and allocation of supplies, the allocation of their services, the scheduling of classes, and, at times, the disposition of student complaints. Such control may in some instances lead to sanctions against a professor by polite reluctance to furnish supplies, ignoring his preferences for the scheduling of classes, and giving others preference in the allocation of services. While the power to make such decisions may easily be removed from the jurisdiction of the lower participant, it can only be accomplished at a cost—the willingness to allocate time and effort to the decisions dealing with these matters. To the extent that responsibilities are delegated to lower participants, a certain degree of power is likely to accompany the responsibility. Also, should the lower participant see his perceived rights in jeopardy, he may sabotage the system in various ways.

Let us visualize a hypothetical situation where a department concludes that secretarial services are being allocated on a prejudicial basis as a result of complaints to the chairman of the department by several of the younger faculty. Let us also assume that, when the complaint is investigated, it is found to be substantially correct; that is, some of the younger faculty have difficulty obtaining secretarial services because of preferences among the secretarial staff. If, in attempting to eliminate discretion by the secretarial staff, the chairman establishes a rule ordering the allocation of services on the basis of the order in which work appears, the rule can easily be made ineffective by complete conformity to it. Deadlines for papers, examinations, and the like will occur, and flexibility in the allocation of services is required if these deadlines are to be met. Thus the need for flexibility can be made to conflict with the rule by a staff usually not untalented in such operations.

When an organization gives discretion to lower participants, it is usually trading the power of discretion for needed flexibility. The cost of constant surveillance is too high, and the effort required too great; it is very often much easier for all concerned to allow the secretary discretion in return for cooperation and not too great an abuse of power.

H7. Other factors remaining constant, the less effort and interest higher-ranking participants are willing to devote to a task, the more likely are lower participants to obtain power relevant to this task.

Attractiveness   Another personal attribute associated with the power of low-ranking persons in an organization is attractiveness or what some call "personality." People who are viewed as attractive are more likely to obtain access to persons, and, once such access is gained, they may be more likely to succeed in promoting a cause. But once again dependence is the key to the power of attractiveness, for whether a person is dependent upon another for a service he provides, or for approval or affection, what is more relevant is the relational bond which is highly valued.

H8. Other factors remaining constant, the more attractive a person, the more likely he is to obtain access to persons and control over these persons.

Location and Position   In any organization the person's location in physical space and position in social space are important factors influencing access to persons, information, and instrumentalities (Thibaut and Kelley, 1959: 39–42). Propinquity affects the opportunities for interaction, as well as one's position with a communication network. Although these are somewhat separate factors, we shall refer to their combined effect as centrality (Leavitt, 1958: 559) within the organization.

H9. Other factors remaining constant, the more central a person is in an organization, the greater is his access to persons, information, and instrumentalities.

Some low participants may have great centrality within an organization. An executive's or university president's secretary not only has access, but often controls access in making appointments and scheduling events. Although she may have no great formal authority, she may have considerable power.

Coalitions It should be clear that the variables we are considering are at different levels of analysis; some of them define attributes of persons, while others define attributes of communication and organization. Power processes within organizations are particularly interesting in that there are many channels of power and ways of achieving it.

In complex organizations different occupational groups attend to different functions, each group often maintaining its own power structure within the organization. Thus hospitals have administrators, medical personnel, nursing personnel, attendants, maintenance personnel, laboratory personnel, and so on. Universities, similarly, have teaching personnel, research personnel, administrative personnel, maintenance personnel, and so on. Each of these functional tasks within organizations often becomes the sphere of a particular group that controls activities relating to the task. While these tasks usually are coordinated at the highest levels of the organization, they often are not coordinated at intermediate and lower levels. It is not unusual, however, for coalitions to form among lower participants in these multiple structures. A secretary may know the man who manages the supply of stores, or the person assigning parking stickers. Such acquaintances may give her the ability to handle informally certain needs that would be more time-consuming and difficult to handle formally. Her ability to provide services informally makes higher-ranking participants in some degree dependent upon her, thereby giving her power, which increases her ability to bargain on issues important to her.

Rules In organizations with complex power structures lower participants can use their knowledge of the norms of the organization to thwart attempted change. In discussing the various functions of bureaucratic rules, Gouldner maintains that such rules serve as excellent substitutes for surveillance, since surveillance in addition to being expensive in time and effort arouses considerable hostility and antagonism (1954). Moreover, he argues, rules are a functional equivalent for direct, personally given orders, since they specify the obligations of workers to do things in specific ways. Standardized rules, in addition, allow simple screening of violations, facilitate remote control, and to some extent legitimize punishment when the rule is violated. The worker who violates a bureaucratic rule has little recourse to the excuse that he did not know what was expected, as he might claim for a direct order. Finally, Gouldner argues that rules are "the 'chips' to which the company staked the supervisors and which they could use to play the game" (1954: 173); that is, rules established a punishment which could be withheld, and this facilitated the supervisors' bargaining power with lower participants.

While Gouldner emphasizes the functional characteristics of rules within an organization, it should be clear that full compliance to all the rules at all times will probably be dysfunctional for the organization. Complete and apathetic compliance may do everything but facilitate achievement of organizational goals. Lower participants who are familiar with an organization and its rules can often find rules to support their contention that they not do what they have been asked to do, and rules are also often a rationalization for inaction on their part. The following of rules becomes especially complex when associations and unions become involved, for there are then two sets of rules to which the participant can appeal.

What is suggested is that rules may be chips for everyone concerned in the game. Rules become the "chips" through which the bargaining process is maintained. Scheff, as noted earlier, observed that attendants in mental hospitals often took on responsibilities assigned legally to the ward physician, and when attendants refused to share these responsibilities the physician's position became extremely difficult (1961).

> The ward physician is legally responsible for the care and treatment of each ward patient. This responsibility requires attention to a host of details. Medicine, seclusion, sedation and transfer orders, for example, require the doctor's signature. Tranquilizers are particularly troublesome in this regard since they require frequent adjustment of dosage in order to get the desired effects. The physician's order is required to each change in dosage. With 150 patients under his care on tranquilizers, and several changes of dosages a week desirable, the physician could spend a major portion of his ward time in dealing with this single detail.
>
> Given the time-consuming formal chores of the physician and his many other duties, he usually worked out an arrangement with the ward personnel, particularly the charge (supervisory attendant), to handle these duties. On several wards, the charge called specific problems to the doctor's attention, and the two of them, in effect, would have a consultation. The charge actually made most of the decisions concerning dosage change in the back wards. Since the doctor delegated portions of his formal responsibilities to the charge, he was dependent on her good will toward him. If she withheld her cooperation, the physician had absolutely no recourse but to do all the work himself (Scheff, 1961: 97).

In a sense such delegation of responsibility involves a consideration of reward and cost, whereby the decision to be made involves a question of what is more valuable—to retain control over an area, or to delegate one's work to lower participants.

There are occasions, of course, when rules are regarded as illegitimate by lower participants, and they may disregard them. Gouldner observed that, in the mine, men felt they could resist authority in a situation involving danger to themselves (1954). They did not feel that they could legitimately be ordered to do anything that would endanger their lives. It is probably significant that in extremely dangerous situations organizations are more likely to rely on commitment to work than on authority. Even within nonvoluntary groups dangerous tasks are regarded usually as requiring task commitment, and it is likely that commitment is a much more powerful organizational force than coercive authority.

The Hierarchy of Authority in Organizations*

PETER M. BLAU

.   .   .

A theory of formal organization, as distinguished from a theory of group life in a bureaucratic context, seeks to explain why organizations develop various characteristics, such as a multilevel hierarchy or decentralized authority. To furnish these explanations requires that the characteristics of organizations are not taken as given but the conditions that produce them are investigated. Thus one may ask how the qualifications of an organization's staff influence the structure of authority in it, or generally what conditions affect the shape of the hierarchy, which are the two problems posed in this paper. In order to answer this kind of question, it is necessary to compare different organizations and not merely to study the influence exerted on behavior by the conditions found in a single case. The method of comparison might involve analyzing bureaucracies in different historical periods, which was Weber's approach; or intensive examination of two contrasting forms of organization, as in Stinchcombe's study (1959) or quantitative comparisons of many organizations and multivariate analysis of their characteristics. The last procedure is adopted here.

. . . The analysis of the authority structure to be presented is based on data collected from several hundred government agencies. Only agencies of a specific type are directly compared, to eliminate the disturbing influence of differences between types; but the results of one such study are confronted with those of another, to discern

* Reprinted from *The American Journal of Sociology, 73* (January 1968), pp. 453–467, with omissions, by permission of the author and The University of Chicago Press. Copyright © 1968 by the University of Chicago. All rights reserved. In reprinting the article, parts of text and all expository footnotes are deleted.

whether conclusions are confined to a single type. The inquiry is restricted to the formal attributes of organizations, since it was not possible to collect data on informal patterns and individual attitudes in hundreds of government agencies. . . .

Professional and Bureaucratic Authority

The relationship between the expert qualifications of a professional staff and the bureaucratic authority vested in a hierarchy of offices poses an interesting theoretical issue. Professionalism and bureaucracy have much in common, such as impersonal detachment, specialized technical expertise, and rational decision making based on universalistic standards. There are also divergent elements, however, and professional principles often come into conflict with the requirements of bureaucratic authority. Weber implied that the professional authority rooted in expert technical knowledge and the bureaucratic authority rooted in a hierarchy of offices with legitimate claims to disciplined compliance tend to occur together, both being distinctive characteristics of complex rational organizations. "The role of technical qualifications in bureaucratic organizations is continually increasing" (1947: 335). But, in addition, "each lower office is under the control and supervision of a higher one" (1947: 331). The assumption that professional expertness and bureaucratic discipline are simply two aspects of the rational organization of large-scale tasks not only conflicts with the prevailing impression that professional work suffers if subjected to bureaucratic discipline but also has been questioned on both systematic theoretical and empirical grounds.

In a well-known footnote, Parsons criticizes Weber for confounding two analytically distinct types of authority (1947: 58–60). Professional authority rests on the certified superior competence of the expert, which prompts others voluntarily to follow his directives because they consider doing so to be in their own interest. Bureaucratic authority, in contrast, rests on the legitimate power of command vested in an official position, which obligates subordinates to follow directives under the threat of sanctions. Superior knowledge is not required for bureaucratic authority (expert knowledge is not what authorizes the policeman to direct traffic, for example, or what induces us to obey his signals), whereas it is essential for professional control, and mandatory compliance is enforced by coercive sanctions in the bureaucratic but not in the professional case. Gouldner similarly stresses the difference between the influence exerted on the basis of technical competence and the compelling authority in a bureaucratic hierarchy, and he derives from this distinction two contrasting forms of bureaucracy—"representative" and "punishment-centered" (1954: 21–24). . . .

The present paper addresses itself first to this problem of how variations in the qualifications of the personnel affect the authority structure in formal organizations, and it then turns to the question of how other conditions affect the hierarchy of authority.

A simple working hypothesis for investigating the first problem can be derived from a few plausible considerations. Entrance requirements that assure that the agency staff (meaning all personnel, in line as well as "staff" positions) has relatively high minimum qualifications might be expected to lessen the need for guidance and close supervision. The implication is that such expert requirements widen the span of control of managers, increasing the number of subordinates under each (Janger, 1960: 9), and therefore reduce the proportion of managerial personnel in the organization, because each superior can supervise more subordinates if they are experts than if their lower skills necessitate much guidance and checking. These inferences, which appear straightforward and perhaps even self-evident, suggest as an initial hypothesis that expert requirements decrease the ratio of managerial to non-supervisory personnel in organizations, which widens the average span of control. . . .

Study of Government Finance Departments

A study of 254 finance departments of state and local governments made it possible to test the hypothesis that staff expertness leads to decentralization of responsibilities, and further to explore the conditions that influence the structure of authority in organizations. Original data were collected for the purpose of this study by N.O.R.C. interviewers from informants (senior managers) in the major finance department of each government. The universe consists of the departments in all states, all counties with a population of more than 100,000, and all cities with a population of more than 50,000, in the United States, except those with a staff of fewer than twenty or with no subdivision of responsibilities into two or more units. The sample comprises the entire universe, and information was obtained from 96.6 percent of these organizations. Although responsibilities vary, nearly all departments maintain financial records and pre-audit disbursements, and the majority are also responsible for post-auditing other departments, investments, investment management, and fixed-asset accounting. The median department has a staff of sixty, six major subdivisions, and four hierarchical levels. . . .

The basic finding reported from the study of public personnel agencies is confirmed by this research on another type of government agency; a high ratio of managerial personnel is more often found in finance departments with a large proportion of college-trained experts than in those with comparatively few employees so qualified (Table 1, row 1). The more extensive data of the second study make it possible to stipulate the structural implications of the higher ratio of managers in organizations with many experts. The employment of an expert staff seems to give rise to vertical differentiation, increasing the number of managerial levels in the organization. The number of hierarchical levels tends to be larger in departments requiring of its personnel relatively high educational qualifications than in those with lower requirements (row 2). The span of control of first-line supervisors is, on the average, somewhat narrower if the staff has superior qualifications (row 3) than if it does not (Bell, 1967: 100–109). The span of control of middle managers (those between the top executive and first-line supervisors) is, by contrast, wider in agencies with well-trained personnel than in others (row 4). But these middle managers have many fewer subordinates in any case, averaging less than two, than first-line supervisors, whose median is six subordinates. Managers have typically broader responsibilities than operating officials, and very few managers report to a single superior; expert qualifications presumably broaden the responsibilities of operating employees, which is reflected in a parallel reduction in the number reporting to a single supervisor. This consistent inverse association between scope of responsibilities and width of span of control clearly indicates that a narrow span of control must not be assumed to be indicative of closeness of supervision (Bell, 1967: 106).

The utilization of employees with superior qualifications raises the proportion of managers in an organization, apparently because it tends to increase the number of managerial levels and decrease the span of control of first-line supervisors without decreasing that of higher managers. The question arises how the extra managerial manpower is utilized in departments with a highly qualified staff. The time estimates of informants permit tentative answers to this question. If much of the staff is college trained, managers are less likely to spend most of their time in actual supervision than if it is not (Table 1, row 5, based on the mean for all managers), and this is the case for first-line supervisors as well as higher managers. The finding that superiors of experts devote comparatively little time to actually supervising them helps to explain why their narrow span of control does not imply close supervision. Managers in departments with highly qualified personnel seem to spend more time than other managers on professional work of their own which keeps them in touch with the problems encountered by the operating level. Such greater involvement in actual operations on the part of managers of an expert staff, compared to other managers, may well improve their qualifications to discuss technical problems of the work with their subordinates and thus to take full advantage of the greater opportunities for communication that the smaller numbers of subordinates per superior create.

The question of prime interest is whether the hypothesis that expertness promotes decentralization, which rested merely on inferential conjecture, is confirmed by the directly pertinent data from finance departments. This is in fact the case. Responsibilities of various kinds

TABLE 1. TRAINING REQUIREMENTS AND AUTHORITY STRUCTURE

Percentage of finance departments (in cols. [1] and [2]) in which:	Proportion of staff required to have B.A.*		Yule's Q (gamma) (3)
	Low (1)	High (2)	
1. The proportion of managers exceeds one-quarter of the total personnel	35 (147)	48 (106)	.27
2. The number of levels is four or more	36 (148)	51 (106)	.29
3. The mean span of control of first-line supervisors is six or more	56 (147)	44 (106)	—.23†
4. The mean span of control of middle managers is 1.6 or more	38 (135)	54 (100)	.32
5. The average manager spends more than two-fifths of his time supervising	52 (145)	38 (106)	—.29
6. Division heads make budgeting or accounting decisions	40 (122)	54 (86)	.26†
7. An official below the director recommends promotions and dismissals	30 (147)	45 (104)	.32

* Since this variable is not associated with size, it is not necessary to control size.
† All relationships are significant below the .05 level except these two, which are significant on the .08 and .06 levels, respectively.

tend to be delegated by management to lower levels in agencies where the staff has relatively high qualifications. Thus budgeting and accounting decisions are more likely to be made by division heads rather than the department director himself if the staff includes many college-trained men than if it includes few (Table 1, row 6). The likelihood that an official below the top executive recommends promotions and dismissals is also greater in agencies with many experts than in others (row 7). Parallel relationships with expertness, though they are somewhat less pronounced, are revealed by other indications of decentralization of responsibilities, such as the top executive's policy to let his division heads make most decisions, and the fact that first-line supervisors, not higher officials, formally evaluate the performance of non-supervisory employees. In sum, managerial authority over decision making appears indeed to be more decentralized in organizations with large proportions of trained experts than in others.

Multilevel Hierarchies

The finding that superior qualifications of the personnel in government agencies encourage delegation of responsibilities is not surprising. But what is unexpected is that such superior qualifications are also associated with vertical differentiation into multilevel hierarchies. It is generally assumed that the proliferation of hierarchical levels in organizations is a sign of overbureaucratization and an impediment to rational operations, and the results of Udy's study of primitive production organizations point to this conclusion (1959: 791–795), whereas the opposite is implied by the association obtained here between levels and training requirements, since superior training undoubtedly entails more rational decision making. The question arises of what conditions in contemporary American agencies promote hierarchical differentiation.

A multilevel hierarchy is associated with several basic characteristics of finance departments. (1) The number of levels increases with increasing size, that is, the number of employees (Pearsonian zero-order correlation, 51). (2) Although the zero-order correlation between number of levels and number of major subdivisions is virtually zero (−.05), there is an inverse association between the two when size is controlled (−.34). (3) The wider the average span of control of middle managers, the larger is the number of levels in the hierarchy (.27). (4) Automation in the form of computers is associated with multiple levels (.34). (5) Explicit written promotion regulations encourage hierarchical differentiation (.22). (6) The number of levels increases the more weight written examinations have for promotions (.24), and it decreases the more weight seniority (−.22) and supervisory evaluations (−.16) have for promotions. (7) Decentralization of responsibility for promotions and dismissals is correlated with multiple levels (.18). (8) The larger the proportion of employees required to have college degrees, finally, the larger the number of levels (.16).

Since so many factors are associated with hierarchical levels, partial correlations were computed between each of the eight and number of levels holding constant the other seven. The results of this analysis, which provide the basis for the further discussion, are presented in Table 2. The multiple correlation between all eight factors and levels is .65. These characteristics of finance departments explain 43 percent of the variance in hierarchical levels, with most of the difference being due to three factors—size, divisions, and automation.

Some reflections on the considerations that probably influence the decision to add new levels in the hierarchy can serve as a starting point for interpreting these associations. As an organization expands in size and complexity, it is likely that additional major divisions are established, which increases the number of officials directly responsible to the department director and overburdens him with supervisory

TABLE 2. CORRELATIONS WITH NUMBER OF LEVELS IN THE HIERARCHY

Independent variable	Zero-order correlation	Partial correlation	Standar-dized B*	Regression error	Data on employment agencies: zero-order correlation
1. Number of employees	.51	.50	.53	.06	.60
2. Number of major divisions	−.05	−.32	−.30	.06	.19
3. Span of control of middle managers	.27	.11	.09	.05	.31
4. Automation (computers)[a]	.34	.23	.19	.05	.53
5. Explicit promotion regulations[a]	.22	.04	−.03	.06	.33
6. Weight of examinations in promotions	.24	.13	.12	.06	[b]
7. Decentralization of promotion decisions[a]	.18	.12	.09	.05	.19
8. Proportion of staff required to have B.A.	.16	.03	.02	.05	−.00

[a] These three factors are dichotomous and were used as dummy variables in the regression analysis. All others are continuous variables except weight of examinations, which was coded in four categories.
[b] No corresponding variable is available for the employment security study.

responsibilities. To lighten this administrative load of the top executive and free him to devote more time to his primary executive functions, a few assistant directors may be installed on a new level to whom the division directors report and who in turn report to the director, just as the creation of the U.S. Secretary of Health, Education, and Welfare constituted an intermediate level between the President and officials who formerly reported directly to him. The introduction of such a new level of assistant directors would account for the inverse association observed between levels and major subdivisions because the few "superdivisions" headed by the assistant directors, not the former divisions, would be defined as the "major subdivisions" by the criterion used. This change would also help to explain why number of levels and span of control of middle managers, which includes assistant directors, are correlated without controls (.27) but are no longer significantly related once size, subdivisions, and other conditions are controlled (.11). The assumptions here are that the assistant directors, whose establishment increases levels, have a particularly wide span of control—hence the zero-order correlation—but that the introduction of this new level occurs usually in large agencies and reduces the number of major subdivisions—hence the considerably lower correlation under these controls.

Differentiation into a multilevel hierarchy has evident advantages for expanding organizations, according to these conjectures. In fact the number of levels in finance departments increases with increasing size, as previously noted; so does the number of major subdivisions, however (the zero-order correlation between size and subdivisions being .43, nearly as large as that between size and levels, .51). Not all large agencies have many levels and few major divisions. The inverse association between levels and subdivisions when size is controlled implies the existence of two contrasting departmental structures, one that is primarily differentiated horizontally into many major divisions and one that is primarily differentiated vertically into many levels. The question is what conditions discourage horizontal differentiation—which places an excessive administrative burden on top management—and encourage vertical differentiation instead.

The clue for answering this question is provided by the other major correlate of number of levels, namely, automation, which reveals a substantial association with it (.34) that persists when other conditions are controlled (.23). Although extending the hierarchy has administrative advantages for the top executive of a large organization, it also removes him increasingly from the operating level and makes it difficult for him directly to control operations and keep tight reins on them. This loss of close contact with the operating level is a serious disadvantage for a director who relies largely on direct supervision for control, but it is not such a disadvantage if top management has instituted indirect mechanisms of control and can exercise with their aid sufficient influence on operations by setting policies and formulating programs. The automation of accounting procedures through computers is just such an impersonal mechanism of control in finance departments. It places much controlling influence over operations into the hands of the top executives whose decisions determine the over-all setup of the automated facilities and the nature of the computer programs, thereby obviating the need for much direct supervision. The assembly line serves similar functions in factories (Blau and Scott, 1962: 176–178). Since automation serves as a control mechanism that greatly reduces the main disadvantage of multilevel hierarchies, it furthers their development.

The general principle suggested is that conditions in organizations that make the reliable performance of duties relatively independent of direct intervention by top management further the development of multilevel hierarchies. Advanced technological equipment, inasmuch as it mechanizes operations and makes them to some degree self-regulating, often serves this function. The mechanization of facilities is not the only condition that affects the reliability of performance, however. Regardless of how automated operations are, top management must rely on its managerial staff to implement its objectives and administer its policies. Herein lies the significance of promotion procedures for the hierarchy. Explicit promotion regulations furnish uniform standards that all higher officials must have met. But these standards assure top management that higher officials will have adequate qualifications for their responsibilities only if they stipulate that promotions be based primarily on examinations designed to test these qualifications rather than on seniority or the possibly idiosyncratic evaluations of supervisors. A significant correlation between the weight of written examinations in promotions and number of levels remains when other conditions are controlled (.13), but the correlation between the existence of promotion regulations and levels disappears when the weight of examinations and other conditions are controlled (.04). The reason probably is that only promotion regulations that give merit examinations much weight guarantee that all managerial officials have certain minimum qualifications and thus reduce top management's reluctance to lose direct contact with the operating level by establishing intervening layers in the hierarchy.

The more top management trusts the middle managers who constitute its administrative arm to discharge their responsibilities in accordance with its guidelines and directives, the more inclined it will be in all likelihood to delegate responsibilities to them. The implication is that the degree of confidence top executives place in their managerial assistance will promote decentralization of authority as well as multilevel hierarchies. If this surmise is correct, it could explain why the zero-order correlation between number of levels and decentralization (.18) is reduced to a point that falls just short of significance at

.05 when other conditions that affect management's trust are controlled (.12).

Entrance requirements that demand comparatively high qualifications of employees undoubtedly improve their abilities to perform their duties without close supervision. The interpretation advanced implies, therefore, that the proportion of the agency personnel expected to have college degrees and the number of levels in the hierarchy are positively related. As a matter of fact, such a positive zero-order correlation has been observed (.16), but controlling other conditions reduces this correlation to the vanishing point (.03). The proportion of employees with college training is not strongly associated with any of the other control variables under consideration, but it is somewhat correlated with four of them (between .12 and .14), its most pronounced zero-order correlation being that with decentralization (.14). A plausible explanation of this pattern of findings can be derived if expert qualifications are viewed as simply one element in a configuration of conditions indicative of operations that are relatively self-regulating and independent of direct intervention by management. As part of this configuration, the qualifications of employees are associated with the development of multilevel hierarchies. But once the other factors that manifest independence of managerial intervention are controlled, including those to which expert qualifications directly contribute, such as decentralization, the entire significance of qualifications for the hierarchy has been taken into account, and they are no longer associated with the number of levels.

Two Contrasting Types

In conclusion, some inferences about two contrasting types of formal organization will be drawn from the associations with multilevel hierarchy observed. One of these types may be considered the modern organization governed by universalistic standards; the other represents the old-fashioned bureaucracy.

A fundamental issue confronting the executives of organizations is whether to manage primarily by means of direct or indirect controls. Management through direct controls entails keeping in close touch with operations and issuing corrective orders whenever necessary. Management through indirect controls involves devising impersonal control mechanisms that constrain operations to follow automatically the policies and programs specified by top executives. The substitution of indirect mechanisms of control for direct control requires that an orientation to abstract universalistic standards replace reliance on personal judgments. The development of these impersonal control mechanisms is most likely if technical considerations and effective performance are supreme values, whereas ideological commitments and particularistic solidarities have little significance.

Today the prototype of an impersonal control mechanism is the computer, which dramatically illustrates how technological facilities automate operations and simultaneously give top management—whose decisions govern the basic computer setup—much control over them without requiring frequent direct intervention. Not only the operations themselves but also the recruitment of employees and that of managerial staff tend to become standardized in the modern organization in terms of universalistic principles of effective performance. Explicit personnel regulations stipulate merit criteria for employment and for advancement to managerial positions, relieving top management of administrative tasks, lessening the influence of personal bias and variations in judgment over personnel decisions, and assuring minimum qualifications. Both the automation of the work process and the merit standards that the managerial and operating staff must meet contribute to the reliable performance of duties and help to make operations comparatively self-regulating within the framework of the organization's objectives and management's policies. These conditions reduce management's need to keep close direct control over operations and, consequently, often give rise to major changes in the hierarchy. To wit, vertical differentiation creates a multilevel hierarchy, which usually decreases the number of major divisions whose heads report to the agency director and increases the span of control of these division heads, and responsibilities become decentralized. The strongest pressure to institute impersonal mechanisms of control, and thus the conditions that facilitate these structural changes, comes from the expanding size of organizations.

In short, the modern organization is characterized by a tall, slim hierarchy with decentralized authority. The opposite type, an old-fashioned bureaucracy, has a squat hierarchy with authority centralized at the top. In this case, which is most prevalent in smaller organizations, the top executive maintains tight control over operations by directly supervising many division heads, assigning each of them only few subordinates, refraining from introducing intermediate levels that would increase his distance from the operating personnel, and delegating few responsibilities. The lesser interest in impersonal mechanisms of control under these circumstances is reflected in the rare instances of automation and in the nature of the personnel policies. Explicit regulations that specify personnel qualifications are infrequent; promotions are largely left under the discretion of management; and insofar as promotion standards do exist, they tend to give weight to seniority and personal judgments of superiors rather than objective merit criteria, thus implicitly placing the importance of loyalty above that of technical competence. . . .

Dimensions of Organization Structure*
D. S. PUGH, D. J. HICKSON, C. R. HININGS, AND C. TURNER

A major task of contemporary organization theory is the development of more sophisticated conceptual and methodological tools, particularly for dealing systematically with variations between organizations. Udy (1965), for example, feels that "comparative analysis is an appropriate initial, boundary-setting approach to general organizational theory." Without it, case studies remain haphazard and generalizations remain dubious. Mayntz (1964: 3) is of the same mind, but she fears that to regard all organizations as comparable systems is so abstract that "propositions which hold for such diverse phenomena as an army, a trade union, and an university, must necessarily be either so trivial or so abstract as to tell hardly anything about concrete reality." There is as yet insufficient evidence to support or refute this view.

This paper reports attempts to investigate and measure structural differences systematically across a large number of diverse work organizations, using scalable variables for multidimensional analysis. A previous paper (Pugh et al., 1963: 289–315) described the conceptual framework upon which the present studies are based, which accords closely with that which Evan (1963: 468–477) has advocated, and with concepts from which Hage (1965: 289-320) derives his axiomatic theory.

From an examination of the literature on organizations, six primary dimensions of organization structure were defined: (1) specialization, (2) standardization, (3) formalization, (4) centralization, (5) configuration, (6) flexibility. These "constitutive" definitions, as Kerlinger (1964) has termed them, were then translated into operational definitions, and scales constructed. Scales were also constructed for aspects of organizational context, and these were used as independent variables in a multivariate analysis to predict structural forms. The present paper describes the methods and results of scaling the structural variables.

Sample

Data were collected on 52 organizations in the Birmingham area. Of these, 46 were a random sample stratified by size and product or purpose, according to the Standard Industrial Classification of the British Ministry of Labour. They include firms making motor cars and chocolate bars, municipal departments repairing roads and teaching

* Reprinted from *Administrative Science Quarterly, 13* (June 1968), pp. 65–105, with omissions, by permission of the authors and the publisher.

TABLE 1. SAMPLE: ORGANIZATIONS STUDIED (*N* = 46)

Number of employees		
251–500	501–2,000	2,001+

Metal manufacture and metal goods

Components	Metal goods	Nonferrous
Components	Metal goods	Metal automobile components
Research division	Metal goods	
Components	Domestic appliances	

Manufacture of engineering and electrical goods, vehicles

Components	Engineering tools	Automobile components
Vehicles		
Components	Repairs for government department	Commercial vehicles
Components		Vehicles
	Automobile components	Carriages
	Engineering components	

Foods and chemicals, general manufacturing, construction

Food	Civil engineering	Confectionery
Paper	Glass	Public civil engineering department
Toys	Printer	
Abrasives	Food	Brewery
		Automobile tires

Services: public, distributive, professional

Government inspection department	Public water department	Public education department
	Department store	Public transport department
Public local savings bank	Chain of retail stores	Bus company
Public baths department		
	Chain of shoe repair stores	Cooperative chain of retail stores
Insurance company		

arithmetic, large retail stores, small insurance companies, and so on. These 46 organizations were distributed as shown in Table 1 (three organizations of the original sample felt unable to cooperate and were replaced in the present sample).

Primary Dimensions of Structure

Specialization Specialization (Hinings *et al.,* 1967) is concerned with the division of labor within the organization, the distribution of official duties among a number of positions (Pugh *et al., op. cit.*). Analysis of data from a pilot survey of organizations in terms of the Bakke activity variables made it possible to construct a list of sixteen activities that are assumed to be present in *all* work organizations, and on which any work organization may therefore be compared with any other. These activities or functions exclude the workflow activities of organization, and so are not concerned with operatives in manufacturing, sales clerks in retailing, and similar activities.

Standardization Standardization of procedures is a basic aspect of organizational structure, and in Weber's terms would distinguish bureaucratic and traditional organizations from charismatic ones. The operational problems here revolve around defining a procedure and specifying which procedures in an organization are to be investigated. A procedure is taken to be an event that has regularity of occurrence and is legitimized by the organization. There are rules or definitions that purport to cover all circumstances and that apply invariably (Pugh *et al.,* 1963).

Formalization Formalization denotes the extent to which rules, procedures, instructions, and communications are written (Pugh *et al.,* 1963). Definitions of 38 documents were assembled, each of which could be used by any known work organization.

Although filing is characteristic of a bureaucracy, an attempt to discriminate between organizations in this respect failed. Once a document is in existence, copies of it appear to be filed for a very long time.

Centralization Centralization has to do with the locus of authority to make decisions affecting the organization (Pugh *et al.,* 1963). Authority to make decisions was defined and ascertained by asking, "Who is the last person whose assent must be obtained before *legitimate action* is taken—even if others have subsequently to confirm the decision?" This identified the level in the hierarchy where executive action could be authorized, even if this remained subject to a routine confirmation later, for example by a chairman or a committee. A standard list of 37 recurrent decisions was prepared covering a range of organizational activities. For each organization, the lowest level in the hierarchy with the formal authority to make each decision was determined.

Configuration Configuration is the "shape" of the role structure (Pugh *et al.,* 1963). Its data would be contained in a comprehensive and detailed organization chart that included literally every role in the organization. The assessment of the configuration of this hypothetical chart requires the use of a combination of selected dimensions, each of which provides a measure of the development of a particular aspect of the structure.

Intercorrelations of Structural Scales With scales to represent the postulated primary dimensions of structure, one can explore the relationships between the dimensions and search for underlying similarities.

TABLE 2. PRINCIPAL-COMPONENTS ANALYSIS OF SELECTED SCALES OF STRUCTURE AFTER GRAPHIC ROTATION

Scale	Factor I' Structuring of activities	Factor II'' Concen-tration of authority	Factor III' Line con-trol of workflow
Standardization	0.89*	−0.01	−0.21
Role specialization	0.87*	−0.33	0.01
Formalization	0.87*	0.14	−0.21
Chief executive's span	0.42‡	0.23	−0.07
Non-workflow personnel (%)	0.58†	−0.43‡	0.06
Vertical span	0.69*	0.03	0.08
Clerks (%)	0.40‡	−0.09	0.42‡
Subordinate ratio	−0.05	−0.19	−0.80*
Workflow superordinates (%)	−0.23	0.60*	0.50†
Centralization	−0.33	0.83*	0.01
Autonomy of the organization	0.10	−0.92*	0.00
Variance (%)	33.06	18.47	12.96

* Weightings > 0.06
† Weightings > 0.5
‡ Weightings > 0.4

Intercorrelating the 64 scales of structural variables produces a large matrix of 2,016 coefficients. A list of the major indices is found in Table 2. Many of the measures of structure are highly intercorrelated. For example, Overall Role Specialization has a correlation of 0.80 with Overall Standardization, of 0.68 with Overall Formalization, of 0.66 with Configuration, Vertical Span, and of 0.56 with Configuration, Percentage Non-Workflow Personnel. In other words, an organization with many specialists tends also to have more standard routines, more documentation, and a larger supportive hierarchy. A hypothesis on this process is that as specialists increase in number, they introduce procedures to regulate the activities for which they are responsible— the personnel specialist his selection procedure, the inspector his quality control—resulting in documentation—the application forms for vacancies and the inspection reports. A tall hierarchy results to encompass the specialists and the large number of non-workflow jobs.

This intercorrelation of these five scales contrasts markedly with the correlations between Centralization and these scales, which are all *negative,* and much smaller. This appears to disprove the hypothesis (Pugh *et al.,* 1963), drawn from the Weberian tradition and the notion that bureaucracies pass decisions to upper levels, that specialization, formalization, and centralization would be highly positively correlated. Hage, too, incorporates in his axiomatic theory the proposition that "the higher the centralization, the higher the formalization" (standardization) (Hage, 1965: 300). On the other hand, the correlations support his proposition summarizing Thompson, Gouldner, and Blau and Scott: "The higher the complexity, the lower the centralization" (Hage, 1965: 300), "complexity" for Hage being specialization of tasks plus the length of training required for the task.

Standardization of Selection Procedures is even more interesting. It breaks the pattern of a strong positive relationship within specialization, standardization, formalization, and many configuration variables, correlating only 0.09 with Overall Role Specialization and 0.37 with Overall Formalization.

The meaning of patterns of structural scores should be kept in mind when interpreting these correlations. An organization that scores high on specialization, standardization, and formalization (which is probable in view of the intercorrelations among these variables) would have gone a long way in the regulation of the work of its employees. As an organization, it would have gone a long way in *structuring* its activities; that is, the intended behavior of employees has been structured by the specification of their specialized roles, the procedures they are to follow in carrying out those roles, and the documentation of what they have to do. In short, what these three associated variables are exploring is the range and pattern of *structuring*.

The scales of centralization cannot be regarded as measures of structuring in this way. To assess structuring in terms of centralization would require measurement of how specific the loci of authority are; that is, how definite it is that authority for decision X rests in role Y. But the centralization scales treat this as a constant and measure only the vertical distribution of authority over the hierarchy. That one organization scores as centralized, whereas another scores as decentralized, does not necessarily bear any relationship to how specific the allocation of authority is within the two. Basing the measures of centralization upon a conceptual basis different from the rest of the structural variables has a very important effect upon the results.

Underlying Dimensions of Structure   The intercorrelations suggested that the interpretation would be improved by a search for basic dimensions of organizational structure by the method of factor analysis. Principal-components analysis was applied to the variables listed in Table 2, and four factors were extracted, accounting in turn for 33, 19, 14, and 8 percent of the variance after rotation.* These factors are orthogonal to one another, that is, mutually independent. The loadings of the variables on the factors are given in Table 2.

The meaning of the factors is readily apparent. Factor I can be seen to be most highly loaded on the variables of standardization,

---

* The fourth one, "Relative size of supportive component," is not shown in Table 2.

specialization, and formalization. This dimension therefore is called *structuring of activities.* The concept of the structuring of organizational activities has the advantage of applying to any or all parts of the organization; whereas it is a question whether the Weberian concept of bureaucracy can or cannot be applied outside the administrative hierarchy to the workflow operatives. Both clerical activities and shop floor activities can be more or less structured; whether they can both be bureaucratized is open to question (Caplow, 1964: 287). Structuring therefore includes and goes beyond the usage of the term bureaucracy. It has the further advantage of being conceived and defined as an operationalized dimension, and not as an abstract type.

This usage accords with Etzioni (1964: 4), who prefers to avoid terms such as bureaucracy, formal organization, and institution in favor of using the term organization "to refer to planned units, deliberately structured." Etzioni does not go on to use this definition to examine organization theory from the standpoint of variations in *structuring,* but this approach follows from Hickson's (1966: 225–237) argument that a common thread of this kind runs through the subject, which he calls the varying "specificity of role prescription." Specificity has a very close affinity to structuring. Thus standardization may be considered as the specificity of procedures to cases, specialization as the specificity of tasks to roles, and so on. Hickson's linking of the approaches of twenty-two organization theorists by the concept of specificity also suggests that measures of structuring are prerequisite to further development in the subject.

Factor II is marked by the opposition of centralization and autonomy and is thus concerned with *concentration of authority.* Specialization is in the direction of dispersed authority, as would be expected; with more specialization, authority is likely to be distributed to the specialists. "Non-workflow personnel" also has a definite weighting toward dispersed authority, but the percentage of workflow superordinates is firmly weighted in the direction of concentrated authority. Thus the greater the percentage of the line hierarchy, the more concentrated is the authority, and the less decentralized are the decisions down the line. Standardization of selection procedures is also positively loaded on this factor, as would be anticipated from its correlation with centralization.

The third factor is characterized by the heavy positive loading of Percentage of Workflow Superordinates and negative loading of Subordinate Ratio, and is concerned with the line hierarchy. Formalization of role performance records has a high negative loading, and inspection of the items of this scale (for example, record of work, record of time, record of maintenance) indicates that these records are those prepared on the workflow personnel for control purposes. The factor may thus be considered as that of *line control of workflow* (rather than impersonal control). This characterization is supported by the significant positive loading of Standardization of Selection Procedures for selection, advancement, and so on, the bipolar scale. This is a bipolar scale and a high score on it means not only that there *are* procedures for selection, and so on, but also that there are not procedures for controlling the workflow. Thus control would be expected to rest in the hands of the workflow personnel themselves and their line superordinates.

Thus it must be presumed that there are a number of distinctive underlying dimensions of structure—this particular trial produces four. Since these are mutually independent, an organization's structure may display all these characteristics to a pronounced degree, or virtually none at all, or display some but not others. Insofar as the original primary dimensions of structure, specialization, standardization, formalization, centralization, and configuration were drawn from a literature saturated with the Weberian view of bureaucracy, this multifactor result has immediate implications for what we have elsewhere called the Weberian stereotype (Hinings *et al.,* 1965: 468–477). It is demonstrated here that bureaucracy is *not* unitary, but that organizations may be bureaucratic in any of a number of ways. The force of Blau's criticism of the "ideal type" can now be appreciated: "If we modify the type in accordance with the empirical reality, it is no longer a pure type; and if we do not, it would become a meaningless construct" (Blau, 1963: 305–316). The concept of *the* bureaucratic type is no longer useful.

4
THE INTERNAL CONTROL PROCESSES OF ORGANIZATIONS

Besides the analysis of the impact of organizational resources on structure, another rapidly growing area of theory and research is the analysis of coordination and control processes. This focus was the inevitable outcome of a series of developments both in and out of the field, which revealed that as organizations become larger, and more complex, the issue of coordination becomes problematic rather than axiomatic. In particular, the conflicts generated in the rapidly growing universities, as evidenced by symptoms such as the breakdown in communications, taught that although coordination may be a functional necessity, it does not necessarily prevail in all organizations all of the time (Baldridge, 1971). With these developments, the problem of control also became a serious issue to consider. Part of this shift in interests from structure to control reflects the popularity of process analysis as opposed to the more static view of structure, a criticism leveled against sociology but equally applicable to the area of organizational analysis. Partly, it reflects an increasing interest in system analysis, a form of process thinking ideally suited to the problems of conflict and control, which were becoming empirically evident.

Theoretically, the problems of coordination and integration become more apparent as appreciation of the extent of differentiation in organizations grows. Victor Thompson (1961) was one of the first to call attention to this problem, when he observed that creating a team of specialists also means bringing them together into a meaningful whole. Beyond the problem of how to coordinate and integrate the parts of an organization—whether staff and line, specialists, or departments—lies the other troublesome issue of how to gain control over the human beings who work in the organization. Weber earlier recognized this problem (1947) and in a different context Parsons (1961) made much of the issue of control. Likewise, the people problem of conformity and consensus increasingly became a significant issue in the study of organizations.

Although control, coordination, and integration are used interchangeably, there are certain nuances in the meaning of each. Those who study control tend not to be concerned with coordination, and vice versa, since the concepts apply to different organizational levels. Coordination denotes integration between departments and/or occupations, and the various devices used to interrelate and reconcile the parts of an organization. Control implies the various means for making people and personalities conform to orders and rules, focusing more directly on the wielding power behind particular commands and the reasons for accepting work directives. Integration has been used to mean both instrumental (task) and expressive (social) ties between people or parts of an organization.

Apart from the twin problems of coordination and control, several other variables deserve special attention in that they have been studied independently as problems in their own right. Communications and conflict are two topics that have greatly fascinated organizational sociologists, especially during the past few years. As a result, researchers at first attributed to the two variables consequences and causes at variance with later conceptions, when communications and conflict were considered aspects of coordination and control. Indeed, it is interesting to observe that early work on communications did not focus on it as a mechanism of coordination and control but instead concentrated on what causes a breakdown in communication. The critical issue in the fifties was barriers to communication (see Ronken and Lawrence [1952] and note McCleery and Julian's selections in this chapter as well). Studies on conflict followed a similar pattern. The phenomena were of interest in their own right—everyone likes a story about a fight—and thus seen as independent of the theory of coordination and control. Such juxtaposition can be informative and helpful in expanding our understanding, however. For this reason, we have separated the topics as follows: (1) the problem of coordination and integration, (2) the problem of control, (3) the problem of communications, and (4) the problem of conflict and consensus.

THE PROBLEMS

The Problems of Coordination and Integration

An early, lucid discussion of coordination, especially the difficulty involved in achieving it, is by Victor Thompson (1961), who phrased the problem, however, more in a traditionally Weberian way, viewing the hierarchy of authority as a mechanism. From another standpoint, the case study of prison reform by McCleery, our first selection in this chapter, provides an excellent description of how changes in power distribution relate to changes in communications; but it is also a study of the breakdown in coordination between guards and rehabilitators and the consequences for organizational effectiveness. In system analysis terms, it is a study of organizational disequilibrium. The conflict between the guards and the rehabilitators also illustrates how basic intraorganizational conflicts bring on and increase the power of other organizations, in this instance, the legislature.

By far the best work on the problem of coordination is our second selection, by Lawrence and Lorsch (1967a). They tie together both the internal problem of how best to integrate an organization and the external one of how to cope effectively with the environment. Their definitions of differentiation and integration are somewhat atypical, but the contrast with other existing definitions is instructive. In particular, one can contrast their description of different behaviors and attitudes, as measured by them, with the definitions of complexity, specialization, and structural differentiation provided by Hall *et al.*; Pugh *et al.*; Blau; Hage, Aiken, and Marrett in their various selections. Presumably, different levels or departments or, perhaps most importantly, occupations exhibit these various forms of behavior and attitudes. Similarly, Lawrence and Lorsch's definition of integration as mechanisms for resolving conflict is informative and should be contrasted with the idea of integration expressed in the Hage, Aiken, and Marrett selection.

The data selected for inclusion from the Lawrence and Lorsch article on the differences between departments and on the various mechanisms used to achieve integration make concrete many of the more theoretical discussions to follow. What has not been included in the selection, for lack of space, is the authors' demonstration that the more differentiated organizations could be successful if they had more mechanisms of integration. For those interested in this aspect of Lawrence and Lorsch's work, their book *Organizations and Environment* (1967b) is highly recommended.

Whereas the first two selections focus on the integration of departments (thus largely on managers) the third selection, by Fullan, accents worker integration. Indeed, a careful reading of the latter reveals a shift in the concept of integration; that is, as we move down the hierarchy, interest in coordinating the parts of the organization gives way to concern for integrating the people. In short, Fullan's conceptualization of the problem moves from an instrumental to an expressive interpretation. Similarly, the work of Blauner (Chapter Two) and of Crozier (Chapter Three) is representative of those who study workers as opposed to managers. Crozier's case study also presents an excellent description of the kind of worker isolation that can occur, giving concrete realization to the statistical tables of Fullan.

An unanswered question is whether a synthesis of two perspectives—one with an emphasis on the worker and the other on the organization—would lead to a finding that worker integration is more likely to occur when the organization is more differentiated and integrated in the sense of Lawrence and Lorsch. Crozier's and McCleery's case studies suggest that, indeed, this is precisely what would happen. As yet, however, there has been little empirical research on this problem.

Hage, Aiken, and Marrett study coordination and integration at both the bottom and the top of the pyramid, but only in professional organizations. Furthermore, they focus expressly on the problem of task integration, especially as reflected in the volume and direction of communications and in programming. The Lawrence and Lorsch piece, moreover, descriptively illustrates a variety of ways in which either information feedback or programming can be instituted. What determines the coordinational mechanisms used? Although Hage, Aiken, and Marrett present an explicit theory of coordination and control, their premises describe largely structural factors. Lawrence and Lorsch look to the environmental factor—as would Burns and Stalker—while Fullan, in conjunction with Blauner, Crozier, and perhaps even McCleery, see the technology or work-flow as key aspects of the explanation. There is nothing inherently contradictory about these intellectual perspectives. They can be synthesized by observing how the environment relates to the resources of the organization, thereby influencing its structure. Further, these divergencies in point of view themselves create a feeling for the complexities of organizational analysis.

Outside of these few pieces by Lawrence and Lorsch, Hage *et al.,* Blauner, and Fullan, not too many others exist, in part because of the newness of the topic of integration and in part because of some difficulties in studying it. For those wanting additional reading, perhaps the most important work is James Thompson's (1968) *Organizations in Action* (Chapter Five). Here a causal link is made between technology and various ways of achieving coordination. The approach is quite unique and raises some fundamental issues. In addition, Victor Thompson's earlier work (1961) can still be read with profit and is particularly accessible to the less advanced student. A paper by Klatzky (1970), although not specifically measuring coordination, does make some interesting inferences about it and other factors that might affect it. From a different perspective, Price's (1972) informative discussion of how to measure coordination includes a review of a study that attempted to do so. Finally, for those wishing to read more about social integration, the Peter Smith, Moscow, Berger, and Cooper (1969) study suggests an alternate approach to that of Fullan, Blauner, and Crozier.

The Problem of Control

Although the issues of coordination and integration are relatively new formulations of an organizational problem, the idea of control has its beginnings in the tenets of Weber and in the empirical findings of the first case studies using his model. Weber felt that the triumph of rational–legal authority, and thus of bureaucracy, lay precisely in superior discipline and control; under such a regimen, mistakes were to be at a minimum. As soon as the first few case studies were completed, however, it became clear that even bureaucratic control might be more difficult than Weber envisioned it. For example, Gouldner's (1954) case study of a gypsum plant is a classic illustration of the truism that workers obey some of the rules some of the time. It is also interesting in that it suggests what happens when a new head of a plant tries to exert control over individuals who, for whatever reasons, do not accept him. Although considerations of space prohibit its inclusion here, this study can still be read with profit. Another early example, the case study by Blau (1956), focuses on the use of statistical records as a way of getting social workers to conform to certain production standards. This study calls into question the perfect impartiality of bureaucracies; it also demonstrates the difficulties of anticipating all the ways in which the spirit of the law can be violated.

The McCleery selection offers some rich and fascinating data about the nature of authoritarian control, and how it differs from that found in a more equalitarian model. Further, the Hage, Aiken, and Marrett piece provides a theoretical skeleton for analyzing both an organization's choice of sanctions—whether reward or punishment—and its choice of socialization, such as the rehabilitation program. In general, much has been made of the close similarity between centralization and control; in fact, the two are often considered the same. How power is distributed among various groups and departments and/or individuals is clearly distinguishable from how much power is applied. Centralization is a measure of the former and coercion is a measure of the latter. While it may be true that centralization leads to coercion, it is a hypothesis to be tested, rather than an accepted fact. Dornbush *et al.* (1967) have suggested that the right to evaluate or sanction is power. The Julian and the Warren selections stem from traditions that tend to see the distribution of power (centralization) and the exercise of power (control) as essentially the same. Julian's work is based on Etzioni's conception that different types of sanctions give rise to different types of compliance structures, which, once perceived, become the bases of understanding other aspects of organizations. What is especially interesting about Julian's article is that the problem of control applies to the client, in this case, the patient. In the same vein, Warren (1969) builds on the famous French and Raven discussion of the bases of power, exploring how much they interrelate. What is interesting is that essentially, he finds two major bases, at least in terms of the intercorrelations. Warren does a very fine piece of research in distinguishing between attitudinal and behavioral conformity. He also focuses on a major problem: does more control lead to more conformity? The answer is, it does.

Still another approach to the problem of control is presented in the piece by Price (Chapter Five), where he analyzes the different sanctioning systems and their consequences for conformity and productivity. Another important aspect of this work is the attempt to discern the consequences of a particular sanctioning system, the resulting conformity in performance and, more particularly, the ensuing effectiveness of the organization. Like Lawrence and Lorsch, Price observes not only cause and effect but also what might be called payoff, a point that may seem obvious, but, nevertheless, is seldom mentioned in discussions of control and conformity. In a theoretical analysis of several case studies, Price suggests that perhaps organizations have little choice in the types of controls employed. Given a certain construction, they must exercise certain controls or else lose their effectiveness. We have seen this in operation in Woodward (Chapter Two) and it is certainly the point of the Lawrence and Lorsch work, even though not included in the edited selection contained in this chapter.

Two readings are highly recommended to those especially interested in the problem of control. First is Etzioni's (1961b) discussion on compliance structures. However, a shorter, clearer version of his work appears in the *Handbook of Organizations* edited by March (1965). The second reading is a study using French and Raven's distinctions, a research effort by Bachman, Bowers, and Marcus, which is reprinted in Tannenbaum (1968). Both books provide bibliography, and both are worth examining; the former is theoretical and the latter empirical.

Also worth reading in connection with the problem of control are the many articles on the span of control. We have placed our discussion of this organizational property in the preceding chapter, since, in the past, span of control usually has dealt with the measurement of the supervisory–subordinate ratio and not the exercise of control per se. Usually, however, inferences about the latter are made from the former. Certainly, the issue of supervision, in some hierarchy of power, and the exertion of control to ensure conformity blend together, as can be seen by reading the specific items used by Hall (see Price's [1971] and Hall's index of hierarchy of authority) for a discussion of centralization.

Perhaps the major issue is under what circumstances we will observe either more or less control exerted. Blau and Scott (1962) advance in their text a number of insightful ideas on the subject, especially on the use of the indirect mechanisms of control such as the assembly line. Blauner's (1964) case studies, including our selection, can be read in this light as well. Warren (1969) suggests a different answer, namely, that professionalism (in teachers) seems to lessen the effects of various forms of control. Other literature on professional autonomy tenders the idea that the professional, as a qualified expert in his own right, is given protection from the exertion of control. Here again, Warren's article is helpful, suggesting that even within the same profession, immunity from control may vary, depending upon the extent of training and professional involvement. Hage and Aiken (1967a) elsewhere found approximately the same pattern.

What happens to the client or customer appertaining to the organization when control is not being exerted? Here we have perhaps located one of the sources of difficulty during the decade of the sixties. Unfortunately, possibly because sociologists, too, are professionals, little research has accumulated on the issue of whether or not professional autonomy leads to deterioration in services for the client, whether university student, hospital patient, or welfare recipient.

Another reason why the problem of professional control, especially as it affects the client, may have been passed over, is a tendency, as revealed in Julian's research, to see the client as part of the organization. This impression arises out of Etzioni's definition of the *organizational members,* a perspective which has obscured this problem. When we define students or patients or welfare recipients as clients and no longer as members of the organization, we begin to ask questions about who is controlling the professionals or quasi-professionals, the real members of the organization. We begin to ask about the quality of the service they provide. This shift in focus might be all to the good.

The Problem of Communications

For some strange reason, communications was a favorite topic for discussion by management consultant firms during the fifties. One of the better case studies, Ronken and Lawrence (1952), was completed by a team of researchers at a graduate school of business. Yet the topic was largely ignored by sociologists during much of the sixties. The major exceptions are the work of Landsberger (1961) and of Georgopoulos and Mann (1962).

McCleery makes clear in his case study that communications can be viewed as an important mechanism of control; but, more importantly, he suggests that changes in communications processes can affect the distribution of internal power. In contrast, the Hage, Aiken, and Marrett selection suggests that such a cause-and-effect relationship might run in the opposite direction.

Perhaps the most interesting work on communications has disclosed its impact on various kinds of organizational performances. Of a number of studies relating communications to one or more other variables, Pelz and Andrews (1966) in their series of studies found that individual patterns of communication are related to creativity; Clagett Smith (1970) studied the same problem on an organizational level of analysis and found basically the same associations; finally Price (1967) notes that communications is related to effectiveness.

What is interesting about all of these studies is that they indicate that the associations between communications and organizational performance are not simple one-to-one relationships. In general, it would seem that too much communication is as undesirable as too little, something the management consultant firms began to observe during the sixties. Furthermore, the pattern or direction of communications, as noted in the Hage, Aiken, and Marrett article, is a complex one. What appears critical is the horizontal communication between departments. These, perhaps more than others, allow for the cross-fertilization of ideas and the linking together of perspectives and personalities.

Besides change, the other major theme with which conflict has been linked is communications. Generally, studies advocate the use of communications as a way of reducing conflict. Thus in the Lawrence and Lorsch selection we see communications as one of the integration mechanisms. This idea has a long tradition and had much to do with the interest in communications in business organizations. Starting with Coch and French (1948), there developed a social-psychological approach to the study of organizations called the human relations school. Its adherents have advocated what is essentially the decentralization of power and plenty of upward communications. With this shift in emphasis comes understanding and appreciation of each level's problems. In turn, this development has led to a large body of applied lessons about organizations. Perhaps the best known are the T-groups. These unstructured training groups were the forerunners of sensitivity training and the group therapy movement.

While T-groups can resolve conflicts and other problems through the use of communications, the opposite effect can also result. For example, the role of conflict study by Kahn et al. selected for this chapter demonstrates how this particular kind of conflict can lead to a withdrawal of communication. Of course, role conflict is of a different origin than most, emerging out of the disparity between personal standards and expectations imposed by the nature of one's position in the organization. With this inner conflict come stress and tension, which are then met by lessened interaction, where this is an option open to the individuals involved. In the end, for some, communication all but loses its effectiveness. Hopefully, others in the field will build on this work, indicating when differences can be resolved by communication and when they cannot.

The Problem of Conflict and Consensus

The resolution of differences is perhaps the essential requisite for the removal of conflict.

This perspective is well illustrated in our first selection, by McCleery, and is implied by Lawrence and Lorsch in the second as well. We seldom have a chance to study organizations in the midst of conflict, as McCleery has done; for this reason, there is much to learn from his case study. In somewhat the same vein is Baldridge's (1971) case study of student conflict in a university. Here we see the application of interest group theory to political science and the articulation of interests via conflict. This study can represent a whole new approach to the conflict problem, while also serving as another argument for reviving the case study approach. The first traditional approach to the study of conflict is contained in the selection by Kahn *et al.* Building on a long tradition in the literature on role, they explore some of the interactional consequences of role conflict as described in the preceding section. We have included accounts of some concrete cases uncovered in their research to lend appreciation both to the substances and the prevalence of this problem. For those who are especially interested in role conflict, their book is a classic. Perhaps more than anyone else in the organizational literature that we are aware of, Kahn *et al.* synthesize sociology and psychology effectively. Not only do they identify types of roles that create problems—the ambiguous role, the man in the middle, the man on the boundary—but they also ascertain that different personalities respond in alternative ways. While the latter is a truism, it is one not frequently documented by research, and not with their competency.

Additional reading other than *Organizational Stress* (1964) by Kahn *et al.* can be found in the study of the school superintendent (1958) by Gross, Mason, and McEachern, and, of course, in the theoretical discussion of the role-set by Merton (1957: Ch. 9). The latter is well worth extended study in that it notes the essential protection that exists because of lack of visibility.

A second, more recent approach to the study of conflict is represented in the selection by Corwin, who attempts to document, in a large survey, a variety of school conflicts. The several variables considered as potential causes of conflict suggest that conflict, as Corwin has measured it, is endemic to large-scale, complex organizations or, at least, to schools. More importantly, the different associations between variables are suggestive. Corwin has opened up a whole new way of studying the problem of conflict empirically. For interested readers, Corwin has devoted an entire book (1969) to detailing more of his research.

One more very important study, which we were unable to include, is Clagett Smith's "A Comparative Analysis of Some Conditions and Consequences of Intra-Organizational Conflict" (1966). It is a difficult article both because of its many ideas and because its measures vary, but the results are informative. The beauty of this paper lies in the author's consideration of several alternative chains of hypotheses relative to the cause of conflict, each one helping to explain part of the data. Again, we note the necessity for synthesizing several perspectives to obtain a more complete picture.

Corwin focuses mainly on the structural causes of conflict, using a several stage cross-sectional design. The earlier case studies, because they observed organizations across time, had an opportunity to see conflict as a process. Both the McCleery and the Chandler selections (Chapters Four and Five, respectively) indicate that one cause of conflict is a change in the social structure. What is interesting about both studies is that change toward decentralization was resisted, in the first case, by prison guards, and in the second, by a chemical corporation president. We will need comparative longitudinal research designs before we can generalize enought to determine if change inevitably produces conflict. Most organizational sociologists would already accept this as fact. However, social psychologists believe their human relations techniques can go far in reducing the magnitude of association. The other side of the picture, does conflict produce change, as far as we know, has been little studied in the context of organizations by sociologists.

If conflict is disagreement then consensus, the opposite, is agreement. The Clagett Smith and Ari article (Chapter Five) is superb, viewing consensus as the intervening link between structure, in this case the measure of influence, and effectiveness, measured by several variables. The linking together of three different parts of the organization is rare in research. For a theoretical linking of consensus, by far the best work is *Organizational Effectiveness* by Price (1967), who offers numerous propositions. In Chapter Five we have selected from Price's book a chapter which includes propositions on the sanctioning system, consensus, and effectiveness.

THE READINGS

Disequilibrium in Changing from a Mechanistic to an Organic Model of Structure*

RICHARD H. MC CLEERY

The immediate focus of this study is on administration and the management of men in a situation which presents power relations with naked clarity—the prison. The bulk of administrative theory notwithstanding, the administrator is strictly limited in the sanctions which he can apply to sustain authority, and even the power of summary dismissal is a relic from a more primitive economic era. These limitations do not apply to prison management where force and fear stand ready as instruments of control. The task of analysis here is to weigh the role of force in comparison to the communication patterns as the basis of power. Implications of the analysis go beyond the governing of prisons to the management of men in any setting. They extend to the issues of free expression in a democracy and censorship in the authoritarian state.

The Authoritarian Prison

Organization and Communications The formal organization and official policy of the traditional prison recognizes industry as a goal and reform as a hope along with the objective of custodial control. However, one basic proposition emerging from this study is that formal organization is modified by the location and control of communication channels. Thus, while the prison had a work program, its inmates were sentenced to "hard labor," and the economic self-sufficiency of the institution was an ideal, the effective roles of industry and the industrial supervisor were institutionalized in their relations with the custodial force.

The Warden and his Deputy were the only policy-making officials of the institution. At the beginning of this study the main divisions of the staff were the custodial force, organized in three watches under a Senior Captain, and the work line supervisors. Past attempts to vitalize a treatment program had atrophied by that time into a single position —an ex-guard supervised recreation. There were other functions performed within the walls—a kitchen, an admissions and records

* Reprinted from *Policy Change in Prison Management* (East Lansing: Social Science Research Bureau, Michigan State University, 1957), pp. 7–39, with omissions, by permission of the author and publisher.

office, and a hospital—but these seemed to have no independent organizational status.

The entire staff accepted those implications for organizational structure which were institutionalized in the custodial force. The structure of that force was borrowed directly from military organization. The steps in its uniformed and disciplined hierarchy served as the measure by which those who performed non-custodial services determined their own status within the structure of formal organization. Hence the admissions officer insisted upon the rank of Captain which he had earned through many years of custodial service.

The nerve center for all institutional communication lay in the office of the Captain of the Yard. This location was dictated by the primary interest of custodial officials in the hour-by-hour reports on the location and movement of men. However, it was not just the report of counts and the time books of the work line supervisors but all orders, requests and reports which passed through this communications center. With the issuance of orders and the assignment of men channeled through a communication system controlled by custody, the perceived status of work line supervisors was below that of the guards from whom, in effect, they took their orders.

The Captain's office had a primary interest in reports accounting for the presence of the men and for their discipline. Perfect control involved a knowledge of where every man was at any moment, and much of the overt work of custody consisted in the balancing of books which indicated, after the fact, that the men had been in their appointed places. The keeping of these records assumed certain characteristics of a ritual, and every gate pass issued became a part of the permanent archives of the institution. Hence, the type of information required and returned through the communication system gave constant reassertion to custodial values in every aspect of institutional life. Record items of costs, production, or the needs of the men might be ignored, but control information was never overlooked. The institutional pressures which dominated the office in which communication centered dictated its content and use. Custodial control of communications, and the interactional patterns thus established, imposed custodial attitudes, values and behaviors throughout the industrial program, negating its formal position and purpose.

Work supervisors had little contact with the Director of Industry but daily contact with the guards. Their ability to communicate their day-to-day needs depended on the influence involved in that contact. But contact normally involves effective communication only to the extent that shared attitudes and values are present.[1] As a result,

---

[1] There is no effective execution of orders in an agency except as some motive or sentiment appears in connection with and in support of the activity. In the absence of some more complex sentiment, the desire to earn wages may be enough to gain a tolerable level of activity, but the activity itself seems to produce sentiments in respect

supervisors came to think, act, and dress like the guards. They justified labor in terms of disciplinary rather than productive or training results, maintained sharp class distinctions on the job, and repressed the rare examples of initiative which appeared among their inmate employees. Accepting that definition of labor and the status of the supervisor, inmates opposed the industrial program and gave the minimum tolerable effort to it. Supervisors, in turn, borrowed custodial attitudes which explained failures of production on the basis of the malice and incompetence of the inmates. The institutionally shared belief in the limited possibilities of prison industry further reduced its role.

The status of other functions performed in the prison was subverted in a similar way, and this may be illustrated most clearly in respect to professional services. Psychological diagnosis and medical treatment were carried on in the institution. Referral to and reports from these services were passed through custodial channels which emphasized security considerations above all else. Psychological services seemed to the inmates to be an adjunct of disciplinary control, and medical treatment appeared to be geared to the detection of malingering. Consequently, inmates believed, with some justification, that these services were subordinated to custody, and the prison community in general regarded the professional with a contempt inconsistent with his formal status and the real motive of his work.[2] The "bug doctor" was considered lower than a "screw." That contempt, in turn, reduced the actual function of professional services to insignificance.

Thus, its control of communication permitted custody to co-opt the efforts of other institutional units to the support of its own function and status. In addition to this mechanical routing of all orders and reports through the Captain's Office, that center also censored all mail and passed on requests by inmates for interviews with other institutional officials. These duties implied additional discretionary control and command over the flow of information. The custodial force enjoyed an actual power to negate or compromise other institutional functions which held independent status or equal rank.

The custodial hierarchy, the central power structure of the institution, was the basic route to advancement from guard through Sergeant, Watch Officer, and Senior Captain or to positions such as Admissions Officer, Recreation Officer, and Mess Steward. Within that structure, it was necessary to resolve the basic paradox of authoritarian control—

---

to the work among the employees. The manner in which the work is then carried on and the aspects of the work which gain emphasis in time are colored by the sentiments held about it and the manner of their communication. For a careful analysis of the relationships between activity, interaction and sentiment, note Homans (1950).

[2] The contrast between the formal and the effective status of professionals in penal work has been generally noted. Powelson and Bendix discuss the conflict with custodial forces and the attitudes of inmates which negate the work of the professional in prisons (1951).

the restraint of discretion within the narrowest limits but the unqualified support of officers in their relationships with inmates.

There is an anarchic tendency in the principle of backing up the subordinate which would seem to maximize discretionary authority throughout an organization. The absence of two-way communications controlled that tendency in the authoritarian prison. All communication flowed upward, leaving each superior better informed than his subordinate and limiting the information on lower levels on which discretion could be based. Official definitions alone are not enough to establish the legitimacy of senior officials and enforce discipline in a strict hierarchy of rank. The patterns of communication in the authoritarian institution established the official hierarchy as a relative intellectual elite and legitimized the assumption that the superior was correct on any question. The superior was always better informed. As a means of control, the Captains of the Yard perpetuated with good success a myth of their own omniscience. Where the ruler knows all that is known within the given system, it is a short jump to the idea that he knows everything.

Decisions are influenced as much by withholding information as by injecting it into communication channels. However, subordinate officers hesitated to stop reports or deny requests where there was any possibility of being reversed later. Each superior reinforced his place in the hierarchy with a wider sphere of movement and access to personal contact than those of his subordinates. While the fundamental basis of status in both inmate and official societies was power to command others, prestige was closely related to freedom of movement. The power to exert influence was directly proportioned to one's access to communication channels and information. Inmates plotted to enlarge their sphere of movement in the prison as they would plot to escape.

The situation, as it has been described so far, would seem to place the Senior Captain in a power position superior to that of the Warden. As seen from the perspective of the inmate in the yard, or to judge by the tenure of men in the two positions, that would appear to be true. The Warden signed all policy decisions. His Deputy endorsed punishment orders. But these actions were based on the record as submitted by the Captain's Office, and that is where effective control of internal policy lay. The actual superiority of the Warden's position appeared in regard to external policy. All communication to and from the prison crossed his desk, giving him the broadest perspective and hence, widest discretion in external affairs. The respect accorded to the Warden by the prison community was far above that given to his Deputy. Within the institution, however, the power to define and to decide followed control over the information on which decision was based.

In the authoritarian prison, the exercise of coercive power based essentially on force constituted one foundation of social control. But this power was, perhaps, least effective when it took the form of punitive sanctions imposed on individuals. A high degree of discipline was maintained with the minimum of direct sanctions. A vital basis of social control lay in procedures of regimentation—frequent counts and assemblies—which imposed a psychology of domination and placed the subject in a posture of silence, respect and awe. Recognition of distinctions in rank was imposed in all inmate–official contacts by the requirements of a salute and special forms of address.

More punitive forms of control rested on summary procedure and a few rules as broad in their import as the officer's sense of insubordination. Control, rather than "justice" in the familiar sense, was the object. Hence, there was no place for a body of principles or "constitutional" rights to restrain disciplinary procedure. Secret accusation was the rule, and the accused had no notice, hearing, counsel or appeal. The resulting atmosphere of "terror," produced as much by secrecy as by the actual use of informers, was vital to formal control and a key to values and social structures in inmate society. All governments use exemplary punishment. Uncertainty, rather than force, is the heart of "terror" as a political instrument in any authoritarian system.

The distinguishing characteristic of ordinary operations in the authoritarian prison was the absence of alternatives for behavior permitted to or provided for the inmates. Rewards went only for ritual conformity, and initiative was as suspect to the static inmate community as to the officials. This accent on conformity did not prevent—in fact, seemed to require—the emergence of a complex organization in inmate society. Silence was imposed wherever inmates congregated, but the patterns of inmate organization and communication could not be suppressed by even the most rigid silent system. They could only be controlled.

Not just the inmates, but subordinate officers as well, were forbidden to mention institutional affairs to outsiders. Contacts between inmates and subordinate officers were closely regulated. At the foundation of the system of security was a careful censorship of all contacts with the free world. Any attempt to evade that censorship provided the most serious punitive sanctions.

The Liberal Revolution

Three phases can be distinguished in the prison's period of transition. The first runs from the death of the old Warden in 1946 to the end of 1950. In that period, a liberal group appeared in the administration, gained formal authority, and revolutionized the policies of the institution. In the next phase, from 1950 through 1953, the liberal group engaged in a contest with the guards for control over operating procedures and, in effect, for control over the population. The present section will trace these developments. A following section will outline that contest, in which control was nearly lost, to its result in the defeat of the "old guard." The final period from 1954 through 1955 was one of reconstruction, adjustment, and, as stated by the officials, "tightening up the organization."

The seeds of revolution were contained in the appointment of five men from 1946 through 1949 who had no previous penal experience and who would not or could not adjust to traditional processes by which custody had become fixed as the dominant institutional goal. While these appointments were policy acts, they did not, in themselves, indicate a policy change, and the consequences which were to follow from altered patterns of behavior were not anticipated. The extent to which these new men injected inconsistent patterns of behavior from the free community into the prison, as much as their democratic policy statements later, marks the change as a liberal or democratic revolution. The character of this congenial group and the types of changes they introduced are indicated briefly in examples of their impact on the interactional system of the prison.

The new Warden was conscious of his inexperience and did not try to act the part of institutional autocrat. Drawing on his experience as an agricultural agent and teacher, he felt that his task was less to make decisions than to create an environment in which informed decisions would emerge. Except for a personal commitment to frankness and fair play, he arrived without plans for policy change. However, his easy personal accessibility and open-door policy of management constituted a change in the decision-making process which had radical policy implications.

Reformulation of Policy The disciplined traditions of the custodial force and the attitudes toward authority held by its members blocked their access to the open door of the new Warden. Those who took advantage of that access were the new employees who were conscious of the traditional chain of command only as a device by which their functions were frustrated. Other non-custodial employees in the past had resigned in the face of these frustrations or had accepted the attitudes and goals of custody with their acceptance of its communication channels. This group was spared the custodial orientation (with its narrow definition of purposes, roles and possibilities within the prison) by a practice of turning to one another and the license it took in turning to the Warden for definitions. The new men were members of the official staff, but they were not members of the official community in the same sense of sharing the goals and values which gave an integrity to that group.

The prison staff in the authoritarian period was not greatly different from the inmate body in the sense that it functioned on the basis of orders rather than reasons provided from above. Its militant traditions and the practice of limiting control of information to the top of the hierarchy left the bulk of guards doing only "what they were told." The system left the guards, as it left the inmates, to supply their own reasons, rationale, or justification for what they did. The system created the conditions for a grapevine among employees as well as among inmates by failing to supply justifying rationalizations for the activities it required. The concepts of the guard force, once generated, functioned with an energy of their own, coloring the interpretation of further orders given. In the failure of the new staff members to share these prevailing custodial concepts, a basis was laid for conflicting interpretation of orders given later.

As the new men by-passed conventional channels and turned to the Warden for definitions, they found that officer sensitive to the limits on his discretion imposed by custodial control of communication. His efforts to inquire through the custodial force into rumors of corruption in the prison had been frustrated for a year, forcing him to employ an outside investigator. The dismissal of several guards as a result of that inquiry, based in part on testimony taken from inmates, had lowered custodial morale and strained relations with that group. In this situation, the new men were able to form themselves into a policy caucus around the Warden and participate in the making of the definitions they sought. In turn this gave the functions represented by the new men (industry, education, and treatment) a hearing in policy decisions which they had not previously enjoyed.

When other units gained a share in policy definitions, the techniques of controlling decision by controlling the information on which it was based reacted against custodial officials. The new group was able to inject a wider range of pertinent considerations for policy than had reached the Warden in the past. As officials charged with treatment responsibilities gained access to the decision-making forum, this constituted a virtual representation of the interests and welfare of the inmates. This representation was reflected in a number of minor policy changes.

One of the first projects of the liberal group was to establish a clear conception of its own functions in the institution. To that end it produced a formal diagram of the organization. In contradiction to the actualities of custodial domination and the effective goals of the agency, the organizational chart placed the functions of treatment and industry on a level with the guard force. This, in itself, was a critical redefinition of roles if not of powers. Then, discarding its advisory capacity, the next step of the liberal group was to formalize its position as a policy agency for internal affairs. The guard force, the largest numerical group of employees, had only minority representation on the policy committee, and other officials of importance in the old power hierarchy were excluded altogether.

The next project of the liberal group was a Policy and Philosophy Manual. There was little formal statement of policy in the traditional prison between the establishing statute and the descriptive "wake 'em, work 'em, etc." of the guards. An authoritarian system is necessarily weak in operational ideology because it must resolve issues by appeal to the superior official rather than by appeal to principle. Authoritarian discipline is subverted by the publication of principles to which an appeal from persons can be made. Given a constitution or a law of the twelve tables, the weakest man in the community is armed with a weapon against the strongest. However, a Manual was published for the institution, and it asserted "rehabilitation through treatment and constructive industry" as the primary institutional purpose. It stated that "the democratic approach to management is the soundest" and contained commitments to:

> The delegation to lower management levels of all possible responsibility and authority commensurate with sound management.
>
> A practice of constant consultation, dissemination of information, and discussion of problems up and down the management chain.

These concepts were directly inconsistent with authoritarian hierarchy and control. Custodial officers were members of the council that produced the document, but they made no effective resistance to its publication. Unable to communicate effectively in the new policy forum, suspicious and on the defensive, the guard force withdrew from the area of general policy and fell back on its control over the actual operations, procedures and communications in the prison yard. The liberal group had no impact on that area until it could translate its formalized principles into operating procedures.

The Procedural Revolution   From a legalistic point of view, it would seem that the revolution in the prison had been accomplished by 1950. The liberal group had gained formal status, drafted a "constitution" and seized control of the policy-making centers thus created. In terms of the daily operating procedures of the institution, however, the change had scarcely begun. While work supervisors continued to report and take orders through the guards, their programs and the emphasis of their work continued along essentially traditional lines. The policy-making group had gained status without gaining influence. It wrote new regulations and the guards continued to enforce the old. At this point—one not uncommon in the administration of penal or other institutions—reformulation of general policy had exerted little visible impact on actual procedures.

While efforts of the policy group to legislate patterns of behavior and standards of action were defeated in the execution, that group was able to adjust institutional patterns of communication to the new policy.

The principle that all those affected by a decision should have an understanding of the issues and a voice in their determination dictated the holding of discussion meetings in several sections of the organization. Led by the treatment director, these discussions proved most effective in the newly established and more complex units of the industrial program. There they provided a means by which the interests of the work supervisors were advanced past the custodial hierarchy, and the supervisors responded briskly to the chance. As an outcome of these meetings, prison rules were revised to abandon the time-honored salute in all contacts between inmate and supervisor and to give up other elements of regimentation on the work line which had hindered productivity in the past. The abandonment of these status distinctions at work opened the way to more active communication on the job, improved production, the development of workshop communities of interest, and habits of interaction quite inconsistent with the continuing demands of life in the cell blocks. The more open contacts between supervisors and inmates provided a basis for turning later to the supervisors rather than the guards for direct reports on the men. As might be expected, efforts to conduct similar discussion sessions with the custodial force brought little response.

At the start of 1951, an inmate council was established with a right to debate any issue and advance proposals for staff consideration. This Council, with an adviser from the treatment unit, formed working committees for such areas as food, hobby, and craft work, education, recreation, and public relations. It would seem especially significant in terms of the type of analysis advanced here that the Council called itself "the voice of the inmates."

Later developments began to challenge the realities of custodial control in one area after another. In times past, punishment, inmate promotions, job assignments, good-time allowances, and every type of petty privilege had been administered by custody in terms of consideration of control. Seniority and the appearance of adjustment within the walls were used as a basis for the distribution of privilege. This reinforced the dominance of conservative and con-wise old prisoners. When the administration of privileges was, in effect, delegated to senior inmates, that served the interest of control as much by strengthening the inmate social structure as by applying sanctions to individuals. The administrative processes involved in this management of incentives were mainly informal and summary. That does not mean, however, that the operating decisions were not rational on the criterion of custodial control. A basic tactic of the liberal group was to alter the method and, hence, the dominant motive by which those operating decisions were made.

The treatment office claimed a voice in decisions on privilege and punishment on the grounds that privilege should be "meaningful" and that incentives should be concentrated behind their recently defined "goals of the institution." In defense of treatment-oriented personnel, it must be admitted that they had little conception of how all operations had been geared to the goals of security. By failing to share in institutional goals as defined by the guard force, they failed to comprehend the rationale of traditional procedures. They had little understanding of the economy of scarcity which prevailed in the yard or the extent to which a privilege or a larger sphere of movement extended to the "wrong" inmate could disturb the prison's social order. The philosophy of the treatment unit accented the importance of the individual, and this is the crucial basis on which the changes introduced may be called a "democratic" revolution. The focus of treatment men on the individual—a focus permitted by their lack of custodial responsibilities—was crucial in their conflict with the authoritarian tradition.

Participation in the expanding group of activities sponsored by treatment became the basis of a record. At the same time, the more complex processes of production required work supervisors to reward inmates on the basis of productivity as well as conduct. A report of the inmate's work record was channeled directly to the treatment office. Such records were inserted as relevant to daily operating decisions, and the decisions responded to the interests which were communicated most effectively. The traditional "time off for good behavior" became a committee decision in which six factors, only one of which was conduct, were weighted equally. The interest of teaching men a trade was taken as a ground for moving the administration of transfers to the treatment unit and away from custodial administration. By that time, the terminology and ideology of "individual development" rather than "good conduct" had been imposed on the reports of supervisors.

The treatment unit, armed with an expanding record, first asserted an informed interest and then assumed the management of functions in one area after another, extending finally to recreation and entertainment. These changes in the location of effective discretion within the agency tended to leave the custodial force with nothing but its guns as a basis of control. Rising disorder in the inmate community indicated that such a basis is weak indeed. The present section had indicated that the range of discretion possessed by a unit of administration tends to be as wide and no wider than the store of information on which decision is based. The administrative concept of a staff unit, specializing in information and communication but without authority, can be dismissed as an improbable fiction.

The Impact of Administrative Change

The Revolt of the "Old Guard"   While significant changes took place elsewhere in the institution, the custodial force retained the traditional

patterns of communication from an earlier day. Just as the new officials had avoided indoctrination with custodial attitudes, the bulk of
the guard force remained isolated from the new concepts and principles of the policy manual. Three years after its publication, few of
the guards knew of its existence. Written declaration from above
proved incapable of challenging the rationalizations which emerged
within the group. Men whose daily work required them to be constantly ready to shoot an inmate arrived at a conception of inmates as
persons who might justifiably be shot.

The system of limited communication to subordinates, which supported an authoritarian hierarchy in both official and inmate groups,
was supplemented by a grapevine which supplied each level of the
hierarchy with self-justifying and conservative values. Acceptance of
these values as legitimate was the price of peer group acceptance in
all ranks. Thus, a limited communication pattern within the guard
force protected the traditional set of custodial attitudes from challenge
or criticism. At the same time, their isolation frequently left watch
officers less well-informed than the inmates they guarded, reversing
the conditions of the past and removing the legitimate basis of the
guard's authority.

The guards tended to blame the treatment unit and its programs
for the decline in their status which inevitably followed. The over-all
consequences of procedural change were to flatten the status pyramid
of the prison community by providing equal access to influence and
information, narrowing the gaps of social distance which made up a
formal hierarchy of authority.

In order to understand the resistance of the custodial force, it
is necessary to see the situation as the guards viewed it. New officials
violated the chain of command at every turn and dismissed the traditional prerogatives of rank. The failure of treatment officers to maintain distinctions of class threatened the psychology of domination so
central to control, and led guards to see the treatment officials as on
a level with the inmates themselves. Policy discussions with the Inmate Council challenged control based on secrecy and fear simply by
supplying the rational basis for actions which had appeared to be
arbitrary before. The inmates had more direct and effective representation in policy than the guards. Custodial accounting for the movement of men was confounded by the treatment activities. Finally, the
guards felt with some reason that they knew far more about the behavior of prisoners in the authoritarian institution than did treatment
officials. The guards were in the most favorable position to see inmates exploiting new activities in pursuit of the old goals of dominance
and power.

The treatment officials, who thought of themselves as performing
professional functions, took their work as its own justification and
ignored considerations of rank. Guards, however, had no conception

of an authority of function as opposed to an authority of rank. They regarded the powers of the treatment office as improperly assumed and irresponsibly employed. As the guards had rationalized the old order, they saw it as right and just. When the liberal revolution redistributed power and status in the institution, it challenged the moral order of the custodial universe, provoking an organized and effective resistance. The custodial revolt was based on a deep conviction of righteousness and a sense that the liberal program was a compromise with criminals and with sin.

The old guard launched a counterattack with the only weapons remaining to it. The Inmate Council, meeting with its staff adviser in the yard, was free from harassment. However, completely literal enforcement of old regulations against movement and communication brought the follow-up activities of Council committees and treatment-sponsored clubs to a halt. Inmates who were "getting out of their place" through participation in new activities were the subject of disciplinary reports. Gaining access to the treatment office was made so complex and, for selected inmates, so humiliating that many who valued their self-respect in the yard abandoned the effort. Requests sent through the custodial channels to the treatment office were often lost. The custodial force perpetuated a distinction in the yard between "right inmates" and "politicians," who were assumed to be using contact with the treatment office for their own advantage. Guards manipulated traditional inmate values by asking men returning from the treatment office how much they had "beaten their time." In the face of those pressures, inmates employed in the Treatment Unit arranged for passes to work until lock-up and stayed out of the yard. In spite of the expanding number of privileges which could be manipulated by contacts in the treatment office, the influence of its inmate employees was neutralized.

By the beginning of 1953, the revolt of the old guard reached the height of its effectiveness. Conservative inmates had withdrawn from the Inmate Council, and the younger men who replaced them were exploiting the Council to an extent which challenged the faith of even the liberal officials. The inmate clubs and associations sponsored by the Treatment Unit had collapsed, and voluntary class attendance was in decline. Violence and escape had risen to a point at which new emphasis on custodial values of repression and control was required. The Deputy Warden, once a leader for liberal changes, sided with custody in the staff conferences and threatened a split in that group.

For all practical purposes, the guard force had regained control over the operation of the prison. However, it had lost control over formal policy statements as it lost its monopoly over communication channels. The old guard, ambitious for legitimacy as well as practical success, sought alliances outside the prison with men discharged earlier and with community groups which supported their position.

Represented by a minority bloc in the legislature which was seeking an issue, the old guard took its policy contest into the field of politics.

Legislative hearings on the prison opened with a series of charges which indicated, by their nature, their source in the active custodial force. A stand was taken on those matters which seemed most like mismanagement to the old guard: promotion and discipline. However, what the guards called favoritism was proved to be a sound promotion on the basis of "merit." What the guards considered abuses of discipline in the failure to back up subordinates was defended as a policy of judicial fairness. The staff was able to meet the legislative inquiry with a convincing mass of records and documentary material while the guards, in making the charges, were limited to the information they could leak. Hence the position of the old guard, which had a great deal of merit from the standpoint of authoritarian control or custody and a strong prospect of success in the conflict with the institution, was flatly rejected in the more democratic forum of the legislature. By pressing for a definition of policy in a forum beyond the range of their effective influence and communication, the guards gained only the endorsement of the liberal position and a final repudiation of their own.

The prison had changed in its character from a military dictatorship to an institution in which the role of armed force was subordinated to the objective of treatment. The extent of that power shift and its general recognition is illustrated by a number of voluntary personnel changes. Key figures who had supported the traditional position went into retirement and others accepted the new role of custody in the best spirit they could muster. One man died shortly after the hearings. A senior Captain asked for a reduction to Sergeant after 15 years in grade, and he was replaced by another officer who had been the first to accept treatment unit techniques. The Deputy Warden resigned in the following year and was replaced by the Director of Treatment in a position then enlarged and reclassified to Superintendent. While some guards persisted in their belief that all control over the inmates had been lost, a decline in escape, violence and disorder indicated, and the inmate community generally recognized, that the treatment unit had assumed control.

Postscript: Since this was written, McCleery has had a chance to observe yet another upheaval, this time brought about by changes in the prison's environment. This second time the warden lost and the guards won, illustrating anew the role of other organizations and their impact on the autonomy of an organization, see McCleery (1968).

Differentiation and Integration in Complex Organizations*

PAUL R. LAWRENCE AND JAY W. LORSCH

Basic Research Design

The basic concepts used in this examination of the internal functioning of large organizations are *differentiation* and *integration,* the key research question being: What pattern of differentiation and integration of the parts of a large organizational system is associated with the organization's coping effectively with a given external environment? The concepts as used here in relation to organizational studies suggest a return to the central concern of early organizational theorists; i.e., the optimal division of labor given a general organizational purpose (Fayol, 1930; Gulick and Urwick, 1937; Mooney and Reiley, 1939). More recently, Miller has used these concepts in theorizing about complex organizations and Rice has made use of them in the description of his work with an Indian textile firm (Miller, 1959; Rice, 1963).

It is helpful to look first at the relation between the development of specialized attributes of subsystems and the task of each subsystem in coping with the relevant segment of the external environment (Dill, 1958).

The Organization and Its Environment Since the primary concern was with the internal functioning of organizations, it appeared that one useful way to conceive of the environment of an organization was to look at it from the organization outward. This approach is based on the assumption that an organization is an active system which tends to reach out and order its otherwise overly complex surroundings so as to cope with them effectively. Then as the organization becomes differentiated into basic subsystems, it segments its environment into related sectors. As Brown has pointed out, industrial organizations usually become segmented into three essential major subsystems here termed basic subsystems to distinguish them from integrative subsystems. These are the sales subsystem, the production subsystem, and the research and development subsystem (1960: 143–145). By the definition given, this segmentation indicates that the organization is undertaking a whole task. In this division of tasks, the organization is also ordering its environment into three sectors: the market subenvironment, the technical–economic subenvironment, and the scientific subenvironment. It is readily apparent that each of these environments can range from highly dynamic to extremely stable. The importance of this variability can easily be obscured by the usual

* Reprinted from *Administrative Science Quarterly, 12* (June 1967), pp. 1–47, with omissions, by permission of the authors and the publisher.

approach of thinking of an organization's environment as a single entity. Here, each major subsystem was seen as coping with its respective segment of the total external environment. It was hypothesized that each subsystem would tend to develop particular attributes which would be predictably related to characteristics of its relevant external environment.

It was hypothesized that four attributes of an organizational subsystem would vary with the relevant subenvironments. Although many other attributes of organizations could be related to the environment, prior research led to a special interest in structural attributes and the pattern of cognitive and normative orientations held by the members of each subsystem.

Degree of structure. Prior experimental and field studies indicated that an important attribute of any subsystem that could be expected to be related to its relevant environment was its degree of *formalized structure.* Structure here refers to those aspects of behavior in organizations subject to pre-existing programs and controls. We wanted to compare the degree of formalized structure in different organizations and subsystems, that is, the extent of pre-existing programs and controls. Leavitt, as well as other researchers working with experimental groups, found that groups working on relatively simple and certain tasks tended to perform the task better when the groups had more structure (i.e., preplanned and limited communication nets), whereas groups working on uncertain, more complex tasks tended to perform better with less structured communication nets (1958: 546–563). In field studies, Burns and Stalker found that organizations that were profitably coping with uncertain, changing environments had a low degree of formalized structure ("organic"), instead of the higher degree of formalized structure ("mechanistic") associated with financial success in more certain environments (1961: 1–10). Woodward also found a relationship between the nature of the task and the structure of the organization. More significantly she found that more profitable organizations tended to adopt structures consistent with the requirements of their technological environments (1958: 16–24). Similarly, Hall found that departments with routine tasks tended to have a higher degree of bureaucracy (structure) than departments with less certain tasks (1962). These findings suggested that subsystems in any organization could be expected to develop different degrees of structure in relation to the certainty of their subenvironment. It was therefore, hypothesized that:

Hypothesis 1 The greater the certainty of the relevant subenvironment, the more formalized the structure of the subsystem.

Orientation of members toward others. Moment and Zaleznik, and Leader suggested a second attribute of subsystems that could be expected to be related to the task of coping with different subenvironments (Moment and Zaleznik, 1963; Leader, 1965). This is a cognitive and affective orientation toward the objects of work, which is manifested in a person's interpersonal style. The objects can be either people or inanimate tools and instruments, and the concern of members with them tends to polarize along a task-social dimension. Subsystem members in their interpersonal relationships will be primarily concerned with either task accomplishment or with social relationships. Fiedler in studies of group effectiveness found task-oriented leadership associated with effective task performance under the extreme conditions of high and low task certainty, while more socially oriented styles were associated with effective performance under conditions of moderate uncertainty (1960). Although Fiedler was focusing particularly on leadership behavior, whereas the interest here is in the wider interpersonal orientation of members of an organizational unit, his findings are relevant if one recognizes that leadership behavior is closely related to the interpersonal norms of the unit in which the leader functions. Based on these earlier findings it was hypothesized that:

Hypothesis 2 Subsystems dealing with environments of moderate certainty will have members with more social interpersonal orientations, whereas subsystems coping with either very certain environments or very uncertain environments will have members with more task-oriented interpersonal orientations.

Time orientation and members. A third attribute of subsystems can best be understood by considering the definition of certainty used in conceptualizing the characteristics of the different subenvironments. Three indicators of subenvironmental certainty were used: the rate of change of conditions over time in the subenvironment, the certainty of information about conditions in the subenvironment at any particular time, and the modal time span of definitive feedback from the subenvironment on the results of subsystem behavior. It was predicted that structure and interpersonal orientation would be related to all three environmental indicators, while the members' time orientation, the third subsystem attribute, would be related to the timespan of definitive feedback. For example, a production subsystem that received feedback about its efforts on an almost daily basis could be expected to have members with a short-term orientation, whereas a research unit coping with a subenvironment where feedback might occur only on the completion of a project lasting well over a year would be apt to have members with a more long-term orientation. It was hypothesized that:

Hypothesis 3 The time orientations of subsystem members will vary directly with the modal time required to get definitive feedback from the relevant subenvironment.

This attribute has apparently not been empirically studied in organizations, but it has been used as an important dimension of the comparative study of cultures (Kluckholn and Strodbeck, 1961; Caudill and Scarr, 1962; McArthur, 1955).

Goal orientation of members. The fourth attribute that subsystems were expected to develop in relation to their subenvironments was the *goal orientation* of members. Following the empirical research done by Dearborn and Simon on this subject, it was hypothesized that:

Hypothesis 4   The members of a subsystem will develop a primary concern with the goals of coping with their particular subenvironment (1958).

Thus marketing managers could be expected to be more concerned with customer and competitor actions, while production executives would be more oriented toward the operation of equipment and the actions of suppliers.

One might question whether the development of these four different attributes in subsystems is not so obvious as to make it unnecessary to test for them. The testing can be sufficiently justified, however, on the grounds of establishing a factual base line for the testing of more debatable hypotheses to be described shortly. Furthermore other factors can be expected to counteract the tendency of subsystems to become differentiated in relation to their relevant subenvironment. The only counterforce to be dealt with formally in this study is the tendency to reduce differences between subsystems to achieve integration between them. Finally, it needs to be emphasized again that the particular attributes selected for measurement and examination in this study are not the only ones related to differences in subenvironments. Other attributes were seriously explored for inclusion, but were excluded because of methodological problems. The first was the linguistic or semantic orientation of the subsystems. The specialized languages that develop around certain tasks and environments are reputed to complicate the relations between subsystems (March and Simon, 1958: 162–163). The second was concerned with supplementing the goal-orientation of the subsystems, since some studies indicate that various motivational orientations toward achievement, power, or social rewards are related to environmental characteristics (McClelland, 1961: 266–267). The four attributes selected for this study, however, were considered both operationally feasible and based on prior research.

Means of Achieving Integration   Much of the theorizing about integration has suggested that the achievement of integration is the task of top management. Barnard has indicated that this is one of the principal functions of an executive (1938: 136–137). More recently, both Haire and Rice, among others, have made a similar point (Haire, 1959: 302–303; Rice, 1958: 35). Although coordination is undoubtedly an important part of the top manager's job, there is considerable evidence that many organizational systems develop integrative devices in addition to the conventional hierarchy. Litterer recently suggested three main means of achieving integration: through the hierarchy, through administrative or control systems, and through voluntary activities (1965). It is our view that these "voluntary" activities, which managers at lower echelons develop to supplement the hierarchical and administrative systems, are becoming increasingly formalized. One has only to note the proliferation of coordinating departments (whether called new product, marketing, or planning departments), task forces, and cross-functional coordinating teams to find evidence that new formal devices are emerging to achieve coordination.

It was predicted that in the industry studied, the high degree of subsystem differentiation required and the environmental requirements for a high degree of integration between the differentiated subsystems would make integrative devices necessary for effective performance. Top managers in these organizations would not be able to deal with the many technical and market factors that had to be assimilated in making well-coordinated decisions. It was therefore hypothesized that:

Hypothesis 5   When the environment requires both a high degree of subsystem differentiation and a high degree of integration, integrative devices will tend to emerge.

The effectiveness of these integrative devices is questionable. Burns and Stalker reported that such devices observed in their study were not effective (1961: 9). However, if an organization was both highly differentiated and highly integrated, and yet these two processes were antagonistic, then these integrative devices would have to be functioning effectively. This raised another question: If the presence and effective functioning of these devices was necessary for high system performance, what were some of the determinants of the effectiveness of these devices? Before this question can be answered, it is necessary to consider the findings about the relationship between differentiation and integration, and the relation of these to the ability of the organization to cope with its external environment.

Research Findings

Research Setting   The six organizations studied were all operating in a chemical processing industry, which was characterized by relatively rapid technological change and product modification and innovation. According to top executives in these organizations, the dominant competitive issue confronting them was the development of new and improved products and processes in this rapidly changing environment. The organizations were selected for study because these environmental conditions, particularly the importance of innovation, seemed to require organizations to achieve a high degree of both differentiation and integration.

Subenvironments. Since the six organizations were operating in the same environment, efforts to characterize this environment were limited to an examination of the requirements of the three subenvironments: the market subenvironment, the scientific subenvironment, and the technical–economic subenvironment. Data about these subenvironments were collected in interviews with the top executives in each organization. From these interviews it was concluded that the certainty of these subenvironments could be measured by: (1) the rate of change in environmental conditions, (2) the certainty of information at a given time about environmental conditions, and (3) the time span of definitive feedback from the environment. The ranking of each of the subenvironments along these three dimensions is presented in Table 1. The total score obtained by summing the three columns provides at least a crude estimate of the relative certainty of these subenvironments; science being the least certain and the technical–economic the most certain.

The scientific subenvironment was characterized by relatively uncertain information at any given time about the nature of the materials being investigated. This was further complicated by the rapid rate of change in knowledge; new materials and formulations continually being developed might antiquate present methods and products. Definitive feedback from this subenvironment was only secured after a project was entirely completed; only then was there concrete evidence to evaluate the success of the organization in coping with its scientific subenvironment.

TABLE 1. RANKING OF SUBENVIRONMENTS ALONG THREE DIMENSIONS

Subenvironment	Certainty of information	Rate of change	Time span of definitive feedback	Total
Science	1*	1.5	1	3.5
Market	2	1.5	2	5.5
Technical–economic	3	3	3	9

* 1—least certain or longest in time span; 3—most certain or shortest in time span.

The rate of change in the market subenvironment was also relatively high; however, the executives seemed to feel somewhat more certain about market information than about scientific data. They indicated that they received feedback from the market subenvironment on a regular basis, and often as frequently as once a week.

In the technical–economic subenvironment, there was much more certainty about conditions in this subenvironment at a given time than in the others. Machine capacities, raw material specifications, and similar conditions could be accurately assessed. Also the rate of change was less rapid, since processes change only after thorough testing had indicated they were warranted economically as well as technically. Finally feedback from this subenvironment was very rapid; information about processing costs, quality, and the like, being available on a daily basis.

Requisite integration. In addition to the characteristics of these subenvironments, interviews with the top executives also provided information on the requirements for integration in this environment. A high degree of integration was required primarily because of the necessity for developing new processes and products and constantly modifying old ones. The executives indicated that the requirement for effective integration was particularly acute between the sales and research subsystems and between the production and research subsystems, as well as between these units and the integrative departments intended to link them. Sales and research needed to maintain an effective liaison first, so that the sales subsystem could provide researchers with information about market needs and requirements; and second, so that the research subsystem could make sales and marketing managers aware of the characteristics of new products. In addition to this flow of technical information, a close bond was necessary to achieve relationships that motivated salesmen to sell new products and researchers to undertake scientific investigations to meet market requirements.

Similarly close collaboration was needed between production and research so that researchers would be aware of processing capabilities and limitations as they developed new and modified processes, while production personnel would understand how to set up and maintain new and modified processes. Here too, collaboration was required to maintain close interpersonal ties between these groups, so that researchers would be motivated to investigate processing problems, and production personnel would be receptive to changes in production processes originating in the research subsystem.

All the organizations studied had segmented the research subsystem further into two subsystems: one for applied research and the other for more fundamental long-range investigations. Of these two units, the fundamental research subsystem, both because of the longer time span of definitive feedback and the less certain information with which it dealt, was coping with the least certain portion of the scientific subenvironment. Also, in each organization, an extra subsystem had been established to integrate the activities of the basic subsystems. These were one type of integrative device that was expected to emerge, and they will be discussed in more detail later.

The presence of two research subsystems and the integrative subsystem in each organization complicated the question of where high integration was required. In some of the organizations, the top executives indicated that integration was also required between the two research subsystems; in other organizations, this was not required. This depended largely on the function assigned to the integrative subsystem. Since we were interested in studying subsystems of equal requisite integration, attention was focused on the relationship between sales and applied research and between production and applied research, as well as the relation of these subsystems to the integrative subsystems, where high requisite integration was defined as necessary by all of the top executives. In determining which subsystems had comparable requisite integration with the fundamental-research subsystem, the special circumstances of each organization as defined by the top executives involved, served as a guide.

Attributes of Basic Subsystems and Requirements of Subenvironments
It was predicted that each of these basic subsystems would develop four attributes (structure, members' interpersonal orientation, members' orientation toward time, and members' orientation toward goals) in relation to the specific requirements of the relevant subenvironment, particularly its certainty.

Structure. To measure the structure of the subsystems, dimensions suggested by Hall, Woodward, Evan, and Burns and Stalker that could be operationally measured were used: the span of supervisory control, number of levels to a supervisor shared with other subsystems, the specificity of review of subsystem performance, the frequency of review of subsystem performance, the specificity of review of individual performance, and the emphasis on formal rules and procedures (Hall, 1962; Woodward, 1958; Burns and Stalker, 1961; Evan, 1963). The more levels to a shared superior, the tighter the span of control; the more frequent and specific the reviews, and the more emphasis given to rules, the higher the formalized structure of the particular subsystem. Data on these characteristics for each subsystem were gathered from organizational documents (organization charts, procedural manuals, and the like), or when these were not available, by interviewing subsystem managers about organizational practices.

A four-point scale, ranging from most controlling to least controlling, was developed for each structural characteristic, and a structural score was computed for each subsystem in all organizations by

**TABLE 2.   SUBSYSTEM STRUCTURE SCORES RANKED FROM
LOW TO HIGH STRUCTURE***

Subsystem	Organizations					
	I	II	III	IV	V	VI
Fundamental research	(8) 1	(13) 1.5	(12) 1	(8) 1	(16) 1.5	(8) 1
Applied research	(16) 2.5	(13) 1.5	(13) 2	(16) 2	(16) 1.5	(15) 2
Sales	(16) 2.5	(17) 3	(17) 3	(18) 4	(19) 3	(16) 3.5
Production	(18) 4	(22) 4	(21) 4	(17) 3	(23) 4	(16) 3.5

* Number in parentheses is structure score: low score indicates low structure; high score indicates high structure. Other numbers are rank order.

adding the scores on all six characteristics. While there was some variation within individual subsystems, scores for one characteristic were generally consistent with those for others. Although space precludes discussing all these scores in detail, the important finding was that subsystems within each organization did tend to rank from low to high structure in relation to the uncertainty of their subenvironments, as is apparent from Table 2.

Production, with a more certain subenvironment, tended to have the highest structure in all but one organization (IV). Fundamental-research subsystems tended to have the least structure. Sales subsystems with moderately certain tasks tended to be more structured than research subsystems, but usually less structured than production. Although these rankings were found within all organizations, it is important to emphasize (as the raw scores indicate), that the degree of structure varied considerably between organizations. For example, the fundamental research subsystems in organizations I, IV, and VI tended to be considerably less structured than the counterpart subsystems in the other three organizations. We will return to the significance of this point later.

These data indicate, as predicted, that subsystems tend to develop a degree of formalized structure related to the certainty of their relevant subenvironment. This also, of course, indicates that the subsystems within each of these organizations were differentiated from each other in their internal structure.

Interpersonal orientation. The interpersonal orientation of members of the several subsystems in these organizations was measured by using the Least Preferred Coworker instrument developed by Fiedler (1960). This semantic differential scale measures the respondent's interpersonal style on a continuum from primary concern with task accomplishment to primary concern with social relationships. The results are presented in Table 3.

Although the interpersonal orientations of the various subsystems

TABLE 3.   SUBSYSTEM INTERPERSONAL SCORES RANKED FROM TASK CONCERN TO SOCIAL CONCERN*

Subsystem	Organizations						Average rank all organi- zations
	I	II	III	IV	V	VI	
Sales	(103) 2	(100) 1	(90) 2	(92) 2.5	(118) 1	(92) 2	1.8
Applied research	(85) 3	(96) 2	(86) 4	(99) 1	(93) 2.5	(98) 1	2.3
Fundamental research	(112) 1	(94) 3	(87) 3	(90) 2.5	(88) 4	(78) 4	2.9
Production	(71) 4	(83) 4	(98) 1	(83) 4	(93) 2.5	(90) 3	3.1

* Numbers in parentheses are mean scores: high score indicates social concern; low score indicates task concern. Other numbers indicate rank order from social to task.

were generally differentiated in a direction consistent with their environmental tasks, the relationship was not as clear as in the case of structure. The sales subsystem, with a moderately certain subenvironment, did tend to have members who preferred a more socially oriented interpersonal style. The data also suggest that production personnel, whose task was most certain, preferred a more task-oriented style. In five organizations, fundamental-research personnel, confronted with a highly uncertain subenvironment, seemed to prefer a more task-oriented style, though less intensively than production personnel.

The findings for the applied-research subsystems are even less clear. In some organizations, members of these subsystems preferred a more social orientation; in others, a task orientation. The explanation may be because the applied-research task in the six organizations differed more than the tasks of any of the other basic subsystems. In some organizations, the applied-research subsystem was doing long-range research; in other organizations it was directly involved in short-range process development and technical service activities. This made it difficult to establish the subenvironmental requirements for applied research subsystems. It is also possible, as Fiedler (1960) has pointed out, that situational factors other than the nature of the task were also influencing the preferred interpersonal style in all of these subsystems. Nevertheless, the findings about the interpersonal orientation of members of subsystems in these organizations appear to follow the curvilinear relationship consistent with their subenvironmental requirements, as interpreted by Fiedler's contingency model. The clearest evidence of this is seen in the average ranking of units for all six organizations.

Time orientation of members. The time orientation of members of the different units was measured with a question which asked for an estimate of the percentage of total time used working on activities

TABLE 4.   DOMINANT TIME ORIENTATION OF BASIC SUBSYSTEMS*

Subsystems	Organizations					
	I	II	III	IV	V	VI
Sales	S	S	S	S	S	M
Production	S	M	S	S	S	M
Applied research	M	L	S	L	L	L
Fundamental research	L	L	L	L	L	L

* S = one month or less; M = one month to one year; L = one year to five years.

affecting the organization's profits within a specific time period: less than one month, one month to one year, and one year to five years. The results (see Table 4) clearly support the prediction that the time orientation of members of each subsystem would be related to the time span of definitive feedback of the relevant subenvironment. Sales and production subsystems tended to have the shortest time orientations, consistent with the shorter time span of definitive feedback in the market and technical–economic subenvironments. The research subsystems tended to have a long-term time orientation, which was congruent with the longer time span of feedback in the scientific subenvironment. The time orientation of the applied-research subsystems was somewhat less consistent than that of the fundamental-research subsystems, which, again, seemed to be due to the differences in the division of the research task within each organization. For example, in organizations I and III the applied-research subsystem worked primarily on immediate customer and process problems, whereas in the other organizations they focused on more complex applied problems. Thus, in organizations I and III the members of the applied-research subsystems tended to have more short-termed time horizons.

Goal orientation of members.   Finally, it was predicted that each subsystem would develop a goal orientation toward its relevant subenvironment. A list of ten criteria which managers might consider in making decisions relevant to product and process innovation was developed to measure this goal orientation. Three of these criteria related to factors in each of the three subenvironments; for example, competitive action (market), processing costs (technical–economic), and developing new knowledge (scientific). One criterion, which was related to the total environment, was not used in this analysis. The respondents were asked to select from these ten criteria the three most important considerations in making decisions, and then the next three most important.

The primary goal orientation of the sales and production subsystems (see Table 5) was as predicted. Sales personnel were more concerned with the market subenvironment, whereas production per-

TABLE 5.   GOAL ORIENTATION OF BASIC SUBSYSTEMS*

	Organizations					
Subsystem	I	II	III	IV	V	VI
Sales	M	M	M	M	M	M
Production	TE	TE	TE	TE	TE	TE
Applied research	S	TE	TE	TE	TE	TE
Fundamental research	S	TE	TE	S	TE	S

* M = market; TE = technical–economic; S = science.

sonnel were concerned primarily with the technical–economic sub-environment. In five of the organizations, however, the research personnel in the applied-research subsystems were concerned mainly with the technical–economic subenvironment. Among the fundamental-research subsystems the primary goal orientation was equally divided between the scientific subenvironment and the technical–economic subenvironment. This finding is not too surprising, since much of the activity of research subsystems was dealing with process improvements and modifications. However, where members indicated a primary goal orientation toward the technical–economic subenvironment, they also indicated a strong secondary orientation toward the scientific subenvironment. In goal orientations, then, the subsystems in these six organizations generally tended to develop a primary concern with their relevant subenvironment.

The basic subsystems were therefore differentiated in these four attributes, and the differentiation was generally in a direction consistent with predictions. Although these findings are not surprising, since they had been strongly suggested by earlier studies, they are important, because they suggest that these attributes within each subsystem are related to the particular requisites of the relevant subenvironment. They are also important because it was possible to measure these four attributes in each subsystem, at least crudely, so that the relationship of the differentiation in these four attributes to integration between the subsystems could be examined.

Achieving Differentiation and Integration

Emergence of Integrative Devices   Hypothesis 5 predicted the emergence of integrative devices. As indicated, in all the organizations except organization II, there were integrative subsystems whose members had the function of integrating the sales-research and the production-research subsystems. In organization II there was also a formally established integrative subsystem, but it functioned somewhat differently from the others and might be termed an integrative role set.

In addition to these integrative subsystems, four of these organizations (I, IV, V, and VI) had integrating teams with representatives from each of the basic subsystems and the integrative subsystems. The function of the teams was to facilitate the coordination of these activities of the various subsystems by providing formal machinery for discussing and resolving mutual problems.

Thus the hypothesis that integrative devices would emerge in organizations with environments which required both high differentiation and integration was confirmed; however, we were interested in examining these devices to understand the factors related to their effectiveness in achieving integration in the face of varying degrees of subsystem differentiation. Preliminary and prior research pointed to several factors that might be partial determinants of the effectiveness of these devices, and these were investigated further.

Structure and Orientation of Integrative Subsystem   It was predicted that one partial determinant of effective integrative devices would be that the orientations of members of the integrative subsystem would be intermediate between those found in subsystems they were to coordinate. An effective coordinator working between research and sales, for example, could be expected to be oriented equally toward long-term problems (the requisite time orientation of researchers) and short-term problems (the requisite time orientation of sales personnel) and to have an equal concern with market goals and scientific goals. Similarly, it was expected that effective coordinators would have interpersonal orientations between those of the groups they were linking. Finally, it was expected that the structure of the integrative subsystem would be intermediate between those of the basic subsystems being linked. This determinant was derived from the work of Sherif (1958) and of Seiler (1963).

The methods used for measuring structure, and time, goal, and interpersonal orientations were also used for this analysis. The midpoint of the range of scores in each attribute was computed for the basic subsystems being integrated. The difference between the score for the integrative subsystem and the midpoint was then computed, to determine how closely the integrative subsystem approached an intermediate position.

These difference scores indicate that the integrative subsystem in organization I was the only one to be intermediate in all four attributes. All other organizations, except organization V, appeared to be intermediate in two of the four attributes. Data gathered in interviews suggested that in all the organizations not intermediate in all four attributes (except organization II), the failure to meet this condition made it difficult for the members of the integrative subsystem to communicate effectively.

The time and goal orientations seemed to cause the most difficulty. Members of the basic subsystems in organizations III, V, and

VI complained frequently that the members of the integrative subsystems, who were not intermediate in time orientation, were too preoccupied with current problems to be helpful in coordinating long-range activities. Typical comments from sales, production, and research personnel in these organizations follow:

> I am no coordinator, but I can see that one of our troubles is that they [integrative] are so tied up in day-to-day detail that they can't look to the future. They are still concerned with '64 materials when they should be concerned with '65 markets.

> We get lots of reports from them [the integrative subsystem] and we talk to them frequently. The trouble is that all they present to us [in research] are short-term needs. They aren't the long-range things we are interested in.

> They [the integrative unit] only find out about problems when they find out somebody has quit buying our material and is buying somebody else's, and this keeps you on the defense. A lot of our work is catch-up work. We would like more future-oriented work from them.

Similarly members of the basic units in organizations IV and V frequently complained about the lack of balance in the goal orientation of the members of the integrative subsystem:

> Our relations with them [the integrative subsystem] are good, but not as good as with research. They [integration] are not as cost-conscious as the laboratory people. They are concerned with the customer.

> He [the integrator] is under a lot of pressure to work with the salesmen on existing products in our product lines. What he [the integrator] should be and often tries to act like is a liaison person, but in reality he is not. He is too concerned with sales problems.

> What's lacking is that they [the integrators] are so busy that they continually postpone working with research. They work closely with applied research on minor modifications, but the contact with basic research is minimal.

We are not implying that the other attributes (structure and interpersonal orientation) were unimportant, but only that they operated more outside the awareness of the members of the organization. In any case one can conclude from these data that organization I, with the most effective integration, had an integrative subsystem that was consistently intermediate in structure and orientation, whereas organizations II, III, IV, and VI had integrative subsystems that were only moderately intermediate, and organization V, a low-integration organization, had an integrative subsystem that was intermediate only to a very limited extent.

Influence Attributed to Integrative Subsystem   A second partial determinant of effective integrative devices was also derived from the work of Seiler, and from a preliminary analysis. Seiler reported that intergroup relations tend to be characterized by open collaboration when high-status groups were initiating for lower-status groups (1963: 196–197). Preliminary analysis suggested that many of the activities would be initiated by the integrative subsystem; therefore an effective integrative subsystem would be perceived to be legitimate in initiating activities for the basic subsystems. Seiler had discussed this legitimacy in terms of status, but the internal organizational status of a subsystem can be measured in terms of the influence attributed to members of that subsystem by members of the rest of the organization. We thus predicted that the members of effective integrative subsystems would be perceived by other organizational members as having high influence in decision making relative to the members of other subsystems.

To measure the influence of the several subsystems, members of each organization were asked, "How much say or influence do you feel each of the units listed below has on product-innovation decisions?" Each subsystem was included, and responses were made on a five-point scale ranging from "little or no influence" to "a very great deal of influence." The mean scores for each subsystem within each organization were then ranked.

The integrative subsystem was ranked first out of the five subsystems, in organizations I, IV, and VI; second in organizations II and V, and tied for first ranking in organization III. Since all integrative subsystems appeared to have relatively high influence, it was concluded that this particular determinant did not discriminate among these organizations and it was not used further in this analysis.

Basis of Influence   A separate but related partial determinant is that the basis for influence be appropriate to the task of achieving integration. Influence can be based either on professional expertise or on hierarchical authority. As Blau and Scott have pointed out, influence based on hierarchical position is not appropriate where professional judgment is required for decisions related to coordination (1962: 185). In the organizations studied, where integration often had to be achieved around complex, unprogrammed problems involving technical issues, it was predicted that integrators whose influence stemmed from their professional competence would be more effective than those whose influence was based on their position in the organization.

Data about the basis of influence was collected in interviews from responses to questions about the role of the integrative subsystem. In organizations I and II, the integrative personnel were seen as having influence primarily stemming from their knowledge and competence in dealing with problems associated with the environment.

In the other organizations the influence of the integrative personnel was almost entirely attributed to their position.

Typical comments made by personnel in the basic subsystems in organizations I and II are:

> He [the integrator] has a powerful job if he can get the people to work for him. A good man in that job has everybody's ear open to him. A good coordinator has to be thoroughly oriented to his market or to his process. Whichever area he is working in he has to be able to make good value judgments in his area.

> The way we operate we feel that we get suggestions rather than directions from him [the integrator]. In my relations with him there is 100 percent freedom of action. He may tell me what to work on, but in the day-to-day operations I am never really aware of it.

> We usually talk to him [the integrator] on the nature of two things. We are asking him that since we have such and such a material, how does it work as a new product? He might tell us what kind of product the market is looking for. We get a flow of information both ways.

> They [the integrators] are the kingpins. They have a good feel for our [research's] ability and they know the needs of the market. They will work back and forth with us and the others.

> It [the integrative subsystem] is on the border of research, so we work together closely. The integrative people are just a step away from the customer, so when I make a change in a material I let them know because they may have a customer who can use it. The good thing about our situation is that it [the integrative unit] is close enough to sales to know what they are doing and close enough to research to know what we are doing.

It is clear from these comments that the coordinators were seen as people who had knowledge about different aspects of the environment, and this knowledge appeared to be the basis of their high influence.

In the other four organizations, the comments about the integrator's role were quite different:

> We [in the integrative subsystem] are in the thick of activities here. We are in control of the experimental material. When we feel that things are ready, we can transfer to sales. In this respect we are in the driver's seat.

> We [in research] have to go by what they [the integrative subsystem] say. They have the upper hand. If we can't get their approval, we have to shut up.

> He [an integrator] will tell you what material he thinks will work, and if you don't agree there isn't much you can do except beat your head against the wall and continue to work. If you aren't getting anywhere, then eventually he may listen to you.

We [the integrators] are staff men, but I like to feel we are line men. I take authority and initiative. If a salesman has a problem I go directly to him; then I tell his boss. When I talk to the laboratory director I like to feel I am his boss, even though the organization chart doesn't say so.

In setting up a coordinator, what you have done is set up a staff position where [the general manager] is able to go to a man and beat him on the head to get information and get things done.

A good coordinator is a guy with a red hot bayonet. He doesn't take no for an answer on anything. He also is in an enviable position since he reports to the general manager and he finds very little opposition to what he wants to do.

Nobody wants to pull the wool over the coordinator's eyes, since he reports to the general manager. That would be disastrous. I don't think anybody could be a coordinator and have many friends. You have to be too aggressive.

For a man to move into a coordinating role should be a big thing. But it isn't now. My guys say "I know more than that guy [in the integrative subsystem]." People compare their skills and often the comparison is not favorable.

He [the integrator] is supposed to know the field and he may think our product isn't any good. This is fine if you have confidence in him, but we have had a bad experience with some of them. As the knowledge of chemistry grows, his [the integrator's] knowledge of the market must grow. I guess I would appraise the situation this way: just because they [integrators] have had twenty years' experience doesn't mean they have twenty years of knowledge.

In these organizations, the coordinators were seen as having influence stemming from their positions, either because of the formal authority of their position or because of their close proximity to top management; the only comments about the knowledge and competence of the coordinators tended to be negative ones. These excerpts from interviews suggest that organizations I and II met the hypothesized condition for good integration and the other four organizations did not.

Perceived Basis of Rewards for Integrators   A third partial determinant of effective integrative devices was suggested by the work of Zander and Wolfe (1964). They found that members of groups conditioned experimentally to be concerned with group performance, "generated more emphasis on providing successful scores for others and less concern about personal rewards or costs involved, more motivation to achieve a good score, more trust in others, and less strain in interpersonal relations." On this basis, it was predicted that integrative devices would be most effective when the integrators perceived themselves to be rewarded for the performance of the total set of activities they were integrating; that is, effective integrators were expected to perceive that they were being rewarded for the achievement *with* others of a superordinate goal.

One of the questions included in the questionnaire asked respondents to select from a list of possible criteria for evaluation, the three most important factors used by their supervisors to evaluate their performance. The criteria used were: your own individual accomplishments, performance of your subordinates, performance of the product group, how well you get along with others in your own department, and how well you get along with members of other departments. The respondents were asked to rank their three choices: most important (1), second most important (2), and least important (3). The mean score for the integrators in each organization was then computed. The criteria by which personnel were being evaluated indicated to them the basis on which they were being rewarded; therefore, the basis of evaluation may be used as a measure of the perceived basis of rewards.

The data indicated that integrative personnel in the two least integrated organizations, V (with a score of 2.5) and VI (with a score of 3) saw themselves as being significantly less rewarded for the performance of the product group with which they were associated than did the integrators in organizations II (with a score of 1.8) and III (with a score of 1.1). Organizations V and VI were significantly different from organizations II and III at the .01 level. Although the difference between organizations V and VI and organizations I and IV (both with a mean score of 2.0) was not significant, it was clearly in the predicted direction. The integrators in organizations V and VI also perceived themselves to be significantly more rewarded for their individual performance than did the integrators in organizations III and IV. In organizations V and VI, then, this determinant was not present. In organizations II and III, two of the high-integration organizations, it was clearly operating; while in organizations I and IV, this determinant was operating to a moderate extent. From this, one can conclude that this factor generally discriminated between the organizations which were lowest in achieving integration and the other organizations.

Total Influence in the Organizational System   The fourth partial determinant of effective integrative devices was derived from the work of Smith and Ari (1964), who found a relationship between the total amount of perceived influence among organizational members and organizational effectiveness. They concluded that, "The significant exercise of control by both members and leaders leads to a high degree of identification and involvement in the organization." Horwitz's findings (1964) about influence and hostility carried this point a step further. Organizations with subsystem members who feel that they have high influence in the organization would be likely to feel that their point of view was being given adequate weight by other groups and therefore would not feel hostility toward the members of other subsystems. This suggested that another factor related to effective integrative devices would be a high total amount of perceived influence in the organization.

The question used to determine the relative influence of the integrative subsystem was also used to derive the data for this determinant. The scores ranged from "little or no influence" (1) to "a very great influence" (5). Organizations I, II, and IV had mean influence scores of 3.6; organization III, a mean influence score of 3.5. The two organizations with the lowest integration scores—V with a total influence score of 2.5, and VI with a total influence score of 3.1—had significantly less total influence than the other four organizations. These two organizations were significantly different from the other organizations at the .05 level using an orthogonal comparison and did not meet this determinant.

Locus of Influence in Subsystems   A fifth partial determinant of effective integrative devices was also suggested by Smith and Ari. In the same study they predicted that "democratic" influence (high influence at lower levels of the organization) would be associated with high organizational performance (1964). Although their findings in the organization they studied did not support their hypotheses, they concluded that:

> It is conceivable that a positively sloped distribution of control [high influence at lower echelons] might lead to a system of shared norms and consequently concerted action on the part of the organization in a different type of organization with different organizational conditions. This might occur in a "mutual benefit" type of organization such as some voluntary organizations where the interests and objectives of members and leaders are more widely shared, and where decision-making is of a judgmental nature (1964: 638).

As these authors point out, Tannenbaum (1962) found that this condition was present in a voluntary organization. Although the organizations we studied were not voluntary, they had managers and professionals at several levels of the organizational hierarchy whose interests and objectives might be more highly shared than in the organization studied by Smith and Ari. Furthermore, the environmental demands made it necessary to have the influence for decision making and conflict resolution at the management levels, where the knowledge about technical and market factors was available. We therefore predicted that another partial determinant of effective integrative devices would be the presence of a sufficient degree of influence to resolve interdepartmental conflicts at the level in each subsystem where the most knowledge about subenvironmental conditions was available; that is that better integration would be achieved if the persons who had the knowledge to make decisions also had sufficient influence to do so.

Data about the locus of pertinent knowledge was obtained in interviews with top managers in all six organizations. There was widespread agreement that in both the fundamental- and applied-research subsystems, the knowledge required to make product decisions was found among personnel at the lower levels of the organizational hierarchy. In the sales and production subsystems, where the subenvironment was more certain, the required knowledge was at the upper levels of the hierarchy. In the integrative subsystems, the respondents indicated that the required knowledge was to be found among members at the lower levels of the hierarchy. Since in all six organizations, high influence in the integrative subsystems was at the lower levels, as consistent with the task requirements, the integrative subsystems were not considered in this analysis.

To measure influence in each subsystem, respondents were asked to indicate for their own subsystems, "How much say or influence each of the levels has on product innovation decisions?" The scale used was five points ranging from "little or no influence" to "a very great deal of influence." These data were analyzed to determine if the levels where influence was concentrated were also the levels with the required knowledge.

Organizations V and VI (the low-integration organizations) did not have the highest influence at the required level in two subsystems. In organization VI, influence was centered at too high a level in the applied-research subsystem and at too low a level in the production subsystem hierarchy.

In both the applied- and fundamental-research subsystems of organization V, the highest influence was too far up the organizational hierarchy. Organizations II, III, and IV each had one subsystem in which influence was not concentrated at the required level. In organization II influence was centered at too low a level in the production hierarchy. The concentrated influence in the applied-research subsystem in organization III was at too high a level in the hierarchy, while in organization I the locus of high influence was consistent with the required knowledge in all four subsystems. Thus organization I, which achieved the highest integration, met this condition completely; organizations II, III, and IV met it partially, and organizations V and VI, with the lowest degree of integration, met it the least.

Modes of Conflict Resolution   The sixth determinant was suggested by the work of Blake and Mouton (1964), who emphasized that the mode of conflict resolution used in organizations was an important variable in intergroup collaboration. Initially they had identified five possible modes of resolving conflict: win–lose power struggle, smoothing over, withdrawal, compromise, or confrontation. They suggested that organizations placing greater emphasis on confrontation or problem-solving modes of conflict resolution would have effective intergroup relations.

In complex organizations having differentiated subsystems with different goals, norms, and orientations, it appeared that intergroup conflict would be an inevitable part of organizational life. The effective achievement of integration through the use of teams and other interpersonal contacts, therefore, would be closely related to the ability of the organization to resolve these conflicts. It was therefore predicted that the use of confrontation as the typical mode of conflict resolution would be an effective integrative procedure. The more confrontation and problem solving that occurred within an organization, the more effective would be its integrative procedures. Although this determinant is the last to be discussed it is not the least important. The differentiated subsystems often have quite different interests and objectives, so that the resolution of conflict between them may well be the most important function of integrative devices.

Limitations of space make it impossible to describe in detail the method used to measure the modes of conflict resolution, but a short description may be useful. The instrument to measure modes of conflict resolution used aphorisms or traditional proverbs, which described various methods of resolving conflict. It was assumed that these modes could be classified into the five types identified by Blake: confrontation, compromise, smoothing, forcing, and withdrawal, and the aphorisms were selected to match these modes (1964). Aphorisms were used, because they represent folk wisdom about useful methods of handling conflict and because they avoided the use of biased phraseology and social science jargon.

Respondents indicated on a five-point scale (from "very typical behavior, usually occurs" to "behavior which never occurs") to what extent each of twenty-five aphorisms described typical ways of handling conflict in their organization. The data were factor analyzed using an orthogonal rotation. Three factors were identified. Factor I described the forcing mode of conflict resolution while factor II described the smoothing mode and factor III described the confrontation mode. No other interpretable factors were present.

The scores for these three factors provide several important findings. Although all organizations used confrontation more than other modes, organizations I and II used confrontation to a significantly greater degree than the other organizations and organizations III and IV used it to a significantly greater extent than organizations V and VI. As predicted, the effectiveness of each organization in achieving integration seemed to be clearly related to the extent that its members relied on problem-solving behavior to resolve conflicts.

These data also provide an interesting additional finding. Organizations IV and VI were doing significantly more smoothing than the other organizations. Organizations III and VI were using significantly less forcing behavior than the other organizations. This, together with the data about smoothing, suggests that a large amount of smoothing behavior or a small amount of forcing behavior can also hinder effective integration. For example, organization VI, with the lowest integration, was not only doing less confrontation than the more effective organizations, but was also doing more smoothing and less forcing. This suggests that while heavy reliance on confrontation to handle conflict is important, it is also important to have a supporting mode of handling conflict which relies on some forcing behavior and a relative absence of smoothing behavior.

Summary   One of the main broad hypotheses of this study was that those organizations with integrative devices that more clearly met the six hypothesized partial determinants would be able to achieve both high integration and high differentiation, and that these in turn would be associated with high performance. All of the data relevant to this general hypothesis have now been presented and are summarized in Table 6. This indicates the extent to which organizations met the conditions for each of the six partial determinants. We have no adequate theory or empirical data at present to guide us in gauging the relative impact of each of these conditions on overall effectiveness of integration, nor on how these conditions affect one another. There certainly is no reason to think they are simply additive. However, the entire configuration of these conditions in relation to our measure of overall integration is highly suggestive of a close causal relationship. Experimental methods will probably be necessary to develop an understanding of these relationships further.

The relation between these six partial determinants and the degree of differentiation is not so clear. One can see by inspection that organizations I and II present patterns that fit the entire sequence of hypothesized relations very closely. They met most of the six conditions, achieved high differentiation as well as high integration, and were the two high companies in total system performance. This suggests that, as predicted, integrative devices that meet the six conditions tend to increase both overall integration and differentiation, which then leads to high performance in this industrial environment.

The data on organizations III and IV suggest that they achieved their medium level of overall performance by emphasizing different states. Organization III was the higher of the two in integration, but did not achieve a very high degree of differentiation. In contrast, organization IV seems to have emphasized achieving a fairly high degree of differentiation at the expense of integration. This kind of a potential exchange is, of course, consistent with our finding that these two states are essentially antagonistic.

The final pair (V and VI) were low in overall performance. Orga-

TABLE 6. SUMMARY OF PARTIAL DETERMINANTS OF EFFECTIVE INTEGRATIVE DEVICES RELATIVE TO DIFFERENTIATION, INTEGRATION, AND PERFORMANCE

Organization	Intermediate position of integrative subsystem*	Influence of integrators derived from technical competence*	Integrators perceive rewards as related to total performance*	High influence throughout the organization*	Influence centered at requisite level*	Modes of conflict resolution	Degree of differentiation	Degree of integration	System performance
I	H	H	M	H	H	H	H (9.4)	H (2.3)	H
II	M	H	H	H	M	H	H (8.7)	H (2.4)	H
III	M	L	H	H	M	L	L (7.5)	H (2.7)	M
IV	M	L	M	H	M	L	H (9.0)	L (2.9)	M
V	L	L	L	L	L	M	H (9.0)	L (3.1)	L
VI	M	L	L	L	L	L	L (6.3)	L (3.3)	L

* H = high, M = medium, L = low; indicates relative extent to which each organization met this condition.

nization V achieved a higher degree of differentiation than is consistent with its failure to meet the six conditions and its level of performance, but its level of integration is consistent with these variables. This, along with the other data, suggests that integration is a better single predictor of performance than differentiation alone. Organization VI presents a pattern that is again consistent with all hypothesized relationships. It failed to meet almost all of the conditions for integrative devices that were predicted to be associated with high integration and differentiation, and is, in fact, the lowest company on both of these scores.

General Conclusions

In initiating this study the researchers wished to make a contribution to the theory of complex organizations based on empirical research. To do this, the study was designed to examine a fairly wide-ranging set of variables on a comparative basis in a set of complex organizations. It was necessary therefore to develop a number of new and relatively crude measures which were used together with established ones. The research strategy was to attempt to relate such diverse variables as environmental characteristics and modes of conflict resolution in a single study, even at the expense of methodological nicety. This strategy made it possible to draw on a wide variety of earlier works to provide theoretical leads that could be tested further. Almost all previous findings, particularly in regard to achieving intergroup integration were given further support.

This study has demonstrated the feasibility and usefulness of simultaneously examining the differentiation and integration of major subsystems in complex organizations. This is of particular importance for future research. It clearly suggests the desirability of studying these phenomena under other environmental conditions to learn more about the relationship between organizational states and different environmental requirements.

This study also has a number of implications for practitioners concerned with administration of complex organizational systems. Increasingly, modern organizations are being expected to cope with heterogeneous environments that have both highly dynamic and quite stable sectors. While the advances of science are increasing the tempo of change in some subsystems the requirements for regularity and standardization remain in others. This continually increases the need for differentiation in organizations; yet the requirements for integration to achieve a unified effort are at least as great as ever. The findings of this study indicate, that, other things being equal, differentiation and integration are essentially antagonistic, and that one can be obtained only at the expense of the other. Modern administrators are very familiar with this issue. They are constantly struggling with the difficulty of reconciling the need for specialization with the need for coordination of effort. But the data also provide some clues to the conditions that seem able to make it possible to achieve high differentiation and high integration simultaneously. These clues, in combination with an emerging methodological capacity to quantify states of differentiation, integration, and environmental attributes, provide concrete direction for the deliberate design of organizations that can cope more effectively with the turbulent environments that science and technology are creating.

Industrial Technology and Worker Integration in the Organization*

MICHAEL FULLAN

Various writers in recent literature have suggested that the type of technology employed in an industrial organization has an important effect on its organizational structure and on the relationship of the worker to his work (Touraine, 1955, 1962; Mann and Hoffman, 1960; Blauner, 1964; Faunce, 1965; Woodward, 1965; and Harvey, 1968). These relationships will be further explored in this paper by examining how industrial workers' integration in the organization varies according to the type of technology characteristic of the organization. By technology I mean the manual and machine operations performed on an object in the process of turning out a final product (Blauner, 1964: 6; Perrow, 1967: 195). Organizational structure refers to the patterns of social interaction involved in the coordination of this work process.

Following the above authors, I identify three basic types of industrial technology: craft, mass, and continuous process production. Briefly defined, the *craft system* is characterized by a production system in which individual workers require a high level of traditional skill for the manipulation of physical materials with tools (Blauner, 1964: 37). *Mass production* has at least four traits: a high degree of repetitiveness in work tasks, minimum skill requirements for workers, standardization of tools and techniques, and minute subdivision of product worked on (Walker and Guest, 1952: 12). Thus, skill is "built into" the machines with the worker performing a few simple operations. *Continuous process* involves the automatic, centralized control of an integrated production system. Production and materials handling are

* Reprinted from *American Sociological Review 35* (December 1970), pp. 1028–1039, with omissions, by permission of the author and the publisher, The American Sociological Association.

done by automatic regulation and remote control of processing units. The worker becomes a monitor of a panel of instruments which control the integrated system.

Past research has concentrated on the relationship between technology and the worker's job tasks (Blauner, 1964) or between technology and organizational structure (Woodward, 1965). The distinctive focus of this paper is the relationship between the worker and the organization as it varies by type of technology. I will argue that factors concomitant with variations in the three types of technology are significantly related to integration of the worker in the organization, with the continuous process worker being most integrated and the mass production worker least integrated. Integration is defined in terms of the extent to which people perceive themselves as isolated or linked together through interaction. It will be examined in five areas: (1) relationship with fellow workers, (2) relationship with first-line supervisors, (3) labor-management relations, (4) the status structure, and (5) evaluation of the company.

Data and Methods

The data are drawn from a large survey of Canadian industrial workers carried out in 1968 for the Task Force on Labour Relations of the Federal Government of Canada (Loubser and Fullan, 1970). The following industries were included in the original study: automobile, chemical, electrical equipment, oil, printing, and steel. The analysis in this paper is based on the printing, automobile, and oil industries which I have selected to represent the craft, mass production, and continuous process systems, respectively.

The sample consists of 1491 Canadian manual industrial workers from twelve plants representing three industries: five printing, two automobile (a car assembly plant, and an engine plant), and five oil. The size of the plants (in terms of total number of employees) ranges from 120 to 1100 within the printing industry, 1400 and 7000 in the automobile industry, and between 80 and 1200 in the oil industry.

The problem of nonresponse in the use of mailed questionnaires is a critical one. In our sample, one possibility is that the level of worker integration in the organization may be lower for nonrespondents. If this is true for nonrespondents in general, it should not affect comparisons across industries. Whatever the case, it is important to emphasize that I do not have a randomly selected sample of industrial workers.

Type of Technology and Integration

In a number of recent studies, there has been an interesting convergence from two different perspectives in the emphasis on investigating firms and industries on the basis of type of technology. One group—

Touraine (1955, 1962), Mann and Hoffman (1960), Blauner (1964)—takes the individual worker as the main point of reference; the other—Woodward (1965), Harvey (1968)—focuses on organizational structure. Although these authors sometimes use different labels and sometimes prefer further subdivisions, the one common aspect of these studies is the characterization of industrial technology roughly into three basic types: craft, mass, and continuous process production.

Although there has been a direct concern with the individual worker in some of the above studies (Blauner, 1964), this has mainly been in terms of the relationship of the worker to his *immediate job.* That is, the emphasis has been on the orientations and attitudes of the worker to the nature of his job tasks—the amount of skill required, control over the pace and quality of work, degree of repetitiveness, etc. No one has yet systematically investigated the relationship of the worker to various aspects of the *organization* as this may vary according to type of technology. I propose to do this in terms of the individual's attitudes toward his fellow workers, his first line supervisor, the labor–management relations, the status structure of the organization and the company. The argument can be most clearly developed by first describing the continuous process systems as a basis for considering the other two systems.

Many authors have suggested that the technology of process industry demands an integrated production system because the production process involves the *continuous* flow of material, not a series of separate operations (Faunce, 1965). This integration of the technical process has very important consequences for the social structure of the organization.

First, process production increases the interdependence of work activities. The tremendous costs of breakdowns and errors require a high degree of individual and collective responsibility (Mann and Hoffman, 1960). Moreover, automated plants tend to be based on small team operations (Blauner, 1964: 143). This collective responsibility and small team production foster the social cohesion of the work group.

A second characteristic of process industry is that the ratio of managers and supervisors to nonsupervisory personnel is lower than in other types of production. More specifically, there is an increase in interaction and communication between supervisory and nonsupervisory personnel. Touraine *et al.* (1965: 45) claim that "the need for the rapid exchange of information increases contacts and communication and calls for close cooperation at all levels." Blauner (1964: 147–148) concurs that in automated production "consultation with supervisors, engineers, chemists and other technical specialists becomes a regular natural part of the job duties." Mann and Hoffman (1960: 64) found in a more automated power plant "an increase in satisfaction with the amount of communication from the top of the plant organization to the non-supervisory employees." In short, the increase in interaction and exchange of information between supervisory and nonsupervisory levels is another factor which contributes to the integration of the worker in the automated system.

A third feature of continuous process technology affecting the structure of the organizational system is that the proportion of labor costs to total costs decreases with level of automation (Woodward, 1965: 53–54). When labor is a small proportion of total costs, paying workers a few cents more an hour or offering greater employee welfare benefits are not major issues. Woodward (1965: 55) found in her study that the ten firms (mostly process) in which labor costs were less than 12.5% of total costs spent the greatest amount per capita on employee welfare and services. There was also a tendency for firms in which labor costs were low to spend more money on the employment of specialists in the personnel management and human relations field. Perhaps this is a reflection of the value placed on integration. In any case, in addition to more cooperative relations between workers and supervisors, industrial relations also seem to be more integrated in process industry.

A fourth factor which affects the integration of the worker in the continuous process organization is the status structure, in particular, the career orientation of the worker (Blauner, 1964: 148 ff.). The typical production worker in the oil refinery enters the organization as a general laborer, and the expectation is that he will progressively move from third operator to second operator and then to head the production team as first operator. Elaborate on-the-job training, including formal courses, is a standard company-sponsored program for all workers in the oil industry. In a word, the institutionalization of mobility increases the integration of the worker in the company.

By way of contrast, there is a distinct lack of integration of the auto worker in the organization due to the extreme subdivision of labor in mass production. First, the conditions of work on the assembly line restrict close social contacts. Noise level may be high. The constant speed of the line requires close attention in order to keep up. Physical mobility is also restricted. On the whole, the technology of the assembly line does not require functionally interdependent work groups, and in fact inhibits the formation of close knit social units. In Blauner's words "on an assembly line a worker may be able to talk with the men on both sides and those across from his work station, but each man is in contact with a different set of workers" (Blauner, 1964: 114; also Walker and Guest, 1952, Ch. V).

Conveyor-belt technology also deters social interaction between the worker and supervisor. The fixed nature of the line and the extreme standardization of tasks reduce the need for interaction or exchange of information between worker and supervisor. In a sense, supervision to a large extent is built into the technology. The day-today contacts between worker and supervisor that do occur usually take the form of downward directives rather than exchanges of information. Besides a loose relationship with his immediate foreman, the auto worker has virtually no contact with higher level supervisors in the organization (Walker and Guest, 1952: Ch. VII). This low degree of interaction between worker and supervisors in the auto industry contributes to the worker's sense of an impersonal, i.e., unintegrated relationship to the organization (Walker and Guest, 1952: Ch. VII).

The third area of difference between process and mass production industries is related to the proportional costs of labor. Volume in mass production depends on a large labor force. Consequently, wages, welfare services to employees, etc., are very important cost factors for management. The U.A.W. has been an effective agent for workers' interests, particularly in attaining relatively high wages. Labor–management relations in the auto industry have been more a power struggle and rule-making affair than in the oil industry. In this atmosphere workers are less likely to feel a sense of integration with the organization.

The status structure, in particular the "massified" wage and skill distribution in the auto industry, is a final element contributing to the worker's lack of identification with the organization (Blauner, 1964: 112–113). The extensive subdivision of labor and the standardization of tasks in assembly line production have resulted in low wage and skill distribution among workers. The maximum wage spread, including virtually all production jobs, is only about 15 cents an hour. Thus there are few better jobs for the manual worker to aspire to in the auto industry and no natural progression from one job to another as is the case in the oil industry. The relatively undifferentiated status structure of mass production systems is another aspect of the "depersonalization" and the lack of social integration of the production worker in the auto industry.

Oil and auto workers should be highest and lowest, respectively, on degree of integration at the various levels of organization just discussed. Workers in the printing industry should fall in between—they should be closer to oil workers than auto workers.

Printers will be less likely than oil workers to identify with the organization, because the technology of the organization does not require close functional relationships. First, the "made to orderness" of the product and the functional autonomy of the work do not require a high degree of interdependence between workers. Unlike the auto industry, however, social contacts are not *inhibited* by work arrangements.

Printers as craftsmen have a high degree of autonomy regarding standards of workmanship for carrying out their tasks. Consequently, there is little need for close interaction with foremen. Blauner (1964: 43) reports that "craftsmen with their strong sense of independence and dignity, resent close supervision and are likely to resist it more militantly and successfully than other manual workers." On the other hand, foremen are often the most experienced journeymen and respected for their expertise. In short, the relationship between craftsmen and foremen may be one of mutual respect.

Labor costs are high in the printing industry, but the union's craft orientation and pride in the quality of work of its members provide more of a bond with management than would be the case in mass production systems. This is not to say that issues of wages are not hard fought over. Moreover, mechanization has been a bone of contention between the union and management in recent years.

Finally, formal apprenticeship leading to journeyman status builds a certain level of status advancement into the system. This is more likely to endear the occupation and the union to the worker rather than the organization. For one thing, the large number of firms in the printing industry provides many alternative sources of employment to the printer, whose skills are readily transferable from firm to firm (Blauner, 1964: 48). Strong identification with any particular employer is less likely under these conditions.

In conclusion, the argument is that technology influences the type of relationship that a worker has with the organization. The main hypothesis is that the level of integration of the worker in the organization will be highest for oil workers, followed by printers, and lowest for automobile workers.

Findings

Five aspects of worker integration in the organization are examined: relationship with fellow workers, relationship with first line supervisors, labor–management relations, the status structure, and evaluation of the company.

Work Group Integration with fellow workers is partly a function of structural conduciveness of social arrangements. Workers who have to work with others in the course of their tasks and who have time to talk with fellow workers on the job have more opportunity to develop cohesive work group attachments. Similarly, the smaller the work group, the more opportunity for close social relations. The more these structural conditions obtain, the more likely a worker will identify with his work unit.

The data on these matters, by industry, are as follows. We asked respondents how much contact they had with other workers on the job. We found that oil workers were much less inclined to say that they worked alone than workers in the other industries. Only 9% of the oil workers saw themselves as working alone compared to 49% and 44% of printers and auto workers, respectively (Cramer's $V =$

.275). This confirms our impression that working with others on the job is the predominant social arrangement in oil refining. In the other industries, auto workers are slightly less likely than printers to say that they work alone. This may be partly a function of the continuous nature of the assembly line with workers in physical proximity to each other. While such a configuration may mean more contacts with others, I suggest that these contacts will be more superficial in nature and hence will less often develop into close-knit groupings.

Another structural condition concerns whether or not workers have time to talk with other men on the job. Here the results more closely follow the expected order. Only 6% of the oil workers have little time or no time to talk with others on the job, compared to 18% of the printers, and 43% of the auto workers ($V = .356$). Clearly then, oil workers have much more of an opportunity to socialize on the job than auto workers.

A third element that will probably influence the degree of integration with fellow workers is the size of the work group. As expected, oil workers tend to specify small work units, and auto workers large work groups. Forty-six percent of the oil workers who said that they were in a work group report that the size of the work group consists of only two to four people. Printers at 28% and auto workers at 22% are much less likely to report work groups this size. At the other extreme, mass production workers are more likely to report work groups of greater than 15 people.

Identification with one's work group should reflect these varying work conditions. In fact, 90% of the oil workers, compared to 74% of the printers and 72% of the auto workers, feel that they are really a part of the work group ($V = .201$). Although in the expected direction, these differences are not very large.

Similar results are obtained when we look at responses of workers who say that their work groups are very competitive ($V = .144$). Only 4% of the oil workers give this response, followed by printers at 7%, and auto workers at 18%.

Comparing the extremes, we note that social arrangements in the oil industry are more conducive to contacts with fellow workers than is the situation in automobile manufacturing, although the last two measures of identification with one's work group did not show very large industry differences.

Supervision   One of the most important structural indicators of the frequency and type of worker–supervisor relations is the ratio of non-supervisors to supervisory personnel (Woodward, 1965). The lower the ratio, the more contact that workers have with supervisors, the greater the two-way communication and hence the greater the integration between workers and supervisors. To test these ideas in our sample, I will examine worker–supervisor ratios in each industry, the type of communication from the foremen, and the overall evaluation of the foreman.

The automobile industry, as we expected, has the highest ratio of manual workers to supervisors (23.1 direct production and skilled maintenance workers to one supervisor). Printing has the next highest (8.2 to one). In the oil industry, the ratio of 2.6 workers for every supervisor reflects earlier findings about continuous process systems.

I also suggested above that one-way downward communication (commands) would not be functional for integration and that continuous process technology seems to require more two-way communication between worker and supervisor than the other technologies. A question on whether the foreman tells, asks, or explains to the worker when he wants something done provides some information on this issue. First, auto workers are most likely to receive direct commands (tells) and oil workers least likely (50% versus 36%, respectively). Second, oil workers are twice as likely as other workers to say that their foreman explains to them what he wants done (35% versus 18% in each of the other two industries).

Overall evaluation of foreman should also reflect differences in identification with first-line supervisors. Sixty-one percent of the auto workers have a low evaluation of their foreman, compared to 53% of the printers, and 49% of the oil workers ($V = .096$).

Another item which refers more directly to the aspect of communication upward asks how much influence the worker has on how the plant is run. Only 14% of the oil workers say they have no influence, compared to 26% printers and 31% auto workers ($V = .140$).

Finally, in the organization that has greater integration at all levels, we would expect the foreman to have more say in how the firm is run. We have these data from the manual worker's perspective. Sixty-eight percent of the auto sample say that their foreman has little or no say, while 37% printers and 32% oil workers give this response ($V = .221$). A marked difference thus occurs between auto workers and the others.

Labor–Management Relations Labor–management relations is another important facet of organizational integration. Conflict is likely an indication of lack of integration (Faunce, 1968: 9). One obvious measure of conflict is the number and length of strikes or walkouts in the firm in the past five years. During the last five years, the auto assembly plant experienced walkouts or strikes on seven occasions lasting a total of 33 days. Two of these occurred during the only two occasions of contract negotiations in this five-year period. The auto engine plant, also represented by the U.A.W., was on strike during the two periods of contract negotiations. By contrast, only two of the five oil refineries experienced strikes (one each) during the past five years. None of the four printing firms on which we have data reported strikes.

This may be partly due to the rapport that the International Typographical Union has established over the years with management. In short, the automobile plants experienced more strikes than the others.

Kerr and Siegel (1954: 212) in their well-known study on inter-industry propensity to strike also classified the auto industry in the United States as high on propensity to strike. The oil industry was classified as medium; and printing, as low.

The number of strikes or walkouts obviously does not tell the whole story of labor–management relations. In an attempt to ascertain the manual worker's general impression of labor–management relations in the firm, we asked respondents simply whether they saw these relations mainly marked by conflict or cooperation. The results confirm our predictions. Auto workers (59%) are substantially more likely to report a conflict atmosphere than oil workers (26%) and printers (19%).

Another item which asks respondents whether they have to "fight" for what they get in the company strongly supports the view that conflict is greater in the auto industry. Seventy-three percent of the auto workers say that they usually have to fight for what they get, while only 32% each of the oil and printing workers give this response ($V = .325$).

Status Structure   The one aspect of status structure that seems most relevant to integration is the possibility for career advancement. If workers perceive good chances for promotion, they are more likely to develop a career orientation and identification with the firm. I have already argued that this institutionalization of mobility is mainly evident in the oil industry. In the other industries, it is only present to a limited extent in the apprenticeship training of printers. Manual workers in the three industries were asked to describe their chances for promotion as good, fair, or poor. Twenty-six percent of the oil workers say that their chances for promotion are good, compared to 14% of the printers and 18% of the auto workers ($V = .130$). At the other end of the scale, only 39% of the oil workers say that their chances are poor, while 60% of the printers and 56% of the auto workers feel that their chances are poor. This is an aspect of integration that apparently only operates in the oil industry.

The Company   The underlying theme in the previous sections is that certain aspects of work conditions facilitate integration of the worker in the organization. The overall measure of integration is the worker's identification with or evaluation of the company. Five items were identified by factor analysis as referring to evaluation of the company. The five questions refer to whether the company is better or worse than most places to work; whether the company is more interested in cutting costs than in its people; whether employees have to fight for what they get in the company; how well the firm is managed; and how satisfied the respondent is with the amount of information he gets about what is going on in the company. These items were combined to form an index of company evaluation.

An examination of the variations by industry on the index of company evaluation substantially confirms the main hypothesis. Seventy percent of the oil workers and 65% of the printers score high on the index of company evaluation while only 32% of the auto workers score this way.

The data analysis so far combines all workers in each industry. Since the proportion of production and skilled maintenance workers differs by technology, I examined these categories of workers separately to see if there were important intraindustry differences. There were no large differences. Both oil maintenance and oil production workers are substantially higher on level of integration than auto maintenance and auto production workers.

In order to consider the possible effects of other variables on the above relationships, it is necessary to control for a number of other factors. Three work related factors—size of firm, length of time with the company, and unionization—and three prejob factors—age, education, and place of birth—were selected as possibly influencing the level of integration of workers in the organization. In examining these variables, I will use the index of company evaluation as the best single indicator of integration in the organization.

Size (total number of employees) is so closely related to type of technology that Blauner (1964: 109) considers it as part and parcel of the technology of the assembly line. In this sense, size is not a control factor, but rather is an aspect of technology. I would tend to agree with this position, but, since there is some variance in size within industries in our sample, it is worthwhile considering this factor as it relates to the index of company evaluation.

There is no systematic relationship between size and tendency to score positive on the index of company evaluation. In fact, the larger firms tend to have larger proportions scoring positive on this index. The only exception to this is in the auto industry where 27% in the car assembly plant ($N = 7000$) score positive on the index of company evaluation, compared to 50% in the engine plant ($N = 1400$). I suggest that this difference may be related to technology differences as well as to size, because in the car assembly plant nearly all production workers work on the assembly line (which greatly inhibits integration), while in the engine plant many workers operate comparatively automated machinery.

There are two aspects of length of time with the company that I would like to consider: (1) the possibility that it may be another indicator of integration in the organization; (2) even controlling for length of time with the company, integration should be much higher in the oil industry than in the auto industry.

If the organization inhibits integration of the worker, we would expect higher turnover rates, and a consequent smaller proportion of workers who have been with the company for a long time. The average turnover rate per annum during the last three years for production workers in the auto assembly plant (reported by the company) is 15%. In the auto engine plant it is 16.5%. By contrast, only one of the five oil refineries reports a turnover figure above 12.5%. The largest oil refinery reports an average turnover rate of 2.3%. Figures for the other refineries are 2.1%, 7.2%, 12.5%, and 27%. We have turnover rates for only two of the five printing firms: 10.3% and 11.5%. The main point is that the auto plants included in this study report higher turnover rates, in general, than the oil refineries.

The proportion of workers who have been with the company a long time should reflect turnover rates. Here we find that 69% of the oil workers in the achieved sample have been with the company over 15 years, compared to 34% of the printers, and 20% of the auto workers.

The second question asks if these differences in length of time with the company account for industry differences in worker integration. They do not. Regardless of length of time with the company, auto workers are lowest by far on company evaluation.

Unionization cannot be strictly controlled for because all auto workers are unionized. Comparing the other two industries, we see a striking difference on company evaluation between the unionized and nonunionized firms. Only 50% of the unionized printers score positive on the company index, compared to 81% of the nonunionized printers. Similarly, 57% of the unionized oil workers, compared to 77% of the nonunionized, are positive toward the company. There would seem to be at least two reasons why the presence of a union would inhibit integration of the worker in the organization. First, the union competes with the company for the loyalty of the worker. Lipset et al. (1962), for instance, analyze in some detail what they call the occupational community of printers which is fostered by the union and which inhibits strong identification with the organization. A second reason why the union might hinder integration is that it may articulate or crystallize an anticompany philosophy.

We have seen that unionized printers and oil workers are much lower on company evaluation than their nonunionized counterparts. However, expected interindustry differences remain among the unionized workers in the three industries. The rank order of industries on the company index corresponds to the main hypothesis. Unionized oil workers have 57% who score positive on the company index, followed by unionized printers at 50% and unionized auto workers at 32% ($V = .234$).

Finally, age, education, and whether the respondent was born in Canada were controlled for. The strength of the association between industry and company evaluation was about the same for each control category.

The examination of the above control factors gives us more confidence that we have observed real interindustry differences. Of course, this does not rule out the possibility that other unmeasured factors account for the findings.

Discussion

There is no claim in this paper that technology is the only determinant of worker integration in the organization. That plants within the same industry can have radically different levels of integration dispels this notion. The evidence presented, however, suggests that technology is one of the important factors which at least facilitates or inhibits worker integration in the organization.

The findings can only be taken as suggestive for further research because type of technology was not directly measured. Rather, certain industries were selected on the basis of their approximation to the basic types of technology. There are a number of possible problems here. First, the fit between the ideal type of technology and the industry selected to represent it was not satisfactory in every case. The most obvious discrepancy was the selection of the printing industry to represent the craft system. Furthermore, it was not possible to separate the effects of industry from those of technology since only one industry represented each technology. A study of a number of industries employing similar technologies would be an important step in sorting out some of the effects of these two variables.

A second basic question is whether the typology of technologies can be readily applied to the wide range of industrial settings in our society. Most industries are not as technologically homogeneous as the auto and oil industries. It is probable that most industrial manufacturing employs a mixture of the technological types. Is the threefold typology useful for studying heterogeneous systems? What seems to be required in future research is the further specification of types of technology and their application to a wide range of industries, perhaps using a more precise definition of technology such as level of mechanization.

If technology does influence worker integration, this would have important implications for the study of at least two central problems in the field of industrial sociology, namely, worker receptivity to industrial change and alienation from work.

On the first point Faunce (1968: 9) has stated that the degree of social integration "refers to the extent to which role definitions either isolate people from each other and bring them into conflict, or link them together in conflict-free interaction." Lower degrees of conflict between workers and management could provide a more conducive atmosphere for the introduction and acceptance of industrial changes. In other analyses on the same data, we did find that the more integrated workers in each industry had more positive attitudes toward specific changes which had occurred in their company and were more likely to score high on an index of general evaluation of technological change (Fullan, 1969).

There is, of course, considerable evidence that technology directly effects the degree of alienation from the job (Blauner, 1964). There is also some evidence that social integration can mitigate the effects of objectively alienating work. Blauner (1964: 75) found this to be the case among textile workers. Blum (1953) in his study of a meat packing plant found that integration in the organization lessened the impact of work which was objectively highly alienating (see also Kornhauser, 1965: 180–182). In our own work this may be true for oil workers, who despite the fact that certain aspects of their work are potentially alienating (e.g., the lack of control over the work process), score lowest on an index measuring the degree of subjectively experienced alienation (Fullan, 1969: 134). On the other hand, it does seem plausible that high alienation from the job inhibits integration. There is no doubt a reciprocal relationship between the two factors, and this should be investigated more systematically in future research.

In the meantime, the aim of this paper has been to explore the role of technology as it relates to various aspects of the integration of workers in three types of industrial organizations. The findings point to the desirability of further utilizing and developing the comparative framework of technologies which should lead to much more systematic and fruitful research, not only on integration of workers but also on the whole complex relationship of man to his job and to the work organization.

Organization Structure and Communications*

**JERALD HAGE, MICHAEL AIKEN, and
CORA BAGLEY MARRETT**

In a few insightful pages March and Simon (1958: 158–169) suggest that there are two basic ways in which organizations can be coordinated: feedback and plan. Coordination is here defined as the degree to which there are adequate linkages among organizational parts, i.e., specific task roles as well as subunits of the organization so that organizational objectives can be accomplished (cf. James Thompson, 1967). Coordination by plan is based on preestablished schedules while coordination by feedback involves the transmission of new information. Building on the work of March and Simon, James Thompson (1967) discusses three types of coordination: standardization, plan, and mutual adjustment, although the first appears to be an aspect of coordination through planning. The point here is that there seem to be two major types of linkage mechanisms in organizations: linkages through preestablished rules, routines, blueprints, or schedules (coordination by standardization, plan, programming) and linkages through the transmission of new information (coordination by feedback or mutual adjustment). The basic question with each type of coordination is concerned with how a variety of task roles and/or organizational subunits are articulated into a coherent whole so that organizational objectives can be accomplished.

In a different context, Parsons (1951) has noted that social control over individuals can be maintained either by socialization or by sanctions. In the application of these ideas to professional organizations, Blau and Scott (1962) noted that professionals conform to organizational norms either because of peer pressures or because of certain rewards and punishments. Social control, however, is not the same as coordination; the first refers to the adequacy of achieving conformity with expectations of behavior and standards of work while the latter refers to the method by which task roles are articulated together to accomplish a given set of tasks. At the same time, there does seem to be some consistency between these ideas; i.e., coordination through planning or programming is more likely to imply use of sanctions to achieve social control; coordination through feedback is more likely to rely on socialization. Of course, we do not want to suggest that there is an identity here, since there are many other mechanisms of social control such as performance records, reliance on hierarchy, or recruitment practices that are also used to insure predictability of performance in organizations.

* Reprinted from *American Sociological Review, 36* (October 1971), pp. 860–871, with omissions, by permission of the authors and the publisher, The American Sociological Association.

TABLE 1.   PREMISES AND HYPOTHESES ABOUT ORGANIZATIONAL CONTROL

Premises

    I. All organizations need coordination.

   II. There are two basic mechanisms for achieving coordination. Programming with emphasis on sanctions and feedback with emphasis on socialization.

  III. The greater the diversity of organizational structure, the greater the emphasis on coordination through feedback.

  IV. The greater the differences in status and power in an organization, the greater the emphasis on coordination through planning.

Derived Hypotheses

  1. The greater the degree of complexity, the greater the rate of task communications.

  2. The greater the degree of complexity, the greater the proportion of horizontal task communication.

  3. The greater the degree of formalization, the less the rate of task communications.

  4. The greater the degree of formalization, the higher the proportion of vertical task communication.

  5. The greater the degree of centralization, the less the rate of task communication.

  6. The greater the degree of centralization, the higher the proportion of vertical task communication.

Both feedback and programming involve the articulation of a variety of task jobs and their occupants in a division of labor in which each fulfills his respective tasks. Both mechanisms are intended to achieve the same result—the integration of the task roles, but the question remains as to how this is accomplished. Implicit in all of these writings is the premise that all organizations need coordination. This becomes our first assumption in our theory of organizational structure and communications. (See Table 1.)

Our second assumption, following March and Simon (1958) and James Thompson (1967) is that coordination can be achieved in two basic ways. First, the activities of each job occupant can be programmed and then a system of rewards and punishments can be utilized to insure conformity to the basic organizational scheme. A clear blueprint of action would make departures from the plan immediately obvious, and a system of rewards would provide the muscle or force behind the basic plan. Standards would leave little ambiguity about whom to punish and whom to reward (whichever the case might be). Second, organizations can rely more upon continuous flows of information (feedback or mutual adjustment) as a method for coordinating the organization. Under this system, errors, when detected, are often seen as a problem of improper socialization or training; one method of correcting this situation is through the provision of new information. Also, implied in this approach is that pressure comes not so much from formal sanctions, in the strict sense of the term, but more from peer pressures and inner standards of quality that have been developed through socialization. The first approach relies upon external control, whereas the latter is more concerned with internal control, or what is called self-control.

Thus, two basic processes to achieve coordination can be distinguished: feedback and programming. In practice, most organizations would use some mixture of the two mechanisms. For us, the most interesting, as well as most important question is the specification of the organizational circumstances under which one or the other of these two mechanisms will be emphasized. March and Simon (1958) provide no suggestions about the structural concomitants of these mechanisms of coordination, although they do suggest that the uncertainty of the task may affect the choice, but Thompson (1967) does suggest some structural concomitants of various types of interdependencies and coordination. The internal structure of an organization should have an important relationship to the form of coordination that is most dominant, and hence, to the way in which communications are designed.

We assume that there are two major structural factors that affect the patterns of internal verbal communication: diversity and the distribution of power and status. These are basic axes of organization structure that Victor Thompson (1961) and others have noted. As the diversity of an organization increases, it becomes more difficult to plan a successful blueprint for the organization. As the variety of tasks in an organization increases, the number of potential connections among parts increase even more rapidly; the articulation of organizational parts by a set of predetermined rules becomes more complicated; and the application of sanctions becomes more difficult because each of the jobs may require a different set of standards. The decision-makers in such organizations are likely to be forced to rely more upon feedback mechanisms than upon rigidly programmed mechanisms of communication. This whole process is further enhanced if the nature of most jobs in the structure is very complex and involves a variety of activities, which is often the case with professionals. This should affect the intensity of feedback. Here it should be noted that we are suggesting that the variety of tasks, in addition to the degree of uncertainty, is an important determinant of the degree of communications (March and Simon, 1958; James Thompson, 1967; Perrow, 1967; Hage and Aiken, 1969).

In addition, great differences in power and status among job occupants in an organization are likely to inhibit the rate of feedback communications. As social distance between organizational levels increases, the free flow of information is reduced (Barnard, 1964).

Similarly, the threat of sanctions from the top discourages the frank discussion of problems and, therefore, organizational decision-makers are unlikely to learn of problems until a crisis has developed, as Blau and Scott (1962) have suggested and as Barnard (1964) explicitly argued.

The degree of organizational diversity propels the organization toward attempts to coordinate through information feedback while status and power differences propel the organization toward attempts to coordinate through programming. Together they influence the probabilities of the adoption of either programming or feedback, or more precisely the particular combination, since each of these factors can be operative at the same time. We assume that organizational elites attempt to program some interaction in the form of regular reports. Even where they have made a conscious decision to rely only upon a feedback mechanism of coordination, there will always be some feeble attempts to rationalize parts of the organization. What is critical here is the differential emphasis on coordination through feedback and coordination through planning or blueprints.

A number of testable hypotheses can be deduced from our theoretical framework but, before discussing some of them, we should note that feedback is itself an involved and complicated concept. For us, the simplest way of understanding feedback is to see it as a high volume of task communication, that is, the communication of information relevant to the work of the organization. One would not want to include gossip, rumors, jokes, and other forms of expressive communication. In addition, feedback carries the notion that it is information coming from different parts of the organization. Thus direction, as well as volume, is a critical factor. Traditionally, the literature has tended to distinguish between the sheer rate of communication and its direction. The latter is frequently broken down into horizontal and vertical communication (Landsberger, 1961; Guetzkow, 1965; Price, 1967). For these reasons, the volume of task communication and the direction of task communication become two excellent derivations from the broader idea of feedback.

Diversity of organizational structure can be interpreted in a variety of ways. For us, the major idea is the complexity of occupations, that is, their sheer number. The idea here is that of personal specialization as contrasted to the microdivision of labor implied by task specialization (Victor Thompson, 1961). A secondary idea is that as occupations become more complex, that is, more professional, one can say that the organizational structure is more diverse. This leads to the following hypotheses:

1. *The greater the degree of complexity, the greater the rate of task communications.*

2. *The greater the degree of complexity, the greater the proportion of horizontal task communications.*

The key idea here is that greater diversity of occupations internally as well as greater professional activism among the incumbents of these roles is likely to mean greater reciprocal interdependence, and thus coordination through feedback, which should be reflected in a greater volume of communications overall as well as heightened horizontal communications.

The concept of programming can be caught by the idea of formalization, that is, the importance of job descriptions and the specificity of their content. If our reasoning is correct, a formalized set of jobs should reduce the need for communications between the different parts of the organization. This supplies two additional hypotheses:

3. *The greater the degree of formalization, the less the rate of task communications.*

4. *The greater the degree of formalization, the higher the proportion of vertical task communication.*

Social distance is created by concentration of power (or centralization) in an organization. There is less need for feedback when power is concentrated at the top of the organization hierarchy, since the role of subordinates is to implement decisions rather than to participate in the shaping of those decisions. Therefore, as the concentration of power becomes greater, and consequently as the degree of participation becomes less, we would expect inhibitions on communications in an organization (Crozier, 1964; Ronken and Lawrence, 1952). Therefore, the following hypotheses are additionally suggested:

5. *The greater the degree of centralization, the less the rate of task communication.*

6. *The greater the degree of centralization, the higher the proportion of vertical task communication.*

One could logically derive hypotheses regarding the relationship between frequency of communication and the degree of stratification, but since we did not measure this variable, we do not include such hypotheses here.

Findings

Complexity and Communication   Two measures of organizational complexity are used—the number of occupational specialties and the

TABLE 2. PEARSONIAN CORRELATION COEFFICIENT BETWEEN INDICATORS OF COMPLEXITY, FORMALIZATION, CENTRALIZATION, STRATIFICATION, SIZE, AND ECOLOGICAL SPREAD AND MEASURES OF SCHEDULED AND UNSCHEDULED COMMUNICATIONS AMONG SIXTEEN HEALTH AND WELFARE ORGANIZATIONS

1.	2.	3.	4.	5.	6.	7.	8.	9.	10.	11.
	Complexity			Formalization		Centralization		Stratification	Size	Ecological spread
Scheduled Communications										
A. Organization-wide Committee Meetings										
1. Average number attended per month	.66***	.32	.48*	−.30	−.31	.60**	.10	−.31	.34	.50*
2. Proportion of staff involved	.31	.20	.14	−.40	−.29	.61**	.03	−.39	.16	.41
B. Departmental Meetings										
1. Average number attended per month	.20	.25	.00	−.09	−.57**	.45*	−.39	−.06	.04	.62**
2. Proportion of staff involved	.13	.30	.07	−.06	−.30	.37	−.09	−.42	−.01	.23
Unscheduled Communications										
C. Frequency of Communications										
1. Interdepartmental, higher level	.34	.52*	−.07	−.41	−.08	.51*	.33	−.62**	.07	.23
2. Interdepartmental, same level	.67***	.62**	.40	−.61**	−.20	.53**	.19	−.57**	.37	.39
3. Interdepartmental, lower level	.40	.19	.05	−.45*	−.42	.42	−.26	.00	.28	.45*

TABLE 2. (Continued)

1.	2.	3.	4.	5.	6.	7.	8.	9.	10.	11.
	Complexity			Formalization		Centralization		Stratification	Size	Eco-logical spread
4. Intradepartmental, higher level	.29	.26	.22	−.15	.28	.18	.52*	−.53**	.16	−.26
5. Intradepartmental, same level	−.04	−.36	.01	.15	.30	−.36	−.03	.19	.12	−.22
6. Intradepartmental, lower level	−.19	−.31	−.28	−.52*	−.34	−.24	−.47*	.47*	−.08	.07
7. All unscheduled communications	.51**	.42	.28	−.50*	−.12	.36	.00	−.42	.44*	.19
D. Proportion of Communications										
1. Interdepartmental, higher level	.20	.40	−.19	−.19	−.14	.49*	.27	−.42	−.13	.36
2. Interdepartmental, same level	.48*	.46*	.48*	−.30	.06	.39	.37	−.52*	.18	.30
3. Interdepartmental, lower level	.25	.17	.30	−.04	.00	.22	−.06	−.22	.27	.10
4. Intradepartmental, higher level	.00	−.23	.12	.33	.42	−.12	.30	.02	.15	−.29
5. Intradepartmental, same level	−.42	−.72***	−.08	.46*	.47*	−.62*	−.10	.59**	−.01	−.37
6. Intradepartmental, lower level	−.22	.09	−.37	−.23	−.54**	−.08	−.42	.20	−.27	.03

* P .10; ** P .05; *** P .01.

Indicators of complexity
Col. 2. Number of occupational specialties
Col. 3. Professional activity
Col. 4. Number of departments

Indicators of formalization
Col. 5. Presence of job specifications
Col. 6. Index of job specificity
Indicators of centralization
Col. 7. Index of participation in decision-making

Col. 8. Index of hierarchy of authority
Indicator of stratification
Col. 9. Proportion of non-supervisory profess. staff
Organizational size (Rank order): Col. 10.
Ecological spread: Col. 11.

377

degree of professional activity. The first is simply the number of specific occupational specialties that exist in each organization. The second reflects the degree to which staff members are active in professional activities outside the organization. The first two empirical hypotheses are that the intensity of communications will vary directly with the number of occupational specialties and the degree of professional activity and that these factors are most likely to be associated with communications in a horizontal direction. Looking just at the relationships between occupational diversity and the intensity of communication, we note that the more diversified the occupational structure of an organization, the higher the intensity of overall unscheduled communications ($r = .51$) and the greater the involvement in organization-wide committees ($r = .66$) as shown in Panels C7 and A1 of Column (1), Table 2. The relationship between the diversity of the occupational structure and the frequency of attending departmental meetings is in the predicted direction, but quite weak as shown in Panel B1, Column (1) ($r = .20$), indicating that while complexity is positively associated with the overall rate of scheduled communications, it is more strongly associated with horizontal communications, namely organization-wide committee meetings, than with vertical communications, i.e., departmental meetings.

Professionalism was measured by the degree to which staff members were involved in professional associations, including number of associations, frequency of attendance, number of offices held, and number of papers given. This measure has weak relationships with most of the intensity of communications measures, although each is in the predicted direction; in the case of the intensity of overall unscheduled communications, the relationship is quite high as shown in Panel C7, Column (2) of Table 2 ($r = .42$).

To the extent that organization-wide committee meetings provide opportunities for horizontal communications, the second hypothesis above is supported. However, it requires some interpretation. Horizontal communications, as suggested earlier, can mean at least two things. First, it can simply mean communications across departmental boundaries. But second, it can mean communications with someone at the same status level, regardless of whether the communication is in the same or a different department. If we ask, however, whether such interdepartmental interactions are with someone at the same level, at a higher level, or at a lower level, we find that the frequency of such interdepartmental communications is greatest with others at the same status level for both the number of occupational levels ($r = .67$) and for the degree of professional activity ($r = .62$), although there is some suggestion that it can also be upward ($r = .34$ and $.52$, respectively) in other departments as well.

The conclusion we reach is that complexity—as measured both by the number of occupational specialties and professional activism

—tends to be positively associated with the intensity of organizational communications, both organization-wide committees as well as all unscheduled communications. Looking more closely at this latter relationship, however, we find that it is the flow of communications with people *on the same status level in different departments* that is most highly associated with these two measures of complexity. Horizontal relationships with people in the same department are actually inversely related to the two measures of complexity. Thus, the word horizontal in our hypothesis should be modified to mean interdepartmental communications with persons on the same status level. However, this is exactly the intent of our original premise regarding the meaning of feedback. In particular, communication between departments is more likely to be of this kind. Regardless of this interpretation, it is clear that the volume of communications is higher in more complex organizations; and this is especially true of communications between departments, both scheduled and unscheduled.

Formalization and Communication The measures of formalization included here are, first, the degree to which respondents reported there is a complete job description for their job, and secondly, the degree of job specificity. The latter measure was an index which included a number of additional items reflecting the programming of jobs such as the existence of specific procedures for various contingencies, written records of job performance, and well-defined communication channels. The hypothesis here is that the greater the degree of formalization, the lower the rate of communications, and second, the direction is likely to be upward and downward within the same department, not between departments.

   In general, we find that the correlations between formalization and measures of both the scheduled and unscheduled communications are not as strong as those between measures of complexity and communication rates. The existence of job descriptions tends to be negatively associated with the average frequency of participation on organization committees ($r = -.30$), as shown in Panels A1 and A2, Column (3) of Table 1. The existence of job descriptions has no relationship with the intensity of participation in departmental meetings, however. Job specificity also has weak negative relationships with these same measures of communications. On the other hand, job specificity has a strong negative relationship with the frequency of attending departmental meetings, meaning that the greater the degree to which jobs are programmed, the less frequently staff members attend departmental meetings, which reflects in part that there are fewer departmental meetings in such organizations. The greater the degree to which there are job descriptions in an organization, the fewer overall unscheduled interactions there are ($r = -.50$), although there is no relationship between job specificity and this measure of communication $(r = -.12)$. The small size of these correlations, especially between the measures of formalization and scheduled communication, may reflect that we have poor measures of the degree of planning of the work flow. Both of our measures are specific to individual tasks, and neither reflects the degree of programming or coordination. This may explain why our measures work better with unscheduled communication than scheduled communication since unscheduled communications are more likely to reflect discussions about particular jobs than organization-wide coordination.

Looking more closely at the categories of unscheduled communication, we see that the presence of job descriptions is negatively related to the frequency of interaction in each category with the exception of communications on the same status level within the same department. The presence of job descriptions is especially strongly related (in a negative direction) in the case of communications between individuals at the same status level in different departments $(r = -.61)$. Similarly, job specificity tends to affect the frequency of communications, although there are positive relationships between intradepartmental communications with superiors and colleagues on the same status level.

Centralization and Communication   The measure of centralization utilized here is the Index of Participation in Decision-making. It reflects the degree to which organizational members report participating in decisions about the hiring of personnel, the promotion of personnel, the adoption of new organizational policies, and the adoption of new programs or services. A high score on this measure reflects the degree to which strategic organizational decisions, in contrast to decisions about work assignments and the like, are decentralized. Conversely, a low score on this measure means that there is a high degree of centralization in such organizations. Our hypotheses are that participation in decision-making is positively related to the intensity of communications and that there are more horizontal communications in such organizations.

The degree of participation in these strategic organizational decisions was found to have strong positive relationships with the frequency of communications (see Column (5), Table 1). There is a strong positive relationship between the degree of participation in these strategic organization decisions and the frequency of attending both committee meetings $(r = .60)$ and departmental meetings $(r = .45)$. The relationship between participation in these decisions and the frequency of unscheduled interactions is in the predicted direction $(r = .36)$, but not strong.

Looking more closely at the relationship between the index of participation in decision-making and each category of unscheduled interaction, we note first that organizations with wide participation in decision-making have a higher degree of interdepartmental communication. This is true for information flows upward, on the same level, and downward ($r = .51$, $.53$, and $.42$, respectively). In decentralized organizations, there is greater interdepartmental communications in all directions—i.e., at a higher level, the same level, and at a lower level in the chain of command and this is generally true for staff members on all organizational levels. In decentralized organizations, there are fewer intradepartmental communications on the same level and downward.

Discussion

Together these findings suggest the following story about the patterns of communications within organizations. As organizational structure becomes more diversified and, in particular, as personal specialization increases, the volume of communication increases because of the necessity of coordinating the diverse occupational specialists. The major direction of this increased flow of information is horizontal, especially cross-departmental communications at the same status levels. In this sense, committee meetings represent a greater emphasis on horizontal information flows than do department meetings because the former involve other departments. But there is also an increased horizontal flow of unscheduled task communication. Conversely, insofar as organizational leaders attempt to coordinate the organization via programming as reflected in job descriptions and specified task procedures, the necessity for interaction declines. The interaction that exists is probably concerned with the interpretation of a particular regulation. Concomitantly, if power is dispersed in the organization, not only does the volume of communication increase, but the flow of communications across departmental boundaries is also increased. Similarly, organization-wide committees and department meetings, both scheduled mechanisms of interaction, are likely to be increased as well. As organizations have more and more of a sharp status pyramid, upward communication tends to be considerably inhibited just as it is when the power is concentrated in the hands of a small elite.

If one accepts our theoretical framework, then there are some interesting implications of our findings. These findings suggest that as organizations become more diversified, more specialized (personal specialization, not task specialization) and more differentiated, they have to rely less on a system of programmed interactions to achieve the necessary linkages between parts of the organization and more on a system of reciprocal information flows to achieve coordination. We have also suggested that such organizations would more likely rely on socialization rather than use of sanctions as a key mechanism of social control.

It may well be that findings such as ours are greatly affected by the nature of the technology in the organization or characteristics of the environment. That is, we might expect that an organization with a non-routine technology would have a more diversified, more specialized (i.e., more reliance on knowledge), and more differentiated structure, would more likely achieve coordination through feedback or mutual adjustment, and consequently would have a greater volume of communications (cf. Perrow, 1967). Similarly, we might expect that the consequences of an organization's having an environment that was unstable, heterogeneous, and characterized by uncertainty would be similar (cf. James Thompson, 1967; Lawrence and Lorsch, 1967). If this were true, it would suggest that the processes described here are only part of a larger system of interrelated forces. Future work might also explore the relative effectiveness of organizations using feedback as opposed to programming to achieve organizational goals, given similar structural characteristics. In these ways, the approach here might be extended and made more complete.

Compliance Patterns and Communication Blocks in Complex Organizations*

JOSEPH JULIAN

Compliance involves the relationship between the different means of influencing behavior and the kind and amount of affect generated by these means. Compliance analysis assumes that the axis for the systematic explanation of organizational phenomena is the linkage between the social structure and the individual. This framework incorporates a wide range of organizational research under a single rubric.

The primary focus of this paper is on the differences among five hospitals in compliance relations. Moreover, I shall examine the extent to which different compliance patterns are related to the degree of obstacles to communication between patients and hospital staffs. Following Etzioni (1961: 66–67), it is expected that general hospitals will have normative compliance patterns, i.e., predominantly normative power structures and patients who evince a positive involvement toward the hospital; whereas hospitals with a more custodial orientation will be characterized by coercive power structures whose patients

* Reprinted from *American Sociological Review, 31* (June 1966), pp. 382–389, with omissions, by permission of the author and the publisher.

have a relatively unfavorable attachment to the hospital. Furthermore, it is hypothesized that, as the compliance relations of hospitals move along the continuum from normative to coercive, the degree of communication blockage increases.

Sample and Method

One hundred and eighty-three patients in five hospitals—a university hospital, a medium-sized general voluntary hospital, a large general voluntary hospital, a tuberculosis sanatorium, and a veteran's hospital —located within the metropolitan area of a large western city were interviewed. These patients represent an availability and density sample in selected hospital units, that is, persons who were willing and physically and intellectually able to participate. In general, the patients in the five hospitals were similar in age, sex, marital status, and number of children under eighteen years of age living with the patient. However, in terms of years of school completed, length of hospitalization, and expected release, the patients did vary from hospital to hospital. The range and distribution by occupation were fairly similar between hospitals. The same was true for medical diagnosis with the exception, of course, of the primary care of tuberculosis in one hospital.

Results

The power structures of the five hospitals are represented in Table 1. The rate of reported occurrences of normative sanctions ranges from .58 to .79. In all five hospitals, normative sanctions are applied in well over half of the possible reported occurrences, suggesting that in these hospitals the utilization of normative power prevails.

TABLE 1. RATE OF REPORTED OCCURRENCE OF THREE TYPES OF SANCTIONS BASED ON PATIENT PERCEPTION

Hospitals	N	Sanctions[1]			Total amount of control[2]
		Normative	Coercive	Neutral	
A (University)	40	.67	.34	.39	.47
B (Medium-size general)	30	.58	.35	.32	.43
C (Large general)	39	.72	.46	.42	.55
D (TB sanatorium)	39	.76	.54	.45	.60
E (Veteran's)	35	.79	.54	.49	.62

[1] The higher the proportion, the more frequent the occurrence.
[2] This index is determined in the following manner: (1) multiply the ratio of reported occurrence of the three types of sanctions by the number of indicators of each type of sanction, (2) total the multiplied ratios, and (3) divide by the total number of sanction indicators.

Table 1 further reveals that coercive sanctions are reported less frequently in Hospitals A (a university hospital), B (a medium-sized general hospital), and C (a large general hospital) than in D (a tuberculosis sanatorium) and E (a veteran's hospital). Coercive sanctions are reported less than half of the time in Hospitals A, B, and C (.34, .35, and .46, respectively), while in Hospitals D and E coercive sanctions are applied in over half of the possible reported cases. These data lead me to conclude that the tuberculosis sanatorium and the veteran's hospital constitute dual structures, because they exercise two types of power—a normative type as well as a coercive one. Further justification for characterizing the structures of these hospitals in this manner is provided by the fact that the number of coercive sanctions available to Hospitals A, B, and C is limited, whereas Hospitals D and E have available a wider range. In Hospitals D and E, for example, greater use is made of passes and leaves, and facilities for isolation are available.

Compliance and Communication

Having established the compliance relations of the five hospitals, we turn our attention to an examination of the relationship of compliance to the organizational variable of communication flow. It will be recalled that the flow of communication in a normative organization is predicted to be smoother than in a normative-coercive organization.

Table 2 presents a set of six indicators to examine this proposed

TABLE 2. PERCENTAGE OF PATIENTS EXPERIENCING SIX TYPES OF COMMUNICATION BLOCKS IN FIVE HOSPITALS

Type of communication block	Percentage					Rank				
	A	B	C	D	E	A	B	C	D	E
1. Not told enough about personal illness and progress	18	10	18	39	23	2.5	1	2.5	5	4
2. Staff holds back information on case	0	10	24	26	11	1	2	4	5	3
3. Doctor makes the rounds too fast	8	7	24	31	6	3	2	4	5	1
4. New treatment, etc., not explained ahead of time	20	13	20	24	26	2.5	1	2.5	4	5
5. Hesitate to speak up, to ask questions	15	10	15	14	23	3.5	1	3.5	2	5
6. Staff does not spend good deal of time talking with patients	40	50	36	44	43	2	5	1	4	3

relationship. The first set of figures represents the percentage of patients responding to the items. The second set of figures represents the hospital's rank on communication blocks. Rank one indicates low communication blocks, and rank five denotes high communication blocks.

A higher percentage of patients in normative-coercive hospitals than in normative hospitals indicate that they are not told as much as they would like or that they are not told many important things about their illness or how they are coming along—nearly four times as many patients in the tuberculosis sanatorium (Hospital D) than in the medium-sized general hospital (Hospital B) report that they are not told enough about their personal illness and progress.

The percentage of patients who feel that the hospital staff holds back certain information about their case "very often" or "fairly often" (item 2) is highest in Hospital D. No patients in Hospital A reported incidents of this kind, while over one-fourth of the patients in Hospital D mentioned this occurrence.

The percentage of patients "who don't get to talk to or ask questions of their physicians 'almost always' or 'fairly often' " is highest in one of the two normative-coercive hospitals (D), and in one of the three normative hospitals (C). The factors which might account for Hospitals C and E being deviant cases will be discussed in a subsequent section.

"Not usually" or "hardly ever" having new treatment, medication, tests, etc., explained to them ahead of time (item 4) occurs more often in normative-coercive hospitals (D and E) than in normative hospitals (A, B, and C). Examination of the rank order of this item reveals a fairly direct relationship.

Hospital E has a higher percentage of patients who "almost always" or "usually" hesitate to speak up and ask questions of the hospital staff than the other four hospitals. In point of fact, the other four hospitals appear to have equal percentages of patients who always or usually hesitate to speak up and ask questions. This item suggests that at least one of the normative-coercive hospitals has a relatively high percentage of patients who feel inhibited about initiating contact toward the staff.

The last item in Table 2 indicates that the lowest percentage of patients whose hospital staffs do "not usually" or "hardly ever" spend a good deal of time talking with them are found in Hospital C, whereas Hospital B has the highest percentage. The other three hospitals are rather similar. The relationship between this indicator and the type of hospital compliance pattern is not consistent.

These six indicators allow at least one conclusion to be drawn. When the overall rankings of hospitals on each of the six indicators are considered, it will be observed that Hospital A (normative organization) ranks low or middle on all six items; Hospital B (normative organization) ranks low on five of the six items; Hospital D (normative-coercive organization) ranks high or middle on five of the six items; Hospital E (normative-coercive organization) ranks high or middle on five of the six items; but Hospital C (normative organization) ranks low or middle on only three of the six items. Apart from Hospital D, which is a mixed case, it is concluded that normative hospitals have fewer communication blocks than normative-coercive hospitals.

Discussion

Why is the flow of communication generally smoother in normative organizations than in normative-coercive organizations? What accounts for the few specific instances in which this relationship did not hold up as measured by the present study?

Etzioni states that prisons, which are prototypes of pure coercive organizations, tend to follow a communication policy which withholds information from the general inmate population and allocates it to a selected few in a manner that will turn information into a source of reward and control (1961: 139). This is further substantiated by McCleery (1957), who points out that order is maintained in a custodial prison through the use of arbitrary power, combined with allocation of valid information to a selected elite of inmates in tacit exchange for their support of order in prison.

Blau and Scott suggest that the restriction of communication, which is often a function of hierarchical differentiation, improves the performance of organizations when the task is essentially one of co-ordination (1962: 243). Within the framework of this study, normative-coercive hospitals, which control and block patient activities to a greater extent than normative hospitals, restrict communication for coordinative purposes. In a more general way, normative-coercive organizations have more communication blocks because they are more effective for realizing the goal of control or coordination.

The work of Strauss and his colleagues on two psychiatric hospitals bears on the relationship of communication and control, particularly in normative-coercive organizations. Strauss *et al.* (1963: 160), argue that:

> When patients are closely observed "operating around" the hospital, they will be seen negotiating not only for privileges but also for precious information relevant to their own understanding of their illness.

Roth's studies of tuberculosis hospitals also bear on this issue. He takes the position that (1963: 313):

> A doctor, nurse, or aide never tells a patient "everything." Though exactly what a staff member will tell a patient will vary with the individual and with the situation, there is always some informa-

tion that is considered a threat to the control of treatment or hospital management if known to the patients.

All the research cited above clearly indicates that the *amount* as well as the *type* of organizational control is related to the degree and nature of organizational communication blocks. This proposition accounts for one rather unexpected result of the present research, and is reinforced by other results.

The unexpected result involves the relatively high percentage of patients in Hospital C reporting blockages in the communication system. The control-communication proposition mentioned above suggests that Hospital C should have a relatively higher frequency of coercive as well as all types of sanctions. Table 2 presents an index of the total amount as well as the type of control exercised in the five hospitals. These data clearly show that Hospital C has a higher reported frequency of coercive sanctions and a higher amount of total control exercised than either Hospital A or B. In point of fact, C is closer to Hospitals D and E in kind and amount of control than it is to A and B. These data give considerable support to the notion that the kind and amount of control exercised in organizations is closely related to the degree of communication blocks.

The present research also provides some support for the notions of Roth and Strauss *et al.,* regarding the nature of communication blocks in what is here considered as normative-coercive organizations. Two items, which are part of the power and involvement scales, bear particularly on the functional effectiveness of communication blocks in organizations with coercive and/or relatively high amounts of control. Hospitals C, D, and E have a higher percentage of patients who indicate that staff "withholds information from patients in order to elicit compliant behavior" than Hospitals A and B. Forty-three, forty-one, and forty-six percent of the patients in Hospitals C, D, and E, respectively, indicated that they had either witnessed this practice or thought it would occur.

Offering information to the patient in exchange for his cooperation was reported by 33, 31, and 48 percent of the patients in Hospitals C, D, and E, respectively. Only 17 percent of the patients in Hospital A and 10 percent in Hospital B reported this practice. Furthermore, the majority of patients in Hospitals C, D, and E approve of this practice, whereas the majority of patients in Hospitals A and D disapprove.

The above data offer considerable evidence to the effect that blocks in downward communication occur more often in organizations with relatively high degrees of both coercive and general control. Since this is the case, the question arises, are there blocks in upward communication?

A further look at Table 2 (items 3 and 5) suggests that downward and upward communication blocks are related. The familiar "doctor's rounds" has as one of its many functions the opportunity for patients to initiate contact with the physician. The questions that patients ask can be therapeutic for the patient, and a useful diagnostic device for the physician. The fact that over three times as many patients in Hospitals C and D do not get to talk to or ask questions of their physicians "almost always" or "fairly often," points to the possibility that normative-coercive and quasinormative-coercive organizations can structure relationships so as to establish obstacles in upward communication.

Hospital E was expected to be more like Hospital D, but was not. However, the highest percentage of patients who "almost always" or "usually" hesitate to speak up and ask questions is found in Hospital E. This points to the possibility that patients in some normative-coercive organizations, such as Hospital E, have the feeling that their comments and questions are not important.

The data suggest that the restriction of information and communication is related to the effectiveness of organizations that utilize coercive sanctions and generally exercise relatively high degrees of control to attain their objectives. Conversely, therefore, the free flow of communication is related to the effectiveness of organizations that utilize normative sanctions and exercise relatively low degrees of control.

Role Conflict in Organizations*

**ROBERT L. KAHN, DONALD M. WOLFE,
ROBERT P. QUINN, J. DIEDRICK SNOEK,
and ROBERT A. ROSENTHAL**

Only one out of six men in the labor force of the United States reports being free of tension on the job. For some, of course, the tensions are relatively mild and can readily be taken in stride. But for many the tensions are sufficiently severe to impose heavy costs for the person and for the organization in which he works. Because role conflicts constitute a major source of such tensions, this chapter is devoted to a more detailed analysis of the nature and immediate consequences of role conflict.

Table 1 indicates the variety of sources of opposing role pressures in *inter-sender* conflicts as reported by respondents in the national survey. Only those respondents who report having such conflicts are represented there; entries in the cells indicate the percentage

TABLE 1.   MATRIX OF INTER-SENDER ROLE CONFLICTS[1] (FROM THE NATIONAL SURVEY, WEIGHTED)

First Party to Conflict	Second Party to Conflict						
	(a)	(b)	(c)	(d)	(e)	(f)	(g)
(a) Management or company in general	2%	5%	8%	3%	20%	17%	2%
(b) Person's direct supervisor(s)	(5)	4	8	8	3	7	1
(c) Co-workers within organization	(8)	(8)	3	—	—	—	2
(d) Person's subordinates	(3)	(8)	(—)	—	—	1	—
(e) Union or its representatives	(20)	(3)	(—)	(—)	—	—	1
(f) Extraorganizational associates[2]	(17)	(7)	(—)	(1)	(—)	2	1
(g) Other (family, friends, etc.)	(2)	(1)	(2)	(—)	(1)	(1)	2
Totals (%)[3]	57	36	21	12	24	28	9

[1] The column and line headings indicate persons or groups whom the respondents identify as contributing to inter-sender conflicts. Cell entries reflect the percentage of all those reporting conflict who feel "in the middle" between the two groups defining the cell.
[2] Extraorganizational role senders include such business contacts as clients, customers and suppliers, and outsiders who have regulatory or advisory relations with the company.
[3] Totals represent the percentage who report the person or group at the head of the column to be a party to the conflict, regardless of who represents the other party. Figures in parentheses below the main diagonal repeat corresponding cells above. Total $N = 259$; "no conflict" and "not ascertained" cases are omitted.

of cases in which the opposition is between members of the categories which the row and column represent. Several points of interest are to be found in this table.

First, the importance of organizational superiors is clearly evident; combining categories (a) and (b), 88 percent of all inter-sender conflicts involve pressures from above. This is hardly surprising since the major directives and constraints in one's role come down the chain of command. Fifty-seven percent of the respondents speak of these pressures from above as coming from some impersonal source—"the company" or "management." Thirty-six percent, still a substantial number, implicate their own direct supervisors. By contrast, only 12 percent of the conflicts involve pressures from the person's subordinates, and these are almost always in opposition to pressures from superiors. In evaluating this finding, however, one must bear in mind that most people in the labor force hold nonsupervisory jobs and have no subordinates.

Intraorganizational conflicts—those involving pressures that stem from within the organization—account for 41 percent of the inter-sender conflicts reported. All but 3 percent involve superiors, and 25 percent involve the person's direct supervisor as one party to the conflict. The following cases represent examples of intraorganizational conflicts.

> *Production control supervisor*—We have to control material and there's a difference between what production control wants and what the superintendent and management want.
>
> *Truck driver*—The dispatcher dispatches trucks at a certain time. The store manager wants the goods delivered at a certan time. So, the driver is in the middle between the two.
>
> *Electronics technician*—I was transferred from one department to another and there is conflict between the two departments. My loyalty should lie with the second department, but it lies with the first.
>
> *Assistant art director, advertising department*—Salesmen request special types of promotional material. My boss feels that it's not desirable. So, I'm not pleasing our salesmen in this respect.
>
> *Design engineer*—It's between what the engineers want and what the shop people want.

Even more common are conflicts induced in part by pressures from persons or groups outside the organization—59 percent of all inter-sender conflicts reported in the national survey. Two major forms are common: those involving pressures from labor unions or their repre-sentatives (24 percent) and those in which outside business associates play a part (28 percent). The following examples illustrate difficulties stemming from union–management conflicts.

> *Pipefitter*—Between union and management. Can't do electrical work like management wants—I have to get an electrician to do that or break the contract with the union.
>
> *General supervisor, automobile assembly*—Management demands certain work standards and union rejects them. I'm right in the middle.
>
> *Machine operator*—Production rate used to be 330 units per hour, the women worked hard and could do that. Since we made 400 they've changed the production rate to that, and the women can't get 400. That bothers me because the union *and* the women hold it against us for getting 400.

Relations between customer and company often contain the seeds of role conflict, as indicated in the following cases.

> *Oil furnace repair man*—Between the office and the customer—

customer may feel she's entitled to one thing; office says she's not; I have to explain to customer.

Drug store manager—In between help and owner, customers and boss. How much credit to allow—it's something all the time.

Farm machinery mechanic—Between customers and boss on free service. Also, two girls in the office will promise repair service involving me for the same time.

Waitress—Customer is supposed to be right but boss sometimes thinks *he* is, and you're in the middle.

Pharmacist—A doctor will write a prescription and tell the patient it will cost "x" amount of money, but I have to charge "y" amount to stay in business—this makes the patient unhappy. Also, one neighbor benefits from some medicine so another wants me to give her the same thing. I must use my judgment and try to tell her it might not be good for her.

Salesman—A customer will want a better price. I can't do it but feel it should be better and management won't allow it.

Similar problems are found for those who deal with special kinds of clients.

Teacher—Between parents and administration. Occasionally I have to carry out orders that parents and children do not like but those in authority request it—discipline and retention of first graders.

Physician at U.S. Public Health Hospital—Employee with the company—patient and the company, I'm in the middle. Coast guardsmen want me to tell them they are ill—Companies want me to say they aren't ill—I'm constantly in a dilemma.

Role overload stands out as another type of role conflict confronting sizable numbers in the labor force. Forty-five percent of male wage and salary workers indicate being disturbed about "feeling that (they) have too heavy a workload, one that they can't possibly finish during an ordinary work day," and 43 percent are distressed by "thinking that the amount of work (they) have to do may interfere with how well it gets done." An accounting manager summarizes well, "I have more work to do than I can get done well enough to satisfy my standards of quality."

Person-role conflicts—conflicts between the demands of the role and such personal properties as needs and values and personal abilities—also apparently arise in substantial numbers. "Feeling that you have to do things on the job which are against your better judgment" is a source of some concern to 45 percent of the men in our sample, and some 22 percent are bothered by "feeling that (they) are not fully qualified to handle (their) jobs." The data for women show similar patterns, although the percentages are somewhat smaller. Consider the following cases.

Waitress—I'm often troubled because a customer comes in and spends but he also misbehaves. (She has to be pleasant to people who make degrading advances toward her.)

Social worker—In the area of personnel standards and practices, there is a conflict between the Board's policies and the employees' aspirations.

Secretary—Sometimes it's hard to make the younger ones see things the way we older ones do. Our experience has taught us certain things and sometimes the younger generation think their way is best. (This woman is conflicted because in fact she fears her younger co-workers may be right and that her skills are becoming obsolete.)

Conflicts within the structure of the work role are major sources of stress, but conflicts also arise between the work role and other roles of importance both to the men and to society in general. Nearly a third of the men in the national sample are at times disturbed by the extent to which their jobs interfere with their family life. Thus, *inter-role* conflicts are also found in significant numbers. In Table 1, the 9 percent category (g) is largely of this nature.

In short, there is substantial evidence to indicate that problems of occupational role conflict abound in America today. For many these problems stand as minor and occasional irritants. Many others face them as chronic stresses. And for some the personal costs reach disastrous proportions.

Personal and Organizational Costs of Conflict

Some of the conflicts described above may seem petty and transient at first glance, hardly matters for major concern. All of us are faced with minor conflicts and frustrations throughout our lives and we seem to take most of them in stride. One might well make a case for interpreting some conflict as essential for the continued development of mature and competent human beings. Why, then, such concern about role conflicts in industry? What are the consequences of conflict which need to be understood and dealt with?

Answers to these questions are strikingly apparent, but also in some respects subtle and complex. Of most immediate concern are the personal costs of excessive emotional strain. Of more far-reaching import, perhaps, is the fact that common reactions to conflict and its associated tensions are often dysfunctional for the organization as an ongoing social system and self-defeating for the person in the long run. Let us look more closely at the evidence for these conclusions.

Tension, Dissatisfaction, and Inner Conflicts   Various forms of emotional turmoil—anxiety, tension, frustration, and a sense of futility—have long been associated with psychological conflict. These symp-

TABLE 2. EMOTIONAL REACTIONS TO ROLE CONFLICT (FROM THE INTENSIVE STUDY)

Emotional Reaction	Degree of Role Conflict		
	High	Low	p^1
(a) Intensity of experienced conflict	3.3	1.9	<0.07
(b) Job-related tensions	5.1	4.0	<0.03
(c) Job satisfaction	4.4	5.6	<0.02
(d) Confidence in organization	5.7	7.3	<0.001
N^2	(27)	(26)	

[1] The p-values are based on t-tests of differences between means.
[2] The total N for the intensive study is 53. Occasional nonresponse to individual items creates small reductions in the effective N for certain specific comparisons.

toms should be similarly related to objective role conflicts to the extent that these conflicts are internalized, that is, to the extent that the objective role pressures generate conflicting psychological forces in the person. Some evidence for this qualifying phrase is given in Table 2(a). In this and the following tables, the sample of focal persons from the intensive organizational study has been divided at the median on the composite index of role conflict. The mean intensity of experienced conflict, as judged from the protocols of the second interview with focal persons, is substantially higher for those in high conflict roles than for those who face little or no environmental conflict. In fact, only 28 percent of those in low conflict roles mention any feelings of conflict in the open-ended interview, while 58 percent under high conflict discuss such problems and frequently point to them as being severe and taxing. The presence of conflicting role expectations in one's social environment tends to produce internal motivational conflicts. Persons so exposed tend to be conflicted in the psychiatric sense of the term [Horney, Karen, *Our Inner Conflicts* (New York: Norton, 1945)], as well as in the social–psychological sense in which role conflicts are defined.

The presence of conflicting role pressures may influence the affective experience of the person in a variety of other ways as well. Table 2(b) indicates that tension associated with various aspects of the job increases under high degrees of conflict. Under such conditions the person tends to worry more about and feel more bothered by various conditions and events in his work life than does one whose role involves less conflict. Moreover, role conflicts tend to reduce one's general satisfaction with the job (Table 2(c)) and the conditions surrounding it, and to undermine one's confidence in his superiors and in the organization as a whole (Table 2(d)). These data are based on standardized attitude scales developed in earlier industrial research by the Survey Research Center. The attitudes reflected are important components of employee morale and have been shown under certain conditions to have significant effects on work performance, absenteeism, and staff turnover. It is clear that chronic conditions of conflict in one's work role tend to be demoralizing as well as tension provoking.

But the evidence for the emotional costs involved in role conflicts goes well beyond the data presented in Table 2. More intense and debilitating emotional reactions are sometimes found. Some people experience a rather marked sense of futility when confronted with conflict. A loss of self-esteem is often apparent. Others show symptoms of acute anxiety, and of confusion and indecision, which may leave them immobilized for a time. And for a few, symptoms of hysteria and psychosomatic disorders seem to be connected to the tensions engendered by role conflicts.

Role conflicts, then, tend to be quite stressful for those who face them, and at times the emotional strain reaches serious proportions.

Interpersonal Relations and Communication   The impact of role conflicts only begins with the emotional experience of the person. Unfortunately, the effects of conflict also carry over into one's interpersonal life. Social relations with one's work associates tend to deteriorate under the stress of conflict. In part, this reaction reflects the person's general dissatisfaction with the work situation. Attitudes toward those role senders who create the conflict become worse, just as do those toward the job and the organization in general.

Three types of such attitudes toward role senders were measured: trust, respect, and liking. Each focal person was asked the following questions concerning his role senders: "Suppose you were having some sort of difficulty in your job. To what extent do you feel each of these people would be willing to go out of his way to help you if you asked for it?" (Trust)

"We all respect the knowledge and judgment of some people more than others. To what extent do you have this kind of respect for each of these people?" (Respect)

"How well do you *like* each of these people personally?" (Liking)

Each focal person was presented a series of fixed alternatives with which to answer these questions. A role-set average for each of these attitudes was then obtained by taking the mean scores for trust, respect, and liking over all interviewed role senders in a particular role set. These averages were subsequently converted by means of a linear transformation to an eight-point index representing the degree to which a particular person tended on the average to trust, respect, and like his role senders.

The evidence in Table 3(a) should come as no surprise. When role senders impose conflicting pressures on the focal person, it is

TABLE 3. INTERPERSONAL CONSEQUENCES OF ROLE CONFLICT (FROM THE INTENSIVE STUDY)

	Degree of Role Conflict		
Interpersonal Bond	High	Low	p^1
(a) Trust in senders	4.5	5.8	<0.01
(b) Respect for senders	4.2	5.9	<0.001
(c) Liking for senders	4.8	5.2	<0.05
N	(27)	(26)	

[1] The p-values are based on t-tests of differences between means.

little wonder that his trust in their cooperativeness is undermined. Under conditions of high conflict there is apt to be little indication that others are looking out for one's welfare; the focal person may well doubt that they would be willing to go out of their way to help him. In the extreme case his doubt goes well beyond the reality of his associates' untrustworthiness. Something akin to paranoid suspiciousness may develop, in which the person attributes to his associates more base intentions toward him than they in fact hold. Even short of this extreme reaction, the absence of trust makes it unlikely that the person will openly seek help from his senders toward finding a mutually satisfactory resolution to their conflict. Some substantial degree of mutual trust is required for free and open communication and for integrative problem solving.

Table 3(b) and (c) give still further reason to doubt that constructive collaboration and coordination will be forthcoming in the face of strong role conflicts. Not only does the focal person under conflict trust his role senders less, he also likes them less well personally and holds them in lower esteem. But the problem extends beyond the affect and perception of the person into his overt behavior. People communicate less with their associates when under strong conflicts than when they are relatively free of them (Table 4(a)). This would be expected, considering the weakening of such affective interpersonal bonds as trust, respect, and attraction. There is also a direct instrumental reason for this curtailment of communication. Role pressures are exerted for the most part by oral communications from role senders. When these inductions prove stressful, the stress can be reduced by withdrawing from the inducers, by avoiding interaction with those who create the conflict.

The evasiveness of the conflicted person is further demonstrated by Table 4(b). Those in high-conflict clusters attribute less power to their role senders than do those who suffer little conflict. This response appears largely autistic, in view of the substantial evidence that the expectations of senders in high-conflict clusters have a marked effect

TABLE 4. INTERACTIONAL CONSEQUENCES OF ROLE CONFLICT (FROM THE INTENSIVE STUDY)

| Interaction Variable[1] | Degree of Role Conflict | | |
	High	Low	p[2]
(a) Communication frequency	3.9	5.8	<0.001
(b) Power attributed to others	3.8	5.6	<0.001
N	(27)	(26)	

[1] Indications of interaction between the focal person and his role senders are taken from his responses to the following pair of questions asked about each of his senders: "First, I'd like you to tell me how important each of these persons is in determining how you do your job." (Attributed Power); "How often do you talk with each of them?" (Communication Frequency). . . . For each focal person the mean Attributed Power and Communication scores were computed over all role senders named by him—a group which included all senders interviewed plus a number not interviewed. Averages of scalar responses were converted by means of a linear transformation of averages for the role set, based on an eight-point scale.
[2] The p-values are based on t-tests of differences between means.

on the focal person, though it may not be the one these senders intend. They may not gain conformity to their wishes, but they "get through" to him sufficiently to disrupt his emotional life and to elicit strong defensive responses. Attributing less power to one's associates, discounting the importance of their recommendations and directives, is a kind of psychological withdrawal paralleling the social withdrawal of reduction in communication.

There is reason to doubt whether any of these all too common responses to conflict—the weakening of interpersonal bonds, the curtailment of interaction, or the denial of power—is truly effective. All make it unlikely that the person under conflict will seek out the counsel and cooperation of his role senders in finding solutions for his problems. It is even less likely that he will volunteer his aid in working on their problems. Resolutions are less probable and the conditions for more serious conflicts are present. We should expect this first because the usual response of role senders to a withdrawal from their influence efforts is to press the point harder. If the focal person does not seem to "hear" what he is being told, perhaps they have to "shout" all the louder—and to invoke stronger sanctions. Second, since the usual affective bonds tend to be replaced by negative feelings, conflicts around new issues are more apt to arise.

The reduction in the person's cooperative orientation toward others is costly for the organization as a whole as well as for the more immediate group. To the extent that coordination of behaviors within the role set is required for meeting organizational objectives, the effectiveness of the unit is impaired when role conflicts are present. And this is all the more serious because conflicts, through these common reactions to them, beget conflicts; the circle tightens.

Patterns of Organizational Conflict*
RONALD G. CORWIN

Writers have called attention to the compelling need for models of
organization that take conflict into account (Litwak, 1961; Dahrendorf,
1958b; Coser, 1957; Barnard, 1950). Such a model would include many
types of variables, but at least some conflict might be expected to be
related to the organizational structure itself (Dahrendorf, 1958a). This
paper deals with structural differentiation and structural integration,
focusing on some patterns of relationship between selected characteristics of high schools as organizations and rates of staff conflict
among teachers. This should help to identify variables that deserve
priority in the model and point the way to more fruitful research.

Several types of structure that seem to be related to conflict have
been identified. A few of these have been selected for analysis here:
structural differentiation, participation in the authority system, regulating procedures, heterogeneity and stability of personnel, and interpersonal structure. Relationships between one or more indices of
each of these five variables and several indices of organizational conflict are then described, controlling for other relevant variables.

The data were taken from a larger study of routine staff conflicts
in 28 public schools (Corwin, 1969). Because the study was exploratory
and the emphasis was on discerning general patterns among various
dimensions of organizations, the initial field work was confined to a
relatively small number of organizations, which could be analyzed in
detail along various dimensions. In addition to the small sample size,
the crude measures necessarily limit generalization from these data,
and make the propositions advanced here tentative. It is hoped, however, that they may lead to a more secure foundation with more precise
measures.

Variables

Structural Differentiation   The degree of differentiation within an organization is reflected in the number of administratively distinct but functionally interdependent subunits. It can be assumed that problems of
defining the boundaries and responsibilities of subunits typically arise
at the linkage points (Dubin, 1959). Accordingly, the division of labor
has been identified as one of the major sources of conflict (Thompson,
1960). Some subunits of an organization develop a degree of autonomy
from the others. Having distinct functions, they develop their own
objectives and norms and compete with other units, even though they
must also cooperate (Katz, 1964). The amount of tension is likely to

* Reprinted from *Administrative Science Quarterly 14*, 4 (December 1969), pp. 507–520,
by permission of the author and publisher.

vary with the proximity of departments, with the relationships among the key members of each department, and with the need for joint decision making (March and Simon, 1958). White (1961) found that both the drive for departmental autonomy and interdepartmental hostility was greatest where the interrelation of tasks was highest.

This instability is aggravated by the fact that departments within an organization seldom have control over outsiders (even though subject to criticism from them) and by the inconsistent practices and role conceptions among the members of the separate subunits (Kahn, 1964). Complex linkage systems tend to contribute to a general sense of uncertainty, which some authors (White, 1961; Crozier, 1964; March and Simon, 1958) believe is a major source of conflict. However, the anomie may result from structural characteristics rather than the affective state of the members.

In short, a differentiated structure requires a delicate system of linkages, which becomes a source of strain and accommodation. The greater the number of interrelations, the greater is the likelihood that the organization will break down at some point (Argyris, 1954). It is proposed that *conflict will increase with the degree of differentiation in an organization.* Here the level of specialization of personnel, the number of levels in the hierarchy of authority, and a total measure of organizational complexity are considered in addition to size. Size alone is not a sufficient condition for differentiation.

Specialization. Specialization has the effect of accentuating differences among employees and delineating group boundaries. It seems reasonable to assume that specialists are more likely than nonspecialists to develop interests and monopolistic claims over certain spheres of work, which they are then ready to defend from encroachment. Specializations supported by the authority of distinctive competences are particularly identifiable as targets for hostility (Gamson, 1966). It therefore might be expected that *specialization will be positively associated with the incidence of conflict.*

Levels of authority. The number of echelons also contributes to the complexity of the organization. It is often difficult to achieve adequate communication between socially isolated levels of authority, and each echelon in turn presses on its incumbents distinct role conceptions, problems, objectives, and vested interests. It can be expected then that members of the more hierarchical organizations will not identify closely with persons in different echelons, nor share their perceptions and attitudes (Smith and Ari, 1964; Thompson, 1961), and that persons in different echelons frequently compete as special-interest groups for more favorable allocations of rewards, i.e., status, prestige, and monetary returns (Thompson, 1960; Katz, 1964). Also new levels of authority may be instituted as a means of mediating existing conflicts between subordinate levels, which would have the effect of intensifying the relationship between this characteristic and conflict (Boulding, 1964).

Both supervisors and professional employees are subject to special forms of tension because of anomalies inherent in their positions (Kahn, 1964). Pressures from superiors for efficiency and technical competence may be inconsistent with the professional's value for technical procedure, and executives in complex organizations typically are less qualified than some of their own subordinates to judge the specialists below them (Gouldner, 1959). It is expected that *organizational tension and conflict will increase with the number of levels of authority in an organization.*

Organizational complexity. The overall complexity of an organization then, is a product of the horizontal division of labor as well as the hierarchical division of authority. Interdependent units develop distinctive role conceptions and objectives, and compete for resources and rewards (Wilson, 1966). The differences of interest between functionally differentiated groups may be largely responsible for organizational conflict (Landsberger, 1961). It can be hypothesized the *organizational tension and conflict will be positively associated with organizational complexity.*

Participation in the Authority System Several writers have noted problems that authority systems create for employed professionals (Ben-David, 1958; Corwin, 1961; Francis and Stone, 1956; Goss, 1961; Reissman, 1949). A study of an electrical factory, for example, indicated that a small group of design engineers felt that managers sometimes made arbitrary decisions (Arensberg and MacGregor, 1942). Becker (1953) reported a conflict between school principals and teachers because of teachers' desires for autonomy.

Coleman (1957) argued that conflict was encouraged when channels of legitimate political expression were closed, but this seems to assume that discontent accumulates in reservoirs. Gamson (1966) questions this; he maintains that open channels can simply encourage the expression of any existing tensions, so that if there is strain, participation in the decision-making process provides employees who are already discontented with the channel and the opportunity to communicate grievances that otherwise might remain hidden.

In addition to giving subordinates influence against administrators, making routine decisions can promote disagreement among subordinates themselves. Since decisions represent compromises between contending groups and must be implemented under pressure, conflict is likely to accompany the responsibility to make decisions, wherever that responsibility resides. For these reasons, members of an organization will have more opportunity and more reasons to disagree among themselves, when the decision-making process is decentralized than when it is centralized. The more frequently subordinates participate in decision making, the greater the likelihood for disagreement; therefore, *organizational tension and conflict will be positively associated with the participation of subordinates in the authority system.*

Regulating Procedures   The existence of tension and conflict probably encourages more organizational control. The precise balance between the divisive condition and efforts to control divisiveness will fluctuate as power shifts. This makes it very difficult to anticipate how effective particular control procedures will be in regulating conflict.

Since standardization and supervision generally are intended to narrow the discretion of subordinates, to clarify situations, and to protect spheres of authority, it might be expected that they would serve to minimize conflict, especially conflict arising from misunderstanding. Kahn (1964), for example, found that role conflict was highest where there was low emphasis on rules and less close supervision. Close supervision, in particular, could serve as a channel for resolving differences informally before they develop into major problems.

But there are also compelling reasons to expect that controls will be positively associated with conflict. First, the very rules that limit the discretion of some groups can protect other groups and provide them with support and a sense of independence (Gouldner, 1954). This protective function gives rules a strategic role in conflict. Each group in conflict, said Crozier (1964), supports the rules and presses the other group to follow the rules, while at the same time preserving its own area of freedom. A study of teachers' sense of power supports the conclusion that certain bureaucratic characteristics of school systems provide teachers with a sense of power (Moeller and Charters, 1966). A predictable organization helps individuals to anticipate and influence possible consequences of their actions.

Secondly, if a group subscribes to a professional ideology, in which self-determination of work is central, regulations which specifically restrict their freedom will be resisted. Subordinates may react to rules not only by withdrawing their loyalty (Gouldner, 1959), but also by rebelling. For example, the professionally oriented employees of a public welfare agency, in comparison to those oriented to the bureaucracy, more frequently agreed that agency rules and procedures sometimes interfered with professional performance, and they were more likely to deviate from agency rules (Blau and Scott, 1962: 73). Gouldner (1957) reported that professionally oriented faculty members were less willing to rely on formal rules as a means of controlling students.

Finally, control procedures are likely to be introduced into situations that are already troubled and where the control on interdependent and semiautonomous units is already difficult. Threatened groups will place more emphasis on rules during periods of conflict than during periods of harmony (Rushing, 1966). Schools must perform many nonroutine tasks, which are likely to cause disagreement (Corwin, 1965), and teachers have become increasingly militant in their drive to increase their authority. Attempts on the part of administrators to exercise more control under these circumstances might only provoke further conflict. For these reasons, it is proposed that organizational tension and conflict are positively associated with emphasis on procedures for regulating organizational conflict. Three major types of regulating procedures are examined: standardization of procedures, emphasis on rules, and close supervision.

Heterogeneity and Stability   Recruitment of members from outside the organization makes the organization more or less vulnerable to unofficial influences. Because "people take culture with them" (Becker and Geer, 1960), latent roles arise from differences in training, age, religion, sex, and ethnic backgrounds. Such roles were identified by Thompson (1960) as one of three major sources of organizational conflict and adaptability.

Heterogeneity.   It seems reasonable to assume that when divergent cultural backgrounds are represented among the members of an organization, they will hold different cultural values and have divergent perspectives toward common organizational problems. Moreover, their backgrounds may be systematically related to their status and authority within the organization. On the other hand, conflict can be expected to diminish when personnel are drawn from the same backgrounds—a preferred teacher's college, a specific regional background, a specific sex, religion, ethnic, or social–economic background. Therefore, heterogeneity of personnel backgrounds should be positively associated with the organizational tension and conflict. Becker and Geer (1960) propose, however, that latent culture operates in those areas that are less critical for an organization and that are not covered by the formal and informal structural roles. Consequently, the association between heterogeneity and conflict will be lower in more standardized organizations than in less standardized ones.

Staff additions.   Adding new staff members can be a tension-producing process, irrespective of their backgrounds. The influx of new members can disrupt both informal and formal procedures, and the recruitment of new members may reflect the existence of other problems, particularly turnover among the leadership (Levenson, 1961; Carlson, 1961: 30–35). It is expected that *the number of staff members added to an organization will be positively associated with organizational tension and conflict.*

Past experience.   March and Simon (1958) hypothesized that the greater the past experience that members have had with a situation, the less likely is intraindividual conflict. Older and more stable faculties and administrations may have solved many problems that new faculties confront, and they may have expelled nonconforming members. Therefore, *the length of time that members are part of an organization will be inversely associated with organizational tension and conflict.*

Interpersonal Structure Regardless of the tension-producing conditions, overt incidents are not likely to develop, unless the members of an organization have the means, as well as the desire, to participate in the official system. Informal channels of communication can function in the same way as official channels to provide occasions for expressing problems. Interaction among peers is more conducive to the expression of discontent than is social distance (Gamson, 1966).

It can be hypothesized that the more frequently faculty members associate with one another on social occasions, the greater the likelihood that discontent will be expressed as overt incidents. More generally, it is proposed that *the rate of informal interaction among a faculty, the rate of interaction between a faculty and its administration, and the degree of participation in employee associations are positively associated with organizational tension and conflict.* Two facilitating channels of interaction are considered: the proportion of faculty who lunch together and the proportion of faculty who see each other socially.

Procedures

Data on 28 high schools in Pennsylvania, Ohio, Michigan, and Indiana were collected between 1962 and 1965. Over 1500 teachers and administrators, representing a stratified sample of more than three-fourths of the faculty, returned lengthy questionnaires. Over 700 of these respondents, stratified by position and subject matter taught, were randomly selected for tape-recorded interviews lasting from 30 to 60 minutes. The people involved are reasonably representative of Ohio and national norms for teachers' ages, years of experience, years of education, marital status, and activity in professional organizations; however, the proportion of males and the salary levels of the sampled teachers are a little higher than the national averages. The sample proportion of teachers with master's degrees is underrepresentative for Ohio, but it is representative for the nation as a whole. The schools represent all size categories, but were chosen to overrepresent the larger schools in the region, because it was felt that it was more important to maximize the variability of organizational characteristics than to have a representative sample.

Findings

Size Authority structures appear to be less stable in larger schools. [This and other results of the analyses are presented in Table 1.]

TABLE 1. RANK-ORDER CORRELATIONS BETWEEN ORGANIZATIONAL CHARACTERISTICS AND INDICES OF TENSION AND CONFLICT

Organizational characteristics	Degree of tension averaged across all roles and all respondents	Rates of disagreement	
		Total disagreements per faculty member	Severe disagreements per faculty member
Organizational size	.22*	.16	.35†
Structural differentiation			
1. Specialization			
Did not major in course	.08	.02	—.18
Did not major or minor in course	—.07	—.23*	—.12
2. Levels of authority	.30*	.18	.37†
3. Organizational complexity	.19	.16	.32†
Participation in the authority system	.14*	.17	.17
Regulating procedures			
1. Standardization of work	.28*	.20	.26*
2. Emphasis on rules	.10	.24*	.06
3. Close supervision	—.04	.13	.12
Heterogeneity and stability			
1. Heterogeneity of staff	.03	—.08	.10
2. Staff additions during the past 5 years	.34†	.30*	.37†
3. Average age of faculty	—.26*	—.06	—.40†
Interpersonal structure			
1. Lunching patterns	.09	—.03	.15
2. Social contact outside of school	.26*	.15	.29*

* Rank-order correlation significant at $p < .05$.
† Rank-order correlation significant at $p < .01$.

Both the number of conflicts reported involving authority and the rate of conflict between teachers and administrators increase with the size of school; however, conflicts among teachers do not appear to be influenced by size of school.

    Controlling for the emphasis that schools place on rules (by using a partial correlation) did not appreciably alter the conclusions; but, when the number of staff additions during the past five years was controlled, reductions occurred in the correlations with total tension and the rate of severe disagreement. This latter finding indicates that conflict is not the result of size in itself; it is probably heavily influenced by factors that are associated with size.

Structural Differentiation

Specialization. Most of the correlations between conflict and specialization indicate a positive relationship. However, only a few of these are statistically significant. The lack of specialization (as reflected in the proportion of a faculty assigned to courses in which they had neither majored nor minored) is inversely associated with total rate of disagreement and with the ratio of disputes, and the rate of major incidents declines with the proportion of teachers assigned to courses outside of their majors. These correlations remain after school size has been controlled for.

But if specialization is associated with the incidence of certain types of conflict, it does not appear to have a bearing on the members who become involved. It is not associated with the volume of conflict occurring either among teachers or between teachers and administrators, and it is not associated with the incidence of authority problems.

The 28 schools were dichotomized on two different variables: total bureaucratization and mean professional orientation. With one exception, the positive relationships between specialization and certain types of conflict were accentuated in the 14 more bureaucratic schools and in the 14 more professional schools. However, there was an inverse, but not statistically significant, relationship with major incidents in the 14 less professional schools ($\tau = -.28$) and the 14 less bureaucratic schools ($\tau = -.30$), suggesting that conflict among specialists was likely to become uncontrolled in settings where neither bureaucracy nor professionalism dominated.

Levels of authority. Ten of the 12 school systems having six or seven levels of authority reported high rates of severe disagreement, in comparison to only one of the seven systems with three or fewer levels of authority (X^2 significant at $p < .05$). The more hierarchical organizations appear to have relatively unstable authority structures; both the rate of authority problems and rate of conflict between teachers and administrators increase with the number of authority levels. When schools were divided on the basis of their total bureaucratization scores, however, only in the 14 less bureaucratized schools were authority problems associated with length of the hierarchy. The rate of conflict among teachers themselves does not appear to be associated with the hierarchy.

Departmentalization. The number of officially recognized departments in a school, one aspect of organizational complexity, was associated with the number of moderate and severe disagreements among the faculty (X^2 significant at $p \leqslant .01$). Seven of the eight schools

with more than six departments reported high rates of moderate disagreement in comparison to only three of 15 schools without department heads. There was a similar pattern for severe disagreements.

Organizational complexity. Indicators of conflict that increase
significantly with the index of organizational complexity are: rates of
severe disagreement, total incidents, and conflicts between teachers
and administrators. In the 14 more professionally oriented schools,
complexity was particularly associated with conflict between teachers
and administrators.

When the mean age of the faculty was controlled, the relationships held for all age levels, which perhaps indicates that experience
in itself does not necessarily compensate for the problems associated
with complexity. Since organizational complexity was associated with
school size, controlling for size lowered the correlation, but it did not
eliminate it.

Participation in Authority System

Teachers' participation in decisions about their classrooms is
positively associated with the rate of disputes, but it is inversely associated with the number of major incidents. The fact that the number
of major incidents in a school decreases with faculty authority, even as
the rate of other forms of dispute increases, suggests that the conten-
tions of Gamson (1966) and Coleman (1957) may both be correct in
certain respects. The authority to make routine decisions permits more
opportunity for the expression of existing disputes and provides more
occasions for disputes to arise; however, this opportunity to participate
in the decision-making process, by providing occasions for expressing
minor forms of conflict, might prevent minor irritations from developing
into major incidents.

Regulating Procedures

Standardization. Although it is assumed that standardized procedures are introduced in order to clarify the structure and minimize
conflict, standardization is positively associated with the rate of conflict between teachers and administrators, incidents involving authority
issues, the total tension within the school, rates of severe disagreement,
the number of total incidents, and the rate of disputes.

The correlation between standardization and conflicts between
teachers and administrators over authority issues, apparently is confined to the 14 more professionally oriented schools and to the 14 less
bureaucratized ones; standardization is not associated with conflict
over authority in either the less professional or more bureaucratic
organizations. Also, although conflicts among teachers themselves do
not increase with standardization in the sample as a whole, among the
14 more professional schools there is a positive association ($\tau = .41$),
whereas among the less professional schools the relationship is nega-

tive ($\tau = -.41$). Standardization tends to reduce conflict among subordinates in less professional schools, and to increase it in the more professional schools. But since most of these correlations drop below statistical significance when school size is controlled, factors other than standardization are probably contributing to these relationships.

Emphasis on rules. As with standardization, the rates of severe disagreement, disputes, heated discussions, and total incidents increase with the emphasis on rules. Since these variables are related to the number of new staff members added over the preceding five years, they drop appreciably when that factor has been controlled for (except for heated discussions). Also, neither conflict over authority issues nor teacher–administration conflict is prevalent in schools where rules are emphasized.

As with standardization, the rate of total disagreement correlates with emphasis on rules only in the 14 more professionally oriented schools ($\tau = .32$); the correlation between emphasis on rules and major incidents also approaches statistical significance in the more professionally oriented schools ($\tau = .30$). The correlation between the emphasis on rules and rate of total disagreement, on the other hand, holds only in the 14 less bureaucratic schools ($\tau = .33$). Among the more bureaucratic schools, emphasis on rules is correlated with a decrease in authority problems.

Close supervision. The evidence here provides only limited support for Gamson's contention that rules are more likely than close supervision to be used in conflict-laden situations, because interpersonal relations tend to be aggravated in difficult situations. Although correlations between close supervision and several of the conflict measures are in the positive direction, only the number of disputes is statistically significant and remains so after school size has been controlled.

There is a very low negative association between close supervision and the ratio of major incidents, which apparently pertains primarily in less professional schools ($\tau = -.42$). Disputes are directly associated with close supervision in the more professional ($\tau = .34$).

Heterogeneity and Stability

Age of the faculty. Faculties seem to become more peaceful as they grow older. As the mean age of a faculty increases, the incidence of conflict declines on 9 of the 10 measures examined. Most of these relationships remain after controlling for complexity and the number of staff additions, although the latter control lowers the correlations with total incidents and disputes.

Staff additions. Most of the conflict measures (except for conflict among teachers and major incidents) are positively associated with the number of staff members added during the preceding five years. As staff additions increase, so do open disputes, heated discussions, total tension, total disagreements, and severe disagreements. The rate of conflict involving authority issues also increases. Both total incidents and incidents between teachers and administrators show relatively high correlations, and these measures remain significant after organizational size has been controlled for. The correlations with conflicts over authority and between teachers and administrators are higher in the less bureaucratic schools than the more bureaucratic ones. These findings suggest that it might be more difficult to integrate new members into the administrative system than into the peer group system.

When organizational size was controlled, the correlation between staff additions and major incidents was negative and statistically significant ($\tau_p = -.21$). Insofar as additions of staff replace members who have left, the more discontented faculty members may be replaced before conflicts develop into major incidents. This correlation is probably strengthened by the association of staff additions with other variables (i.e., routine decision-making and close supervision), which are also negatively related to major incidents.

Heterogeneity. Heterogeneity is positively associated with conflict among teachers; and when organizational size is controlled, the positive association with incidents reaches significance ($\tau_p = .25$), as does the association with disputes ($\tau_p = .21$). The association with major incidents, however, is negative ($\tau = -.21$).

It is not immediately clear why there are fewer major incidents in heterogeneous schools. Perhaps one answer is that heterogeneity tends to be associated with close supervision and also with the proportion of faculty seeing each other socially, both of which are inversely related to the occurrence of major incidents.

Interpersonal Structure

Lunching patterns. The proportion of a faculty who lunch together "very frequently" is significantly associated only with the number of disputes. Controlling for school size, the correlation with heated discussions is also significant, but then the correlation with disputes decreases. The positive relationship with the dispute ratio holds up only in the less professional schools. Major incidents occur less often in more sociable schools, the relationship being stronger in less professional ($\tau = -.35$) and in less bureaucratic schools ($\tau = -.25$) than in the more professional and more bureaucratic schools. Apparently the situation that provides an opportunity for open discussion—in the absence of other tension-producing factors, such as those associated with the more professional and more bureaucratic organizations—also helps to counteract the development of major incidents.

The schools were divided into high and low groups on the proportion of their faculty who had been in the school more than four years. The positive correlations between lunching frequency and each measure of conflict (except major incidents) apply only to the more experienced faculties; in less experienced faculties, the relationships are all negative. It is in more experienced faculties, therefore, that frequent lunching is associated with conflict. In less experienced faculties, most conflict (again except for major incidents) tends to decrease with interaction.

Social occasions. The facilitating effects of interaction can be seen even more clearly when the proportion of faculty who "very frequently" see one another socially is used as an index of the informal interaction system. That measure is positively associated with total tensions, severe disagreements, total incidents, disputes, heated discussions, conflicts between teachers and administrators, conflicts among teachers, and conflicts involving authority issues. The association with major incidents reaches statistical significance when professional orientation of the faculty is controlled ($\tau_p = .25$). However, this association is found primarily in less bureaucratic organizations ($\tau = .36$), compared to $\tau = -.12$ in more bureaucratic organizations. Controlling for professional orientation reduces some of the other associations, notably the correlation with disputes ($\tau_p = .14$).

Since both social interaction and conflict were associated with organizational size, this variable was taken into account. It was expected that personnel in smaller, undifferentiated schools would be more likely to face similar problems than personnel in larger schools, where social life tends to form around cliques rather than to reflect school-wide cohesiveness. Controlling for size reduces the correlation of sociability with disputes ($\tau_p = .14$) and with conflicts between teachers and administrators ($\tau_p = .17$). The positive direction of the correlation remains, however, and in four of the correlations, the correlation remains statistically significant. The correlation between sociability and heated discussions is not affected by size ($\tau_p = .38$). Sociability, therefore, seems to be connected with conflict independently of organization size.

Discussion

The results reported here are necessarily tentative and exploratory; but descriptive studies which consider a large number of variables are needed to identify variables that deserve priority in a conflict model. Such studies reveal complexities that must be incorporated in the model. At the very least, further consideration needs to be given to developing (1) a typology of organizational variables based on their relation to conflict, (2) a catalogue of contextual properties that influence the relationship of each variable with conflict, and (3) a typology of organizational conflict.

Typologies of Variables This paper has concentrated on internal structural variables, rather than social–psychological or contextual variables. Clearly, future studies should compare the relative significance of these different classes of variables in explaining conflict, but the data reported here indicate that structural variables are relevant to organizational conflict.

Gamson (1966) proposed that three types of structural variables are relevant in explaining community conflict:

1. *Conductive variables* which permit or facilitate conflict.
2. *Variables associated with organizational strain:* i.e., structural variables that generate conflict.
3. *Integrative variables:* i.e., structural variables that inhibit or prevent conflict.

A correlational analysis using a small number of cases cannot demonstrate whether a particular variable is a cause or a consequence of conflict. However, based on the consistency between these data and other interpretations in the literature, a tentative first approximation can be attempted.

For example, organizational size, specialization, hierarchy, complexity, staff additions, and heterogeneity seem to contribute to organizational *strain;* participation in decision-making and cohesive peer relations seem to *facilitate* conflict if it is present. Close supervision also might be included in this category, except for major incidents. Experience and close supervision (to the extent that the latter is associated with reductions in major incidents) are *integrative* variables. Standardization and rules logically might be integrative as well, but under some conditions they appear to be more closely associated with strain than with integration.

Contextual Properties The indeterminateness of some of the variables in the preceding classification highlights the fact that the same variable may be a source of strain in one context and integrative in another. For example, in both the less professional and the more bureaucratic schools, as bureaucratization increased most forms of conflict diminished; while in the more professional and the less bureaucratic schools, the bureaucratization was positively associated with conflict.

Standardization, emphasis on rules, and close supervision all seem to be associated with tension under conditions where they are least compatible with an organization's tradition and with the belief of employees in their right of self-direction, that is, in the less bureaucratic and in the more professional schools. It is possible that rules are created where a high level of tension already exists, and that attempts to impose rules in professionally oriented, relatively bureaucratic settings may be further provocations. On the other hand, attempts to control conflict seem to be more effective in the more bureaucratic settings, where rules are likely to reinforce other control measures, and in the less professional schools.

Gamson (1966) argues that rules are more likely to be used in conflictful situations, because close supervision aggravates intrapersonal problems in difficult situations. However, the data reported here indicate that a supervisory practice that is effective in reducing major incidents in the less professional and less bureaucratic schools fails to contain conflict—and perhaps may aggravate it—in more professional and more bureaucratic schools. While supervision may reduce major incidents in the more bureaucratic and less professional schools, it will be less effective in the opposite types of schools. Moreover, close supervision was positively associated with both standardization ($\tau = .26$) and emphasis on rules ($\tau = .26$).

The extent of hierarchy and staff expansion were more closely associated with conflict in less bureaucratic schools than in more bureaucratic ones. An organization becoming bureaucratized may be more vulnerable than one already bureaucratized to changes in personnel and in its hierarchical structure. Furthermore, both specialization and complexity were more closely associated with conflict in the more professional schools than in the less professional ones; and in the case of complexity, the correlation was higher in the more bureaucratized organizations.

Finally, the conflict-facilitating effects of peer-group interaction appeared to be limited to the less professional schools and to schools with older faculties; in the younger and professionally oriented faculties, peer-group interaction is associated with less conflict.

Types of Conflict The various structural variables were associated with conflict in different ways, depending on the type of conflict, i.e., the members involved, and the form and intensity of conflict. Minor disagreements tended to differ from overt disputes; more important, major incidents formed a pattern which tended to be in a direction opposite from that of most other forms of conflict. Since this study considered only routine staff conflicts arising during the normal course of work, it is possible that teacher strikes might show a different pattern.

Moreover, the data repeatedly indicated that a given organizational characteristic affected relationships among teachers in very different ways from the way it affected relationships between teachers and administrators. For example, although organizational size, staff additions, standardization, and complexity were all positively associated with conflict between teachers and administrators, none of these variables was associated with conflict among teachers themselves. On the other hand, the effect of the heterogeneity of faculty backgrounds was more evident in the increased rate of conflict among teachers than between teachers and administrators.

Conditions such as these complicate the relationship between organizational characteristics and conflict, but their identification illustrates one way in which exploratory descriptive research can contribute to the development of a model that can explain organizational conflict. It is very probable that an accumulation of such empirical evidence must precede the development of an adequate model.

5
THE PERFORMANCES AND GOALS OF THE ORGANIZATION

One might assume that with the success of Robert McNamara's cost-effectiveness techniques in the Defense Department, the best developed area in the study of organizations would be the research on performances and goals. The practical benefits are easy to see. If one can demonstrate that centralization does increase production, this has wide import for directors, presidents, superintendents, and others interested in maximizing this performance. But there has been a major stumbling block in research both on performances, such as effectiveness, and on goals. It has proved difficult to find measures, especially such as would apply to more than one kind of organization (Price, 1972). This does not betoken an absence of interest in low various models of structure affect performance and policies; sufficient theoretical interest is seen in the works of Hage (Chapter Three), Price (Chapter Five), and others. But the relative number of research studies is surprisingly small, especially when contrasted to the amount of theoretical work.

With speculation ample, but confirmed hypotheses in scarce supply, we can nevertheless frame our discussion of the selections around some current problems facing organizational sociologists. The most important issues are (1) the goals approach vs. the structural–functional approach to the analysis of organizations and (2) the general problem of effectiveness. The analytical approaches represent ways of thinking which, although frequently blended, are fundamentally different, especially respecting cause-and-effect relationships. The importance of effectiveness is obvious. At least, everyone in management wants to give lip service to this concept as either a goal or an achievement, or both; but the crux of the problem is to be able to discern if the averred effectiveness is a fact or only a gleam in the mind's eye of management.

Beyond the immediate issue of effectiveness are several performances which are sometimes subsumed under the variable of effectiveness: morale or alienation, innovation, and efficiency. The first two have accumulated a sizable literature because they have been studied in their own right. Paramount to the foregoing issues and, indeed, comprehending all the problems discussed so far in this text–reader, is the problem of survival, how an organization endures through time, altering in the light of changing conditions and responding to new situations. It is owing to this problem more than to any other that we have begun to see the advantages of a system perspective as well as the usefulness of the concepts of feedback, both positive and negative. As we reach this point in our analysis, we are again forced to relate the environment to the organization, bringing us back to where we started in Chapter One.

THE PROBLEMS

The Problem of Goals

Organizational sociologists have found it useful to assume that organizations are purposive. Our own definition of an organization as a social collective designed to achieve some specific objectives illustrates this thinking. However, it has been much more difficult to actually measure the goals of an organization (Perrow, 1961; Zald, 1963). Researchers find the purposive image helpful but somehow elusive. For example, when reading the selection by Chandler, it is easy to think in terms of goals. Presumably, the management of DuPont was interested in achieving the goal of a profit—more specifically, a return of 15 percent. Similarly, the concept is useful to Price, who summarizes a number of case studies while searching for propositions that can predict the extent of effectiveness in an organization. But it is in reading the third selection, by Perrow, when we come to realize that the problem of goals is indeed a complex one. He notes that an organization can have several different kinds of goals, and that they should be carefully distinguished, something usually not done. On one level, he reports, General Motors has the goal of producing cars and on another, making a profit. Even more complicated is the fact that car manufacturers differ in their objectives of emphasizing quality or quantity and of wanting to make a large or a small profit. Other manufacturers are similarly at variance; for example, some companies during the period prior to the First World War would have been shocked to learn that DuPont was interested in only a 15 percent return.

Perrow is largely responsible for advancing goal analysis, a long-term interest of his (1960, 1961a, 1970). Particularly important are his suggestions about more general goals and what these might comprise. Here, there seems to be some consensus. Perrow's basic dimensions of stability vs. risk, quantity vs. quality, growth, etc., are not so different from performance as suggested in the important selections by Hage (Chapter Three) and Price in this chapter.

Another way of conceiving goals is to view them as organizational policies or, to use Chandler's term, strategies. The advantage of the selection by Chandler is that he very carefully keeps clear in the mind of the reader the dialectic between structure and goals. An example of how policy changes can lead to structural changes, or the reverse, is recorded by McCleery in his case study of the prison.

The two case studies just cited represent a considerable advance over the traditional way that goals have been used to explain organizational structure and operation. Usually the argument goes that schools, hospitals, various business organizations, government agencies, etc., were different because they had different kinds of goals. An example of this kind of reasoning runs through the various sections on types of organizations in March's *Handbook of Organizations* (1965). Chandler's and McCleery's discussions can be applied to organizations outside the specific confines of a business firm or a prison. Organizational sociology seeks propositions that transcend common organizational classifications, and one can clearly see such an attempt in Perrow's work (1967), where he moves from specific to general dimensions, which apply to all kinds of organizations. Once such general applications emerge, organizational sociologists can begin to test propositions in a variety of contexts.

The best measurement work on goals has been accomplished by the Aston group (Pugh *et al.*) in the selection in Chapter Two. Rather than using the word "goals," they have selected to call the same variable "charter," and this has helped to obscure their contribution. They have truly operationalized goals by deducing two general dimensions, which they call operating variability and operating diversity. It well may be that their disclosure is the key to the development of complexity or specializations, although their correlations are somewhat small. Variability and diversity may also be the key that Lefton and Rosengren (1966) advocate as the source of a more complex division of labor in the people-processing organizations. Note that this variable was ascertained on the organizational level and not by way of summarizing the perceptions of the people in the organization. In fact, this approach characterizes the Aston group (Pugh, Hickson, *et al.*), in contrast to the approach of Hage and Aiken who also tried to operationalize goals. Hage and Aiken have relied upon the views of the staff as to whether there was more or less emphasis on effectiveness, efficiency, and morale; program change vis-à-vis each other; and quantity of clients vs. the quality of service. They found that technology did not predict well in respect to these goals as measured.

At the end of the selection by Perrow, he briefly mentions two major problems that are as yet unresolved. The first might be called the causes of organizational goals. Although he suggests a number of interesting possible causes, generally these insights result from case studies, for which there is little comparative research to date. More typically, goals have been thought of as a "given" and then related to a number of other factors. Perrow notes this oversight arguing that goals, like structure and technology, are an important independent factor in helping to predict the performances and operations of an organization. This remains the major intellectual question: just how independent are goals and policies? More than any other, it is this question that separates structural-functionalism from goal analysis as a way of thinking about organizational cause and effect. The case studies of Presthus (Chapter One), Selznick (Chapter Two), and McCleery (Chapter Four) in various ways indicate the complexities of analyzing goals. Organizations from without and occupations from within each impose conflicting and competing priorities. Naturally, one would expect an admixture of both internal and external goals, but it becomes increasingly difficult to decide which goals are intrinsic to the organization and which stem from other causes.

For those who would like to read more in this area, we especially recommend two theoretical articles, one by Simon (1964) and the other by Warner and Havens (1968). The former is significant for suggesting that (1) an organization may pursue a multiple number of goals simultaneously, (2) organizational goals are distinct from individual goals and motivations, and (3) organizational goals may be ascertained through observing decision-making processes, because they indicate the various constraints that are present. Some of the constraints are induced by organizational roles and some by individual motivations, and the decisions thus reached reflect the net balance of the goals pursued. The latter article, by Warner and Havens, raises a fundamental problem, namely, that some goals are more tangible than others, with the possible consequence of a displacement of objectives. We saw the problem of goal displacement in the Selznick selection (Chapter Two). But his explanation is that structure, in this case, centralization and cooperation with local agencies, is the cause of the alteration in objectives. Warner and Havens suggest that inherent in some goals or policies are objectives that are more difficult to measure and, as a consequence, one begins to shift to objectives whose achievement is more visible. The book by Perrow (1970) from which we have extracted the selection in this chapter is also worth reading for additional examples and cases.

The Problem of Effectiveness or Success

This is easily one of the most critical issues. Whether trying to raise support for ending the war in Vietnam or building a tank or fighting cancer or any instrumental task that man hopes to accomplish, he wants to be effective. Indeed, a constant cry of the past few years has been the complaint of ineffectiveness. Everyone can agree on the necessity for more research, and yet it is difficult to decide how to proceed. For the problem of effectiveness suffers from all the same difficulties as does goals, and naturally the two are related. As Price demonstrates in this chapter, to say *effective* is to mean *effective at something,* and herein lies the catch. How important this connection is, is grasped by rereading both Presthus' (Chapter One) and Selznick's (Chapter Two) case studies. The former notes that a bureaucracy can be effective as an absorber of the unemployed and thus become inefficient. The latter notes that the process of displacement means that ineffectiveness in achieving one set of goals is the price for achieving another.

The Price selection is also excellent for demonstrating a form of thinking: structural-functionalism. He even uses the terms functions and dysfunctions, words that have become unfashionable because of the many critiques against this form of analysis. The essential reasoning is quite simple and straightforward. Some aspect of structure—span of control, complexity, centralization, etc.—is related to some aspect of performance—effectiveness, efficiency, or morale. If the structure seems to facilitate the performance, one says that it is functional; and if the reverse is true, then the structure is said to be dysfunctional. It should be noted here that the argument is that structure to some extent determines the kinds of performances obtained, a hypothesis made explicit in the work of Price and of Clagett Smith and Ari in this chapter and of Hage in Chapter Three.

This concept of structure is true even for those such as Woodward, who belong to the technological school. Her selection (Chapter Two) indicates that different spans of control have different consequences for success. What distinguishes her article from the typical structural–functional analysis is her use of technology in combination with structure and function. In the same vein, Perrow's article on routine technology (1967) is a theoretical attempt to bridge and unite these perspectives, which can be realized precisely because they represent different parts of an overall system.

Although many similarities exist between the goal perspective and the structural–functional approach (in fact, we see them both to a certain extent in the selection by Price), a fundamental difference still prevails, which should be kept in mind regardless of the labels attached to the thinking. The latter sees structure as primarily determining performances and goals, whereas the former sees goals as being independent. Which way one points the causal arrow is critical. This is not to say that feedback of information from performances to structures is impossible, as illustrated in the Chandler selection to follow and in Davis and Dolbeare's work (Chapter One), and as suggested in Hage's (Chapter Three). But this is quite different from the argument made by Perrow for the relative independence of goals or policies in determining structure. Again, the distinction between performances, what is accomplished, and goals, what is to be accomplished, is not trivial and maintains the primacy of causality. In simple terms, the question is: how much can leaders or management set policies? The McCleery case (Chapter Four) is an example where policy, despite conflict, eventually prevailed, but Chandler's report on DuPont is an argument for the triumph of structure over strategy. On this fundamental issue, there are many shades of opinion, but probably the majority would agree with Perrow's finding that goals have an independent force. Besides, no one really cares for the idea that determinism allow the elite little room to maneuver; some elites find this idea particularly difficult to accept.

The Price selection is also critical in its attempt to solve some of the problems of measuring effectiveness by noting certain intervening variables that are probably related and more easily measured. Thus, he relates a series of control devices to conformity, morale, and productivity and, where possible, connects these in turn to effectiveness. He notes both functions and dysfunctions. In the same way, we see Clagett Smith and Ari relate the control graph to consensus and this in turn to several variables, which for them are indicators of effectiveness. Both of these selections, the one theoretical and the other empirical, are important because they provide three variable links between three parts of the organizational system. For the same reason, the Woodward selection is worth rereading at this point. Although she does not tell us what her measures of success were (and she did measure this), the combining of variables from three parts of the organization system provides some good insights into how an organization operates as a total unit.

Those who are especially interested in the problem of effectiveness will find Price's book (1967) the best place to begin reading further. Also of interest is the attempt by Seashore and Yuchtman (1967) to measure effectiveness. They approach the problem by reckoning the amount of resources the organization can gain. Finally, we recommend one of the first empirical comparative studies to have appeared (Georgopoulos and Tannenbaum, 1957); it is still one of the best.

The Problems of Morale and Alienation

Although organizations are viewed by sociologists as composed of jobs articulated into some coherent whole, the fact remains that it is people who fill these jobs, work at them, and invariably come under organizational control. Consequently, special problems emerge, which might be called organizational morale and alienation.

Sometimes these two ideas are confused (Aiken and Hage, 1966), in spite of the difference between them. As Price (1972) notes in his book of measures, morale or job satisfaction typically refers to how happy the workers or managers or, in short, all the members of the organization are with their work, pay, fringe benefits, and so on. Alienation is more related to whether the work has any meaning and whether the individual works for extrinsic reasons such as money or intrinsic reasons such as enjoyment of the job.

We have already seen a discussion of alienation among chemical workers in the selection by Blauner. In addition to other chapters in his book *Alienation and Freedom* (1964), the following articles might be of interest: Miller's (1967) work on professionals in bureaucracy, Pearlin's (1962) work on nurses, and the Shepard (1971) book on alienation among plant and office workers. The Crozier selection (Chapter Three) gives us an excellent description of work, isolation, and apathy. (Elsewhere in his book [1964], there is an extended discussion of job satisfaction.)

In contrast to alienation, job satisfaction and satisfaction with fellow workers, the two measures of morale reported in the Hage and Aiken selection, depict the more common notion of worker contentment. This article's interest lies in the attempts to interrelate both structural and performance variables with morale. In another paper, Aiken and Hage (1966) more specifically analyze the impact of structure on job satisfaction. They find, as the human relations school has long argued, that decentralization and elimination of formalization makes professionals more satisfied with their work and with their co-workers. This has been well documented by Tannenbaum and his colleagues (1968), as exemplified in the selection by Smith and Ari, who also find that the more democratic structure leads to higher morale.

Job satisfaction has been of interest largely to social psychologists, who have most frequently related it to the problem of productivity. Whether morale increases productivity or not is still one of the most debated points in the literature, even though it is one of the most researched. Undoubtedly, much of the disagreement could be cleared up through multivariate research, that is, the analysis of three or more variables at one time. Outside of productivity and centralization, the variable to which morale has been most frequently related is innovation or change. The Hage and Aiken selection represents this approach and also reviews related literature.

The Problems of Innovation and Efficiency

These two performances have received much less scrutiny, probably in part because of measurement difficulties. However, they are still somewhat easier to measure than effectiveness. The selection by Hage and Aiken represents one line of intellectual attack, namely, that of examining an organization's structure to explain the different levels of program innovation employed. For the theoretical discussions one can read, in addition to Hage and Aiken's book on the subject, *Social Change in Complex Organizations* (1970), the very fine work by Victor Thompson (1965 and 1969), who also has been much interested in the problem of maximizing innovation. Empirically, one of the best studies recently published is by Clagett Smith (1970). Whereas Hage and Aiken infer various communication processes linking structure and function, Smith actually demonstrates the existence of such processes in a research organization, together with their impact on innovation in the organization.

Some of the better work on this problem has been done by social psychologists interested in how to relate the job per se to greater or lesser creativity. In a number of studies, Pelz and Andrews (1966a), with careful attention to the meaning of creativity and with reference to various attempts at validating measures of creativity, provide a series of insights. For a summary of the insights, one may consult the last page of Pelz (1956) in which he specifies seven conditions promoting an individual's scientific performance. Especially interesting is the suggestion that having colleagues with a variety of values and disciplines promotes one's creativity.

Perhaps the best article on efficiency as an organizational problem—not as a problem of productivity on particular jobs—is by Blau, Heydebrand, and Stauffer (1966). They associate size, professionalism, and efficiency, indicating some complex relationships because of positive and negative feedbacks. Specialists, they find, help increase efficiency but after a certain point are more costly. This argument is diagrammed in the first selection by Blau, in Chapter Two (see Figure 3). Here we see organizational sociology moving toward the acceptance of a marginal utility curve, certainly a more sophisticated way of understanding organizations and probably a more accurate one as well. Descriptively and theoretically, the Davis and Dolbeare and the Terreberry selections (both in Chapter One) give an extended idea of feedback as well.

Empirically, the same point is made (but without the terms of economics or system analysis) in a very early article by Tsouderos (1955), selected for inclusion here because it, more than other recent works, indicates how the answer to efficiency must be sought in both short-term and long-term effects. Unfortunately, this article is seldom referenced, perhaps because it was too far ahead of its time. Now we can truly appreciate the advantages of longitudinal comparative research in that it is the necessary next step to unveiling some of the complexities of organizational life.

The Problem of Adaptation and Adjustment

The Tsouderos selection naturally leads to a consideration of the largest issue in the literature but, again, little can be said because present thinking and research is not sufficiently advanced. This is the problem of how organizations adapt and adjust to changing circumstances in order to survive. We assume that all organizations desire to survive, save those initially meant to be temporary; the latter usually are called projects (such as the Manhattan Project) rather than organizations (Miles, 1964: 437–490). More complicated is the question of how organizations adjust or adapt to the changes, both internal and external, that continually occur. Burns and Stalker, and Hage, in their respective models at least point to some of the answers. But these can only be considered a beginning.

The Tsouderos selection suggests that organizations may run into long-term difficulties if they formalize too much, because while they gain in efficiency, they lose in membership participation. Then again, an organization may run into trouble because it grew via a policy of diversification and then discovered its structure of decision-making to be inappropriate, as seen in the case of DuPont, which Chandler reports. Or the environment may have different characteristics, as suggested in the work of Lawrence and Lorsch (Chapter Four). Or as a consequence of changed programs of education, new personnel may enter an organization with new conceptions of structure and new policies regarding goals, as illustrated in the case study by McCleery. Regardless of the source of change, external or internal, organizations clearly have to adapt and to adjust to change.

Unfortunately, we know little about how adaptation and adjustment occur, and particularly why some organizations are so slow in adapting to different circumstances whereas others get the message so quickly. Some organizations appear to be finely tuned to negative reports; others seem to ignore the handwriting on the wall. For some adaptation is easy; for others it is a crisis. We are just beginning to observe these problems in organizational analysis, but one work that may be consulted is Buckley (1967).

Part and parcel of the issue of organizational survival is a question posed in Chapter Three. Are some organizational models destined for the future because they are better adapted for future environments? This a tough problem, one which we know little about. Solving it requires not only knowing what future environments will be like but also understanding which organizations are best suited to which environments. The ability to predict organizational evolution would have handsome payoffs for practical men who must propel organizations into the future. Unfortunately, we need more syntheses, more system analyses, much better research, and stronger theories before we can make valid predictions. Hopefully, these developments also lie in the future, and the near future at that.

THE READINGS

Structure, Performance, and Policy*
ALFRED D. CHANDLER, JR.

Wartime expansion was to increase greatly the problem of excess capacity in the smokeless powder operations, for the giant European orders were largely for smokeless powder to propel shells rather than for high explosives that accounted for the lion's share of the company's normal business. Starting with a capacity of 8,400,000 pounds a year, the three existing plants at Carney's Point, Haskell, and Parlin—all in New Jersey—increased to a production of 200,000,000 pounds a year by the end of 1915. By April 1917, this had reached 455,000,000 pounds a year, or fifty-four times that of the October 1914 rate. Moreover, in 1915, Major William G. Ramsay and his Engineering Department completed in record time the construction of the largest guncotton plant in the world at Hopewell, Virginia. At the same time, at Repauno and other plants devoted to making high explosives for commercial purposes, there was a smaller, but by older standards, still extremely rapid expansion in the production of T.N.T. and other explosives based on toluene, tetryl, picric acid, ammonium nitrate, and ammonium picrate. Similarly, the output of special explosives and accessories like caps, fuses, and ignition pellets grew enormously.

Also because of the unexpected increase in volume, the du Ponts

* Reprinted, with omissions, from *Strategy and Structure: Chapters in the History of the Industrial Enterprise* by Alfred D. Chandler, Jr., by permission of the author and The M.I.T. Press, Cambridge, Massachusetts. Copyright © 1962 by Massachusetts Institute of Technology.

began to manufacture more of their raw materials than they had in the past. In these years the company produced vast quantities of sulphuric, nitric, and lactic acids, alcohol, toluene, and such new items as diphenylamine, ammonium picrate, and analine, as well as purifying cotton linters and making ice machinery to recover alcohol and acids. The new demand led the company's research laboratories to concentrate on improving its supplies of acids and semiraw materials as well as making its processes more efficient. The need for assured supplies demanded increasing vertical integration.

The total number of men working for du Pont rose from 5,300 in the fall of 1914 to over 85,000 in the fall of 1918, while the managerial or administrative group (men receiving salaries of $4,200 or more) grew from 94 to 259. The gross capital employed by the company increased from $83,500,000 in 1915 to $309,000,000 by the end of 1918. Profits—which grew comparably—provided ample funds for any program developed for the postwar use of this greatly enlarged plant and personnel.

The company began to consider the details of such a program as soon as powder-plant construction was far enough along to assure the filling of military orders. An enlarged Development Department had the responsibility for planning the postwar diversification, but the final strategic decisions on where and when to move were those of the Executive Committee. From the first, all agreed that the Department must focus its attention on industries whose processes were based on the science of chemistry. There the company was technologically strong and the market opportunities particularly inviting. "In mechanical manufactures," the Development Department pointed out, "the United States is far in advance at present of any country in the world. In chemical manufacture Germany is undoubtedly in advance of any country in the world." And the war had closed the American market to German goods.

The planning of postwar diversification went through two distinct stages. First, the Department's new Excess Plant Utilization Division concentrated on finding uses for the greatly enlarged smokeless powder facilities, since "only a portion of the present equipment will be useful after the European Wars are settled." Then, in 1917, the Department began to consider its resources as more than physical plant and facilities. Its planners began to think about the use of its laboratories, its sales organization, and particularly its personnel trained in the complex processes of nitrocellulose technology and in the administration of great numbers of men and large amounts of money and materials.

The resulting diversification program into chemical-based industries developed along three lines. First, there was expansion in industries in which the company had already entered—artificial leather (Fabrikoid) and pyroxylin. Growth in the pyroxylin field was hastened when the Arlington Company, makers of Pyralin, a high-grade pyroxylin, approached the du Ponts with an offer to sell. Their management was old and had been troubled by internal dissensions as well as labor and competitive difficulties. The du Pont Company quickly accepted the offer, for the Arlington firm, one of the largest celluloid producers in the country, was an integrated firm with valuable properties and a well-established name. Its plants at Arlington, New Jersey, Poughkeepsie, New York, and Toronto, Canada, were well located for easy coordination with the existing du Pont operations. Moreover, its paper mill in New York and camphor plantation in Florida assured it of supplies which the European war was making difficult to obtain. In the following year, the du Pont Company enlarged its Fabrikoid Production through the purchase of the Fairfield Rubber Company in Fairfield, Connecticut, a concern whose major product was rubber-coated automobile and carriage tops. In January, 1917, to assure itself of adequate supplies, it moved further toward vertical integration by purchasing the Marokene Company of Elizabeth, New Jersey, makers of the "gray goods" base for the Fabrikoid products.

Second, the company entered areas where the European war had caused critical scarcities. Of these, the most important was dyes. The du Pont Company went into dyemaking hesitantly even though many of its products, such as diphenylamine and anthracene, were used as "intermediates" in dye manufacturing. Despite urgings of the textile industry, the American government, and the Allied powers, the Development Department as late as December 1915, made adverse recommendations. The company at the moment had neither the experience nor plant capacity to go into dye production. Walter Carpenter, as Director of Development, noted the specific reasons: "First, as all our plant capacity is fully occupied, we would have to build a complete new plant for the production of intermediates. Second: Due to the scarcity of crude material. Third: Due to the time of our technical men being fully occupied." Carpenter further commented that Pierre du Pont did not altogether agree with his position. A little later, Pierre and the Executive Committee decided that a start should be made. With the assistance of German dye chemists recruited by the State Department, a dye-manufacturing operation was set up at Deepwater, New Jersey, where several acid plants had been built. The development of a satisfactory product was slow as was the development of plant and personnel. Dyestuffs continued to be a costly drain on the company's treasury until long after the end of the war.

Third, the Development Department continued to study a variety of new products that could use postwar capacity. At first, it hoped to do this by manufacturing chemicals which the company was "making or could make with very slight expenditure" and which should have a wide market as raw materials in the rubber and chemical industries.

Quickly it decided that the demand for these could not employ many of the existing resources.

By 1919, the du Pont Company was rapidly changing the nature of its business. Where before the war it had still concentrated on a single line of goods, by the first year of peace it was fabricating many different products whose manufacture was closely related to the making of nitrocellulose for smokeless powder but which sold in many very different markets and in some cases used new types of supplies and materials. This strategy of product diversification was a direct response to the threat of having unused resources. The need to find new work for existing resources, beginning with the loss of government orders in 1908 and greatly intensified by the coming of World War I, made senior executives increasingly aware of the potentialities of nitrocellulose technology for the development of new products that might employ existing plant and personnel more profitably than the making and selling of explosives. These potentialities became clearer as the company's top command came to realize that their personnel, trained in the techniques of nitrocellulose technology and in the methods of administrating far-flung industrial activities, was an even more valuable resource than their physical plant and equipment. Yet, in carrying out a policy of diversification to assure the long-term use of existing resources, the same executives failed to see a relation between strategy and structure. They realized clearly that structure was essential to combine and integrate these several resources into effective production, but they did not raise the question of whether a structure created to make and sell a single line of goods would be adequate to handle several new and different products for new and different markets.

New Structure for the New Strategy

The essential difficulty was that diversification greatly increased the demands on the company's administrative offices. Now the different departmental headquarters had to coordinate, appraise, and plan policies and procedures for plants, or sales offices, or purchasing agents, or technical laboratories in a number of quite different industries. The development of plans and the appraisal of activities were made harder because executives with experience primarily in explosives were making decisions about paints, varnishes, dyes, chemicals, and plastic products. Coordination became more complicated because different products called for different types of standards, procedures, and policies. For although the technological and administrative needs of the new lines had many fundamental similarities, there were critical dissimilarities.

The central office was even more overwhelmed than the departments by the increased administrative needs resulting from diversification. Broad goals and policies had to be determined for the resources allocated to functional activities, not in one industry but in several. Appraisal of departments performing in diverse fields became exceedingly complex. Interdepartmental coordination grew comparably more troublesome. The manufacturing personnel and the marketers tended to lose contact with each other and so failed to work out product improvements and modifications to meet changing demands and competitive developments. Coordinating the schedules of production and purchasing on the basis of market demand was more difficult for several lines than for one, particularly when the statistical offices at du Pont had no experience in estimating types of markets other than explosives and when little of this sort of analysis had been tried by anyone in the industries du Pont had entered. Also in 1919, no one in the du Pont Company had been assigned the overall responsibility for compiling and acting on these forecasts in order to maintain an even and steady use of company facilities by preventing the piling up of excessive inventories in any one department. Each of the three major departments—Purchasing, Manufacturing, and Sales—made its own estimates and set its own schedules.

New Problems Created by New Strategy

While these administrative strains became quickly apparent, the adoption of a new structure came only when the sharp depression of 1920 and 1921 made its need painfully obvious. The poor performance of some of the company's new ventures provided the first warning of these difficulties. Even in the boom year of 1919, many new products had failed to return the expected profits. Paints were actually showing serious losses. In 1917, the company recorded a loss of $108,720 on a gross sale of $1,265,328 in its paint and varnish business. In 1918, the loss was $321,492 on a gross of $2,958,999, and in 1919, the final reckoning was to show a still larger loss on a larger gross—$489,337 on $4,015,769. "The more paint and varnish we sold," one report wryly noted, "the more money we lost."

Such performance was especially disturbing because the du Ponts had assumed that large volume would bring profits through lowering unit costs. This was indeed one reason why they had moved so readily into the paint business. The industry at that time was made up of many small, nonintegrated, highly competitive firms. Sherwin-Williams was the only large integrated enterprise. Du Pont had anticipated an "opportunity for consolidation and economy in such an industry, as there were no particular secret processes, patents, or other causes which would interfere with a new concern engaging in that business, but that the advantages of careful business management on a large scale would be fully realized." Yet in 1919, when they were losing money, many of the smaller paint companies were enjoying one of their most profitable years.

While the story in other new businesses was less bleak, profits were still well below expectations. Those products which, like paints, were sold in small lots to retailers or ultimate consumers, were turning in the poorest showing. For example, the small return on finished articles helped bring the estimated return on investment in the du Pont pyroxylin business down from an estimated 21.06 percent in 1916 to 10.95 percent in 1917 and 6.60 percent in 1918.

Selling, nearly all agreed, raised the most difficult problems. The manufacturing of the new lines used many of the same materials and processes as explosives, but there was little similarity in their marketing. Frederick W. Pickard, the Vice-President in Charge of Sales, therefore urged the Executive Committee appoint a subcommittee of representatives of four grand divisions—Production, Sales, Treasurer's, and Development—to make a thorough study of the problems and possible solutions.

These men, the heads of the divisions, too busy to give the necessary attention to the critical problems, then selected a sub-subcommittee of one able representative from each department plus one of the President's assistants. After six months of fairly intensive work, these five men submitted a report to their seniors on March 16, 1920. Their work and the resulting report had an impact far beyond the company's immediate marketing difficulties: for the first time a new form of management structure was proposed.

The investigation had been carried out in the methodical, rational manner that had become a hallmark of the du Pont way of doing business. First, both the subcommittee and its sub-subcommittee were careful to define just what they meant by merchandise, industrial, and jobbers trade. Then they made a detailed study of outside experience. Next, after examining a list of companies with market activities comparable with their own, the members of the sub-subcommittee decided to study the activities and to interview the managers of eight leading industrial enterprises. These included Armour and International Harvester, which the Haskell Committee had looked into the previous winter, and also Johns-Manville, Scovill Manufacturing, Aluminum Company of America, Procter & Gamble, Colgate & Company, and United States Tire Company.

The sub-subcommittee came to the conclusion early in 1920 that the underlying problem was not one of selling but organization. In the paint and varnish business and in the making of finished Celluloid articles, the company's competitors had "no advantage over us in the purchase of raw materials, and no secret process, no patents preventing us from using the best method of manufacture." Therefore, the sub-

subcommittee concluded, "the factor or factors making this great difference between our success in the articles and paint and varnish lines are entirely within ourselves."

"The method of carrying on the business is through its organization," the committee continued in its final report. In the du Pont Company's paint and articles business it found "an excellent line of responsibility for carrying on each of the functions of the business," but "we have been unable to find the exact responsibility for profits." In other words, the activities of each line within each functional department were effectively managed, but no one was responsible for administering them so as to assure a profit on each individual line of products.

Thereupon, the sub-subcommittee recommended strongly a fundamental change in structure: make product rather than function the basis of the organization; take the offices handling purchasing, manufacturing, marketing, and accounting for paints and varnishes and for Pyralin and Celluloid articles out of existing offices and place each of the two lines under one executive responsible for all four functions as well as for profit and performance. The committee then drew up an organization chart to indicate how these two divisions could be "practically self-contained" units. In each unit, the managing director would have his own purchasing, accounting, manufacturing, and sales departments. The last two offices the committee subdivided into merchandising and bulk operations, each headed by an assistant manager (see Figure 1).

Under the new plan, the Executive Committee would have general supervision over the managers of the proposed divisions. These new units would be line organizations; that is, the line of authority would run from the President to the division's General Manager and then through him and his assistants to the heads of the functional units within the division. The staff departments in the central office would have an advisory relationship to the new divisions.

These recommendations made by relatively young but experienced departmental executives provided the basic conception not only for the present du Pont management structure but for the multidivisional structure that has become widely used in American industry. But a year and a half had to pass before the proposals were accepted and put into action. Members of both the subcommittee on the marketing problem and the Executive Committee itself had strong objections to them. One senior member made his views clear in penciled notations on the margin of the report. In this critic's opinion, the proposed structure ran counter to "the theory of our present organization," based as it was on functional specialization. Second, the subcommittee had failed to show exactly: "Where is the benefit of the reorganization?" A week later he, or another critic, said: "The report cites the agency for solving ills (namely, change in organization) though does not cite ills or how [they are] to be cured by a change in organization."

FIGURE 1. FIRST PROPOSAL OF A DECENTRALIZED STRUCTURE (in Report of Sub-Committee, March 16, 1920)

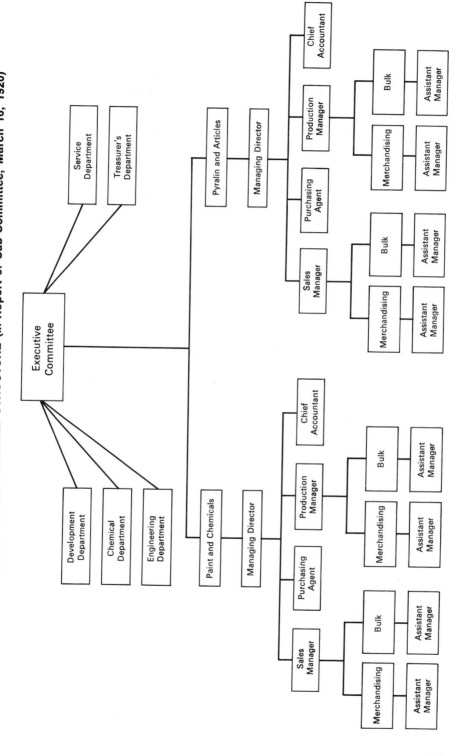

Moreover, this executive was certain that the recent losses were the almost inevitable result of moving into new businesses and that they would be rectified with the development of proper administrative procedures and reliable information. "We have carried excessive stock," he noted, "we have made several unfortunate guesses on the purchase of raw materials," or have been "working against orders rather than setting up appropriate stocks." Selling expenses have been too high, the company has taken too many small orders, and "while our business has been large enough for economical business, we have been scattered ver a [sic] wide field." Finally, the rationalizing and systemizing of the new manufacturing processes had been expensive and were still not completed. "Our rearrangements, repairs, renewals, and replacements of plants have been high." There were still "miscellaneous shortcomings in factory operations such as poor routing, and inefficient piece-work, pay schedules, short-runs, etc."

The answer was not reorganization but better information and knowledge. It was not the development of new offices and new lines of authority and responsibility but rather the fashioning of more effective inventory controls, or more accurate volumes, sales, and market figures, and of other data to flow through the existing lines of communication. Such information would help prevent unnecessary purchasing and make it possible to find just where the high manufacturing and selling expenses were located. Because of these views, the subcommittee's senior members deleted all of the sub-subcommittee's analyses and recommendations on organization when it forwarded the report to the Executive Committee.

President Irénée du Pont raised objections to the findings in this report. He disliked abandoning the proven "principle of specialization." The steady growth of the company's efficiency had resulted, he maintained, from "having specialists in charge of the various departments." So he turned the report back to the committee for further study. When that body resubmitted an enlarged report with substantially the same proposals in November 1920, the President, traditionally having the final say on organizational matters, again vetoed them.

Irénée had strong justification for his position. The old ways had, until very recently, worked exceptionally well. Any professional writer or expert on organization of that day would have endorsed his views completely, as, indeed, did many men in the company, including both his brothers, Pierre and Lammot. Moreover, as President, he, not the men proposing them, would have to carry the responsibility for these fundamental changes.

A Compromise Structure Adopted

Faced with such skepticism about the radical new plan, Pickard and other executives began to seek ways to administer more effectively the activities of those units that handled the same line of products in the different functional departments. During the fall, Pickard and Walter Carpenter had encouraged three men—one from the Sales Department, another from the Manufacturing, and a third from the Development Department—to meet "unofficially and without portfolio" to consider ways of improving the company's performance in the paint business. One of the three, Frank S. MacGregor, had been the Development Department's representative and chairman of the sub-subcommittee that had made the initial proposals for reorganization. This informal "council," as the three called themselves, had worked up some detailed plans by November, 1920. Then, at the Executive Committee meeting of the 23rd of that month, four days after Irénée had turned down for the second time the organization committee's recommendations, Pickard suggested and the Executive Committee agreed to formalization of this paint "council." On December 10, Pickard forwarded the report of the group to the Executive Committee.

The council's report did not concern itself explicitly with organization. Instead it was encouragingly titled "A Plan to Make 10% on Our Paint and Varnish Net Sales." The report began by pointing out that in 1919, the company had "lost nearly $500,000 which made a total loss of income to the Company of nearly a million," and that most of these losses were on over-the-counter merchandising sales. The performance for the current year was little better, and the forecast for 1921 indicated a probable loss of $800,000. The council then suggested a number of specific ways by which to turn this loss into a profit. It provided excellent detailed figures on the costs of raw materials and production and selling expenses, and indicated just how these might be cut. Such action, however, would require that "the responsibility of profits and the control of the business be in [the] same place," and this place should be "a council composed of the paint sales director, the paint production assistant director, and a neutral member."

The Executive Committee, apparently impressed by the specific nature of the suggestions, approved the plan. It is not surprising that the same men who had written the report were appointed to the new council or, as it came to be called, the Paint Steering Committee. MacGregor, as its chairman, was given full responsibility for du Pont's performance in the paint and varnish business.

Only a week after the Paint Steering Committee had been approved, Pickard and his associate on the subcommittee on organization, William Spruance, broadened the council idea to include most of the company's activities. Again they did not raise the question of organization, but rather made their recommendations in a report on statistical controls. That October (1920), Treasurer Donaldson Brown, the third member of the subcommittee on organization, had pointed out that the growing postwar recession was showing deficiencies in current statistical methods. These had, after all, been developed to meet the requirements of the explosives industry, not those of the new businesses. Inventory control based on three-month forecasts had failed to prevent losses from overbuying of gray goods for Fabrikoid production and from similar overstocking of both raw materials and finished goods in other products. Moreover, several executives had been insisting that the company's present need was for better information rather than for a new organization. At Brown's urging, Spruance and Pickard were assigned to study the existing statistical controls. Brown did not join these men in their final report to the Executive Committee on December 22, for he was then preparing to leave the company to join Pierre du Pont, who three weeks earlier had taken over the presidency of General Motors. As their colleagues undoubtedly expected, Pickard and Spruance insisted that the real problem was not statistics but organization.

The current data were adequate enough, but were not properly utilized. The channels for the flow of this information for the different product lines were not yet clearly defined. This was primarily because each major functional department developed its own statistics.

Also under the 1919 plan, the Manufacturing Department had been given full responsibility for inventory control, but such control, the report pointed out, must be the joint responsibility of all three departments. Therefore, in order to "obtain the maximum benefit from the statistical scheme," the two men proposed the creation of "industry councils" for each major product similar to the one already started in paints. Each related line of goods would be managed by a Divisional Council that would include the Executive in the Sales, Manufacturing, and Purchasing Departments most concerned with that line:

> These Divisional Councils by uniform, proper, and definite delegation of authority by the Heads of these Departments respectively, and without in any way interfering with the functional responsibility or authority of the Departments in their own spheres of action, can exercise the necessary joint control of the business program which is embodied in the quarterly forecasts and harmoniously and effectively carry it out.

To check on the Divisional Council's work and to resolve any issues arising among the junior executives, Pickard and Spruance further proposed similar councils of Departmental Directors and Vice-Presidents.

The plan for Divisional Councils was thus under attempt to redefine the channels of authority and communication in order to assure more effective administration of the company's diversified product lines. Pickard and Spruance proposed that sufficient authority be delegated to the members of the Divisional Councils to permit them, when there is complete agreement, to settle problems concerning the immediate control of the particular industry. In reaching a conclusion it would be their duty to call upon appropriate individuals in other functional departments of the Company, such as the Assistant Treasurer (Forecast and Analysis), the Economic Statistician, the Assistant Director of Materials and Products Division of the Service Department, or the Development, Chemical, or Engineering Department's representatives when these representatives were needed.

Where the members disagreed, after consulting the staff executives, the matter was to go to the Departmental and, if necessary, to the Vice-Presidential Councils. In this way the Councils, in much the same way as the divisions proposed earlier by the sub-subcommittee on marketing problems, were to assure coordination of the different functional activities for each "industry" or major product line. They were to be responsible, for example, for the coordination of product flow through the departments by deciding the level of inventories and volume of orders within each functional department's headquarters.

The Councils were to appraise and to plan as well as to coordinate. They were to develop and apply standards of controls over capital expenditures, apply budget systems for controlling operating expenses, outline plans for chemical and engineering experimental work, and devise "additional plans for expansion of the business." In fact Pickard and Spruance believed the interfunctional product committees could administer all the company's operational activities and make most of its tactical decisions. These committees could handle "nearly all the routine matters concerning immediate control of each industry, with the minimum of delayed decisions or failures to agree on action," and would further "ensure the desirable degree of exchange of ideas and information of mutual direct and indirect interests."

The three members of each Divisional Council were to meet frequently, in fact daily, if possible. A permanent secretary would keep a record of the meetings and make brief monthly reports to the Executive Committee on important decisions taken during the previous months, on general current conditions, and on the outlook for the future. The Councils differed from the Paint Steering Committee and from the divisions proposed earlier in that no departmental representative was made chairman or general manager of the Council, and in that the members were under the supervision of their seniors rather than given full autonomy. The Councils, indeed, would create a type of committee government for most of the du Pont Company's activities.

The Executive Committee immediately accepted the Pickard and Spruance proposals. As 1921 opened, the du Pont Company was beginning to move toward a *de facto* structure based on product divisions rather than functional departments. The senior executives soon came to consider the new Divisional Councils (High Explosives, Blasting Powder, Blasting Supplies, Commercial Smokeless, Colors and Pigments, Pyralin, Acids and Chemicals, Pyralin Chemicals, and Fabrikoid), the Paint and Varnish Steering Committee, and the Dyestuff Department as similar units. For example, in March 1921, all of these groups were asked to submit the same type of uniform monthly reports.

Of the new coordinating committees, the Paint and Varnish was the most active, and this was because one man alone had full responsibility for its work. MacGregor began by making a number of organization changes—eliminating and combining offices in the sections dealing with paints in the Sales, Production, and Purchasing Departments. Under this control, the paint and varnish business began to improve. At least, the losses lessened. Nevertheless no one suggested, during the winter and spring of 1921, that the example of the paint unit be followed by giving a single executive full responsibility for any one of the nine Councils. In fact, the subcommittee on organization agreed in May that the new Council system was working well, and on its recommendation the Executive Committee voted to continue the current scheme for at least a year.

Crisis and the Acceptance of the Multidivisional Structure

This compromise structure lasted, however, only until September. The company's financial statement for the first half of 1921 provided the shock that finally precipitated a major reorganization. In those six months, as the postwar recession became increasingly severe, the company had lost money on every product except explosives. At the end of the first six months, the profits from explosives had been close to $2,500,000, but the losses for the other products had been over $3,800,000. The largest deficit, over a million, came from the Dyestuffs Department. Paints added a loss of $717,356; cellulose products $746,360; and Fabrikoid $863,904. When other items, such as interest, were taken into account, the total net loss for the six-month period was $2,433,491.

The Executive Committee's regular review of the semiannual operating statistics brought home to it the need for structural changes. Before that meeting, however, H. Fletcher Brown, manager of the Smokeless Powder Department from 1911 to 1919, had written a letter based on his second thoughts and probably those of some of his colleagues. His letter, clearly outlining the situation and the alternatives, became a guide for the top committee's major decisions in the following weeks. After going over the company's financial position, Brown emphasized that: "The trouble with the Company is right here in Wilmington, and the failure is the failure of administration for which we, as Directors, are responsible." Du Pont had had little trouble until it began to diversify. After the war it "made money for a year because of a temporary spurt in business. It is now losing money very fast, partly on account of inventory losses which still continue, partly on account of our inexperience in the dyestuffs business, and partly because of the failure of our organization to adjust itself to present conditions." The adjustment, Brown continued, called for two remedies. The centralized functionally departmentalized organization structure should be completely replaced by the one recommended in the previous year. Second, the Executive Committee should not be made up of operating executives.

The Executive Committee was weak, Brown believed, largely because it could not be objectively critical and analytical and because its members were unable to get an overall picture of the company's needs and problems. The present emergency, Brown concluded, demanded the abolition of the present Finance and Executive Committees and the appointment of a new small combined top committee. This committee should be of five men, "no one whom shall be the Head of any Department of this Company." In this way the Department Head would be able to "give his undivided attention to the details of his own Department," and "the Executive Committee will direct and control the operations of the Company as a whole."

On August 22, 1921, nearly all the senior executives in the company met at a joint meeting of the Executive and Finance Committees. Even Pierre du Pont and Raskob left their busy General Motors affairs to attend. The group quickly agreed on Fletcher Brown's suggestions and then asked him to draw up, with Pickard and Spruance, members of the old subcommittee on organization, plans for a structural reorganization. The three immediately brought forth from the subcommittee's files the earlier proposals for dividing the company into five product or Industrial Departments and eight staff or Auxiliary Departments plus the Treasurer's Department. The only additional change proposed was to reshape the Executive Committee in the way Brown had outlined (see Figure 2).

Their final report fully described the functions of the proposed divisions and the new general office. The report did not follow Brown's suggestion of uniting the Finance and Executive Committees, but rather specifically recommended that they remain separated. This was probably because Pierre, and other du Pont officials and large stockholders no longer actively connected with day-to-day affairs of the company, still wanted to have a place to check on its activities and performance. No department head or other executive with operating responsibilities was to sit on the new Executive Committee for the very reasons Brown had proffered. Nor was any member except for its Chairman to sit on

FIGURE 2. PROPOSED ORGANIZATION OF THE DUPONT COMPANY, AUGUST 31, 1921

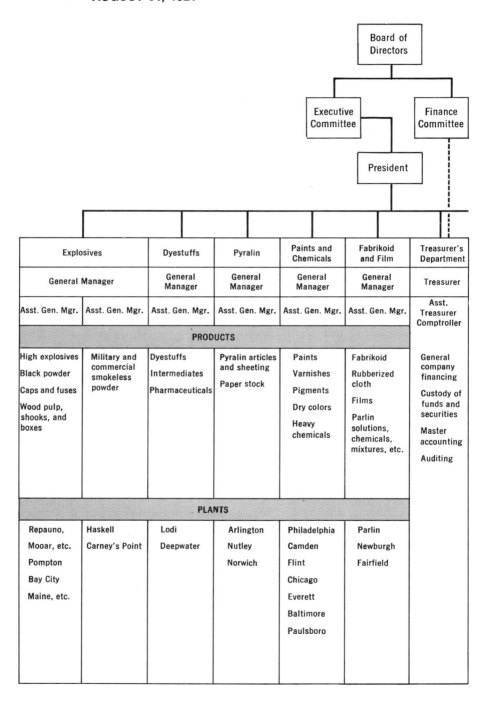

Explosives		Dyestuffs	Pyralin	Paints and Chemicals	Fabrikoid and Film	Treasurer's Department
General Manager		General Manager	General Manager	General Manager	General Manager	Treasurer
Asst. Gen. Mgr.	Asst. Gen. Mgr.	Asst. Gen. Mgr.	Asst. Gen. Mgr.	Asst. Gen. Mgr.	Asst. Gen. Mgr.	Asst. Treasurer Comptroller
PRODUCTS						
High explosives Black powder Caps and fuses Wood pulp, shooks, and boxes	Military and commercial smokeless powder	Dyestuffs Intermediates Pharmaceuticals	Pyralin articles and sheeting Paper stock	Paints Varnishes Pigments Dry colors Heavy chemicals	Fabrikoid Rubberized cloth Films Parlin solutions, chemicals, mixtures, etc.	General company financing Custody of funds and securities Master accounting Auditing
PLANTS						
Repauno, Mooar, etc. Pompton Bay City Maine, etc.	Haskell Carney's Point	Lodi Deepwater	Arlington Nutley Norwich	Philadelphia Camden Flint Chicago Everett Baltimore Paulsboro	Parlin Newburgh Fairfield	

Legal	Purchasing	Development	Engineering	Chemical	Services	Traffic	Advertising
Chief Counsel	Director of Purchasing	Director	Chief Engineer	Director	Director	Director	Director
Legal and legislative matters	Major purchases and those not special or routine within industrial departments	Expansion and development studies	Major construction and engineering in the experimental and operative activities	Research laboratory and consulting chemical in the operative and experimental lines	Medical Welfare Real Estate Protection Publicity Salvage and recovery Safety Fire protection General inspection Stationery and printing Mailing	Traffic activities, rate adjustment not carried out within the departments	Advertising

the Finance Committee. The Executive Committee was to concentrate on the administration of the company as a whole and was to be responsible for its ultimate performance.

While the members of the new committee, with no direct operating duties, were to concentrate on overall planning, appraisal, and coordination, each was also to help oversee one set of functional activities in all five of the new product divisions. In carrying out these last duties, the committee members were to act only in an advisory way.

The report next took up the duties of the General Managers of the new Departments:

> According to this plan, the head of each Industrial Department will have full authority and responsibility for the operation of his industry, subject only to the authority of the Executive Committee as a whole. He will have under him men who will exercise all the line functions necessary for a complete industry, including routine and special purchasing, manufacture, sales, minor construction, normal and logical chemical and engineer operative and experimental laboratory activities, work supplies, cost-keeping routine and analysis, finished products standards and complaints, orders, work planning, routine traffic, trade records and sales expense.

A General Manager was to report to the Executive Committee, which on a regular schedule would analyze departmental reports and discuss them with the manager and his assistants. The Manager's work was to be evaluated on the basis of financial performance in terms of return on investment as defined by Donaldson Brown's formula. Therefore, interdivisional billing appears to have been based on current market prices as first proposed in the sub-subcommittee's report on "Merchandising versus Tonnage Sales."

With the General Managers handling day-to-day administration and the Executive Committee charged with overall coordination, appraisal, and policy planning, the duties of the eight more specialized functional departments now became wholly [subject] to the provision of advice and services, to both the divisional and general offices. The eight departments included Legal, Purchasing, Development, Engineering, Chemical, Service, Traffic, and Advertising. Only the Treasurer's Department continued to have some line authority. It would set overall accounting practices and prescribe the forms for statistical and other regular reports. However, the details of cost accounting were to be left to the General Managers.

Throughout these meetings in late August and early September 1921, Irénée du Pont remained skeptical about the underlying concept of the committee. He disliked the abandoning of administration by functional specialists, and he was unhappy about the prospect of group management at the top. "No man on the Executive Committee," he said at one meeting, was "to have individual responsibility." This lack of responsibility would cause difficulties, he felt. Despite this, in deference to the strong opinion of the majority of his colleagues he voted at the same meeting to institute the new committee. Possibly Irénée's protest encouraged the appointment of the President to the Executive Committee, for the President continued to be the individual entrusted with the final responsibility and authority for the company's affairs.

Once the role of the Committee and the Treasurer's Department was decided, the one other point at issue was purchasing. Irénée, Lammot, and most of the other members of the existing top committees agreed that the General Managers should have "full control" over their purchasing. Only Edge, the Vice-President in Charge of Purchasing and Traffic, made a strong plea for continuing centralized purchasing through the existing organization. During a week between meetings on the new plan, he had one of his assistants study the purchasing practices of eleven large companies as well as those of New York City and the federal government. All the institutions investigated, Edge reported, had, or were about to institute, centralized purchasing. Edge's arguments convinced the Committee, and the Purchasing Department was made a separate unit somewhat similar to the Treasurer's Department. However, it was to "close no contract affecting any Department except with the approval of the General Manager and/or the Assistant General Manager." If the department head was certain he could buy to better advantage and was unable to convince the Purchasing Department, then the question would go to the Executive Committee for decision.

Since there was general agreement on all matters except purchasing, the new plan was quickly adopted. The Executive Committee approved it on September 8 and then voted the men for the new posts. Two weeks later the Board of Directors approved all changes. In September 1921, the du Pont Company put into effect this new structure of autonomous, multidepartmental divisions and a general office with staff specialists and general executives. Each division had its functional departments and its own central office to administer the several departments.

Unencumbered by operating duties, the senior executives at the general office now had the time, information, and more of a psychological commitment to carry on the entrepreneurial activities and make the strategic decisions necessary to keep the overall enterprise alive and growing and to coordinate, appraise, and plan for the work of the divisions. As the Executive Committee noted in their report to the Board of Directors on the proposed changes, the members of the new committee could "give all their time and effort to the business of the

Company as a whole. Being connected with no . . . [division], they will be able to consider all questions or problems without bias or prejudice."

If the general officers were better equipped to handle overall strategic decisions, the division managers had full authority and the necessary facilities to make the day-to-day tactical ones. As each controlled the functional activities needed for making and selling one major line of products, each could determine, within the framework set and funds allotted by the Executive Committee, the most efficient ways to use the resources at his command. "This type of reorganization fixes responsibility," the final report to the Board continued. "When a man is made responsible for result, his interest is stimulated —hard and effective work follows, which brings success. We believe that the adoption of this plan will bring a tremendous improvement in the morale of the du Pont employees." This was, incidentally, the first time that the planners had suggested that the new type of organization might improve managerial psychology.

The structure accepted in September 1921, has served the du Pont Company effectively ever since. Losses were soon converted into profits and never again—not even in the middle of the depression of the 1930's—did the company face a crisis as severe as that of 1921.

Organizational Goals*

CHARLES PERROW

The concept of organizational goals, like concepts of power, authority, or leadership, has been unusually resistant to precise, unambiguous definition. Yet a definition of goals is necessary and unavoidable in organizational analysis. Organizations are established to do something; they perform work directed toward some end. We must examine the end or goal if we are to analyze organizational behavior.

When research concerns the behavior of groups or individuals who happen to function within an organization, attention to the goals of the organization as a whole is not necessary. Much investigation that goes under the name of organizational research is of this type; it is really concerned with how groups or individuals function in certain settings. It is assumed that increasing productivity, raising morale, and reducing conflict are legitimate goals, and attention is directed toward

* Excerpted from *Organizational Analysis: A Sociological View* by Charles Perrow. Copyright © 1970 by Wadworth Publishing Company, Inc. Reprinted by permission of the publisher, Brooks/Cole Publishing Company, Monterey, Calif.

whatever promotes these ends. But we are ultimately concerned with formal organizations rather than with group processes, so attention to the goals of the organization as a whole, or some major part of it, is necessary.

Goals, in this latter view, are problematical; it must be established that increasing productivity is, indeed, an important goal. It might appear to be obvious that all organizations seek to increase productivity, but organizations actually vary a great deal in their emphasis upon productivity (or morale, or reducing conflict). The concept of goals implies aims foregone as well as those which are sought; otherwise all that remains is a set of Boy Scout maxims. Quality may take precedence over productivity in one organization, while the reverse is true in another organization.

Among the many problems associated with the concept of organizational goals are the following: (1) It can be argued that, strictly speaking, organizations do not have goals; only individuals do. (2) Goals are hard to observe and measure. For example: should we focus upon the behavior of all members of the organization or only on the powerful ones? Should we take at face value the statement of goals of top officials, or should we ignore these and examine only what they actually do? (Perrow, 1961a). (3) How do we distinguish between a goal and a means? What one observer calls a goal, another may equaly well designate as a means toward some higher or more general goal. Profit, for example, may be viewed as a goal, or as a means of rewarding stockholders or ensuring growth (the "real" goals). These and several other problems have made the goals concept one of the most ambiguous in the literature, yet it remains essential to define the ends to which organizational behavior is addressed.

For our purposes we shall use the concept of an organizational goal as if there were no question concerning its legitimacy, even though we recognize that there are legitimate objections to doing so. Our present state of conceptual development, linguistic practices, and ontology (knowing whether something exists or not) offers us no alternative.

As we examine specific organizations, we shall infer goals from a number of empirical traces. We hope that our discussion will convince the reader that the inferences are reasonable. Sometimes we will use the statements of top executives if they appear to be frank and consistent with other information. Sometimes the evidence of decisions regarding such matters as budgets, product changes, and dividend payments will be used to infer goals.

Five Types of Goals

The problem of what is a means and what is a goal will be minimized to some extent by distinguishing five types or levels of goals. But our main reason for distinguishing types of goals is to deal with the question of whose point of view is being recognized—society's, the customer's, the investor's, the top executives', or others'. For society, the justification of a steel company's existence may be to produce needed goods; for customers, the goal of a firm may be to produce certain kinds of steel and deliver them on time; for the investors, the aim may be to pay out large dividends; for top executives, the purpose may be to run a stable, secure organization where life is fairly predictable and not too stressful; for a division manager the goal may be to make the best damn steel around. From the manager's point of view, delivery, price, profits, and stability all take a back seat, just as all goals except dividends may be secondary to investors. Note that this means that organizational goals are not only multiple but may also be conflicting, and that they can be pursued all at once or in sequence.

We shall distinguish five categories of goals.

1. Social goals. Referent: society in general. Examples: produce goods and services; maintain order; generate and maintain cultural values (Parsons, 1960: 17). This category deals with large classes of organizations that fulfill societal needs. We will not discuss this group since it has little to do with functioning organizations.
2. Output goals. Referent: the public in contact with the organization. This category deals with types of output defined in terms of consumer functions. Examples: consumer goods; business services; health care; education. Our concern will be with shifts in output categories, as when a producer of consumer goods also undertakes to train Job Corps applicants or when penal establishments seek to control the sentencing of offenders.
3. System goals. Referent: the state or manner of functioning of the organization, independent of the goods or services it produces or its derived goals. Examples: the emphasis upon growth, stability, profits, or upon modes of functioning, such as being tightly or loosely controlled or structured. Organizations have options in these respects, and the way the system functions and what it generates irrespective of products can become goals for the members.
4. Product goals (or, more exactly, product-characteristic goals). Referent: the characteristics of the goods or services produced. Examples: an emphasis upon quality or quantity, variety, styling, availability, uniqueness, or innovativeness of the products. Organizations vary widely and deliberately in this respect.
5. Derived goals. Referent: the uses to which the organization puts the power it generates in pursuit of other goals. Examples: political aims; community services; employee development; investment and plant-location policies which affect the state of the economy and

the future of specific communities. Organizations generate considerable power which they may use in consistent ways to influence their own members and the environment. This power is used independently of product goals or system goals.

Unfortunately, this scheme is not as neat as one might like, and some goals could be classified into one or another category. Since our major purpose is to illustrate the variety of goals organizations pursue and since some system of classification is needed to make our discussion orderly, this is not an important problem.

Another complication is that it is frequently necessary to distinguish the goals pursued by investors from those pursued by management. Sometimes members of top management are the major investors, but this is not generally true in large organizations. Therefore we shall examine some cases where the system and product goals of investors and managers appear to differ.

Before discussing the categories in detail, it is useful to use the case of the National Foundation for Infantile Paralysis to provide a brief, concrete example of the categories. After polio was substantially eliminated, in part through the research sponsored by the Foundation, the organization was confronted with the question: what to do next? It considered going into mental health and a variety of other activities, but settled finally upon childhood diseases in general. This has been analyzed in the literature (Sills, 1957) as a case of goal succession. It was, if we consider only product goals. The shift was from one childhood disease (polio) to all childhood diseases. But from the standpoint of output goals, there was no change: the organization's goal continued to be the financing of research and limited treatment in connection with human diseases or, more generally, it was still concerned with health. In terms of system goals, there was again no change. Even though the particular task of eradicating polio was accomplished, the goal of the Foundation continued to be organizational growth, as well as to continue to operate with the same distinctive structure: a highly centralized and powerful national office and highly decentralized local leadership with open membership. Finally, in terms of derived goals, one might say that the real goal was otherwise; the new arrangements were merely a means of providing the Foundation's top executives with positions of power and prestige in the national health field so that they could shape the nature of the country's health activities. Shifting from polio to other diseases was merely a means to this end, as was the decision to retain the same form of organizational structure. In sum, all these goal categories are useful and relevant. Which is chosen depends upon what is to be analyzed—the health system, the shift in products, organizational growth and structure, or the power accruing to the leaders themselves.

Output Goals

Output goals, it will be recalled, refer to the general sector of the society or consumers toward which the products are directed. They include such examples as the production of consumer goods, business services, health care, and education. It is interesting to note the increasing tendency for organizations to include in their output matters which were previously handled by quite separate organizations or to add functions which had never before been performed by large, complex organizations. For example, organizations usually have some internal training program for their employees. But when an electronics company concerned with an output goal of producing an industrial product to be sold in the marketplace also undertakes to operate a Job Corps program to train the unskilled and unemployed in a ghetto area (as some companies are doing), it has added a new output goal. As we shall speculate, such an action may affect the organization in a variety of unintended ways. Most conglomerates do not change output goals when they add new products; their goal continues to be the production of goods. If such an organization begins to buy advertising companies, however, we might be inclined to say that they have added a new output goal—producing commercial services—to their original goal of production of goods.

Since a change in output goals is rare, the value of this category for organizational analysis will not be great. But it is useful for understanding the organization's relationship to the environment, national policy issues, and the nature of our "organizational society." However, even at the organizational level, attention to these goals can alert us to some massive problems of change which organizations may face. For example, prisons are becoming somewhat more involved in probation work and even crime prevention. While the "client" is perhaps the same in some cases, his location is quite different depending on whether he is in prison, on parole, or a free citizen in a crime-inducing environment. It may be difficult for prisons to think in terms other than custody and perfunctory attempts at treatment, but they are being pressured to do so. State departments or bureaus which operate prisons are beginning to argue that they should have more control over the judicial function of sentencing offenders, so that they may control their volume. Such a change is resisted on the ground that the two functions should be separate. Police departments are engaged not only in crime detection and prevention, but in social services (such as providing emergency health facilities, breaking up family quarrels, preventing self-destructive acts, and giving information and advice on a wide variety of matters). Because of these different output goals, the selection and training of a "peace" officer becomes more difficult as are supervisory practices, promotion criteria, resource allotment, and the like.

In our society there is a strong belief that organizations should not assume too many diverse functions and that if many organizations each do one of a number of different jobs, there will be healthy checks and balances. One of the bases on which liberals criticized the old company towns, where all facets of the community—religion, recreation, housing, consumer goods—were controlled by the corporation, was that industry should stick to its own output sector and leave these others in the hands of independent groups of citizens. Businessmen and conservatives attacked the Tennessee Valley Authority not only because it was competing with private business, though there the question of output goals entered since the businessmen believed the government's output goal should not include commodities like electric power and fertilizer. The attack also centered about the fact that due to the massive effects of building dams and producing cheap power and fertilizer, the TVA drew into its orbit of control large segments of planning that had always been the province of the private sector. These included such matters as the establishment of recreation areas (telling private firms in the recreation business where they could and could not set up business), the relocation of towns and people, the design of newly built towns, the uses of timber and watershed areas, the training and subsidization of independent farmers, and the farming techniques that would be employed. As in socialism, a variety of output goals were being fused into one large agency. (Due to the survival goals of TVA, most of its power in these areas was transferred to local economic and political interests, so the consequences were not as dire as businessmen had feared (Selznick, 1949).

This issue of the public or private control of certain kinds of output is still quite alive, though now the controversy does not center about company towns or "socialism" and federal planning. Ironically, the roles have shifted. Now the dispute concerns the intrusion of business into the public areas of education and community facilities. Liberals have criticized business for taking on the tasks of socializing and training the hard-core unemployed; for investing in, establishing, and controlling the planned communities, or "new towns"; for exercising, through business-dominated boards of trustees, too much control over the universities; for creating, in former President Eisenhower's words, a military–industrial complex, and even, in the words of Michael Harrington, a social–industrial complex (Harrington, 1968). The issue is one of limiting organizations to certain broad output goals in the interest of a pluralistic society. Conservatives, with their cry of "creeping socialism," rail as much as liberals over this issue.

It is obvious that taking on a new function will have a considerable effect upon an organization, but we cannot go much beyond that generalization. The Ford Motor Company found it quite difficult to include even the production of appliances in its output goals, let alone training hard-core dropouts or remaking the dreary city of Detroit. Ford bought Philco as a diversification measure and fully expected to rehabilitate the sickly company through the infusion of talent and capital, which Ford had in abundance (Siekman, 1955). Within a short time, all but three of the top 25 men at Philco had left, voluntarily or otherwise, and Ford brought in 18 young managers in the first six months, including seven at the vice-presidential level. Within four years there were about 50 Ford men working in the Philco division. But the patient did not respond to all this new blood. Henry Ford II contended that "a good manager can run anything." But, according to *Fortune*, the man now running Philco says: "This is not true, and Ford has paid a fat price to learn it." If the shift from autos to appliances is so difficult, how about the shift to social programs?

Present experience with such goals is still too limited to draw final conclusions, but it seems likely that there could be internal reverberations if the new output goals were to command very much in the way of organizational resources and talents. Routes to the top can change, and those who take the novel assignments and do them well might well achieve rapid promotion in the company. But managers who are effective in traditional roles may easily falter in novel jobs, and few may wish to take the risk. Attitudes toward "bungling, inefficient government" may change as companies experience the recalcitrance of clients or the complexities of total community planning. Those outside the corporation who decry the lack of social responsibility of business may be alarmed when they see what the product of such ventures looks like. What a business concern may conceive of as socially desirable, the liberal critic may feel is quite undesirable.

We have explored this subject at such length because it promises to be a controversial one for the next few decades. As the economy becomes more complex and interrelated, as there are more and more joint ventures of government and business, and as business expands its activities to include matters traditionally defined as belonging to the public sector, there will be shifts in output goals. One can see this shift in output taking place in the universities today. Originally concerned with training ministers, universities later assumed public-sector responsibilities, such as training teachers, doctors, and government officials. There followed an increasing number of programs for engineers and businessmen. More and more, the engineering, agricultural, and business schools began to define the output goal. Now, when the "intellectual" has become a distinct class or status group (Lasch, 1965), the demand is that universities be concerned primarily with knowledge rather than with training. In this view their clients are not the churches, public schools, and corporations, but society as a whole. Social commentary and criticism are held to be the vital tasks, rather than training. Such a shift in goals will be hard won, if it is to occur, and perhaps it can only be accomplished by means of specialized institutions that will train intellectuals to continually subject society to critical analysis. At the same time, most universities and colleges will continue to train the specialists needed to man a high-energy technology and a complex society. But there is no doubt that in the meantime this controversy over the proper goals of universities contributes to an unprecedented turnover of university presidents, who are caught between the demands of business-oriented trustees and legislators, on the one hand, and faculty and student intellectuals, on the other.

System Goals

System goals pertain to desired conditions of the organization as an organization, rather than to the goods or services it produces. A high rate of profit for the organization would be a system goal, as would a high rate of growth. An emphasis upon stability for the organization is a system goal—it says something about the organization as a whole—and this emphasis varies by organizations. Some other typical system goals are an emphasis upon a particular kind of structure or process—e.g., some organizations are committed to centralized, bureaucratic, tight-ship operations for their own sake, while others are not. Rapid product change or innovation, or being judged an industry leader, are possible system goals. Managers have choices in these matters and can say: "This is the best way for this organization to function." To some extent, some system goals are simply constraints—survival is not a preoccupation of most successful organizations, but it is a necessity for any organization if it is to be an organization. But for some organization, what might have been a constraint can become a goal in itself, and organizational behavior is thereby affected. Organizations, of course, can also choose not to survive, but we are more likely to know about those which survive than about those which do not.

For economic organizations the major areas in which goals are established, relating to the system or organization as a whole, concern stability, fiscal policies, size and growth, method of internal operation, and relationship to the environment. The decisions taken in these areas may be clear-cut determinations by one man or an executive team, or they may result from incremental policies built up over a long period of time, where "no one really decided it; it just came to be the way things are done here." But they are important decisions; they are difficult to change; change would generally involve some internal pain and substantial adjustment, and they often provide a shorthand clue to the character of the organization.

Stability and Risk

Stability may subsume several of the other goals, but is worth emphasizing in its own right. Some organizations place a premium upon stable operation, few risks, and gradual and incremental change. Generally, their technology and market situation makes this feasible, or even dictates it. If an organization has enormous "sunk costs"—fixed investments which are relatively immovable—or resources which can only be exploited over a long period of time, as in mining, there will be a corresponding emphasis upon stability in all phases of the operation and in fiscal and even community areas. The railroads were in such a position until trucks and airlines began cutting in on their monopoly; many of them still behave as if there were no competition. Those rails which have emphasized and risked change and have sought innovations not only in technology but in organizational structure and in relationships with the environment of communities, competitors, customers, and regulatory agencies, have done so with high consciousness of their maverick status in the industry. Incidentally, even though the railroads are saddled with inefficient and inflexible rate structures, overregulated, and generally out of tune with current transportation needs, they are not necessarily unprofitable. They have enormous reserves in land and other capital investments which make them truly sleeping giants. While their return on investment is small, their net profit is quite respectable. The net income as a percent of operating revenues of the seven largest in 1966 was 11.4 percent, quite good for an ailing and wailing industry.

On the other hand, some industries cannot expect to survive without the system goals of change, innovation, and risk. In this connection, one frequently hears, "If we have been doing it the same way for five (or two) years, we must be doing it wrong by now." An organization with this attitude places a premium on change or even makes a virtue of change, rewarding it for its own sake. Lines of communication must be flexible and open and in steady use; investment risks are considered to be part of the overhead. One expects them and hopes that there will not be too many.

An organization which lives with and accepts risks adopts a different criterion of performance from one which does not. In such organizations the statement may be heard that if a man has not made a few bad and costly decisions, he is probably not making enough decisions, or taking enough risks. At times this heretical criterion is employed in hospitals among doctors. They say there should be a certain (small) percentage of cases where the examination of tissue removed during surgery reveals that the organs were not, in fact, diseased and there was no need of surgery. The argument is that unless this happens, some patients will suffer or die because the doctor was uncertain and reluctant to order surgery, when in fact it was necessary. Similar reasoning is employed by sophisticated social agencies. If there are no instances of "welfare chiselers," then too much money is being spent on determining eligibility and on policing; such a situation is uneconomical. It may also mean that the organization is only handling very sure "risks" and thus not offering service to others who need it;

allowing for a small percentage of clients who may be misusing aid is considered a small price to pay for complete coverage.

This willingness to take and live with risks may seem ridiculous to those who favor a highly stable and conservative system. Such people need several very good reasons for taking a new step, but only one for not taking it. This position is realistic if the organization is very secure or if risky actions can be extremely dangerous. The position is also popular, of course, with those who stand outside the organization and demand of it a perfect decision record. It is hard to justify errors that may serve the organization in some vague "long run."

Eastern Airlines

Even though he owned only 3 percent of the stock (no one owned more), it was quite clear that Eddie Rickenbacker, the World War I ace, controlled Eastern Airlines from 1935 to 1959 and ran it as if he owned it all. No one was disposed to quarrel with his leadership, for the company was the most consistent money-maker in the volatile airline business. For 25 years it had a record of uninterrupted profits; this included very large gains at a time when the other airlines were losing money. According to *Fortune,* Rickenbacker ran a one-man show, and the main act was economy: "Despite his dashing war record and flamboyant exterior, he had the cautious soul of a greengrocer when it came to spending money." His frugality became an industry legend. He actually lectured his employees on the importance of saving not just pennies, but mills (a mill is one-tenth of a cent). His main goal for the company appeared to be cost reduction, and it worked for a good many years.

Organizations are likely to be particularly concerned with cost reduction when they are in a monopoly situation. Further expansion of the monopoly is risky, but a dynamic leader can always stress cost reduction. Since the market is more or less guaranteed, this becomes a significant lever. Many public agencies operate in this environment— their market or domain is established by some parent body, such as the legislature, and they are expected to carry out the mandate at the lowest posible expense to the public. Eastern was in such a situation, with a near monopoly on its most profitable routes, particularly the lush New York–Miami run. Its only competitor there was small and could not field as many flights as Eastern. For Eastern, its route structure meant that it was easy to make money as long as costs were kept under control, and this is what Rickenbacker did.

However, cutting costs meant reducing services. The airline was slow in introducing faster and more comfortable aircraft, which started to come along every three or four years. Tight scheduling, to ensure maximum use of aircraft, and careful control of maintenance saved money, but this meant that scheduling and maintenance were at the convenience of the company, not the customers, and less desirable departure and arrival times were utilized. Service aboard the plane was spartan; given the cost of a ticket, the saving on a midmorning snack was really pinching pennies. Coffee and cookies were served instead of breakfast. Seating was five abreast in contrast to four on other lines. While other airlines were hiring pretty stewardesses, Eastern retained male stewards on the grounds that they could perform a wider range of duties and would not give up their jobs to get married. Errors in reservations were frequent, as was overbooking. Airlines count on some no-shows, and therefore on some runs they sell more seats than they have. But Eastern did it more frequently and blatantly. In one celebrated instance *nine* more passengers than could be accommodated showed up with confirmed reservations. Seven of them accepted their fate stoically, but two decided they had had enough of this treatment from Eastern. They stood under the plane's propellers for more than an hour, preventing take-off. (You can understand how the airport security guards might be reluctant to drag away forcibly two businessmen in front of a gathering crowd.) The newspapers covered the story, and soon an informal organization called Wheals—We Hate Eastern Air Lines—came into existence and appealed to the Civil Aeronautics Board.

Meanwhile, the competition, investing in newer planes, nonstop service conveniently scheduled, pretty girls, and good food started to cut into Eastern's near-monopoly. The final straw was the decision of the Civil Aeronautics Board to strengthen smaller lines and competition by giving them a chance at the more profitable and busy routes. This step affected all large airlines, but Eastern was already performing poorly. With old equipment, poor service, and inconvenient schedules at Eastern, the interlopers did well and Eastern started to go under. The line lost increasing amounts of money from 1960 to 1963, and its share of trunk-line traffic was cut by one-third. Rickenbacker had retired in 1959, just before the deluge. In 1964, he commented, with his usual crispness: "It took 25 years to build Eastern and only three and a half years to tear it apart."

Rickenbacker held the largest single block of stock in the corporation, and his investment had grown enormously over the years. He had been able to run the organization as if he owned it all and to pursue the system and product goals that he desired (for example, low-cost operation as a system goal, and minimal service as a product goal). An interim executive did what he could from 1959 to 1963, but Rickenbacker was still active as chairman of the board. The new executive introduced innovations, such as the shuttle service out of New York, and he managed to secure massive refinancing. But it was only after Floyd Hall took over in 1963, and Rickenbacker had left the board, that company policies and system and product goals were changed. Hall did not own a substantial interest in the company and thus did not have much interest in high dividends and short-term profits. He bought new planes and introduced nonstop routes, substantially increasing debt; sold off unprofitable feeder lines; stressed customer service (reducing short-run efficiency), and undertook the then unsentimental and unusual step of changing the advertising agency in order to create a new image. The "new look" at Eastern paid off, and remarkably quickly. The worst year had been 1963; *Fortune,* writing in 1964, estimated that it might lose 15 million dollars in 1964, while the new president dared hope for only a five million dollar loss. It turned out to be 5.8 million dollars. The company has not done as well since. Its ten-year growth rate in earnings is still far below the big four, ranking about eleventh among the airlines, according to figures for 1967. Still, it managed to make 24 million dollars in 1967.

One way to look at this example is to say that the airline was mismanaged by Rickenbacker and allowed to get out of step with the times. From this viewpoint, the company's goal was and continued to be high profits. But this tells us little; it says Eastern's goals were just like the goals of other airlines, and the difference was that they used different means. Eastern's methods no longer worked in the 1960s, so it changed them. But referring to means and "poor management" only begs the question. Nor does the line's near-monopoly status explain too much. As Joseph Schumpeter once pointed out, the only successful monopoly is one that does not behave as if it is a monopoly. Furthermore, the other large airlines had their own protected routes.

A more telling explanation would be that mismanagement was not the problem and that, rather, the system goal pursued by Rickenbacker deserved analysis. Given the goal of maximizing profits through cost reduction, his preoccupation with frugality served the company extremely well for 25 years. Had the environment not changed and had his successors continued his policy, there would have been no question that the company had been extremely well-managed. The other airlines, we presume, had no such goal. For them, profit itself, from a short year-to-year perspective, appeared to have been more of a constraint on their activities, and not a very strong one, at that. *They* pursued goals of growth and innovation. We know very little about the other companies, but it does not appear that they were all mismanaged while Eastern made money, or that they were all well-managed when Eastern lost money. The other companies simply had different goals, and when their goals of growth and product innovation began to pay off, Eastern had to change its goals, too (Ross, 1964).

Growth

Growth is another possible system goal. Again DuPont provides an example. The company executives repeatedly stress, in their official statements to security analysts and other influential groups, that growth is not a goal of DuPont; instead, their goals are profitability and a high return on invested capital. In doing so they implicitly and sometimes explictly contrast themselves with those firms that are regarded as the very models of progressive management. Growth has become such a preoccupation of American business and is held by so many commentators to be the true goal of professional managers, that it is well to remind ourselves of firms like DuPont. Growth comes at a cost, and some firms are not willing to pay the price.

In my experience, many family-controlled manufacturing firms of modest size (around 30 to 50 million dollars in sales volume) are glad to grow *if* growth doesn't make life too difficult, cause them to be targets for mergers, dilute their control of the stock if the firm is public, force them to go public if it is not, or threaten their ability to ensure high corporate positions for sons and relatives. In view of all these risks, growth is not very highly valued. Yet these firms can be quite profitable, well managed, and even exciting places in which to work. (One cannot climb too high in them, however, for they will probably remain small, and a vice-presidency in a modest-sized firm is not as "high" in status as a department head in a large firm.)

Of course, growth is desirable for many other reasons. It is a validation of success and thus a sign of prestige. Perhaps incorrectly, it suggests security for all concerned. It certainly provides status escalators for managers, since it opens up promotions. It makes the top-management positions higher because, as the pond grows larger, so does the size of the frog. It provides more options for talent, as well as more places to hide whenever more sophisticated younger people come along. As the economy grows, there is room for all organizations to grow. But should the economy falter in the future, we may find that other criteria are held up by social scientists as the goal of the professionally managed firm. Growth may appear at the present time to be an inevitable goal of professionally managed firms in the view of social scientists, merely because it was achieved with relative ease in the 1960s.

Method of Operation

In some organizations the method of operation achieves the status of a goal; it becomes something to be protected at all costs and is seen as an end in itself. The statement, "We believe in running a tight ship here," is reinforced by personnel policies, structural arrangements, and by other means, so that when the organization needs to loosen up to adjust to change, it finds it can't alter the commitment to this system goal. (Other organizations, of course, have no such commitment and thus no goals in this area.) General Motors was apparently so profoundly affected by the revolutionary changes in structure carried out by Alfred Sloan in the 1920s that its decentralization of operations, with centralized fiscal and policy controls, has become an article of faith. Since General Motors does all right in its gargantuan way, and since these policies may indeed still have a great deal to do with its performance, there is no need to change.

But across the street, Ford Motor Company has pursued a quite different strategy for much of its stormy life. At one point it hired away a top G.M. executive with the avowed intention of modeling itself upon the G.M. organization. Somehow, while the whole structure was adapted in many aspects, it did not work, or at least it did not "take." Ford is an "open system" corporation, so to speak, where a man can move up rapidly if he is aggressive and makes a couple of highly visible, good decisions, and where he can go down or out just as rapidly as a result of one bad move. At G.M. such a posture would be heresy. People rise slowly; presumably, top-notch talent is stacked three or four deep behind every position of at least moderate importance—where they wait. (Of course, at G.M., this is well-paid waiting. With its commanding position and high profits it can afford this practice.) People are not fired; they are just moved aside. Some saw the costs of such a philosophy appearing in performance reports in the late 1960s. Ford had the jump on G.M. with Thunderbirds, Falcons, and Mustangs; G.M. found it must respond to Ford, rather than the other way around. Ford managers spoke of a policy of flexibility and of hit-and-run guerrilla warfare in the product line, while they tried to outdistance G.M. in the "Buck Rogers stuff" of econometric models of the firm and elaborate dealer-inventory simulation studies (Cordtz, 1967). It is clear that quite different managerial styles are operating here, and it would appear that General Motors' style has been entombed as a system goal.

Product Characteristic Goals

Two organizations may have identical output goals, such as making steel, but may nevertheless differ markedly in terms of their product goals or, more exactly, their goals regarding the characteristics of their products. Such characteristics are quality, quantity, type, cost, styling, availability, and so on. One often hears product goals mentioned in the following terms: "We don't go in for those kinds of fancy steels; we are only interested in producing the basic stuff that industry needs." Or, "We are the Cadillac of the steel industry—we produce the high-quality steels in small quantity and leave the easy stuff to the others." Two different product goals are being invoked here.

For other examples, consider these typical statements:

We thought of getting into that, and had the patents, but we sold them off; that is not our dish of tea.

We should never have gotten into this line; it is foreign to the rest of our operation, and we just don't have the experience or the skills.

If we start to turn this stuff out in quantity, now that we know how to make it, it is going to change the whole character of this company; we will become a production outfit, and our top R and D men will leave.

We engineer everything to death around here; by the time we get it on the market the others have sewed the market up. So what if our product is 10 percent better? It is two years too late. This kind of thing is all right if you are in aerospace, but not in our business.

Product-goal decisions are being invoked in these cases. Such goals become built into the company and denote a degree of specialization and distinctive competence that shapes the behavior of the organization.

The distinction between "producing" juveniles who have (hopefully) learned how to obey adults and those who have (hopefully) developed insight into their own characters and ways of dealing with things is a product-goal distinction. Part of the difference between Dick and Inland, the institutions we described in the second chapter, is in their product goals. (Dick also had a system goal of stability and little change, while Inland prized change and did not value stability.) Both sought to reform delinquents, but the characteristics of their products differed markedly.

As with other types of goals, decisions about product characteristics are not susceptible to handy slogans or rules-of-thumb. More than one company has found that it did not have the capability to go from low-volume, high-cost quality items to high-volume, low-cost standard items. The whole character of the company can change with such a shift, and unanalyzed or unknown competencies and market situations that were highly favorable can evaporate.

The Great A & P

Until recently, the Great Atlantic and Pacific Tea Company had been the largest grocery chain in the nation; for as long as most people could remember it had been the most successful and profitable one as well (*Fortune,* March 1963). It had built up its commanding position by an emphasis upon foodstuffs of uniform and good quality, priced low to ensure high volume. Then consumer habits and tastes shifted, and other stores found that consumers also wanted non-food items in the stores. These stores found the higher markup on these items very attractive. According to the *Fortune* story in 1963, A & P had dabbled in items such as drugs, cosmetics, kitchenware, and nylons but "with extreme caution and considerable distaste." A divisional president expressed the attitude in this way: "I think our primary purpose is to sell food cheaply, and tangents tend to hurt the food operation. There is a higher profit margin on non-foods, but it's *just not our business.*"

It was also "not their business" to engage in promotional devices such as Sunday openings, stamps, and loss leaders, except in unusual circumstances. The other chains were growing fast on these techniques. However, the 1963 *Fortune* article describes an imminent change in strategy. Three new executive vice-president positions were created for "younger men" to placate a board restive with low profits and aggressive competitors. The "younger" men were aged 51, 59, and 62; on the other hand, the chief executive officer was 73, and the president was 67. One of the new vice-presidents was Melvin Alldredge, who was quoted as saying that he thought A & P was slow to take on non-foods, and he was not against this new step. His own contribution had been an emphasis upon modernizing the stores by means of glamour and all sorts of conveniences. He had even experimented with a discount-house–supermarket combination, a revolutionary undertaking for A & P. There were, then, signs of change.

Product Versus System Goals in the Textile Industry

Forstmann and Product Identification   What is only a small part of the dynamics of supermarket retailing—the willingness to sell whatever the customer might buy rather than to maintain product goals—appears to be a matter of almost life and death in the textile industry. This old, technologically backward industry, protected by high government tariffs, government subsidies upon subsidies, and complex two-price systems, is still the haven of strong product identification among the executives. Their attachment to fibers such as wool, cotton, or silk and their resistance to new synthetic fibers, was so strong in the early 1960s that, at a meeting of the Fashion Institute of Technology, an executive of one large textile company was hissed by "silk men" in the audience when they felt that their true love had been slurred (Whalen, 1963). When the demand for long-established, high-quality goods evaporates, many old-line companies just fold in preference to adopting new fibers or cheap versions of the old fiber. This happened to the old Forstmann Woolen Company of New Jersey. They continued to turn out five-dollar-a-yard quality goods on 500 looms when the market would support the production of only 50 looms. Stricken by debt, they were taken over by J. P. Stevens, a company whose chairman said in 1963: "If the public wants straw, we'll weave straw. We're not wedded to any particular product or fiber."

This particular take-over is worth examining in a little more detail, for it nicely illustrates how a strictly fiscal goal of profit (a system goal) allows one to turn debts into assets . . . whereas a product goal ("We're in the wool business," or "We are in the business of producing high-quality wool at a price that will provide us with a reasonable return on investment") would render such a strategy unacceptable or even unperceived. I do not pretend to fully understand the matter myself, so I will just quote from the *Fortune* article, whose author, Richard J. Whalen, presumably knows what he is talking about.

> Forstmann was acquired for 280,000 shares of Stevens' stock, which was selling at $23 a share at the time, and its assets were transferred to Stevens' records at book value. Stevens tried to operate Forstmann but soon concluded its old mills could not be run competitively and would have to be liquidated. In anticipation of losses involved in running out and selling the Forstmann mills, a reserve fund was created. The proceeds of the liquidation, plus the reserve, produced a cash flow of $11 million for Stevens. In effect Stevens realized $41 a share for its 280,000 shares of stock. "It took two years of hard work and a lot of explanation to the board," said Kenneth W. Fraser, Stevens' financial vice president, "but this deal enhanced our equity by $11 million."

Indian Head and Profits

In direct contrast, in many respects, is the equally successful Indian Head Mills company, which has somewhat different system goals, although this company, too, is not enticed by any particular product-characteristic goals (Rieser, 1962). Indian Head Mills had been losing money badly, like most of the many modest-sized textile companies, when it was acquired by Textron in an effort to put together an integrated textile empire. Textron failed and began to sell off its textile property. The trade name of Indian Head was worth a good deal, and it was bought by an enterprising "professional manager," James E. Robinson, a Harvard Business School graduate with no experience in textiles. He proceeded to run it strictly in terms of that bedrock tenet of capitalism: money must flow in the direction in which it will earn the greatest profit. He began by selling off a good deal of Indian Head property and then buying more declining mills and selling off parts or most of them. This is easy to do. Even today, there are nearly unlimited possibilities for buying textile companies that have problems and can be acquired at less than book value. The losses thus incurred can be used to great advantage for tax purposes, as was suggested in the case of J. P. Stevens. Furthermore, with an unsentimental eye and no commitments to any products, Robinson retained those parts of the companies that were making money—thread here, lace there. He was able to put together an unintegrated but highly profitable group of companies strongly entrenched in their specific and narrow fields.

It is remarkable just how profitable the venture was. The new return on invested capital was more than double that of the industry as a whole, and in 1960 it was almost 20 percent. The stocks of eight of the ten leading publicly owned textile companies sold for less than book value; Indian Head stock sold for 2.7 times book value. The book value of a share went from $2.72 in 1954 to $60.00 in 1962. However, and this is the revealing figure, the company's *operating* profit in 1961 was only five percent of sales. Indicators such as return on invested capital and book value reflected something other than the company's ability to produce goods at a profit. One reason these indicators were so high was that from 1955 to 1959 the firm paid no federal income taxes at all, despite a high return on invested capital, and in 1961, when the return was 17.6 percent, it paid only a pittance in taxes. It was still carrying forward $1,400,000 of unused tax credits. Thus, its profitability was based largely on nonrecurring profits.

Fiscal sleight of hand? Paper profits? Not at all. These figures reflect the system goals of the company; it has no product goals. As expressed by the president, the goal is not to produce textiles, let alone to manufacture products of particular quality, variety, or novelty. Nor is growth the goal. According to the policy manual prepared by the president, "the objective of this company is to increase the intrinsic value of the common stock." *Fortune* goes on:

> The manual then explains that the company is in the business *not* "to grow bigger for the sake of size, nor to become more diversified, nor to make the most or best of anything, nor to provide jobs, have the most modern plants, the happiest customers, lead in new product development, or to achieve any other status which has no relationship to the economic use of capital.
>
> "Any or all of these may be, from time to time, a means to our objective, but means and ends must never be confused. Indian Head Mills is in business solely to improve the inherent value of the common stockholders' equity in the company."

The list of things for which the company is *not* in business is fairly representative of the variety of goals that companies can pursue: growth, diversification, quality, employment, technological advance, happy customers, and new products. But Indian Head is not even in business to make money out of production of goods. Its sole aim is to increase the value of the stock.

"We have no emotional involvement in the textile industry. We're in it through happenstance," said Robinson in 1961. Other members of the textile industry both on the business and labor side have assailed this philosophy. According to the *Fortune* article:

> They complained that Robinson does not try to save some of these situations by putting money into mechanization and automation in order to cut costs. A top official of one of the oldest and largest U.S. textile companies asked bitterly, "Is he trying to build up a textile business or just to make money?" Told of the comment,

Robinson replied, "He has the money. I don't have three generations of accumulated capital with which to protect the status quo."

What have been the consequences of Indian Head Mills' goal?
We have already noted the dramatic increase in the value of common
stock and the very substantial dividends paid out to stockholders. In
addition, however, Robinson was hung in effigy in at least one textile
town whose major source of employment was closed down. Also,
many plants both in New England and in the South were closed, with
resulting dislocation of labor and local economic problems. Viewed
abstractly, on the broad macroeconomic plane of capitalism, there
is a good deal of force in Robinson's logic. Money should go where it
will earn the greatest profit.

Thus, Robinson would disagree on a number of points with the
leadership of J. P. Stevens, which is also very successful. Robinson
believes in the elimination of subsidies and tariffs in the textile industry
on the ground that the industry needs to be thoroughly shaken up
before it can become healthy, whereas Stevens has led the trek to
Washington for tariffs and subsidies. Robinson feels the answer to
industry problems lies in neither mechanization nor automation because such steps merely increase the glut of goods in an oversupplied
market and lower the price. But Stevens is a leader in mechanization,
automation, R and D, and high-volume production. Indian Head rarely
invests in new equipment or attempts to improve efficiency in the firms
it buys, but simply writes off the inefficient segments, leaving the rest
as they are. In contrast, Stevens, which has itself made quite a few
acquisitions, invests further in their improvement.

Quality as a Product Goal

One of the most common examples of product-characteristic goals that
shape an organization concerns the degree of attention to quality. All
organizations proclaim their aim to be quality goods or services, but
what is generally meant is the degree of quality necessary to prevent
a decline in sales or customer acceptance. When we discuss quality as
a goal, however, we are speaking of those organizations that attempt
to provide goods or services whose quality exceeds that of competitors, or, in some cases, quality higher than the minimum demanded by
controlling agencies, such as legislators. Quality becomes a problem
at Ford Motor Company only when it appears to dip below the standards of its competitors. For Daimler-Benz, the makers of Mercedes
cars, quality is a goal in itself. That company has infinitely higher
quality standards than Detroit or the mass producers in Europe.

Organizations which are known for the quality of their goods or
services appear to have certain characteristics in common. They draw
upon a special pool of labor skills and management talent or have a

long history of employing talented people. They are conscious of their quality, pride themselves on it, talk about it a good deal, and often sacrifice short-run gains to maintain this goal. They cater to a select segment of the market—an upper-class neighborhood, in the case of schools; middle-class clients, in the case of welfare agencies; well-to-do customers, for business firms; or, in the case of industrial firms, customers that supply products to highly technical, specialized, and often government-related operations. These characteristics are not produced overnight in an organization or upon the stern warnings of an executive; it is difficult to move from a low-quality product to a high-quality product.

The case of Gar Wood industries illustrates how difficult it also is to move in the reverse direction, from high to low quality. After having produced high-quality custom boats, Gar Wood decided to compete with Chris Craft in the market for cheap, mass-produced boats. It found that it could not induce its workers to shift over to the new techniques and lower quality standards. The company finally had to give up production of the new lines at the base plant and build a new one in a location many miles away, hiring new people. Quality had been built into the old producing organization, and the shift in goals required a new organization with new people (Selznick, 1949: 53–54).

A glimpse of an organization with a product goal of quality is provided by the *Fortune* story of "Daimler-Benz: Quality uber Alles" (Sheehan, 1961). The firm built the world's first practical automobile and has been building quality cars in small numbers for over 75 years. The chief engineer of the company described the 75-year-old traditions as "constant experimentation, concentration on new developments, and continuous improvement." This has meant that the Mercedes has incorporated, as standard equipment, all significant innovations as soon as they appear, whether the public demands them or not and without regard to the increase in the cost of the car. For example, Daimler-Benz introduced such innovations as four-wheel suspension, fuel injection, and joint rear swing axle long before they were adopted by other manufacturers. The company is dominated by engineers and has an adequate pool of skilled labor. Its workers have lived and worked for generations in the German towns where the cars are produced, and they take a fierce pride in their skilled craftsmanship.

Not all firms which emphasize high quality need be small operations with highly skilled craftsmen. Magnavox has produced TV sets, radios, and hi-fi sound systems for years on a volume basis, while competing most successfully with the giants in the field (Brown, 1964). Here again a decision was made to emphasize product quality, and the marketing and production aspects were made to conform to that decision. While sales in the consumer electronic industry were standing still from about 1958 to 1963, Magnavox sales nearly doubled (to

200 million dollars in 1962). In 1963, it lead in many areas (stereo hi-fi phonographs, big-screen TV sets, and combinations). Its return on invested capital was a neat 26.5 percent in 1962—only eight of the 500 largest industrial corporations had a higher return. Magnavox managed all this by selling only "big-ticket" (high-priced), high-quality products through franchised dealers at an absolutely firm price. Zenith, for example, had about 30,000 retailers in 1963; Magnavox had no middlemen and only 2,200 dealers—in the best department and music stores, strategically located around the country. Discount sales are endemic to the industry, but unheard of for Magnavox. The company does little innovating, but waits for others to develop long-play records, stereo, and color TV. However, it is insistent on quality.

Incidentally, Magnavox violates many prescriptions of progressive management as well. It is run single-handedly by a perfectionist president, who is the largest stockholder (8 percent), with a very small administrative staff, no committees, and a small executive team that he brought in from the outside. "I have not had the time or patience to develop management," the president admits. There is no emphasis upon growth *per se,* and only with a great deal of reluctance did the company "compromise" itself by introducing a low-priced "second set." A salesman, the president said, would be a fool to push it when he can make much more on the higher priced sets. An inexpensive phonograph was developed, only to be junked by the president when he heard its tone. An emphasis upon high quality need not be associated with one-man rule, but perhaps it helps when high volume is involved.

Derived Goals

Finally, let us at least mention a somewhat residual category, one rarely dealt with explicitly in these terms, but of great importance for understanding organization—derived goals. We tend to forget, or neglect, the fact that organizations have an enormous potential for affecting the lives of all who come into contact with them. They control or can activate a multitude of resources, not just land and machinery and employees, but police, governments, communications, art, and other areas, too. That is, an organization, as a legally constituted entity, can ask for police protection and public prosecution, can sue, and can hire a private police force with considerably wider latitude and power than an individual can command. It can ask the courts to respond to requests and to make legal rulings. It can petition for changes in other areas of government—zoning laws, fair-trade laws, consumer labeling, and protection and health laws. It determines the content of advertising, the art work in its products and packages, the shape and color of its buildings. It can move out of a community, and it selects the communities in which it will build. It can invest in times of imminent recession or it can retrench; support or fight government economic policies or fair employment practices. In short, organizations generate a great deal of power that may be used in a way not directly related to producing goods and services or to survival. Presumably, organizations need most of these powers to function, but there is also a great deal of latitude in how the power is exercised.

We explored many of these issues at the end of the last chapter, when we spoke of the organization's impact upon its environment. They are discussed to some extent in books and courses dealing with the "social responsibilities" of business and businessmen. These issues also constitute a topic which is appended to the business-school training program with little enthusiasm, many generalities and much oracular moralism. The whole question deserves better, not only because economic organizations have an enormous impact upon our society, but because derived goals become embedded in organizations and should be closely examined if we wish to understand organizations. Neither the simplicities of the radical left nor the mushy self-congratulation of the business community will suffice. But if these two have failed us in understanding how power is utilized, so has the social scientist. Organizational analysis has been wary of dealing with organizational goals in general, let alone with the subtle, submerged, and latent area of derived goals.

Goals and Organizational Character

I have paid so much attention, and devoted so many pages, to the neglected area of goals because I believe that they provide a key, not found elsewhere, to an organization's "character," and thus to its behavior. The concept of technology can tell us much; the examination of structure can tell us more. But goals are, to some unknown but perhaps substantial degree, independent of these factors. At the least, they provide a quick conceptual entry to the organization. Finally, they reflect more readily the uniqueness of organizations and the role of specific influences within the more general technological and structural categories. For goals are the product of a variety of influences, some of them enduring and some fairly transient. To enumerate some of these influences: the personality of top executives, the history of the organization, its community environment, the norms and values of the other organizations with which it deals (e.g., the "mentality of the steel industry"), the technology and structure of the organization, and ultimately the cultural setting.

Few organizations, like few individuals, have peripheral vision, enabling them to single out and accurately assess all the events that might be important to them. Some successful organizations, like some successful individuals, have tunnel vision—they see only in one direction, and they see a narrow bit of the world at that. The range of vision can be altered. Expanding a sales department into a marketing department and conducting market surveys and systematic studies of competitors' behavior is a way of broadening vision. Some other ways include diversifying the board of directors, recruiting middle and upper management from other industries, doing basic research, and participating in trade associations. But only to a limited extent can the organization rely upon these techniques, for even with expanded vision the goals of the organization still provide highlights and blinders. Montgomery Ward did not "see" the extent of the move to the suburbs (Sears did), not because of faulty intelligence information, but because the diversification and investment that would be required with suburban stores was incompatible with fiscal beliefs and centralized authority (or was thought to be). A & P did not miss the obvious shift in consumer preferences because no one observed what the competition was doing, but because such a change in strategy would have meant a threatening change in management expertise and the need to introduce new people. A & P's goal was not to adjust to such changes, but to do what the company could do well: sell food in a straightforward manner at very low margins. (Actually, the situation was more complicated. A & P is also a substantial *producer* of foods, thus reinforcing its concern with high-volume food items; major investments, and thus much organizational power, lay in the production side of business.)

Goals become built into organizations, making change difficult. Personnel at all levels construct their organizational life around the reality of goals. Elaborate checks and balances can be constructed where risks are not favored, and these become justifications or, mistakenly, explanations for caution. Where risks are expected, the decision-making machinery is simplified and communication lines are direct and multiple; but when operations are conducted this way, it is difficult to ensure adequate analysis even when it is desired. Personnel who cannot adapt to the prevailing goals leave or find their advancement blocked; those who do adapt recruit others of similar views. Technical people are recruited for work on specific products, limiting the company's ability to shift to other markets. It is easier to buy a company in a different market than to break into it. In a sense, "people" do not resist change but, rather, patterns of interaction, relationships, bargains, negotiations, mutual adjustments, and, above all, forms of solutions or ways of handling problems resist change. The concept of goals, or organizational character, directs us to these types of formulations rather than to those relating to techniques or training.

Goals, in this sense, are necessary for concerted effort. It is possible for an organization to lack important goals, or to lack a distinctive character. Without firm goals, such organizations are subject to vagrant pressures from within and without, even as they may grow and prosper. There is, of course, a direction of effort, but it may be changeable, vulnerable, and not firmly anchored in the organizational structure. While this gives the organization flexibility, it also provides few resources for unusual effort of a concerted kind. Organizations are tools; system, product, and derived goals shape the form of the tool, indicating for what it can or cannot be used. An organization with weakly held goals is a poor tool for accomplishing ends, so that it may be shaped by opportunistic forces in the environment (Selznick, 1949: 74–75). Thus, goals represent a positive resource to organizations.

This is not to say that all goals are "good" or desirable; some may bring about the decline or demise of the organization, as we have seen in a number of instances (Isbrandtsen, A & P, Endicott, Forstmann). Generally, their goals were adequate in a different environment, but they did not change in time. Indeed, the problem is often that the past appropriateness of goals prevents executives from seeing their present inappropriateness.

Finally, it is clear that goals are multiple and conflicting, and thus the "character" of an organization is never stable. We have emphasized dramatic examples of goals and have generally singled out only one in a particular organization. But organizations pursue a variety of goals, sometimes in sequence, sometimes simultaneously. DuPont, for example, is both innovative and conservative; it is large enough to emphasize quality in some areas and quantity in others. At times these aims conflict; at other times the conflicting goals can be segregated, just as we have seen that organizations may include varying structures and technologies. It would even appear that tension among conflicting goals can be as healthy for an organization as the differentiation of subunits. Despite inevitable costs, such tension helps ensure ready channels for changes in goals, when appropriate (Wilensky, 1967).

We began this book by stressing the variety of organizational forms that exist and emphasizing that there is no one best way to run organizations. We have looked at varying technologies, structures, and leadership styles, and different means of relating to the environment. To all this we can now add that goals also vary and that "successful" organizations do not have identical goals. The *Fortune* profiles—the best single source of general material on specific organizations—illustrate the variety of goals that can be pursued by successful organizations. Presumably a complex society that values a plurality of means and ends will depend upon a variety of organizations that differ in their technologies, structures, and goals. For any one organization, the problem is to ensure that technology, structure, and goals are in harmony. This is what good management or good leadership is all about.

Sanctions and Effectiveness*
JAMES L. PRICE

This inventory has already indicated the types of economic and political systems which have the greatest likelihood of increasing the effectiveness of an organization. However, it is not sufficient that an organization have components which produce an output and make decisions; it must also have components which will motivate the members of the organization to conform to its decisions. *Control* system may be defined as the components of a social system which motivate conformity to norms.

Proposition 1. Organizations which have a high degree of sanctions are more likely to have a high degree of effectiveness than organizations which have a low degree of sanctions.

Definition A *sanction* may be defined as role performance, the primary significance of which is gratificational–deprivational (Gross *et al.,* 1958: 65). *Positive* sanctions are gratificational and *negative* sanctions are deprivational. Examples of sanctions are the use of physical force, material resources, praise, and criticism. Material about sanctions is frequently found in discussions of "rewards," "punishments," and "incentives." One of the functions which primary groups are supposed to have for effectiveness is the reduction of tensions (sometimes called "tension management"). Since one of the functions of "grievance procedures" is supposed to be the reduction of tensions, the material about "grievance procedures" is also relevant to sanctions.
    Melman's study (1958) of the Standard Motor Company and Warner and Low's study (1947) of the seven shoe factories in Yankee City provide contrasting illustrations of the proposition. Sanctions have a negative impact on *communication,* that is, the transmission of the information of a social system. (The next chapter will discuss communication.) Blau's study (1955) of a department of a federal enforcement agency provides an illustration of this dysfunction.

Proposition The Standard Motor Company was an English firm which produced motor vehicles and tractors to make a profit. Melman provides data about the profit of the company (1958: 168–170, 248–257). The amount of profit earned per vehicle produced, the size of total profit, the amount of profit on total assets employed—all indicate a relatively low degree of profit. However, if the earning of profit is measured by market penetration, the growth of net assets, or the rate

* Reprinted with slight omissions from *Organizational Effectiveness: An Inventory of Propositions* (Homewood, Illinois: Richard D. Irwin, Inc., 1968), pp. 137–162. By permission of the author and the publisher.

of dividends paid as a percent of the par value of its stock, then the company was satisfactorily achieving its profit goal. Since all of these indicators are valid measures of profit, and since Melman presents no data from which to determine how the major decision makers in the company measure achievement of their profit goal, it is not possible to evaluate the company's success in making a profit. In short, the effectiveness of the company cannot be unequivocally determined. (Since Melman was not basically interested in explaining variations in profit—his main concern was productivity—it is not surprising that his information about profit is ambiguous.)

He does, however, provide information about productivity and turnover. With respect to productivity, the Standard Motor Company's number of man-hours per tractor decreased 14 percent between September, 1948, and August, 1950; the output per employee in 1953 was 10 percent higher than the average for the industry; and the number of vehicles produced per thousand pounds sterling of stock and work in progress was higher than that of its competitors in the British motor vehicle industry during 1953–1954 (1958: 164–170). Consequently, the company appears to have had a high degree of productivity. The company also appears to have had a low degree of turnover (pp. 163–164). Melman states: "In 1951, the turnover rate per 100 workers in the motor vehicle industry was 29.9. This meant that for every 100 workers employed in 1951, on the average, in the plants of the industry 29.9 changed employment during that year. The turnover rate in the Standard Motor Company for 1951 was 17.5 per 100 employees . . . (p. 163). This inventory assumes that the company's low degree of turnover indicates a high degree of morale. Since turnover is proscribed by the management (because, among other things, turnover increases the cost of maintaining a trained work force), it can also be interpreted as an example of deviant behavior. This inventory, for reasons which will soon be evident, interprets turnover as a measure of morale *and* deviant behavior.

Melman, in his attempt to explain the company's high degree of productivity, notes that the "terms of employment" for the nonsupervisory production workers were determined by collective bargaining between management and trade-union representatives of the workers (pp. 41–80). Included in the terms of employment were such issues as who might participate in the work force, amount of work time, movement of workers among jobs in the plant, work loads of the different jobs, and all aspects of payment by the employer. Melman calls collective bargaining "bilateral decision making" to distinguish it from the "unilateral decision making" of the remaining segments of the company.

The company's bilateral decision-making process for determining the terms of employment increased the relative cost of labor to machinery (pp. 141–177). The workers, through their elected trade-union representatives, made decisions to improve their conditions of work; these improvements were a cost to the management, and, since the rise of machinery costs was not as rapid as the increase in labor costs, the result was an increase in the relative cost of labor to machinery. Because labor became relatively more expensive, compared to machinery, and because alternative forms of production could still be selected by the management, the management was motivated to increase mechanization. The company's high degree of productivity was a result of the increased degree of mechanization.

The Standard Motor Company also offered its production workers an impressive array of benefits. The company paid the highest wage in the British motor vehicle industry. In 1950, the average hourly earnings in the company were 69 pence per hour; the average hourly earnings for the whole motor vehicle industry were 46 pence per hour (p. 29). The company also offered its wage workers a shorter workweek than the rest of the motor vehicle industry (p. 51), it compared very favorably with other British plants in terms of physical facilities (such as spaciousness, height of ceilings, overall cleanliness, lighting, layout of machines on the plant floor, and attention to safety considerations) (p. 72), and it provided important nonwage payments (such as a clubhouse and athletic field near the principal plants of the firm, a subsidized cafeteria, payments during periods of sickness, payment to shop stewards for the time they devoted to collective bargaining during regular working hours, and the right to purchase company products at a discount) (pp. 150–151). Since the primary significance of these benefits is gratificational, this inventory suggests that the company dispensed a high degree of positive sanctions to its production workers.

Absolute wage levels assume little importance in Melman's explanation of the company's high degree of productivity. As just indicated, he argues that the company's bilateral decision making with respect to the terms of employment increased the *relative* cost of labor to machinery, and thus *motivated the management* to mechanize their plants more extensively. The company improved its productivity because of the increased mechanization. This inventory also suggests that the high relative cost of labor to machinery *motivated the workers'* high degrees of morale and conformity, because the high *relative* cost gave the workers a high degree of *absolute* benefits. The high degrees of morale and conformity probably added a small increment to productivity. There are a multitude of opportunities for the members of an organization to sabotage its operations and thereby to increase its cost. By and large, it would appear that a labor force with a high degree of morale will more often decide for the benefit of the organization, at the points where they are free to make decisions, than a labor force with a low degree of morale; and, every reduction in cost means an increased degree of productivity. With respect to conformity, a labor force which is characterized by the small turnover preferred by the management reduces the cost of maintaining a trained labor force and thereby increases the degree of productivity.

Proposition   Warner and Low are aware of the fact that the economic situation of the shoe factory workers in Yankee City had deteriorated (Warner and Low, 1947: 8–30). In summarizing the grievances of the workers, they state:

> The three major specific grievances of the operatives of all Yankee City shoe factories at the beginning of 1933 were: (1) that wage rates had been cut so much that operatives not only could not maintain a decent standard of living, but were unable to obtain even the bare necessities of life; (2) that the workers spent most of their time in the factories waiting for work, for which time they received no pay since most operatives were paid on a piece-work basis; and (3) that they were required to make, without extra pay, mostly novelty shoes which involved a great deal of extra work and militated against fast work because of constant style changes . . . (p. 24).

Not only are Warner and Low aware of the workers' grievances, but they believe that the economic situation was of "prime importance" in explaining the successful strike (p. 53). Since the successful strike indicates low degrees of morale, conformity, and effectiveness, and since declining wages were deprivational for the workers, it appears that one variable which contributed to the successful strike was the low degree of positive sanctions for the workers in the shoe factories. The shoe factories did not have sufficient positive sanctions to maintain high degrees of morale and conformity; the result was a decrease in effectiveness.

In summary, the Standard Motor Company was characterized by high degrees of productivity, morale and conformity, and a high degree of positive sanctions. Although Melman does not emphasize the significance of the *absolute* level of sanctions (he focuses on the *relative* cost of labor to machinery), this inventory suggests that a large supply of positive sanctions was a determinant of the company's high degree of productivity. The positive sanctions increased productivity by increasing morale and conformity. Since the shoe factories in Yankee City had a low degree of positive sanctions at their disposal, they could not obtain high degrees of morale and conformity, and, consequently, effectiveness decreased.

Dysfunction   The goal of the department of the federal agency studied by Blau was enforcement of practices designed to bring about uniform application of the provisions of two federal laws in two eastern states (1955: 99–101). The key role occupants in achieving this goal were agents who were responsible for investigating the degree of conformity to the federal laws by business firms. Any problem that any agent encountered in his investigation was supposed to be discussed with the supervisor; agents were officially prohibited from consulting with other agents about the cases they were investigating. However, because the supervisor was a major figure in the distribution of sanctions, and because discussion of problems with the supervisor would have revealed some lack of competence on the part of the agents, and thus adversely affected his evaluation by the supervisor, the agents did not generally seek the assistance of the supervisor. Since an adverse evaluation by the supervisors would be deprivational to the agents, it is a negative sanction.

In defiance of the norm prohibiting consultation, an informal system of consultation developed among the agents, and this pattern, by destroying the anxiety which pervaded the decision-making process, contributed to improved role performance by the agents (pp. 99–118). In short, the effectiveness of the agency was increased. However, because the supervisor's assistance was not sought, communication was weakened. Since control depends on the communication of information, the weakening of communication reduced the supervisor's control over the agents. In this instance, the supervisor's lack of information did not decrease the degree of effectiveness. Since the supervisor is such a key figure in attaining a high degree of effectiveness, the lack of information might be more serious in other situations. Therefore, the existence of a sanction system appears to be generally accompanied by the difficulty of insuring accurate collection of information about the membership of the organization.

Discussion 1   The agents in the federal enforcement agency deviated from the "no-consultation norm," and this deviation increased the effectiveness of the agency. This inventory does not assume that *all* instances of deviant behavior are dysfunctional for effectiveness; the assumption is that *more often than not* deviant behavior is dysfunctional for effectiveness. One instance of deviant behavior which increases the degree of effectiveness does not invalidate the general assumption. It is also possible that the agency, despite this *instance* of deviant behavior, had a *generally* low degree of deviant behavior.

Discussion 2   The sanction system of an organization complements its system of decision making. A high degree of centralization, for example, will not increase the degree of effectiveness, no matter how well these decisions are designed to achieve the goals of the organization rather than the goals of the subsystems, unless the decisions can be enforced. Sanctions, as has just been indicated, are a key mechanism to secure this enforcement.

Explicit mention of sanctions was omitted in the previous discussion of decision making to simplify the presentation of the propositions.

Sanctions were, however, implied in the phrasing of the propositions, "other things being equal."

Proposition 2.   Organizations whose norm enforcer-norm conformer relationships are basically secondary are more likely to have a high degree of effectiveness than organizations whose norm enforcer–norm conformer relationships are basically primary.

Definition   A *norm enforcer* may be defined as a role occupant who is responsible for the enforcement of the norms of a system; conversely, a *norm conformer* may be defined as a role occupant who is responsible for conforming to the norms of a system. The typical pattern in organizations, for example, is a high degree of correspondence between the norm enforcer–norm conformer relationship and the superordinate–subordinate relationship: the norm enforcer is generally a superordinate, and the norm conformer is generally a subordinate. However, not all norm enforcers are superordinates, and superordinates do more than enforce norms. Norm enforcement is sometimes assigned to role occupants who are not officially designated as superordinates; and decision making is an important element of superordinate behavior not included within norm enforcement. Therefore, although there is frequently a correspondence, there is not complete identity, between a norm enforcer–norm conformer relationship and a superordinate–subordinate relationship.

A relationship is *primary* to the degree that it is diffuse, emotionally involved, biased, and governed by ascribed criteria. The clearest example of a primary relationship is a family in a rural area, especially in a society little touched by industrialization and urbanization. A relationship is *secondary* to the degree that it is specific, emotionally neutral, impartial, and focused on achieved criteria. The relationship between a doctor and patient in a large, urban, university-affiliated hospital in a highly industrialized society is perhaps the best approximation of a secondary relationship. Blau's previously cited study of a department of a federal enforcement agency illustrates this proposition.

Proposition   As previously indicated, the goal of the federal agency was enforcement of practices designed to bring about uniform application of the provisions of two federal laws in two eastern states (Blau, 1955: 99–101). The key role occupants in achieving this goal were agents who were responsible for investigating the extent of conformity to these federal laws by business firms. Investigation involved an audit of the books and records of the firm; interviews with the employer and a sample of the employees; determination of the existence of legal violations and of the appropriate action to be taken with respect to these violations; and negotiations with the employer.

Each case processed by an agent had to be written up and checked for errors, first by the supervisor, and then by a special review section (pp. 161–162). Reviewers were expected to return all cases involving errors to the agents who conducted the investigation; each error was supposed to be accompanied by a rejection slip, which was to be placed in the file of the agent who had made the mistake. To place a rejection slip in the agent's file was to evaluate unfavorably the agent's role performance; therefore, the reviewers were supposed to dispense sanctions to the agents. (The deprivational nature of unfavorable evaluations was indicated in the previous summary of Blau's material about the federal enforcement agency.) Since the disposition of sanctions is one way to enforce conformity, the reviewer–agent relationship was, in effect, a norm enforcer–norm conformer relationship.

Blau's investigation revealed that the reviewers officially found very few errors in the cases they examined (pp. 162–167). If a small error was found, the reviewer usually did not return the case through official channels but took the case instead to the agent who had made the mistake, and told him to correct it. This assured accuracy, without harming the agent's record. However, the reviewer's rating suffered, because his rating largely depended on the proportion of cases he had rejected officially.

However, Blau notes three types of situations in which the reviewers officially found more errors in the cases they examined (pp. 162–167). First, the reviewers found a higher percentage of errors in the cases submitted by agents of departments located out of the city (15 percent) than in cases submitted by agents of departments located in the city (5 percent). There was no reason, according to Blau, to assume that the agents located out of the city were any less competent than the agents located in the city. Second, *permanent* reviewers officially rejected more cases than *temporary* reviewers. The temporary reviewers were agents from the departments serving a six-month assignment in the review section; after the completion of their assignment in the review section, these agents returned to their original departments. The permanent reviewers were, of course, the officials assigned permanently to review work. Third, temporary reviewers who were not affiliated with friendship groups in their departments before going to work in the review section found more official errors than temporary reviewers who were affiliated with friendship groups in their departments before going to work in the review section.

This inventory suggests that Blau describes an example of deviant behavior: sanctions (the official rejection slips) which were supposed to be used by reviewers in the reviewer–agent relationship (in this instance, a norm enforcer–norm conformer relationship) were not used. As previously indicated, this inventory assumes that deviant behavior generally indicates a reduced degree of effectiveness.

Blau explains these differences in conformity (though he does not conceptualize the data in terms of conformity and deviance) by the nature of the relationships between the reviewers and the agents (pp. 162–167). Where friendships existed between the reviewers and the agents, conformity was less (the prescribed sanctions were less frequently used) than when the reviewers and the agents were not friends. The norm was generally not followed, because most of the agents assigned temporarily to the review section maintained friendly relations with their former co-workers. Conversely, the norm was conformed to (the prescribed sanctions were more frequently used) in those situations where friendly relationships did not exist between reviewers and the agents. Contact between the reviewers and the agents from departments located out of the city, contact between the permanent reviewers and the agents from departments located in the city, contact between the socially isolated temporary reviewers and the agents from departments located in the city—all were examples of nonfriendly relationships in which there was more conformity to the norm about officially reporting rejections.

Blau does not use the term "friendship" to characterize the relationship between the reviewers and the agents. What this inventory calls "friendship" Blau calls "informal relations" and "cordial relationships." This inventory suggests that relationships which are "informal" and "cordial" are probably friendly; and friendships are an important class of primary relationships, which, like familial relationships, are diffuse, emotionally involved, biased, and governed by ascribed criteria. Therefore, where primary relationships existed between the reviewers and the agents, the reviewers did not use the sanctions they were supposed to use (did not conform to the norm about officially noting mistakes); contrarily, where primary relationships did not exist between the reviewers and the agents, the reviewers did use the sanctions they were expected to use. In brief, norm enforcement duties which should have been fulfilled (and the exercise of official sanctions is a duty of a norm enforcer) were not fulfilled when the norm enforcer–norm conformer relationship (the reviewer–agent, in this case) was primary.

This illustration, taken from Blau's study of the federal enforcement agency, does not constitute a large section of his book. Consequently, Blau does not indicate the link between primary relationships and deviant behavior. This inventory suggests that primary relationships result in deviant behavior, because the roles in organizations are secondary. In Blau's study, the reviewer–agent relationship was supposed to be a secondary relationship; therefore, since the reviewer–agent relationship was primary, the relationship deviated from the secondary role prescribed by the agency. Organizations prescribe secondary roles for their members, because these roles are believed (correctly, as far as this inventory is concerned) to increase productivity to a greater degree than primary roles.

The federal enforcement agency, in summary, was characterized by an association between the use of sanctions and the existence of primary relationships. Where primary relationships existed in the norm enforcer–norm conformer relationship, socially prescribed sanctions were not used; conversely, where primary relationships did not exist in the norm enforcer–norm conformer relationship, socially prescribed sanctions were used. This inventory suggests that primary relationships are deviant, because organizations prescribe secondary relationships in order to increase their degree of effectiveness.

Discussion   Mann and Hoffman's study of two power-generating plants contains some data which seem to contradict Proposition 2 (Mann and Hoffman, 1960). The study will be summarized and an attempt made to reconcile its findings with Proposition 2.

The power-generating plants probably had a profit goal, because they were business firms operating in American society. However, because such information was not pertinent to their theoretical concern, Mann and Hoffman include no data about the definition, measurement, and achievement of profit.

However, the researchers provide data about productivity. Their data reveal greater productivity in the newer of the two plants (pp. 10–20). It required 171 employees to generate 664,000 kilowatt-hours of electricity in the newer plant; in the older plant, it required 300 employees to produce 515,000 kilowatt-hours of electricity.

Mann and Hoffman also provide data about the role orientation and role performance of the workers in the two plants. The workers in the newer plant had a higher degree of role satisfaction than the workers in the older plant. The most pertinent general finding was that 80 percent of the workers in the newer plant said they liked their jobs; 40 percent in the older plant said they liked theirs (pp. 77–85). The rate of absenteeism was also higher in the older plant (pp. 217–220). Since "satisfaction" means the same thing as "morale," and since absenteeism is a measure of morale, this inventory suggests that the newer plant had a higher degree of morale than the older plant.

The dimension of morale which is relevant for Proposition 2 is the morale of the employees in reference to their supervisors. Employees in the two plants were asked: "Taking all things into consideration, how satisfied are you with your immediate supervisor?" (p. 147). A significantly greater proportion of the men at the newer plant (called "Advance") than at the old plant (called "Stand") felt "very or quite satisfied" with their immediate supervisors. The exact figures were 66 percent at Advance and 36 percent at Stand (p. 147).

Mann and Hoffman distinguish three dimensions of supervisory competence: technical, administrative, and human relations (pp. 141–151). The authors define each of these areas by specifying the kinds of knowledge, or behavior, considered to belong in that area. Technical competence is measured (and also at the same time, defined) by the following question: "How well does your foreman *know* the *technical side* of his job—the operation and maintenance of the equipment for which he is responsible?" (p. 145). Administrative competence is measured (and again, defined) by the following question: "How well does your foreman *do* the *administrative side* of his job— by this we mean planning and scheduling the work that is done, etc. (p. 145)?" Human relations competence is measured (and defined) by the following question: "How well does your foreman *do* the *human relations side* of his job—getting people to work well together, getting individuals to do the best they can, giving recognition for good work done, letting people know where they stand, etc.?" (p. 146). (The emphases in the quotations are Mann and Hoffman's.) After making these distinctions, Mann and Hoffman attempt to relate supervisory competence to employee satisfaction with supervision.

In the two plants, the proportions of the men who rated their foreman as having an adequate knowledge of the technical and administrative sides of their jobs were approximately equal (p. 145). However, a significantly greater proportion of the men in Advance (the newer plant) than Stand rated their foremen as performing their human relations tasks extremely or very well (49 percent in Advance compared to 32 percent in Stand) (p. 146). Mann and Hoffman then state the point made earlier in this discussion: A significantly greater proportion of the men at Advance than at Stand felt very or quite satisfied with their immediate supervisors. The plant where the foremen had greater competence in human relations was also the plant where the employees indicated greater satisfaction with their supervisors. Mann and Hoffman argue, after a far more sophisticated analysis than is indicated by this sketchy summary, that human relations competence was more important in determining worker satisfaction with supervision than technical or administrative competence.

The researchers then indicate the specific foreman behavior included by the term "human relations" (pp. 151–159). Specific foreman behavior was correlated with foreman competence in technical and human relations dimensions. After a very elaborate analysis, Mann and Hoffman state ". . . a foreman who was considerate of his employees' feelings, was a *warm and friendly person,* and was reasonable in what he expected of his subordinates was considered to be competent in the human relations aspects of his job . . ." (p. 155). (Emphasis supplied.) Since being a "warm and friendly person" undoubtedly includes some emotional involvement, and since emotional involvement is one component of a primary relationship, a primary superordinate–subordinate relationship was a variable which increased morale.

The relevance of Mann and Hoffman's data for Proposition 2 should now be apparent. (To simplify the discussion, a norm enforcer–norm conformer relationship is equated with a superordinate–subordinate relationship.) The proposition indicates that the relationship should be basically *secondary* to insure the greatest likelihood of a high degree of effectiveness. Yet, the supervisors Mann and Hoffman studied had a *primary* relationship with their subordinates, and this relationship appeared to be functional for effectiveness. Mann and Hoffman's material thus appears to contradict Proposition 2.

The findings can be reconciled when primary and secondary relationships are viewed as a matter of *degree.* A superordinate–subordinate relationship can be *basically* secondary and still exhibit some *features* of a primary relationship. In other words, basically secondary does not mean *totally* secondary. This inventory suggests that the superordinate–subordinate relationship Mann and Hoffman describe was basically secondary; the warm and friendly superordinate probably allowed only an element of a primary relationship to enter the superordinate–subordinate relationship. Had the superordinate–subordinate relationship which Mann and Hoffman described been basically primary, it is very unlikely that this relationship would have been functional for effectiveness. Blau's data about the federal enforcement agency illustrates how a superordinate–subordinate relationship which is basically primary is dysfunctional for effectiveness.

Proposition 3. *Organizations which have sanction systems with a high degree of grade are more likely to have a high degree of effectiveness than organizations which have sanction systems with a low degree of grade.*

Proposition 4. *Organizations which have sanction systems which are primarily collectivistic are more likely to have a high degree of effectiveness than organizations which have sanction systems which are primarily individualistic.*

Definition   A sanction system is *graded* to the degree that service to the social system is positively sanctioned, and lack of service is negatively sanctioned (Parsons, 1954: 34–49). The greater the service to the social system, the greater should be the positive sanctions; conversely, the less the service, the fewer should be the positive sanctions. Material relevant to graded sanction systems appears under many different headings: "distributive justice," "operation by achieved rather than ascribed criteria," "vertical mobility," "promotion from within rather than lateral promotion," "open and closed systems," "social stratification," "circulation of the elite," and "careers."

A sanction system is *collectivistic* to the degree that it is based on group output; conversely, a sanction system is *individualistic* to the degree that it is based on individual output. In a life insurance sales office, for example, salesmen's income can be designed to vary with the amount of insurance sold by single salesmen or with the amount sold by the entire membership of the sales office. If an individualistic means of payment were used, there would be wide variations in individual incomes, because not all salesmen would sell the same amount of insurance. However, if the collectivistic means of payment were used, all the salesmen would receive the same income, despite variations in individual performance. Fluctuations of income exist with the collectivistic means of payment, but the fluctuations are contingent upon the amount of insurance sold by the entire sales agency, rather than by individual salesmen.

Melman's previously cited study of the Standard Motor Company and Shih's study of a Chinese factory illustrate the proposition about a graded sanction system (Melman, 1958; Shih, 1944). The relationship between a collectivistic sanction system and effectiveness is also illustrated by Melman's data. Unfortunately, none of the studies surveyed contains an illustration of an individualistic sanction system and a low degree of effectiveness.

Proposition 3   Melman examines the Standard Motor Company's sanction system in his attempt to explain its high degree of productivity. One facet of the sanction system which he examines is the nature of the wage payments received by the production workers.

The wage payments of the workers consisted of two components, a guaranteed weekly wage and a bonus (Melman, 1958: 11–14, 37–40, 48, and 61–62). Irrespective of a plant's output, the workers received their guaranteed weekly wage. However, the bonus fluctuated with the plant's output: the greater the output, the greater the bonus. The bonus payments were of significance to the workers, because approximately half of their average weekly earnings depended upon the plant's output. Since wage payments are sanctions, and since output is a service to the organization (the greater the output, the greater the likelihood of increased productivity), and since wage payments varied directly with output (sanctions varied directly with service), this inventory suggests that the company had a graded sanction system for its production workers.

Melman does not focus primarily on the bonus system. However, his frequent citation of the bonus system suggests that he believes that a sanction system (of which the bonus system is a part) should be related to output, if productivity is to be increased. Consequently, the greater output of the Standard Motor Company may have been partially a result of the fact that the workers received higher average weekly earnings (due to the increased bonus payments) when output was higher. In brief, some of the company's high productivity was possibly due to the fact that the production workers had a graded sanction system.

Since Melman does not conceptualize his material in terms of a graded sanction system, he does not raise the question of how a graded sanction system increases effectiveness. This inventory suggests that there is a norm of "social justice" which closely corresponds to what has been called a graded sanction system. The norm of social justice requires that those who conform should be positively sanctioned, and those who deviate should be negatively sanctioned. Colloquially, the norm requires that the "good guys" should prosper, and the "bad guys" should suffer. Since the official norms of an organization are designed to increase achievement of the goal(s) of the organization (and, when conformed to, probably have this effect), those who conform are rendering a service to the organization; and, the greater the conformity, the greater the service. Consequently, when the Standard Motor Company varied wage payments with output (created a graded sanction system), it was establishing the kind of system which corresponded to the norm of social justice internalized by the workers. Because the company conformed to their norms, the workers had high degrees of morale and conformity which, in turn, increased productivity.

Proposition 5.3 The Chinese factory (called the "Kunming Factory") studied by Shih was government owned and operated and did not regard profit as its only goal (Shih, 1944: xxii–xxiii). The Kunming Factory produced electrical supplies; its apparent goal was to produce the electrical equipment as efficiently as possible in order to contribute to the war against the Japanese. (The research started August 25, 1940, and ended November 10, 1940.)

In a very brief discussion of "working efficiency" (pp. 60–62) Shih states: *"The opinion that workers, generally speaking, are not efficient is held both by management and workers.* The chief reason that led managers to welcome our investigation was that they are anxious to improve the working efficiency . . ." (p. 60). (Emphasis supplied.) After citing anecdotal material, Shih concludes: ". . . if we compare it [the Kunming Factory] with the factories in Shanghai in the pre-war period, *we must admit that the general circumstances of the war have brought about a lower working efficiency"* (p. 62). (Emphasis supplied.) Shih's "efficiency" means the same thing as this inventory's "productivity." Therefore, compared to the productivity of pre-war factories in Shanghai, the Kunming Factory had a low degree of productivity.

Shih presents systematic data about turnover among the production workers (pp. 132–139). He states: "The turnover of unskilled labor for the entire seven months under study came to about 18 percent per month. The turnover for skilled workers averaged 10 percent per month . . ." (pp. 134–135). The unskilled workers thus had a yearly turnover rate of 210 percent; the rate for the skilled workers was 120. The production employees of the Kunming Factory thus appear to have had a very high rate of turnover. If turnover is a valid indicator of morale, then morale was relatively low in the Kunming Factory.

The wage payments of the Chinese workers were not related to the factory's output (Shih, 1944: 63–77). Workers were paid on a fixed hourly basis; the rate remained constant, irrespective of the plant's output. If the workers exerted great effort, and managed to increase significantly the factory's output, they received no higher wages than they would have received had they put forth little effort and had the factory's output remained low. Therefore, the Kunming Factory did not have a graded sanction system.

Shih does not argue that the factory's system of wage payments adversely affected its productivity and morale. *The shortage of material and the lack of sanctions, two variables which Shih cites, were the major variables influencing productivity and morale.* However, the Kunming Factory did lack a graded sanction system and was characterized by low degrees of productivity and morale. This inventory suggests that the productivity and morale of the workers would have been increased if greater service to the factory (greater output, for example) had been connected with greater positive sanctions (higher wages, for example).

Proposition 4 In the Standard Motor Company, the production workers were grouped into gangs, and their bonuses were tied to the output of the gangs (Melman, 1958: 11–14, 34–36, and 65–71). Some plants of the company had 1 gang, other plants had as many as 15. The size of the gangs varied. In the plant with 15 gangs, the sizes ranged from 50 to 500 workers. Direct and indirect production workers were included in the membership of the gangs. The inclusion of the indirect production workers meant that membership was not restricted to individuals working on the assembly line but extended to the maintenance employees who kept the line in good repair.

This inventory suggests that the Standard Motor Company was characterized by a collectivistic, rather than an individualistic, sanction system. An individual worker, for example, could not increase his wages by increasing his output; individual incomes only increased as the output of the group increased.

Melman believes that the company's collectivistic sanction system (its "gang system" of wage payment) was a major variable influencing its productivity (pp. 65–73, 85–87, 110–113, and 120–128). The collectivistic sanction system contributed to lower cost by reducing the administrative overhead in two ways. First, since the earnings of the workers depended on group output, there was a built-in pressure favoring cooperative activity among the workers. Workers who failed to contribute their fair share to the production process were harming all the workers, and were, therefore, informally prodded to produce more by the other workers. Since the workers, in effect, supervised themselves, fewer supervisors were needed, and since supervisors were part of the administrative staff, administrative overhead was reduced. With a smaller administrative staff, the output per employee for the entire company (not just for the production workers) was greater. Second, the bookkeeping associated with a collectivistic sanction system was greatly simplified. Had the company tied its wages to variations in individual output, the bookkeepers would have had to maintain production records for each worker. However, with a collectivistic system, only the output of the group had to be recorded. Since a smaller volume of bookkeeping activities meant a smaller number of clerks, and since clerks were part of the administrative staff, the collectivistic system again contributed to productivity by reducing the administrative overhead and thereby increased the output per employee for the entire company (again, not just for the production workers).

In summary, productivity and morale were high in the Standard Motor Company, and the factory had a graded sanction system; on the other hand, productivity and morale were low in the Kunming Factory, and the factory did not have a graded sanction system. The illustrations thus reveal a positive correlation between effectiveness and a graded sanction system; it is also assumed that a graded sanction system was a determinant of effectiveness. This inventory suggests that a graded sanction system increases effectiveness, because it increases morale by being in conformity to the norm of social justice. The Standard Motor Company had a collectivistic sanction system for its production workers. Melman believes that the collectivistic sanction system increased output per worker, because it reduced the size of the administrative staff. This inventory assumes that increased productivity generally results in increased effectiveness.

Discussion 1 This inventory does not intend the Melman and Shih illustrations to resurrect the idea of "economic man." It is mere happenstance that both illustrations use money as the example of a sanction. The important point is that degrees of service and nonservice should be related to degrees of positive and negative sanctions. And it so happens that money is *one* example of a sanction. As previously indicated, sanctions include the use of physical force, material resources, praise, and criticism. Money would, more often than not, be classified as a "material resource."

Discussion 2 When role performance is highly professionalized, application of the idea of a graded sanction system requires a departure from the traditional pattern of organizations. Traditionally, organizations have implemented a graded sanction system by categorizing their employees, by assigning different ranks to these categories (thus obtaining a "stratified" organization), and by proportionately allocating sanctions to the different categories (the higher the rank, the higher the positive sanction). In the traditional pattern, supervisory employees are ranked higher than nonsupervisory personnel and, consequently, receive more positive sanctions. In the typical business firm or government agency, the traditional pattern probably is functional for effectiveness, because the supervisory employees are rendering services of a decision-making and enforcement nature which are vitally important to the effectiveness of the organizations.

The traditional efforts to implement a graded sanction system are probably dysfunctional when role performance is highly professionalized. Consider a university as an example of an organization with a high degree of highly professionalized role performance. (A medical hospital, a research laboratory, or a therapeutic mental hospital would serve equally well as an example.) Assume the following simplified system of stratification: president, deans, department chairmen, and professors. Assume further that sanctions are perfectly correlated with supervisory duties: all department chairmen have higher incomes and prestige than all professors. Since individuals seem to seek positive sanctions and avoid negative sanctions, were such an arrangement to characterize all universities (and this is not the case), the professors would be highly motivated to occupy administrative roles.

Such professional motivation, if sufficiently general, would probably be dysfunctional for effectiveness because of the strategic service which professors render to the university. Not only are the professors key figures in directly producing the output of the system (the educated student and the original research), but they also exercise a major responsibility in determining the nature of that output (what will be taught and researched, for instance), and in maintaining proper performance standards relative to the output (motivating conformity to professional norms of acceptable teaching and research). In short, the role performance of a professor constitutes essential elements of the university's economic, political, and control systems. When role performance is not so highly professionalized, as in a business firm or government agency, no single role occupant performs so many vital services for the organization. Therefore, because of the many strategic services which professors perform for the system, it would not do for universities to spur their academicians to occupy administrative roles.

The strategic services of professors (their performance of crucial economic, political, and control activities) require some modifications of the traditional efforts to implement a graded sanction system. One such modification is the creation of "alternate career patterns" for the professional employees. One career sequence could be as follows: professor, department chairman, dean, and president; a second series could consist of differentiation within the professional role: instructor, assistant professor, associate professor, and full professor. If it is to be truly an *alternative* career pattern, this second sequence should be so structured that not all administrators (presidents, deans and department chairmen) receive more money (this being one important kind of sanction) than all nonadministrators (the professors, for instance). Considerable flexibility is required to develop other procedures to implement a graded sanction system in situations where role performance is highly professionalized.

Discussion 3   It has previously been suggested that highly professionalized role performance should be concentrated in specialized divisions. For instance, in a business firm with an elaborate system of research and development, the scientists, who perform the bulk of the research and development work, rather than being assigned to the different production divisions, should be assigned to a special division of the firm devoting itself exclusively to research and development. The advisability of this type of arrangement has been indicated by the previous propositions dealing with economic and political variables; the nature of the control system would also seem to favor such an arrangement.

Consider again the business firm with an elaborate system of research and development. If the firm decides to create an alternate career pattern for its scientists, some of the scientists will receive more positive sanctions than some of the administrators. If this alternate career pattern exists only for the scientists, and if these scientists are dispersed among production departments where this system is not in effect, this arrangement is likely to influence effectiveness adversely. The egalitarian norms of the production employees will predispose them to react negatively to any "special treatment" (as the alternate career pattern will be interpreted) accorded the scientists; and negative reactions of this kind are an essential ingredient of low morale, which, in turn, is likely to decrease effectiveness.

These complications are avoided by creating a division specializing in research and development. The preferred type of career pattern can be established for the scientists, and the remaining employees (those exposed to the traditional manner of implementing the idea of a graded sanction system), because they will probably be less aware of the advantages accorded the scientists, will exhibit little or no decline of morale and effectiveness. Therefore, the type of economic, political, and control system most likely to allow the organization to make the best use of its professional staff can be best approximated in differentiated divisions devoted primarily to the performance of these professional employees.

Discussion 4   The construction of a graded sanction system requires the solution of an important problem, the measurement of service to the organization. The solution of this problem was apparently relatively easy in the Standard Motor Company, because the number of motor vehicles and tractors produced could easily be counted; and service would be directly proportional to output. However, in many situations, and especially for highly professionalized occupations, the construction of valid measures of a role occupant's (or a class of role occupants') contribution to effectiveness is an exceedingly complex task. Unless the measurement problem is reasonably well solved, a graded sanction system cannot be implemented. This probably means that it will be difficult to apply the idea of a graded sanction system to many roles in organizations.

Discussion 5 At least three unusually complex problems exist in devising a collectivistic system of sanctions. First, there is the difficulty of measuring group output. The solution of this problem was relatively easy in the Standard Motor Company, because the number of motor vehicles and tractors produced could easily be counted. However, in many organizations, such as organizations with a relatively large number of professionals, the measurement problems would be more troublesome. Second, there is the difficulty of selecting the proper subsystem to use as the basis for the measurement of group output. Many subsystems exist within an organization, and each could conceivably be used as the basis for calculating group output. This problem was apparently not particularly difficult for the Standard Motor Company, because Melman merely notes that different plants had gangs of various sizes. However, in many organizations, and organizations with a relatively large number of professionals may again be cited as examples, selection of the "number of gangs" probably will be more complex. Third, there is the difficulty of reconciling the propositions referring to graded and collectivistic sanction systems. If the members of a group are sanctioned on the basis of group performance, and if there are wide variations in what different individuals contribute to the group's performance, then *for each person,* degrees of service will not be related to degrees of sanction. This problem was not unusually acute in the Standard Motor Company, because there was apparently little variation in the contributions of the different workers. However, where there are wide variations in individual performance, such as among a group of scientists in a university, the problem of reconciling a graded sanction system with a collectivistic sanction system is a very complex task. These complexities in constructing a collectivistic sanction system probably will somewhat limit its use.

Program Change and Organizational Properties: A Comparative Analysis*

JERALD HAGE AND MICHAEL AIKEN

Our purpose in this paper is to relate the organizational characteristics of complexity, centralization, formalization, and job satisfaction to the rate of program change. We hypothesize that the rate of program change is positively related to the degree of complexity and job satisfaction, and negatively related to the degree of centralization and formalization (Hage, 1965). The rationale for each hypothesis is discussed below as the data are examined.

Study Design and Methodology

The data upon which this study is based were gathered in sixteen social welfare agencies located in a large midwest metropolis in 1964. Ten agencies were private; six were either public or branches of public agencies. These agencies were all the larger welfare organizations that provide rehabilitation, psychiatric services, and services for the mentally retarded as defined by the directory of the Community Chest. The agencies vary in size from twelve to several hundred. Interviews were conducted with 314 staff members of these sixteen organizations.

Organizational Properties and Rate of Program Change

Following the work of Pugh *et al.,* we find it useful to make a distinction between structural variables and performance variables as two special kinds of organizational properties (1963: 289–316). The former refers to the arrangements of positions or jobs within the organization, for example, the utilization of different professional specialties or the degree of complexity, the distribution of power or the degree of centralization, the utilization of rules or the degree of formalization. The latter refers to the outcomes of the arrangements of positions, for example, the rate of program change, the degree of job satisfaction, the volume of production. In addition we examine a personality characteristic of the individuals who work in the organization, namely, their attitudes toward change. Since we are interested in rates of program change, it is entirely possible that this is affected not only by the structural and performance characteristics of the organization but also by the general orientations of the individual members. Admittedly these are not the only distinctions that can be made, but they provide

* Reprinted from the *American Journal of Sociology,* 72 (March 1967), pp. 503–519, with omissions, by permission of the authors and The University of Chicago Press. Copyright 1967 by the University of Chicago. All rights reserved.

a useful framework for distinguishing among major kinds of variables, helping to isolate the characteristics that are part of the system.

Structural Variables: The Degree of Complexity

Since the publication of the English translation of Durkheim's *The Division of Labor,* the degree of complexity, or specialization, has been a key concept in the organizational literature (Durkheim, 1933: Part I; also Preface to 2nd ed.). For our purposes, we define organizational complexity with three alternative empirical indicators: occupational specialties, the length of training required by each occupation, and the degree of professional activity associated with each occupation. The greater the number of specialties, the greater the length of training required by each occupation; and the greater the degree of professional activity, the more complex the organizational structure. The term "specialization" has frequently been used to describe both this phenomenon and the minute parceling of work such as that of an assembly line where training of job occupants is minimized. From our perspective, the latter is the opposite of complexity. In order to avoid terminological confusion, we prefer to use the word "complexity" to refer to the former phenomenon, since we feel that this is more consistent with Durkheim's usage of the term (V. Thompson, 1964: Ch. 3).

A recently published axiomatic theory hypothesizes a direct relationship between complexity and the rate of program change (Hage, 1965: 303). There are several reasons why these two properties should be related in this way. The addition of new programs frequently necessitates the addition of new occupations. Job occupants of such occupational specialties often have a particular organizational perspective which leads to the introduction of still other new programs. Further, the professional activities of job staff members function as communications links between the organization and its competitiors, providing a source of information about new ideas and techniques. In addition, conflicts among the different occupational specialties in an organization act as a further dynamic force for the creation of new programs. The more professionalized the occupations, the greater the struggle to prove the need for expansion (Durkheim, 1933: 269–270). There is a correlation of .48 between the number of occupational specialties and the rate of program change. A variety of occupational perspectives is associated with a higher rate of change.

The amount of professional training is another indicator of the complexity of organizations. This was measured by computing an index reflecting the degree of formal training and other professional training for each social position in the organization. As can be seen from Table 1, there is a weak but positive correlation between the organization score of professional training and the rate of program

**TABLE 1.   RATE OF PROGRAM CHANGE AND OTHER
ORGANIZATIONAL PROPERTIES**

	Pearson Product-Moment Correlation Coefficients of Each Organizational Characteristic with Rate of Program Change*
Structural variables:	
1. Degree of complexity:	
a) Measure of the number of occupational specialties	.48
b) Measure of the amount of extra-organizational professional activity	.37
c) Measure of the amount of professional training	.14
2. Degree of centralization:	
a) Measure of the degree of participation in organizational decision making	.49
b) Measure of hierarchy of uthority	—.09
3. Degree of formalization:	
a) Measure of the degree of job codification	—.47
b) Measure of the degree of rule observation	.13
Performance variables:	
1. Degree of satisfaction:	
a) Measure of job satisfaction	.38
b) Measure of expressive satisfaction	—.17
Personality variables:	
1. Motive of self-interest and negative attitudes toward change	—.04
2. Motive of values and positive attitudes toward change	—.15

* The measures of association reported here are Pearson product-moment correlation coefficients. The units of analysis in this report are the sixteen organizations in our study, not our 314 individual respondents. Product-moment correlation coefficients are highly sensitive to even slight modifications of numerical scores with so few cases. We rejected the use of non-parametric measures of association because our scales are lineal and not ordinal; non-parametric statistics necessitate our "throwing away" some of the magnitude of variations in our data. Since those sixteen organizations represent a universe of organization, tests of statistical significance are inappropriate.

change ($r = .14$). Thus the amount of professional training in an organization is positively associated with the rate of program change.

To measure the extent of the extra-organizational professional activity of members of each organization, the respondents were asked to report the number of professional associations to which they belonged, the proportion of meetings attended, the number of papers given, and offices held, all of which represent professional involvement. The higher this score, that is, the greater the extra-organizational professional activities of members of the organization, the more likely it was to have a high rate of program change, as shown in Table 1

$(r = .37)$. It should be noted that the amount of professional involvement is more highly related to program change than the amount of professional training.

Involvement in extra-organizational professional activities evidently heightens awareness of programmatic and technological developments with a profession (V. Thompson, 1965: 10–13). Professionally active job occupants introduce new ideas into the organization, and the outcome is a high rate of program change. Similarly, r ɔw programs require the addition of new job occupants who are highıy trained. A plausible line of reasoning is that greater extra-organizational professional activity implies a greater emphasis on the improvement of the quality of client service. Such an emphasis requires a continual application of new knowledge, whether reflected in new programs or in new techniques. The number of occupational specialties and the amount of extra-organizational professional activity were themselves related; the correlation coefficient was .29. The sheer presence of different occupational perspectives, implying the idea of occupational conflict, appears to heighten professional involvement, as was suggested by Durkheim (1933).

Structural Variables: The Degree of Centralization

There are many debates in the organizational literature about the relative merits of centralization as opposed to decentralization of decision making. On the one hand, Weber argued that strict hierarchy of authority increased both the volume of production and the efficiency of an organization (1947: 334–340). On the other hand, the human relations specialists have argued that decentralization increases job satisfaction and reduces resistance to change (Coch and French, 1948; Reimer, 1955). Both arguments are probably correct.

In our study the staff members were asked how often they participɛ.ed in organizational decisions regarding the hiring of personnel, the promotions of personnel, the adoption of new organizational policies, and the adoption of new programs or services. The organizational score was based on the average degree of participation in these four areas of decision making. As can be seen from Table 1, the greater the participation in agency-wide decisions, the greater the rate of program change in the organization $(r = .49)$. Decentralization allows for the interplay of a variety of occupational perspectives. As Thompson has suggested, a centralized organization is one in which change can be, and frequently is, easily vetoed (V. Thompson, 1965: 13–18).

Agency-wide decisions are not the only kind that are made. Other decisions are those concerning the performance of a specific job. Agency-wide decisions are basically decisions about the control of resources, while job decisions are basically decisions about the control of work. It is at least logically possible that the centralization of the former kind of decision making can be associated with the decentralization of the latter kind of decision making. We measure the degree of decision making about work with a scale called the "hierarchy of authority" (Hall, 1963). This scale was found to have little relationship with the rate of program change, although it was in the predicted direction ($r = -.09$). It is the centralization of decisions about organizational resources, not the centralization of work control, that is highly related to low rates of this kind of organizational change.

Structural Variables: The Degree of Formalization

Rules or regulations are important organizational mechanisms that may be used to insure the predictability of performance. There are two aspects of the use of rules as a mechanism of social control; one is the number of regulations specifying who is to do what, where, and when; we call this the degree of job codification. Another is the diligency in enforcing these rules that specify who is doing what, where, and when; this we call rule observation. The latter is important because many organizations may not enforce all regulations. The degree of formalization is defined as both the degree of job codification as well as the degree of rule observation.

While it has been commonplace to argue that bureaucracies retard change, there have been few studies that have examined this proposition in a comparative framework. One of the essential elements of bureaucracy is its emphasis on formalization. Our hypothesis is that the two aspects of formalization outlined above retard the adoption of new programs because they discourage individual initiative (Merton, 1957a: 195–206). Clearly codified jobs that are closely supervised to insure conformity also reduce the search for better ways of doing work. Such a use of rules encourages ritualistic and unimaginative behavior.

As indicated by Table 1, job codification is inversely related to the rate of organizational change ($r = -.47$). The relationship between the degree of rule observation and the rate of program change is much weaker and is in a direction opposite from our prediction ($r = .13$).

Performance Variables: The Degree of Satisfaction

Since the famous French and Coch experiment, the advocates of the human relations approach to organizational analysis have emphasized the importance of morale as a factor in understanding differential acceptance of change and, therefore, implicitly differential rates of program change. We developed two different measures of morale—an index of job satisfaction and an index of satisfaction with expressive relations. There is a correlation of .38 between job satisfaction and rate of program change. On the other hand, satisfaction with expressive relations is negatively correlated, albeit the size of the correlation is small ($r = -.17$). This suggests a plausible explanation for several contradictory viewpoints in the literature concerning morale and organizational change. The work of Coch and French suggests a positive relationship between morale and change, but a series of studies by Mann, Hoffman, and others at the University of Michigan have noted that change creates social strain in the organization (Mann and Williams, 1960; Mann and Hoffman, 1960; Ronker and Lawrence, 1952; Walker, 1957). One may infer, not necessarily from our data, that job satisfaction may be a necessary precondition for the introduction of changes, but after this change has been introduced it may have disruptive and negative effects on social relationships among members in an organization. It is also plausible to argue that the organizational conditions that facilitate the introduction of change, namely, occupational diversity and decentralization, reduce satisfaction with expressive relationships because of the conflicts they engender.

Personality Variables: General Orientation to Change

It is argued by some social psychologists and psychologists that all collective properties of organization, such as the degree of centralization, the degree of formalization, or the degree of complexity, are ultimately reducible to psychological factors. Since this is a common argument, we attempted to measure several personality variables that might account for differences in organizational rates of program change. It could be argued that change occurs in organizations because the organization has a high proportion of individuals who are favorably oriented to social change. Selznick (1961) has suggested the idea of selective recruitment of certain personality types; that is, when an organization needs new job occupants, the attempt is made to recruit individuals who have personality attributes consistent with organizational needs. Mann and Hoffman (1960) have hypothesized the obverse of this process, namely, that individuals who cannot tolerate change will leave changing organizations and seek work in more stable ones (1960). Finally, Homans (1964) and others have argued that sociological variables are fundamentally reducible to psychological variables. While we do not accept this argument, we included measures of individual orientations toward change developed by Sister Marie Augusta Neal (1965) in an attempt to test the validity of such assertions.

The Neal batteries of self-interest motives, value motives, pro-change motives, and anti-change motives were factor analyzed and yielded two clear factors; one factor contains items representing attitudes of self-interest and a negative attitude toward change, while the second factor contains items representing attitudes of ideals and a positive orientation toward change. We would expect the former to be *negatively* associated with rate of program change and the latter to be *positively* associated with program change. We found only a modest relationship between these measures of attitudes toward change and the amount of organizational program change.

The measure of self-interest and anti-change was virtually unrelated to program change ($r = -.04$), while the measure of ideals and pro-change was related to program change opposite from the expected direction ($r = -.15$).

An organization can have a high proportion of job occupants who are favorably disposed toward change in their personal orientations, and yet the organization does not necessarily adopt new programs. The reverse pattern is equally true.

What this suggests is that the personality attributes included in our study add little to our understanding of organizational change as we have measured it. On the other hand, there is the possibility that there are other personality variables that are appropriate for the understanding of organizational change.

Contextual Variables, Organizational Properties, and Rate of Program Change

The fact that there are varying rates of program for our different kinds of agencies suggests that there may be disparate situations faced by each of our organizations. The rate of technological change may be faster in rehabilitation than in social casework agencies.

In particular, the organizations in our study vary considerably in their ease of access to resources, whether personnel or finances. They differ considerably in their age and autonomy. These and other indicators of their environmental situation can have an impact on the organization and its ability to adopt new programs. By studying the impact of such variables as auspices, size, and function, it becomes possible to view the process by which organizations are likely to develop one or another system. It also allows us some insight into the generalizability of our findings. If one of these variables accounts for most of the observed relationship between the rate of program change and the organizational properties, then we are aware of a significant limitation on our findings.

In a recent review of the organizational literature, Pugh and his associates suggest a number of contextual variables that can be used either as controls or as independent variables when examining the relationships among organizational properties. The variables that they discuss are: origin and history, ownership and control, size, charter, technology, location, resources, and interdependence.

To explore the relative importance of these environmental factors for the relationships discussed above, we employed partial correlations. A fourth-order partial correlation was computed between each of the organizational properties and rate of program change, controlling for *size,* auspices, age of organization, and major function.

Not all of the four contextual variables are related to the rate of program change. Both age ($r = -.03$) and aupices ($r = -.06$) were unrelated to this kind of organizational change as we have measured it. But size ($r = -.61$) and function ($r = .58$) were highly related to the rate of program change. The larger the size of the organization and the more time the client spends in the organization, the higher the rate of program change. Since these contextual factors are themselves interrelated (larger organizations were much more likely to be total institutions) and since these factors do have an impact on rate of program change, the question remains whether the relationships between our dependent variable and the other organizational properties will be maintained if we simultaneously control for all four of the contextual variables. To put it another way, we want to know if our results are a consequence of organizational arrangements or a consequence of the environmental situations.

In general, the observed relationships between rate of program change and the organizational properties remain, even after simultaneously controlling for these contextual factors. That is, even though the context or environment affects the organization, most of the organizational properties examined are still related to the rate of program change.

Another way of determining the generalizability of these findings is the examination of other studies of organizations to see if they found similar results. In a study of large business firms in the United States, Chandler suggests (1962) that increases in complexity as measured by product diversification led to the decentralization of decision making. This was especially likely to occur after the introduction of professional managers. These firms were also more likely to allocate a much larger proportion of their budget to research, indicating a higher rate of program change. Woodward's study (1965) of some ninety industrial firms in South Essex, England, suggests that those firms that made small batches of products or custom models were more likely than the assembly-line manufacturers to have professional managers, skilled labor, decentralized decision making, higher job satisfaction, and less routinization of procedures. While this study does not have a direct measure of the rate of program change, both of these studies are at least supportive of the findings reported here.

Conclusions and Discussion

Our findings suggest the following two stories about the rate of program change. One line of reasoning is as follows: Given that there is a high rate of program change, there is likely to be relatively decentralized decision making because of the necessity for discussions about the problems of change. There is a variety of decisions involving the allocation of personnel and funds attendant to the addition of new programs. In addition, the implementation of programs inevitably indicates contingencies not considered and engenders conflicts that must be resolved. Similarly, the high rate of program change will necessitate the relaxation of rules in order to solve the problems of implementation. There will be conflicts between the demands of the new program and previous regulations that will make rule observation difficult. The addition of new programs is likely to attract better-trained and active professional personnel who will like the challenge of change. And new programs can require, in many cases, new skills or areas of expertise relative to the organization. The high rate of job satisfaction can flow from the satisfaction of being a member of a dynamic organization. But the high rate of change creates strain in interpersonal relationships.

Another line of reasoning is as follows: If an organization is relatively decentralized, it is likely to have a variety of information channels which allow the consideration of both the need for new programs and their appropriateness. The sheer number of occupational specialties also increases the diversity of informal channels of communication. This is likely to lead to conflict among competing ideas for organizational resources. In contrast, the amount of job codification reduces the diversity of informal channels of information by circumscribing the occupants' perspectives, including the recognition of needs and the choice of remedies. Given that an organization is complex, decentralized, and non-formalized, then it is likely to be high in rate of program change. Such an organization is also likely to have high job satisfaction but low satisfaction with expressive relations. High job satisfaction evidently facilitates the introduction of changes, but the changes themselves are evidently disruptive of interpersonal relationships. The structural arrangements that facilitate change seem to generate conflicts among staff members. The diversity of occupational specialties, the power struggles in a decentralized arrangement of decision making, and the lack of clear work boundaries—consequences of the lack of formalization—are all conducive to organizational conflicts that are manifested in dissatisfaction with expressive relationships.

The nature of our data does not allow us to choose between these two lines of reasoning. It is our belief that both are correct and reflect again the system nature of organizations. However, future research should be directed to verifying which line of reasoning is more pervasive, but this will require longitudinal studies. Our analysis indicates that rate of program change is associated with configurations on other organizational properties, supporting the basic assumption that an organization is best viewed as a system of variables. While program change is only one kind of change within the system, future research should be directed to the question of whether other changes within the system, such as changes in rules as opposed to changes in degree of job codification, changes in who makes decisions as opposed to changes in emphasis on hierarchy, changes in techniques as opposed to changes in technology, can be analyzed in the same way. We feel that this study provides an illustration of how change within the system and change of the system can be differentiated.

Our analysis indicated that different empirical indicators of the three structural properties of organizations, that is, centralization, complexity, and formalization, are related differently to the rate of change in new programs, at least among the sixteen organizations in this study. The number of occupational specialties in the organization, an indicator of complexity, is a better predictor of program change than professional training or professional activity. Participation in agency-wide decision making is a more powerful predictor of organizational change than the degree of hierarchy of authority. Finally, the degree of job codification, an indicator of formalization, is a more powerful predictor of program change than the rule observation.

A partial correlation analysis simultaneously controlling for size, auspices, age of organization, and function demonstrated that most of the organizational properties have associations with rate of program change which are independent of variations in these contextual factors. However, function and auspices, to a lesser extent, were so strongly related to the number of occupational specialties that the relationship between number of occupational specialties—one indicator of complexity—and rate of program change disappears. Future research should attempt to consider additional contextual variables besides the ones included here.

A major theme contained in this paper is that it is important to view organizations from a sociological viewpoint. Our method for drawing the sample and the procedure for computing scores for organizational properties conceive of organizations as a collection of social positions (or jobs), not simply as an aggregate of individuals. Several different collective properties of organizations were found to be related to the rate of change. When individual orientations toward change were measured, they were found to be relatively unrelated to the rate of organizational change, at least as we have defined it. Our findings are supportive of Durkheim's famous phrase that "social facts must be explained by other social facts." That is, we were able to explain the rate of organizational change better with other organizational properties, such as degree of centralization, degree of complexity, or degree of formalization, than with measures of attitudes of organizational members toward change. Certainly this does not constitute definitive proof, but it does suggest that emphasis on structural and performance variables in organizations may be a more fruitful way to study organizational change.

Organizational Control Structure and Member Consensus*

CLAGETT G. SMITH AND OĞUZ N. ARI

Recent research in several organizations, including a clerical organization, several union locals, a service organization, and a voluntary association, has indicated that the manner in which control is structured, at least as reported by members, is related to organizational effectiveness (Morse and Reimer, 1956: 120–129; Tannenbaum, 1956: 536–545; 1961: 33–46; Likert, 1960: 214–227; Smith and Tannenbaum, 1963: 299–316; Tannenbaum, 1962: 236–257; Likert, 1961). These studies suggest the importance in some organizations of high rank-and-file control relative to leadership control and, more generally, the importance of a high amount of control exercised by members at all echelons in the organization. The interpretations offered of these findings suggest that these patterns of control may be conducive to high organizational effectiveness, in part, through the uniformity with respect to organizational standards and policies which they promote. Likert, for example, has suggested that significant influence exercised by persons at all levels, the leaders as well as the rank and file, provides the basis of the effective coordination of organizational activity. Such coordination is derived, in part, from the shared goals and agreement on the means to these goals which this pattern of control promotes. Similarly, the exercise of control by lower echelons is likely to bring with it greater acceptance of jointly made decisions as well as an increased sense of responsibility and motivation to further the goals of the organization. Such motivational effects are very likely to be reflected in increased uniformity concerning the decisions and goals of the organization. A relationship between a high amount of control exercised by persons at all echelons ("high total control") and member uniformity (as a criterion of organizational norms) was suggested in a study of local unions (Tannenbaum, 1956: 536–545). Furthermore, amount of total control and member uniformity were related to "union power," that is, effectiveness. The hypothesis was offered that a high level of total control is part of an organizational power syndrome including uniformity and effectiveness.

These interpretations seem to suggest one particularly significant process explaining the efficacy of these patterns of control in promoting high organizational performance, namely, the coordination and regulation of member behavior with respect to organizational norms. The resulting uniformity derives its significance from the fact that it is basic to the concerted member effort underlying effective organiza-

* Excerpted from the *American Journal of Sociology, 69* (May 1964), pp. 623–638, by permission of the authors and The University of Chicago Press. Copyright 1964 by the University of Chicago. All rights reserved.

tional performance (Georgopoulos, 1957). It is the purpose of this paper to consider further the relationships of patterns of control to member uniformity and to evaluate their implications for organizational effectiveness.

Theory and Hypotheses

"Control" refers to any process by which a person (or group or organization of persons) determines or intentionally affects what another person (or group, or organization) will do. In organizations this process may include formal aspects, such as formulating policy and making decisions, exercising authority in implementing decisions, and applying rewards and sanctions for conformity or deviance. It may also include informal mechanisms and techniques, such as non-legitimated pressures, informal discussion, and decision-making.

The "structure of control" designates the relatively enduring pattern of influence within an organization. Most generally, this consists of the pattern of influence of persons or groups upon the organization. This entails, in large part, influence *between* persons or groups of persons within the organization. We shall employ as a measure of aspects of control structure the technique of the "control graph," which has been discussed and illustrated in a number of earlier publications (Tannenbaum, 1956: 50–68; Tannenbaum and Georgopoulos, 1957: 44–50; Tannenbaum and Kahn, 1957: 127–140; Tannenbaum, 1961: 33–46). The horizontal axis of the graph represents the hierarchical levels of an organization from the top to the bottom. The vertical axis represents the amount of control exercised by those at each of these hierarchical levels, that is, how much influence each of these levels has in determining the behaviors in question, such as the actions of the organization or certain behaviors of members. Two aspects of organizational control described by the control curve are (1) the hierarchical distribution of control, represented by the shape or slope of the curve and (2) the total amount of control exercised by all levels in the organization, represented by the average height of the curve (Tannenbaum, 1961: 33–46). A curve which rises with hierarchical ascent is negatively sloped and might be said to fit the "autocratic" prototype, while one declining with hierarchical ascent is positively sloped and describes the "democratic" model. A low, flat curve, indicating relatively little control by any level would illustrate a "laissez faire" situation, while a high curve, indicating a high level of control by all levels, fits the "polyarchic" model.

In addition to specifying the pattern of influence of the various levels upon the organization in general, the control graph further permits a more specific description of organizational control in terms of patterns of influence existing between members of various levels. This pattern of influence may be specified both in terms of exercising control ("active control") and of being controlled ("passive control"). Thus the amount of control which persons at a given level exercise over those at other levels may be ascertained, as well as the extent to which persons at a given level are controlled by those at other levels. This permits a description of where in the hierarchy a given level directs its control, as well as the determination of the sources from which control over any given level originates.

Control and Uniformity

The relationship between control and member uniformity has been traditionally subsumed under the concept of social norm. This concept can be defined simply as the continuous uniformity in expectations, attitudes, or behavior within a group (or organization) regarding an activity developed and maintained by processes of control (Allport, 1962: 3–30). Central to this definition of norms is the premise that they are a function of control. While this constitutes the basic premise of the present formulation, the subject of our inquiry is more specifically the relationships of varying patterns of organizational control to member uniformity. We shall be concerned with uniformity in perceptions and attitudes which will be referred to as "consensus." The focus will be upon consensus within the work group and between members of the work group and those at higher echelons in the organization. Two general hypotheses can be stated:

Hypothesis I. Consensus within the work group and between members and supervisors will be related directly to the degree to which the control curve is positively sloped.

Hypothesis II. Consensus within the work group and between members and supervisors will be related directly to the amount of total control.

The first hypothesis is a restatement in terms of the control graph that "democratic control" will be conducive to a system of shared norms. The rationale for this hypothesis is based on several processes. Rank-and-file involvement in decision-making, especially in a society that extols democratic values, tends to foster conditions of identification, motivation, and loyalty to the organization. Such effects result, in part, from the satisfaction that individuals may derive from participation in decision-making, that is, exercising significant control contributes to their sense of importance and personal worth. It may also provide important pragmatic or material rewards to the members, and it may be expected to enhance attraction and loyalty of rank-and-file members to the work group. Loyalty to the work group, coupled with involvement and identification with the organization, should give rise to increased uniformity with respect to organizational and work-group standards. They tend also to promote a high level of participation and a greater amount of accurate communication and influence, permitting members to see what the norms of the organization and the work group are, as well as facilitating their determination. Further, relatively high rank-and-file influence in decision-making may permit members to develop policies and practices which represent the interests of a fairly broad segment rather than merely the interests of the leaders, and thus may further enhance acceptance of these decisions by both the rank-and-file members and the leaders.

While high rank-and-file control relative to that of the leadership may have these positive consequences under certain conditions, other authors have pointed up the necessity of control from above to insure efficient organizational functioning. Despite its detrimental effects, "hierarchical control" (negative slope) is viewed as necessary to insure shared organizational norms, effective coordination, and concerted member effort. Indeed high rank-and-file control relative to that of the leaders (i.e., positive slope) may result in a lack of consensus and conflict between echelons, if the rank-and-file members act simply in terms of their own self-interests, do not possess the skill to exercise control effectively, or do not accept the contributions of members at higher echelons (Maier, 1952; Selznick, 1948: 25–35; Tannenbaum, 1961: 33–46). The hypothesis as formulated assumes that these circumstances are not present.

The second hypothesis offers an approach to the dilemma stated above by considering the necessity of control by upper echelons *together* with the favorable effects of control by the rank-and-file members. This hypothesis states that a high amount of control exercised by persons at all levels in the organization will contribute to high member consensus within the organization. The hypothesis is based on a set of interrelated processes accompanying a high amount of total control previously elaborated by Tannenbaum and Likert (Tannenbaum, 1956: 536–545; 1961: 33–46; Likert, 1961). Part of these processes derive from the high rank-and-file influence per se inherent in a high level of total control, and thus the predicted effects in promoting high consensus are similar to those specified in Hypothesis I.

Likert suggests that the efficacy of a high amount of total control in an organization may be explained in terms of the existence of an "effective interaction-influence system," that is, a system in which there is high reciprocal influence and free communicative exchange throughout the organization. Such an interaction-influence system permits members to understand clearly what the norms of the organization are, as well as fostering their *joint* determination and enforcement. Furthermore, this process provides the basis of the effective coordination of organizational activity, in part, by facilitating the integration of the interests of both the rank-and-file members and the leaders. As a consequence, there is wider acceptance of policies and practices, and cooperative relations between members at different levels tend to be enhanced. This is likely to be reflected in a set of shared norms, in the form of means and goals, adherence to which tends to be "promotively interdependent" for all the parties involved (Zald, 1962: 335–345; 1962: 22–49). Furthermore, utilizing the contributions of both the members and the leaders provides the basis for better policies and decisions which, in turn, are likely to result in higher organizational effectiveness. Consequently, acceptance of such decisions tends to redound to the advantage of both members and leaders, because of the greater stock of disposable rewards accruing to the more effective organization.

In summary, it is these sets of interrelated processes arising from, or associated with, a positively sloped distribution of control and/or a high amount of total control which provide the bases for expecting relationships between these patterns of control and member consensus.

The present study is based on a survey of a nationwide service organization having operations in several metropolitan areas of the United States (Georgopoulos, 1957; Likert, 1961; Indik, Georgopoulos, and Seashore, 1961: 357–374). The primary function of the organization is to transport and deliver articles from central locations to homes. Each area is organized as a "plant" with two or more major divisions, and each division has several operating units or "stations." A typical station has a station manager, a supervisor, an assistant supervisor, several leaders who work at night, and about twenty-five drivers who work days delivering packages on their respective routes. The stations are geographically separate from one another, each one serving an exclusive territory. They are quite similar in facilities, operating policies, work methods and procedures, but differ considerably in performance and somewhat in size. Thirty-two such stations, representing five company plants, together including twelve hundred employees, comprise our population.

Results

The two hypotheses predicting relationships between degree of positive slope and amount of total control on the one hand and member consensus on the other assume that slope and total control are independent of each other. However, a high negative correlation ($r = -.67$) exists between degree of positive slope and amount of total control in the stations under study (Tannenbaum, 1961; 33–46). A high level of total control obtains in these stations through high managerial control relative to that of the rank and file; conversely high rank-and-file control relative to that of the supervisors is associated with the low amount of control exercised by the various levels in the station. In order to provide independent tests of Hypotheses I and II,

TABLE 1.   PARTIAL CORRELATIONS OF DEGREE OF POSITIVE SLOPE AND AMOUNT OF TOTAL CONTROL WITH MEMBER CONSENSUS

	Control structure	
Member consensus	Degree of positive slope*	Amount of total control†
Work-group consensus:		
Work standards	—.02	—.17
Morale	—.03	.50§
Adequacy of supervisory planning	—.27	.11
Trust and confidence in supervisor	.36‡	.65§
Influence desired for various levels	—.43	—.13
Hierarchical consensus:		
Work standards	.06	.38‡
Morale	.06	.23
Influence desired for various levels	—.37	—.17
Perceived consensus:		
Everyday operations	.37‡	.66§
Absence of conflict	.13	.53§

* Partial correlations between member consensus and degree of positive slope; log size and amount of total control held constant.
† Partial correlations between member consensus and amount of total control; log size and degree of positive slope held constant.
‡ Significant at .05 level of confidence, one-tailed test.
§ Significant at .01 level of confidence, one-tailed test.

partial correlations of degree of positive slope with work-group and hierarchical consensus were computed holding amount of total control constant; partial correlations of amount of total control with these measures of consensus hold degree of positive slope constant. These partial correlations are presented in Table 1.

Hypothesis I is not substantiated. Degree of positive slope is not generally associated with either work-group consensus or hierarchical consensus. The results suggest even that degree of positive slope may be associated in some instances with lack of consensus, specifically concerning ideal control. It is apparently under conditions of high influence of the managers relative to that of the rank-and-file members (i.e., negative slope) that norms regarding the control which members feel the various levels should exercise are likely to occur. High rank-and-file influence relative to that of the managers does have the effect of promoting the perception that people at different levels see "eye-to-eye" concerning the operation of the station irrespective of whether in fact they do.

The results suggest that a high amount of total control is the effective pattern conducive to both work-group and hierarchical consensus, furnishing partial support for Hypothesis II. Considered from the point of view of specific behavioral areas, the results by no means give unequivocal support for the hypothesis. Amount of total control is related to work-group consensus concerning morale and trust in the supervisor—areas of particular importance to the workers. It is related to hierarchical consensus concerning work standards—an issue of vital significance for the effectiveness of the station. And in part because of consensus with respect to so basic an issue as the fairness of work standards, high total control is associated with the perception of consensus regarding the everyday operation of the station and with a felt absence of conflict between people at various echelons.

The influence of the various echelons upon the station and the specific influences existing between the work groups and other levels are correlated with degree of positive slope and amount of total control. Again, because of the significant negative correlation between degree of positive slope and amount of total control, partial correlations between slope and the measures of specific influence are computed holding total control constant; correlations involving total control hold slope constant. As expected, degree of positive slope is highly negatively related to the influence of the station manager and highly positively related to the influence of the men on the station. However, degree of positive slope is related neither to the influence of the work group upon various levels, including the work group itself, nor to the influence upon the work group from upper levels. The fact that positive slope is not associated with a high degree of control *between* members at different levels may explain the absence of the predicted relationships between positive slope and the measures of consensus, that is, high positive slope is not associated with an effective pattern of mutual influence involving rank-and-file members and those at higher echelons which would be expected to facilitate consensus.

In contrast, amount of total control suggests a pattern of high influence within the station. Amount of total control is highly correlated with influence of all echelons upon the operation of the station. High degrees of influence by the men, the supervisors, and the station managers tend to go together in this situation (Tannenbaum, 1961: 33–46). The correlation between the influence of the station manager and that of the supervisors is .65; the influence of the station manager and that of the men correlate .83; however, the correlation between the influence of the supervisors and that of the men is .05. Of particular significance for the achievement of consensus, amount of total control is associated with a system of high mutual influence between members at different echelons, and specifically with the extent to which the workers exercise control upon the work group itself ($r = .72$). In effect, high total control means high self-determination by the workers (but not at the expense of the supervisors).

In an attempt to further interpret the manner in which the pattern of organizational control is related to member consensus in these stations, the various measures of specific interlevel influences involving the work group were correlated with the measures of work-group and hierarchical consensus. The results show that consensus derives in part from the influence of the supervisors upon the workers. It is apparently in response to such "hierarchical control" that work-group norms develop concerning morale, supervision, and the control desired. Such hierarchical control also has the effect of promoting perceived consensus throughout the station, even though in fact it may not exist. However, the direct influence upon the men by the supervisors is not sufficient in itself to guarantee consensus between the workers and the supervisors. In contrast, and consistent with the findings obtained with regard to positive slope, the control of the men upon the upper level is not associated with either work-group or hierarchical consensus. Such influence may have positive motivational effects for the workers, resulting in a feeling that consensus does exist in the station, but it is not sufficient to promote actual consensus. Rather, the results indicate that it is the extent to which the rank-and-file members exercise control upon the station and particularly upon the work group itself which facilitates the development of a high degree of consensus in these stations. When high mutual influence among the workers is coupled with some say by the workers concerning the operation of the station, it constitutes a partial basis for at least a minimum of agreement between the workers and the supervisors, namely, with respect to the critical issue of work standards.

Table 2 assesses the implication of the control–consensus relationship for organizational effectiveness. The results summarize, in part, those previously reported by Likert, Georgopoulos, and Smith and Tannenbaum (1960; 1957; 1963: 299–316). As seen from the findings, the control–consensus relationship that emerges is part of a larger pattern characteristic of the effective station. Not only are amount of total control and general consensus in the station related, but each factor also has significant implications for the effectiveness of the station. Amount of total control is highly correlated with both member morale ($r = .72$) and station productivity ($r = .43$). General station consensus is also significantly correlated with member morale ($r = .32$) and station productivity ($r = .45$). Together, amount of total control and general station consensus yield a high prediction of station productivity; the multiple correlation is .54. The multiple correlation of total control and general station consensus with member morale is even higher, .72. The high-producing station, in contrast to the low-producing station, is characterized by high total control, high member consensus, and high member morale. In contrast, while positive slope

TABLE 2. INTERCORRELATIONS AMONG MEASURES OF CONTROL STRUCTURE, CONSENSUS, AND ORGANIZATIONAL EFFECTIVENESS

Variable	1	2	3	4
1. Positive slope*				
2. Total control†	—.67‡			
3. General station consensus§	—.22	.35‖		
4. Member morale	.55#	.72#	.32‖	
5. Station productivity	.14	.43#	.45#	.34**

* All correlations involving positive slope are partial correlations, holding total control constant (with the exception of r_{12}).

† All correlations involving total control are partial correlations, holding positive slope constant (with the exception of r_{12}).

‡ Significant at the .01 level, two-tailed test.

§ The measure of general station consensus is based on an index derived by pooling the five measures of work-group consensus and the three measures of hierarchical consensus. All correlations involving general station consensus are partial correlations, holding log size constant.

‖ Significant at the .05 level, one-tailed test.

Significant at the .01 level, one-tailed test.

** Significant at the .05 level, two-tailed test.

may have significant implications for the morale of the members ($r =$ .55), the findings have shown that it is unrelated to consensus in the station. It may be for this reason that positive slope is not related to the productivity of these stations. It is not conducive to a high level of order and uniformity which is associated with the high-producing station. The fact that high total control is associated with such uniformity may explain to a large degree its significant implications for the productivity of these stations.

Discussion

In general, the findings suggest that the pattern of control which tends to be associated with member consensus in this organization is that predicted by Hypothesis II: a high amount of control exercised by members at all echelons, leaders as well as rank-and-file members. High total control tends to be conducive to consensus both within the work group and between the rank-and-file and the supervisory levels. However, considered more specifically, the findings are not uniform in their support of the hypothesis. They suggest that high total control facilitates consensus among rank-and-file members with respect to particularly salient and significant aspects of the work situation such as morale or feelings about the supervisor, areas concerning which the workers could also most readily reach an understanding and obtain agreement. Furthermore, high total control tends to promote consensus between rank-and-file members and those at higher echelons with respect to those critical areas, particularly work standards, which are highly relevant to the operation of the station and concerning which procedures might be expected to exist for reaching consensus. Amount of total control is unrelated to either work-group or hierarchical consensus regarding ideal control. This may be due simply to the unreliability of the measure or to the fact that ideal control is not a pertinent area for the development of consensus. Or it may be that it is more difficult to reach consensus about such a controversial area despite its relevance to the operation of the station (Smith and Tannenbaum, 1963: 299–316). Moreover, consensus in the essential areas mentioned is reflected in the perception that people in different positions see eye-to-eye regarding the operation of the station and in a felt absence of conflict between members at various echelons. Thus amount of total control, in part because of the actual basic agreement that it establishes, tends also to foster the feeling of cooperative relations in the station. The latter, in turn, may act to reinforce such basic agreement.

The findings further suggest that high total control is efficacious in promoting member consensus in these stations because it is associated with significant influence by the rank-and-file members upon the operation of the station. They have a part in determining organizational norms and consequently may be expected to be more motivated to accept them. This is substantiated, in part, by the significant relationship between total control and the morale of the members and by the significant relationships between the influence of the rank and file upon the operation of the station and the measures of work-group and hierarchical consensus. Equally important, under conditions of high total control, the direction provided by an effective leadership is utilized in determining consensus as well as the control of the rank-and-file members. Such *joint* control has the effect of facilitating an integration of interests and promoting a shared, acceptable system of norms.

Furthermore, a high amount of total control is conducive to member consensus because it is accompanied by an effective system of high mutual influence *within* the work group and *between* members at the rank-and-file and supervisory levels. The system of control is effective because it reflects *both* significant control by the supervisors upon the rank-and-file members and substantial control by the rank-and-file members upon the work group. The data suggest that it is the control of the rank-and-file members themselves within the work group which contributes to an important extent to work-group and hierarchical consensus. It is understandable that such control by workers themselves would particularly facilitate acceptance of the norms of the work group. When complemented by structure which the supervisors provide, there is the insurance that the control by the rank-and-file members within the work group also functions to enhance consensus between the rank-and-file and supervisory levels. In effect, given this system of control, promoting acceptance of the norms of the work group also has the result of reinforcing acceptance of the norms of upper echelons.

Finally, high total control is associated with the acceptance by the rank-and-file members of this pattern of organizational control as legitimate. A significant positive correlation exists between amount of total control and an index of the extent of correspondence between the actual control exercised by the various levels and that desired for these levels based on member responses ($r = .35$, $p < .05$). Such acceptance facilitates the exercise of effective leadership as well as encouraging the influence of the rank-and-file members in determining and enforcing consensus.

In contrast, while high control by the rank and file *relative* to that of higher echelons may have positive motivational effects for the former and promote the perception of consensus in these stations, it is not in itself a sufficient condition to promote consensus in the work group or to guarantee that the norms of the work group will actually complement those of higher echelons. The absence of the predicted relations between positive slope and member consensus may run counter to the argument of many observers who have discussed the positive effect of "democratic" control or "democratic" decision-making (if by these terms we mean relatively high rank-and-file as compared to leader influence) without considering their full implications in terms of *both* the distribution and amount of control exercised. The insignificant results obtain in these stations primarily because positive slope is not associated with an effective interaction-influence system. High rank-and-file control relative to that of the supervisors is not associated with a high level of control within the work group, which was found to be a highly significant determinant of member consensus, nor is it associated with any appreciable rank-and-file control upon the supervisors or manager. It is furthermore associated with a low amount of control by the supervisors upon the station and the work group. Hence an effective leadership which might provide structure and direction to the relatively high rank-and-file control, and thereby promote and expedite consensus, is absent. This lack of effective leadership under conditions of positive slope is accentuated by the fact that relatively high rank-and-file control may be accompanied by a rejection of the existing pattern of control, that is, by work-group norms regarding ideal control counter to those of the supervisory levels. This may have the effect of reducing the significance of the control exercised by either the rank-and-file or supervisory levels.

While the findings appear to support one of the two major hypotheses, a note of caution should be injected. In our conceptualization we have implied certain causal relationships between control structure and member consensus. However, in view of our cross-sectional data, we are unable to specify with certainty the direction of the relationship. It may be a reciprocal one. Not only may the system of control determine member consensus, but the nature and extent of member consensus may condition the type of organizational control (Thompson and Tuden,

1959: 195–216). It is readily conceivable that a system of work-group norms counter to those of a higher echelon might increase the tendency toward hierarchical control, that is, negative slope. Or lack of consensus within an organization may be so dysfunctional that a low amount of control is exercised by the various conflicting groups.

Control, Consensus, and Organizational Effectiveness

The thesis of this investigation has been that the effects of certain patterns of control on organizational performance derive partially from the uniformity with respect to organizational standards and policies which these patterns of control promote. In turn, the regularity, orderliness, and predictability deriving from such uniformity were viewed as being essential to the concerted action underlying the highly effective organization.

Our findings indicate that this is indeed a tenable explanation for the effects of total control upon organizational performance which we have found in these stations. The significant exercise of control by both members and leaders leads to a high degree of identification and involvement in the organization. All organization members are more motivated to develop a set of shared policies and practices, to accept jointly made decisions, and to act on behalf of the organization. The system of high mutual influence which this pattern of control signifies provides an opportunity for members and leaders to reconcile their interests and facilitates an atmosphere of cooperation. This further bolsters common loyalties and promotes shared objectives which are reflected in the wider acceptance of organizational norms. The conditions thus exist for effective decision-making and improved coordination in carrying out organizational objectives in a concerted manner. Finally, it may be inferred that the joint contributions of members and leaders facilitate better and more acceptable policies and decisions insuring their translation into concerted action of an adaptive nature characteristic of the highly effective organization.

The findings also suggest that "democratic control" (i.e., positive slope) does not have the predicted effect of promoting high organizational performance in these stations partially because it does not promote a system of shared organizational norms which we have found to be associated with the high-performing station. While this pattern of control may lead to high rank-and-file morale, it does not appear to promote basic identification with organizational objectives and practices or motivated action leading to high performance. It appears that in this organization high rank-and-file control relative to the leaders may have the effect of members' acting simply in terms of their own self-interests and not accepting the contributions of the leaders. Furthermore, this pattern of control is not associated with a system of high reciprocal influence in which structure is provided by the leaders.

Such structure would help to insure a system of shared organizational norms. In the absence of shared organizational norms and a system of high mutual influence (i.e., high total control) to regulate and coordinate member action with respect to these norms, it is not surprising that democratic control is not conducive to high organizational performance.

It is conceivable that a positively sloped distribution of control might lead to a system of shared norms and consequently concerted action on behalf of the organization in a different type of organization with different organizational conditions (Tannenbaum, 1961: 33–46). This might occur in a "mutual benefit" type of organization, such as some voluntary associations, where the interests and objectives of members and leaders are more fully shared, and where decision-making is of a judgmental nature (Thompson and Tuden, 1959: 195–216). Other necessary conditions would include a prevailing ideology sanctioning "democratic" control and a formal structure, including authority and decision-making, that would facilitate the control of the rank-and-file members. If such a structure is also associated with high mutual influence between the members and the leaders, the basis is provided to achieve the necessary coordination and to translate rank-and-file control into effective action. In the present organization such conditions do not exist and their absence may account in large part for the lack of the predicted effects of positive slope.

Organizational Change in Terms of a Series of Selected Variables*

JOHN E. TSOUDEROS

The study presented in this paper takes its point of departure from the working hypothesis that institutional and cultural change can be empirically observed through the growth of a number of selected variables. In his writings F. Stuart Chapin has demonstrated the possibility of studying the successive values of certain strategic institutional variables over a period of time and establishing the "law of change" by the well-known statistical method of fitting a logistic curve to the time series (1928: Chs. 11 & 12; 1935: 58–59, 296–299; also Rice, 1931: 307–352). Chapin has linked this time series analysis to one type of broad generalization on the cultural and social change in the social group

* Reprinted from the *American Sociological Review*, 20 (May 1955), pp. 206–210, by permission of the author and the publisher.

which he calls the "cycle of the social process" or the "societal reaction pattern."

An attempt will be made in this paper to summarize some of the findings made in an empirical investigation of a number of quantitative variables related to the organizational growth of ten voluntary associations. Theoretical considerations suggest that these variables are important in understanding the processes of organizational growth and formalization which constitute the topic of this paper.

In the course of conducting the field work, three sources of information were used: (1) the financial statements of the associations; (2) the membership lists and statistics; (3) service statistics mostly compiled by the administrative staffs on the volume of service activities discharged.

The variables subjected to time series analysis were: (1) total annual income; (2) total annual expenditures; (3) value of the property from year to year; (4) annual membership figures; and (5) the number of administrative employees from year to year.

It was seen in the case histories that the initial acquisition of property takes place when an association furnishes a meeting place for the membership and provides equipment to facilitate the discharge of administrative tasks. As the membership increases, a larger home is required by the association; more furniture is needed; real estate becomes desirable. Simultaneously, the growth of the membership group is accompanied by an increase in the volume of administrative tasks and expenditures; more office equipment is needed, especially after the first administrative worker has been hired (Chapin, 1951: 835–836).

Figure 1 is a graphic and composite representation of the relationship of these organizational variables, summarizing our findings (Tsouderos, 1953). The key points of the findings are formulated here as tentative generalizations. As can be seen from the graph there is a definite functional relationship between the growth in membership of an association and other variables such as income, administrative expenditures, property and staff workers; that is, when one of these variables is modified in time the other undergoes a corresponding modification. However, certain qualifications should be made in terms of a general growth pattern of the organizational development: (1) The membership growth precedes the growth of incomes. Even though we find a positive relationship between the increase of membership and growth of income this relationship does not seem to be continuous. With a decline of the membership in an organization there is no immediate or actual decline in income. (2) There is a positive relationship between the growth in total income of an organization and its administrative expenditures. However, the administrative expenditures have a much lower rate of growth than income. It can be noted then that the administrative expenditures increase rapidly after the peak of total income has been passed. (3) Property and administrative office

FIGURE 1. GRAPHIC REPRESENTATION OF THE RELATIONSHIP OF CERTAIN ORGANIZATIONAL VARIABLES

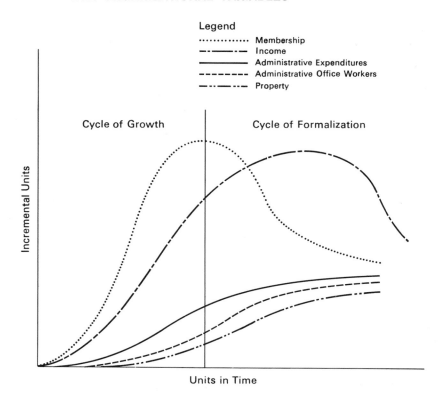

workers continue to accumulate while membership and total income begin to shrink. However, property increases more rapidly in periods of rapid rise in income. We find also a close correspondence between the growth of administrative expenditures and increases in the property of the association.

In general, the above findings demonstrate that there is a certain tendency for the process of formalization to continue in the period when the social group contracts. Evidence shows that in this period of a contracting membership, the administrative staff expenditures, staff workers, and property, rise cyclically. The association which in the past has learned to cope effectively with its many problems by formalization and rationalization of its structure, attempts to survive by continuing the process of formalization.

The question arises as to why there is a functional relationship between the growth of membership, income, administrative expenditures, property, and staff workers. Why do voluntary associations have a tendency to increase their membership to a certain point and then reach a point of maximum growth? Furthermore, why does membership decline after a period of time? Why is it that with a decline in membership there is no immediate or actual decline in income, and, finally, why do property, administrative expenditures and office workers continue to accumulate while membership and total income begin to shrink? Before attempting to answer any of these questions we must clearly have in mind that the material presented above represents only an empirical study of a small selected group of voluntary associations and that the generalizations and interpretations might not fully conform to a more representative sample. It was attempted here merely to explore and suggest a possible method of observation, and, in addition, to present a set of hypotheses which would guide and offer some insight for further research in this field.

In general, then, the above can be conceived as an *ideal type construct* for use as a comparative guide in research on the manifest structural differentiation of small groups. With these limitations in mind let us try to answer these questions in a series of interrelated and tentative propositions:

1. The number of members and the continued growth of the membership group are the result of both the success of an association in coping with the internal functional problems posed by an expanding membership and the total adjustment or adaptation of an association as a functioning organizational unit to its social environment (including success in the enlistment of new members from this environment).

2. The less specialized and segmental the role the members play in the association, the more pronounced is the tendency to regard participation in the association as an end in itself. This leads to a greater solidarity of the group and lessens the possibility of a decline in membership. The more specialized the role each member plays in the association, the more pronounced will be his tendency to regard participation as the means to an end. The loyalty of the members to their association can be stabilized when participation is regarded not merely as a means to the attainment of specified ends, but as the preservation of the association as an end in its own right. It is then to the advantage of the association to encourage primary group relations in the membership. However, a qualifying statement should be made here. We must not overlook on the other hand the stabilizing effect of the specialization and formalization of roles within an organization. That is to say, when the functional position or roles as such are abstracted from concrete persons and codified and defined by symbols, the organization acquires in general greater stability and flexibility than when it is under the personal authority of one or more charismatic leaders. However, the problem of formalization versus lack of it is this: the members most affected by the specialization and

formalization of roles are those "who run the show," i.e., are actively engaged as leaders of the organization, and they are less likely to withdraw their membership. The greatest turnover of the membership is observed in the passive membership *after formalization,* whose roles have been the least specialized. The passivity of this non-specialized group might be due to the disparity that exists between it and the highly formalized segment of the association. Thus, a balance between sociability and formalization must be attained to prevent the disintegration of the association.

3. Certain associations may serve very specific interests and it is precisely for this reason that their appeal is limited to certain types of individuals. This imposes a maximum size on any one organization in any given area.

4. With the increasing need of a service rendered by a voluntary association there is a corresponding increase of membership, and with the fulfillment or partial fulfillment of such service there is a corresponding decrease in membership.

5. With an increased membership, however, there is a corresponding increase in the heterogeneity of the group in terms of sentiments, interests, dedication to the "cause," etc., and a corresponding decline in a feeling of intimacy and frequency of interaction. More specifically, there is a decline of membership in meetings and volunteer work. As a consequence, the membership becomes extremely passive and increasingly removed from the leadership of the association. As the membership expands, the group as a whole is likely to lose its primary character. This is not to say, however, that the primary group disappears; certain clusters of individuals are found to interact with one another more frequently than they do with the rest of the membership. Sub-groups appear which retain the primary character previously extending over the entire membership. These sub-group clusters are integrated into the manifest social structure and the membership is organized in membership units. At the same time the need for control arises out of the fact that some of these membership units tend to become relatively autonomous from the rest of the organization. In varying degrees loyalty of the members is diverted from the association to the membership units so that the basis for a conflict with the organization has been laid.

6. The loss of membership in the organization might be due then to several reasons, such as: increased secondary contacts, competing associations with similar functions, conflict within the association resulting from the heterogeneity of the group members, ineffectiveness of intracommunication, a decrease of the material or symbolic incentives offered by the association, a relative de-

crease in the need of a function or functions rendered by the association to its members or to the community and the extent to which the association is able to coordinate its formal and informal relationships.

7. There is evidence that the formalization and contraction of the social group constitute a "vicious circle." In order to cope with its financial problems and declining membership, the association streamlines its structure and procedures according to modern organizational principles by introducing higher membership dues, professional help, and other means. These new organizational features alienate portions of the membership which had joined the association at an earlier and more informal stage, and lead to secession *en masse.* This mass separation creates even greater problems with which the association attempts to cope by formalizing its organization even more.

8. With a declining membership, efforts are made to control the drop by introducing new incentives, added services, professional and administrative staff in order to discharge and supervise such services. Special communicative devices appear with the declining frequency of face-to-face interaction, preceded by the increasing structural differentiation and the separation of various functional activities. Furthermore, the association is confronted with the problem of enforcing the pertinent features of its program through a relatively expensive outlay. Thus with an increase of controls there is a corresponding increase of staff and administrative expenditures. This phenomenon of increased controls, efforts to improve communication, and the use of additional professional help can be found emerging not only when the membership declines, but also when the membership increases at a rapid rate.

9. Increase of expenditures can also be explained in terms of increased capital outlay to improve facilities in order to maintain organizational prestige.

10. With a decline in the membership of an organization, there is no immediate or actual decline in income. This phenomenon is due primarily to the greater efficiency of the organization in collecting dues and carrying out financial drives.

11. Material property will increase over a period of time, and this increase is closely related to the expenditures for staff and upkeep. Unless the material property is withdrawn from use or permitted to deteriorate, these service expenditures cannot be reduced below a certain level.

6
TOWARD
A SYNTHESIS:
A SYSTEMS
PERSPECTIVE

Out of the many continuing debates and discussions—the theses and antitheses—a consensus is slowly emerging on at least some of the issues. Regarding many of the key variables, or what we might call the coordinates of the system, there is much agreement. Moreover, under-lying the discussions and encompassing the many problems of organi-zational analysis, four basic components of the system, four dimensions, are visible: power, knowledge, rules, and rewards. Taken together, these components or dimensions aid in arranging many, if not all of the variables into a typology of system coordinates. The typology, in turn, will enlighten us concerning which areas to pinpoint for future research and theoretical development. A review of these basic components might crystallize in sharper detail the present stage of knowledge.

A Set of System Coordinates

Running through a number of discussions are the themes of power, knowledge, rules, and, to a lesser extent, rewards. By cross-classifying these themes with the basic features characteristic of an organization —its inputs, processes, and outputs—we are able to delineate many of the variables which organizational sociologists have come to agree are among the most important. Although the typology does not subsume all the variables discussed and, moreover, some of the variables in-cluded seem somewhat forced, the typology is nevertheless a long step toward a needed synthesis. It provides a simple device for ordering many of the ideas and issues in the field. Furthermore, we can see more clearly what has been emphasized most and what least, the peculiar tastes of particular authors as well as their blindspots, and consequently, the direction the field should take in the future. With so many possibilities, the typology would necessarily represent a considerable extent of agreement—some might feel preoccupation—about the nature of an organization, at least in a sociological sense. In any case, the typology is a useful summary of what has been said and what has to be remembered.

Before a general theory of organizations can emerge, we need to make clear what the critical variables are. The typology, while in part induced from what has been studied, is still a rather helpful guide as to the most important variables to study. As apparent in the following discussion, some of the interrelationships between these variables have been examined and others have not. Thus, the typology also serves to call our attention to areas that have been ignored. The typology is an organizing device, again propitious to the development of a general theory, one that might work at least in industrialized societies of the West. By perceiving the similarities in the concepts of various writers (despite some differences in terminology), we can begin to integrate various theories, a topic to be discussed below.

Why four dimensions and particularly these four? The ideas of power, rewards, and rules have been a major focus of much sociological work and thought since the turn of the century. Knowledge is a more recent arrival but, again, implicit in the concern for education as a variable has been an interest in how knowledge affects the distribution of power and rewards. Rules, whether in the guise of norms or regulations in organizations have been a long-time concern of sociologists. Together these four themes represent traditional concerns. They are not the only ones but certainly four important ones.

The Inputs, or Social Resource Variables   The resources of an organization are nothing more than its inputs, what the organization has to work with. When this part of the system is combined with our four basic dimensions, we obtain four basic resources. We begin to speak of the inputs of knowledge, of power, of rules, and of rewards. These represent three of the major issues discussed in Chapter Two.

The inputs of knowledge correspond to the ideas of technology, training, and production continuity, as well as to other variables which, in various ways, tap what is known relative to the production processes of the organization. In various ways, organizations use skills and tools, and the variables are used in an attempt to measure this aspect of organizational reality. Listed in Table 1 are the different names for these variables and the reading selections in which they are described.

Different organizations have various amounts of power. Whether given to them by legislatures or coordinating agencies or whether taken by the organization in its struggles vis-à-vis various publics, organizations have an input of power. This term refers to how much they can do what they want without any restrictions being imposed

TABLE 1. CLASSIFICATION OF READING SELECTIONS FOR FOUR RESOURCE VARIABLES

Basic dimension	Variables of resources	Selections
Knowledge	Types of technology	Blauner; Woodward; Fullan
	Work flow integration production continuity	Hickson *et al.*
	Professional training	Hage and Aiken
	Operating diversity	Pugh *et al.* (Chapter Two)
Power	Autonomy	Berliner; Davis and Dolbeare; Selznick; Pugh *et al.* (Chapter Three)
	Public accountability	Selznick; Pugh *et al.* (Chapter Two)
	Concentration of ownership	
Rules	Size	Hall *et al.*; Pugh *et al.* (Chapter Two); Blau (Chapters Two and Three); Hickson *et al.*; Corwin; Hage and Aiken
Rewards	Investment	Pugh *et al.* (Chapter Two)

from the outside. Whether described as autonomy, public accountability, or concentration of ownership, this idea is discussed in several of the selections.

The next category in Table 1 is less obvious and perhaps somewhat forced. The input of rules we shall call size or the number of members in the organization. It is the presence of human beings that results in the development of that distinctive human phenomenon "red tape" and that necessitates a considerable amount of regulation. Therefore, we have placed size in this row as the input of rules.

The last cross classification is between rewards and resources and represents the concept of investment or, to use the economists' term, capitalization. This has not been a popular topic in the sociological literature on organizations, perhaps precisely because it appears to belong more to classic economic conceptions of organizations. However, it does appear, usually as another indicator for size, that is, as the scale of operation.

Some of the input or resource variables that have been discussed are not included in the cross classification of these themes. It is important to list these as well, both as a check on our procedure and as a critique of its generality. The two main variables not included are age and number of operating sites, which interestingly enough really belong to another tradition, namely that of ecological analysis. To our mind they are also not input variables.

The Structural Variables The concept of structure is a simple one. In various ways, jobs are arranged into a team. These arrangements can

TABLE 2. CLASSIFICATION OF READING SELECTIONS FOR FOUR STRUCTURAL VARIABLES

Basic dimensions	Structural variables	Selections
Knowledge	Complexity, specialisms, structural differentiation	Hall *et al.*; Pugh *et al.* (Chapter Three); Blau (Chapter Two); Lawrence and Lorsch; Hage; Hage, Aiken and Marrett; Hage and Aiken
	Division of labor, technical qualifications	Hall
	Professionalism, activity	Hage and Aiken
Power	Centralization, participation	Presthus; McCleery, Pugh *et al.* (Chapter Three); Hage; Hage and Aiken; Crozier; Hage, Aiken, Marrett; Corwin; Chandler
	Control curve	Smith and Ari; Mechanic
	Number of levels	Blau (Chapter Three); Crozier
	Hierarchy of authority	Hall; Hage and Aiken
	Span of control	Woodward; Hickson *et al.*; Blau (Chapter Three); Pugh *et al.* (Chapter Three)
Rules	Formalization, programming	Hall *et al.*; Hage; Hage and Aiken; Hage, Aiken, Marrett, Pugh *et al.*
	Standardization	Pugh *et al.* (Chapter Three), Corwin
	Rules, job codification, rule observation	Hall; Hage and Aiken
Rewards	Stratification	Blauner; Hage
Not Included:		
	Configuration	Pugh *et al.* (Chapter Three); Hickson *et al.*

be described by our four basic dimensions. Thus, power is distributed among a number of jobs, and this provides the variables of centralization, hierarchy of authority, etc. (See Table 2.) Likewise rewards are distributed, and this generates the idea of stratification in organization. It is in the discussion of the various structural variables that one can most easily observe the emerging consensus. Since structure is the area where most of the work has been accomplished, this is perhaps an encouraging sign.

Whether one uses the term complexity or specialization or structural differentiation, the structure of an organization is divided into different occupations or jobs that form the components of the team. The members of the organization are specialists in some body of knowledge. Closely akin to this concept are the ideas of the division of labor, technical qualifications, and professionalism, other terms employed to tap the same essential coordinates of the system.

Even more popular, at least as measured by frequency of appearance in our selections, is the structure of power: the variable of centralization. In one form or another, this has appeared explicitly in over half the articles. The measures differ, but all agree that this is one of the major coordinates of any organizational system. Some, like Crozier (1964), have argued that the distribution of power is the most important coordinate.

The cross classification of rules with structure provides the familiar variables of formalization, standardization or job codification, and other similar scales. While less common than centralization, the concept of formalization still has been a popular focus of much organizational research. Again this may only reflect the field's debt to Max Weber and his model of bureaucracy. But it also may indicate that the presence of rules and procedures is one of the more important facts about organizations.

The last variable generated in this column of our typology—stratification—is the most important specialty in sociology and yet, surprisingly, it has hardly even been studied within the context of organizations. However, one advantage of a typology in organizational sociology, just as that of the periodic table in chemistry, is to indicate new directions of research.

Again we note that one variable discussed in the selections, configuration, is not included in the system of coordinates shown in Table 2. Although various aspects of configuration have been studied as indicators of complexity, centralization, and even stratification, they have been studied also as a separate aspect of organizational structure, namely, its size and shape. We have therefore listed them separately to call attention to this quite different conception of organizational structure, one that describes the physical distribution of people in various levels and departments. Configuration is not in the typology precisely because it is not a variable and because it is devoid of content.

The Control Process Variables An important component in a system approach is an analysis of the major mechanisms of control. Long before system analysis became popular, this part of the organization system was receiving attention from organizational sociologists and social psychologists. Here our four dimensions appear to cover all of the variables that have been discussed in our selections, as is evident in Table 3.

Involved in communications or information feedback is the theme of knowledge. Less certain is whether social integration, a topic appearing in some five selections, should be placed in the same category. For one reason, social integration as opposed to instrumental communication, is more concerned with the problem of the group in

TABLE 3. CLASSIFICATION OF READING SELECTIONS FOR FOUR CONTROL PROCESS VARIABLES

Basic dimensions	Variables of control processes	Selections
Knowledge	Communications, interaction, information feedback	McCleery; Lawrence and Lorsch; Hage, Aiken, Marrett; Julian; Khan *et al.*
	Social integration	Blauner; Crozier; Fullan; Kahn *et al.*; Corwin
Power	Sanctions, rewards, and punishments	Julian; Price
	Programming	
Rules	Conformity	Kahn *et al.*; Price
Rewards	Consensus	Smith and Ari
	Conflict	McCleery; Lawrence and Lorsch; Kahn *et al.*; Corwin

organizations and, in this sense, is not an organizational problem. However, it has been frequently combined with the analysis of the work integration of an organization. We have placed social integration in this segment of the typology because, like communication, it involves social interaction; they are both part of the broader idea of interaction. Therefore, there are common elements in these concepts if not common causes.

The cross classification of control and power produces the familiar topic of sanctions. Also included are the various conceptualizations about the bases of power. Correctly speaking, two of these bases (expert power and referent power) should be included in the previous segment, just as this one contains the idea of programming. Together the control by knowledge and the control by power in its various manifestations represent the two major procedures for ensuring integration and coordination.

The intersection of rules and control, the concept of conformity, is another popular topic. Here we have only referenced those selections that have measured this variable as opposed to those that have merely discussed this idea. If the latter criterion had been used, then most of the other references in Table 3 would be applicable as well. For it is almost impossible to discuss the subject of control without including the concept of conformity, the idea of individuals obeying orders and rules.

Finally, rewards control generates the variable of consensus, for those who like the accent on the positive, or conflict, for those who prefer the negative side of the coin, namely, the breakdown of control.

This variable has appeared in a number of selections, both individual case studies and comparative ones. The Lawrence and Lorsch selection is categorized in this segment of the table because their definition of integration is the elimination of conflict.

It should be noted that the first two categories are mechanisms of control whereas the last two concern what is being regulated or controlled. Thus the relationship in the typology between these four variables is somewhat different than it is in the other three components of the organizational system.

The Outputs, or Performance and Goal Variables If we understand performance to be what occurs and goals to represent what one desires to occur, then goals and performances can be seen as two sides of the same coin. This does not eliminate their essentially different causal interpretations.

The cross classification of knowledge and performance generates the variables of innovation or program change (Table 4). Innovation or adaption seems to come as a consequence of the cross fertilization of ideas or of knowledge. This is why it seems appropriately classified. The goal of the power row would appear to be effectiveness or production or what might be called goal achievement to use Parsons' term for it (1954, 1959). When rules and performance are cross-classified, we obtain the output of morale or motivation. This is the direct counterpart to the input of size and represents the ability to maintain the participation of the members in the organization. Again, it is perhaps somewhat forced. Finally, the conservation of rewards we call efficiency. To-

TABLE 4. CLASSIFICATION OF READING SELECTIONS FOR FOUR PERFORMANCE AND GOAL VARIABLES

Basic dimensions	Variables of performance	Selections
Knowledge	Program change	Hage and Aiken
	Innovation, adaptiveness	Perrow; Hage
Power	Effectiveness, goal achievement	Price; Perrow
	Volume of production	Hage
	Success	Woodward
Rules	Morale	Smith and Ari; Hage; Hage and Aiken
	Alienation	Blauner; Fullan; Crozier
Rewards	Motivation	Presthus
	Productivity, efficiency	Hage; Price; Smith and Ari; Tsouderos

gether these four dimensions cover much of the same ground as delineated by Perrow in his selection, although the terms are different.

A Typology of Organizational Variables   Although the classification is not always as accurate and exact as one would like, the typology given in Table 5 does have the advantage of at least beginning the process of synthesizing the literature. The reader should note the words "toward a synthesis" in the title of this chapter. Much work remains to be done and this typology is only a first step in categorizing the critical coordinates in a system analysis.

But even this first approximation has several advantages. We see highlighted in Table 5 many, if not all, the major themes in this reader. While it is true that the typology was itself an idea in the prefiguration of the text–reader, many important problems have been covered nonetheless. *By arranging organizational problems according to major dimensions and system components, we can better appreciate their interrelationships and more easily begin to comprehend a much more complex conceptualization of an organizational system.*

The typology allows us to classify what has been emphasized the most and what the least, at least relevant to these sixteen variables. One major dialectic is apparent, and that is between the relative importance of knowledge and power variables. Technology, complexity, or communications vs. autonomy, centralization, or control by sanctions have been major foci of interest. Oddly enough the row of rewards, except for the issues of conflict and consensus, recent arrivals to the repertoire of organizational analysis, has been much less appreciated. Perhaps this reflects a desire for an approach different from prevailing economic concepts of this facet of organizational analysis. But it may

TABLE 5.   A TYPOLOGY OF SYSTEM COORDINATES FOR ORGANIZATIONS

Basic dimensions	Social resources	Social structure	Control processes	Performances and goals
Knowledge	Technology	Complexity, specialization	Communication	Program innovation
	Education	Differentiation		
Power	Autonomy	Centralization	Sanctions	Effectiveness
	Accountability	Hierarchy of authority		Goal achievement
Rules	Membership size	Formalization	Conformity	Morale
Rewards	Investment	Stratification	Consensus	Efficiency
	Scale of operations		Conflict	

also represent an intuition about a truth: It may well be that some variables of knowledge and power are more important than those of rules and rewards for understanding and predicting organizational behavior. Only time will tell, but the typology helps us to appreciate this problem and to focus future research properly.

Authors' tastes also can be classified in terms of the particular columns and rows. An inspection of particular selections indicates that most, if not all, of the authors have by and large concentrated on two columns or three parts of the system at most. There are particular preferences for some themes as opposed to others. Some authors have clearly emphasized power and others knowledge. None has focused on rewards, and hardly anyone on rules, to the exclusion of the other themes. To know what the author has not included is the first major insight about his work. Frequently, there is an implicit assumption that all other things are being held equal. The typology begins at least to spell out what some of these other variables might be. Thus, it can be employed as a check list when we read the work of others. It is also apparent what the typology has left out. Perhaps the most glaring omission is the problem of the environment. We could use the same four dimensions and note that they generate kinds of interorganizational relationships, kinds of supplies of resources, and kinds of customers. But this step is left until more work has been done on the impact of the environment on the organization and vice versa.

Likewise, one can generate still more concepts by noting that a number of special terms exist in the literature for changes in one or more of the concepts. For example, change in formalization has been called the process of institutionalization; change in size is frequently called growth; change in personnel is turnover. In the same vein, many of Terreberry's ideas of turbulence (Chapter One) represent the rapidity of change in the rate of exchange between the organization and its environmental agents. But these refinements are best left until these concepts become more critical. For now, a better utilization of the typology is to assess what research has to be done to reach the stage of development where these kinds of concepts will be useful.

But the remaining advantage of the typology of variables is the most important one. As we noted in the previous section, we can begin to synthesize the theories and the empirical regularities of particular authors. Thus, Blau's theory of structural differentiation can be integrated with Hage's axiomatic theory of social structure and social performances. In turn, both of these can be combined with Price's theory of control and effectiveness and Hage, Aiken, and Marrett's theory of structure and coordination. Likewise, many of the empirical findings can be fitted into a larger theory of organizations.

This does not mean necessarily that these theories will work in every society. As we observed in Chapter One, we have much to learn about the environment and how it will affect the organization. But once key variables describing the environment are identified, they can be interpolated into the general theory in much the same way that we synthesized the above theories. Thus our knowledge can grow systematically and at the same time move to ever greater complexity and subtility.

Areas for Future Research

If we construct a large matrix of 16 by 15 variables, then we can start to see which associations have not been explored. When this appraisal has been made, several patterns become clear. First, a large amount of work relating the resources to the structure of the organization has already been done. But, second, very few findings interrelating inputs with either control or performance variables are accessible. Third, structure has been related to either control or performance variables, but seldom have the three domains been combined. Of the few exceptions, some are already noted in Chapters Four and Five. Perhaps the most underdeveloped area is in the associations between performances and coordinates in each of the other parts of the system. Also, the systematic interrelating of four parts of the system represents another area for future research.

One major problem for research is to continue building upon the work of Pugh *et al.* and Blau (both in Chapter Two). In particular, we need to know the *relative* importance of autonomy (or dependence to use the Aston group's term) vs. size vs. knowledge technology vs. investment or scale of operations in predicting organizational measures of structure. Beyond this, it also would be beneficial to know how important these resource variables are in predicting control variables. Although the connection between technology and control has been suggested (Blau and Scott, 1962, and Blauner, 1964), it has not been studied in a comparative framework. Some possible lines of attack are as follows. One can imagine that knowledge technology as reflected in many different kinds of professionals should result in an increase in communications. This might be beyond the relationship between complexity and communications. What is being suggested here is a kind of path analysis. In general terms, one looks at how resource variables affect control variables holding structure constant. Another plausible area of research in the same vein is to test whether a lack of autonomy leads to greater emphasis on punishment (and rewards) as a mechanism of control, holding constant the degree of centralization.

Despite the tradition of Michel (1915) and his seminal work on what he called the iron law of oligarchy, the association between size and centralization has not been much explored. In particular, given the current controversy over the relationship between size and complexity or structural differentiation, it might be worth studying the effects of size on centralization, controlling for complexity. Likewise, one could study size vis-à-vis formalization in the same way. What is being suggested is a simple idea, namely, that the effects of variables are probably quite complicated, requiring us to hold constant some of the other variables in the typology. We know—indeed, it is perhaps one of the few things about which we are sure—that complexity leads to decentralization. But because size could be related to increases in both complexity and centralization, the impact may be obscured. This same model of reasoning applies in a large number of other possible multivariate combinations. It seems reasonable to assume that perhaps some of the controversy, the thesis and antithesis, derives from more complicated associations.

Another area for building would seem to be the follow-up of Corwin's work. Given some measures of conflict, the question of cause becomes fascinating, especially in light of the assumptions of the need for coordination and control. One possible line of attack is to look for interaction effects. Since we know that complexity is associated with decentralization, then perhaps the combination of complexity with centralization produces conflict, a struggle to alter the power distribution toward a more equalitarian participation in decision making. If so, then the exception would prove the rule about the association and also provide another piece of evidence about coordination and control: that their breakdown only occurs in exceptional circumstances.

Another kind of research to build upon what is known and to help clarify our understanding of organizational dynamics is to focus on the processes by which change in one variable leads to change in another. This will require longitudinal comparative research, that is, a panel study of organizations, but its payoff is potentially great. For example, we do not know the exact causal mechanisms by which change in size leads to change in structural differentiation or how increases in the latter lead to increases in decentralization. By having multiple waves of interviewers in combination with observers, we might begin to tease this kind of information out. A particularly important area for this research design is the analysis of feedback. We need to measure if an increase in conflict is followed by an attempt to exert more control, or if a change in the environment is noted and then the structure of an organization adapts. Only comparative longitudinal research will be successful in attacking the process of dynamic change in variables that are the great strength of system analysis.

As we have noted, the measurement problems of performance variables are formidable. But the potential for social engineering is so great that we should redouble our efforts. In particular, the relationship between input and output, controlling for structure, seems like an area with much potential for future research. Most managers and executive directors want to know how to make their organizations function better —whether in terms of higher morale, more innovative programming, higher production, greater quality, etc. Organizational sociology can make an important contribution here. But to do so, we need to break away from our previous modes of analysis. Too often we have considered only one or two variables in attempting to predict morale, for example. We now need to explore not only mere predictors—centralization, formalization, and stratification for different levels of complexity is one possibility—but more complicated conceptualizations. Small group research (Bales, 1956) has argued for a phase movement. One can imagine that the same phenomenon works in organizations. They can shift in emphasizing performances over the course of several years or even perhaps throughout several leaders' terms of office. (Again the need for a comparative longitudinal design.) If this is so, then simple linear analysis is not the answer.

The above areas of research are not likely to be what is emphasized during the early seventies. The area that will be studied most is in all probability the impact of the environment on the organization and vice versa. This is a lacuna recognized by many, whereas the above problems are perhaps less popular or at least less visible. The environment was the main focus at the 1971 American Sociological Association national convention and in all probability will receive a great deal of attention in the next few years, as it undoubtedly should. It is clear from Chapter One how little has been done in this area. But however much we need research on the interaction between the environment and organizations, it would be unfortunate not to consolidate the gains of the previous decades. And this is the main hope of a text–reader such as this one: that it will make our analysis and research designs much more complex. Organizations are not simple affairs as everyone knows. But until the work of the last decade was completed, most sociologists were at a loss as to where to begin their studies. What has been accomplished so far is to establish some important points of reference. The typology of 16 coordinates provides the shopping list that can enrich our data collection and its analysis. The work of the last decade makes clear the areas where we need more data and more sophisticated analysis. Now we want to build upon this. Time to go to work!

Bibliography

Aaronovitch, S.
1961   *The Ruling Class.* London: Lawrence and Wishart.

Adler, Lee
1966   "Symbiotic Marketing," *Harvard Business Review, 44* (November), 59–71.

Aiken, Michael, and Jerald Hage
1966   "Organizational Alienation: A Comparative Analysis," *American Sociological Review, 31* (August), 497–507.

Aiken, Michael, and Jerald Hage
1968   "Organizational Interdependence and Intra-Organizational Structure," *American Sociological Review, 33* (December), 912–930.

Aiken, Michael, and Jerald Hage
1971   "Organic Organization and Innovation," *Sociology,* 5 (January), 63–82.

Akers, Ronald L., and Richard Quinney
1968   "Differential Organization of Health Professions," *American Sociological Review, 33* (February), 104–121.

Alderfer, E. B., and H. E. Michl
1957   *The Economics of American Industry* (3rd ed.). New York: McGraw-Hill.

Aldrich, Howard E.
1971   "Organizational Boundaries and Inter-Organizational Conflict," *Human Relations, 24* (August), 279–293.

Aldrich, Howard E.
1972   "Technology and Organizational Structure: A Re-Examination of the Findings of the Aston Group," *ASQ, 17* (March).

Allport, F. H.
1955   *Theories of Perception and the Concept of Structure.* New York: Wiley.

Allport, Floyd H.
  1962   "A Structuro-nomic Conception of Behavior: Individual and Col-
            lective. 1. Structural Theory and the Master Problem of Social
            Psychology," *Journal of Abnormal and Social Psychology,* LXIV,
            3–30.
Amber, G. S., and P. S. Amber
  1962   *Anatomy of Automation.* Englewood Cliffs, N. J.: Prentice-Hall.
Anderson, T. R., and S. Warkov
  1961   "Organizational Size and Functional Complexity: A Study of Ad-
            ministration in Hospitals," *American Sociological Review, 26*
            (February), 23–28.
Andrews, Frank M.
  1964   "Scientific Performance as Related to Time Spent on Technical
            Work, Teaching, or Administration," *Administrative Science Quar-
            terly, 9* (September), 182–193.
Ansoff, Igor
  1965   "The Firm of the Future," *Harvard Business Review,* 43 (Septem-
            ber).
Archibald, Katherine
  1947   *Wartime Shipyards.* Berkeley and Los Angeles: University of Cali-
            fornia Press.
Arensberg, C. M., and R. Macgregor
  1942   "Determinants of Morale in an Industrial Company," *Applied An-
            thropology, 1,* 12–34.
Argyris, Chris
  1954   "Human Relations in a Bank," *Harvard Business Review, 32,*
            63–72.
Argyris, Chris
  1954   *Organization of a Bank.* New Haven, Conn.: Yale University Press.
Argyris, Chris
  1964   *Integrating the Individual and the Organization.* New York: Wiley.
Ashby, W. Ross
  1960   *Design for a Brain* (2nd ed.). London: Chapman and Hall.
Azumi, Koya
  1969   *Higher Education and Business Recruitment in Japan.* New York:
            Teachers College Press.
Bakke, E. W.
  1959   "Concept of the Social Organization," in Haire, M. (ed.), *Modern
            Organization Theory.* New York: Wiley.
Baldridge, J. Victor
  1971   *Power and Conflict in the University.* New York: Wiley.
Bales, R. F.
  1950   *Interaction Process Analysis.* New York.
Bales, Robert F., Fred L. Strodtback, Theodore M. Mills, and Mary E. Rose-
borough
  1951   "Channels of Communication in Small Groups," *American Socio-
            logical Review, 16,* 461–468.

Bales, Robert F.
1955   "Adaptive and Integrative Changes as Sources of Strain in Social Systems," in Hare, A. Paul, Edgar F. Borgatta, and Robert A. Bales (eds.), *Small Groups*. New York: Alfred Knopf.

Bales, Robert F., and Edward F. Borgatta
1955   "Size of Group as a Factor in the Interaction Profile," in Hare, A. Paul, Edward F. Borgatta, Robert F. Bales (eds.), *Small Groups: Studies in Social Interaction*. New York: Knopf.

Banfield, E.
1958   *The Moral Basis of a Backward Society*. New York: Free Press.

Banfield, Edward C.
1962   "Ends and Means in Planning," in Mailick, Sidney, and Edward H. Van Ness (eds.), *Concepts and Issues in Administrative Behavior*. Englewood Cliffs, N. J.: Prentice-Hall.

Barber, Bernard
1965   "Some Problems in the Sociology of the Professions," *Daedalus* (Fall).

Barlow, Walter
1965   "Discontent Among Engineers," *Journal of College Placement*, XXV.

Barnard, Chester I.
1938   *The Functions of the Executive*. Cambridge, Mass.: Harvard University Press.

Barnard, Chester I.
1939   *Dilemmas of Leadership in the Democratic Process*. Stafford Little Lectures. Princeton: Princeton University Press.

Barnard, Chester
1964   "Functions and Pathology of Status Systems in Formal Organizations," in Whyte, William Foote (ed.), *Industry and Society*. New York: McGraw-Hill.

Barnard, Jessie
1950   "Where is the Modern Sociology of Conflict?" *American Journal of Sociology, 56,* 11–16.

Barth, Ernest A. T.
1963   "The Causes and Consequences of Inter-agency Conflict," *Sociological Inquiry, 33* (Winter).

Barton, A. H.
1958   "Legitimacy, Power, and Compromise Within Formal Authority Structures—A Formal Model." *Bureau of Applied Social Research*, New York: Columbia University. Mimeographed.

Barton, Allen
1961   *Organizational Measurement*. New York: College Entrance Examination Board.

Bauer, Raymond A., *et al.*
1956   *How the Soviet System Works: Cultural, Psychological, and Social Themes*. Cambridge, Mass.: Harvard University Press.

Baumgartel, H.
1956   "Leadership, Motivations, and Attitudes in Research Laboratories,"
        Journal of Social Issues, 12, No. 2.

Baumol, William J.
1959   *Business Behavior, Value and Growth.* New York: Macmillan.

Bavelas, Alex
1950   "Communication Patterns in Task-Oriented Groups," *Journal of
        the Statistical Society of America, 22.*

Bavelas, Alex
1952   "Communication Patterns in Problem Solving Groups," in von
        Foerster, H. (ed.), *Cybernetics, Transactions of the Eighth Confer-
        ence 1951* (Josiah Macy, Jr. Foundation).

Becker, Howard S.
1953   "The Teacher in the Authority System of the Public School," *Jour-
        nal of Educational Sociology, 27,* 128–141, reprinted in Etzioni, A.
        (ed.), *Complex Organizations.* New York: Holt, Rinehart & Win-
        ston, 1961, 243–251.

Becker, H. S., and J. Carper
1956   "The Elements of Identification with an Occupation," *American
        Sociological Review, 21,* 341–348.

Becker, Howard, and Blanche Geer
1960   "Latent Culture: A Research Note," *Administrative Science Quar-
        terly, 5* (September), 304–313.

Beer, John J., and W. David Lewis
1963   "Aspects of Professionalization of Science," *Daedalus,* XCII.

Belknap, Ivan
1956   *Human Problems of a State Mental Hospital.* New York: McGraw-
        Hill.

Bell, D.
1959   "The 'Rediscovery' of Alienation," *Journal of Philosophy, 56.*

Bell, D.
1960   *The End of Ideology.* New York: Free Press.

Bell, Gerald D.
1967   "Determinants of Span of Control," *American Journal of Sociol-
        ogy, 73,* 100–109.

Ben-David, Joseph
1958   "Professional Role of the Physician in Bureaucratized Medicine:
        A Study in Role Conflict," *Human Relations, 11,* 255–274.

Ben-David, Joseph
1962   "Scientific Productivity and Academic Organization in Nineteenth-
        Century Medicine," in Barber, Bernard and Walter Hirsch (eds.),
        The Sociology of Science. New York: Free Press of Glencoe,
        305–328.

Bendix, R.
1947   "Bureaucracy: The Problem and Its Setting," *American Sociolog-ical Review, 12,* 493–507.

Bendix, Reinhard
1956   *Work and Authority in Industry.* New York: Wiley.

Benne, Kenneth D.
1962   "Deliberate Changing as the Facilitation of Growth," in Bennis, Warren G. *et al.* (eds.), *The Planning of Change.* New York: Holt, Rinehart & Winston.

Bennis, Warren G., N. Berkowitz, M. Affinito, and M. Malone
1958   "Reference Groups and Loyalties in the Out-Patient Department," *Administrative Science Quarterly, 2* (March), 481–500.

Bennis, Warren G.
1959   "Leadership Theory and Administrative Behavior: The Problem of Authority," *Administrative Science Quarterly, 4* (December), 259–301.

Berelson, Bernard, and Gary Steiner
1964   *Human Behavior.* New York: Harcourt, Brace and World.

Berger, Morroe
1957   *Bureaucracy and Society in Modern Egypt.* Princeton, N. J.: Princeton University Press.

Berle, A. A., and G. Means
1937   *The Modern Corporation and Private Property.* New York: Mac-millan.

Berliner, Joseph
1956   "A Problem in Soviet Business Administration," *Administrative Science Quarterly,* I (June), 86–101.

Berliner, Joseph
1957   Factory and Manager in the USSR. Cambridge, Mass.: Harvard University Press.

Bettelheim, Bruno
1943   "Individual and Mass Behavior in Extreme Situations," *Journal of Abnormal and Social Psychology, 38* (October).

Biddle, Bruce J.
1964   "Roles, Goals, and Value Structures in Organizations," in Cooper, William W., Harold J. Leavitt, and Maynard W. Shelly II (eds.), *New Perspectives in Organization Research.* New York: Wiley.

Biersted, Robert
1950   "An Analysis of Social Power," *American Sociological Review, 15,* 730–738.

Black, Bertram J., and Harold M. Kase
1963   "Inter-agency Cooperation in Rehabilitation and Mental Health," *Social Service Review, 37* (March).

Black, D.
  1948   "On the Rationale of Decision-Making," *Journal of Political Economy, 56.*

Blackstone, Sir William
  1902   *Commentaries on the Law of England,* ed. W. D. Lewis. Philadelphia.

Blake, R., and J. Mouton
  1964   *The Managerial Grid.* Houston: Gulf Publishing Co.

Blalock, Hubert M., Jr.
  1960   *Social Statistics.* New York: McGraw-Hill.

Blalock, Hubert M., Jr.
  1965   "Theory Building and the Statistical Concept of Interaction," *American Sociological Review, 30,* 374–380.

Blankenship, L. V., and R. H. Elling
  1962   "Organizational Support and Community Power Structure: The Hospital," *Journal of Health and Human Behavior,* III, No. 4.

Blau, Peter
  1955   *The Dynamics of Bureaucracy.* Chicago: The University of Chicago Press.

Blau, Peter
  1956   *Bureaucracy in Modern Society.* New York: Random House.

Blau, Peter M.
  1960   "Structural Effects," *American Sociological Review, 25* (April), 178–193.

Blau, P. M.
  1963   "Critical Remarks on Weber's Theory of Authority," *American Political Science Review, 57* (June), 305–316.

Blau, Peter M.
  1968   "The Hierarchy of Authority in Organizations," *The American Journal of Sociology, 73,* 453–467.

Blau, Peter M.
  1970   "A Formal Theory of Differentiation in Organizations," *American Sociological Review, 35* (April), 201–218.

Blau, Peter
  1964   *Exchange and Power in Social Life.* New York: Wiley.

Blau, Peter M., Wolf V. Heydebrand, and Robert E. Stauffer
  1966   "The Structure of Small Bureaucracies," *American Sociological Review, 31* (April), 179–191.

Blau, Peter M., and William R. Scott
  1962   *Formal Organizations.* San Francisco: Chandler.

Blau, Peter M., and Richard A. Schoenherr
  1970   *The Structure of Organizations.* New York: Basic Books.

Blauner, Robert
  1964   *Alienation and Freedom: The Factory Worker and His Industry.* Chicago: The University of Chicago Press.

Blum, F.
  1953   *Toward a Democratic Work Process.* New York: Harper.

Bossard, J. H. S.
1945   "The Law of Family Interaction," *American Journal of Sociology, 50, 292–294.*

Bottomore, T. B., and M. Rubel (eds.)
1956   *Karl Marx: Selected Writings in Sociology and Social Philosophy.* London: Watts.

Boulding, K. E.
1953   *The Organizational Revolution.* New York: Harper & Row.

Boulding, Kenneth E.
1955   *Economic Analysis* (3rd ed.). New York: Harper.

Boulding, Kenneth
1964   "'A Pure Theory of Conflict Applied to Organizations," in Kahn, Robert L. and Elise Boulding (eds.), *Power and Conflict in Organizations.* New York: Basic Books, 136–145.

Boulding, Kenneth E.
1965   "The Economies of Human Conflict," in McNeil, Elton B. (ed.), *The Nature of Human Conflict.* Englewood Cliffs, N. J.: Prentice-Hall.

Braithwaite, Richard B.
1953   *Scientific Explanation.* Cambridge, England: Cambridge University Press.

Bramson, Leon
1961   *The Political Context of Sociology.* Princeton, N. J.: Princeton University Press.

Braybrooke, David, and C. E. Lindblom
1963   *A Strategy of Decision.* Glencoe, Ill.: Free Press.

Brech, E. F. L.
1953   *Principles and Practice of Management.* London: Longmans.

Brech, E. F. L.
1957   *Organization: The Framework of Management.* London: Longmans.

Bright, James, R.
1958   *Automation and Management.* Cambridge, Mass.: Harvard University Press.

Brogden, H. E.
1949   "A New Coefficient: Applications to Biserial Correlation and to Estimation of Selective Efficiency," *Psychometrika, 14,* 169–182.

Brown, M.
1966   *On the Theory and Measurement of Technological Change.* Cambridge, England: Cambridge University Press.

Brown, P.
1954   "Bureaucracy in a Government Laboratory," *Social Forces,* XXXII.

Brown, S. H.
1964   "Magnavox Goes Its Own Golden Way," *Fortune* (February).

Brown, W.
1960   *Explorations in Management.* London: Heinemann.

Buley, Hilton
1947   "Personnel Characteristics and Staff Patterns Associated with the

Quality of Education." Unpublished Ed.P Project, Teachers College, Columbia University.

Burin, F. G.
1952   "Bureaucracy and National Socialism," in Merton, Robert, *et al.* (eds.), *Reader in Bureaucracy.* Glencoe, Ill.: Free Press, 33–47.

Burnham, J.
1962   *The Managerial Revolution.* London: Penguin.

Burns, Tom
1960   *Management in the Electronic Industry—a Study of Eight English Companies.* Edinburgh: Social Science Research Centre, University of Edinburgh.

Burns, Tom
1954   "The Directions of Activity and Communication in a Departmental Executive Group," *Human Relations, 7.*

Burns, Tom
1958   "The Idea of Structure in Sociology," *Human Relations, 9.*

Burns, Tom, and G. M. Stalker
1961   *The Management of Innovation.* London: Tavistock Publications.

Burns, T.
1967   "The Comparative Study of Organizations," in V. H. Vroom (ed.), *Methods of Organizational Research.* Pittsburgh: Pittsburgh University Press.

Burack, E. H.
1966   "Technology and Some Aspects of Industrial Supervision: A Model Building Approach," *Journal of Academy of Management, 9,* 43–66.

Burack, Elmer H.
1967   "Industrial Management in Advanced Productive Systems: Some Theoretical and Preliminary Findings," *Administrative Science Quarterly, 12* (December), 479–500.

Burack, E. H., and F. H. Cassell
1967   "Technological Change and Manpower Developments in Advanced Production Systems," *Academy of Management Journal,* 293–308.

Burling, Temple, Edith M. Lentz, and Robert N. Wilson
1956   *The Give and Take in Hospitals.* New York: G. P. Putnam's Sons.

Cangelosi, Vincent E., and William R. Dill
1965   "Organizational Learning: Observations Toward a Theory," *Administrative Science Quarterly, 10* (September), 175–203.

Caplow, Theodore
1957   "Organizational Size," *Administrative Science Quarterly, 1* (March), 484–505.

Caplow, Theodore, and Reece J. McGee
1958   *The Academic Marketplace.* New York: Basic Books.

Caplow, Theodore
1964   *Principles of Organization.* New York: Harcourt, Brace and World.

Carlson, Richard O.
1961   *Executive Succession and Organizational Change: Place-Bound and Career-Bound Superintendents of Schools.* Chicago: Midwest Administration Center, The University of Chicago.

Carter, C. F.
1954   "A Revised Theory of Expectations," in Carter, C. F., G. P. Meredith, and G. L. S. Shackle (eds.), *Uncertainty and Business Decisions.* Liverpool: Liverpool University Press.

Carter, Launor, William Haythorn, Beatrice Meirowitz, and John Lanzetta
1951   "The Relation of Categorizations and Ratings in the Observation of Group Behavior," *Human Relations, 4.*

Cartwright, D., and L. Festinger
1943   "A Quantitative Theory of Decision," *Psychological Review, 50.*

Cartwright, D., and A. Zander
1953   *Group Dynamics: Research and Theory.* New York: Harper & Row.

Cartwright, Dorwin
1959   "The Potential Contribution of Graph Theory to Organization Theory," in Haire, Mason (ed.), *Modern Organization Theory.* New York: Wiley, 254–271.

Catton, William R., Jr.
1962   "Unstated Goals as a Source of Stress in an Organization," *The Pacific Sociological Review, 5* (Spring).

Caudill, William
1961   "Tsu Kisoi in Japanese Psychiatric Hospitals," *American Sociological Review, 26* (April), 204–214.

Caudill, W., and H. Scarr
1962   "Japanese Value Orientations and Culture Change," *Ethnology, 1,* 53–91.

Centers, Richard
1949   *The Psychology of Social Classes: A Study of Class Consciousness.* Princeton, N. J.: Princeton University Press.

Chandler, Alfred D., Jr.
1956   "Management Decentralization: An Historical Analysis," *The Business History Review, 30.*

Chandler, Alfred D., Jr.
1962   *Strategy and Structure.* Cambridge, Mass.: The MIT Press.

Chapin, F. Stuart
1928   *Cultural Change.* New York: Appleton-Century-Crofts.

Chapin, F. Stuart
1935   *Contemporary American Institutions.* New York: Harper.

Chapin, F. Stuart
1951   "The Growth of Bureaucracy: An Hypothesis," *American Sociological Review, 16* (December), 835–836.

Chein, I.
1943   "Personality and Typology," *Journal of Social Psychology, 18,* 89–101.

Cherry, C.
1957   *On Human Communication.* New York: Wiley.

Christie, L. S., R. Duncan Luce, and J. Macy, Jr.
1952   *Communication and Learning in Task-Oriented Groups.* Research Laboratory of Electronics, Massachusetts Institute of Technology Technical Report No. 231.

Cillié, François
1940   *Centralization or Decentralization.* New York: Teachers College, Columbia University.

Clapham, J. H.
1932   *Economic History of Modern Britain, Vol. II: Free Trade and Steel 1850–86.* London: Cambridge University Press.

Clapp, Gordon R.
1945   "The Administrative Resources of a Region: the Example of the Tennessee Valley," in *New Horizons in Public Administration.* University, Ala.: University of Alabama Press.

Clark, Burton R.
1956   "Organizational Adaptation and Precarious Values," *American Sociological Review,* 21, 327–336.

Clark, Burton R.
1965   "Interorganizational Patterns in Education," *Administrative Science Quarterly, 10* (September), 224–237.

Clark, Peter B., and James Q. Wilson
1961   "Incentive Systems: A Theory of Organizations," *Administrative Science Quarterly, 5* (September), 129–166.

Clemmer, Donald
1950   "Observations on Imprisonment as a Source of Criminality," *The Journal of Criminal Law and Criminology, 41* (September–October).

Clemmer, Donald
1940   *The Prison Community.* Boston: The Christopher Publishing House.

Coch, Lester, and John French, Jr.
1948   "Overcoming Resistance to Change," *Human Relations,* I, 512–532.

Cohen, Arthur
1962   "Changing Small-Group Communication Networks," *Administrative Science Quarterly, 6* (March), 443–462.

Cohen, Harry
1965   *The Demonics of Bureaucracy: Problems of Change in a Government Agency.* Ames, Iowa: Iowa State University, Part III.

Coleman, James
1957   *Community Conflict.* Glencoe, Ill.: Free Press.

Coleman, James S.
1961   *The Adolescent Society.* New York: Free Press of Glencoe.

Coleman, James S.
1964   "Research Chronicle: The Adolescent Society," in Hammond, Phillip E. (ed.), *Sociologists at Work.* New York: Basic Books.

Comrey, A. L., J. M. Pfiffner, and W. S. High
1954   *Factors Influencing Organizational Effectiveness.* (Final Technical Report, The Office of Naval Research.) Los Angeles: University of Southern California.

Cooms, C. H.
1964   *A Theory of Data.* New York: Wiley.

Cordtz, D.
1967   "There's Another Generation of Whiz Kids at Ford," *Fortune,* (January).

Corwin, Ronald G.
1961   "The Professional Employee: Study of Conflict in Nursing Roles,"
        American Journal of Sociology, 67, 604–615.
Corwin, Ronald G.
1965   "Militant Professionalism, Initiative and Compliance in Public
        Education," *Sociology of Education, 38,* 310–331.
Corwin, Ronald G.
1969a   "Patterns of Organizational Conflict," *Administrative Science
        Quarterly, 14* (December), 507–520.
Corwin, Ronald G.
1969b   *Staff Conflict in the Public Schools.* New York: Appleton-Century-
        Crofts.
Coser, Lewis
1956   *The Functions of Social Conflict.* Glencoe, Ill.: Free Press.
Coser, Lewis
1957   "Social Conflict and the Theory of Social Change," *The British
        Journal of Sociology, 7,* 197–207.
Coser, Rose L.
1958   "Authority and Decision-Making in a Hospital," *American So-
        ciological Review, 23* (February), 56–63.
Coser, Rose L.
1961   "Insulation from Observability and Types of Social Conformity,"
        American Sociological Review, 26 (February), 28–39.
Coser, Rose L.
1962   *Life in the Ward.* East Lansing, Mich.: Michigan State University
        Press.
Coser, Rose L.
1963   "Alienation and the Social Structure: A Case Analysis of a
        Hospital," in Freidson, Eliot (ed.), *The Hospital in Modern Society.*
        New York: Free Press.
Cressey, Donald R.
1965   "Prison Organizations," in March, James G. (ed.), *Handbook of
        Organizations.* Chicago: Rand-McNally, 1023–1070.
Crozier, Michel
1964   *The Bureaucratic Phenomenon.* Chicago: The University of Chi-
        cago Press.
Cummings, Larry L., and Aly M. ElSalmi
1970   "The Impact of Role Diversity, Job Level, and Organizational Size
        on Managerial Satisfaction," *Administrative Science Quarterly, 15*
        (March), 1–11.
Cyert, R. M., and J. G. March
1956   "Organizational Factors in the Theory of Oligopoly," *Quarterly
        Journal of Economics, 70.*
Cyert, Richard M., and James G. March
1959   "A Behavioral Theory of Organizational Objectives," in Haire,
        Mason (ed.), *Modern Organization Theory.* New York: Wiley, 76–90.
Cyert, Richard M., and James G. March
1963   *A Behavioral Theory of the Firm.* Englewood Cliffs, N. J.: Prentice-
        Hall.

Dahl, Robert A.
  1957   "The Concept of Power," *Behavioral Science, 2.*

Dahrendorf, R.
  1958a   *Class and Class Conflict in Industrial Society.* Stanford, Calif.:
          Stanford University Press.

Dahrendorf, Ralf
  1958b   "Out of Utopia: Toward a Reorientation of Sociological Analysis,"
          American Journal of Sociology, 64 (September), 115–127.

Dalton, Melville
  1950   "Conflicts Between Staff and Line Managerial Officers," *American
          Sociological Review, 15* (June), 342–351.

Dalton, Melville
  1959   *Men Who Manage.* New York: Wiley.

Davis, Arthur K.
  1952   "Bureaucratic Patterns in the Navy Officer Corps," in Merton,
          Robert K., *et al.* (eds.), *Reader in Bureaucracy.* Glencoe, Ill.: Free
          Press, 380–395.

Davis, James A., J. L. Spaeth, and C. Huson
  1961   "A Technique for Analyzing the Effects of Group Composition,"
          American Sociological Review, 26 (April), 215–225.

Davis, James W., Jr., and Kenneth M. Dolbeare
  1968   *Little Groups of Neighbors: The Selective Service System.* Chi-
          cago: Markham Publishing Co.

Davis, R. C.
  1954   "Factors Related to Scientific Research Performance," in *Inter-
          personal Factors in Research, Part I.* Ann Arbor: Institute for Social
          Research, University of Michigan.

Davis, R. C.
  1956   "Commitment to Professional Values as Related to the Role Per-
          formance of Research Scientists." Unpublished doctor's disserta-
          tion, University of Michigan.

Dearborn, D. C., and H. A. Simon
  1958   "Selective Perception: A Note on the Departmental Identifications
          of Executives," *Sociometry, 21,* 140–144.

Delany, William
  1963   "The Development and Decline of Patrimonial and Bureaucratic
          Administrations," *Administrative Science Quarterly, 7* (March),
          458–501.

Demerath, N. J., III
  1968   "Trends and Anti-Trends in Religious Change," in Sheldon,
          Eleanor Bernert and Wilbert E. Moore (eds.), *Indicators of Social
          Change.* New York: Russell Sage Foundation, 349–445.

Dent, James K.
  1959   "Organizational Correlates of the Goals of Business Management,"
          Personnel Psychology, 12 (Autumn).

Deutsch, Morton
  1949   "An Experimental Study of the Effects of Co-operation and Com-
          petition upon Group Processes," *Human Relations, 2.*

Dill, William
1958   "Environment as an Influence on Managerial Autonomy," *Administrative Science Quarterly, 2* (March), 409–433.

Dill, William R.
1962   "The Impact of Environment on Organizational Development," in Mailick, Sidney, and Edward H. Van Ness (eds.), *Concepts and Issues in Administrative Behavior.* Englewood Cliffs, N. J.: Prentice-Hall, 94–109.

Dimock, Marshall E.
1959   *Administrative Vitality.* New York: Harper & Bros.

Dornbusch, Sanford M.
1955   "The Military Academy as an Assimilating Institution," *Social Forces, 33.*

Downs, Anthony
1967   *Inside Bureaucracy.* Boston: Little, Brown.

Drucker, Peter F.
1954   *The Practice of Management.* New York: Harper.

Drucker, Peter F.
1964   "The Big Power of Little Ideas," *Harvard Business Review, 42* (May).

Dubin, Robert
1951   *Human Relations in Administration.* Englewood Cliffs, N. J.: Prentice-Hall.

Dubin, R.
1958   *The World of Work.* Englewood Cliffs: Prentice-Hall.

Dubin, Robert
1959   "Stability of Human Organization," in Haire, Mason (ed.), *Modern Organization Theory.* New York: Wiley, 218–251.

Dubin, Robert
1965   "Supervision and Productivity: Empirical Findings and Theoretical Considerations," in Dubin, Robert, George C. Homans, Floyd C. Mann, and Delbert C. Miller, *Leadership and Productivity.* San Francisco: Chandler.

Duggan, T., and C. Dean
1968   "Common Misinterpretations of Significance Levels in Sociological Journals," *American Sociologist, 3,* 45–46.

Duncan, O. D., W. R. Scott, S. Lieberson, B. Duncan, and H. Winsborough
1963   *Metropolis and Region.* Baltimore: Johns Hopkins University.

Dunham, H. Warren, and S. Kirson Weinberg
1960   *The Culture of the State Mental Hospital.* Detroit: Wayne State University Press.

Dun's Review
1963   "Long Range Planning and Cloudy Horizons," *81* (January).

Durkheim, Emile
1947   *Division of Labor in Society,* trans. George Simpson. Glencoe, Ill.: Free Press.

Durkheim, Emile
1958   *Professional Ethics and Civic Morals.* Glencoe, Ill.: Free Press.

Dynes, R. R.
    1957   "The Consequences of Sectarianism for Social Participation," *Social Forces, 35.*

Easton, David
    1965a   *A Framework for Political Analysis.* Englewood Cliffs, N. J.: Prentice-Hall.

Easton, David
    1965b   *A Systems Analysis of Political Life.* New York: John Wiley.

Eccles, C.
    1958   "The Physiology of Imagination," *Scientific American, 99,* No. 3 (September).

Edelman, Murray
    1964   *The Symbolic Uses of Politics.* Urbana: University of Illinois Press.

Edwards, Ward
    1953   "Probability-Preferences in Gambling," *American Journal of Psychology, 66.*

Eisenstadt, S. N.
    1958   "Bureaucracy and Bureaucratization," *Current Sociology, 7,* No. 2.

Eisenstadt, S. N.
    1959   "Bureaucracy, Bureaucratization, and Debureaucratization," *Administrative Science Quarterly, 4* (December), 302–320.

Elling, R. H., and S. Halebsky
    1961   "Organizational Differentiation and Support: A Conceptual Framework," *Administrative Science Quarterly, 6,* 185–209.

Emerson, Richard M.
    1962   "Power-Dependence Relationships," *American Sociological Review, 27* (February), 31–41.

Emery, F. W., and E. L. Trist
    1965   "The Causal Texture of Organizational Environment," *Human Relations, 18* (February), 21–31.

Etzioni, Amitai W.
    1960a   "New Directions in the Study of Organizations and Society," *Social Research, 27,* 223–228.

Etzioni, Amitai W.
    1960b   "Two Approaches to Organizational Analysis: A Critique and a Suggestion," *Administrative Science Quarterly, 5* (September), 257–278.

Etzioni, Amitai
    1961a   *A Comparative Analysis of Complex Organizations.* New York: Free Press.

Etzioni, Amitai
    1961b   *Complex Organizations: A Sociological Reader.* New York: Holt, Rinehart & Winston.

Etzioni, Amitai
    1963   "The Epigenesis of Political Communities at the International Level," *American Journal of Sociology, 68,* 407–421.

Etzioni, Amitai
    1964   *Modern Organizations.* Englewood Cliffs, N. J.: Prentice-Hall.

Etzioni, Amitai
1965   "Organizational Control Structure," in March, James G. (ed.), *Handbook of Organizations.* Chicago: Rand-McNally, 650–677.

Etzioni, Amitai
1968   "Organizational Dimensions and Their Interrelations: a Theory of Compliance," in Indik, Bernard and S. Kenneth Berien (eds.), *People, Groups and Organizations.* New York: Teachers College Press.

Evan, W. M.
1963   "Indices of the Hierarchical Structure of Industrial Organizations," *Management Science, 9* (April), 468–477.

Evan, William M.
1966   "The Organization-Set: Toward a Theory of Interorganizational Relations," in Thompson, James D. (ed.), *Approaches to Organizational Design.* Pittsburgh, Pa.: University of Pittsburgh Press.

Faunce, William
1958   "Automation and the Automobile Worker," *Social Problems, VI.*

Faunce, W.
1965   "Automation and the Division of Labor," *Social Problems, 13,* 149–160.

Faunce, W.
1968   *Problems of an Industrial Society.* New York: McGraw-Hill.

Fayol, H.
1930   *Industrial and General Management,* trans. C. Storrs. London: Pitman.

Fensham, P. J., and D. Hooper
1964   *The Dynamics of Changing Technology.* London: Tavistock.

Festinger, Leon
1950   *Social Pressures in Informal Groups: A Study of Human Factors in Housing.* New York: Harper & Row.

Fichter, J. H.
1954   *Social Relations in the Urban Parish.* Chicago: The University of Chicago Press.

Fiedler, F.
1960   Technical Report No. 10, Group Effectiveness Research Laboratory, Department of Psychology, University of Illinois.

Florence, P. S.
1961   *Ownership, Control and Success of Large Companies.* London: Sweet and Maxwell.

Follett, Mary P.
1941   *Dynamic Administration,* eds. Metcalfe & Urwick. Management Publications Trust.

Form, William H., and Sigmund Nosow
1958   *Community in Disaster.* New York: Harper & Row.

Fortune
1963   "Pinching 500,000,000 Pennies." (March).

Fortune
1966   "How Seven Employees Can Be Made to Do the Work of One."
        (March).
Fox, Harland
1960   "Employee Savings Plans in the Oil Industry," *Management Record,* XXII.
Francis, Roy G., and Robert C. Stone
1956   *Service and Procedure in Bureaucracy.* Minneapolis: University of
        Minnesota Press.
Freidson, Eliot
1964   "The Organization of Professional Behavior." Paper read at the
        1964 Annual Meeting of the American Sociological Association.
French, John R. P., Jr., and Bertram Raven
1960   "The Bases of Social Power," in Cartwright, D. and A. Zander
        (eds.), *Group Dynamics.* New York: Harper & Row.
Friedrich, Carl J.
1949   "Some Observations on Weber's Analysis of Bureaucracy," in
        Reader in Bureaucracy, ed. R. K. Merton *et al.* Glencoe, Ill.: Free
        Press, 27–33.
Friedrich, C. J. (ed.)
1958   *Authority.* Cambridge, Mass.: Harvard University Press.
Fromm, Erich
1941   *Escape from Freedom.* New York: Holt, Rinehart & Winston.
Fullan, M.
1969   "Workers Receptivity to Industrial Change in Different Techno-
        logical Settings." Unpublished Ph.D. dissertation, University of
        Toronto.
Fullan, Michael
1970   "Industrial Technology and Worker Integration in the Organiza-
        tion," *American Sociological Review, 35* (December), 1028–1039.
Gallie, W. B.
1954   "Uncertainty as a Philosophical Problem," in Carter, Meredith,
        and Shackle (eds.), *Uncertainty and Business Decisions.* Liver-
        pool: Liverpool University Press.
Gamson, William A.
1966   "Rancorous Conflict in Community Politics," *American Sociolog-
        ical Review, 31,* 71–81.
Gamson, William A.
1966   "Reputation and Resources in Community Politics," *American
        Journal of Sociology, 72* (September), 121–131.
Gardner, John W.
1963   *Self-Renewal.* New York: Harper & Row.
Gendell, Murray, and Hans L. Zetterberg (eds.)
1961   *A Sociological Almanac for the United States.* New York: Bed-
        minster.
Georgescu-Roegen, N.
1958   "The Nature of Expectation and Uncertainty," in Bowman, Mary J.
        (ed.), *Expectations, Uncertainty and Business Behavior.* New York:
        Social Sciences Research Council.

Georgopoulos, Basil
  1957a "The Normative Structure of Social Systems: a Study of Organiza-
          tional Effectiveness." Unpublished doctoral dissertation, Univer-
          sity of Michigan.

Georgopoulos, Basil S., and Arnold S. Tannenbaum
  1957b "A Study of Organizational Effectiveness," *American Sociological
          Review, 22* (October), 534–540.

Georgopoulos, Basil S., and Floyd C. Mann
  1962 *The Community General Hospital.* New York: Macmillan.

Gerth, Hans, and C. Wright Mills
  1958 *From Max Weber: Essays in Sociology.* New York: Oxford Univer-
          sity Press.

Gibb, J. R.
  1951 "The Effects of Group Size and of Threat Reduction upon Crea-
          tivity in a Problem Solving Situation," *American Psychologist, 6.*

Gibbs, J. P., and H. L. Browning
  1966 "The Division of Labor, Technology, and the Organization of Pro-
          duction in Twelve Countries," *American Sociological Review, 31,*
          81–92.

Gilbert, Doris C., and D. J. Levinson
  1957 " 'Custodialism' and 'Humanism' in Staff Ideology," in Greenblatt,
          M., D. J. Levinson, and R. H. Williams (eds.), *The Patient and the
          Mental Hospital.* New York: Free Press.

Glaser, Barney G.
  1964 *Organizational Scientists.* Indianapolis: Bobbs-Merrill Co.

Glaser, William A.
  1971 "Cross-National Comparisons of the Factory," *Journal of Com-
          parative Administration, 3* (May), 83–117.

Glock, Charles Y., and Benjamin B. Ringer
  1956 "Church Policy and the Attitudes of Ministers and Parishioners on
          Social Issues," *American Sociological Review, 21,* 148–156.

Goffman, Erving
  1961 *Encounters.* Indianapolis: Bobbs-Merrill.

Gold, D.
  1969 "Statistical Tests and Substantive Significance," *American Sociol-
          ogist, 4,* 42–46.

Goldner, Fred H.
  1961 "Industrial Relations and the Organization of Management." Un-
          published Ph.D. dissertation, University of California, Berkeley.

Goldner, Fred H.
  1965 "Demotion in Industrial Management," *American Sociological Re-
          view, 30* (October), 714–724.

Goldthorpe, J.
  1959 "Technical Organization as a Factor in Supervisor–Worker Con-
          flict," *British Journal of Sociology, 10,* 213–230.

Goodman, Leo A.
  1961 "Modifications of the Dorn-Stouffer-Tibbits Method for 'Testing the

Significance of Comparisons in Sociological Data,' " *American Journal of Sociology, 66,* 355–363.

Gordon, C. Wayne, and Nicholas Babchuk
1959   "A Typology of Voluntary Associations," *American Sociological Review, 24,* 22–29.

Goss, Mary E.
1961   "Influence and Authority Among Physicians," *American Sociological Review, 26,* 39–50

Gouldner, Alvin
1950   *Studies in Leadership.* New York: Harper & Bros.

Gouldner, Alvin W.
1954a   *Patterns of Industrial Bureaucracy.* Glencoe, Ill.: Free Press.

Gouldner, Alvin W.
1954b   *Wildcat Strike.* Yellow Springs, Ohio: Antioch Press.

Gouldner, Alvin
1957   "Cosmopolitans and Locals: Toward an Analysis of Latent Social Roles—I," *Administrative Science Quarterly, 2* (December), 281–306

Gouldner, Alvin
1958   "Cosmopolitans and Locals: Toward an Analysis of Latent Social Roles—II," *Administrative Science Quarterly, 2* (March), 444–480.

Gouldner, A. W.
1959a   "Organizational Analysis," in Merton, R. K., L. Broom, and L. S. Cottrell (eds.), *Sociology Today.* New York: Basic Books, 400–428.

Gouldner, Alvin
1959b   "Reciprocity and Autonomy in Functional Theory," in Gross, Llewellyn (ed.), *Symposium on Sociological Theory.* New York: Harper & Row.

Graicunas, V. A.
1933   "Relationship in Organization," *Bulletin of the International Management Institute* (March).

Granick, David
1961   *The Red Executive.* Garden City, N. Y.: Doubleday.

Gross, Bertram
1965   "What Are Your Organization's Objectives? A General-Systems Approach to Planning," *Human Relations, 18* (August).

Gross, Edward
1953   "Some Functional Consequences of Primary Controls in Formal Work Organizations," *American Sociological Review, 18* (December), 368–373.

Gross, Neal, Ward S. Mason, and Alexander W. McEachern
1958   *Explorations in Role Analysis.* New York: Wiley.

Gross, Neal, and Robert E. Herriott
1965   *Staff Leadership in Public Schools.* New York: Wiley.

Grusky, Oscar
1959   "Role Conflict in Organizations," *Administrative Science Quarterly, 3* (March), 452–472.

Grusky, Oscar
1961   "Corporate Size, Bureaucratization, and Managerial Succession," *American Journal of Sociology, 67* (November), 261–269.

Grusky, Oscar
1970   "The Effect of Succession: A Comparative Study of Military and Business Organizations." In Grusky, Oscar, and George Miller (eds.), *Sociology of Organizations.* New York: Free Press, 439–454.

Guest, Robert
1960   "Work Careers and Aspirations of Automobile Workers," in Galenson, Walter, and Seymour M. Lipset (eds.), *Labor and Trade Unionism.* New York: Wiley.

Guetzkow, Harold
1950   "Interagency Committee Usage," *Public Administration Review, 10* (Summer).

Guetzkow, Harold, and Herbert Simon
1960   "The Impact of Certain Communication Nets upon Organization and Performance in Task-Oriented Groups," in Rubenstein, Albert H., and Chadwick J. Haverstroh (eds.), *Some Theories of Organization.* Homewood, Ill.: The Dorsey Press.

Guetzkow, Harold
1965   "Communications in Organizations," in March, James (ed.), *Handbook of Organizations.* Chicago: Rand-McNally, 534–573.

Guetzkow, Harold
1966   "Relations Among Organizations," in Bowers, Raymond V. (ed.), *Studies on Behavior in Organizations.* Athens, Ga.: University of Georgia Press.

Gulick, L. H., and L. Urwick (eds.)
1937   *Papers on the Science of Administration.* New York: Institute of Public Administration, Columbia University.

Gusfield, Joseph R.
1955   "Social Structure and Moral Reform: A Study of the Woman's Christian Temperance Union," *American Journal of Sociology, 61* (November), 221–232.

Gusfield, Joseph R.
1957   "The Problem of Generations in an Organizational Structure," *Social Forces, 35.*

Guttman, L.
1950   Chapters 1–4 in Stouffer, S. A. *et al., Measurement and Prediction* (Vol. IV of Studies in Social Psychology in World War II series). Princeton, N. J.: Princeton University Press.

Haas, Eugene, and Linda Collen
1963   "Administrative Practices in University Departments," *Administrative Science Quarterly, 8* (June), 44–60.

Haas, Eugene, Richard Hall, and Norman Johnson
1963   "The Size of the Supportive Component in Organizations: A Multiorganizational Analysis," *Social Forces, 42* (October), 9–17.

Haas, J. Eugene, Richard H. Hall, and Norman J. Johnson
   1966   "Toward an Empirically Derived Taxonomy of Organizations," in Bowers, Raymond V. (ed.), *Studies on Behavior in Organizations.* Atlanta: University of Georgia Press.

Haberstroh, Chadwick J.
   1965   "Organization Design and Systems Analysis," in March, James G. (ed.), *Handbook of Organizations.* Chicago: Rand-McNally, 1171–1217.

Hage, Jerald
   ——   "Centralization, Specialization, Effectiveness, and Efficiency in Professional Organizations." Unpublished manuscript, University of Wisconsin.

Hage, Jerald
   1963   "Organizational Response to Innovation: A Case Study of Community Hospitals." Unpublished Ph.D. dissertation, Columbia University.

Hage, Jerald
   1965a   "An Axiomatic Theory of Organizations," *Administrative Science Quarterly, 10* (December), 289–320.

Hage, Jerald, and Michael Aiken
   1967a   "Program Change and Organizational Properties: A Comparative Analysis," *American Journal of Sociology, 72* (March), 503–519.

Hage, J., and M. Aiken
   1967b   "Relationship of Centralization to Other Structural Properties," *Administrative Science Quarterly, 12* (June), 72–92.

Hage, Jerald, and Michael Aiken
   1969   "Routine Technology, Social Structure and Organizational Goals," *Administrative Science Quarterly, 14* (September), 366–376.

Hage, Jerald, and Michael Aiken
   1970   *Social Change in Complex Organizations.* New York: Random House.

Hage, Jerald, Michael Aiken, and Cora Bagley Marrett
   1971   "Organization Structure and Communications," *American Sociological Review, 36* (October), 860–871.

Hage, Jerald, and Gerald Marwell
   1965b   "Research Towards the Development of Role Theory—A New Approach." Paper read at the American Sociological Association, 60th annual meeting, August.

Hagstrom, Warren O.
   1965   *The Scientific Community.* New York: Basic Books.

Haire, M.
   1956   *Psychology in Management.* New York: McGraw-Hill.

Haire, Mason
   1959   "Biological Models and Empirical Histories of the Growth of Organizations," in Haire, Mason (ed.), *Modern Organization Theory.* New York: Wiley.

Hall, Douglas T., and Edward E. Lawler
1970   "Job Characteristics and Pressures and the Organizational Integration of Professionals," *Administrative Science Quarterly, 15* (September), 271–281.

Hall, Richard H.
1961   "An Empirical Study of Bureaucratic Dimensions and Their Relation to Other Organizational Characteristics." Unpublished Ph.D. dissertation, Columbus, Ohio State University.

Hall, Richard H.
1962   "Intraorganizational Structural Variation: Application of The Bureaucratic Model," *Administrative Science Quarterly, 7* (December), 295–308.

Hall, Richard H.
1963a   "The Concept of Bureaucracy: an Empirical Assessment," *American Journal of Sociology, 69* (July), 32–40.

Hall, Richard H.
1963b   "Bureaucracy and Small Organizations," *Sociology and Social Research, 48* (October).

Hall, Richard H.
1967   "Some Organizational Considerations in the Professional-Organizational Relationship," *Administrative Science Quarterly, 12* (December), 461–478.

Hall, Richard H.
1968   "Professionalization and Bureaucratization," *American Sociological Review, 33* (February), 92–104.

Hall, Richard H.
1969   *Occupations and the Social Structure.* Englewood Cliffs, N. J.: Prentice-Hall.

Hall, Richard H., J. Eugene Haas, and Norman J. Johnson
1967a   "Organizational Size, Complexity and Formalization," *American Sociological Review, 32* (December), 903–911.

Hall, Richard H., J. Eugene Haas, and Norman J. Johnson
1967b   "An Examination of the Blau-Scott and Etzioni Typologies," *Administrative Science Quarterly, 12* (June), 461–478.

Hall, Richard H., and C. R. Tittle
1966   "A Note on Bureaucracy and Its Correlates," *American Journal of Sociology, 72,* 267–272.

Harbison, Frederick H., and Robert Dubin
1947   *Patterns of Union–Management Relations.* Chicago, Ill.: Science Research Associates.

Harbison, Frederick H., E. Kochling, F. H. Casell, and H. C. Ruebman
1955   "Steel Management on Two Continents," *Management Science, 2,* 31–39.

Hare, A. Paul
1952   "A Study of Interaction and Consensus in Different Size Groups," *American Sociological Review, 17,* 261–267.

Harmon, H. H.
1960   *Modern Factor Analysis.* Chicago: The University of Chicago Press.

Harrington, M.
1968   *Toward a Democratic Left.* New York: Macmillan.

Harris, Frank W.
1964   "A Modern Council Point of View," *Social Work, 9,* 34–41.

Harrison, Paul
1959   *Authority and Power in the Free Church Tradition.* Princeton, N. J.: Princeton University Press.

Hartford, Ellis F.
1941   *Our Common Mooring.* Prepared for the Advisory Panel on Regional Materials of Instruction for the Tennessee Valley. Athens, Ga.: University of Georgia Press.

Harvey, Edward
1968   "Technology and the Structure of Organizations," *American Sociological Review, 33,* 247–259.

Havens, A. Eugene
1965   "Social Factors in Economic Development." Research Paper No. 5. Madison: University of Wisconsin, Land Tenure Center (May).

Hawley, Amos, Walter Boland, and Margaret Boland
1965   "Population Size and Administration in Institutions of Higher Education," *American Sociological Review, 30* (April), 252–255.

Hayner, Norman, and Ellis Ash
1939   "The Prison Community as a Social Group," *American Sociological Review, 4* (June), 362–369.

Heady, Ferrel
1959   "Bureaucratic Theory and Comparative Administration," *Administrative Science Quarterly, 4* (March), 509–525.

Hempel, Carl G., and Paul Oppenheim
1948   "The Logic of Explanation," *Philosophy of Science, 15,* 135–175.

Henry, W. G.
1958   Comment on G. P. Meredith's paper in Bowman (ed.), *Expectations, Uncertainty, and Business Behavior.* New York: Social Science Research Council.

Herbst, P. G.
1962   *Autonomous Group Functioning.* London: Tavistock.

Heydebrand, Wolf
1971   "New Directions in Research on Organizations." Paper presented at the Annual Meetings of the American Sociological Association, Denver, Colorado, September 2. (mimeo.)

Heydebrand, Wolf V.
1965   "Bureaucracy in Hospitals; An Analysis of Complexity and Coordination in Formal Organizations." Unpublished Ph.D. dissertation, Department of Sociology, University of Chicago.

Hickson, D. J.
1966   "A Convergence in Organization Theory," *Administrative Science Quarterly, 11* (September), 225–237.

Hickson, David J., D. S. Pugh, and Diana Pheysey
    1969   "Operations Technology and Organization Structure: An Empirical Reappraisal," *Administrative Science Quarterly, 14* (September), 378–397.

Hinings, C. R., D. S. Pugh, D. J. Kickson, and C. Turner
    1967   "An Approach to the Study of Bureaucracy," *Sociology, 1* (January).

Homans, George
    1950   *The Human Group.* New York: Harcourt.

Homans, George
    1958   "Social Behavior as Exchange," *American Journal of Sociology, 63* (May), 597–606.

Homans, George C.
    1961   *Social Behavior: Its Elementary Forms.* New York: Harcourt, Brace and World.

Homans, George
    1964   "Bringing Men Back In," *American Sociological Review, 24* (December), 809–819.

Hood, Robert C.
    1962   "Business Organization as a Cross Product of Its Purposes and of Its Environment," in Haire, Mason (ed.), *Organizational Theory in Industrial Practice.* New York: Wiley.

Hopkins, C. Howard
    1951   *The History of the YMCA in North America.* New York: Association Press.

Hopkins, Terence K.
    1961   "Bureaucratic Authority: The Convergence of Weber and Barnard," in Etzioni, A. (ed.), *Complex Organizations.* New York: Holt, Rinehart & Winston.

Hopkins, T. K.
    1966   Review of *Industrial Organization* by Joan Woodward. *Administrative Science Quarterly, 11,* 284–289.

Horney, Karen
    1945   *Our Inner Conflicts:* Norton.

Horwitz, M.
    1964   "Hostility and Its Management in Classroom Groups," in Charters, W. W., and N. L. Gage (eds.), *Readings in the Social Psychology of Education.* Boston: Allyn and Bacon, 196–212.

Hughes, Everett C.
    1952   "Memorandum on Going Concerns." Unpublished paper read before the Society for Applied Anthropology.

Hughes, Everett C.
    1958   *Men and Their Work.* Glencoe, Ill.: Free Press.

Indik, Bernard P., Basil Georgopoulos, and Stanley E. Seashore
    1961   "Superior–Subordinate Relationships and Performance," *Personnel Psychology, XIV.*

Indik, Bernard P.
    1964   "The Relationship Between Organization Size and Supervision Ratio," *Administrative Science Quarterly, 9* (December), 301–312.

Inkson, J. H. K., R. L. Payne, and D. S. Pugh
   1967   "Extending the Occupational Environment: the Measurement of Organizations," *Occupational Psychology, 41,* 33–47.

James, John
   1951   "A Preliminary Study of the Size Determinant in Small Group Interaction," *American Sociological Review, 16,* 474–477.

James, John
   1953   "The Distribution of Free-Forming Small Group Size," *American Sociological Review, 18,* 569–570.

Janger, A.
   1960   "Analyzing the Span of Control," *Management Record,* XXII (July–August).

Janowitz, Morris
   1959   "Changing Patterns of Organizational Authority: The Military Establishment," *Administrative Science Quarterly, 3* (March), 473–493.

Janowitz, Morris
   1961   "Hierarchy and Authority in the Military Establishment," in Etzioni, A. (ed.), *Complex Organizations.* New York: Holt, Rinehart & Winston, 198–212.

Janowitz, Morris, Deil Wright, and William Delaney
   1958   *Public Administration and the Public: Perspectives Toward Government in a Metropolitan Community.* Ann Arbor: University of Michigan Institute of Public Administration.

Jaques, Elliott
   1951   *The Changing Culture of a Factory.* London.

Jaques, Elliot
   1959   *The Measurement of Responsibility.* Cambridge: Harvard University Press.

Johnson, Harry M.
   1960   *Sociology.* New York: Harcourt, Brace.

Julian, Joseph
   1965   "On Organization Involvement: Patients' Orientations Toward Hospitals." Paper presented at the meeting of the Midwest Sociological Society, Minneapolis, April.

Julian, Joseph
   1966   "Compliance Patterns and Communication Blocks in Complex Organizations," *American Sociological Review, 31* (June), 382–389.

Jünger, E.
   1932   *Der Arbeiter.* Hanseatische Verlag.

Kahn, Robert L.
   1964   "Field Studies of Power in Organizations," in Kahn, Robert L., and Elise Boulding (eds.), *Power and Conflict in Organizations.* New York: Basic Books, 52–66.

Kahn, Robert, Donald M. Wolfe, Robert P. Quinn, J. Diedrick Snoek, and Robert A. Rosenthal
   1964   *Organizational Stress.* New York: Wiley.

Kaplan, Abraham
1964   *The Conduct of Inquiry.* San Francisco: Chandler.

Kaplan, Morton
1957   *System and Process in International Politics.* New York: Wiley.

Karsh, Bernard, and Robert E. Cole
1968   "Industrialization and the Convergence Hypothesis: Some Aspects of Contemporary Japan," *Journal of Social Issues 24,* 4 (October), 45–64.

Katz, Daniel
1964   "The Motivational Basis of Organizational Behavior," *Behavioral Science, 9* (April).

Katz, Daniel, and Robert Kahn
1951   "Human Organization and Worker Motivation," in *Industrial Productivity* (ed.) L. Reed Tripp. Madison, Wis.: Industrial Relations Research Association.

Katz, Daniel, and Robert L. Kahn
1966   *The Social Psychology of Organizations.* New York: Wiley.

Katz, Daniel, Nathan Maccoby, and Nancy C. Morse
1950   *Productivity, Supervision and Morale in an Office Situation.* Ann Arbor, Mich.: Survey Research Center, Institute for Social Research.

Katz, Elihu, and S. N. Eisenstadt
1960   "Some Sociological Observations on the Response of Israeli Organization to New Immigrants," *ASQ, 5,* 117–133.

Katz, Fred E.
1964   "The School as a Complex Organization," *Harvard Educational Review, 34,* 428–455.

Kaufman, Herbert
1960   *The Forest Ranger.* Baltimore: Johns Hopkins Press.

Kaufman, Herbert, and David Seidman
1970   "The Morphology of Organizations," *Administrative Science Quarterly, 15* (December), 439–452.

Kelley, Harold H., and Thibaut, John W.
1954   "Experimental Studies of Group Problem Solving and Process," in Lindzey, Gardner (ed.), *Handbook of Social Psychology.* Cambridge, Mass.: ——.

Kelman, Herbert C.
1958   "Compliance, Identification, and Internalization: Three Processes of Attitude Change," *Journal of Conflict Resolution, 2* (March).

Kennedy, Van D.
1954   "Grievance Negotiation," in Kornhauser, Arthur, Robert Dubin, and Arthur M. Ross (eds.), *Industrial Conflict.* New York: McGraw-Hill.

Kephart, William M.
1950   "A Quantitative Analysis of Intragroup Relationships," *American Journal of Sociology, 55,* 544–549.

Kerlinger, F.
　1964　　*Foundations of Behavioral Research.* New York: Holt, Rinehart & Winston.

Kerr, C., and A. Siegel
　1954　　"The Inter-Industry Propensity to Strike—An International Comparison," in Kornhauser, A., R. Dubin, and A. Ross (eds.), *Industrial Conflict.* New York: McGraw-Hill, 189–212.

Kerr, Clark
　1963　　*The Uses of the University.* New York: Harper TorchBooks.

Keynes, John Maynard
　1936　　*The General Theory of Employment, Interest, and Money.* New York: Harcourt, Brace.

Klapp, Orrin E.
　1948　　"The Creation of Popular Heroes," *American Journal of Sociology, 54* (September), 135–141.

Klatzky, Sheila R.
　1970a　　"Organizational Inequality: The Case of the Public Employment Agencies," *American Journal of Sociology, 76* (November), 474–491.

Klatzky, Sheila R.
　1970b　　"Relationships of Organizational Size to Complexity and Coordination," *Administrative Science Quarterly, 15* (December), 428–438.

Klein, J.
　1956　　*The Study of Groups.* London: Routledge.

Kluckholn, F., and F. Strodbeck
　1961　　*Variations in Value Orientations.* New York: Row, Peterson.

Knight, F. (trans.), Weber, Max
　1950　　*General Economic History.* Glencoe, Ill.: Free Press.

Kornhauser, A.
　1965　　*Mental Health of the Industrial Worker.* New York: Wiley.

Kornhauser, A., R. Dubin, and A. M. Ross
　1954　　*Industrial Conflict.* New York: McGraw-Hill.

Kornhauser, William
　1959　　*The Politics of Mass Society.* Glencoe, Ill.: Free Press.

Kornhauser, William
　1962　　"Strains and Accommodations in Industrial Research Organizations," *Minerva,* I.

Kornhauser, William, with the assistance of W. O. Hagstrom
　1962　　*Scientists in Industry: Conflict and Accommodation.* Berkeley: University of California Press.

Kovner, Anthony
　1966　　"The Nursing Unit: A Technological Perspective." Unpublished Ph.D. dissertation, University of Pittsburgh.

Krathwohl, David R., Benjamin S. Bloom, and Bertram B. Masia
　1964　　*Taxonomy of Educational Objectives, The Classification of Educational Goals, Handbook H: Affective Domain.* New York: David McKay.

Kuethe, James L., and Bernard Levenson
1964   "Conceptions of Organizational Worth," *American Journal of Sociology, 70* (November), 342–348.

Lambert, Edmund H., Jr.
1949   "Labor and the Chemical Industry." Master's Thesis, University of California, Berkeley (in files of the Institute of Industrial Relations, Berkeley).

Landsberger, Henry A.
1961   "The Horizontal Dimension in Bureaucracy," *Administrative Science Quarterly, 6 (*December), 299–322.

Larson, Henrietta M., and Kenneth Wiggins Porter
1959   *History of Humble Oil and Refining Company.* New York: Harper and Bros.

Lasch, C.
1965   *The New Radicalism in America.* New York: Knopf.

Lasswell, Harold, and Abraham Kaplan
1950   *Power and Society.* New Haven: Yale University Press.

Lave, L. B.
1966   *Technological Change: Its Conception and Measurement.* Englewood Cliffs, N. J.: Prentice-Hall.

Lawrence, Paul R., and Jay W. Lorsch
1967a   "Differentiation and Integration in Complex Organizations," *ASQ, 12* (June), 1–47.

Lawrence, Paul R., and Jay W. Lorsch
1967b   *Organization and Environment.* Boston: Graduate School of Business Administration, Harvard University.

Lazarsfeld, Paul F.
1958   "Evidence and Inference in Social Research," *Daedalus, 87* (Fall).

Lazarsfeld, Paul F., and Herbert Menzel
1961   "On the Relation Between Individual and Collective Properties," in Etzioni, Amitai (ed.), *Complex Organizations: A Sociological Reader.* New York: Holt, Rinehart & Winston.

Lazarsfeld, Paul F., and Wagner Thielens, Jr.
1958   *The Academic Mind.* Glencoe, Ill.: Free Press.

Leach, E. R.
1954   *Political Systems of Highland Burma.* London: Bell.

Leader, G.
1965   "The Determinants and Consequences of Interpersonal Competence in a Bank Setting." Unpublished D.B.A. thesis, Graduate School of Business Administration, Harvard University.

Leavitt, Harold J.
1958   "Some Effects of Certain Communication Patterns on Group Performance," in *Readings in Social Psychology,* Maccoby, Eleanor *et al.* (eds.). New York: Holt, Rinehart & Winston, 546–563.

Lefton, Mark, and William Rosengren
1966   "Organizations and Clients: Lateral and Longitudinal Dimensions," *American Sociological Review, 31* (December), 802–811.

Lerner, Daniel
1959   *The Passing of Traditional Society.* Glencoe, III.: Free Press.

Lester, Richard
1959   "The New Dimension of Industrial Employment," in Gray, Robert
         (ed.), *Frontiers of Industrial Relations.* Los Angeles: California In-
         stitute of Technology.

Levenson, Bernard
1961   "Bureaucratic Succession," in Etzioni, Amitai (ed.), *Complex Or-
         ganizations: A Sociological Reader.* New York: Holt, Rinehart &
         Winston, 262–275.

Levine, Sol, and Paul E. White
1961   "Exchange as a Conceptual Framework for the Study of Inter-
         organizational Relationships," *Administrative Science Quarterly,
         5* (March), 583–601.

Levine, Sol and Paul E. White
1963   "The Community of Health Organizations," in Freeman, Howard E.,
         S. E. Levine, and Leo G. Reeder (eds.), *Handbook of Medical
         Sociology.* Englewood Cliffs, N. J.: Prentice-Hall.

Levine, Sol, Paul E. White, and Benjamin D. Paul
1963   "Community Interorganizational Problems in Providing Medical
         Care and Social Services," *American Journal of Public Health, 53*
         (August).

Levitt, Theodore
1966   "Innovative Imitation," *Harvard Business Review, 44,* 63–70.

Levy, Marion J., Jr.
1952   *The Structure of Society.* Princeton, N. J.: Princeton University
         Press.

Levy, P., and D. S. Pugh
1969   "Scaling and Multivariate Analyses in the Study of Organizational
         Variables," *Sociology, 3,* No. 2, 193–213.

Lewis, Earl L.
1956   "Wage Dispersion in Manufacturing Industries, 1950–1955,"
         Monthly Labor Review, LXXI.

Lieberman, S., and L. Meltzer
1954   *The Attitudes and Activities of Physiologists.* Ann Arbor: Survey
         Research Center, University of Michigan.

Lieberson, Stanley
1971   "An Empirical Study of Military–Industrial Linkages," *American
         Journal of Sociology, 76* (January), 562–584.

Likert, Rensis
1960   "Influence and National Sovereignty," in *Festschrift for Gardner
         Murphy,* Peatman, John G., and Eugene L. Hartley (eds.). New
         York: Harper, 214–227.

Likert, Rensis
1961   *New Patterns of Management.* New York: McGraw-Hill.

Lilienthal, David E.
1936   Transcript of TVA lecture. Knoxville, Tenn., June 12 (mimeo.).

Lilienthal, David E.
  1939   "The TVA: An Experiment in the 'Grass Roots' Administration of
            Federal Functions." Address before the Southern Political Science
            Association, Knoxville, Tennessee, November 10. Knoxville: TVA
            Information Office, n.d.
Lilienthal, David E.
  1940   "The TVA: A Step Toward Decentralization." Address before the
            Graduate Faculty of Political and Social Sciences, New School for
            Social Research, New York City, April 3 (mimeo.).
Lilienthal, David E.
  1942   "The Partnership of Federal Government and Local Communities
            in the Tennessee Valley." Address before gathering of community
            leaders of northern Alabama, sponsored by Decatur Chamber of
            Commerce, Decatur, Ala., July 30 (mimeo.).
Lilienthal, David E.
  1945   *TVA: Democracy on the March.* New York: Pocket Books.
Lilienthal, David E., and Robert H. Marquis
  1941   "The Conduct of Business Enterprises by the Federal Govern-
            ment," *Harvard Law Review, 54* (February).
Lippitt, Ronald
  1958   *The Dynamics of Planned Change.* New York: Harcourt, Brace and
            World.
Lipset, Seymour M.
  1950   *Agrarian Reform.* Berkeley: University of California.
Lipset, Seymour M.
  1960   *Political Man.* Garden City, N. Y.: Doubleday.
Lipset, Seymour M.
  1961   "Trade Unions and Social Structure," *Industrial Relations, 1*
            (October).
Lipset, Seymour M.
  1963   "Democracy and the Social System," in *The First New Nation.* New
            York: Basic Books.
Lipset, Seymour, Martin Trow, and James Coleman
  1956   *Union Democracy.* Glencoe, Ill.: Free Press.
Litterer, J.
  1965   *The Analysis of Organizations.* New York: Wiley.
Litwak, Eugene
  1961   "Models of Organization Which Permit Conflict," *American Jour-
            nal of Sociology, 67* (September), 177–185.
Litwak, Eugene
  1968   "Technological Innovation and Theoretical Functions of Primary
            Groups and Bureaucratic Structures," *American Journal of So-
            ciology, 73* (January), 468–481.
Litwak, Eugene, and Lydia F. Hylton
  1962   "Interorganizational Analysis: A Hypothesis on Coordinating
            Agencies," *Administrative Science Quarterly, 6* (March), 395–420.

Lodahl, T. M.
1964   "Patterns of Job Attitudes in Two Assembly Technologies," *Administrative Science Quarterly, 8* (March), 482–519.

Lord, F. M.
1963   "Biserial Estimation of Correlation," *Psychometrica, 28,* 81–85.

Lorsch, Jay W.
1965   *Product Innovation and Organization.* New York: Macmillan.

Loubser, J., and M. Fullan
1970   *Industrial Conversion and Workers' Attitudes to Change in Different Industries.* Task Force on Labor Relations, Study No. 12, Ottawa: Queen's Printer.

Maier, Norman R. F.
1952   *Principles of Human Relations.* New York: Wiley.

Maniha, John, and Charles Perrow
1965   "The Reluctant Organization and the Aggressive Environment," *Administrative Science Quarterly, 10* (September), 238–257.

Mann, F. C., and L. R. Hoffman
1960   *Automation and the Worker.* New York: Holt, Rinehart & Winston.

Mann, Floyd C., and Lawrence Williams
1960   "Observations on the Dynamics of a Change to Electronic Data-Processing Equipment," *Administrative Science Quarterly,* V (September), 217–257.

March, James, and Herbert Simon
1958   *Organizations.* New York: Wiley.

Marcson, Simon
1961   "Organization and Authority in Industrial Research," *Social Forces,* XL.

Marcson, Simon
1960   *The Scientist in American Industry.* Princeton, N. J.: Princeton University Industrial Relations Section Report No. 99.

Marvick, D.
1954   *Career Perspectives in a Bureaucratic Setting.* Ann Arbor: Institute of Public Administration, University of Michigan.

Matthews, A. T. J.
1954   "Emergent Turkish Administrators." Ankara: Faculty of Political Science.

Mayntz, Renate
1964   "The Study of Organizations: a Trend Report and Bibliography," *Current Sociology, 13.*

Mayo, Elton, and George F. F. Lombard
1944   *Team-work and Labor Turnover in the Aircraft Industry of Southern California.* Boston: Division of Research, Graduate School of Business Administration, Harvard University.

McArthur, C.
1955   "Cultural Values as Determinants of Imaginal Productions." Unpublished Ph.D. thesis, Harvard University; abstract in *Journal of Abnormal and Social Psychology, 50* (March), 247–254.

McCleery, Richard H.
1957   *Policy Change in Prison Management.* East Lansing, Mich.: Social Science Research Bureau, Michigan State University.

McCleery, Richard H.
1968   "Correctional Administration and Political Change," in Hazelrigg, Lawrence (ed.), *Prison Within Society.* Garden City, N. Y.: Doubleday, 113–149.

McCorkle, Lloyd, and Richard Korn
1954   "Resocialization Within Walls," *The Annals, 293* (May).

McNulty, James E.
1962   "Organizational Change in Growing Enterprises," *Administrative Science Quarterly, 7* (June), 1–21.

Mead, Margaret
1951   *Soviet Attitudes Toward Authority.* New York: McGraw-Hill.

Mechanic, David
1962   "Sources of Power of Lower Participants in Complex Organizations," *Administrative Science Quarterly, 7* (December), 349–364.

Meier, Dorothy L., and Wendell Bell
1959   "Anomia and Differential Access to the Achievement of Life Goals," *American Sociological Review, 24* (April), 189–202.

Meissner, M.
1969   *Technology and the Worker.* San Francisco: Chandler.

Mellinger, G.
1956   Manuscript for *Interpersonal Factors in Research, Part II* (in process; Ann Arbor: Institute for Social Research, University of Michigan.)

Melman, Seymour
1951   "The Rise of Administrative Overhead in the Manufacturing Industries of the United States, 1899–1947," *Oxford Economic Papers, 3.*

Meredith, G. P.
1949   "A Revision of Spearman's Neogenetic Principles," *Proc. Aristotelian Society, 49* (N. S.).

Meredith, G. P.
1958   "The Surprise Function and the Epistemic Theory of Expectations," in Bowman (ed.), *Expectations, Uncertainty and Business Behavior.* New York: Social Science Research Council.

Merton, R. K.
1945   "The Role of the Intellectual in Public Bureaucracy," *Social Forces,* XXIII (May).

Merton, R. K.
1946   *Mass Persuasion: The Social Psychology of a War Bond Drive.* New York: Harper & Row.

Merton, R. K.
1957a   *Social Theory and Social Structure.* Glencoe, Ill.: Free Press.

Merton, Robert
  1957b   "The Role-Set: Problems in Sociological Theory," *British Journal of Sociology, 8,* No. 2.
Merton, R. K.
  1959   "Social Conformity, Deviation, and Opportunity-Structures: A Comment on the Contributions of Dubin and Cloward," *American Sociological Review, 24* (April), 177–189.
Merton, R. K., *et al.*
  1957   *The Student Physician.* eds. Reader, George, and Patricia L. Kendall. Cambridge: Harvard University Press.
Merton, Robert K., L. Broom, and L. S. Cottrell (eds).
  1959   *Sociology Today.* New York: Basic Books.
Merton, Robert K., and Alice S. Kitt
  1950   "Contributions to the Theory of Reference Group Behavior," in Merton and Lazarsfeld (eds.), *Continuities in Social Research.* Glencoe, Ill.: Free Press.
Merton, R. K., and Paul Lazarsfeld (eds.).
  1950   *Continuities in Social Research.* Glencoe, Ill.: Free Press.
Messinger, Sheldon L.
  1955   "Organizational Transformation: A Case Study of a Declining Social Movement," *American Sociological Review, 20* (February), 3–10.
Meyer, Marshall W.
  1968a   "Two Authority Structures of Bureaucratic Organization," *Administrative Science Quarterly, 13* (September), 211–228.
Meyer, Marshall W.
  1968b   "Automation and Bureaucratic Structure," *American Journal of Sociology, 74* (November), 256–264.
Meyer, Marshall W.
  1968c   "Expertness and the Span of Control," *American Sociological Review, 33* (December), 944–950.
Meyers, H. B.
  1967   "The Sweet, Secret World of Forrest Mars." *Fortune* (May).
Michels, Robert
  1949   *Political Parties.* Glencoe, Ill.: Free Press.
Miles, Matthew B., ed.
  1964   *Innovation in Education.* New York: Columbia University Press.
Mill, John Stuart
  1926   *Principles of Political Economy.* London and New York: Longmans.
Miller, D. C., and W. H. Form
  1951   *Industrial Sociology.* New York: Harper.
Miller, E.
  1959   "Time, Technology, and Territory," *Human Relations, 7.*
Miller, George A.
  1967   "Professionals in Bureaucracy: Alienation Among Industrial Scientists and Engineers." *American Sociological Review, 32* (October), 755–768.

Miller, James G.
1955   "Toward a General Theory for the Behavioral Sciences," *The American Scientist, 10.*

Mills, C. Wright
1951   *White Collar: The American Middle Classes.* New York: Columbia University Press.

Mills, C. Wright
1956   *The Power Elite.* London: Oxford University Press.

Minnis, Mhyra S.
1953   "Cleavage in Women's Organizations: A Reflection of the Social Structure of a City," *American Sociological Review, 18,* 47–53.

Moeller, Gerald H., and W. W. Charters
1966   "Relation of Bureaucratization to Sense of Power Among Teachers," *Administrative Science Quarterly, 10* (December), 444–465.

Moment, D., and A. Zaleznik
1963   *Role Development and Interpersonal Competence.* Boston: Graduate School of Business Administration, Harvard University.

Montagna, Paul D.
1968   "Professionalization and Bureaucratization in Large Professional Organizations," *American Journal of Sociology, 74* (September), 138–145.

Mooney, J. D., and A. C. Reiley
1939   *The Principles of Organization.* New York: Harper.

Moore, W. G.
1947   *Industrial Relations and the Social Order.* New York: Macmillan.

Morgan, H. A.
1941   "Some Objectives and End Results of TVA." Address before annual meeting of the American Society of Agricultural Engineers, Knoxville, Tenn., June 23 (mimeo.).

Morgan, H. A.
1942   "The Common Mooring," in *Applications of the Common Mooring,* compiled and edited by Howard P. Emerson, Chairman, sub-committee on Presentation of the Common Mooring, Advisory Panel on Regional Materials of Instruction for the Tennessee Valley, Knoxville, Tenn., June (hectographed).

Morris, Robert, and Ollie A. Randall
1965   "Planning and Organization of Community Services for the Elderly," *Social Work, 10* (January), 96–103.

Morse, Nancy C.
1953   *Satisfactions in the White-Collar Job.* Ann Arbor, Mich.: Survey Research Center, University of Michigan.

Morse, Nancy C., and Everett Reimer
1956   "The Experimental Change of a Major Organizational Variable," *Journal of Abnormal and Social Psychology, 52,* 120–129.

Myrdal, Gunnar
1960   *Beyond the Welfare State.* New Haven: Yale.

Nadel, S. F.
1957   *The Theory of Social Structure.* Glencoe, Ill.: Free Press.

Nath, R.
1968   "A Methodological Review of Cross-Cultural Management Research," *International Social Science Journal, 20,* 35–62.

National Industrial Conference Board
1960   *Economic Almanac,* 1960. New York: National Industrial Conference Board.

Neal, Arthur G., and Salomon Rettig
1963   "Dimensions of Alienation Among Manual and Non-Manual Workers," *American Sociological Review, 28* (August), 599–608.

Neal, Ernest E.
1957   "Community Development in the Philippines," *Community Development Review,* No. 6 (September).

Neal, Sister Marie Augusta
1965   *Values and Interests in Social Change.* Englewood Cliffs, N. J.: Prentice-Hall.

Neumann, Franz, and Julian Franklin
n.d.   "The Democratic Approach to Bureaucracy," *Readings in Culture, Personality and Society.* New York: Columbia, University.

Newell, A., and H. A. Simon
1962   "The Processes of Creative Thinking," in Gruber, H. E., G. Terrell, and M. Wertheimer (eds.), *Contemporary Approaches to Creative Thinking.* New York: Atherton.

Niebuhr, R.
1953   "Coercion, Self-Interest, and Love," in Boulding, K. E., *The Organizational Revolution.* New York: Harper & Row.

Nimkoff, M., and R. Middleton
1960   "Is the Joint Family an Obstacle to Industrialization?" *International Journal of Comparative Society, 1,* 109–118.

Noda, Kazuo
1959   "Keieisha no Soshiki," in Takemiya, Susumu (ed.), *Manejimento.* Tokyo: Chikuma Shobō.

Norman, W. H.
1958   *Administrative Action, The Techniques of Organization and Management.* New York: Pitman.

Ogburn, William F., and Meyer F. Nimkoff
1964   *Sociology* (4th ed.). Boston: Houghton Mifflin.

Ohlin, Lloyd E.
1958   "Conformity in American Society Today," *Social Work, 3.*

Palumbo, Dennis J.
1969   "Power and Role Specificity in Organizational Theory." *Public Administration Review, 29* (May–June), 237–248.

Parsons, Talcott
1937   *The Structure of Social Action.* New York: McGraw-Hill.

Parsons, Talcott
  1947   Introduction to Weber, Max, *The Theory of Social and Economic Organization.* New York: Oxford University Press.

Parsons, Talcott
  1951   *The Social System.* Glencoe, Ill.: Free Press.

Parsons, Talcott
  1954   *Essays in Sociological Theory.* Glencoe, Ill.: Fress Press.

Parsons, Talcott
  1956   "Suggestions for a Sociological Approach to the Theory of Organizations, I and II," *Administrative Science Quarterly, 1* (June and September), 63–85, 225–239.

Parsons, Talcott
  1957   "The Distribution of Power in American Society," *World Politics, 10.*

Parsons, Talcott
  1960   *Structure and Process in Modern Society.* Glencoe, Ill.: Free Press.

Parsons, Talcott
  1966   *Societies: Evolutionary and Comparative Perspectives.* Englewood Cliffs, N. J.: Prentice-Hall.

Parsons, Talcott, Robert Bales, and Edward Shils
  1958   *The Working Papers in the Theory of Action.* Glencoe, Ill.: Free Press.

Parsons, T., E. A. Shils, *et al.*
  1952   *Toward a General Theory of Action.* Cambridge, Mass.: Harvard University Press.

Peabody, Robert L.
  1962   "Perceptions of Organizational Authority: A Comparative Analysis," *Administrative Science Quarterly, 6* (March), 463–482.

Peabody, Robert L.
  1964   *Organizational Theory: Superior-Subordinate Relationships in Three Public Service Organizations.* New York: Atherton.

Pearlin, Leonard I.
  1962   "Alienation from Work: A Study of Nursing Personnel," *American Sociological Review, 27* (June), 314–326.

Pelz, Donald C.
  1956   "Some Social Factors Related to Performance in a Research Organization," *Administrative Science Quarterly, 1* (December), 310–325.

Pelz, Donald C., and Frank M. Andrews
  1966a   *Scientists in Organization.* New York: Wiley.

Pelz, Donald C., and Frank M. Andrews
  1966b   "Autonomy, Coordination, and Stimulation in Relation to Scientific Achievement," *Behavioral Science, 11,* 89–97.

Perrow, Charles
  1960   "Authority, Goals and Prestige in a General Hospital," unpublished Ph.D. dissertation, University of California, Berkeley.

Perrow, Charles
1961a   "The Analysis of Goals in Complex Organizations," *American Sociological Review, 26* (April), 854–866.

Perrow, Charles
1961b   "Organizational Prestige, Some Functions and Dysfunctions," *American Journal of Sociology, 66* (January), 335–341.

Perrow, Charles
1965   "Hospital: Technology, Structure and Goals," in March, James (ed.), *Handbook of Organizations.* Chicago: Rand-McNally, 910–971.

Perrow, Charles
1966   "Reality Adjustment: A Young Institution Settles for Humane Care," *Social Problems, 14* (Summer), 69–79.

Perrow, Charles
1967   "A Framework for the Comparative Analysis of Organizations," *American Sociological Review, 32* (April), 194–208.

Perrow, Charles
1970   *Organizational Analysis: A Sociological View.* Belmont, Calif.: Wadsworth.

Pondy, Louis R.
1969   "Effects of Size, Complexity, and Ownership on Administrative Intensity," *Administrative Science Quarterly, 14* (March), 47–60.

Popper, Karl R.
1959   *The Logic of Scientific Discovery.* New York: Basic Books.

Porter, L. W., and E. E. Lawler, III
1965   "Properties of Organization Structure in Relation to Job Attitudes and Job Behavior," *Psychological Bulletin, 64,* 25–51.

Powelson, Harvey, and Reinhard Bendix
1951   "Psychiatry in Prison," *Psychiatry, 14* (February).

Pragen, Otto
1955   "Automation and Technological Change," *Hearings, Subcommittee on Economic Stabilization,* 84th Congress, 1st Session. Washington: U.S. Government Printing Office.

Presthus, Robert V.
1949   "British Administration: The National Coal Board," *Public Administration Review, 9,* 200–210.

Presthus, Robert V.
1950   "Financial Aspects of Britain's National Coal Board," *Journal of Politics, 12,* 348–370.

Presthus, Robert V.
1958   "Towards a Theory of Organizational Behavior," *Administrative Science Quarterly, 3* (June), 48–72.

Presthus, Robert V.
1959   "The Social Bases of Bureaucratic Organization," *Social Forces, 19,* 103–109.

Presthus, Robert V.
1961a   "Weberian v. Welfare Bureaucracy in Traditional Society," *Administrative Science Quarterly, 6* (June), 1–24.

Presthus, Robert V.
    1961b   "The Sociology of Economic Development," *International Journal of Comparative Sociology, 2.*

Price, James
    1967   *Organizational Effectiveness.* Homewood, Ill.: Irwin.

Pringle, J. W. S.
    1956   "On the Parallel Between Learning and Evolution," *General Systems, 1.*

Pugh, D. S., D. J. Hickson, C. R. Hinings, K. M. Macdonald, C. Turner, and T. Lupton
    1963   "A Conceptual Scheme for Organizational Analysis," *Administrative Science Quarterly, 8* (December), 289–315.

Pugh, D. S., D. J. Hickson, C. R. Hinings, and C. Turner
    1968   "Dimensions of Organizational Structure," *Administrative Science Quarterly, 13* (June), 65–105.

Pugh, D. S., D. J. Hickson, C. R. Hinings, and C. Turner
    1969a   "The Context of Organizational Structures," *Administrative Science Quarterly, 14* (March), 91–114.

Pugh, D. S., D. J. Hickson, and C. R. Hinings
    1969b   "An Empirical Taxonomy of Structures of Work Organizations," *Administrative Science Quarterly, 14* (March), 115–126.

Raphael, Edna
    1967   "The Anderson-Warkov Hypotheses in Local Unions: a Comparative Study," *American Sociological Review, 32* (October), 768–776.

Reader, George G., and Mary E. W. Gross
    1959   "Medical Sociology with Particular Reference to the Study of Hospitals," *Transactions of the Fourth World Congress of Sociology, 2.*

Reiss, Albert J.
    1961   *Occupations and Social Status.* New York: Free Press of Glencoe.

Reissman, L.
    1949   "A Study of Role Conceptions in Bureaucracy," *Social Forces, 27* (March), 305–310.

Rice, A. K.
    1958   *Productivity and Social Organization.* London: Tavistock.

Rice, A.
    1963   *The Enterprise and Its Environment.* London: Tavistock.

Rice, S. A. (ed.)
    1931   *Methods in Social Science.* Chicago: The University of Chicago Press.

Richardson, Stephen
    1956   "Organizational Contrasts on British and American Ships," *Administrative Science Quarterly, 1* (September), 189–207.

Ridgeway, V. F.
    1959   "Administration of Manufacturer–Dealer Systems," *Administrative Science Quarterly, 1* (June), 464–483.

Rieser, C.
    1962   "The Chief Shows Them at Indian Head," *Fortune* (May).

Roethlisberger, F. V.
  1941   *Management and Morale.* Cambridge, Mass.: Harvard University Press.

Roethlisberger, F. J., and W. J. Dickinson
  1939   *Management and the Worker.*

Rogers, L. E.
  1959   *The Measurement of Status Relations in a Hospital.* Columbus, Ohio: The Ohio State University Engineering Experiment Station, Bulletin No. 175, May.

Ronken, Harriet, and Paul Lawrence
  1952   *Administering Changes: A Case Study of Human Relations in a Factory.* Cambridge, Mass.: Harvard Graduate School of Business.

Rose, Arnold
  1954   "Voluntary Associations in France," in *Theory and Method in the Social Sciences.* Minneapolis, Minn.: University of Minnesota Press.

Rosen, Bernard C.
  1956   "The Achievement Syndrome: A Psychocultural Dimension of Social Stratification," *American Sociological Review, 21,* 203–211.

Rosengren, William R.
  1964   "Communication, Organization, and Conduct in the 'Therapeutic Milieu,' " *Administrative Science Quarterly, 9* (June), 70–90.

Ross, Donald (ed.)
  1958   *Administration for Adaptability.* New York: Institute of Administrative Research, Teachers College, Columbia University.

Ross, I.
  1964   "The Private Turbulence of Eastern Air Lines," *Fortune* (July).

Rossi, Peter
  1961   "The Organizational Structure of an American Community," in Etzioni, A. (ed)., *Complex Organizations.* New York: Holt, Rinehart & Winston.

Roth, Julius
  1963   "Information and Control in Tuberculosis Hospitals," in Freidson, Eliot (ed.), *The Hospital in Modern Society.* Glencoe, Ill.: Free Press.

Rubington, Earl
  1965   "Organizational Strain and Key Roles," *Administrative Science Quarterly, 9* (March), 350–369.

Rushing, William A.
  1966   "Organizational Rules and Surveillance: Propositions in Comparative Organizational Analysis," *Administrative Science Quarterly, 10* (December), 423–443.

Rushing, William A.
  1967   "The Effects of Industry Size and Division of Labor on Administration," *Administrative Science Quarterly, 12* (September), 273–295.

Rushing, William A.
  1968   "Hardness of Material as Related to Division of Labor in Manufacturing Industries," *Administrative Science Quarterly, 13* (September), 229–245.

Samuel, Yitzhak, and Bilha F. Mannheim
1970   "A Multidimensional Approach Toward a Typology of Bureaucracy," *Administrative Science Quarterly, 15* (June), 216–228.

Sayles, L. R.
1958   *Behavior of Industrial Work Groups.* New York: Wiley.

Scheff, Thomas J.
1961   "Control Over Policy by Attendants in a Mental Hospital," *Journal of Health and Human Behavior, 2.*

Scheuner, Ulrich
1970   "Das Grundgesetz in der Entwicklung zweier Jahrzehnte," *Archiv des oeffentlichen Rechts,* No. 3, 353–408.

Schien, E. H.
1956   "The Chinese Indoctrination Program for Prisoners of War," *Psychiatry, 19.*

Schnore, Leo F., and Robert R. Alford
1963   "Forms of Government and Socioeconomic Characteristics of Suburbs," *Administrative Science Quarterly, 8* (June), 1–17.

Scott, W. Richard
1964   "Theory of Organizations," in Faris, Robert E. L. (ed.), *Handbook of Modern Sociology.* Chicago: Rand-McNally.

Scott, W. H., J. A. Banks, A. H. Halsey and T. Lupton
1956   *Technical Change and Industrial Relations.* Liverpool: Liverpool University Press.

Seashore, Stanley E.
1965   "Criteria of Organizational Effectiveness," *Michigan Business Review,* XVII (July).

Seashore, Stanley E., and Ephraim Yuchtman
1967   "Factorial Analysis of Organizational Performance," *Administrative Science Quarterly, 12* (December), 377–395.

Seeman, Melvin
1959   "On the Meaning of Alienation," *American Sociological Review, 24* (December), 783–791.

Seeman, Melvin
1963   "Alienation and Social Learning in a Reformatory," *American Journal of Sociology, 69* (November), 270–284.

Seeman, M., J. W. Evans, and L. E. Rogers
1960   "The Measurement of Stratification in Formal Organizations," *Human Organization, 19* (Summer).

Seeman, Melvin, and John W. Evans
1961   "Stratification and Hospital Care: I. The Performance of the Medical Interne," *American Sociological Review, 26* (February), 67–80.

Seeman, Melvin, and J. W. Evans
1962   "Alienation and Learning in a Hospital Setting," *American Sociological Review, 27* (December), 772–782.

Seiler, J.
1963a   "Toward a Theory of Organization Congruent with Primary Group Concepts," *Behavioral Science, 8* (July), 190–198.

Seiler, J.
1963b   "Diagnosing Interdepartmental Conflict," *Harvard Business Review, 4* (September–October), 121–132.

Selvin, Hanan C.
1960   *The Effects of Leadership.* Glencoe, Ill.: Free Press.

Selznick, Philip
1948   "Foundations of the Theory of Organizations," *American Sociological Review, 13,* 25–35.

Selznick, Philip
1949   *TVA and the Grass Roots.* Berkeley: University of California Press.

Selznick, Philip
1952   *The Organizational Weapon.* New York: McGraw-Hill.

Selznick, Philip
1957   *Leadership in Administration.* Evanston, Ill.: Row, Peterson.

Selznick, Philip
1961   "Critical Decisions in Organizational Development," in Etzioni (ed.), *Complex Organizations: A Sociological Reader.* New York: Holt, Rinehart & Winston.

Shackle, G. L. S.
         "Expectation and Liquidity," in Bowman (ed.), *Expectations, Uncertainty and Business Behavior.* New York: Social Science Research Council.

Shackle, G. L. S.
1949   *Expectation in Economics.* Cambridge, England: Cambridge University Press.

Shackle, G. L. S.
1954   Final Comment in Carter, C. F., G. P. Meredith, and G. L. S. Shackle (eds.), *Uncertainty and Business Decisions.* Liverpool: Liverpool University Press.

Shackle, G. L. S.
1955   *Uncertainty in Economics.* Cambridge, England: Cambridge University Press.

Sheehan, R.
1961   "Daimler-Benz: Quality über alles," *Fortune* (August).

Shepard, Herbert A.
1956   "Nine Dilemmas in Industrial Research," *Administrative Science Quarterly, 1* (December), 295–309.

Shepard, Herbert A.
1958   "The Dual Hierarchy in Research," *Research Management,* I.

Shepard, H. A.
         "Superiors and Subordinates in Research." Paper 12 of the *Symposium on the Direction of Research Establishments.* H. M. S. O.: Department of Scientific and Industrial Research.

Shepard, Jon
1971   *Automation and Alienation.* Cambridge, Mass.: The MIT Press.

Sherif, M.
1958   "Superordinate Goals in the Reduction of Intergroup Conflict," *American Journal of Sociology, 3,* 356–394.

Shih, Kuo-Heng
   1944   *China Enters the Machine Age.* Cambridge, Mass.: Harvard University Press.

Shils, Edward A., and Morris Janowitz
   1948   "Cohesion and Disintegration in the Wehrmacht in World War II," *Public Opinion Quarterly, 12.*

Siekman, P.
   1955   "Henry Ford and His Electronic Can of Worms," *Fortune* (February).

Sills, David L.
   1957   *The Volunteers: Means and Ends in a National Organization.* Glencoe, Ill.: Free Press.

Simmel, G.
   1896   "Superiority and Subordination as Subject-Matter of Sociology," *American Journal of Sociology, 2,* 167–189, 392–415.

Simmel, Georg
   1950   *Sociology,* trans. Kurt Wolff. Glencoe, Ill.: Free Press.

Simon, H. A.
   1953   "Birth of an Organization: the Economic Cooperation Administration," *Public Administration Review, 13.*

Simon, Herbert A.
   1957   *Models of Man.* New York: Wiley.

Simon, H. A.
   1957   *Administrative Behaviour.* New York: Macmillan.

Simon, Herbert A.
   1958   "The Role of Expectations," in Carter, C. F., G. P. Meredith, and G. L. S. Shackle (eds.), *Expectations, Uncertainty and Business Behavior.* New York: Social Science Research Council.

Simon, Herbert A.
   1960   *The New Science of Management Decisions.* New York: Harper.

Simon, Herbert A.
   1962   "The Decision Maker as an Innovator," in Mailick, Sidney, and Edward H. Van Ness (eds.), *Concepts and Issues in Administrative Behavior.* Englewood Cliffs, N. J.: Prentice-Hall.

Simon, Herbert A.
   1964   "On the Concept of Organizational Goal," *Administrative Science Quarterly, 9* (June), 1–22.

Simon, Herbert A.
   1965   *Administrative Behavior: A Study of Decision-Making Processes in Administrative Organization* (2nd ed.). New York: Free Press.

Simon, H. A., G. Kozmetsky, and G. Tyndall
   1954   *Centralization vs. Decentralization in Organizing the Controller's Department.* New York: The Controllership Foundation.

Simpson, Richard L., and William H. Gulley
   1962   "Goals, Environmental Pressures, and Organizational Characteristics," *American Sociological Review, 27* (June), 344–351.

Sloan, Alfred P., Jr.
   1963   "My Years with General Motors—Part I," *Fortune, 68* (September).

Smith, Clagett G., and Arnold S. Tannenbaum
  1963   "Organizational Control Structure: A Comparative Analysis," *Human Relations, 16,* 299–316.

Smith, Clagett, and O. Ari
  1964   "Organizational Structure and Member Consensus," *American Journal of Sociology, 69* (May), 623–638.

Smith, Clagett
  1965   "A Comparative Analysis of Some Conditions and Consequences of Intra-Organizational Conflict," *Administrative Science Quarterly, 10* (March), 504–529.

Smith, Clagett G.
  1966   "A Comparative Analysis of Some Conditions and Consequences of Intra-Organizational Conflict," *Administrative Science Quarterly, 10* (March), 504–529.

Smith, Clagett G.
  1970   "Consultation and Decision Processes in a Research and Development Laboratory," *Administrative Science Quarterly, 15* (June), 203–215.

Smith, Peter B., David Moscow, Mel Berger, and Cary Cooper
  1969   "Relationships Between Managers and Their Work Associates," *Administrative Science Quarterly, 14* (September), 338–345.

Smith, Richard
  1962   "How a Great Corporation Got Out of Control," *Fortune, 65* (January).

Soemardjan, Selo
  1957   "Bureaucratic Organization in a Time of Revolution," *Administrative Science Quarterly, 2* (September), 182–199.

Srole, Leo
  1956   "Social Integration and Certain Corollaries: An Exploratory Study," *American Sociological Review, 21* (December), 709–716.

Stanton, A. H., and M. S. Schwartz
  1954   *The Mental Hospital.* New York: Basic Books.

Starbuck, William H.
  1965   "Organizational Growth and Development," in March, James G. (ed.), *Handbook of Organizations.* Chicago: Rand-McNally, 451–533.

Stephan, Frederick, and Elliot G. Mishler
  1952   "The Distribution of Participation in Small Groups: An Exponential Approximation," *American Sociological Review, 17,* 598–608.

Stewart, R., P. Wingate, and R. Smith
  1963   *Mergers: The Impact on Managers.* London: Acton Society Trust.

Stinchcombe, Arthur L.
  1959   "Bureaucratic and Craft Administration of Production: A Comparative Study," *Administrative Science Quarterly, 4* (September), 168–187.

Stinchcombe, Arthur
1965 "Social Structure and Organizations," in March, James (ed.), *Handbook of Organizations.* Chicago: Rand-McNally, 142–193.

Stouffer, Samuel A., Edward A. Suchman, Leland C. De Vinney, Shirley A. Star, and Robin M. Williams, Jr.
1949 *The American Soldier: Adjustment During Army Life* ("Studies in Social Psychology During World War II." Princeton, N. J.: Princeton University Press).

Strauss, Anselm, Leonard Schatzman, Danuta Ehrlich, Rue Bucher, and Melvin Sabshin
1963 "The Hospital and Its Negotiated Order," in Freidson, Eliot (ed.), *The Hospital in Modern Society.* Glencoe, Ill.: Free Press.

Strauss, George
1963 "Professionalism and Occupational Associations," *Industrial Relations, II.*

Street, David, Robert Vinter, and Charles Perrow
1966 *Organization for Treatment, A Comparative Study of Institutions for Delinquents.* New York: Free Press.

Strodtbeck, Fred L.
1958 "Family Interaction, Values and Achievement," in McClelland, David C. *et al., Talent and Society.* New York: Van Nostrand.

Sudnow, David
1965 "Normal Crimes: Sociological Features of the Penal Code in a Public Defender Office," *Social Problems, 12* (Winter).

Sykes, G. M.
1958 *The Society of Captives.* Princeton, N. J.: Princeton University Press.

Sykes, Gresham M.
1961 "The Corruption of Authority and Rehabilitation," in Etzioni, A. (ed.), *Complex Organizations.* New York.

Tannenbaum, Arnold S.
1956 "The Concept of Organizational Control," *Journal of Social Issues, 12.*

Tannenbaum, Arnold S.
1956 "Control Structure and Union Functions," *American Journal of Sociology, 61,* 536–545.

Tannenbaum, Arnold S.
1961 "Control, and Effectiveness in a Voluntary Organization," *American Journal of Sociology, 67,* 33–46.

Tannenbaum, Arnold S.
1962 "Control, in Organizations: Individual Adjustment and Organizational Performance," *Administrative Science Quarterly, 7* (September), 236–257.

Tannenbaum, Arnold S.
1968 *Control in Organizations.* New York: McGraw-Hill.

Tannenbaum, Arnold S., and Basil Georgopoulos
1957 "The Distribution of Control in Formal Organizations," *Social Forces, 36,* 44–50.

Tannenbaum, Arnold S., and Robert L. Kahn
1957 "Organizational Control Structure: A General Descriptive Technique as Applied to Four Local Unions," *Human Relations, 10,* 127–140.

Taylor, Donald W.
1965 "Decision Making and Problem Solving," in March, James G. (ed.), *Handbook of Organizations.* Chicago: Rand-McNally, 48–82.

Terreberry, Shirley
1967 "The Evolution of Environments." Mimeographed course paper.

Terreberry, Shirley
1968 "The Evolution of Organizational Environments," *Administrative Science Quarterly, 12* (March), 590–613.

Terrien, Frederick W., and Donald L. Mills
1955 "The Effect of Changing Size upon the Internal Structure of Organizations," *American Sociological Review, 20,* 11–13.

Thibaut, John, and Harold H. Kelley
1959 *The Social Psychology of Groups.* New York.

Thomas, E. J.
1959 "Role Conceptions and Organizational Size," *American Sociological Review, 24,* 30–37.

Thompson, James D.
1960 "Organizational Management of Conflict," *Administrative Science Quarterly, 4* (March), 389–409.

Thompson, James D.
1962 "Organizations and Output Transactions," *American Journal of Sociology, 68* (November), 309–324.

Thompson, James D. (ed.)
1966 *Approaches to Organizational Design.* Pittsburgh: University of Pittsburgh.

Thompson, James D.
1967 *Organizations in Action.* New York: McGraw-Hill.

Thompson, James D., and Frederick L. Bates
1957 "Technology, Organization, and Administration," *Administrative Science Quarterly, 2* (December), 325–343.

Thompson, James D., and William J. McEwen
1958 "Organizational Goals and Environment: Goal-Setting as an Interaction Process," *American Sociological Review, 23* (February), 23–31.

Thompson, James D., and Arthur Tuden
1959 "Strategies and Processes of Organizational Decision," in *Comparative Studies in Administration,* ed. Pittsburgh University Administration Science Center. Pittsburgh: University of Pittsburgh Press.

Thompson, Victor A.
1961a *Modern Organization.* New York: Alfred A. Knopf.

Thompson, Victor
1961b "Hierarchy, Specialization and Organizational Conflict," *Administrative Science Quarterly, 5* (March), 485–521.

Thompson, Victor
1965 "Bureaucracy and Innovation," *Administrative Science Quarterly, 10* (June), 1–20.

Thompson, Victor
1969 *Bureaucracy and Innovation.* University, Ala.: University of Alabama Press.

Thornton, Rusell
1970 "Organizational Involvement and Commitment to Organization and Profession," *Administrative Science Quarterly, 15* (December), 417–427.

Toffler, Alvin
1970 *Future Shock.* New York: Random House.

Tolman, Edward C., and Egon Brunswick
1935 "The Organism and the Causal Texture of the Environment," *Psychological Review, 42,* 43–72.

Toulmin, S.
1952 *The Uses of Argument.* Cambridge, England: Cambridge University Press.

Touraine, Alain
1955 *L'évolution du travail ouvrier aux usines Renault.* Paris: Centre National de la Recherche Scientifique.

Touraine, A.
1962 "An Historical Theory in the Evolution of Industrial Skills," in Walker, C. (ed.), *Modern Technology and Civilization.* New York: McGraw-Hill, 425–437.

Touraine, Alain, Claude Durand, Daniel Pecaut, and Alfred Willener
1965 *Worker Attitudes to Technical Change.* Paris: Organization for Economic Cooperation and Development.

Trist, Eric L., and E. K. Bamforth
1951 "Some Social and Psychological Consequences of the Long-Wall Method of Coal-Getting," *Human Relations, 4,* 3–38.

Trist, E. L., G. W. Higgin, H. Murray, and A. B. Pollock
1963 *Organizational Choice.* London: Tavistock.

Tsouderos, John E.
1953 "Formalization Process of Voluntary Associations." Ph.D. thesis, University of Minnesota.

Tsouderos, John E.
1955 "Organizational Change in Terms of a Series of Selected Variables," *American Sociological Review, 20* (April), 206–210.

Tucker, W. T.
1964 *The Social Context of Economic Behavior.* New York: Holt, Rinehart & Winston.

Turner, Arthur N., and Paul R. Lawrence
 1965   *Industrial Jobs and the Worker.* Cambridge, Mass.: Harvard University Press.

Turner, Ralph
 1961   "Modes of Social Ascent Through Education: Sponsored and Contest Mobility," in Halsey, A. H., Jean Floud, and C. A. Anderson, *Education, Economy and Society.* New York: Free Press.

Udell, Jon G.
 1967   "An Empirical Test of Hypotheses Relating to Span of Control," *Administrative Science Quarterly, 12* (December), 420–439.

Udy, Stanley H., Jr.
 1959a   " 'Bureaucracy' and 'Rationality' in Weber's Organization Theory," *American Sociological Review, 24,* 791–795.

Udy, Stanley
 1959b   *Organization of Work.* New Haven: Human Relations Area Files Press.

Udy, S. H., Jr.
 1961   "Technical and Institutional Factors in Production Organization," *American Journal of Sociology, 67,* 247–260.

Udy, S. H.
 1965   "The Comparative Analysis of Organization," in March, J. G. (ed.), *Handbook of Organizations.* Chicago: Rand-McNally, 678–709.

Union Research and Education Projects, University of Chicago
 1956   "Report of a Study on the Organizing Potential of the Bayway Refinery." (mimeo.).

Union Research and Education Projects, University of Chicago
 1956   "A Report on the OCAWIU Organizing Effort and the Representation Election at the Whiting Refinery of the Standard Oil Company of Indiana." September (mimeo.).

U.S. Bureau of the Census
 1960   *Historical Statistics of the U.S.*

U.S. Department of Commerce, Bureau of the Census
 1955   *Occupation by Industry.* Washington, D. C.: U.S. Government Printing Office.

U.S. Department of Commerce
 1961   *Statistical Abstracts of the United States, 1961.* Washington, D. C.: U.S. Government Printing Office.

U.S. Department of Labor, Bureau of Labor Statistics
 1959   *Factory Workers' Earnings May 1958.* Bulletin No. 1252. Washington, D. C.: U.S. Government Printing Office.

U.S. Senate
 1940   *Hearings* before the Committee on Civil Service, on H.R. 960, "An Act Extending the Classified Civil Service," 76th Cong., 3rd sess.

U.S. Senate
 1942   *Hearings* on S. 2361, Committee on Agriculture and Forestry, 77th Cong., 2nd sess. (March).

U.S. Senate
  1939   *Report* of the Joint Committee to Investigate the Tennessee Valley Authority, Senate Doc. 56, 76th Cong., 1st sess.

U.S. Senate
  1940   "Statement on Application of H.R. 960 to the Tennessee Valley Authority." *Hearings* before the Committee on Civil Service, 76th Cong., 3rd sess.

U.S. Senate
  1955   *Hearings* before the Subcommitte on Economic Stabilization, 84th Cong., 1st sess.

Urwick, L. F.
  1947   *The Elements of Administration.* London: Pitman.

Vollmer, Howard M., and Donald L. Mills (eds.)
  1966   *Professionalization.* Englewood Cliffs, N. J.: Prentice-Hall.

Von Bertalanffy, Ludwig
  1956   "General System Theory," *General Systems, 1,* 1–10.

Waldo, D.
  1956   *Perspectives on Administration.* University, Ala.: University of Alabama Press.

Walker, Charles
  1957   *Toward the Automatic Factory.* New Haven: Yale University Press.

Walker, C. R. (ed.)
  1962   *Modern Technology and Civilization.* New York: McGraw-Hill.

Walker, C. (ed.)
  1968   *Technology, Industry and Man.* New York: McGraw-Hill.

Walker, Charles R., and Robert Guest
  1952   *The Man on the Assembly Line.* Cambridge, Mass.: Harvard University Press.

Wallace, Anthony F. C.
  1956   "Revitalization Movements," *American Anthropologist,* LVIII (April), 264–281.

Walton, Richard E., John M. Dutton, and Thomas P. Cafferty
  1969   "Organizational Context and Interdepartmental Conflict," *Administrative Science Quarterly, 14* (December), 522–543.

Warner, W. Lloyd, and J. O. Low
  1947   *The Social System of the Modern Factory.* New Haven: Yale University Press.

Warren, Donald I.
  1968   "Power, Visibility, and Conformity in Formal Organizations," *American Sociological Review, 33* (December), 951–970.

Warren, Roland L.
  1965   "The Impact of New Designs of Community Organization," *Child Welfare, 44* (November).

Warren, Roland L.
  1967   "The Interorganizational Field as a Focus for Investigation," *Administrative Science Quarterly, 12,* 396–419.

Warren, W. Keith, and A. Eugene Havens
  1968   "Goal Displacement and the Intangibility of Organizational Goals," *Administrative Science Quarterly, 12* (March), 539–555.

Warriner, Charles K.
  1965   "The Problem of Organizational Purpose," *The Sociological Quarterly, 6* (Spring).

Weber, Max
  1946   *Essays in Sociology.* New York: Oxford University Press.

Weber, Max
  1947   *The Theory of Social and Economic Organization,* trans. A. M. Henderson and T. Parsons. New York: Oxford University Press.

Weber, Max
  1952   "The Essentials of Bureaucratic Organization: An Ideal-Type Construction," in Merton, Robert *et al., Reader in Bureaucracy.* Glencoe, Ill.: Free Press.

Whalen, R. J.
  1963   "The Double Threads of J. P. Stevens," *Fortune* (April).

White, Carl M.
  1960   "Multiple Goals in the Theory of the Firm," in Boulding, Kenneth E., and W. Allen Spivey (eds.), *Linear Programming and the Theory of the Firm.* New York: Macmillan.

White, Harrison
  1961   "Management Conflict and Sociometric Structure," *American Journal of Sociology, 67,* 185–199.

White, R., and R. Lippitt
  1960   *Autocracy and Democracy: An Experimental Inquiry.* New York: Harper.

Whyte, William Foote
  1948   *Human Relations in the Restaurant Industry.* New York: McGraw-Hill.

Whyte, William F.
  1949   "The Social Structure of the Restaurant," *American Journal of Sociology, 54* (January), 302–310.

Whyte, William Foote (ed.)
  1964   *Industry and Society.* New York: McGraw-Hill.

Wilensky, H. L.
  1956   *Intellectuals in Labor Unions: Organizational Pressures on Professional Roles.* Glencoe, Ill.: Free Press.

Wilensky, Harold L.
  1964   "The Professionalization of Everyone?" *American Journal of Sociology, 70* (September), 137–158.

Wilensky, Harold L.
  1967   *Organizational Intelligence.* New York: Basic Books.

Wilensky, Harold L., and Charles N. Lebeaux
  1958   *Industrial Society and Social Welfare.* New York: Russell Sage Foundation.

Wilson, Bryan
    1959   "An Analysis of Sect Development," *American Sociological Review, 24,* 3–15.

Wilson, B. R.
    1962   "Analytical Studies of Social Institutions," in Welford, A. T. *et al., Society: Problems and Methods of Study.* London: Routledge and Kegan Paul.

Wilson, James Q.
    1966   "Innovation in Organization: Notes Toward a Theory," in Thompson, James D. (ed.), *Approaches to Organizational Design.* Pittsburgh: University of Pittsburgh.

Winch, R., and D. Campbell
    1969   "Proof? No Evidence? Yes. The Significance of Tests of Significance," *American Sociologist, 4,* 140–143.

Wolff, Kurt (ed.)
    1950   *The Sociology of Georg Simmel.* Glencoe, Illinois: Free Press.

Woodward, Joan
    1958   *Management and Technology.* London: Her Majesty's Stationary Office.

Woodward, Joan
    1965   *Industrial Organization: Theory and Practice.* London: Oxford University Press.

Worthy,
    1950   "Organizational Structure and Employee Morale." Indianapolis: Bobbs-Merrill reprint series #321.

Wrong, Dennis
    1961   "The Oversocialized Conception of Man in Modern Society," *American Sociological Review, 26* (April), 183–193.

Yuchtman, Ephraim
    1966   *A Study of Organizational Effectiveness.* Unpublished Ph.D. dissertation, University of Michigan.

Yuchtman, Ephraim, and Stanley E. Seashore
    1967   "A System Resource Approach to Organizational Effectiveness," *American Sociological Review, 32* (December), 891–903.

Zald, Mayer
    1962a   "Organizational Control Structures in Five Correctional Institutions," *American Journal of Sociology, 68* (November), 335–345.

Zald, Mayer N.
    1963   "Comparative Analysis and Measurement of Organizational Goals: The Case of Correctional Institutions for Delinquents," *Sociological Quarterly, 4* (Summer).

Zald, Mayer N., and Roberta Ash
    1966   "Social Movement Organizations," *Social Forces,* XLIV, 327–341.

Zald, Mayer N., and Patricia Denton
    1962b   "From Evangelism to General Service: On the Transformation of the YMCA," *Administrative Science Quarterly, 8* (September), 214–234.

Zald, Mayer N., and Charles S. Kamen
   1964   *Selected Characteristics of the Residents of the Service Areas of the Local Departments of the Metropolitan Chicago Young Men's Christian Association.* Chicago: YMCA of Chicago.

Zald, Mayer N., ed.
   1970   *Power in Organizations.* Nashville, Tenn.: Vanderbilt University Press.

Zaleznik, A., C. R. Christiansen, and F. J. Roethlisberger
   1958   *The Motivation, Productivity, and Satisfaction of Workers.* Boston: Division of Research, Graduate School of Business Administration, Harvard University.

Zander, Alvin, and Donald Wolfe
   1964   "Administrative Rewards and Coordination Among Committee Members." *Administrative Science Quarterly, 9* (June), 50–69.

Zeisel, Hans
   1957   *Say It with Figures* (4th ed.). New York: Harper.

Zelditch, Morris, Jr., and Terrence K. Hopkins
   1961   "Laboratory Experiments with Organizations," in Etzioni, Amitai, *Complex Organizations.* New York: Holt, Rinehart & Winston.

Zetterberg, H. L.
   1957   "Compliant Actions," *Acta Sociologica, 2.*

Zetterberg, Hans L.
   1962   *Social Theory and Social Practice.* Totowa, N. J.: Bedminster.

Zetterberg, Hans
   1965   *On Theory and Verification in Sociology. Totowa,* N. J.: Bedminster.

Subject Index

Name Index

579